Managing Investment Portfolios

A Dynamic Process

Managing Investment Portfolios

A Dynamic Process

Edited by

John L. Maginn, C.F.A.
Donald L. Tuttle, C.F.A.

Sponsored by

**The Institute of
Chartered
Financial Analysts**

WARREN, GORHAM & LAMONT
BOSTON • NEW YORK

Foreword

This is a book about investment portfolios and their management. It came into being as a natural extension of a project undertaken by The Institute of Chartered Financial Analysts (I.C.F.A.) in 1979 when a group of practitioners was brought together to analyze, evaluate, and update the content of the portfolio management area of the Chartered Financial Analyst (C.F.A.) Candidate Program.

The C.F.A. Candidate Program is a key means for achieving the Institute's objective of developing and maintaining high standards of professional investment management. The body of professional knowledge represented in the program includes a number of important subjects—ethical and professional standards, financial accounting, economics, fixed income securities analysis, equity securities analysis, and portfolio management. As candidates move through three separate and progressive examinations, these subjects are covered in increasing depth and breadth. The specific content of the body of knowledge on which the examinations are based and the examinations themselves are determined by highly qualified practitioners in the fields of securities analysis and investment portfolio management who have been identified and appointed by the I.C.F.A.

The 1979 project illustrates the Institute's efforts to periodically revise and update the candidate program to reflect changes and developments in investment management practice. The project was initiated by the appointment of a Portfolio Management Review Committee, with membership consisting of John Maginn, Chairman, and Bill Gray, Bob Morrison, Hal Schwind, Don Tuttle, Jay Vawter, and Jim Vertin. As a result of this group's work, the entire content of the portfolio management curriculum was restructured to reflect a new focus on the management process, and important gaps in the literature of finance were identified, to be addressed through publications that would augment the body of knowledge on which the I.C.F.A., its members, C.F.A. candidates, and other interested parties could draw. This book is the third publication flowing from the Committee's work, following C.F.A. *Readings in Portfolio Management* (published by the I.C.F.A. and distributed to all C.F.A.s and C.F.A. candidates) and *Determinants of Investment Portfolio Policy* (authored by members of the group and provided to candidates as part of their study materials).

While the original thrust of the project that led to this book was aimed primarily at improving the quality and expanding the scope of the study materials available to C.F.A. candidates, the usefulness of the book itself will be seen to apply in a much broader context. For example, it will be of value in each of the following applications:

1. For I.C.F.A. members and other investment professionals, as a refresher and as a source of new information and insight.
2. For aspirants to a portfolio management career, as an introduction to the role and responsibilities of practitioners in this professional function.
3. For trustees, members of investment committees, and administrators of institutional investment portfolios, as an explanation of the portfolio management process, which can facilitate their relationships with investment managers and provide important assistance in determining portfolio policies and in evaluating manager performance.
4. For individual investors, as a means for identification and understanding of portfolio management concepts and for assistance in managing (or reviewing the management of) their personal accounts.
5. For students of investment management, as a comprehensive exposition of important aspects of the subject area.

When the decision was made by the I.C.F.A. trustees to proceed with publication of this volume, certain criteria were established as to its overall content and authorship. The most important of these were that it should:

1. Describe and demonstrate that portfolio management is a dynamic decision-making process, based on fundamentally sound and recognizable investment considerations and one that lends itself to equally sound and recognizable principles of organizational behavior.
2. Demonstrate that this process is applicable to any category or combination of investment assets—stocks, bonds, real estate, mortgages, and so on.
3. Draw heavily on the collective wisdom and experience of well-recognized professionals and be written by and for practitioners.
4. Represent a rigorous combination of theory and practice, but at the same time avoid jargon and ambiguity.
5. Aim from the outset to fill gaps in the useful literature available to practitioners by focusing on content and exposition not comprehensively available elsewhere.

The trustees and the I.C.F.A. take great pride in presenting this book to C.F.A.s, to other professionals, and to the broader public. We believe it to be a significant volume, of importance to members and nonmembers alike, combining the forefront of practitioner experience and knowledge with the output of academic research over the last 30 years, from Markowitz's original portfolio theory article to the present. We earnestly hope that you will find in it the value we sought to put there, and that it will be given a prominent place in the library of useful volumes each of you maintains for reference.

On behalf of the I.C.F.A., we would be remiss if we failed to express in this Foreword the strong feeling of gratitude that flows to the book's editors and authors. Collectively and individually they undertook to turn an idea into solid substance, out of conviction concerning the need for this volume and because they care about their profession. Their reward lies primarily in the fact that they said they could produce the book—and they did. We applaud their accomplishment.

O. WHITFIELD BROOME, JR., *Executive Director*
The Institute of Chartered Financial Analysts

JAMES R. VERTIN, *1981–82 President*
The Institute of Chartered Financial Analysts

October 1982

Preface

The management of investment portfolios is a rapidly growing but not well-documented professional endeavor, serving a broad array of investors—both individual and institutional—with investment portfolios ranging in asset size from thousands to billions of dollars.

Like many areas of business, portfolio management is both an art and a science. It is much more than the application of a formula to a set of data input from security analysts. It is a dynamic decision-making process, one that is continuous and systematic but also one that requires large amounts of astute managerial judgment.

This book documents the portfolio management process, blending academic theory with the experience of noted practitioners. The language of the book is that of the investment community rather than the scholar. It was written by and for portfolio managers and those whom they serve.

Each author was chosen from among the leading professionals in his or her subject area. Each author's contribution was highly directed in order to blend its insights into the context of the portfolio decision-making process logic. The result is a uniquely readable book, rich in its real life perspective and its exposition of the subject.

Such a book represents untold hours of effort by authors, editors, and reviewers who have joined together in this common cause.

The editors wish to acknowledge the contribution of the authors and coauthors and to thank their families for allowing these busy people to share their talents. The members of the Editorial Review Board read and reread manuscripts and contributed greatly to the refinement and polishing of each chapter. Their knowledge of the profession and the process was of great value in the preparation of this book.

The editors also acknowledge the comments, criticism, and guidance provided by the following individuals: John C. Aplin, Jr., Indiana University; Peter L. Bernstein, Peter L. Bernstein, Inc. and *The Journal of Portfolio Management;* Boyd A. Carnaby, United of Omaha Life Insurance Company; Richard A. Cosier, Indiana University; Blake Eagle, Frank Russell Company; William S. Gray, III, C.F.A., Harris Trust & Savings Bank; Jerry Heinrichs, Investors Realty Company; Robert H. Hurwit, The Connecticut Bank and Trust Company; Robert C. Klemkosky, Indiana University; Dennis E. Logue, Dartmouth College; Eric A. Manterfield, American Fletcher National Bank; Richard W. McEnally, C.F.A., University of North Carolina at Chapel Hill; Meyer Melnikoff, Goldman Sachs and Company; Robert W. Morrison, C.F.A., The Canada Life Assurance Company; William L. Nemerever, C.F.A., State Street Bank and Trust Company; Frank K. Reilly, C.F.A., University of Notre Dame; John K. Rutledge, Harris Trust & Savings Bank; Harold A. Schwind, C.F.A., Investors Diversified Services, Inc.; Jay Vawter, C.F.A., Stein, Roe & Farnham; and James R. Vertin, C.F.A., Alpine Counselors. We also want to recognize O. Whitfield Broome, Jr., Executive Director of The Institute of Chartered Financial Analysts, and the Institute's trustees for their strong encouragement and financial support throughout this unique project. We are also appreciative of the physical facilities and staff support of the Indiana University Graduate School of Business. Finally, on a personal note, we want to thank our families, especially Carol and Peg, for their support throughout the many months it took to produce this book.

JOHN L. MAGINN, *Associate Editor*

DONALD L. TUTTLE, *Editor-in-Chief*

October 1982

Contents

Part IV Integration of Portfolio Policies and Expectational Factors

8 Portfolio Construction: Asset Allocation 261
Kathleen A. Condon, C.F.A.

9 Portfolio Construction: Fixed Income 291
H. Gifford Fong

Contributors

Keith P. Ambachtsheer is a principal and cofounder of Pension Finance Associates, a company that provides financial and investment advice to Canadian pension fund sponsors. He holds a B.A. from Royal Military College of Canada, has an M.A. from the University of Western Ontario, and did additional graduate work at McGill University. He entered the investment field with Sun Life in 1969 and joined the institutional broker Canavest House in 1972, becoming a director and manager of research in 1974. He is vice chairman of the Financial Research Foundation of Canada and is a regular contributor to professional journals for investment practitioners. His article, coauthored with James Farrell, "Can Active Management Add Value?" won The Financial Analysts Federation's coveted Graham and Dodd Award as one of the best articles in *Financial Analysts Journal* in 1979.

James H. Ambrose is a principal and cofounder of Pension Finance Associates, an investment advisory firm for Canadian corporate pension funds. He received his B.A. degree from the University of Guelph and his M.B.A. from McMaster University. He began his investment career with Canavest House in 1977 and later taught at Waterloo University, where he remained until Pension Finance Associates was formed in 1982. Mr. Ambrose is a part-time faculty member of the University of Toronto.

Peter L. Bernstein is president of Peter L. Bernstein, Inc., economic and financial consultants to institutional investors and corporations, and editor of *The Journal of Portfolio Management*. He is a graduate of Harvard University, a former member of the research staff of the Federal Reserve Bank of New York, and has also managed the bond portfolios of two New York City banks. In 1951 he joined the investment counsel firm of Bernstein-Macaulay, Inc., serving as president and later as chairman. From 1967 to 1973 he also served as a director, senior vice president, and chairman of the investment policy committee of Bernstein-Macaulay's parent company, Shearson/American Express, Inc. He is the author of four books on economics and finance and has written many articles for professional and popular journals. A former consultant to both the New York and American stock exchanges, he also served as vice president for investments of the American Finance Association. He is a trustee and member of the Finance Committee of the College Retirement Equities Fund, and a member of the New York Society of Security Analysts.

Kathleen A. Condon, C.F.A., is a vice president and manager of the employee benefit consulting section at Bankers Trust Company. She joined the bank in 1970 as an equity portfolio manager and later was involved in the initial development and implementation of index and market inventory funds. Prior to her current assignment, she managed the bank's investment process consulting section, which is responsible for integrating quantitative techniques into the investment process. Ms. Condon graduated from Mount Holyoke College and earned an M.B.A. from New York University. She is a member of the New York Society of Security Analysts and currently serves on the board of the Institute for Quantitative Research in Finance. Her publications include the 1981 *Financial Analysts Journal* article "Measuring Equity Transaction Costs," for which she received a Graham and Dodd Award.

William A. Cornish, C.F.A., senior vice president and director of Duff and Phelps, Inc., has been in charge of the firm's credit rating research division since September 1980, when the firm entered the public fixed income rating business. Prior to that, he was director of its industrial/financial research division. He has been a practicing financial analyst for his entire career, which began in 1956 at the Harris Trust & Savings Bank, and has had analysis responsibilities for a wide range of industries. He joined Duff and Phelps as a senior analyst in 1964. Mr. Cornish has long been active in industry affairs; he is a past president of The Institute of Chartered Financial Analysts and has served as chairman of the Institute's Research and Publications Committee. He was president of the Investment Analysts Society of Chicago and also served on several committees of The Financial Analysts Federation. He is a member of the Investment Analysis Standards Board with responsibility to review the joint F.A.F. and I.C.F.A. Code of Ethics and Standards of Practice. He received his B.A. from Yale University and his M.B.A. from Harvard University.

Peter O. Dietz is senior vice president, director of research and development, and a client executive at Frank Russell Company, adviser to forty large pension fund clients. Dr. Dietz holds an A.B. from Dartmouth College, an M.B.A. from Amos Tuck School of Business Administration, and a Ph.D. from Columbia University. From 1960 to 1969 he taught at the Graduate School of Management, Northwestern University, and from 1969 to 1976 at the College of Business Administration, University of Oregon, becoming department chairman in 1973. He is currently chairman of the research committee and a member of the board of directors of the Institute for Financial and Quantitative Research. In addition to his authorship of *Pension Funds: Measuring Investment Performance* (1966), he has written numerous articles on the subjects of setting investment objectives and measuring investment performance. He is a member of the Seattle Society of Financial Analysts.

Charles D. Ellis, C.F.A., is president of Greenwich Research Associates, a business strategy research and consulting firm. The author of three books (*Institutional Investing, The Second Crash,* and *The Repurchase of Common Stock*) and many articles on business, finance, and investment management, he is the 1982–83 vice president of The Institute of Chartered Financial Analysts and an editor of *Financial Analysts Journal*. He earned his B.A. at Yale, his M.B.A. (with distinction) at Harvard University, where he has twice taught the second-year course in investment management, and his Ph.D. at New York University. Before joining Greenwich Research Associates in 1972, Dr. Ellis was vice president of Donaldson, Lufkin & Jenrette and an associate of Rockefeller Brothers, Inc.

Jeffrey D. Fisher is a partner in Real Estate Evaluation Consultants and is a member of the real estate faculty, Graduate School of Business, Indiana University. He received a B.S. from Purdue University, an M.B.A. from Wright State University, and a Ph.D. from Ohio State University. He is a coauthor of the eighth edition of *Real Estate*. His articles on real estate have appeared in *Appraisal Journal, Real Estate Review, Real Estate Appraiser and Analyst, Real Estate Issues,* and *Journal of the American Real Estate and Urban Economics Association,* among others. He has given seminars for numerous professional organizations and is an instructor at the American Institute of Real Estate Appraisers. A real estate investment analysis computer model developed by Dr. Fisher is used nationwide by universities, government agencies, insurance companies, mortgage bankers, and developers.

H. Gifford Fong is president of Gifford Fong Associates, a California-based firm specializing in investment technology systems and consulting. Previously he held consulting and directorship positions in several institutional research houses and banks in their management science departments. Mr. Fong received his B.S., M.B.A., and J.D. degrees from the University of California at Berkeley. In addition to his participation on the board of directors of the Institute for Quantitative Research in Finance, he serves on the editorial advisory board of the *Handbook of Fixed Income Securities,* to which he is also a contributor. He has made frequent contributions to a number of academic and professional journals.

Daniel J. Forrestal, III, C.F.A., is president and chief executive officer of InterFirst Investment Management, Inc., an investment advisory subsidiary of InterFirst Corporation. Mr. Forrestal has held similar senior management positions with Chase Investors Management, Inc., and Alliance Capital Management Corporation. He received his undergraduate and M.B.A. degrees from Holy Cross College and Washington University (St. Louis), respectively. Mr. Forrestal has served on the board of directors of The Financial Analysts Federation and is a former president of the Dallas Association of Investment Analysts. He also serves on the faculty of the Southwestern Graduate School of Banking, and is a frequent speaker on investment markets and the changing role of institutional asset management.

William S. Gray, III, C.F.A., is senior vice president of Harris Trust & Savings Bank. He joined the bank in 1950 as a security analyst, became an officer in 1955, supervised the securities analysis staff in the early 1960s, and moved to the trust department in 1965. He became head of the trust investment division and chairman of the trust investment committee in 1966. Mr. Gray is currently senior investment officer in the trust department, chairman of the trust investment committee, and chairman of the investment guidance committee. He is also group executive of the trust investment systems group. His professional work includes serving as chairman of The Financial Analysts Federation (receiving its Distinguished Service Award), president of the Investment Analysts Society of Chicago, chairman of the investment committee of the trust division of the American Bankers Association, president of the Financial Analysts Research Foundation, lecturer at the National Trust School, and author of many articles, including the award-winning "Application of Discount Rates in Forecasting Returns for Stocks and Bonds." Mr. Gray holds Ph.B. and M.B.A. degrees from the University of Chicago.

Jeannette R. Kirschman is senior vice president, treasurer, chief financial officer, and a client executive of Frank Russell Company, consultants to pension funds. She has been in the consulting business for more than thirteen years and has specialized in accounting and quantitative analysis of institutional funds, including developing and directing Frank Russell Company's portfolio monitoring and portfolio and performance analysis systems. Ms. Kirschman attended Western Washington State University and the University of Washington. She is a Certified Public Accountant and is a member of the American Institute of Certified Public Accountants, the American Women's Society of Certified Public Accountants, the American Society of Women Accountants, and the Washington Society of Certified Public Accountants.

John L. Maginn, C.F.A., is executive vice president–investments and treasurer of Mutual of Omaha Insurance Company and United of Omaha Insurance Company. He received his B.S.B.A. degree from Creighton University and an M.S. degree from the University of Minnesota. He began his investment career in 1962 as a research analyst at Continental Casualty Company (now CNA Financial Corporation), Chicago. His investment experience has included common stock and bond analysis, as well as the management of insurance company, mutual fund, and endowment fund portfolios. Mr. Maginn is a trustee of The Institute of Chartered Financial Analysts and a member of the Institute's Council of Examiners and Candidate Curriculum Committee. He was chairman of the Institute's Portfolio Management Review Subcommittee, and in that connection was involved in the compilation of *C.F.A Readings in Portfolio Management* and authored the insurance company section of *The Determinants of Portfolio Policy.* Mr. Maginn is a former director of The Financial Analysts Federation and a past president of the Omaha-Lincoln Society of Financial Analysts.

Robert D. Milne, C.F.A., is president of Duff and Phelps Investment Management Company. He is a past president of The Institute of Chartered Financial Analysts, is a trustee of the Financial Analysts Research Foundation, serves as a member of the Editorial Board of *C.F.A. Digest,* and is an associate editor of *Financial Analysts Journal.* He is also a past president of the Cleveland Society of Security Analysts. Mr. Milne received his B.A. degree from Baldwin-Wallace College and his J.D. degree from the Cleveland-Marshall College of Law of Cleveland State University. He is the author of numerous professional articles and is a member of the Ohio Bar.

Jack L. Treynor is a partner and chief investment officer of Treynor-Arbit Associates. From 1969 to 1981 he was editor of *Financial Analysts Journal.* After joining Merrill Lynch in 1966, he conceived and organized what became the first beta service, providing risk and risk-adjusted performance measures to that firm's institutional clients. During the prior ten years his consulting clients included Investors Diversified Services, Chase Manhattan Bank, and Yale University. Mr. Treynor received a B.A. in mathematics from Haverford College and an M.B.A. from Harvard University. In addition to two books, he is author or coauthor of articles in *Harvard Business Review, Journal of Business, Journal of Accounting Research, Journal of Finance,* and *Financial Analysts Journal.* He was a Graham and Dodd scroll winner in 1968 and the plaque winner in 1981. Mr. Treynor is a director of the Institute for Quantitative Research in Finance and a trustee of the Financial Analysts Research Foundation. He was a member of the Investment Advisory Council to the City of New York until he left that city, and he has recently completed a three-year term as a director of the American Finance Association. He is a member of the Indianapolis Society of Financial Analysts.

Donald L. Tuttle, C.F.A., is Professor of Finance, Graduate School of Business, Indiana University. He received his B.S.B.A. and M.B.A. degrees from the University of Florida, and his Ph.D. degree from the University of North Carolina at Chapel Hill. He taught previously at the University of North Carolina and has been a visiting professor at the European Institute of Business Administration (INSEAD), the University of Florida, and the University of Virginia. He has served as an investments and capital markets consultant to corporations, government agencies, and professional organizations. He is the author of twenty-two articles in leading finance journals and three books on security analysis and portfolio management. Dr. Tuttle is a former president and executive director of the Financial Management Association. He is also a former associate editor of *Journal of Finance* and *Financial Management*. He is a member of The Institute of Chartered Financial Analysts Candidate Curriculum Committee (chairman, 1982–83), is on its *C.F.A. Digest* Editorial Board, and is a former member of its Council of Examiners and Portfolio Management Review Subcommittee. He is also a member of the board of trustees of the Financial Analysts Research Foundation and the Bison Money Market Fund, and is on the board of directors of the Federal Home Loan Bank of Indianapolis. He is a member of the Indianapolis Society of Financial Analysts and the New York Society of Security Analysts.

Jay Vawter, C.F.A., is a partner in Stein, Roe & Farnham, investment counselors. He has been in the investment management business for some twenty-five years and has specialized in the management of institutional funds, particularly retirement funds and endowments. Mr. Vawter holds a B.B.A. and an M.B.A. from the University of Michigan. From 1978 to 1982 he served as chairman of The Institute of Chartered Financial Analysts Council of Examiners and is currently a trustee of the Institute, and is its 1982–83 Secretary/Treasurer. He served as a member of the Institute's Portfolio Management Review Committee and as a member of the Editorial Review Board of this book. He has served as a trustee of a public pension plan and of a large religious endowment fund. Mr. Vawter is a frequent speaker and lecturer on the economy, financial markets, and personal and institutional investing. He is a member of the Washington Society of Investment Analysts and the New York Society of Security Analysts.

James R. Vertin, C.F.A., principal, Alpine Counselors, recently concluded a career of thirty years with Wells Fargo Bank, involving security analysis, portfolio management, and business management of Wells Fargo Investment Advisors. Mr. Vertin holds an M.B.A. from Stanford University, is a former president of the Security Analysts Society of San Francisco, a former director of The Financial Analysts Federation, a current officer and trustee of the Financial Analysts Research Foundation, and a current trustee of The Institute of Chartered Financial Analysts, an organization which he served as president in 1981–82. He has been a frequent speaker on matters concerning the investment profession and is the author of a number of articles on pension and other investment topics. He is a member of the Institute's Council for Continuing Education, was a member of its Portfolio Management Review Committee, and is also a member of the Editorial Review Board of this book.

CHAPTER 1

The Portfolio Management Process and Its Dynamics

John L. Maginn, C.F.A.
Donald L. Tuttle, C.F.A.

Investment management is an old profession, the growth of which has paralleled the accumulation of wealth and the evolution of our civilization. Investors have sought assets that would grow in value and/or provide income. Over the centuries the investment assets selected have been encyclopedic, reflecting the culture and commerce of the times. In essence, investment management practices have evolved in a long-term trend with a more populous and prosperous world community of investors. Today, the number of investors and investment managers continues to grow rapidly.

Since the seminal work of Harry Markowitz in the early 1950s, the practice of investment management has undergone revolutionary change. His was a watershed contribution to investment theory, identifying the collective importance of all the investor's holdings—the *portfolio* of investments. The interrelationship of individual asset holdings was identified by Markowitz in the context of the classic investment tradeoff between risk and return. Over the past 30 years, investment management attention has been shifting from primary emphasis on asset selection to a more balanced emphasis on diversification and the interrelationship of individual asset characteristics within the portfolio. Thus, the theory of building portfolios has significantly altered the practice of investment management. In fact, portfolio theory has broadened the concept of investment management to that of portfolio management.

All these changes were taking place at a time when two other trends were unfolding within the investment community: *First*, the emergence of institutional investing as a new, yet very big and rapidly growing business that

largely reflects the growth of pension funds; and *second*, the professionaliza-
tion of the field. Thirty years ago, investment analysts were considered
compilers of statistics and portfolio management was the province of senior
management or committees. The phenomenal growth in investment assets,
coupled with pressure from regulatory bodies such as the Securities and
Exchange Commission, motivated the Financial Analysts Federation in the
early 1960s to establish a professional accreditation program and the Chartered Financial Analysts (C.F.A.) designation under the auspices of The
Institute of Chartered Financial Analysts.

Through the Institute a common body of knowledge has been identified
and continuously updated, as explained by Whit Broome and Jim Vertin in
the foreword of this book. The end result of the analysis of economic,
accounting, and capital market information is an investment decision that
determines the portfolio of the investor. Even a decision to take no action is
a decision. Thus, the culmination of all investment analysis is portfolio
management.

PORTFOLIO MANAGEMENT AS A PROCESS

Despite its growth and importance, the subject of portfolio management
has not been treated comprehensively in the literature. Much of the traditional literature was based on an "interior decorator/catalog approach,"
where management was explained in terms of classes of assets matched with
classes of investors on an almost ad hoc basis. Overlooked was the fact that
through the eyes of the practitioner, portfolio management is a *process*, an
integrated set of activities that combine in a logical, orderly manner to produce a desired product. This concept of portfolio management as a process
is so basic, so intuitively correct, so intellectually satisfying, and so pragmatically useful that it can be accepted under virtually any circumstances. It is a
dynamic concept, and a flexible one. And, it is an accurate description for
any portfolio management function regardless of organizational type—trust
company, investment counsel firm, insurance company, mutual fund, or
whatever; regardless of customer orientation—personal, pension, endowment, foundation, insurance, bank, or whatever; and regardless of manager
location, investment philosophy, style, or approach. Portfolio management
is a process which, complete with feedback loops for monitoring and adjustment, is *continuous* and *systematic*. The process can be as loose or as
disciplined, as quantitative or as judgmental, and as simple or as complex as
its operators wish it to be.

Whatever its construct, in a particular application the process at work is
the same as in every other application: an integrated series of steps undertaken in a consistent manner to create and maintain appropriate combinations of investment assets. The process starts with the identification and
specification of an investor's objectives, preferences, and constraints and

the development of appropriate investment policies and strategies. The next step is the implementation of the process in the marketplace through the choice of an optimal combination of investment assets that are selected on the basis of capital market and individual asset expectations. Then, through the monitoring of market conditions, relative values, portfolio performance, and the investor's own circumstances, the process comes full circle when changes in these variables result in the need to rebalance the portfolio. Then the cycle begins anew.

THE PROCESS LOGIC

Given the process idea, the necessary steps for the conduct of the portfolio management function, the logical sequence of these steps, the nature of the decisions to be made, and the ordering of these decisions is immediately apparent. Different organizations will reach differing conclusions as their unique judgments are applied at various points in the process. These organizations will place different emphases on different aspects of the process, since acceptance of the notion demands no uniformity in decision content. Rather, recognition of the process simply permits *any* manager to organize for, identify, and execute the necessary decisions in an orderly, consistent manner that ensures comprehensive attention to all of the areas relevant to portfolio creation, maintenance, and adjustment.

In sum, the process logic, shown diagrammatically in Figure 1-1, is incorporated in the following definition which is the cornerstone for this book:

Portfolio management is an ongoing process by which

- an investor's objectives, constraints, and preferences are identified and specified to develop explicit investment policies;
- strategies are developed and implemented through the choice of optimal combinations of financial and real assets in the marketplace;
- market conditions, relative values, and the investor's circumstances are monitored; and
- portfolio adjustments are made as appropriate to reflect significant change in any or all of the relevant variables.

This book makes no judgments nor voices any opinions about *how* the process should be organized, about *who* should make *which* decisions, or about any other process *operating* matter. Each management organization—indeed, each manager within an organization—will have a preferred operating course that will be uniquely its own, which is as it should be. What the book does discern, and what the authors wish to call attention to, is that the process itself is common to *all* managers, everywhere. Systematic exploitation of this underlying reality is as readily accomplished by a one-manager

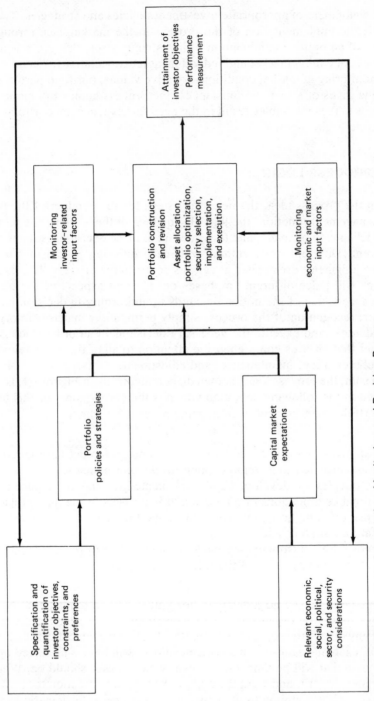

Figure 1-1. The Portfolio Construction, Monitoring, and Revision Process

shop using a hand-held calculator as it is by an industry giant employing the latest in real time, on-line, interactive computer systems. The *dynamic* is there, is useful, and is fundamental.

THE DYNAMICS OF THE PROCESS

One of the truly satisfying things about portfolio management as a professional activity is the existence of the underlying logic and the dynamism illustrated by the definition and the process notion. In the broad sense, the work of analysts, economists, and market strategists is all a matter of "getting ready." The work of portfolio management is where the action is. Taking the inputs and moving step by step through the orderly process of converting this raw material into a portfolio that maximizes expected return relative to the investor's ability to bear risk, that meets the investor's constraints and preferences at the same time that it executes a strategy, and that integrates portfolio policies with expectational factors and market uncertainties—this is where the payoff is because this is where it all comes together. And, of course, it is the result of this process that is judged: the performance of the portfolio relative to expectations and comparative standards.

It is our view that professionalism will be enhanced and practice improved by visualizing *and* operating the portfolio management function as a process that (1) consists of the steps outlined in this book, (2) flows logically and systematically through an orderly sequence of decision making, and (3) moves from the final step of monitoring back to the first step of policy determination in an ongoing way so that, once put in motion with respect to a given investor, the process is continuous. This view sees portfolio management not as a set of separate elements operating by fits and starts as intuition or inspiration but as an integrated whole, where every decision moves the portfolio down the process path and no decision can be skipped without sacrificing functional integrity.

Principles of Asset Management

The building blocks of the portfolio decision-making process are the basic concept of the tradeoff between risk and return. Charley Ellis in Chapter 2 conceptualizes the role of the portfolio manager as a "risk" manager and provides a general description of the risk-return tradeoff. In Chapter 3, Keith Ambachtsheer and James Ambrose provide a concise but comprehensive discussion of the basic financial concepts that are the foundation for portfolio theory.

Determination of Portfolio Policies

With the foundation principles and variables specified, the process begins to unfold in Chapter 4 as Jay Vawter examines the objectives, constraints, and preferences of institutional investors—pension funds, profit-sharing funds, endowment funds, insurance companies, investment companies, and banks—and explains in general how these factors determine portfolio policies for each of these institutional investor groups. Similarly, in Chapter 5 Bob Milne explains how the objectives, constraints, and preferences of individual investors are identified and specified to develop explicit personal investment policies. It is important to note that explicit policy statements are well accepted—although not always well stated—for institutional investors, but typically have not been developed for individual investors, even those who are clients of counselors and bank trust departments. Due to a 1982 change in regulation, investment policy statements are now required for all bank trust customers, so the information and illustrations in these chapters are particularly topical and timely.

Expectational Factors

Investment strategies developed from these policy statements are used, together with the investment manager's expectations for the capital markets in general and for individual sectors and assets in particular, to choose a portfolio of assets in a simultaneous equation type solution process. By focusing on the trend of inflation as the single most important influence in the marketplace over the past decade, Peter Bernstein in Chapter 6 develops some novel insights into the macroexpectational factors influencing the market for bonds, stocks, and real estate. Bill Cornish in Chapter 7 calls on his years of securities research experience to cite microanalytical constructs and causative variables that underlie the prospects for sectors, industries, and individual securities.

Integrating Policies and Expectations

The most difficult and important phase of the portfolio management process is the integration of these expectations with the investor's objectives, constraints, and preferences as defined in the policy statement. This operational phase of the process is covered in four key chapters dealing with the asset allocation decision and the construction of fixed income, equity, and real estate portfolios. Kathy Condon in Chapter 8 discusses in detail the asset allocation considerations that are applicable to any investment portfolio. Gifford Fong in Chapter 9 incorporates some of the newest and most sophisticated fixed income management techniques. Bill Gray in Chapter 10 calls on his years of experience as a portfolio manager to develop a comprehensive description of equity portfolio practices and principles. Jeff Fisher in Chapter 11 provides the Institute's first major thrust into the real estate investment arena. Chapter 11 also demonstrates the applicability of the portfolio management process to asset classes other than bonds and stocks.

The implementation or execution phase of the process is one of the most critical but least understood aspects of portfolio management. This major gap in the literature has been filled by Jack Treynor in Chapter 12, which brings together some nuts and bolts issues, such as measurement of direct and indirect costs of execution, and some new conceptual insights into the transacting process and their implications for portfolio managers, research analysts, and the trading desk.

Restructuring the Portfolio

Despite the fact that portfolio managers spend most of their time monitoring and rebalancing existing portfolios, the literature heretofore has focused almost exclusively on the creation of portfolios. In Chapter 13 John Maginn and Jim Vertin have combined their insights and experience in managing a variety of institutional portfolios to explain how the elements of the portfolio management process are applied to the actual day-to-day monitoring and adjusting of portfolios.

Portfolio managers are not measured by how well they prepare but rather by how well they perform. Chapters 2 through 13 describe a logical, systematic, continuous, decision-making process. In Chapter 14 Peter Dietz and Jeannette Kirschman provide a strong blend of the academic literature and practitioner craftsmanship to examine performance measurement and its uses and abuses. Finally, Dan Forrestal in Chapter 15 has created a unique interpretation of key parts of the professional business management literature to describe the characteristics of effective and successful money management firms and their managers.

It is important for the reader to be aware of the role of the *appendixes* that follow many of the chapters. Traditionally, only technical material is found in the appendix to a chapter; but in this book the editors have also included, where applicable and available, materials extracted from a variety of sources to represent the real world implications and application of the portfolio decision-making process. Thus, the appendixes are designed to provide practical information that complements the authors' treatment of their respective subjects.

PORTFOLIO MANAGEMENT COMES OF AGE

Portfolio management has come of age as a profession in the past quarter century. The evolution and advancement of the theory and practice of portfolio management during this period have been shaped by many factors, including the

- increased institutionalization of money management
- growth in the number and size of investable pools of money, which in turn reflects the growth in population, wealth factors, and social changes—particularly retirement benefits

- increased market volatility reflecting economic uncertainty and instability
- greater use of computers for processing masses of data and as a tool in both the management of information and the performance of functional activities
- increased emphasis on the use of quantitative techniques in the decision-making process of business in general and finance in particular
- larger direct and indirect costs of errors or shortfalls in meeting portfolio objectives

While it is unknown whether these same factors will be the principal shapers of the future investment environment—or if an entirely different set of influences will come into play—change will occur, probably with increasing frequency and severity. Given the enhanced sophistication and competitiveness of the portfolio management community, reaction to change will be increasingly swift and resolute. Only managers with solid grounding in dynamic, systematic, decision-making processes such as those described here will be able to adapt, master, and thrive in such an aggressively changing and competitive environment.

Part I
Principles of Financial Asset Management

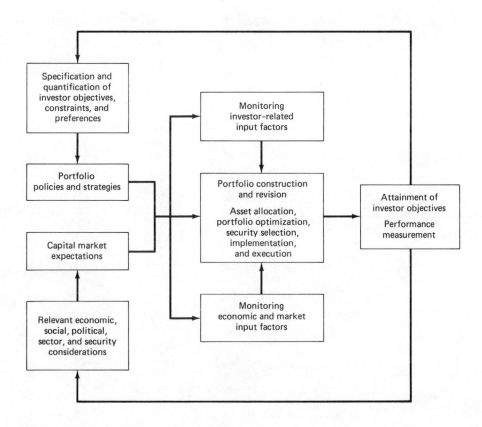

CHAPTER 2

Conceptualizing Portfolio Management

Charles D. Ellis, C.F.A.

Portfolio management is—and always should be—a defensive process.

The goal of the portfolio manager is to control or manage risk in pursuit of wisely determined and explicitly stated objectives of the investor or beneficiaries. No matter that some of the most interesting practitioners style themselves as performance-oriented, the basic responsibility of portfolio managers—since the invention of insurance and pooled risk accounts in merchant shipping on sailing vessels hundreds of years ago—is to control risk.

TYPES OF RISK

Investors are exposed to three kinds of risk, one that cannot be avoided and two that can be eliminated—through careful portfolio management.

Systematic Risk

The risk that cannot be avoided is the risk inherent in the overall market. This risk, which is described as systematic, can be magnified through selection or by using leverage, or diminished by selection of low systematic risk securities, by investing part of net worth in fixed income securities, or by holding cash equivalents, as will be developed later in this chapter.

Despite the enticing appeal of reducing market exposure through astute sales when securities appear to be overpriced and bold commitments when prices appear to have declined to attractively low levels, the overwhelming evidence shows that market timing is *not* an effective way to reduce market risk—for the dour but compelling reason that, on average and over time, it does not work.

The systematic risk inherent in investing in any one market can, of course, be reduced. In a multimarket portfolio one can balance investments in one market with investments in other markets that behave differently. This sort of diversification is an important motivation behind the interest in diversifying internationally. The stock markets of France, Japan, Italy, and Australia fluctuate as much as or more than the American market, but at different times and for different reasons. The multimarket portfolio, with its investments in several different markets, will have reduced the "unavoidable" market risk of any one market. However, for purposes of this analysis, the portfolio will be limited to one market. In this case, the effects of the overall market fluctuations—systematic or market risk—cannot be avoided.

Unsystematic Risk

The two kinds of risk that *can* be avoided or eliminated together constitute unsystematic risk. They are closely associated. One involves the risks associated with individual securities, the other involves the risks that are common to various groups of securities. The former is usually called *specific risk,* while the second is usually called *extra-market risk.*

A few examples will clarify the meaning of extra-market risk. Growth stocks will all move up and down in price *in part* because of changes in investor confidence and willingness to look more or less distantly into the future; interest-sensitive issues such as utility and bank stocks will all be affected by changes in expected interest rates; stocks in the same industry will share market price behavior, driven by changing expectations for the industry; and so on. The number of common causes that affect groups of stocks is surely great, and most stocks will belong to several different groups. To avoid unnecessary complexity, and triviality, portfolio managers will concern themselves only with major forms of extra-market risk.

As will be explained at greater length in Chapter 3, the risk that is identified as either specific or extra-market is the risk that the *price* of an individual stock or group of stocks will behave differently—either favorably or unfavorably—than the overall market over the time period for which performance is measured. Clearly, such risk can be avoided by the simple and convenient strategy of designing a portfolio that replicates the market, wherein no deviations in portfolio composition equate to no deviations in rate of return.

The ease with which specific risk and extra-market risk can be avoided or eliminated is crucial. Why? Because, while risk-averse investors are willing to accept lower rates of return if they can minimize the risks of investing and are willing to allow higher rates of return as an inducement to other investors to accept higher risks, they will *not* pay their risk-taking confreres to take risks that can quite easily be avoided altogether by "buying the market." As a result, for rational investors in a perfectly efficient market, no incremental reward can be earned over the market rate of return for taking either specific risk or extra-market risk.

The lack of reward for taking specific risk or extra-market risk is important because the portfolio manager who takes such risks can only hope to be rewarded by his superior skill—relative to all competing portfolio managers—in selecting individual stocks or groups that are inappropriately priced. Even the most talented investor might wonder how often his competitors will, by incompetence, error, or inattention, provide especially attractive opportunities to buy or sell in size on significantly advantageous terms.

Systematic or market risk is different. Because it cannot be eliminated, risk-averse investors will and must accept a less than market rate of return in order to achieve a less than market risk. And by so doing, they proffer an above-market rate of return to investors willing to accept a greater than market risk. This is why generally investors who accept more than market risk—particularly over time—are rewarded with more than market returns.

Return for Risk Bearing

While it is clear that investors who accept greater systematic or market risk usually acquire higher returns and that return is a function of systematic risk, it is *not* clear that increases in this risk and increases in return are *proportional*.[1]

The question of proportionality in incremental risk and incremental reward is important for many investors because, as implied above, they can use borrowing (or leverage) to *increase* risk and reward, or cash equivalents to *reduce* risk and reward in their own portfolios—without depending upon a proportional progression of higher and higher rewards for higher and higher risks.

It has been suggested that, at the extremes of incremental riskiness, reward does not increase but actually declines. This would be the result if, for example, a sizable number of investors were unrealistic in their appraisal of the potential rewards of high risk stocks and so were to bid up the prices of such stocks to unwarranted levels—from which prices their subsequent rates of return would be insufficient to compensate for the level of market risk taken.

---

[1] An easy test of this question would be to compare the rate of return on a moderate risk, all-equity portfolio with the return on a high risk stock portfolio blended with, say, Treasury bills such that its combined price volatility was equal to the price volatility of a moderate risk, equity-only portfolio. If the high risk stock portfolio's return—after dilution by the Treasury bill return—does not exceed the returns earned in the all-equity, moderate risk portfolio, then incremental return was not worth seeking and the extra risk was not worth taking.

OPTIMAL SYSTEMATIC RISK

The optimal level of systematic or market risk appears to be moderately above the average—for the very long-term investor. This would make sense. Many investors are not free to take a very long-term view because their investments will be liquidated for children's education or at the termination of a trust or for a host of other reasons. Other investors are simply unable to look with calm forbearance on the abrupt and substantial day-to-day and year-to-year changes in stock prices that might be experienced in an aggressive portfolio over the long term. These cautious investors will, as explained above, proffer an above-average rate of return to investors willing to accept—and live with—a greater than average systematic risk level.

The optimal level of systematic risk cannot, however, be very far above the average because it is remarkably difficult to create an efficiently diversified portfolio of large size with significantly above-average market risk. Why? For the simple but compelling reason that there are too few stocks with large market capitalizations and low covariance from which to select the specific stocks with which to build the intended portfolio.

Portfolio managers and institutions managing large, multibillion dollar portfolios will be obliged to make a three-way tradeoff of portfolio volatility (or beta), portfolio diversification, and portfolio liquidity (the ability to sell stock quickly at small price concessions). Practitioners have difficulty finding adequate supplies of stocks with which to build large and efficiently diversified portfolios with betas greater than 1.1 to 1.2. Managers of small portfolios will find the problems of adequate supply far less onerous and may be able to lift portfolio betas above 1.2, and perhaps to 1.3, while still maintaining portfolio diversification and liquidity.

The appropriate level of systematic risk simultaneously integrates (1) what is available in the marketplace and (2) what is right or desirable for the client or beneficiary.

Key Client Characteristics

Determining the level of systematic risk that is desirable for the client is the vital aim of investment counseling. Simplifying for clarity and emphasizing the most important issues, investment counseling seeks to harmonize the portfolio's policy on risk with the goals and perspective of the client on five levels.

First, what are the real risks of an adverse outcome, particularly in the short run? Unacceptable risks should be avoided. For example, it would not make sense to invest all of a high school senior's college tuition savings in the stock market because if—as so often happens—the market went down, the student might not be able to pay the tuition bill. For another example, the worker who is near retirement and will be converting from a company-sponsored profit-sharing plan to an annuity for retirement income should not risk the long-term negative consequences of having to buy a smaller annuity if the market dropped prior to the date of retirement.

Second, what are the probable emotional reactions of clients to an adverse experience? As the axiom goes, some investors care more about eating well and some care more about sleeping well. The portfolio manager should know, and stay well within, the client's risk tolerance.

Third, how knowledgeable about investments is the client? Investing does not always "make sense." Sometimes it seems almost perversely counterintuitive. Portfolio managers can help their clients by explaining the way capital markets behave—and misbehave—and clients can help educate themselves. Lack of knowledge tends to make investors too cautious during bear markets and too confident in bull markets—at considerable cost.

Fourth, what other capital and/or income resources does the client have, and how important is the particular portfolio to the client's overall welfare? Pension funds sponsored by large and prosperous corporations can reasonably accept greater risk than can a college endowment that may have difficulty raising capital to replenish losses, while a retired widow cannot accept as much risk as can her alma mater.

Fifth, what is the time horizon over which the investment portfolio is expected to meet or exceed the investor's return objective? Is there risk of interruption? Time is by far the most important—and often least attended—dimension of investing. Investing for a period of days or weeks should, of course, be limited to high quality money market instruments such as Treasury bills, bankers' acceptances, certificates of deposit, and commercial paper. On the other hand, a portfolio that was certain to remain invested for a very long time, such as 40–50 years, should be invested entirely in equity investments—at least until the horizon date for disinvesting was within a dozen years or so of being reached.

Decisions on the appropriate asset mix for the portfolio and on the market risk appropriate to a particular client or group of clients are an essential preliminary to the propitious management of a portfolio.

Having determined the appropriate systematic or market risk to accept in the portfolio, the portfolio manager's second consideration is the composition of the portfolio. The best prescription in theory is: Start with a fully diversified portfolio that is managed passively at the chosen level of systematic risk and then deviate, *if at all*, only for compelling opportunities to increase return or reduce risk.

Active Management

Remember that deviating from the "market portfolio" incurs either specific risk or extra-market risk and is, therefore, a zero-sum game with, in theory, no reward for taking these avoidable risks. Under these circumstances, the portfolio manager will concentrate any deviation from the market portfolio on either increasing investments in securities with a high probability of incremental return for incremental risk borne or decreasing investments in securities with a negative incremental return relative to incremental risk. The incremental return referred to here is called *alpha*. Managers seek positive alpha securities and attempt to avoid negative alpha securities.

There is remarkably little evidence that would encourage portfolio managers to pursue a highly active portfolio management process. It is very difficult for a portfolio manager regularly to outmaneuver his competitors, and the difficulty increases substantially as assets under management get larger and larger. The investing game includes, after all, transactions costs. It is not just a zero-sum game where the investor achieves a return equal to the benchmark comparison portfolio, but can be a negative-sum game where the net return is reduced by an amount equal to transactions costs.[2]

Some portfolio managers have apparently achieved above-average rates of return in the portfolios they manage by concentrating year after year on a particular concept or style of investing. Some emphasize earnings and dividend growth, some choose stocks with prices that are low in relation to book value, and some focus on other concepts. Interestingly, the successful proponents of the various concepts usually have one characteristic in common: low portfolio turnover. Turning it around, one reason for the low portfolio turnover of these successful investment managers is their fidelity to a particular concept of investing. Another reason is that low turnover allows more time and care to be devoted to each investment decision, which reduces the need to revise opinions and change holdings time and again.[3]

FORMING EQUITY PORTFOLIOS

Each investor has a large number of common stocks from which to choose, representing virtually an infinite number of combinations of expected risk and return. Because higher risk stocks typically promise higher returns, the distribution of returns versus risks will trend up and to the right, as in Figure 2-1.

Portfolios composed of various *combinations* of stocks (including the appropriate dollar amounts invested in each) would have expected returns equal to the weighted average of the expected returns of the constituent stocks. The expected portfolio total risk would be *less* than the weighted average of the risks of the individual stocks, however, because specific risk and extra-market risk can be reduced or even eliminated through diversifica-

---

[2] The nature and implications of the investing game discussed here are contrasted with the nature and implications of the zero-sum trading game described in Chapter 12. I have written more extensively on investing as a negative-sum game in an article titled "The Loser's Game," which appeared in the July/August 1975 issue of the *Financial Analysts Journal*.

[3] Note that low turnover is substantially more important for large institutional investors than for smaller ones. Because the block buying and selling activity of larger institutions tends to move securities' prices up and down, respectively, before a position is established or eliminated, increased institutional trading activity usually will result in adverse price action that is only partially offset by lower negotiated commission rates.

Figure 2-1. Risk-Return Plots for Individual Common Stocks

tion. The factor that measures the degree to which the portfolio's risk and return characteristics are explained and reproduced by the market's rate of return is the coefficient of correlation between the two returns series, *rho*.[4] Much more will be said about this in Chapter 3.

Efficient Portfolios

In Figure 2-2 on page 18, the solid line shows the outside boundary of the risk and return characteristics of the feasible portfolios. Any other combination within the solid line can also be achieved by one or more portfolios. However, an informed and rational investor will want the portfolio that provides the most return for any given level of risk (or the minimum risk for any given level of return). The portfolios that meet these requirements lie along the curved line *AB*. All of the other feasible portfolios are inferior to those on curve *AB* because—as the reader can readily see—at any specified level of *risk* (the horizontal axis), the feasible portfolios *not* on curve *AB* offer a lower expected return, and the rational investor will not want a portfolio that has the same risk but offers a lower expected return. Rather, the investor will want—at that level of risk—the portfolio with the highest feasible expected return, i.e., the one on curve *AB*.

Similarly, at any particular level of expected *return* (the vertical axis), the feasible portfolios *not* on curve *AB* offer a higher risk, and the rational investor will reject a portfolio that offers the same return with greater risk. He will prefer the portfolio with the lowest risk among those with the same expected rate of return. And that "best" portfolio is, again, on curve *AB*.

The efficient portfolio has greater return than any other feasible portfolio with equal risk and less risk than any other feasible portfolio with equal expected return.

---

[4] When portfolio returns are totally explained by market returns, the correlation coefficient, ρ, equals $+1.00$.

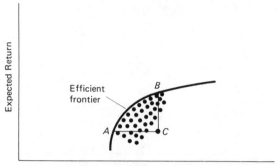

Figure 2-2. Risk-Return Plots for Portfolios of Common Stocks

Borrowing and Lending Portfolios

With the introduction of what is called a "risk-free" asset, an asset located on the vertical axis and therefore having a positive expected return but no risk, the notion of lending and borrowing portfolios can be considered. When this new risk-free asset is introduced, the efficient frontier becomes a straight line running from the risk-free asset on the vertical axis to the point of tangency of the old efficient frontier. This is shown in Figure 2-3.

Lending portfolios—typically consisting of a combination of cash equivalents and common stocks—will be located between points X and Y in Figure 2-3. The proportion of cash to stock will be directly related to how close the portfolio is to the vertical axis.

Assuming the investor can borrow and use leverage in designing the portfolio, the feasible set of portfolios will be located on line XYZ between Y and Z in Figure 2-3, if Z represents the maximum allowable use of leverage.

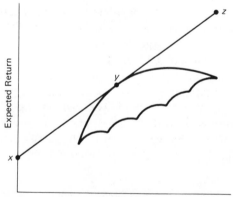

Figure 2-3. Borrowing and Lending Portfolios of Common Stocks

The specific portfolio that should be established for a given investor will depend on the investor's risk and reward objectives, but the mix of stocks will be the same in every case: a fully diversified portfolio, *Y,* which offers the highest achievable reward per unit of risk at the point of tangency of *XYZ* and the original curvilinear efficient frontier.

CHOOSING OPTIMAL PORTFOLIOS

Selecting the specific portfolio for a particular investor will depend upon the investment counseling process outlined above. In general, it would be instructive for the client and the portfolio manager to examine together the probable path of experience a proposed portfolio—chosen from the efficient set of portfolios arrayed along the line *XYZ* in Figure 2-3—would have had in the actual markets experienced over the past 10 or 20 years. This examination should concentrate on the most disagreeable periods so the client and the portfolio manager can assess how distressing the experience would have been for the client, and whether the client's risk tolerance would have been exceeded by the probable experience. If so, the portfolio manager and client may decide to increase the proportion of risk-free assets in the portfolio, moving along the *XYZ* line to a portfolio somewhat closer to *X,* so that the chosen portfolio better matches the client's risk tolerance.

Remember, the most important factor in these decisions will be time, that is, the probable time horizon of the investment program. Thus, for example, a young unmarried executive with no financial obligations may appropriately invest entirely in common stocks with an average beta of 1.3 or use some "margin" to add leverage to his portfolio; then, ten years later, as the head of a young family, he may use less leverage but stay invested entirely in aggressive equities; then, as children approach college age, he should probably shift to more conservative equities and bonds; after the children have grown up, he might move more assertively into common stocks, perhaps again using leverage; and finally in retirement he should move toward a conservatively balanced stock and bond portfolio.

ACTIVE MANAGEMENT

Once the optimal passive portfolio has been constructed to satisfy the investor's needs and objectives, the portfolio manager and client can consider actively managing the portfolio, attempting to capture incremental rates of return over the market average rate of return. Consideration can be given to any of three types of decisions: tactics, strategy, and philosophy.

Tactical Decisions

The first of these, tactical decisions—often called "stock picking"—absorbs most of the time, skills, and energy of most portfolio managers and analysts.

Through financial analysis or field studies of competitors and suppliers, as well as management interviews, investors seek to attain a better understanding of the investment *value* of a security or group of securities than that represented by the market consensus. When investment managers find significant differences between the *value* of a security (as they appraise it) and the *price* of that security (as the overall investment community appraises it), they will buy or sell, as appropriate, to capture the differential between market price and investment value for their clients' portfolios.

Strategic Decisions

The second type of decision making, strategy, involves major commitments that affect the overall structure of the portfolio. They are made to exploit insights into major industry groups or major factors such as changes in interest rates or anticipated shifts in the valuation of major categories of stocks—e.g., "emerging growth" stocks or "basic industry" stocks—each of which would involve what has already been described as extra-market risk.

For example, in 1980 portfolio managers who invested heavily in oil and technology stocks had very favorable results, while investors who chose instead to invest heavily in utilities and other interest sensitive stocks or in consumer stocks were heavily penalized. In the early 1970s portfolio managers who invested heavily in large-capitalization growth stocks—the "nifty fifty"—experienced exceptionally favorable results as the notorious two-tier market developed. This was a market where an inordinately large demand for top-tier large-capitalization growth stocks occurred at the expense of normal demand for smaller-cap nongrowth issues. In the later 1970s large positions in these same securities produced exceptionally negative results when institutions became disenchanted with the concept and dumped their holdings. As the saying goes, it is not a stock market but a market of stocks—one that invites portfolio managers (not without peril) to make major strategic decisions on groups of stocks in the portfolios they manage.

Philosophic Decisions

The last category, philosophic decisions, involves the enduring investment commitments—through cycle after cycle in the stock market and in the business economy—to which a portfolio manager or an entire investment management organization adheres with persistence and fidelity. An organization that is committed to growth stock investing will concentrate upon and build important experience in such skills as: evaluating new technologies, understanding the management capabilities required to guide the strategies and practices of rapidly growing organizations, analyzing the financial requirements of investing in new markets and new products to sustain growth, and learning from experience—no doubt sometimes painful experience—

how to discriminate between ersatz growth stocks that fizzle out and true leading growth companies that achieve success over many years.

Other investment management organizations have taken the view that among the many large corporations in mature and often cyclical industries there are always some that have considerably greater investment value than is recognized by other investors. They believe that with an astute research capability these superior values can be isolated and that by buying good values at depressed prices they can achieve superior returns for their clients with relatively low risk. Such organizations will develop considerable expertise in "separating the wheat from the chaff," avoiding the low priced stocks that *ought* to be low priced and ferreting out insights into investment value that other investors have not yet recognized.

Among the variety of concepts of investing that can be pursued over many years, one emphasizes medium-sized growth companies in specialized industries while another focuses on assets rather than earnings, with confidence that carefully chosen, well-positioned assets can be redeployed to earn greater profits. Another group of investors—contrary opinion investors—will concentrate on stocks that are clearly out of favor with other investors, confident that, with prices depressed, they will find bargains if they analyze the companies dispassionately.

The important test of a philosophy or style is a manager's ability to adhere to it for valid, long-term reasons, even when the short-term results are most disagreeable and frightening. Persistence can lead to mastery and development of an important distinctive competence in the particular kind of investing in which the manager specializes. More will be said about constructing equity portfolios in Chapter 10.

FIXED INCOME MANAGEMENT

Thus far our discussion has concentrated on equity investments. Bond portfolio management is somewhat different but basically the same.

The portfolio manager should start with a passive portfolio that will meet the client's feasible goals and objectives. This portfolio would be diversified across numerous issues to protect against the credit risk of individual issuers and would use some defensive or *immunization* strategy to defend against adverse changes in interest rates. A naive version of such a strategy might be an evenly spaced schedule of maturities. The overall quality (or rating) of the portfolio will be set in concert with the beneficiaries' risk preferences and potential liquidity needs. In this writer's view the historical evidence is quite persuasive that the specific risk of individual bonds—which dominate the rating agencies' ratings—can be substantially eliminated through diversification with the result that *in portfolios,* medium to lower grade issues do—after adjustment for all actual losses through defaults on either interest or principal or both—provide higher net returns *over time* than higher grade issues.

As in stocks, bonds present extra-market risks to the investor. For example, bonds issued by companies in a particular industry will change in value with major changes in industry economics; the normal difference in yield (and therefore price) between otherwise identical corporate and government bonds tends to change gradually in undulating long-wave patterns; bonds with particular call or refunding features in common will rise and fall together in relative market popularity.[5] The portfolio, of course, should be diversified against this risk of unexpected price behavior.

Having established a well-diversified portfolio, the manager and beneficiaries may decide to deviate deliberately from the normal or baseline portfolio in an effort to increase returns or reduce risk or both by: (1) buying or selling individual issues in anticipation of a recognition by other investors of a change in quality rating, (2) switching from a sector of the market that is relatively high in price relative to historical norms to a sector that is relatively low in price, (3) selling an issue that is temporarily high in price (perhaps because of a market imperfection) and simultaneously buying an equivalent issue that is lower in price (the so-called arbitrage swap), or (4)—and this is where the greatest impact on return can be effected—changing the average maturity of the entire portfolio, going for long maturities (and call protection) when interest rates are expected to fall and shortening up on maturity when interest rates are expected to rise, both to an extent not already anticipated in the market's yield curve; or shortening maturities when large yield and price volatility is anticipated that will be counter to the portfolio beneficiary's objectives. More will be said about constructing bond portfolios in Chapter 9.

ASSET MIX CONSIDERATIONS

Typically investors manage the bond and stock portfolios as separate entities—each separately composed—and then they combine the two in proportions that give the overall portfolio an asset mix suitable to the investor's objectives.

An important exception to this practice should be made whenever the portfolio manager has made an important *equity* portfolio commitment based on an expected change in interest rates. The overall portfolio should be hedged against the possible failure of the manager's prediction to come true. So, if the expectation is that interest rates will fall substantially and interest sensitive stocks are being bought heavily in the equity portfolio, the manager should not fall unwittingly into the easy trap of also lengthening the maturities of the *bond* portfolio—doubling the portfolio's exposure to the possible risk of interest rates *not* falling—but should instead balance the equity portfolio bet on a drop in rates with a bond portfolio hedge bet on a rise in rates. Much more will be said about the asset mix decision in Chapter 8.

---

[5] It should be noted that rating agencies have found most of their rating errors caused by the difficulty inherent in estimating such extra-market risks.

A CONCLUDING REMARK

Portfolio management is the central work of investment management, and it is only in the context of a particular portfolio—and the realistic objectives of the particular portfolio beneficiary—that individual securities and specific investment decisions can be fully and correctly understood. And it is in the portfolio context that investors have learned to appreciate that their objective is not to manage reward but to control and manage risk.

CHAPTER 3

Basic Financial Concepts: Return and Risk

Keith P. Ambachtsheer

James H. Ambrose

The preceding chapter provided an overview of the major issues in portfolio management. In this chapter a careful building block approach to explain portfolio management as a multipart, logical, systematic process is begun. To tell the whole story we need to begin with an explanation of the basic concepts of risk and return.

The idea that both risk and return can be decomposed into components or factors is introduced. Most securities have attributes that can be segmented into those unique to the security and its issuer, and those it has in common with other securities and/or their issuers. Generally, unique factor risks can be diversified away and may not be rewarded with excess or unique return. Common factor risks, on the other hand, cannot be diversified away and hence should produce return premiums if investors are risk-averse.

The chapter continues with discussions of market efficiency and predictive ability and their potential effects on prospective return and risk. Clearly, in a world of perfect clairvoyance there would be no uncertainty and hence no risk. But what about a world where some are more clairvoyant than others? Can the same security have different risk/return characteristics for different investors? Those readers who answer yes to this question correctly anticipate our message.

The entire chapter has an important underlying premise. Research has provided and will continue to provide us with a wealth of information about return realization. While this knowledge should contribute to a better understanding of financial market behavior, it should never become a substitute for the creative process of anticipating future capital market prospects.

However derived, expressions of prospective risk and return always have been and always will be based on subjective judgments. Although the quantification of risk and return prospects is a valuable exercise, it does not change the reality that the derivation of these prospects is at least as much art as it is science.

Time—As a Factor in Investment Management

Earning a return on investment requires the passage of time. Only two types of time passage are important in investment management: time that has already passed and time that has yet to pass. The former permits objective measurement of the rate of investment return that has been achieved; the latter, dealing with results not yet achieved, requires subjective or expectational expressions of investment return. Ideally, these expressions deal not only with the investment return most likely to be achieved but also with how widely the actual result might depart from that deemed to be most likely.

The organization of this chapter flows naturally from the two types of time reality. It will rapidly become apparent to the reader that no single investment return measure can answer all possible "What happened?" questions. Indeed, a single set of investment results can produce many different return measures, all equally correct. The reasons for these differences lie in the question "Who is asking 'what happened' for what reason?" Taxes, inflation, fees, and the timing of cash flows can all play major roles in the correct return calculation. Whether the inclusion of any one or some combination of these factors is appropriate can be judged only in the context of the answer to the question posed above.

In moving to *future* passages of time, the investor must leave behind the objective world of return realization, or *ex post* known past returns, and enter the subjective world of return prospects, or *ex ante* unknown and uncertain future returns. Extra equipment is needed to deal with this new world. In this chapter we show how measures such as expected return, return standard deviation, and correlation can be useful in describing prospective returns and their associated degree of uncertainty. The potential effects of inflation and taxes on these measures are also discussed.

RETURN REALIZATIONS

The word *return* for most people conjures up an image of some number that is both correct and exact. Very seldom is this the case.

While return, whether expected or realized, is one of the most important attributes of any financial asset, actual usage and application can often be misleading. There are numerous return calculations, most of which are specific to particular assets.

For example, two of the commonly used bond return measures are current yield (coupon divided by purchase price) and yield to maturity (the rate of discount that equates the present value of all future interest and principal repayments with the purchase price).

Measures of return on stocks include dividend and earnings yield (dividend or earnings divided by current or purchase price). Returns on real estate can be calculated on the total cost of the asset or on the net cost after a mortgage.

Total Return Measure

These traditional measures of return all have their uses. But how can return be expressed so that a unique, rational, and comparable measure results, no matter what the asset class? The best candidate is probably *total return* or *holding period return* (*R*):

$$1 + R = \frac{\begin{array}{c}\text{income payments received}\\\text{during period in dollars}\end{array} + \begin{array}{c}\text{value at end of}\\\text{period in dollars}\end{array}}{\text{value at beginning of period in dollars}}$$

The advantage of this return measure is that it can be used for both historical data and future expectations. It measures the total return over any time period and permits a rational comparison across all asset classes.

If you own a stock that was purchased on January 1 for $10, received $1 in dividends at year-end, and the stock's value is $11 on December 31, then its total return or holding period return is:

$$R = \frac{1 + 11}{10} - 1 = .2, \text{ or } 20\%$$

Ibbotson and Sinquefield [1982] have shown that $1.00 invested in the Standard & Poor's 500 Composite Stock Index (S&P 500) at the end of 1925 would have grown to $133.60 by the end of 1981 if all dividends had been reinvested and no taxes or transaction costs paid. The overall 56-year total return then is:

$$R = \frac{133.6}{1} - 1 = 132.6, \text{ or } 13.260\%$$

This can be converted into an annual total return by solving for:

$$R = \sqrt[56]{1 + 132.6} - 1 = 9.1\%$$

This 9.1% can also be shown to be the geometric mean of the 56 one-year total returns that turned a single dollar into $133.60. Hereafter, when the word *return* is used, it will be used in the context of total or holding period return.

Arithmetic Mean Return

Ibbotson and Sinquefield also report an annual *arithmetic mean* return of 11.4 percent for the same investment experience. There is an important conceptual difference between annual geometric and arithmetic mean returns. The former is a measure of the per period growth rate of the original investment. (In our example, the original $1.00 grows at 9.1 percent compounded annually to become $133.60 56 years later.) By contrast, the arithmetic mean return measures the average return on a dollar invested in *each* of the 56 years.

A two-period example will help to clarify the difference. Ibbotson and Sinquefield report stock returns of −26.47 percent and 37.2 percent for the years 1974 and 1975, respectively. By the end of 1973 the $1.00 investment at the end of 1925 had become $72.50. The negative return in 1974 of −26.47 percent would produce a value of $72.50(1 − .265) = $53.31 at the end of 1974. The value at the end of 1975 would have been $53.31(1 + .372) = $73.14. In those two years of the 56-year holding period, the investment grows from $72.50 at the end of 1973 to $73.14 at the end of 1975, for a compound annual return (i.e., geometric mean return) of 0.4 percent. The correctness of this number can be verified: $72.50(1.004)(1.004) ≈ $73.14. By contrast, the average annual return on a dollar invested in each of the two years is simply (−26.47% + 37.2%) divided by 2, or 5.36 percent. Note that the arithmetic mean return cannot accurately measure long-term growth in the value of an investment, especially if year-to-year returns fluctuate significantly.

The major benefit of both return measures is their applicability across different types of investments. See Table 3-1 below for a comparison of long-term returns on four key asset categories and the rate of inflation.

Making Return Adjustments

While the pretransaction cost, premanagement and custodial fee, pretax, preinflation adjusted total returns discussed above can serve many useful purposes, they are obviously less well suited to others.

TABLE 3-1. **Total Annual Returns 1926–1981**

	Geometric Mean	Arithmetic Mean
Common Stocks	9.1%	11.4%
Corporate Bonds	3.6	3.7
Treasury Bonds	3.0	3.1
Treasury Bills	3.0	3.1
Inflation	3.0	3.1

SOURCE: Ibbotson and Sinquefield [1982]

TABLE 3-2. Sample Portfolio Accounting
Statement

Total Value

1. Beginning of year $1,000,000
2. End of year $1,200,000

Cash Flows

End-of-year total value includes the following
cash flows:
1. $75,000 was received in dividends and inter-
est during the year, net of $15,000 in custo-
dial and management fees.
2. The balance represents capital gains.

Other Information

1. The client's tax rate on investment income is
a maximum of 50 percent, on capital appreciation a maximum of 20 percent.
2. The Consumer Price Index increased 14
percent during the year.

A portfolio accounting statement (see Table 3-2) lends itself to not just one but many return calculations. Gross (before fee deductions) calculations can be made by adding the fees back to the net market values. After-tax calculations can be made by adjusting market values for taxes payable. Finally, real return calculations can be made by adjusting the nominal results for inflation.

Consider the case of a portfolio manager who has just been asked to report last year's return on a client fund. The manager has the information shown in Table 3-2. Set out below are descriptions of the various return measures, evaluations of their usefulness, and return calculations based on the portfolio accounting statement data.

Types of Returns

Gross Return. This measure is the one most commonly used by tax-exempt funds such as pension funds to compare the performance of managers. It does *not* deduct managerial and custodial fees, as these vary with fund size.

$$R = \frac{1,200,000 + 15,000}{1,000,000} - 1 = 21.5\%$$

Hence, the one-year return achieved by the manager, before expenses, was 21.5 percent.

Net Return. This measure costs out the management and custodial fees. It is used most frequently in measuring mutual fund performance where fees are a fixed percentage of assets.

$$R = \frac{1,200,000}{1,000,000} - 1 = 20.0\%$$

Net After-tax Return. The before-tax return does not take into account the $37,500 in tax liabilities on investment income (50% × $75,000) and $25,000 in potential tax liabilities on unrealized capital gains (20% × $125,000) that have accrued.

$$R = \frac{1,200,000 - 37,500 - 25,000}{1,000,000} - 1 = 13.75\%$$

Net After-tax Real Return. High nominal returns may merely reflect a high inflation rate. The sample portfolio accounting statement reported that a 14 percent return was required just to maintain purchasing power during the year.

$$R = \frac{1,200,000 - 37,500 - 25,000}{1,000,000 \, (1.14)} - 1 = -0.2\%$$

In answering the fund annual return question, 21.5 percent, 20.0 percent, 13.75 percent, and −0.2 percent all constitute technically correct answers. In a comparative tax-exempt world, the gross before-tax return, 21.5 percent, is probably most useful. Taxes are not a factor here. Inflation affects all funds equally and, therefore, does not affect return comparability.

A 21.5 percent response will be highly misleading, however, when made to a taxable client wishing to ascertain if the investment is earning a positive net after-tax real return. In this context the real, after-tax, and management cost-adjusted return of −0.2 percent is the most appropriate number.

RETURN EXPECTATIONS

Measuring return realizations accurately and with the appropriate return measure is of obvious importance. One must know what has happened in the past. This activity can, however, never serve as a substitute for activity that focuses on returns that may be realized in the *future*. The former deals with past realizations, the latter with expectations.

Possible Scenarios

Having been informed that last year's net after-tax real return realization was −0.2 percent, for example, the inquisitive client might well ask the manager what fund return he expects for *next* year. The manager explains that his organization sees the following four basic longer term scenarios as possible environments in which the capital markets might have to function.

- **STAGFLATION (SF).** This is a "muddle through" period of relative capital market stability with little change in interest rates, stable price/earnings ratios, and earnings maintaining a constant share of national income.
- **DEFLATION (DEF).** This scenario is characterized by a combination of policy errors and bad luck, setting off a worldwide financial crisis, which in turn leads to a collapse of real output and a break in inflation psychology. Stock prices and interest rates collapse.
- **RUNAWAY INFLATION (RAI).** In this situation the flight from money into real assets takes another turn for the worse as new policy initiatives founder. Interest rates continue to climb. Stock price behavior is mixed, with share performance directly related to the perceived inflation immunity of earnings.
- **BETTER TIMES (OK).** Here new policy initiatives create a producer society and reduce world tensions. Renewed productivity gains reduce inflationary pressures. Interest rates decline as stock prices hit new highs.

After careful analysis the organization's investment policy committee has constructed a one-year return matrix for stocks, bonds, and Treasury bills. This was done on the assumption that, although none of the scenarios will have totally unfolded by the end of the one-year horizon, it will be evident to investors which one of the four is unfolding and thus they can price securities accordingly. The policy committee assigned best judgment probabilities to the four possible environments. The resulting matrix is reproduced in Table 3-3 on page 32.[1]

The matrix represents an explicit statement by the policy committee of its views about future capital market reward and risk. The standardization of these views into measurements that would facilitate their evaluation and their use in investment policy formation is of obvious benefit.

Expected Return

In his now celebrated article "Portfolio Selection," Harry Markowitz [1952] suggested three such measures. The first of these was the probability-weighted average return, or "expected return." The returns that will actually occur will of course depend on the economic scenario that unfolds. The

---

[1] While the returns in Table 3-3 have been constructed to convey some degree of realism, they should be viewed as hypothetical. Their main purpose is the development of measures of prospective return and risk. Chapters 6 and 7 will deal with the *process* of expectations formation.

TABLE 3-3. One-Year Nominal Before-Tax Returns

| | ECONOMIC SCENARIO | | | |
	SF	DEF	RAI	OK
Probability	0.4	0.2	0.3	0.1
Investment Strategies				
Stocks	18%	−15%	15%	60%
Bonds	14	35	−10	30
T-bills	11	7	18	8

expected return, however, is the best estimate; it is the *probability*-weighted average return. Its calculation for our example is shown in Table 3-4.

Relating this expected return measure back to the return realizations discussion, it is the average annual return expected to be realized over one-year holding periods with capital markets prospects similar to the period about to commence. An important use of expected return is to compare values across asset classes and across time. For example, in the coming holding period the expected excess return of stocks over Treasury bills is 2.7 percent. Ibbotson and Sinquefield report a 1926–1981 average annual realized excess return of 8.3 percent. Why is the expected risk premium for holding common stocks low by historical standards? This is a legitimate question that the investment policy committee must be prepared to answer.

The other important use of expected return is in portfolio construction. Clearly, high return assets are to be preferred to low return assets, all else being equal. However, in capital markets dominated by risk-averse investors, high return assets can only be purchased at the price of accepting commensurate risk. Markowitz's second and third measures quantify this risk. They will be discussed in subsequent sections.

Before leaving this section, let us return to the curious client and the portfolio manager. The nominal, before-tax, expected return matrix produced by the manager's investment policy committee is of limited value to a client interested in real, after-tax returns. From his knowledge of the client's

TABLE 3-4. Calculation of Expected Returns

| Economic Scenario | Probability | INVESTMENT STRATEGIES | | |
		Stocks	Bonds	T-bills
SF	0.4	× 18 = 7.2%	× 14 = 5.6%	× 11 = 4.4%
DEF	0.2	× −15 = −3.0	× 35 = 7.0	× 7 = 1.4
RAI	0.3	× 15 = 4.5	× −10 = −3.0	× 18 = 5.4
OK	0.1	× 60 = 6.0	× 30 = 3.0	× 8 = 0.8
Expected Return =		14.7%	12.6%	12.0%

Note: Sample calculation of expected return for stocks = (0.4)(18) + (0.2)(−15) + (0.3)(15) + (0.1)(60) = 14.7%.

TABLE 3-5. Real, After-Tax Expected Returns

	ECONOMIC SCENARIO				Expected Return
	SF	DEF	RAI	OK	
Probability	0.4	0.2	0.3	0.1	
Investment Strategies					
Stocks	2%	−18%	−8%	36%	−1.6%
Bonds	−3	17	−29	11	−5.4%
T-bills	−4½	−2½	−9	−4	−5.4%

tax status and the committee's projected inflation rates for stagflation, deflation, runaway inflation, and better times of 10, 6, 18, and 8 percent, respectively, the manager can construct (using the manipulations discussed above in "Return Realizations") a real, after-tax, expected return matrix for the client such as that shown in Table 3-5.

These prospects leave the manager and the client with nothing but unhappy choices, ranging from finding a new asset class with a positive, after-tax real expected return, to praying for tax relief, to simply hoping the better times environment actually comes to pass!

RISK AND UNCERTAINTY

The Oxford Dictionary includes in its definition of the word *risk* the following: "chance of bad consequences, . . . exposure to chance of injury or loss." Most people understand the concept—risk refers to the possibility of an unpleasant outcome.

As a measure of risk the definition above is somewhat vague. Traditionally security analysts have looked at the worst possible outcome, or downside risk, versus the upside potential. Although a step in the right direction, it is only a partial answer to describing risk adequately.

Measures of Risk

Another approach is to apply probabilities to the possibility of loss. But if asked which was riskier, a 50 percent chance of a small loss or a 45 percent chance of a large loss, most investors would find the second riskier.

Standard Deviation. There is a measure that takes into account not only the probability and magnitude of a range of outcomes but also the amount the return is likely to diverge from the expected return. The statistical measure *standard deviation* takes all three into account. Standard deviation can be adjusted and used to measure only the unpleasant outcomes if desired. However, as return outcomes tend to be symmetrical about the expected return, we usually simply use standard deviation, which measures a specified proportion of the outcome range of possible returns. This includes both desirable and undesirable outcomes.

Variance. Earlier we referred to three standard measurements proposed by Markowitz to summarize risk and reward. He pointed out that, just as expected return had useful analytical qualities, so did *return standard deviation* (σ) or its square, *return variance* (σ^2). Like expected return, standard deviation and variance can be directly derived from an expected return matrix like the one produced by the investment policy committee in Table 3-4.

In Table 3-6a the nominal, before-tax returns and their probability of occurrence are given. The expected return for each asset class is calculated by multiplying each possible outcome by its probability of occurrence. Adding the results produces the expected return, $E(R)$.

In Table 3-6b the $E(R)$ is subtracted from each nominal return. For example, "stocks in SF," nominal return minus expected return equals: $18 - 14.7 = 3.3$.

In Table 3-6c the numbers produced in 3-6b are squared and multiplied by their probability of occurrence. Thus "stocks in SF" becomes $(3.3)^2 \times 0.4 = 4.4$.

By adding these probability-weighted squared deviations we arrive at the variance of returns. The standard deviation is the square root of the variance (e.g., stocks: $\sqrt{386.0} = 19.6$).

The return standard deviations implicit in the return projections and their assigned probabilities turn out to be 19.6 percent for stocks, 16.9 percent for bonds, and 4.2 percent for Treasury bills. Again, a measure has been created

TABLE 3-6. Standard Deviation

	ECONOMIC SCENARIOS				
	SF	DEF	RAI	OK	E(R)
Probability	0.4	0.2	0.3	0.1	
a. Nominal, Before-Tax Returns					
Stocks	18%	−15%	15%	60%	14.7%
Bonds	14	35	−10	30	12.6%
T-bills	11	7	18	8	12.0%
b. Deviations Around Expected Returns					
Stocks	3.3	−29.7	0.3	45.3	
Bonds	1.4	22.4	−22.6	17.4	
T-bills	−1.0	−5.0	6.0	−4.0	

						σ^2	σ
c. Probability-Weighted Squared Deviations							
Stocks	4.4 +	176.4 +	0.0 +	205.2	=	386.0	19.6
Bonds	0.8 +	100.3 +	153.2 +	30.3	=	284.6	16.9
T-bills	0.4 +	5.0	10.8 +	1.6	=	17.8	4.2

that permits comparisons across asset classes and across time. Ibbotson and Sinquefield report 1926–1981 return standard deviations of 21.9, 5.7, and 3.1 percent for stocks, long government bonds, and Treasury bills, respectively. An obvious question for our investment policy committee is why it sees a much wider range of return outcomes for bonds in the upcoming holding period than that experienced year-to-year during the period 1926–1981 (i.e., a projected standard deviation of 16.9 percent versus an historical standard deviation of 5.7 percent). While we can only speculate on the answer, the committee's uncertainty with respect to the effect of government policies on future inflation is apparent in the scenario descriptions and probability assignments.

Covariance/Correlation. There was a third investment return related measure that Markowitz introduced in his paper. *Return correlation* (ρ) measures the degree to which two asset class (or security) returns are expected to covary with each other. Judgments about covariability are of importance in structuring portfolios. (The basic relationships of covariance to correlation are discussed in the chapter appendix.) Portfolio risk depends not only on the risk of the securities in the portfolio but also on the degree to which diversification can reduce these risks. Correlation coefficients range from +1 to −1 with:

+1 = perfect positive correlation
 0 = no correlation
−1 = perfect negative correlation

Diversification can reduce portfolio risk only if security return covariability is less than perfect (this will be covered in more detail later in this chapter).

As with the expected return and standard deviation measures, the correlation coefficient can also be calculated from the now-familiar policy committee expected return matrix, as demonstrated in Table 3-7. Parts a and b in Table 3-7 (see page 36) are the same as parts a and b in Table 3-6 with two exceptions: the standard deviations are included and the numbers are for stocks and bonds only.

Table 3-7c gives the probability-weighted deviation cross products. These are calculated by multiplying the deviation around expected returns (3-7b) for stocks and bonds, and then multiplying that result by the probability of occurrence. For stocks and bonds under SF, this becomes: (3.3)(1.4)(0.4) = 1.8. This is completed for each scenario; the sum of the four cross products is the covariance.

In 3-7d the covariance of stocks and bonds is divided by the product of the standard deviations of stocks and bonds, producing the correlation coefficient. In this manner the covariability of returns is standardized.

The stock-bond and stock-bill return correlations implicit in the return matrix (see Table 3-8 on page 37) both turn out to be close to zero (−0.16 and 0.13, respectively). These results are consistent with the diversity in return

TABLE 3-7. Calculation of Correlation Coefficients

	ECONOMIC SCENARIOS					
	SF	DEF	RAI	OK	E(R)	σ
Probabilities	0.4	0.2	0.3	0.1		
a. Nominal, Before-Tax Expected Returns						
Stocks	18%	−15%	15%	60%	14.7%	19.6%
Bonds	14	35	−10	30	12.6%	16.9%
b. Deviations Around Expected Returns						
Stocks	3.3%	−29.7%	0.3%	45.3%		
Bonds	1.4	22.4	−22.6	17.4		

c. Probability-Weighted Deviation Cross Products

						Cov
Stocks and Bonds	1.8	− 133.1	− 2.0	+ 78.8	=	−54.5

d. Correlation Coefficients

				ρ
Stocks and Bonds	−54.5	÷	(19.6 × 16.9)	= −0.16

outcomes projected across the four capital market scenarios. Referring again to the 1926–1981 period, the stock-government bond and stock-bill correlations based on one-year holding periods were 0.02 and −0.13, respectively.

While the signs for the two sets of correlations are reversed, both prospective and retrospective numbers suggest little correlation between stock returns and bond or Treasury bill returns. By contrast, the −0.99 bond-bill correlation suggests that, prospectively, high bond returns will almost certainly go hand in hand with low Treasury bill returns and vice versa (this can be easily confirmed by inspecting the original return matrix). The 1926–1981 bond-bill correlation was virtually zero (−0.01). Consequently, the investment policy committee has (as it did with its prospective bond return standard deviation) some explaining to do. We would again speculate that it would contrast its very high uncertainty regarding prospective inflation (and therefore prospective interest rates) with the now "certain," one-way historical phenomenon of steadily rising inflation and interest rates. When interest rates can fall as well as rise, bonds and Treasury bills clearly can become hedging assets with respect to each other.

PURCHASING POWER RISK

The potential impact of taxes and inflation on returns from investments has already been explored. Continuing that exploration in this section, we will show that when (a) the future course of inflation is highly uncertain and

TABLE 3-8. Nominal and Real Return Matrix

| | Nominal Return | | | | Real Return | | | |
| | ECONOMIC SCENARIO | | | | ECONOMIC SCENARIO | | | |
	SF	*DEF*	*RAI*	*OK*	*SF*	*DEF*	*RAI*	*OK*
Probability	0.4	0.2	0.3	0.1	0.4	0.2	0.3	0.1
Returns								
Stocks	18%	−15%	15%	60%	8%	−21%	−3%	52%
Bonds	14	35	−10	30	4	29	−28	22
T-bills	11	7	18	8	1	1	0	0
Inflation	10	6	18	8	—	—	—	—

	Expected Return	Standard Deviation	Expected Return	Standard Deviation
Stocks	14.7%	19.6%	3.3%	19.4%
Bonds	12.6	16.9	1.2	21.4
T-bills	12.0	4.2	0.6	0.5
Inflation	11.4	4.6	—	—

Correlation Matrix

| | NOMINAL RETURN | | | | REAL RETURN | | |
	Stocks	*Bonds*	*T-bills*	*Inflation*	*Stocks*	*Bonds*	*T-bills*
Stocks	1.00				1.00		
Bonds	−0.16	1.00			0.06	1.00	
T-bills	0.13	−0.99	1.00		−0.31	0.64	1.00
Inflation	0.12	−0.98	1.00	1.00	—	—	—

(b) nominal return realizations are expected to be systematically related to inflation realizations, nominal return and risk measures can mislead investors interested in real rather than nominal return prospects.

The investment policy committee's return matrix, shown in Table 3-8, effectively demonstrates this phenomenon. In building the real return matrix the original estimates were merely adjusted by the projected inflation rate in each scenario.

In adjusting the nominal expected returns to real expected returns, there are no surprises: They all decrease by the expected inflation rate. There are changes in the standard deviations, however. Because of the almost perfect negative correlation between bonds and inflation, the range of real returns is magnified. For example, when inflation is high, bonds do badly; the result is a low nominal return, reduced further by high inflation. With the Treasury bills the result is almost the reverse. The expected return drops to 0.6 percent in real terms, but so does the standard deviation. The expected standard deviation for Treasury bills in real terms decreases to 0.5 percent.

Although the correlation coefficient between bonds and bills has changed from −0.99 in nominal terms to 0.64 in real terms, Treasury bills continue to be a good portfolio risk reducer because of their very low real return standard deviation. This very low standard deviation makes the new correlation measure that involves bills and bonds both less meaningful and less important.

In the bonds-bills case, the big correlation swing simply means that, once the inflation impact is removed, the little return variability left in bill returns moves positively with real bond return variability (which, as was noted, is larger than nominal bond return variability).

The outcome that real Treasury bill and bond returns are projected to have a positive correlation is in fact consistent with historical experience.

Let us turn our attention to a real after-tax return using a 50 percent income tax rate and a 20 percent capital gains tax rate (see Table 3-9). The economic scenario returns are produced in Table 3-5 so we will not reproduce them here. While the income tax is based only on nominal income received, the capital gains tax is based on capital gains and losses as if they were realized in each period. Where losses occur, a tax credit is received. These taxes affect the different assets in very different ways. First, they make all the expected returns (in this particular tax bracket) become negative. However, stocks maintain their lead, with the Treasury bill and bond returns being identical. Stocks still have a lower standard deviation than bonds, but the tax effect in this case *increases* the standard deviation of Treasury bill returns.

As we have shown in the foregoing sections moving from nominal to real (both before-tax) to real, after-tax measures of risk and return leads to considerable changes in results. Although inflation has reduced the expected return substantially, it has increased the outcome range of bond returns adjusted for loss of purchasing power. Conversely, the real return outcome range for Treasury bills has become almost insignificant. The addition of taxes further reduced expected returns and the outcome range for stocks and bonds but increased the outcome range for bills. In moving from nominal to

TABLE 3-9. Real After-Tax Summary Statistics

Investment Strategy	Expected Returns	Standard Deviation
Stocks	− 1.6%	14.6%
Bonds	− 5.4	17.2
T-bills	− 5.4	2.7

Correlation Matrix

	Stocks	Bonds	T-bills
Stocks	1.00	—	—
Bonds	0.15	1.00	—
T-bills	0.08	0.97	1.00

real returns, the change in correlation coefficient between bonds and Treasury bills was large but not material because of the insignificant standard deviation of bill returns.

The lesson learned from the foregoing is that it is extremely important for the investor to specify in what terms—nominal or real, before-tax or after-tax—he wishes to have expected returns, standard deviations, and correlation coefficients calculated, because there is no simple, straightforward relationship among the various ways return and risk can be measured.

DISCRETE AND CONTINUOUS DISTRIBUTIONS

The return-risk exposition in this chapter was based on four possible capital market states and their probabilities of occurrence. In statistical terms, judgments about stock, bond, and bill returns were expressed as *discrete* probability distributions. That is, only a finite (four in this case) number of outcomes were considered. The reader should recognize that these discrete probability distributions, while highly useful from a planning and communication standpoint, are approximations of *continuous* distributions. That is, when the investment policy committee produced its return matrix, it identified four sets of forces that would impact on interest rates and stock prices in different ways. The committee should not claim to have identified *all* possible forces, nor should it assume that those that were identified will produce the exact returns projected. For these reasons, return distributions with a continuous relationship between possible return outcomes and their probability of occurrence are sometimes used in investment analysis.

Normal Distribution

The specific continuous relationship most often assumed is a *normal*, or bell-shaped one, as it tends to approximate security return distributions reasonably well. Using the parameters (i.e., the reward-risk measures) derived for prospective stock returns as captured in the return matrix, three ways of describing the associated return distribution are shown in Figure 3-1 on page 40.

One attractive feature of the continuous normal return distribution is that it is completely described by its expected return and standard deviation. Ibbotson and Sinquefield used this feature in projecting the prospects for stock returns from 1982 to 2001. Using an expected inflation rate of 12.4 percent—much higher than assumed in their earlier studies—they simulated the return outcome ranges yearly to 2001 as shown in Figure 3-2 on page 40.

Geometric Mean

The return measure in Figure 3-2 is, appropriately, the annual geometric mean return. Its expected value to the year 2000 worked out to 18.7 percent.

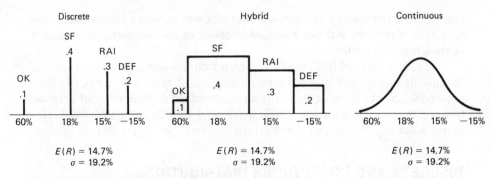

Figure 3-1. Prospective Stock Return Distributions.

In 1982 there was an estimated 5 percent chance the realized return would exceed 26.1 percent. Similarly, there was a 5 percent chance it would be less than 11.4 percent.

While longer and longer time horizons will reduce the range of annualized return outcomes as more and more one-year holding periods are added, the range of terminal values for an original $1.00 invested increases as more and more holding periods are added. This occurs because, as more single-period returns are added, the geometric mean moves closer to its expected

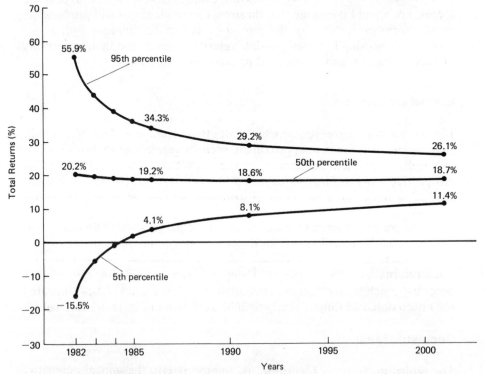

Figure 3.2. Projections of Geometric Mean Returns for Common Stocks for the Period 1982–2001. (SOURCE: Ibbotson and Sinquefield [1982])

value. However, given some dispersion of possible mean returns, the compounding effect of those returns over a long time horizon moves the terminal values further apart.

Terminal Wealth Projections

In terms of terminal wealth projections as shown in Figure 3-3, expected value of a year-end 1981 $1.00 investment in the year 2001 worked out to be

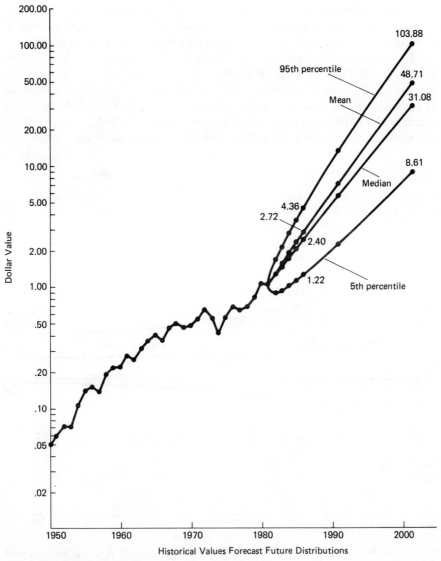

Figure 3-3. Projections of Common Stock Wealth Index Values for the Period 1982–2001 (Year-end 1981 = 1.00). (SOURCE: Ibbotson and Sinquefield [1982])

$48.71; the 90% confidence range was $8.61 to $103.88. Results of this sort must be seen for what they are. The key assumption underlying this type of mechanical projection process is that the original measures of expected return and standard deviation will continue to be appropriate during the entire simulation or projection period. A related assumption in the Ibbotson-Sinquefield projections is that the future will be like the past (adjusted for inflation expectations, as captured by the historical distribution at the time the projections were made) in the sense that the expected return and return variability measures were based on historical experience rather than making judgments based on economic scenarios (as were those made by the investment policy committee in the early sections of this chapter).

By contrast with the nominal common stock forecasted returns distributions and wealth indexes, two additional sets of figures show quite different results. In Figures 3-4 and 3-5, inflation-adjusted common stock projected returns distributions and wealth indexes are produced. The real return distributions and indexes are about as widely dispersed as the nominal, though all of the numbers are uniformly much smaller because they are deflated by the sizeable 12.4 percent assumed inflation rate. Figures 3-6 and 3-7, which show the same phenomenon for nominal long-term corporate bond returns, are

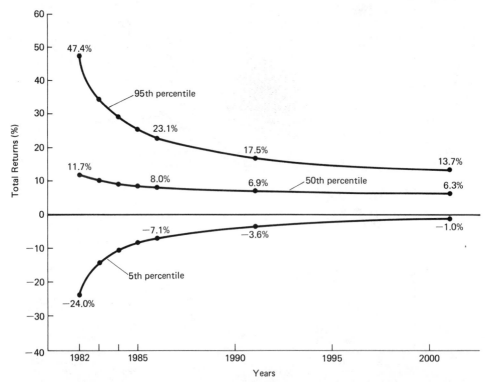

Figure 3-4. Projections of Inflation-Adjusted Geometric Mean Returns for Common Stocks for the Period 1982–2001. (SOURCE: Ibbotson and Sinquefield [1982])

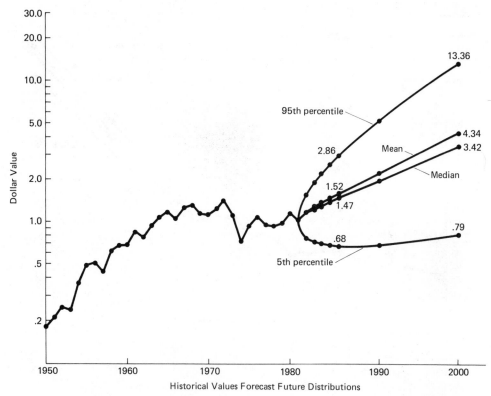

Figure 3-5. Projections of Inflation-Adjusted Common Stock Wealth Index Values for the Period 1982–2001 (Year-end 1981 = 1.00). (SOURCE: Ibbotson and Sinquefield [1982])

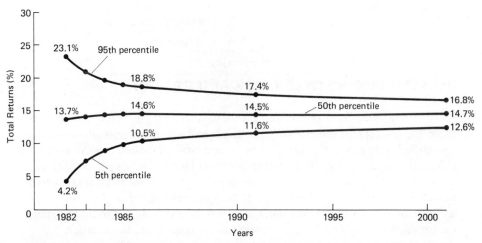

Figure 3-6. Projections of Geometric Mean Returns for Long-Term Corporate Bonds for the Period 1982–2001. (SOURCE: Ibbotson and Sinquefield [1982])

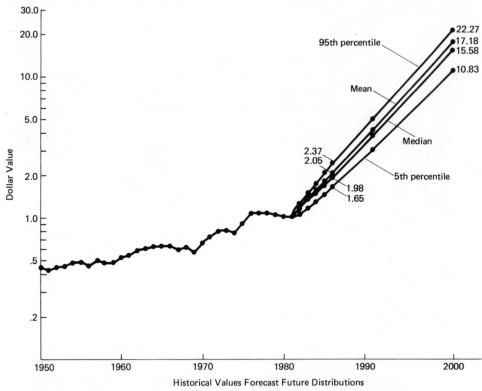

Figure 3-7. Projections of Long-Term Corporate Bond Wealth Index Values for the Period 1982–2001 (Year-end 1981 = 1.00). (Source: Ibbotson and Sinquefield [1982])

somewhat different. While the numbers are lower than those for common stock, the distributions are much narrower because the projected variability of bond returns around a mean or median measure of central tendency is smaller.

RELATIONSHIP BETWEEN RISK AND RETURN

After all that has been said in the previous section about risk and reward, there are a series of unresolved questions and the client is still somewhat unsatisfied. For example, standard deviation has been cited as a measure of risk, and correlation coefficients are noted as having an impact on portfolio construction. But how do these concepts mesh? How do individual securities fit in with the asset class risks discussed previously? Is there only one measure of risk? What causes risk? How much more return should the client get for each unit of risk? By answering these questions, the relationship of risk to return that is relevant to the investor will be revealed.

Modern Portfolio Theory

What follows is a brief explanation of what is commonly referred to as *modern portfolio theory* (MPT) and how it fits in with a more traditional investment framework. The intent here is to provide a nonmathematical, intuitive summary that can bring the reader up to date on current thinking in the area. We mentioned earlier the work of Markowitz. What Markowitz focused on for the first time was the quantification of diversification. There was nothing new to diversification. It could be observed in almost all portfolios; investors just did not put all their eggs in one basket. Markowitz realized that if investors sought only the highest return, they would hold only that asset (security) with the highest expected return. Clearly people diversified to reduce risk—but what was risk, and how did diversification reduce it? The key to Markowitz's contribution was the concept of covariance of returns on individual assets. Although mathematicians resort to a rigorous definition of statistical covariance, an intuitive understanding can be developed by looking at Figures 3-8, 3-9, and 3-10.

Figure 3-8 shows perfect positive dependence. If the total portfolio is split between two securities with perfect positive dependence, there is no benefit from diversification; that is, the portfolio performs the same as the individual securities. Securities A and B have a correlation coefficient of +1 with each other.

Figure 3-9 shows perfect negative dependence. The two securities move in exactly the opposite direction. The proper mix of the two securities can provide us with a perfectly riskless portfolio. Securities C and D have a correlation coefficient of −1 with each other.

Figure 3-10 demonstrates positive but imperfect dependence. It shows some dependence but also an element of randomness; this randomness tends to dampen the extreme returns of the individual securities when combined

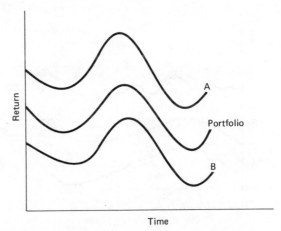

Figure 3-8. Perfect Positive Dependence.

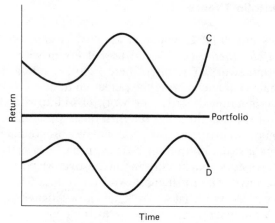

Figure 3-9. Perfect Negative Dependence.

into a portfolio. Securities E and F have a correlation coefficient somewhere between zero and +1 with each other.

Common sense would seem to support Markowitz's observation that managers are usually faced with the problem of investing in securities the returns of which are related to one another but not perfectly so. If the returns on securities were perfectly positively related, then managers would have little incentive to add securities to their portfolio, since doing so would really not add to the portfolio's diversification. On the other hand, if there were *no* relationship at all between security returns, then diversification among a very large number of securities would produce a portfolio with a significantly reduced standard deviation of return. And with perfect negative correlation between security returns patterns, a portfolio can be assembled that would have no risk. The no-relationship situation is analogous to the situation faced

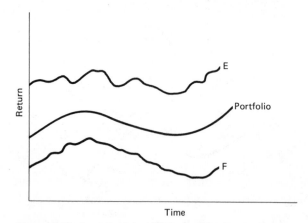

Figure 3-10. Imperfect, but High, Positive Dependence.

by a life insurance company; it does not know the outcome of any particular policy, which is random, but it knows the population's outcome. Given an infinitely large population, it knows how many people will die (provided there is no war), but individual deaths are independent of one another.

If the returns for most securities have some positive but not perfect dependence on one another, how does this affect the portfolio manager? Markowitz continued his paper with a mathematical description of how people can build portfolios with expected returns and standard deviations out of individual securities with particular expected returns, standard deviations, and correlation coefficients. He demonstrated how the standard deviation of the portfolio would be less than the weighted average of the standard deviation of the individual securities. Hence, by combining individual assets optimally, an expected return of the weighted average of expected individual returns can be achieved with a standard deviation less than the weighted average.

Markowitz suggested that this is why individuals should hold diversified portfolios. He further postulated that since individuals are risk-averse wealth maximizers, they should seek the highest level of return for any given level of risk or the lowest level of risk for any given level of return. If total risk reduction is a desired goal, then investors will diversify their holdings until they can reduce risk no further. These optimal portfolios he called *efficient* portfolios. Such portfolios offer the highest level of return at the level of risk assumed.

A principle that falls out of this process is that total standard deviation, while a valid measure of risk for the total portfolio, may not be an appropriate measure of risk for individual securities. Part of the total risk of a single security can be diversified away. Hence, there are two components to total risk: *diversifiable* and *nondiversifiable*.

Diversifiable vs. Nondiversifiable Risk

A number of papers followed Markowitz's, most notably Sharpe [1964] and Lintner [1965], which made the argument that if part of the total risk was diversifiable, then the market would not pay a premium for it. For example, you may pay a fireman a risk premium (danger pay) but be unwilling to pay an additional premium for his running into a burning house naked and without equipment. The argument is that the market does not pay for risks that can sensibly be eliminated.

Figure 3-11 on page 48 shows the relationship graphically between diversifiable (also known as *unsystematic* or *specific*) risk and nondiversifiable (also known as *systematic* or *market*) risk. As more securities are added to the portfolio, total risk falls at a decreasing rate. At the limit, unsystematic risk becomes zero (because of perfect diversification), and the only risk remaining is that associated with the market in general.

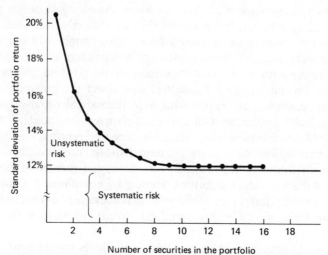

Figure 3-11. Effect of Diversification on Portfolio Standard Deviation. (SOURCE: Evans and Archer [1968])

CAPITAL ASSET PRICING THEORIES

Given for the moment that the market only pays for systematic risk, what then is the relationship between risk and reward?

Components of Return

Let us start by looking at only the components of return. Assuming away purchasing power risk, the risk-free rate is the pure time value of money. It is the price of foregone consumption. Because of their default-free nature and their short time horizon, U.S. government Treasury bills are typically used as the risk-free asset. The government can tax or print more money to pay off the obligations, and the term is so short that there is little or no interest rate risk. This is the rate necessary to lure investors away from current consumption.

To attract investors away from the risk-free asset, there must be some amount required to lure them into "risky" assets. This risk premium is the expected premium component of return.

Given these economic realities, let us now turn to a description of the family of what are commonly called *capital asset pricing theories*. These theories are not presented in chronological order of development; instead they are presented in order from the most general and intuitive to the most specific.

Arbitrage Pricing Theory

The most general theory is probably Ross's [1976] *arbitrage pricing theory (APT)*. Quite simply, it stated that the expected return is the risk-free rate plus a *linear* combination of risk premiums attributable to other "factors." Of importance here is that Ross is looking at only systematic risk.

He assumes investors are both rational and capable of avoiding unsystematic risk, and that the market does not pay for it. He also assumes there is some riskless asset—usually accepted to be short-term Treasury bills, which have no default or interest rate risk. He does not, however, say what the factors are.

Intuitively most individuals view the world as follows: If you have one asset with a particular level of risk and return and if you double the risk, you should receive more than double the return. Ross proves that this is not true.

Consider for a moment the situation where there is only one factor that affects the return on securities. In mathematical notation the expected return on any of these securities, $E(R_i)$, could be expressed as follows:

$$E(R_i) = R_f + [E(R_1) - R_f] \, b_{i1}$$

or, in words,

$$\frac{\text{expected return}}{\text{on security } i} = \frac{\text{risk-free}}{\text{return}} + \left[\begin{array}{c} \text{excess return} \\ \text{on factor 1} \end{array} \times \begin{array}{c} \text{excess return sensitivity} \\ \text{parameter of } i \text{ with 1} \end{array} \right]$$

Note that this model can be presented either in terms of returns or in terms of excess returns. The latter was chosen because it allows richer interpretation of the model's parameters.

Figure 3-12 on page 50 shows why the indicated relationship must hold true. Assume there are three securities, A, B, and C. Given securities A and B, it is possible to construct a portfolio that we will call D. The systematic risk and return of D will be the weighted averages of A and B.

If investors agree on the future concerning A, B, and C, then they will sell their combined holdings of A and B (which when held in combination are portfolio D) and buy C, thereby creating a riskless profit. But by making these transactions they will drive up the price of C (and drive down its expected return) while forcing down the price of D (and push its expected return up). In this way, arbitrage will force securities into equilibrium such that they are producing returns that are some linear function (*b*) of the factor.

In summary, this most general of asset pricing models shows that when using a one-factor case, expected return is a linear function of systematic risk. It also shows that the measure of systematic risk is the term *b*, which is the sensitivity measure of the security's excess return ($R_i - R_f$) to the excess return on the factor(s).

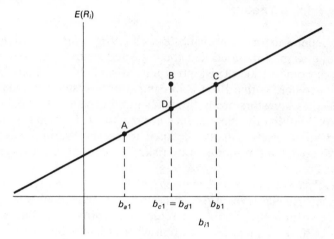

Figure 3-12. One-Factor Arbitrage Pricing Model. (SOURCE: Fuller [1981])

There are numerous other models of the equilibrium condition between risk and reward. Most of them specify a number of other factors. These multifactor models include such factors as the market return, dividend yield, capitalization, or industry group.

Capital Asset Pricing Model

The most specific of the multifactor models is the *capital asset pricing model* (*CAPM*) proposed by Sharpe. Using a set of highly restrictive assumptions, he showed that

$$E(R_p) = R_f + \frac{E(R_m) - R_f}{\sigma_m^2} \text{Cov}_{pm}$$

which in words is

$$\begin{array}{l} \text{expected return on fully} \\ \text{diversified portfolio } p \end{array} = \begin{array}{l} \text{risk-free} \\ \text{return} \end{array} + \left[\frac{\text{excess market return}}{\text{variance of market return}} \right.$$

$$\left. \times \begin{array}{l} \text{portfolio } p\text{'s covariance} \\ \text{with the market} \end{array} \right]$$

$$= \begin{array}{l} \text{risk-free} \\ \text{return} \end{array} + \left[\begin{array}{l} \text{market price} \\ \text{of risk} \end{array} \times \text{Cov}_{pm} \right]$$

In its beta (β) equivalent form, the model becomes

$$E(R_p) = R_f + [E(R_m) - R_f]\beta_p$$

or, in words,

$$\begin{array}{l}\text{expected return on fully} \\ \text{diversified portfolio } p\end{array} = \begin{array}{l}\text{risk-free} \\ \text{return}\end{array} + \left[\begin{array}{l}\text{excess market} \\ \text{return} \\ \qquad \times \begin{array}{l}\text{beta-sensitivity of excess} \\ \text{return on portfolio } p\end{array}\end{array}\right]$$

This is a specific form of the arbitrage pricing theory; in fact, it is identical to the single-factor model used in demonstrating it. The factor is the excess return (the return in excess of the risk-free rate) on the market as a whole.

The CAPM and the other models had all arrived, in different forms, at the same conclusion: Beta, or sensitivity to factors, was the relevant risk measure for an individual security. The CAPM is the easiest model with which to demonstrate what an individual security's beta is. Recall that in the CAPM it is assumed that the only relationship between individual securities is their common relationship to the return on the market portfolio.

Estimating Historical Beta

Figure 3-13 demonstrates the procedure for estimating a security's historical beta. The points shown are the monthly excess returns on the market plotted against the excess returns on the security. The upward-sloping line is called the security's *characteristic line*. It is the best fit to the data points calculated by the least squares regression technique.

The slope of the characteristic line is the measure called beta, which is the *sensitivity* of the excess return on the security to the excess return on the market. The dispersion of data points around the line represents the specific

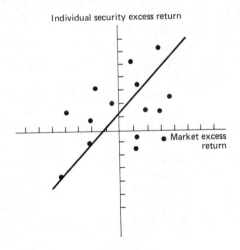

Figure 3-13. Characteristic Line.

risk—the amount of risk that presumably can be diversified away in an efficient portfolio.

The intercept on the vertical axis is called *alpha*. This is the return generated by nonmarket factors over and above the risk-free rate. It has occurred because the security was previously undervalued or because new corporate events have led to a reappraisal of the value of the firm. Clearly, positive alphas are a desirable commodity. In fact, the major mission of the equity security analyst can be stated as identifying positive alpha (i.e., undervalued) common stocks.

Ex Ante vs. Ex Post Measurement

An important difference that must be addressed is that of *ex ante*, before the fact, and *ex post*, after the fact, measurement, which were mentioned earlier in the chapter. The calculation of a stock's beta using historical information, as shown in Figure 3-13, is an ex post measurement, as are the historical standard deviations of stock and bond returns referred to in earlier sections of this chapter.

The APT, multi-factor models, and the CAPM are all ex ante concepts. The only hard data available to estimate standard deviation and beta are historical. Yet, by definition, there is no risk ex post; we know what the return was. By using historical returns to calculate standard deviation and beta, we are assuming future uncertainty can be adequately represented by historical return variability.

When using or considering any of the equilibrium pricing models (whether for portfolio building or performance measurement), care must be taken to remember that the models describe investors' perceptions *today* of the *future*. The use of the historical beta and standard deviation as estimates for future risk must be remembered for what they are—estimates based on history. When standard deviation and beta change over time, it just goes to show that, yes, estimating risk is risky business. Betas and standard deviations, just as with returns, must be forecast and assessed by the analyst. Purely historical risk estimates, like historical returns, are unlikely to be the best ex ante predictions. At best, they represent a starting point that the analyst can then adjust based on personal insights about future prospects.

Looking into the future, three key measures summarize a security's prospects: (1) alpha, which is the extra expected return due to nonmarket factors, (2) beta, which summarizes a security's systematic risk, and (3) a second risk measure, the dispersion of possible outcomes around the characteristic line, which is not associated with the market. This nonmarket (or unsystematic) risk is often broken into two further components: that *specific* to the company and that which is not—usually termed *extra-market* risk.

Extra-Market Risk

Extra-market risk is that risk which, although not correlated to the market as a whole, is related to subgroups of the market. For example, part of the nonmarket risk of steel companies may be related to one another and the singular product they produce. That is, steel companies may covary directly with one another even after their covariance with the market factor has been removed.

The results of these theories were extremely important. Looking at the world from a demand point of view, an individual's risk aversion would require *more* than a doubling of the risk premium for a doubling of risk. However, Sharpe, Ross, and others showed that the equilibrium relationship between risk and return should be linear.

Security Market Line

For the individual security this equilibrium relationship should hold in a return-factor space and is usually called the *security market line* (*SML*). That is, the relationship of individual securities in an SML world is linear in return-beta space. The equation for the SML is:

$$E(R_i) = R_f + \beta_i[E(R_m) - R_f]$$

which, in words, becomes

$$\begin{array}{l}\text{expected return on} \\ \text{security } i\end{array} = \begin{array}{l}\text{risk-free} \\ \text{return}\end{array} + \left[\begin{array}{l}\text{excess market} \\ \text{return}\end{array}\right.$$

$$\left. \times \begin{array}{l}\text{beta-sensitivity of excess} \\ \text{return on security } i\end{array}\right]$$

This relationship can be shown to be linear by the same arbitrage arguments cited earlier. The SML identified the relevant measure of risk for an individual security, one that interrelates the security's return with that of other securities or factors rather than its own variability of return. In fact, this was a reasonable extension of Markowitz's work. The emphasis on the interrelationship between security returns stems quite naturally from his focus on a portfolio approach as opposed to an individual security approach.

Tests of the Capital Asset Pricing Theories

There have been numerous empirical tests of the APT, CAPM, and multifactor models for common stocks (see the chapter's bibliography). In this area, at least, there seems to be support for these theories in that (1) individual security reward is positively related to measures of systematic risk, and (2) rates of return of well-diversified portfolios are positively related to the standard deviation of return. However, most studies have indicated that the return on low-risk stocks has been higher than expected and on high-risk stocks lower than expected.

Traditional Approaches to Risk

Traditionally security analysts and portfolio managers looked at proxies for risk in a rather intuitive fashion. Traditional interest rate risk and market risk are, respectively, embodied in the modern definition of systematic risk for bonds and stocks, while business or credit risk is defined as unsystematic risk. For example, in looking at equities, the analyst might examine volatility of sales, earnings, profit margins, dividend yields, or price/earnings ratios. This approach is not necessarily in conflict with the MPT approach. These traditional proxies of risk influence rather than measure the standard deviation of a stock's return. Standard deviation is not a cause but an effect.

Where MPT does depart radically from traditional thought is in its focus on the risk of the total portfolio. Traditional approaches to risk focused on total security risk rather than the security's contribution to portfolio risk. The newer approaches to risk analysis recognize this distinction and hence attempt to decompose total security and portfolio risk into components or factors that are systematic or nondiversifiable and into factors that are unsystematic or diversifiable. The former types of risk have associated risk premiums; the latter should not.

RETURN AND RISK REVISITED

During much of the 1960s and 1970s, convincing practicing investment professionals of the merits of the more systematic, quantitative approach that later was known as modern portfolio theory was a frustrating and sometimes agonizing process. But, as business school graduates from the post-Markowitz era rose to investment decision-making positions, the quantitative, modeling approach became more accepted. As the quantification of return and risk from probability distributions of returns gained acceptance, users have often come to believe that measures such as standard deviation are objectively determined. That is, if the standard deviation on a stock market index was 18 percent over a particular time period, they concluded that that had become an eternal truth. While historical numbers are valuable for gauging the future, they are just that: representative ballpark numbers. But the investment professional needs a *subjective* judgment about what standard deviation or beta risk will be in the *future*. It's the difference between ex post and ex ante once again.

To carry the exposition one step further, we can posit a situation where two analysts legitimately come up with two very different judgments about a security's standard deviation of return and *both* are right. How can this be? Because one analyst just has more or better information than the other. Both are OK perhaps, but one is better than the other. As a result, when surveying analysts' ex ante judgments, especially about risk—one of the all-important inputs to portfolio management—one must make implicit or explicit judgments about the *degree of insight* the analyst has about risk estimates.

An extreme example of this phenomenon would be the potentially different stock return distribution and therefore estimate of risk that an insider with inside information might have relative to an outsider without such knowledge. Another example is the widely different estimates of beta frequently encountered among various investment information services using the same data and calculation techniques. This occurs because analysts subjectively adjust "raw" betas differently based on differing interpretations of available information. The message is clear. Although modern portfolio theory produces results that appear precise, the methodology and its results are only as good as the information that goes into the process and the interpretation that comes out of it. Obviously, superior insight into investment opportunities should reduce the uncertainty range around expectations. In short, the higher the predictive accuracy for any given expected return, the lower the prospective or ex ante return standard deviation of the investment portfolio constructed with the predictions.

The perceptive reader will now recognize that an investment portfolio embodies two types of risk. The first is the remaining uncertainty of actual portfolio return, given an assumed level of accuracy associated with the security return predictions. The second risk is that the assumed level of predictive accuracy is too optimistic! Readers wishing to delve further into these concepts should consult Treynor and Black's [1973] seminal paper in this area.

SUMMARY

Investment return has both an objective and a subjective side to it. The historical reward associated with investments already made can be measured objectively, with the correct measure to be used dependent on the specific purpose of the return calculation. In contrast, determining the prospective reward of investments not yet made is a subjective exercise. This does not mean that only such terms as "high return, moderate risk" or "accumulate on weakness" are appropriate descriptors of a security's investment prospects. Developments in investment theory during the last 30 years have provided today's investment professional with an impressive kit bag of descriptive tools to communicate a security's or portfolio's investment prospects. Expected return, return premium, return standard deviation, covariance, systematic risk, specific risk, etc., are concepts of genuine value when the investment prospects of a security or a portfolio are being discussed.

Further, the evolution of organized thought regarding capital market efficiency and pricing is an important extension of the basic security return and risk framework that Markowitz introduced in 1952.

The purpose of this chapter was to introduce the reader to the basic descriptive tools of the investment profession: risk and return. The chapters that follow will make extensive use of these tools as the many dimensions of portfolio management are addressed in turn.

FURTHER READING

There are numerous reviews of modern portfolio theory. A few that will help provide supplementary reading (the first is probably the most useful as a state of the art primer) include Fuller [1981], Modigliani and Pogue [1974], Sharpe [1970], Chapters 1–5, and Sharpe [1981], Chapters 6–8.

Summaries of the capital asset pricing theory's empirical tests are given in Fuller [1981], Chapters 2 and 6, Hagin [1979], Chapter 27, and Lorie and Hamilton [1973], Chapters 11 and 12.

BIBLIOGRAPHY

Ambachtsheer, K. P., "Profit Potential in an 'Almost Efficient' Market," *Journal of Portfolio Management,* Fall 1974.

————**, and James Farrell,** "Can Active Management Add Value?" *Financial Analysts Journal,* November/December 1979.

Brealey, R. A., and S. D. Hodges, "Portfolio Selection in a Dynamic and Uncertain World," *Financial Analysts Journal,* March/April 1973.

Evans, J. H., and S. H. Archer, "Diversification and the Reduction of Dispersion: An Empirical Analysis," *Journal of Finance,* December 1968.

Fama, E. F., "Efficient Capital Markets: A Review of Theory and Empirical Work," *Journal of Finance,* May 1970.

Fuller, R. J., *Capital Asset Pricing Theories-Evolution and New Frontiers,* Charlottesville, Va.: The Financial Analysts Research Foundation, 1981.

Hagin, R. H., *Modern Portfolio Theory,* Homewood, Ill.: Dow Jones–Irwin, 1979.

Ibbotson, R. G., and R. A. Sinquefield, *Stocks, Bonds, Bills and Inflation: The Past and the Future,* Charlottesville, Va.: The Financial Analysts Research Foundation, 1982.

Lintner, J., "The Valuation of Risky Investments in Stock Portfolios and Capital Budgets," *Review of Economics and Statistics,* February 1965.

Lorie, J. H., and M. T. Hamilton, *The Stock Market: Theories and Evidence,* Homewood, Ill.: Richard D. Irwin, 1973.

Markowitz, H. M., "Portfolio Selection," *The Journal of Finance,* March 1952.

Modigliani, F., and G. Pogue, "An Introduction to Risk and Return," Part I, *Financial Analysts Journal,* March/April 1974; Part II, *Financial Analysts Journal,* May/June 1974.

Reilly, Frank K., *Investments,* Hinsdale, Ill.: Dryden Press, 1982.
Ross, S., "The Arbitrage Pricing Theory of Capital Asset Pricing," *Journal of Economic Theory,* December 1976.
Samuelson, P. A., "Proof That Properly Anticipated Prices Fluctuate Randomly," *Industrial Management Review,* Spring 1965.
Sharpe, W. F., "Capital Asset Prices: A Theory of Market Equilibrium Under Conditions of Risk," *Journal of Finance,* September 1964.
————, *Portfolio Theory and Capital Markets,* New York: McGraw-Hill, 1970.
————, *Investments,* 2nd Ed., Englewood Cliffs, N.J.: Prentice-Hall, 1981.
Treynor, J., and F. Black, "How to Use Security Analysis to Improve Portfolio Selection," *Journal of Business,* January 1973.

APPENDIX
Covariance and Correlation

It is desirable to develop the key statistical notion of covariance (Cov) and its relationship to more familiar statistical concepts, such as the correlation coefficient (rho or ρ) and standard deviation (σ). This discussion draws heavily on Reilly [1982].

Covariance is an absolute measure of the extent to which two sets of numbers move together over time, i.e., move up or down together. In this regard, move together means they are generally above or below their means at the same time. Covariance between i and j is defined as

$$\text{Cov}_{ij} = \frac{\Sigma(i - \bar{i})(j - \bar{j})}{N}$$

If we define $(i - \bar{i})$ as i' and $(j - \bar{j})$ as j', then

$$\text{Cov}_{ij} = \frac{\Sigma i' j'}{N}$$

Obviously, if both numbers are consistently above or below their individual means at the same time, their products will be positive, and the average product (covariance) will be a large positive value. In contrast, if the i value is below its mean when the j value is above its mean, or vice versa, the product will be a large negative value and you would find negative covariance. The example in Table 3A-1 on page 58 should make this clear. In this example the two series generally moved together, so there was positive covariance. As noted, this is an *absolute* measure of their relationship and, therefore, can range from $+\infty$ to $-\infty$. Note that the covariance of a variable with itself is its *variance*.

To obtain a *relative,* rather than an absolute, measure of the relationship between variables i and j, we use the correlation coefficient rho (ρ_{ij}), which is a normalized measure of the relationship

$$\rho_{ij} = \frac{\text{Cov}_{ij}}{\sigma_i \sigma_j}$$

TABLE 3A-1. Calculation of Covariance

Obs.	i	j	$i - \bar{i}$	$j - \bar{j}$	$i'j'$
1	3	8	−4	−4	16
2	6	10	−1	−2	2
3	8	14	+1	+2	2
4	5	12	−2	0	0
5	9	13	+2	+1	2
6	11	15	+4	+3	12
Σ	= 42	72			34

Mean = 7   12

$$\text{Cov}_{ij} = \frac{34}{6} = +5.67$$

That is, rho is equal to the covariance of i and j relative to or divided by the product of the standard deviations of i's and j's.

Note that since the formula for standard deviations is

$$\sigma_i = \frac{\Sigma(i - \bar{i})^2}{N}$$

if the two series i and j move together completely (i.e., in exact synchronization), the covariance of i and j becomes σ_i times σ_j and

TABLE 3A-2. Calculation of Correlation Coefficient

Obs.	$i - \bar{i}$[a]	$(i - \bar{i})^2$	$j - \bar{j}$[a]	$(j - \bar{j})^2$
1	−4	16	−4	16
2	−1	1	−2	4
3	+1	1	+2	4
4	−2	4	0	0
5	+2	4	+1	1
6	+4	16	+3	9
		42		34

$\sigma_i^2 = 42/6 = 7.00$ $\sigma_j^2 = 34/6 = 5.67$

$\sigma_i = \sqrt{7.00} = 2.65$ $\sigma_j = \sqrt{5.67} = 2.38$

$$\rho_{ij} = \text{Cov}_{ij}/\sigma_i\sigma_j = \frac{5.67}{(2.65)(2.38)} = \frac{5.67}{6.31} = .898$$

$$\rho_{ij} = \frac{\sigma_i \sigma_j}{\sigma_i \sigma_j} = +1.0$$

and the two series are perfectly positively correlated.

It should be noted that although the key variable is Cov_{ij}, because $\text{Cov}_{ij} = \rho_{ij}\sigma_i\sigma_j$, the relationship between data series frequently is stated in terms of the more familiar statistical measure ρ_{ij} rather than Cov_{ij}.

Continuing the example given in Table 3A-1, the standard deviations are computed in Table 3A-2, as is the correlation between i and j. As shown, the two standard deviations are rather large and similar but not the same. Finally, when the positive covariance is normalized by the product of the two standard deviations, the results indicate a correlation coefficient of $+.898$, which is obviously quite large and close to $+1.00$. Apparently these two series are highly related.

Part II

Investor Objectives and Constraints

Determination of Portfolio Policies

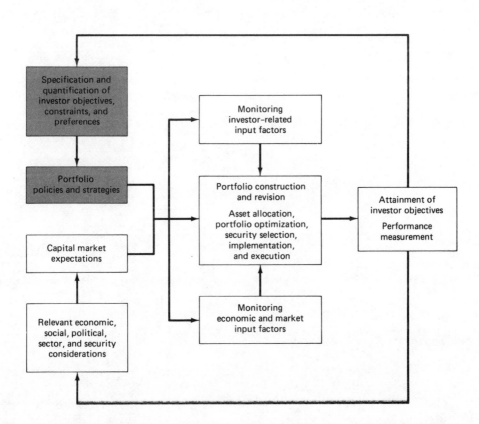

CHAPTER *4*

Determination Of Portfolio Policies: Institutional Investors

Jay Vawter, C.F.A.

Before an appropriate investment program can be established for an individual or institutional investor, careful consideration must be given to the investor's specific objectives, constraints, and policies. Objectives are goals that are generally defined in terms of return requirements and risk tolerance. Constraints are limitations on the portfolio management process within which the investor or his advisor must operate to achieve the objectives. These constraints include liquidity, time horizon, taxes, legal or regulatory matters, and unique needs and preferences. The combining of objectives and constraints leads to the development of a set of investment policies for each investor—an operational statement or set of guidelines that specify the action to be taken to achieve the investment objectives within the constraints imposed.

In other words, behind all investment portfolios lie flesh and blood investors, each of whom is unique. Many of these considerations are qualitative, but all lead to a quantification of risk and return and ultimately to the development of an efficient portfolio geared to the needs and objectives of each investor.

Chapter 5 deals with objectives, constraints, and policies of individual investors, including personal trusts. This chapter focuses on institutional investors, with particular attention being given to retirement funds, endowment funds, insurance companies, banks, and investment companies.

63

EMPLOYEE BENEFIT FUNDS

Although the employee benefit concept was pioneered by Sears Roebuck & Co. in the early part of the twentieth century, it only truly blossomed in the latter half. However, that blossoming has indeed been immense, with total assets of retirement plans in the United States in 1981 reaching a level well in excess of $700 billion (see Table 4-1). Employee benefit plans cover a broad range, including defined benefit plans (pensions), defined contribution plans (pension annuities, profit sharing, thrift and savings plans, and health, accident, and life insurance trusts), Keogh plans for the self-employed, and Individual Retirement Accounts (IRAs). So great, in fact, has the magnitude of funds invested in employee benefit plans become (see Table 4-2 on page 66) that this may have been a major factor in the declining personal savings rates in the United States over the past several decades. Employees, knowing that retirement is at least partially provided for through Social Security and private retirement benefits, have felt freer to spend a higher proportion of personal disposable income, saving less.

Because savings and thrift plans as well as various insurance plans are of relatively minor importance when compared to retirement plans, this chapter will deal in detail only with pension and profit-sharing plans. However, a few comments about the former are warranted. These types of plans tend to be managed conservatively. In the case of thrift and savings plans, which involve substantial employee contributions (usually the employee contributes up to 6 percent of salary, with such amount then being matched by the employer), there are often requirements that funds be invested only in fixed income securities or guaranteed investment contracts (GICs). Insurance trusts, whether life or casualty, often bear greater resemblance to insurance company assets in their investment treatment than they do to retirement plans; or if the actual insurance is carried by an insurance company, these funds may be highly liquid reserves available to supplement premiums against a poor insurance experience in a given year.

Keogh plans are an innovation of the 1960s. They permit self-employed persons who are not otherwise eligible for qualified employee plans to set aside funds for their own retirement in plans qualified under the Keogh Act. Legislation passed in mid-1981 amending the original act permitted a self-employed person to contribute up to 15 percent of his self-employment income to a Keogh plan, with a maximum contribution of $15,000 annually. In 1982 Congress increased this limit to the lesser of 25 percent or $30,000 annually effective in 1983, bringing Keogh plans into parity with corporate contribution rules.

IRAs were originally available only to persons who did not have qualified employee benefit plans available to them. Such employees were permitted to set aside 15 percent of income or $1,500, whichever was the lesser, in a qualified IRA prototype plan. If they chose to include their spouse under a spousal deduction, a total of up to $1,750 annually could be deducted from gross income provided this amount was split equally between the employee

TABLE 4-1. Assets of Private and Public Pension Funds, Year-End Value (billions of dollars)

	1970	1971	1972	1973	1974	1975	1976	1977	1978	1979	1980
1. Insured pension reserves	$ 41.2	$ 46.4	$ 52.3	$ 56.1	$ 60.8	$ 72.2	$ 89.0	$101.5	$119.1	$139.2	$164.6
2. Noninsured pension funds	110.4	130.1	156.1	134.3	115.5	146.8	171.9	178.5	198.6	222.4	286.1
3. Total private pension funds	151.6	176.5	208.4	190.4	176.3	219.0	260.9	280.0	317.7	361.6	450.7
4. State and local government retirement funds	60.3	69.0	80.6	84.7	88.0	104.8	120.6	132.6	153.0	170.1	202.7
5. U.S. government retirement funds	27.5	30.4	33.4	35.5	38.2	41.9	46.4	52.9	59.8	67.7	76.4
6. Total public pension funds	87.8	99.4	114.0	120.2	126.2	146.7	167.0	185.5	212.8	237.8	279.1
7. Total private and public pension funds	239.4	275.9	322.4	310.6	302.5	365.7	427.9	465.5	530.5	599.4	729.8

SOURCE: Securities and Exchange Commission [1981].

TABLE 4-2. U.S. Corporate Business, Profits Before Taxes and Employer Contributions to Private Pension and Profit-Sharing Funds, 1971–1981 (billions of dollars)

	1971	1972	1973	1974	1975	1976	1977	1978	1979	1980	1981
Corporate profits before taxes	$77.4	$91.3	$108.9	$117.3	$114.3	$147.7	$167.3	$203.6	$225.0	$212.1	$209.3
Employer contributions to private pension and profit-sharing funds	15.0	17.8	20.7	24.2	28.1	32.9	38.8	44.8	54.9	54.7	60.2
Profits plus contributions	$92.4	$109.1	$129.6	$141.5	$142.4	$180.6	$206.1	$248.4	$279.9	$266.8	$269.5
Contributions as a percentage of profits	19.4%	19.5%	19.0%	20.6%	24.6%	22.3%	23.2%	22.0%	24.4%	25.8%	28.8%
Contributions as a percentage of profits plus contributions	16.2%	16.3%	16.0%	17.1%	19.7%	18.2%	18.9%	18.0%	19.6%	20.5%	22.3%

SOURCES: Corporate profits before taxes from U.S. Department of Commerce, Bureau of Economic Analysis, *Survey of Current Business*, Table 1.13, "Gross Domestic Product of Corporate Business." Contributions from published and mimeographed material from Bureau of Economic Analysis, *Survey of Current Business*, Table 6.15, "Other Labor Income by Industry and by Type."

and his or her spouse. Under the 1981 legislation, however, IRA qualification was broadened to include all employees, including those covered by a qualified plan, and the annual maximum amount was raised to $2,000. The spousal deduction could increase this to $2,250, which, furthermore, no longer had to be divided equally between the two spouses.

In the early 1980s another type of employee retirement benefit, the salary reduction plan, began to be used more widely. Under this plan an employee could elect to take a salary reduction, which was then contributed to a qualified profit-sharing trust but excluded from taxable income (unlike a voluntary contribution, which is made with after-tax dollars). Unlike an IRA, this plan qualifies for the ten-year averaging tax benefit upon distribution at retirement. Because it is possible to contribute a larger amount to this type of plan than to an IRA, many employees prefer it, although either or both can be used. Many rules govern salary reduction plans; thus great care must be exercised in using them.

Since pension and profit-sharing plans differ considerably in terms of their overall investment objectives and policies, sharp contrasts will be drawn between these two important types of retirement benefit funds.

Return Requirements

Defined Benefit Plans. The return requirement for pension plans is generally referred to as the *actuarially assumed rate of return* or, more simply, the *actuarial return rate*. This rate of return might be defined as the rate that equates the plan's liability stream with the assets necessary to make the required payments to beneficiaries upon their retirement. The liability side of this equation includes not only known benefits payable to each retiree but must also take into account projected future wage increase assumptions. On the other side of the equation, the assets come from contributions made by the plan's sponsor and from earnings on investments during the working lifetime of each beneficiary. Thus, the actuary, knowing the ultimate benefits expected to be paid, establishes a reasonable rate of return to be achieved by the plan and, discounting the expected liabilities by this rate, can determine the amount that the employer must contribute each year to assure benefit payments as they become due.

BENEFIT FORMULAS. It might be useful at this point to examine three methods by which benefits are determined for defined benefit plans.

First, benefits may be a flat percentage of earnings. Annual retirement benefits, for example, may be "equal to 50 percent of the average salary for the last five years of employment." The percentage may vary according to each plan and may also be adjusted so as to present a package of retirement benefits that includes Social Security. In such case the benefit might be defined as "equal to 70 percent of average salary for the last five years of employment, reduced by the amount of Social Security paid to the employee.'' The flat percentage of earnings method is generally used for sala-ried personnel. The percentage chosen will vary by plan and plan sponsor, but generally falls in a range of 50 to 70 percent.

Second, the benefit may be defined as a flat amount per year of service. The monthly retirement benefit, for example, might be stated as "equal to $15 per month times the number of years of service." This method is often used for hourly personnel.

Third, the benefit may be stated as a percentage of earnings per year of service. For example, the annual benefit might be defined as "the sum over all years of service of $1\frac{1}{4}$ percent times each year's earnings."

Regardless of how benefits are determined, if the employer makes the required contributions each year and is able to earn the required rate of return, sufficient funds will accumulate over the lifetime of each beneficiary to provide the benefit guaranteed by the employer.

ACTUARIAL ASSUMPTIONS. Although it would be easy to suggest that the return requirement for any pension plan is its actuarial return rate, this is clearly an oversimplification and, in fact, could lead a portfolio manager down the wrong path. It could be argued, in fact, that determination of required rates of return might best be done by the investment manager rather than the actuary. Although the rate of return assumption is obviously very important, many other actuarial assumptions, all intricately interrelated and dependent upon one another, are involved in determining ultimate benefits to employees.

Another actuarial assumption that has an important bearing on the total return required in a particular pension plan is the *salary progression rate.* In determining the ultimate benefit to be paid to an employee upon retirement, the actuary must take into account the salary likely to be earned by the employee in his later or most highly paid years (since most plan benefits are based on the final few years of salary or the highest level reached), the life expectancy of the employee upon retirement, and the rate of return likely to be earned on contributions set aside for each employee during his working years. In recent years, with the rate of inflation accelerating, salary progres-sion estimates of most plans have lagged well behind actual experience, meaning that the final pay basis of most pensions at retirement will be signifi-cantly higher than that estimated using conservative salary progression rates. Fortunately, largely offsetting this is the fact that many plans have earned significantly higher rates of return than their conservative actuarial return rates. The point here is clear—these two important actuarial assump-tions are interdependent and must be considered together. An overly con-servative salary progression rate (too low) can be offset by an equally con-servative (too low) assumed rate of return. However, such an offset cannot be taken for granted.

Even if one could determine with certainty that the stated actuarial re-turn rate was, in fact, adequate in light of salary progression rates and other actuarial assumptions, by no means would this fix the required rate of return for a particular plan. While it would assure minimum provision for benefits to be paid to retirees, there is clear incentive to earn a higher rate than the actuarial return rate. To the extent that a plan earns above its actuarial return rate, and all other actuarial assumptions are in proper balance, the plan's sponsor can either reduce contributions to the plan to the benefit of shareholders, increase the benefits of employees, or elect some combination of the two. Interestingly, the high inflation rates of recent years have contributed to insufficiency of actuarially assumed salary progression rates—and in many instances have caused actuaries to raise these rates. Should the rate of inflation peak and begin to drop over a period of years, this process could well work in reverse, generating actuarial gains as salaries and payrolls (adjusted for employee turnover) grow more slowly.

Defined Contribution Plans. Profit-sharing plans, the most common form of defined contribution plan, present quite a different problem. In this type of plan the benefit at retirement is unknown and annual contributions are dependent on the profitability of the firm (the annual contribution might be equal to employee's salary divided by total employee payroll times a sliding scale percentage of before-tax profits). These plans were originally devised to create an incentive for employees by allowing them to participate in the profitability of the company. The larger the company, however, the less likely these plans are to serve as a real incentive since employees would likely see their own efforts diluted by the failure of others to perform well. In fact, rather than helping to attract and keep good people, in many instances the outcome is quite the opposite. Employees seeing these rather substantial accumulations building up on their behalf are frequently tempted to leave the company in order to obtain control of their share well before retirement. When this occurs, the profit-sharing plan has instead served as deferred compensation that can be pulled out and spent without regard to any ultimate retirement benefit.

However, for many companies, especially family-owned companies that employ relatively small numbers of outsiders, defined contribution plans have become very purposeful estate-planning tools. The plans may or may not have retirement benefits as the end result, but they nonetheless enjoy substantial tax benefits. Contributions made on behalf of employees are tax deductible to the company, and all earnings on the plan accrue tax-free until drawn down by the employee at retirement. To the extent that such funds are not drawn down but are simply allowed to continue accumulating, they may benefit the participant's heirs; if the participant remains on the payroll until his death, no income tax may even be paid. Thus, whether a defined contribution plan is used as a retirement benefit or an estate-planning tool will depend on the individual employee.

In establishing return requirements for these plans, a careful analysis is required to determine whether the ultimate objective is to provide a retirement benefit or to meet estate-planning goals and objectives. To the extent that a retirement benefit objective is involved, it is probably desirable to accept lower returns in order to reduce risk. On the other hand, a beneficiary viewing the plan as an estate-planning tool may well seek higher returns and accept higher risks. This conclusion may also be affected by whether the profit-sharing plan stands on its own or is an adjunct to a defined benefit pension plan. In the latter case, the pension plan in essence puts a floor under the employee's ultimate retirement benefit and the profit-sharing plan may seek higher returns, thus becoming more of an estate-planning tool and less a retirement benefit.

Risk Tolerance

Defined Benefit Plans. In a defined benefit plan, where the benefit is guaranteed by the employer and known to the employee in advance, it is very important to determine what exactly is meant by risk. Because of the long-term nature of these plans, volatility of returns is of less consequence than it would be with a shorter time horizon, at least insofar as the ultimate effect on beneficiaries. Plan sponsors may wish to avoid high volatility for reasons related to accounting and contributions planning, but in the final analysis corporate considerations must take a back seat to beneficiaries' needs. Under the Employee Retirement Income Security Act of 1974 (ERISA), all pension plans must be managed solely for the benefit of the employees, and the employer's interests are clearly secondary in a legal sense.

However, if one defines risk in terms of the possibility of permanent loss of capital through defaults and bankruptcies or absolute losses of principal through market depreciation, where the beneficiaries' benefits could be jeopardized, risk tolerance becomes a more important factor despite the long-term nature of the plan. Fortunately, under ERISA a portfolio is viewed quite differently than under the standard *prudent man rule*. (Under this concept, which will be discussed in Chapter 5, each item of investment must stand on its own in terms of prudence.) The Labor Department's interpretation of ERISA has clearly established that only the *entire* portfolio must meet prudent man responsibilities; so long as careful attention is paid to the management of the fund and it is properly diversified, a serious loss in one security is not necessarily viewed as imprudent. That is, as long as portfolio concentration and diversification are properly balanced, if a set of securities with favorable return-risk tradeoffs are chosen and maintained, the fact that an actual sizable loss is incurred in some securities relative to a benchmark or comparison portfolio is, in and of itself, not likely to constitute imprudent behavior. However, there is a natural tendency on the part of sponsors, reflected in their risk tolerance, to avoid undue financial risk and thus avoid potential criticism should a serious loss be realized in a security.

The characteristics of the plan itself and the attitudes of the plan's sponsor play an important role in determining risk levels of most pension plans. For example, as discussed earlier, the actual level of the actuarial return rate and its relationship to the salary progression rate are important factors in setting investment policies. To the extent that the rate of return assumption is low relative to the rate actually earned and the assumed salary progression rate is high relative to that actually experienced, resulting in high employer contributions and overfunding of the plan, a greater degree of risk may be assumed in order to generate higher returns without great risk of impairing the ultimate benefit to employees. Contrarily, if the assumed rate is high and the salary progression rate is low relative to actual experience, resulting in low employer contributions and underfunding of the plan, the risk level should be modified downward since the potential of failing to meet required return would be significantly increased.

Actuarial Methods and Assumptions. The method of actuarial asset valuation is also an important factor. Most defined benefit plans try to smooth out fluctuations in market value to avoid increasing contribution costs in bad years. But for those that don't, whether an attempt to smooth was made or not, markets are volatile and where assets are "marked to market," a lower risk level may be desirable to avoid having to increase contributions in bad years, especially since those may be the very years in which the company's ability to make higher contributions is also reduced because of lower profitability.

The funding methods and cash flows of a pension plan also figure importantly in identifying and quantifying risk tolerance and avoidance. While the scope of this book, and especially of this chapter, does not permit detailed discussion of the actuary's role, particularly its highly technical aspects, some understanding of funding methods is necessary because they have a considerable impact on the ultimate investment policies of pension funds. An analysis of how well a plan is succeeding in matching its assets and accrued liabilities will provide useful insights in determining the plan's overall risk tolerance based on its particular financial strengths or weaknesses.

FUNDING FUTURE LIABILITIES. Funding methods can be characterized as either conservative or aggressive. We should keep in mind that both types of methods are designed to do the same thing—to fund the plan and meet its liabilities as they become due. Conservative funding methods build up assets at a faster rate and generally involve greater employer contributions to the plan in the early years; aggressive methods take longer to match assets and liabilities and usually result in smaller contributions in the early years.

The two most common funding methods are called *unit credit* and *entry age normal*. The former is widely used in Canada; the latter is the most popular method in the United States. In order to understand these funding methods it is necessary first to recognize that benefits accrue over the working life of each employee. Thus, since there is less time as each year passes for earnings to be generated on each contribution, the contributions themselves must be higher each year.

Under the unit credit method, contributions are designed to match accruals dollar for dollar; thus they start out rather low and increase over time. Under the entry age normal method, in simplified terms, a level contribution is made each year that is sufficient, along with investment earnings, to accrue to the required benefit at retirement. This is similar to a level premium life insurance policy, in which the premium in the early years is higher than required and in the later years is lower. Because the unit credit method involves lower contributions in the early years, it is the less conservative of the two; and because the entry age normal method involves larger contributions in the early years (thus causing a quicker matching of assets and liabilities), it is the more conservative method. Plans utilizing the unit credit method, then, might well consider conservative investment policies; plans using the entry age normal method might well utilize more aggressive investment policies.

FUNDING PAST LIABILITIES. The funding methods for past service liabilities represent another important factor in an analysis of actuarial funding methods and assumptions. All other things equal, where these liabilities are large, greater pressure is exerted on the sponsor to make larger contributions so that the assets may be built up toward this future liability. A conservative investment policy is consistent with this accelerated funding rate, because if the portfolio itself fails to achieve the returns needed and expected, even greater pressure would be exerted upon the sponsor to make larger contributions.

Likewise, if the funding period of past service liabilities is long, suggesting that the sponsor is contributing less toward meeting its liability for past service, risk tolerance considerations would dictate a conservative investment policy. Again, failure to meet the expected return would put greater pressure on the company. Conversely, if past service liabilities are relatively low or are amortized over shorter periods of time, the investment program can take a more liberal view toward risk and the investment policies accordingly may reflect a more aggressive investment stance. As a rule, if past service liabilities exceed 30–40 percent of plan assets, funding is generally considered aggressive and should be coupled with conservative investment policies; if these liabilities are below 10 percent of plan assets, funding is conservative and there is less pressure to fund quickly and invest conservatively. Also, in general, funding periods in excess of 30 years are aggressive and call for conservative investment policies; funding periods under 20 years are conservative and permit more aggressive investment policies. It should be emphasized that past service liability considerations, while important, are only one of the variables influencing investment policy for a pension fund.

Unfunded vested benefits and their effect on the investment policy is another area where risk tolerance must be taken into consideration. Generally speaking, the higher these unfunded benefits in relation to plan assets, the lower the risk tolerance of the plan from an investment viewpoint. Where there are little or no unfunded vested benefits, risk tolerance is greater, allowing more investment flexibility. On the other hand, when unfunded vested benefits begin to reach or exceed 10 percent of plan assets, increasingly more conservative investment policies should be adopted.

OTHER CONSIDERATIONS. Also important in assessing risk is the average age of the employee universe. That is, the older the average age, generally the lower the risk tolerance of the investment program because the plan is closer, timewise, to a period when benefits will overwhelm plan returns and contributions. Another factor is the degree to which the plan is contributory or noncontributory. That is, if employee funds are involved, plans generally tend to have more conservative investment attitudes. Also to be considered is whether or not there is a cost of living adjustment factor in employee benefits. If there is one, lower risk tolerance is suggested and a more conservative investment posture is advisable.

Another important risk consideration is the ability of the plan's sponsor to fund the plan given the cyclical sensitivity of the company's basic business. Put another way, it is far less likely that an expanding drug company would have difficulty in meeting its annual required contribution than a basic steel company, given the differences in cyclicality and secular growth of these two industries. One should be particularly alert to changes in the plan sponsor's business that might have an impact on its ability to fund its pension needs. For example, a dramatic increase in company leverage would imply increased earnings volatility and, therefore, lower tolerance for risk in the investment of pension assets.

Defined Contribution Plans. In a defined contribution plan attitudes about risk will have a very different effect on investment policy. Risk tolerance will depend on the extent to which the plan is viewed as a retirement benefit or an estate-planning tool, and whether or not a defined benefit pension plan is also involved. In a sense, the spectrum of risk tolerance for a defined contribution plan is probably similar to that of the actual individuals who are the beneficiaries. Compared to situations where there is only one basic policy, this makes setting unambiguous investment policies more complex because there can be such a great diversity of individual objectives among the employees covered.

This is not at all unlike the dichotomy of objectives of a life-income trust, where the income beneficiary views risk quite differently than does the remainderman. Many profit-sharing plans now permit or even require employees approaching retirement age to convert their shares of the plan to more conservative investments, with a strong bias toward short- to intermediate-term fixed income assets. This reduces the risk of the employee having to cash out at retirement during a period of depressed financial markets and values. Others utilize a range of investment alternatives that allow the individual participant to diversify according to his or her own needs and risk preferences.

Investment Vehicles

Once the effect of risk tolerance has been identified, a broad array of investment vehicles consistent with its specific risk tolerance is available to each retirement fund. Whereas at one time these funds invested almost exclusively in stocks and bonds, many now utilize covered call options, real estate, and financial futures. Even some of the more aggressive investment vehicles, such as venture capital, are appropriate for many funds—though in restricted amounts—given the long-term time horizon of these funds and the need, both legal and investment, for the highest possible cumulative return over that time horizon.

Summarizing Investment Objectives

To summarize, the determination of investment objectives for any pension plan must recognize that there are several interdependent aspects that must be considered. As Gray [1981] noted, it is important to recognize the objectives of each of the following:

- *Pension Sponsor*. In a public corporation the pension sponsor desires to enhance the value of the enterprise on a longer term basis.
- *Pension Plan*. The pension plan's objective is to make retirement benefit payments in the amount and at the time they are due. ERISA's intention has been to assure this result.
- *Pension Portfolio*. The pension portfolio's chief goal is to achieve or exceed the actuarial return rate so the funding plan can be realized.
- *Pension Portfolio Manager*. This individual wishes to establish and maintain an efficient portfolio, i.e., maximize the expected return for the amount of risk that is determined to be appropriate or relative to the investment style employed.

It is important to identify and consider the interrelationships noted above for each particular pension sponsor–investment manager situation. Out of this analysis a set of *client factors* should emerge. Although, in practice, there is a great variation in the manner in which such factors are evaluated, their importance justifies a systematic approach to evaluating sponsor attitudes and plan characteristics. According to Gray, some of the more important characteristics include:

- *Plan Provisions*. These include retirement benefit formula, timing and amount of vesting, early retirement adjustments, and so on.
- *Work-Force Characteristics*. These involve employee age distribution, turnover, considerations that might alter normal life expectancy, and so on.
- *Actuarial Inputs*. These usually encompass the salary and wage growth rate assumption, actuarial return rate assumption, method of funding (unit credit, entry age normal), and so on.
- *Cash Flows*. Here consideration is given to contributions and payouts, both historical and expected.

The evaluation process would consist of gathering information on sponsor attitudes and plan characteristics, comparing this information with how it is handled in other pension plans, and then blending this information into an integrated overall statement of plan objectives. Because much of this process is judgmental, the final conclusion will depend on the quality of the information and the relative perspectives developed.

Finally, the unsettled business conditions in the early 1980s have increased the awareness of the importance of sponsor characteristics in developing pension portfolio objectives. The financial characteristics and integrity of the sponsor cannot be taken for granted. They, too, must be subjected to careful and frequent evaluation.

In sum, the determination of return objectives and risk tolerance for a pension plan involves the systematic integration of sponsor attitudes and characteristics along with plan characteristics. The results should be a unique set of objectives, modified by the constraints imposed on the portfolio by liquidity, time horizon, tax, and regulatory/legal considerations.

Liquidity Requirements

Defined Benefit Plans. Liquidity requirements for defined benefit plans tend to fall into three basic categories based on the current age distribution of future beneficiaries.

In the first category, relatively young plans in growing companies tend to have very low liquidity requirements. In fact, all contributions and a significant portion of income are generally reinvested, with only a small amount of income needed to cover present retirement benefits paid out. The second category is in the middle of the maturity scale. These plans may require all or most income to pay benefits to retired employees, but company contributions are available for longer term investment. Finally, there are some plans that have reached a stage of maturity where all income along with at least part of the contributions is needed to pay benefits. It is, of course, possible to have yet a fourth category—plans that have been terminated and in which all earnings, as well as a large portion of the assets of the plan, are required to pay benefits and no contributions are being made. Such plans, of course, are designed to liquidate themselves over the remaining life expectancies of employees covered.

Defined Contribution Plans. Liquidity needs for defined contribution plans may be significantly different from defined benefit plans, even for the same sponsor, depending on the specific circumstances of the plan, especially employee turnover rates, vesting periods, withdrawal provisions, and the average age of the employees. Even with a relatively young employee base, high employee turnover and rapid vesting can result in significant payouts from the fund as employees leave for one reason or another. (This is quite common in many of the high technology fields.) By the same token, a small company operated solely by family members who have no intention of retiring would have relatively low liquidity requirements. Death, of course, represents a liquidity risk for such plans if the average age of the family members is high. Thus, it is very important to project expected retirements, employee turnover, and possible death rates in determining the liquidity needs of defined contribution plans.

Time Horizon

Although the typical defined benefit plan has a very long-term time horizon, with actuarial assumptions based on periods of 30 years or more, it is probably best pragmatically to view the long-term time horizon as being composed of a series of shorter investment planning or evaluation horizons, perhaps five to ten years in length. This view allows for more realistic establishment of investment objectives based on reasonably foreseeable trends and conditions and also for periodic review and modification of investment objectives based on changes in company and plan circumstances. For example, factors such as addition of new benefits or advancing age of the employee base that normally would require a change in investment policy might be ignored with a longer horizon. Certainly, in terms of basic investment objectives, a long-term view should be taken, particularly with regard to the expected volatility of the portfolio.

Unfortunately, especially in recent years, plan sponsors have become increasingly sensitive to volatility and have tended to shorten their investment evaluation time horizons—in many cases to the long-run detriment of the plan. Focusing on short periods of experience has the added disadvantage of putting undue and unnecessary pressure on investment managers and can often be counterproductive if it results in encouraging a higher degree of risk on the part of the manager than might otherwise be called for. Managers more and more are judged on performance on a quarter-by-quarter basis, even though the plan may have objectives focusing on five- and ten-year horizons. This may lead to investment postures that are more aggressive and oriented toward a shorter term than they should be.

As in the case of other constraints discussed earlier, the time horizon aspect of defined contribution plans varies broadly and again is dependent on how the plan is viewed. In general, selection of an appropriate time horizon for a profit-sharing plan is considerably more difficult than it is for a pension plan. The individual time horizons for the employees under the plan vary greatly and, thus, no one time horizon can be singled out as correct. The net result is that some approximation of an appropriate horizon for the plan is made, depending largely on the average age distribution of employees in the plan. Furthermore, selection of the time horizon must be carefully integrated with the liquidity requirements of each plan.

Tax Considerations

Company contributions to both defined benefit and defined contribution retirement plans are tax deductible. Furthermore, earnings—whether from interest, dividends, or capital gains—are exempt from taxation. Benefits paid upon retirement are taxable to the beneficiary and, depending on the way in which they are received, are subject to varying levels of taxation. Thus, tax considerations are not a constraint on the management of retirement plan funds, although for individual members of defined contribution plans tax planning needs to be done, either by the manager, sponsor, employee, or some combination of the three.

Regulatory and Legal Considerations

Retirement benefits are subject to the rules and regulations of the Employee Retirement Income Security Act of 1974 (ERISA). The most important aspects of that act as they apply to investment policy can be quoted from Section 404:

> (a)(1) Subject to sections 403(c) and (d), 4042, and 4044, a fiduciary shall discharge his duties with respect to a plan solely in the interest of the participants and beneficiaries and—
> (A) for the exclusive purpose of:
> (i) providing benefits to participants and their beneficiaries; and
> (ii) defraying reasonable expenses of administering the plan;
> (B) with the care, skill, prudence, and diligence under the circumstances then prevailing that a prudent man acting in a like capacity and familiar with such matters would use in the conduct of an enterprise of a like character and with like aims;
> (C) by diversifying the investments of the plan so as to minimize the risk of large losses, unless under the circumstances it is clearly prudent not to do so; and
> (D) in accordance with the documents and instruments governing the plan insofar as such documents and instruments are consistent with the provisions of this title.

There are a couple of unique aspects to this statement as contrasted to the standard prudent man rule of trusts. First, as mentioned earlier in this chapter, prudence is applied to the *total* portfolio rather than to any individual item within the portfolio. This is a direct response to modern portfolio theory and practice and recognizes the importance and desirability of diversification. Second, the law treats fiduciaries of plans differently according to their own level of skill and experience "with such matters." Thus, the degree or level of responsibility attributed to a fiduciary with little personal investment experience who runs a small plumbing contracting company and who is not very conversant with such matters will be lower than that of a professional investment manager who is hired to manage a larger plan. The latter is frequently referred to as a *prudent expert* and is held to a much higher level of responsibility than is a fiduciary with less skill and experience.

Several other provisions of ERISA affect investment policies of retirement plans. A pension plan may not hold more than 10 percent of the sponsor's own stock. Profit-sharing plans may hold unlimited amounts of the sponsor's stock if clearly provided for in the trust agreement. For pension plans having more than 10 percent in company stock, an orderly liquidation through 1984 of amounts above 10 percent is required to meet this rule. As shown in Section 404, ERISA requires that a fund be properly diversified. The language related to this legal requirement is not very specific and quite properly gives broad discretion to the sponsor and/or manager in deciding how to meet it.

Plan sponsors are specifically encouraged to utilize the services of profesional investment managers in handling their plan investments. Although sponsors are personally liable for imprudent investment judgments, this liability may be significantly reduced by hiring, after careful investigation, a qualified investment manager, who also becomes a fiduciary under the law, and then carefully monitoring the management of the fund by that professional.

To ensure that pensions would be paid if a company should fail, the Pension Benefit Guarantee Corporation (PBGC) was established. Each year sponsors are required to pay a modest amount to PBGC for each covered employee in order to build up reserves to meet this need. Furthermore, PBGC can assess a company up to 30 percent of its net worth to fund pension liabilities should a company fail to properly fund its plan. In 1982 this provision was under review and was expected to be increased. It is also important to note that the liability of multiemployer plans is not limited to 30 percent of their net worth.

Unique Needs, Circumstances, and Preferences

Despite the high level of sophistication of many plan sponsors, personal prejudices and emotions often play an important part in determining investment objectives. Despite the generally long-term characteristics of pension plans, in the mid-1970s many sponsors forced their managers to liquidate stocks and shift over to fixed income securities at the very time, in retrospect, that the reverse policy was called for. At the outset of a professional management relationship it is highly desirable to get sponsors' input as to how they view the plan, particularly with regard to risk assumption. In fact, sponsors generally should be required to participate in the establishment of initial objectives and update them as called for. However, when sponsors have a direct impact on the day-to-day management of the fund, they risk losing personal liability protection of the law that assumes operational independence of the professional portfolio manager.

Determination of Portfolio Policies

The first real issue in determining portfolio policies may in fact center on the question of whether the sponsor is to use a single investment manager or a number of managers. Smaller plans, which are less sophisticated at the sponsor level, probably would utilize a single, broad-based manager. To the extent that only one manager is used, that manager will have great impact on the overall investment policies of the plan. Contrarily, larger plans with more sophisticated sponsors might wish to use multiple managers in order to utilize a variety of investment philosophies and approaches. In this case, each manager will have little input into the overall investment policies and such responsibility will fall upon the sponsor or his outside consultant.

Some large funds, however, have developed new and innovative approaches to asset allocation and determination of investment policies in order to utilize the best skills and abilities of all their managers. This may involve periodic meetings in which each manager updates the group on how he sees his own role for the coming period and decisions can be made to change asset allocations among security types and investment manager style. For a discussion of this approach, see Kent [1979].

It is interesting to note that many of the smaller "boutique" investment management organizations tend to have very high minimum account size requirements, which probably works not only to their benefit but also tends to lead them away from smaller plans where less specialized managers are probably desirable anyway. This also underlines the importance of having a clearly stated and well-defined set of written objectives and guidelines. This will give the manager a path to follow in managing the fund and the sponsor a basis for monitoring the manager and fund.

Particularly in the case of defined benefit plans, investment policies should flow from the careful analysis of risk and return described earlier in this chapter, taking into account the funding requirements of the plan, the actuarial assumptions, the characteristics of the sponsor's own business, and, finally, the basic underlying attitudes, temperament, and prejudices of the plan sponsor (see Figure 4-1 on page 80). Likewise, defined contribution plans—if carefully analyzed in terms of the underlying approach (retirement benefit versus estate planning), plan characteristics such as the average age of the employees, turnover, and sponsor characteristics—can easily and logically establish meaningful investment policies designed to meet the specific objectives determined. It should be noted that investment objectives cannot be determined based on client factors alone, but must also take into consideration the characteristics of potential investment asset alternatives. Chapters 6 and 7 deal with the capital market factors and Chapter 8 exam-

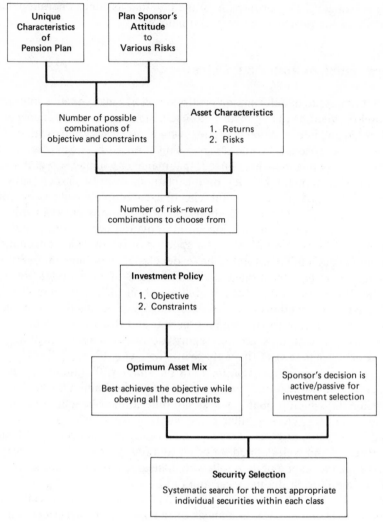

Figure 4-1. The Investment Management Process for Pension Plans.
(SOURCE: Ezra [1979])

ines the integration of client and market factors to determine the asset allocation plan best suited to particular classes of investors.

Portfolio Investment Strategies

Asset Allocations. All of the client factors that go into determining policies must be monitored on an ongoing basis. They can be expected to change over time and should therefore be reflected in changing investment policies. The long-term nature of most plans, particularly pension plans, tends to suggest a normal or base level of common stock investment that is relatively high—in the range of 60 to 90 percent of total assets—except for more mature plans. Despite the poor experience of the mid-1970s, equities over time have provided higher returns than fixed income securities. Thus, so long as the plan is in a position to muddle through difficult periods, the higher returns of equities seem clearly justified in light of the attendant risks. Bendix Corporation, for example, after a careful study of its actuarial and investment policies, determined that up to 90 percent of its non-real estate assets could be invested in common stocks, with the other 10 percent being committed to cash equivalents. While this is perhaps an atypical example, it is illustrative of the trend for many funds toward significantly higher proportions of common stocks and recognizes the higher potential return in stocks over time and a lesser concern by many plan sponsors for higher volatility of those returns. Such long-term asset mix decisions, of course, can be modified on a short- to intermediate-term basis dictated by changing conditions in the economy and financial markets.

Dedicated Bond Portfolios. An interesting innovation of the late 1970s and early 1980s is the *dedicated bond portfolio*, which is explained in detail in Chapter 9. Like so many aspects of pension investing this also is a by-product of high inflation and high interest rates and would be less appropriate should interest rates fall from the level of the early 1980s. Dedicated bond portfolios deal only with that portion of a defined benefit plan relating to retired lives. Because the benefits to be paid to those already in retirement are known and reasonably accurate actuarial assumptions can be made as to their normal life expectancies, actuaries can rather easily determine the cash flows needed to pay benefits to those already retired.

With interest rates during the 1970s and early 1980s exceeding actuarial return rates by rather wide margins and with no need to consider salary progression risks for retirees, a portfolio of fixed income securities could have been constructed to meet all retirement benefits for the known retirees at considerably lower cost to the sponsor than had previously been determined actuarially. There was no reinvestment risk because all income and principal were dedicated to the payment of benefits as they came due. Computer techniques permit a careful structuring of such a dedicated bond portfolio so that cash generated from interest and maturing bonds will very closely match the payment schedule for benefit liabilities. Many investment management firms have developed computer models to make such portfolios readily available to the sponsoring institution at a very modest cost.

The plan assets released by the use of a dedicated bond portfolio may be made available to fund past service liabilities for those yet to retire or unfunded vested benefits, or would permit reduced contributions in future years because of a one-shot overfunding. (More on this topic in Chapter 9.)

Critics of dedicated bond portfolios would point out, however, that much the same result can be accomplished by putting such investment policies into effect as part of the overall investment program and then modestly raising the actuarial rates of return on the entire program to achieve the same advantages for the sponsor. They also point out that dedicated bond portfolios work on the assumption that benefits are known and predictable. In fact, however, many sponsoring companies have given ad hoc cost-of-living increases to their retired employees that would not have been provided for in the dedicated portfolios.

Pension Investment Policy Statement

The net result of all of these investment policy considerations is generally a written investment policy statement that gives the professional manager a road map to follow in developing an investment program to meet the objectives agreed upon and enables the sponsor to monitor the progress of the plan. These policy statements take many forms but the following example of a major U.S. corporation is fairly typical:

THE CONTINENTAL GROUP, INC.
Investment Guidelines for XY Associates*

Guidelines for XY Associates are an integral part of our Plan for the total pension fund. Because of this interrelationship between the role of individual managers and our overall requirements, the first section of these guidelines summarizes the policy framework for our total fund. A second section lists the specific standards that will apply to the portfolio actively managed by XY Associates. A final section defines the method that will be used to evaluate performance of the portfolio.

Policy Framework—Total Fund

The investment objective of our total fund is differentiated from the individual objectives of any one of our active managers. The fund objective, which we have established after careful planning, reflects the trade-off between the risk and expected return considered most appropriate for our total pension fund. The individual objective of each active manager, in contrast, relates to the special role that he has chosen as his best opportunity to add investment value.

Our *Basic Portfolio Plan* provides the broad policy framework required to respond to the investment objective of the total fund. To this end, it assigns each asset category (i.e., stocks, bonds, real estate, and cash equivalents) a "normal" position in the total fund.

The Basic Portfolio Plan contributes directly to the performance of the fund in two ways:

1. It affords downside protection in periods of adversity in the financial markets, since it controls risk at a level consistent with the requirements for our fund. Risks for the individual asset categories partially offset each other to the extent that their returns are out of phase. Combined risks for the diversi-

* XY Associates is a fictitious name for an actual investment manager.

fied mix of assets specified by the Basic Portfolio Plan are therefore considerably less than the weighted average of the risks for the component asset categories.

2. Equally important, the discipline incorporated in the Basic Portfolio Plan enables the total fund to aim at incremental rate of investment return over the longer term. Since overall risk is reduced by asset diversification, the fund is able to include a greater proportion of aggressive investment vehicles than would otherwise be the case. The Basic Portfolio Plan, by our calculations, provides a probability of more than 50 percent that *real* returns will average in excess of 4 percent annually over a ten-year period. Less carefully diversified portfolios, *subject to the same risk limitations*, would have to aim at an average annual return which would be lower by as much as a full percentage point.

Within the broad framework of the Basic Portfolio Plan, each *active manager* is expected to operate in his own *investment universe*. Subject to individually prepared guidelines, each manager will pursue his own strategies within the population of securities that he prefers. Our coordination of guidelines for the individual managers assures that the combined efforts of our managers will be consistent with the overall objective of the fund. The benefits for the active manager of our approach are twofold:

1. Through appropriate definition of his preferred investment universe, the individual manager will be able to concentrate his efforts in those areas where he is best able to demonstrate his strengths. The designated investment universe will exclude those segments of financial markets where research coverage is absent. It will concentrate investment efforts in those activities that are most likely to be advantageous on the basis of the manager's investment philosophy and decision-making process.

2. Once the preferred investment universe is defined, the active manager can enhance opportunities to add value by aggressively exploiting his convictions. The preferred investment universe of each manager will be carefully coordinated with the various investment universes that make up the remainder of the fund. As a result, the sum of our manager's efforts can be controlled to avoid unacceptable deviation from the normal positions specified for the Basic Portfolio Plan. Given careful planning and control for the total fund, the potential negative implications of intensified risk-taking by individual managers will be limited.

Portfolio Standards

Standards for the portfolio of XY Associates follow from identification of the investment universe in which the firm prefers to operate. The investment universe, in turn, is defined by an index and the range of deviation from this index.

The index for the portfolio of XY Associates is designated by XY index. Equities will comprise 90 percent of the weight of the index, with the remaining 10 percent accounted for by 90-day Treasury bills.

The equities included in the index will be drawn from the S&P 500 Index. Based on the Barr Rosenberg risk indexes, issues with unusual financial risk (more than 1.5 standard deviations greater than that of the S&P 500) or low earnings growth (0.1 standard deviations below the growth rate of the S&P 500 or less) will be deleted. Weighting of the remaining issues in the S&P 500 will be based on market capitalization:

1. Equities with market capitalization of $3 billion or more will be equally weighted.
2. Equities with market capitalization of less than $3 billion will be capitalization weighted.

Latitude for implementation of investment strategy within the preferred investment universe is indicated by the range of deviation of the portfolio of XY Associates from the XY index. Portfolio standards are provided for both market risk and equity diversification. Subject to these broad standards, equities that are not included in the index may be purchased from time to time. There is an understanding between XY Associates and the sponsor that, nevertheless, the index will generally represent the median characteristics of the portfolio over an extended period of changes in strategy.

Market risk (systematic risk) will be defined in terms of the portfolio beta. As is the standard practice, beta will be measured against the S&P 500. XY Associates may alter beta within the range shown below as changes in the financial markets are anticipated. Adjustment in beta can be most quickly achieved through adjustment of cash reserves, but may also be attained through modification of the mix of equities held in the portfolio.

	XY Index	*Portfolio Range*
Beta	1.06	0.85–1.25

The beta for each individual equity will be calculated on the basis of the investment fundamentals of the underlying company as provided by Barr Rosenberg Associates. Cash equivalents will be assumed to provide a zero beta. Fixed income securities with maturity over one year will be excluded from this portfolio.

Diversification for the portfolio of XY Associates will be defined by the coefficient of determination (rho-squared or ρ^2) with the managed portfolio measured against the S&P 500.

	XY Index	*Portfolio Range*
Coefficient of determination (ρ^2)	0.97	0.85–0.96

Within the limits specified for diversification, XY Associates is expected to concentrate the portfolio in order to exploit as fully as possible the firm's strategic insights. Where such insights warrant high confidence, the coefficient of determination is likely to approach the low end of the range. During periods when strategic insights are accompanied by low confidence, portfolio diversification will move toward the upper end of the range.

Other standards guiding management of the portfolio by XY Associates are summarized below:

1. Private placements or other investments without active trading markets will not be made without our prior approval.

2. There are no restrictions relating to dividends or earnings of the stocks held in the portfolios.
3. Securities turnover is warranted by the need to alter strategy as prospects for the financial markets change. Since transaction costs represent a reduction of pension assets, and also reflect against the performance of XY Associates, turnover will be maintained at the lowest level consistent with implementation of strategy.
4. There are no requirements for, or restrictions against, realization of net investment gains or losses during the calendar year.
5. No securities of The Continental Group, Inc. are to be purchased.
6. There are to be no short sales, trading on margin, purchase or sale of options, or lending of securities.

Portfolio Evaluation

XY Associates will be evaluated in terms of its demonstrated ability to add value relative to the XY index, which will be calculated on a monthly basis.

A shortfall from the index under favorable market conditions will be regarded negatively, as would failure to attain relative gains under unfavorable market conditions. Over a period of changing market conditions, active management is expected to demonstrate a cumulative net gain over the applicable standard of measurement.

Periodic Review

Standards established for the portfolio of XY Associates reflect our mutual agreement as of the date of the guidelines. Guidelines will be reviewed at least annually, and more frequently as required.

XY Associates will promptly advise us at any time these guidelines no longer seem appropriate. A compelling reason would be significant change in the evaluation by XY Associates of the expected real return or risk over the longer term for the assets that comprise the firm's preferred investment universe. Upon mutual agreement, the standards for the portfolio will be changed to assure the latitude necessary for exercise of special skills of XY Associates in active management.

ENDOWMENT FUNDS

As endowment funds have moved out of the treasurer's back offices, where in many cases they were ignored, ill treated, poorly managed, and generally failed to reach their intended purposes, they have increasingly been recognized by the investment community as a vast and fertile area for professional investment management. Much of the credit for this can be given to the Ford Foundation study conducted in the 1960s, *Managing Educational Endowments*. Although some of the philosophies and approaches espoused by that study have been challenged by endowment experts and found wanting by actual experience, many of the principles have proved to be valid. Of particular note is the strong admonition that such funds utilize professional management, in recognition of the fact that the fund's basic structures and various finance and investment committees have not always successfully managed their assets.

The Ford Foundation's emphasis on utilizing a total rate of return concept for endowment funds proved to be highly controversial, not so much because the concept itself was unsound, but rather because the report, by happenstance, was published virtually at the peak of the late 1960s' bull market. The report emphasized investing in rapidly growing companies where dividends were reasonably low but where capital appreciation and strong growth of dividends were anticipated. The low dividend payouts were to be supplemented by cashing in part of the growth and using it for spending purposes. However, as the stock market declined by some 50 percent through 1974, funds that adopted this approach found they were selling equities at distressed prices in order to supplement income and meet spending requirements. With the subsequent significant recovery of stock prices, the total return concept again gained adherents. However, a number of methods have been developed to smooth out the use of capital and mitigate distress selling. We will discuss some of these techniques later in the chapter.

Scope of Endowment Funds

Endowment funds, which held more than $50 billion in assets in 1981, encompass a broad range of institutions (see Table 4-3). Among these are religious organizations, educational institutions, cultural entities such as museums and symphony orchestras, private social agencies, hospitals, and corporate and private foundations. Another rapidly growing area of endowment investing is nonprofit organizations, such as trade associations, that often have significant endowment or reserve assets.

Although often compared in terms of investment objectives and constraints, endowment funds and retirement funds in fact have only two major similarities: They are both usually long-term in nature and—with few excep-

TABLE 4-3. Total Assets and Number of Endowment Funds
(as of 1981)

	Number of Institutions	Total Assets
ENDOWMENT FUNDS College, private school, museum, and hospital endowments over $2 million	439	$25 billion
FOUNDATION FUNDS Charitable organizations with over $2 million	432	$26 billion
Total	871	$51 billion

SOURCE: Fitzgerald [1982].

tions—are not taxable. But their differences are for more important than their similarities. The range of objectives of such funds is extremely broad and the objectives themselves are often highly qualitative in nature. In this sense, perhaps, they resemble individual investors. One might say that the determination of investment policy for an endowment fund is the resolution of a creative tension existing between the highly demanding need for immediate income and the pervasive and enduring pressures for a growing stream of income to meet future needs. Unfortunately many of the institutions sponsoring these funds, particularly those in the fields of education, health care, and the performing arts, have suffered even greater distress at the hands of inflation than other investors. Religious organizations, too, face demands to provide increasing funds for their various purposes. Thus, perhaps the most important factor in determining endowment investment policies is resolving the tension between short-term and long-term needs and requirements.

Return Requirements

Frequently the determination of an endowment fund return requirement is a tenuous compromise between the sponsoring institution's unrealistic demands for current income and the more realistic probabilities of achieving reasonable returns on invested capital over time consistent with risk-taking ability. This may involve determining specific dollar outlays, with a predetermined progression of income growth, from which the asset mix may fall out naturally depending on the yields available in the various types of investment instruments. For example, a $1 million educational endowment may be required to generate a $60,000 annual income and to increase that income by 7 percent annually. If interest rates were in the range of 14 percent and the portfolio manager's typical stock portfolio for such a fund were yielding 3 percent, the maximum equity position could easily be determined by computing these rates on alternative proportions in stocks and bonds to achieve the desired amount.

In this example, if approximately $700,000 were invested in stocks yielding 3 percent to produce $21,000 of income, and the remaining $300,000 were invested in bonds yielding 14 percent to produce $42,000 of income, the annual income objective of $60,000 would be met with this 70/30 asset mix. Additionally, to meet the 7 percent annual growth rate desired in income, stocks with a strong emphasis on expected dividend growth would be selected, recognizing that the fixed income portion would show no increase in income.

Total Return Approach. However, many endowments have adopted a *total return* approach to their spending policies, using the basic concept suggested by the Ford Foundation. The total return of a portfolio is the combination of interest, dividends, and other current earnings, plus capital appreciation or less capital depreciation for the period. Thus, a fund utilizing the total return concept will not only spend current income from investments but may over time also utilize a portion of capital appreciation as a part of its spending rate.

Relationship to Spending Rate. A variety of formulas have been developed by different endowments to establish a total return objective, generally inclusive of the rate of inflation, and a compatible maximum spending rate. Such formulas indicate how much of the total return will be utilized for the endowment's current needs as opposed to being reinvested. The spending rate may apply a specific percentage of the total return, say 5 percent, to a moving average of the value of the assets over any period desired, such as the last three years, five years, or other period. The rate of return and spending rate desired involve careful consideration and thought, although most endowments tend to pick these rates somewhat arbitrarily.

Some endowment funds take the approach of establishing their total return objective by summing the maximum spending rate—the percentage amount actually taken out of the fund and spent by the endowed institution each year—and the expected inflation rate. This approach assures maintenance of the real value of the endowment if the goal is actually achieved.

In their attempt to reach total return objectives, endowment funds have taken some very creative approaches in determining overall asset mix. Many endowments today are including vehicles that would once have been thought off limits, including venture capital, covered call options, real estate, security lending, and financial futures hedging. A good example of how this total return–spending rate concept can be used is illustrated by the policy of a major university:

INVESTMENT OBJECTIVES
Pooled Marketable Endowment Funds

I. Achievement of a total annual return, measured on a five-year moving average basis, equal to the spending rate (as determined from time to time by official university action) plus the inflation rate (calculated on a consistent basis by national government sources).

II. Within the total return objective, desirability of stability and maximization of current income, consistent with the need and opportunity for long-term capital appreciation.

Definitions

a. *Total annual return* equals the sum of dividend, interest, and current earnings, plus the net impact of price change, time-adjusted for capital additions and withdrawals, all after transaction costs and management fees, for a given fiscal year.

b. *Spending rate,* which is equivalent to the sum distributed annually to pooled marketable endowment fund participants, is calculated as a percentage

(5.5% in fiscal 1982) of the average market value as of the preceding five fiscal year-ends, adjusted for capital additions and withdrawals during the period.

c. *Inflation rate* is the Consumer Price Index as calculated and reported by the U.S. Department of Commerce.

Average for Five-Year Period from Indicated Date

Date	Spending Rate	Inflation Rate	Total Annual Return Objectives
6/77	5.00%	7.21%	12.21%
6/78	5.10	7.90	13.00
6/79	5.20	8.03	13.23

It is important to understand that the return objectives derived from this method are just that—objectives. They may or may not actually be realized in practice, but at least they provide the endowed institution and the investment manager with a known target.

Risk Tolerance

In analyzing and understanding risk tolerance for endowments it may be useful to go back to our creative tension concept discussed earlier (see Figure 4-2). Endowment fund return objectives encompass a broad spectrum, ranging from maximum income at one end to maximum growth at the other. In fact, this spectrum's breadth rivals that for the most risk-heterogeneous of all investors, the individual. Thus, the portfolio manager must be concerned about the *type* of risk assumed as well as the *amount* of risk. For example, where maximum income is the objective, and thus long-term fixed income securities with holding periods to maturity tend to predominate, purchasing power risk generally must be accepted since little or no opportunity for growth in principal is provided. Where maximum growth is the objective, and thus equity-type investments such as common stocks and real estate tend to predominate, market risk generally must be accepted. For a fund with a short time horizon because of a near-term capital outlay or other immediate purpose, preservation of capital is primary and thus principal risk cannot be accepted. In this case, funds would be invested in high quality

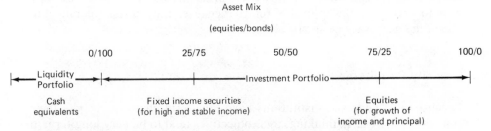

Figure 4-2. Creative Tension in Determining Portfolio Policy.

money market instruments with no chance of default and with little effect on market value even if interest rates rise.

At the other end of our spectrum, where growth is paramount and little income is needed for current purposes, the primary risk is purchasing power risk. These funds are concerned more with a moderate, but growing, stream of income to meet future needs, and they are fully able to accept high volatility of returns in the short run in order to maximize capital appreciation and income growth over the long run.

Most funds fall somewhere between these extremes. Assessing the type and amount of risk such funds can tolerate is really a balancing act in which a variety of risks are considered and investment policies are established to deal with them.

As one can now see, identification of risk tolerance for endowments is quite different from that for defined benefit retirement funds and similar to that for individual investors or defined contribution retirement plans. The net result is that endowments, particularly those at the growth end of the creative tension spectrum, generally use the same financial instruments as retirement funds. As mentioned earlier, even venture capital has been added as an appropriate vehicle for some endowments where long-term growth is an important objective and risk tolerance is high.

An important factor in weighing risk tolerance of endowments is the relative importance of the endowment fund in the sponsoring institution's overall revenue picture. Where the revenues generated, whether from interest, dividends, or capital appreciation, play a relatively minor role in the institution's overall operations, risk tolerance may be relatively high, suggesting more aggressive policies in an effort to build additional reserves against possible future demands greater than those of the present. Contrarily, where the endowed institution is heavily dependent on the return from its endowments (such as one mid-western college that derives about one-half of its operating revenues from its endowments), there is a major risk impact on investment policy, not only in terms of the stability of returns but also their minimum magnitude. While it might be said that all endowment funds seek a stable, growing stream of income, the achievement of this goal over time, and with little straying from the intended trend line, becomes increasingly important where the endowed institution is heavily dependent on the return from its endowments. However, in such case, the institution may have to settle for a lower level of return (because of lower risk tolerance) to obtain the necessary certainty of that return.

Liquidity Requirements

Because most endowed institutions have long-term charters, despite their sometimes short-term thinking, their objectives tend to be very long-term in nature. As a result, little liquidity is needed except, perhaps, to meet emergency needs. Funds have often been contributed by donors in the form of cash or securities with a strong obligation that these donations be kept intact on a more or less permanent basis.

However, there are important exceptions, such as capital contributions made for specific projects where it is known in advance that the funds will be expended (for instance, to build a new hospital, add a new educational wing to the church, and so on). Liquidity is a critical element for such special projects, and investment policies must be clearly established to provide the needed degree of liquidity. Income, while not to be ignored, takes a back seat during the period in which the funds are expended.

Tax Considerations

The endowment income of all but private, nonoperating foundations is tax exempt. Thus, investments such as tax-exempt bonds and preferred stocks are not appropriate investment vehicles for endowments. Private foundations are required by law to pay out investment income equal to 5 percent of their assets annually; to the extent that income is insufficient, the difference must be paid out of principal. Assets used in the normal course of operations—offices, furniture, and the like—are excluded from the asset base for purposes of making this 5 percent calculation. In addition, 1.5 percent of assets may be excluded as a cash balance for normal operating purposes. Investment income of private foundations is taxed at a rate of 2 percent. In determining investment income for tax purposes, long-term capital gains are excluded but short-term capital gains are taxable. Capital gains can be offset by capital losses. Investment management and custodial expenses are deductible from investment income before taxes, as are other reasonable costs. On balance, tax considerations are not a major constraint for the manager.

Regulatory and Legal Considerations

Other than the regulations discussed above concerning taxation of charitable foundations, endowment funds are subject to little in the way of federal regulation. However, many *states* have very specific rules and regulations concerning the management and administration of such funds. Cemetery maintenance funds that provide for perpetual care, for example, generally are very closely scrutinized by state regulatory bodies given the public interest aspects of such funds. The portfolio manager responsible for any endowment fund, therefore, should be aware of state or local regulations and carefully review them with the endowed institution to determine their impact on the investment program. Fortunately, many states that formerly had very rigid rules and regulations concerning the types of investments that could be used by endowments, along with very specific requirements as to dividend history, consecutive years of positive earnings, rating by outside investment advisory services, and so on, have modified these rules largely to encompass the standard prudent man rule.

Unique Needs, Circumstances, and Preferences

Because endowment funds are generally controlled by a broad array of trustees and investment committees, each with different levels of investment skill and understanding, there is also a very wide range of unique needs, constraints, and preferences. This unevenness of approach to endowment administration has a major impact on investment policies as well as on results. Personal prejudices, fears, and anxieties concerning difficult market climates and other emotional elements frequently overwhelm a reasonable, logical approach to the investment management of such funds. Some committees often force liquidation of equities as the market collapses and then jump on the bandwagon once stocks have risen for extended periods.

This is not to say that such emotional elements have no validity. A number of endowments today, particularly in the religious and educational spheres, reflect thoughtful, deep-seated concerns about a variety of social issues in their investment programs. These range from the obvious concerns of a religious organization regarding owning tobacco or liquor stocks to subtle nuances on such concerns as defense policies and racial policies that are often difficult to monitor on a company-by-company basis. Some funds choose to voice their objection by excluding certain investments from their portfolios; others prefer to use their investments in such companies to give them a voice for change. Most professional managers will not accept responsibility for determining which companies may fail to meet the institution's requirements, leaving that to the institution.

All of this points up very clearly the need of such funds to have highly qualified and skilled professional managers and to assure that such managers are not overly constrained by emotional issues. It is likewise very important to develop a clearly defined plan of investment and to stay with it despite other variable factors, so long as the fundamental assumptions on which it is based can be shown to have continued validity.

Determination of Portfolio Policies

The portfolio policies established by endowments will depend on how they resolve the *creative tension*. Such policies may range from a 100 percent position in fixed income securities, in order to maximize current income for present needs, all the way to a 100 percent position in common stocks, with growth as a primary objective and a total concern for future needs. Most endowments fall somewhere in between, trading off present and future needs in some balance specifically designed to meet their own objectives. The greater the focus on immediate demands for current income, the higher will be the fixed income portion of the asset mix; contrarily, the greater the emphasis on long-term growth of principal and income, the greater the emphasis on common stocks.

As discussed earlier, these decisions may all too frequently be arbitrary and based primarily on emotional factors and prejudices of the investment committee. Because endowment investing for many years focused almost entirely on risk aversion in nominal terms, this resulted in not only unproductive but probably counterproductive investment policies. Emphasis on fixed income securities in the overall asset mix and on high yielding stocks in the equity portion resulted in extremely low overall returns in an environment of high inflation and rising interest rates. In many instances this not only was tantamount to *not* preserving capital in nominal terms, but actually contributed toward consuming it. Many of the stocks paying high dividends were, in fact, of companies which borrowed heavily in the fixed income market—essentially to maintain those high dividends—and thus gradually eroded the capital base of the underlying investor. Consider, for example, the return of capital aspect of dividend payments of many utilities. Increasingly, it became apparent that the major risk not being dealt with was the purchasing power of endowment capital and income.

Movement Toward Total Return Approach. But many endowment committees have developed far more imaginative and creative approaches to setting investment policies, establishing a meaningful spending rate and, using a variety of formulas, incorporating these factors into a total rate of return approach. However, because there is still strong reticence on the part of many investment committees to move away from the traditional methods, this itself becomes a major constraint on the investment policy of such institutions. But funds using the newer techniques have benefited from the achievement of higher *usable* returns over time. In terms of the real objective of these funds, risk has truly not been significantly increased, but rather has been modified. One could argue that with hemorrhaging of inflation-adjusted capital values effectively staunched, the risk of greatest concern has been significantly reduced. The damage to the total return approach by the stock market of the mid-1970s may have slowed the process, but in many instances enlightened management has prevailed, with attendant excellent long-term investment results.

Effect of Inflation. One major factor that must be considered by all endowments, however, whether short-term or long-term oriented, is that whatever income is desired should be stable and, hopefully, grow to compensate for inflation.

Perhaps the most obvious difference between endowment investing and retirement investing shows up in this area. Whereas a retirement fund generally does not really depend on current income nor does its value from year to year significantly affect its overall, long-term objectives, endowment funds are very dependent upon their returns on an ongoing, continuous basis. Consider the fixed income portion of the fund, for example. While a retirement fund can change both bond maturity structure and coupon/price relationships—techniques that often result in wide swings of current income—an endowment fund has far less ability to effect these changes. Fluctuation in principal can be tolerated, but fluctuation of income from short-term investments generally cannot because the cash flow volatility of short-maturity instruments that roll over frequently is usually too high a price to pay for the potential of increased total returns. Thus, an endowment fund may emphasize longer term bonds on a more or less permanent basis. This policy is strengthened when the fund has a fairly high cash flow from donations and can take advantage of rising interest rates through new investments. Provided adequate call protection is taken, emphasizing long-term bonds when interest rates are high reduces the risk of significantly lower yield and lower cash flow on maturity rollovers in a prolonged period of declining interest rates.

The disadvantage of this emphasis on longer term bonds is the opportunity cost of income during a period of rising interest rates, such as the 1965–81 period, especially since such a trend is usually the result of rising inflation that adversely affects the operating costs of the endowed institution. An interesting variation of fixed income policy designed to deal with this and maintain the traditional "real" income on bonds—that is, the difference between yield and the inflation rate—is to use a laddered or spaced maturity schedule ranging from short to intermediate, perhaps two to twelve years. During periods of rising interest rates, rollover of maturities would provide funds to take advantage of higher yields and the short average maturity (duration) would limit price decline. Although this would work in reverse during periods of falling interest rates, with rollover occurring at lower and lower yields, presumably this would happen during a period of declining inflation, so the institution's costs would also be expected to fall.

Desire for Income Stability. The desire for income stability will also suggest a policy of purchasing and holding to maturity discount bonds where the interest-on-interest element is of little consequence since all coupon income will be spent and it is desirable to assure returns on a continuing basis. The endowed institution must understand, however, that utilizing discount bonds typically reduces both current yield and yield to maturity somewhat, and the deeper the discount the greater the potential loss of income. This relates to the tax benefit enjoyed by certain taxable entities that can afford to "pay up" (i.e., pay a higher price) for discount bonds given their tax status, since the discount will be taxed at capital gains rates. However, a carefully structured fixed income portfolio with spaced maturities and moderate discounts for call protection can provide a very high and stable level of income to the endowed institution, and that consideration may be decisive.

This also suggests that even with a total return concept there should be a solid anchor of current income to avoid wide fluctuations of spendable returns as would result, given the high volatility of common stock prices, from a great dependence on capital appreciation over time. The farther the total return moves from this income anchor, the greater is its potential volatility and the greater the risk of not meeting the required return. Thus, if a spending rate is established at 6 percent, with an asset mix of 25 percent in bonds yielding 14 percent and 75 percent in stocks yielding 3.5 percent, all or most of the current income needs will be obtained from dividends and interest, leaving all or most of the growth in principal from equities to accumulate and generate a higher level of income in the future. If, however, spending rates were established at 10 percent, with the same mix and yield, nearly half the total return required would have to come from capital appreciation from the equity portion, thus increasing the potential volatility of the income stream. To some extent this can be mitigated by a formula designed to smooth the use of appreciation over a market cycle.

Inherent in this discussion is the implication that the types of securities employed, as well as the asset mix, will also be influenced by the basic policies of the fund with regard to the spending rates, total return, and so on. Thus, a fund with a longer time horizon, emphasizing reasonable current income (but not at the expense of long-term growth of principal and income), may hold more volatile, aggressive securities than a fund in which the time horizon is short term.

Endowment Fund Investment Policy Statement

A statement of investment policy developed from these considerations by the same university as in our earlier example of return requirements follows:

INVESTMENT POLICIES
Pooled Marketable Endowment Funds

I. A portfolio balance, to be averaged over time, of a maximum position of 67 percent in equity-type investments and a minimum position of 33 percent in fixed income-type investments.

II. Qualified equity and fixed income investments to consist of the following:

Equity Related	Fixed Income Related
Common stocks and warrants	Government and agency obligations
Convertible securities	Corporate obligations
Option writing	Preferred stocks
Venture capital participants	Real estate mortgages
Real estate participations	Private placements
Security lending programs	Security lending programs

III. In the case of convertible securities, corporate obligations, and preferred stocks carrying a credit rating, qualified for purchase are such securities rated no less than BBB ("regarded as having an adequate capacity to pay interest/dividends and repay principal") as defined by Standard & Poor or its equivalent as defined by other recognized rating agencies.

IV. No more than 10 percent of the average maximum equity position (7 percent of total marketable endowment funds) to be invested in venture capital and real estate equity participations, combined. No more than 20 percent of the average minimum fixed income position (7 percent of total marketable endowment funds) to be invested in real estate mortgages and private placements, combined.

V. The Office of the Treasurer to have direct responsibility for no more than 50 percent of total marketable endowment funds. Remaining funds to be the responsibility of outside managers as selected from time to time. All managers to have full investment discretion within defined statements of objectives and policies.

To summarize, endowment funds have become an increasingly important factor to the professional investment manager as these funds have found that using outside management is desirable in achieving goals. Investment policies determined by these funds depend on a variety of factors, including temperament and emotional involvement of the trustees or investment committees, the tradeoff between short-term demands for income and long-term needs for a growing stream of income and enhancement of capital in real terms, and an awareness of social issues which may or may not be part of the organization's philosophy.

LIFE INSURANCE COMPANIES

So far this chapter has considered what might be characterized as the two major private, nonprofit institutional investors—retirement plans and endowment funds. Now, attention is directed to the two major financial institutions, insurance companies and banks, that operate for profit and, thus, must reflect in their investment policies the element of competition. While some interesting innovations in both the endowment and retirement fields have been noted, none of these can be considered nearly as revolutionary or far-reaching as the trends in banking and insurance over the past decade or so. As will be seen, the inflation and higher interest rates of the 1970s and early 1980s have caused major changes in the competitive position and investment policies of these major financial institutions.

In a sense, all investing can be thought of as a matching of assets with liabilities. Especially in the case of individual investors, endowments, defined contribution retirement plans, and investment companies (mutual funds), this process may involve a number of highly qualitative judgments because the liabilities are not so obvious or clearly definable for these classes of investor. Contrarily, as has been noted, defined benefit retirement plans generally have more clearly determinable liability structures. This, in turn, leads to more clearly definable investment policies and allocation of invested assets. Perhaps this matching of assets and liabilities is nowhere clearer or more quantifiable than in insurance (especially life insurance) companies and banks, the next two topics of discussion in this chapter. Of particular interest with regard to these two major institutions has been the very dynamic change in the patterns and duration of their respective liability structures, which in turn have caused dramatic responses in terms of asset deployment and investment policy.

For the personal line segment of the life insurance industry, two major developments—which have evolved over the past quarter century but have accelerated in the past ten years as a result of historically high inflation and interest rates—have had a significant impact on the structure of liabilities and the attendant investment policies.

First, life insurance companies have experienced unprecedented disintermediation as interest rates reached such high levels that policyholders took advantage of the unusually cheap policy loan rates (5–9%) available to them based on the cash values of their whole life insurance policies. Such policies involve a combination of insurance and savings, with part of the premiums going to pay for insurance coverage but a major portion being invested in reserves to accumulate cash value and ultimately to pay benefits that will come due upon the death of the policyholder in later years. These reserves are accumulated at very low rates, usually no more than 4 to 5 percent. And an important provision of most whole life policies is that the policyholder can borrow against the cash value at statutorily defined rates. In the past policy loan rates were in line with rates available on passbook savings and other short-term investment vehicles. But as inflation and interest rates rose, these loan rates became cheap and policyholders have taken advantage of the opportunity to borrow their accumulated value at interest rates significantly below the going market rates.

Second, as interest rates have risen, insurance buyers have considered a broader array of financial alternatives, and the philosophy of "buy term and invest the difference" has gained more acceptance. Essentially, this means that the policyholder buys term insurance for risk protection only and takes the significant difference between the premium on term and on whole life and invests it at rates of return considerably higher than the actuarial accumulation rates of the whole life policy. Both these developments are having a major impact on the investment policies of life insurance companies. This section of the chapter will discuss the characteristics and competitive position of the insurance industry as the determinants of portfolio policies for both life and nonlife (casualty) insurance companies.

Size and Scope of the Insurance Industry

Insurance companies are a major source of investment funds for the world capital markets. On a worldwide basis, the 1982 invested assets of insurance companies were estimated to be in excess of $1.5 trillion, with U.S. and Canadian companies accounting for approximately one-half of the total. Insurance companies in four other industrial countries—Japan, West Germany, Great Britain, and France—represent the next largest segment of the industry, accounting for about one-third of the world total. It is interesting to note that although insurance enjoys a world market, only a very small number of the approximately 10,000 insurance companies conduct business on a worldwide basis.

The economic significance of the insurance industry is its unique role as an absorber of personal and business risks. By providing financial protection, the industry plays a key role in the growth and development of a country's economy. Because of the risk aspects of the business and the contractual obligations to policyholders, the traditional investment practices of the insurance industry have been characterized as conservative.

The business of insurance is complex but can be divided into three broad product categories: life insurance, health insurance, and property and liability insurance. For purposes of considering investment policy, it is sufficient to narrow the categories to life and nonlife (casualty) insurance companies. This division of the insurance business is consistent with the major classifications established in the United States by the insurance regulatory bodies and the Internal Revenue Service (IRS).

Insurance companies, whether life or casualty, are incorporated either as stock companies or as mutuals (that is, companies that have no stock and are owned by their policyholders). Mutuals have a long tradition and play a major role in certain segments of the insurance industry, but stockholder-owned companies have become the primary form of entry into the industry. While there is little difference in the investment operations of mutual and stock companies, the differences between life and nonlife companies are substantial, as will be illustrated in the following sections.

Return Requirements

Historically, return requirements for a life insurance company have been specified primarily by the rates used by actuaries to determine policyholder reserves or accumulation rates for funds being held by the company for future disbursement. In effect, an assumed rate of interest is established for each contract and continues for the life of the contract. Interest is then credited to the reserve account at the assumed rate; the latter can thus be defined as the minimum return requirement. Failure to earn the minimum return would result in an increase in liabilities, by accrual of interest, that was greater than the increase in assets. The shortfall would be reflected in a decrease in surplus or surplus reserves, assuming the most simple case. Needless to say, the adequacy of reserve funding is carefully monitored by management, the regulatory commissions, and rating agencies such as Best's *Insurance Reports*.

The assumed statutory accumulation rates (minimum return) for most life insurance contracts range between 3 and 5½ percent. Thus, in the high interest rate environment of the late 1960s and for the entire decade of the 1970s, the return on new investments (the new money rate) and portfolio returns in general have exceeded the minimum returns by a widening margin

TABLE 4-4. Pretax Portfolio Yields of U.S. Life Insurance Companies (ratio of net investment to mean cash and invested assets)

Year	Industry Rate	MAJOR LIFE COMPANIES		
		Prudential	Lincoln National	Equitable—N.Y.
1920	4.30%			
1930	5.05			
1940	3.45		Not Available	
1950	3.13			
1960	4.11			
1970	5.34	5.56%	5.47%	5.32%
1975	6.44	6.47	6.98	6.22
1976	6.68	6.69	7.21	6.64
1977	7.00	7.02	7.55	7.13
1978	7.39	7.44	7.72	7.55
1979	7.78	7.75	8.24	8.06
1980	8.06	7.85	8.09	8.18

SOURCE: *Life Insurance Fact Book* [1982]; *Best's Insurance Management Reports* [1981a].

(see Table 4-4). It should be noted that the prevalence of positively sloped yield curves over the past 40 years has focused life insurance fixed income investment in long-term issues.

Beyond the assumed statutory accumulation rate, the return objectives of life insurance companies have not been well defined, although more and more companies are pricing policies assuming interest rates of 8 percent or more. Consistently above-average investment returns should and do provide a company with some competitive advantage in setting premiums. However, in reality, the returns for most life insurance company portfolios are more similar than different (see Table 4-4). This largely reflects the role regulation plays in constraining the asset mix and quality characteristics of every life company portfolio. Furthermore, the fact that benefits are payable in fixed dollar amounts has limited the motivation to assume additional risk in an effort to achieve portfolio returns in excess of the rate of current inflation or average industry experience. In fact, one could say that high inflation has benefited life insurance sales. As inflation eroded the protection value of existing policies, the policyholder had to buy additional insurance to have the same *real* protection.

More Competitive Returns. It is equally important to note that during the decade of the 1970s competitive investment returns have become a necessity, especially for companies selling annuity and guaranteed investment contract products. This major segment of the life insurance business accounts for 45 percent of total industry reserves (see Table 4-5). For these lines of business, competition comes from outside, as well as from within, the insurance industry. These competitive pressures are requiring insurance

TABLE 4-5. Reserves for Annuities
and Guaranteed Investment
Contracts—Life Insurance Industry

Selected Years	Percent of Total Reserves
1965	23.9%
1970	26.6
1974	29.8
1978	39.7
1979	42.2
1980	45.4
1981	47.9

SOURCE: *Life Insurance Fact Book* [1982].

companies to more closely match assets and liabilities and even consider *segmenting* the portfolio in order to assure maintenance of a competitive rate of return under volatile market conditions. For example, insurance companies issuing guaranteed investment contracts (GICs) must invest cash flow in a portfolio of securities so as to assure the maintenance of guaranteed rates during the life of the contract, which can be up to five years or more. Such bond portfolio techniques as immunization, to be discussed in Chapter 9, have been widely utilized in this regard.

The annuity business presents another set of return objectives. Disintermediation has forced life companies to provide annuity returns that can compete with the higher short-term rates seen in recent periods of inverted yield curves. To achieve these return objectives, many life insurance companies have shifted some segment of their portfolios into shorter term securities, increasing holdings of money market instruments like Treasury bills and commercial paper and/or emphasizing maturities of one to ten years.

New Policy Forms. New life insurance policy forms are being created to stem the surrender of policies, particularly whole life. The most recent and revolutionary are the so-called universal life policies which provide the policyholder with a flexible, investment-oriented package. The policyholder pays a specified amount for the insurance protection desired. For a separate fee, he can deposit funds in a savings-type fund that provides the benefits of a competitive interest rate, the income from which can be tax deferred. In September 1982, the tax status of universal life and single-premium annuities was clarified via Congressional action on life insurance company tax revision.

In essence, a trend toward unbundling insurance risk management and investment management is developing. The investment management segment of these policies requires competitive rates of return—whether they be in the form of an annuity or some other form. Thus, in an environment of volatile interest rates, the return requirements of a life insurance company may well vary by major line of business, the result being that multiple return objectives may be incorporated into a single company's investment policy.

Risk Tolerance

In terms of public policy, the investment portfolio of an insurance company (life or nonlife) is looked upon as a quasi-trust fund. Accordingly, conservative fiduciary principles largely reflect the low risk tolerance of an insurance portfolio. Confidence in the ability of any insurance company to pay benefits as they are due is a crucial element in the financial foundation of the economy. Thus, insurance companies are usually averse to any significant chance of large principal loss.

To absorb some modest loss of principal, life insurance companies are required to maintain a *mandatory security valuation reserve* (MSVR). This is a reserve established by the National Association of Insurance Commissioners (NAIC). The annual contributions and maximum amounts of the reserve are determined by specific "quality tests" delineated by the NAIC for bonds, preferred stocks, and common stocks. Net realized capital gains are also credited to the reserve as long as it is below the maximum. All realized capital losses are charged to the reserve, as are unrealized capital losses on common stock holdings—the only class of assets carried at market value by life insurance companies. The maximum amount of the reserve varies by the class and/or quality of the invested assets: bonds of investment grade—2 percent of their total cost; bonds of lower grade—20 percent; preferred stocks in good standing—10 percent; and common stocks—$33\frac{1}{3}$ percent. These maximum rates suggest a substantial margin for absorbing losses. However, with a growing portfolio and annual contribution rates varying from 0.1 percent (bonds) up to 1 percent (common stocks), most life insurance company security valuation reserves are well below the maximum. Thus, surplus is vulnerable to write-down if significant losses occur.

Valuation Concerns. Such write-downs did occur at the end of 1974 when the cumulative effect of two years of sharply declining common stock prices resulted in a capital adequacy problem for the insurance industry. Unrealized capital losses on stocks exceeded the amount of the MSVR for many companies, with the excess being a direct reduction of surplus. As a result of that experience many insurance companies, willingly or at the urging of the NAIC, reduced the percentage of assets invested in common stocks.

It should be pointed out that, as of early 1982, the surplus of life insurance companies was overstated, because bonds, mortgages, and preferred stocks were not valued at market for statement purposes. For example, the 1980 and 1981 interest rate peaks and consequent declines in the market value of bonds would have wiped out the surplus of the life insurance industry if these fixed income securities had been valued at market value rather than amortized cost.

Cash Flow Volatility. Finally, loss of income or volatility of cash flow from investment is another key aspect of risk for which life insurance companies have low tolerance. Compounding (interest-on-interest) is an integral part of the reserve funding formula and a principal source of surplus growth. The actuaries assume that all investment income will be available for reinvestment at a rate at least equal to the assumed (minimum return) rate. Thus, insurance companies seek investments offering a minimum risk of volatility (disruption) of income and principal.

Reinvestment Risk. For those insurance companies competing for annuity and guaranteed investment contract business, yet another risk factor can be significant—reinvestment. Reinvestment risk is defined as the risk of reinvesting coupon income or principal at a rate less than the original coupon or purchase rate. For GIC or annuity contracts on which no interest is paid out until the maturity (terminal date) of the contract, the guaranteed rate typically includes the insurance company's best estimate of the rate(s) at which semiannual interest payments will be reinvested. Thus, an unexpected decline in interest rates can jeopardize the profitability of these contracts. It should be pointed out that many GIC contracts provide for annual disbursement of interest; this, of course, reduces or eliminates reinvestment risk.

As discussed earlier, competitive conditions dictate maintenance of the guaranteed rate for GICs and the flexibility to adjust the rates paid on annuities. The quest for competitive returns, especially under unbundled policies, may require an increased tolerance for risk on the part of insurance companies and some broadening of asset mix to the extent permitted by regulation.

Liquidity Requirements

Traditionally, life insurance companies have been characterized as needing minimal liquidity. Except during the depression of the 1930s, annual cash inflow has far exceeded cash outflow. Thus, the need to liquidate assets was negligible, reflecting the growing volume of business, long-term liabilities, and rollover in portfolio assets from maturities. Investment focus was concentrated on seeking the highest yield for the longest period of time.

However, times have changed. On four different occasions in the past 15 years (1966, 1970, 1974, and 1979–81), inflation and high interest rates have forced life insurance companies to take measures to accommodate extraordinary cash outflow. Initially, policy loan drains in conjunction with heavy forward commitment positions forced some remedial but temporary change in investment strategies. The ability of policyholders to borrow cash values at interest rates ranging between 5 and 9 percent has long been a sales feature emphasized by companies that concentrate their efforts in the high income sector of the personal insurance market. While policy loans represent approximately 9 percent of industry total assets (see Table 4-6), such loans account for over 25 percent of the assets of some companies.

TABLE 4-6. Policy Loans for the Life Insurance Industry

Selected Years	Percent of Total Assets
1965	4.8%
1970	7.8
1974	8.7
1978	7.8
1979	8.1
1980	8.6
1981	9.3

SOURCE: *Life Insurance Fact Book* [1982].

Disintermediation. The most recent cash flow gap in 1979–81 was further complicated by a disruption of the flow of pension monies into GICs or separate accounts and an increase in surrenders of life insurance and annuity policies. The cumulative effect of these disruptions and policy loan outflows was a scramble for liquidity. Some companies delayed the take-down of previously committed investments, many ceased all new investment for a period of several months, and some sold portfolio assets to raise cash. A few major life insurance companies were even forced to borrow from the banks or issue commercial paper at the prevailing high rates of 15–20 percent.

These volatile economic and capital market conditions have heightened liquidity requirements and thus further constrained insurance companies' ability to utilize a traditional long-term investment media—private placements of long-term bonds. In addition, marketability of investments and the maturity schedule of portfolio investments are receiving increased attention in an effort to ensure ample liquidity. Also, forward commitments have been curtailed, if not suspended, by liquidity considerations. Such commitments represent agreements by life insurance companies to purchase private placement bonds or mortgages, with part or all of the settlement delayed typically over a period of from one to eighteen months. The traditional stability and growth of cash flow fostered this practice, but disintermediation has undermined the predictability of life companies' cash flow. Furthermore, to deal with the change in liquidity requirements, life insurance companies are discussing and in some cases implementing changes in investment policy to more closely match the maturity or duration of assets with liability reserves.

One criticism of this approach is that it tends to look at an insurance company on a liquidating basis. While it is true that liability reserves are not static, it is also true that policyholder disintermediation has been heightened by the pressures of inflation. Thus, the potential for cash flow gaps, plus the experience of 1979–81, is reshaping investment policy, with liquidity requirements assuming a much higher priority. With flat or inverted yield curves, liquidity considerations result in little or no sacrifice in yield and materially reduce the principal risk of the portfolio. A positively sloped yield curve increases the cost of liquidity but, conversely, it should also reduce the need for liquidity as disintermediation pressures subside.

Time Horizon

Life insurance companies have long been considered the classic long-term investor. Portfolio return objectives have been evaluated traditionally within the context of holding periods of as long as 20 to 40 years. Furthermore, with annual cash available for investment ranging from 100 million to several billion dollars for the top 50 life companies (which account for over half of industry assets), putting that much money to work creates an internal pressure to seek an adequate number of investment outlets. Thus, most life insurance companies have traditionally sought long-term maturities for bond and mortgage investments. Real estate ownership, with returns that increase with inflation over longer periods of time, has also been attractive to life insurance companies.

Again, for certain rapidly growing segments of the life insurance business—annuities and GICs—short-term horizons of one to five years are required. Thus, as mentioned earlier, some companies have even gone so far as to segment their portfolios; in effect, they have created a portfolio within the portfolio with a time horizon unique to the return objectives of the annuity and/or GIC. A few life companies have requested regulatory approval for segmentation on a statutory basis.

Essentially, two factors are reshaping investment practices and time horizons for the life insurance industry: (1) an unprecedented high level and volatility of interest rates in the bond and mortgage markets, and (2) significant changes in the liability structure, as evidenced by the increasing percentage of total reserves attributed to shorter term liabilities associated with annuity-type contracts and the increasing role of term insurance, universal life, and variable life policies. As matching of asset and liability maturities or durations becomes more prevalent, these shorter time horizons represent a further constraint.

Tax Considerations

Taxation, in general, is complex, but the tax statutes applying to life insurance companies are especially so. With rising returns on investment, the tax rates of life companies are rising rapidly. Many life insurance companies are faced with the prospect of changing their operating and portfolio policies to minimize the impact of rising marginal tax rates.

In a very simplified context, the investment income of life insurance companies is divided into two parts for tax purposes under the Life Insurance Tax Act of 1959: (1) the policyholders' share—that portion relating to the actuarially assumed rate necessary to fund reserves—and (2) the balance that is transferred to surplus. Only the latter portion is taxed. The tax rate varies essentially with the spread between the interest rate assumed to be earned and the actual yield on the portfolio. With rising interest rates and widening spreads, the marginal tax rates for life insurance companies are rising rapidly. True, the industry's effective tax rate is about 25–30 percent; but for some major companies the effective rate is at or near the 46 percent corporate rate. Under a complex formula (the so-called Menge rule) for taxing "excess earnings," marginal tax rates can exceed the 46 percent corporate rate as the spread between actual portfolio yields and assumed rates widens. Also, it is important to note, tax-exempt income (that is, interest from U.S. municipal bonds) is subject to federal income tax for life companies. This further constrains the life companies' efforts to maximize after-tax portfolio returns.

Rather than belabor the complexities of the tax status of life insurance companies, it is sufficient to point out that taxes are becoming an increasingly important consideration in determining investment policy. Tax considerations are also generating reinsurance agreements and other operating policy changes designed to control or reduce the marginal tax rate. Finally, in 1982 Congress made changes in the life insurance tax code that should have important and favorable implications for the industry.

Regulatory and Legal Considerations

Insurance is a heavily regulated industry. In the United States, state rather than federal regulation prevails; and this regulation pervades all aspects of an insurance company's operations—permitted lines of business, product and policy forms, authorized investments, and the like. Through the NAIC, whose membership covers all 50 states, accounting rules and financial statement forms are promulgated. In Canada, regulation is federal, except for those companies doing business only within a specific province. At either level—federal or provincial—Canadian regulation is as pervasive as U.S. regulation.

These regulations are the primary constraint affecting investment policy. First, state insurance laws determine the classes of assets eligible for investment and the "quality" standards for each asset class. For example, most states require that for a bond issue to be eligible for investment the interest coverage ratio (earnings + interest/interest) must meet minimum standards over a specified time period (e.g., 1.5 times coverage over each of the past five years), and that common stocks must have had a minimum amount of net earnings available for the payment of dividends over each of the past five years.

Second, state laws specify the percentage of an insurance company's assets that can be invested in a specified class of eligible assets. For example, most states limit the cost value of common stock holdings of life insurance companies to no more than 10 percent of total admitted assets. The scope of regulation is far more extensive than these summary comments suggest. For example, the *Investment Law Manual* published by the Life Insurance Association of America contains over 80 pages of references to New York statutes, which are considered the model for most other states. Audit procedures of the state insurance departments and the NAIC ensure compliance with the regulations of the state in which the company is domiciled.

Third, uniform valuation methods are established and administered by the NAIC. In fact, the *Securities Valuation Book,* published at the end of each year, is a compilation of the values or valuation bases to be used by insurance companies for portfolio securities. This book is the source of the valuation data listed in Schedule D of the Annual Statement filed by each company with the insurance departments of the states in which they operate. The schedule is an inventory of all bond and stock holdings at year-end and a recap of all transactions during the year.

Because the primary emphasis of insurance regulation is protection of the interests of policyholders, it limits the broad investment alternatives—in terms of classes of assets, quality factors, and concentration of holdings— available to insurance companies. Regulation, then, has a profound effect on both the risk and return aspects of a life insurance company portfolio, primarily because it constrains the most critical aspect of portfolio management—the asset mix.

Unique Needs, Circumstances, and Preferences

Each insurance company, whether it be life or nonlife, can have unique preferences or needs, attributable to factors over and above the insurance products the company provides, that may further modify portfolio policies. It is also important to note that the size of the company and the sufficiency of its surplus position are among the considerations influencing portfolio policy.

By law, a committee of the board of directors, usually called the investment or finance committee, is required to establish investment policy and oversee its implementation by approving all transactions. This committee's preferences or perception of the company's needs is influenced by the operating goals of the executive management and the size and qualifications of the investment staff.

Determination of Portfolio Policies

As noted, it is clear that life insurance companies' low tolerance for risk is the dominant factor shaping their investment policy. Because of their contractual liabilities, it is prudent that risk be minimized by offsetting assets. Despite the emphasis on safety, the persistence of inflation has distorted normal risk-reward relationships. The result is that life insurance companies have suffered far greater market value volatility in their bond portfolios than regulators and management had ever envisioned. Under these conditions, the traditional definition of a fixed income security as a "safe" asset is less than viable.

We have previously discussed the impact of increased policy loans on investment policy, with its primary effect on liquidity. The impact on investment policy tends to be a transitory one, increasing as interest rates rise and receding as interest rates fall.

Effect of Industry Trends. Of perhaps greater and more fundamental importance to the long-term investment policy of life companies is the accelerating move away from whole life policies toward term and other innovative types of policies, specifically universal life and variable life policies. As the "buy term and invest the difference" trend has developed, insurance companies have found themselves losing investable dollars to other savings and investment outlets such as certificates of deposit, Treasury obligations, and mutual funds. Universal life and variable life can be seen as an effort on the part of the life insurance industry to recapture these investment dollars.

These trends might also be considered to be part of a broad consolidation of financial services developing in the United States. The acquisition of Bache & Company by Prudential and other significant mergers, combinations, and acquisitions within the financial services field are indicative of this trend. Today, life insurance policies are routinely sold by investment brokerage firms. On the other hand, since the 1960s some insurance companies have offered mutual funds to investors through their vast financial distribution networks. It appears that this trend toward one-stop shopping for financial services will accelerate dramatically in the 1980s, and will have a significant impact on the total capital market system of the United States. As the pattern of sales has shifted toward shorter term policies, life insurance companies have significantly reduced their commitment to the long-term corporate bond market; this, in turn, has made such borrowing by U.S. corporations more difficult and expensive. If corporations are forced to borrow funds in the short- and intermediate-term markets, it becomes more difficult for them to forecast interest cost from a budgetary viewpoint.

One major result of these trends is a dramatically changing asset mix for the life insurance industry. Figure 4-3 on page 108 shows clearly the change in asset mix taking place within the industry; one can expect these trends to continue and perhaps accelerate over the next several years.

Effect of New Insurance Products. Universal life, with its important function as a savings instrument, will require insurance companies to invest significant funds in the shorter term debt markets. To the extent that policyholders elect an equity alternative for their universal life policies, this will open up opportunities for life insurance companies to invest more funds in the equity market.

This changing mix of insurance products will have its greatest impact on investment policies in the increased risk that insurance companies assume in

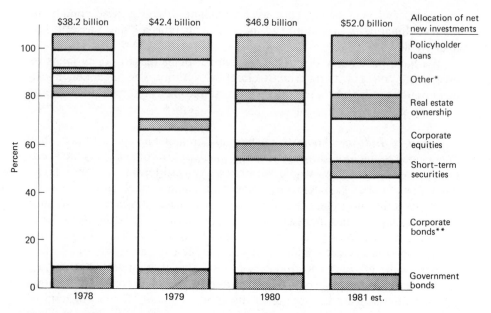

*Including uncollected premiums, oil and gas, cash, leasing, venture capital, etc.
**Includes private placements and mortgages

Figure 4-3. Changing Allocation of Net New Investments of Life Insurance Companies. (SOURCE: "The Changing Life Insurers" [1981]. Reprinted from *Business Week* by special permission, © 1981 by McGraw-Hill, Inc., New York, N.Y. 10020. All rights reserved.)

order to provide competitively attractive returns. At the same time the industry has had to cope with a major asset base worth considerably less than original cost (the long-term fixed income portfolio) held against a liability base that is shortening in maturity (duration) and subject to disintermediation. One of the real problems facing the life insurance industry in recent years is the risk of *cannibalization.* If a company with a large book of whole life actively promotes these new products, it may well encourage present whole life policyholders to cash in and replace their policies with the new products, thus forcing the massive liquidation of long-term bonds at distressed prices the industry is trying so desperately to avoid. One hopes that it is possible to have a smooth transition over a long period of time so that the problems will not seriously impact either on the profitability of the insurers or the safety of the policyholders' benefits.

Portfolio Segmentation. The net result of all of this may well be portfolio *segmentation,* or the creation of subportfolios within the general account portfolio, according to the product mix for each individual company.

Portfolio segmentation is being seriously considered by the management of life insurance companies and the state insurance commissions. In 1982 the return on invested assets in the general account was allocated proportionally to various lines of life insurance business (whole life, annuities, group, and so on) on the basis of *investment year* or, alternatively, on the basis of each line's ratio of reserves to total reserves. (Allocation of investment income by the investment-year method means that the cash flow for investment by line of business is credited with the new money rate or average yield for new investments in that year.) Thus, statutory reports have not permitted or encouraged life insurance companies to match invested assets and their returns with a product line. However, the shift of the product mix to annuity and guaranteed investment contracts (the reserves for which now exceed 45% of total assets) has created a need to identify subportfolios designed to support those product lines. Segmented portfolios provide the investment manager with a clear focus for meeting the return objectives over the time horizon specified for a subportfolio. Regulators and senior management are finding that segmentation provides for more accurate measurement of both profitability by major line of business and suitability of the investment policy defined for these subportfolios. As of year-end 1981, one major New York domiciled life insurance company received regulatory approval to segment its portfolio. Widespread regulatory approval of portfolio segmentation could change life insurance investment practices dramatically and provide the opportunity for flexible and responsive investment policy.

In the final analysis, investment policy must complement the operating policy of any insurance company. Thus, investment portfolio policy seeks to achieve the most appropriate mix of investment alternatives, first, to counterbalance the risks inherent in the mix of insurance products involved, and, second, to achieve the stated return objectives. Numerous factors must be considered in arriving at the appropriate mix, the most important of which are regulatory influences, time horizon, and tax considerations. Finally, competition—both within and outside the insurance industry—is expected to require more flexible and responsive investment management of insurance company portfolios.

Life Insurance Company Investment Policy Statement

The following example shows how a life insurance company might state its investment objectives and policies:

XYZ LIFE INSURANCE COMPANY
Investment Policy Statement

The investment objectives and policies established reflect the long-term nature of most life insurance reserves but also recognize the shorter term characteristics of the reserves for certain products such as annuities. Regulatory, tax, and operating considerations shape the policies and priorities outlined below:

Objective: Obtain a favorable return (in excess of contract accumulation rates) on invested assets through a diversified portfolio of high quality income-producing assets.

Policy: Investment yield (after adjusting for potential tax liability) is emphasized to maximize investment income through investment in fixed income securities and mortgages that are rated or have the financial characteristics to qualify for a rating of A or better.

Liquidity and preservation of surplus considerations are limiting elements in achieving a favorable return on invested assets. Sufficient cash funds are maintained to meet financial obligations, and funds not immediately needed to offset withdrawals are invested in short-term securities as operating conditions require. Balanced (laddered) maturities are maintained to supplement annual cash flow from operations and investment income. In addition, the maturity schedule is a source of liquidity and flexibility to meet changing market, tax, and operating considerations.

Objective: Obtain growth of capital to maintain the purchasing power of surplus, and add to the growth of surplus from operations.

Policy: Capital growth is sought through equity investment in common stocks and real estate.

NONLIFE INSURANCE COMPANIES

The second broad insurance industry category is the nonlife sector, which includes but is not limited to health, property, liability, marine, surety, and worker compensation insurance. For purposes of considering investment policy, these nonlife (casualty) companies are really quite similar although the products they sell are rather diverse. However, the investment policies of a casualty company are significantly different from those of a life insurance company.

Return Requirements

Historically, casualty insurance companies have not taken investment earnings into account in the calculation of premiums, in striking contrast to the accumulation rates factored into life insurance premiums. For this reason, a casualty insurance company is often operated as if it were two separate organizations—an insurance company and an investment company operating a balanced fund.

Since investment returns are not factored into the calculation of casualty premiums, there is no specific minimum return requirement. However, given the underwriting uncertainties inherent in the casualty insurance business, it is obvious that investment income provides financial stability for the insurance reserves. In fact, periodic underwriting losses (claims and expenses in excess of premium income) from the insurance side of the company are expected to be offset by investment earnings. Most products of the casualty insurance business are priced competitively, and thus premium rates are not sufficiently ample or flexible to eliminate the loss aspects of the so-called underwriting cycle (the profit cycle of the business).

A second function of the investment operation is to provide growth of surplus, which, in turn, provides the opportunity to expand insurance vol-

TABLE 4-7. Pre-Tax Portfolio Yields of U.S. Property/Casualty Companies (net investment income as a percent of mean cash and invested assets)

	Average Top 100 Companies	State Farm	Allstate	CNA Financial	Travelers Indemnity	St. Paul Fire & Marine	Continental Insurance
1975	5.7%	5.5%	5.1%	5.3%	7.3%	6.1%	5.5%
1976	5.6	5.5	5.1	5.3	8.1	6.0	5.4
1977	5.9	5.5	5.3	5.7	9.3	6.2	5.7
1978	6.2	5.7	5.6	6.5	7.8	6.3	6.8
1979	6.6	5.8	6.1	7.1	8.6	6.2	6.8
1980	6.9	5.9	6.3	7.3	8.0	6.1	7.2

SOURCE: *Best's Insurance Management Reports* [1981b].

ume. The risk-taking capacity of a casualty company is measured to a large extent in terms of the ratio of premiums to capital and surplus. Traditionally, this ratio is maintained between 2 to 3 times. Thus, each dollar of surplus generated by net investment income or capital appreciation has the potential to support $2 to $3 of additional annual premiums.

Traditional Asset Mix. As the above discussion suggests, casualty insurance companies have traditionally maintained a bond portfolio to offset insurance reserves, with capital and surplus funds largely invested in common stocks. As will be pointed out later, these companies are very sensitive to the after-tax return from the bond portfolio and to the tax benefits of dividend income (through the exclusion of 85 percent of dividends received on other corporations' stock) and capital gains. In contrast to life insurers, the investment returns of casualty portfolios vary significantly from company to company, reflecting the latitude of asset mix permitted by insurance regulations, differences in underwriting results and their tax status, and the use of common and preferred stocks (see Table 4-7).

It is important to note that because of high interest rates and competitive pressures within the industry casualty insurance companies are directing an increased amount of attention to the inclusion of some portion of investment earnings in the calculation of premium levels. Such a change would be expected to more closely integrate the insurance and investment operations. As for life insurance companies this may lead to more precise specification of investment return objectives.

Risk Tolerance

Casualty insurance companies, like life insurance companies, have a quasi-fiduciary role; thus, safety is a dominant consideration influencing investment policy. However, the risks insured by casualty companies are less predictable. In fact, for companies exposed to catastrophic events—such as hurricanes, tornadoes, and explosions—the potential for loss can be significantly greater. Furthermore, casualty policies frequently provide replacement cost or current cost coverage; thus inflation adds to the degree of risk.

Not surprisingly, then, the cash flow from casualty insurance operations can be quite erratic. Unlike the life companies, which traditionally have been able to project cash flow and make forward commitments, casualty companies must be prepared to meet operating cash gaps with investment income and/or maturing securities. Thus, for the portion of the investment portfolio relating to policyholder reserves, the tolerance for loss of principal or diminished investment income is low. Predictability of investment maturities and investment income is necessary and operates as a direct offset to the unpredictability of operating trends.

Interestingly, casualty insurance companies are not required to maintain a security valuation reserve. Evidently, the regulators feel that the surplus requirements (i.e., $1 of surplus for every $2 to $3 of annual premium) are sufficient. The casualty insurer's need for liquidity and the shorter time horizon (as compared to a life company) may be considered by the regulators to be an additional modifier of market valuation risk.

Inflation in the United States and worldwide has further reduced the tolerance for investment risk among casualty insurers. In fact, the volatile stock market conditions of the 1970s, and in particular 1974, persuaded many casualty companies to reduce the percentage of surplus invested in common stocks. Several major companies were forced to liquidate large portions of their common stock holdings near the end of the 1974 bear market because of significant erosion of surplus, which impaired their ability to increase volume. Essentially, the regulators gave such companies the option of reducing common stock holdings or temporarily ceasing or curtailing the issuance of new policies. Needless to say, the experience reduced casualty companies' risk tolerance for the portion of the investment portfolio related to surplus.

Here again it should be pointed out that the surplus of casualty insurance companies, like life companies, is often overstated because bonds are not carried at market value for statement purposes. If bonds had been valued at market rather than amortized cost, the 1980–81 decline in bond prices would have reduced the surplus of the industry by approximately 50 percent.

Liquidity Requirements

Given the uncertainties of the cash flow from casualty insurance operations, liquidity has always been a paramount consideration. As mentioned earlier, this is in sharp contrast with the relative certainties—excluding policy loans—of the cash flow of a life company.

In addition to meeting cash flow needs, liquidity is also a necessary adjunct of the variable tax status of a casualty company. As will be discussed later, casualty companies may find it necessary to shift between tax-exempt and taxable classes of bonds as insurance underwriting cycles swing between profits and losses. To provide portfolio flexibility and maximize after-tax income, at least some portion of the casualty company's bond portfolio must be highly liquid, not a common characteristic of most tax-exempt bonds.

To meet its liquidity needs, the typical casualty company will maintain a portfolio of short-term securities as an immediate liquidity reserve, hold a portfolio of readily marketable U.S. government bonds of various maturities (20% or more, versus less than 5% for life companies), maintain a balanced, spaced maturity schedule to ensure a rollover of assets, match some assets against seasonal cash flow needs, and, finally, concentrate investments in higher quality bonds that are generally more marketable.

Needless to say, such attention to maturity and marketability complements the low risk tolerance and further modifies the return objectives of casualty insurers.

Time Horizon

As the discussion of liquidity suggests, the time horizon of a casualty company is much shorter than that of a life company. Casualty liabilities are relatively short term, as contrasted with the long-term liabilities of life insurers. Emphasis is on maximum current after-tax return on assets to offset liability reserves. Thus, the bond portfolios of casualty companies typically have an average maturity of 10 years or less, as compared with approximately 15 years or longer for the typical life company.

In terms of common stock investments, however, the casualty companies are "classic" long-term investors, with long-term growth of surplus the primary return objective of the stock portion of the portfolio.

Tax Considerations

In contrast with the complex tax structure of the life insurance industry, the tax status of a casualty company is relatively simple and straightforward. The full corporate tax rate, 46 percent in 1982, is applied to profits from insurance underwriting and to investment income. In addition, the full corporate dividend exclusion (85 percent of total dividends received) is applicable for federal income taxes.

Tax-exempt securities (municipal bonds) are often attractive to a casualty company enjoying underwriting profits. Returns on tax-exempt bonds have typically equalled 65–75 percent of the return on fully taxable bonds (actually near 90% in early 1982), while the after-tax retention rate on the latter is only 54 percent. Thus, tax exempts can provide a 20–40 percent after-tax yield advantage. Dividends on common and preferred stocks are also largely tax sheltered, with 15 percent of such dividends taxed at 46 percent, or an actual tax rate of only 6.9 percent.

It is not merely the tax structure that impacts the portfolio policy for a casualty company but also the variability of underwriting results, since the combination determines tax status. Major shifts from tax-exempt to taxable bond purchases are necessitated by unfavorable shifts in the underwriting picture. Since the profit cycle for casualty companies has been as short as four to five years in the past decade, a substantial degree of portfolio flexibility is necessary to maximize after-tax returns. For nonlife companies, underwriting experience has called for active strategies resulting in the periodic sale of taxable or tax-exempt bonds, as well as passive redirection of newly available cash. This means a great need for marketability in the bond portfolios, as compared to life companies whose portfolios are laden with private placements.

Each company seeks the most appropriate balance of taxable and tax-exempt investment income. Tax loss carryforward and carryback provisions of the tax code also play a key role in determining such a balance. Thus, a casualty company may have multiple return objectives based on its current and projected tax status.

Regulatory and Legal Considerations

It bears repeating that while, in general, the insurance industry is heavily regulated, the regulation of casualty company investments is relatively permissive. Indeed, classes of eligible assets and quality standards for each class are specified just as they are for life companies. Also, the New York law, which is considered the most restrictive, requires that assets equal to 50 percent of the unearned premium and loss reserves combined be maintained in "eligible bonds and mortgages." Beyond these general restrictions, casualty companies are permitted to invest the remainder of their assets in a relatively broad array of bonds, mortgages, stocks, and real estate, without restriction as to the amount invested in any particular class of assets (except that certain states impose limitations on real estate holdings).

A casualty company is not required to maintain a valuation reserve but is required to value both preferred and common stocks at market value. (A life company is required to value only common at market.) In essence then, the full impact of increases and decreases in the market value of stocks is reflected in the surplus of a casualty company.

Determination of Portfolio Policies

As in the case of life insurance companies, a low tolerance for risk is the dominant factor determining investment policy for casualty companies. Because of contractual liabilities and difficulty in forecasting the cash flow from insurance operations, casualty companies seek a high degree of safety from the assets offsetting insurance reserves. Indeed, even the willingness to assume investment risk with the assets offsetting surplus has been moderated by the market volatility of recent years.

Over and above liquidity needs, which are clearly important, casualty insurance companies develop a significant portfolio of stocks and bonds to generate a high level of income to supplement or offset insurance gains or losses. Capital appreciation builds the reserve base and supports additional premium income. The structure of the bond portfolio as between taxable and tax-exempt securities will depend on the results from insurance experience. When the insurance operation is profitable (and taxable), tax exempts are sought; when the insurance operation is unprofitable (and taxes have been minimized), taxable bonds are the choice.

To the extent that the insurance operation is profitable and taxes are relatively high, the common stock policy will often emphasize yield to get the benefit of the 85 percent tax exemption on dividends. At the same time, long-term growth is an important objective so that the surplus base can be expanded to support higher aggregate premium income levels. Because of the possibility of having to liquidate stocks under distressed conditions, relatively low volatility is probably desirable and, of course, marketability is essential.

Casualty Insurance Company Investment Policy Statement

The following is a sample statement of investment policy for a casualty insurance company:

XYZ CASUALTY INSURANCE COMPANY
Investment Policy Statement

The investment objectives and policies established reflect the short-term nature of most casualty insurance reserves but also recognize the pricing flexibility the company has with regard to its insurance policy contracts. Regulatory, tax, and operating considerations shape the policies and priorities outlined below:

Objective: Obtain a favorable return (in excess of contract accumulation rates) on invested assets representing policy reserves through a diversified portfolio of high quality income-producing assets.

Policy: Investment yield (after adjusting for potential tax liability) is emphasized to maximize investment income through investment in fixed income securities—taxable, tax-exempt, or some combination thereof—that are rated or have the financial characteristics to qualify for a rating of A or better.

Liquidity is a limiting factor in achieving a favorable return on invested assets. Sufficient cash funds are maintained to meet financial obligations, and funds not immediately needed to offset withdrawals are invested in short-term securities as operating conditions require. Maturity balance is maintained to supplement annual cash flow from operations and investment income. In addition, the maturity schedule is a source of liquidity and flexibility to meet changing market, tax, and operating considerations.

Objective: Obtain a favorable total return (capital and income combined) on invested assets representing capital and surplus to augment the growth of surplus from operations.

Policy: Capital growth is sought primarily through equity investment in common stocks and real estate. Market valuation volatility is a limiting factor that influences the proportion of assets invested in stocks and liquidity.

COMMERCIAL BANKS

Bank investment management is truly unique among the various institutions considered in this chapter. Unlike pension funds, endowment funds, and insurance companies, banks do not deal with essentially cost-free funds that are invested at a rate of return adequate to meet a specific purpose. Rather, they generally must purchase funds, often at considerable cost, with the expectation of reinvesting those funds at a rate higher than the borrowing cost. This spread, or margin, becomes the return to the bank.

Prior to the rapid inflation of the 1970s and 1980s, bank investment of assets was largely a passive exercise. Liabilities, consisting of deposits and savings, were mostly uncontrollable, so asset management involved providing for primary and secondary reserves to meet legal requirements and providing liquidity for deposit withdrawals, then lending the balance either in the form of commercial loans or consumer loans, or investing it in fixed income securities. However, the rapidly increasing rate of inflation starting in the mid-1960s created immense loan demands that could be met only by purchasing liabilities and managing both assets and liabilities to maximize the spread between interest rates. Investment management of banks has been further complicated by changing regulations and increasing competition, both within the banking industry and from insurance companies, brokerage houses, and other financial institutions.

Risk-Return Tradeoff

For practical purposes, money is a commodity and, thus, to a large extent, an undifferentiated product. This means that it is highly price sensitive—and price is the interest rate. In a perfect world, if interest rates were known to be rising, a lending institution would borrow long and lend short, thus freezing the cost of borrowed funds while the price of the product being sold—money—would rise, thus increasing the spread between the borrowing cost and the interest rate realized on assets. Contrarily, if interest rates were known to be falling, one would borrow short and lend long, freezing the return received while the cost of funds fell, again widening the spread between the two. However, we do not live in a perfect world, as the wild fluctuation of interest rates in recent years has demonstrated.

In an effort to maximize profits in terms of the interest spread between borrowed liabilities and investable assets, banks have undertaken to manage carefully both their assets and liabilities. This has led to the development of a *sensitivity ratio,* which is the ratio of interest sensitive assets to interest sensitive liabilities. The definition of interest sensitivity is somewhat arbitrary. Some consider it to be 90 days or less term to maturity, others up to one year. Whatever the definition, the lending institution will make its projections for interest rates and establish this sensitivity ratio accordingly. For example, if interest rates were expected to rise, the ratio could be raised above parity (1.0), to a point where interest sensitive assets exceeded interest sensitive liabilities, thus freezing the cost of liabilities (by borrowing more longer term funds) while allowing the interest rate on earnings assets to rise on the faster rollover to widen the spread between the two. Contrarily, if interest rates were expected to fall, the proportion of interest rate sensitive assets should be below parity, thus maximizing the returns on the asset side (lending long) while allowing the cost of liabilities to fall more rapidly (borrowing short).

The risks inherent in these strategies are obvious. If the interest rate forecast is incorrect, the opposite result of what is intended will occur. During periods of unstable or uncertain interest rates, lending institutions will generally try to equalize interest sensitive assets and liabilities to maintain the spreads at a constant level and reduce the risk of error. But this is not quite as simple as it seems because interest rates on assets tend to be more sensitive to change than are rates on liabilities. For example, many loans are tied to the prime rate; as the prime rate fluctuates so does the return on assets. Contrarily, interest rates on CDs are fixed for the entire maturity of the CD, and the lending institution must wait until maturity before that rate can be adjusted. Many banks are developing instruments with variable rates to deal with this problem.

As the sensitivity ratio concept evolved, there has been a greater effort on the part of banks to manage spreads across specific maturity categories, not just in those that are purely interest rate sensitive by changing the terms of the asset mix to conform more closely to the liability mix. In 1982 some banks even established variable interest rates on their credit card operations as another way to match rates on assets with those on liabilities.

Liquidity Requirements

Banks maintain liquidity primarily to meet withdrawals of funds by depositors or provide loans to customers. In the latter case this may be controllable by the bank, e.g., in the case of making a new loan, or uncontrollable, e.g., in terms of customers drawing down lines of credit. There are two forms of liquidity for banks—internal and external. Internal refers to highly liquid assets that can be converted to cash quickly and made available to meet liquidity demands. However, banks are generally in the fortunate position of having access to considerable external liquidity, either by borrowing under standby loan agreements with other institutions or by issuing securities such as CDs.

Banks, however, must be careful not to overuse these various external sources or they may well impair their overall capital position to the detriment of the shareholders and perhaps even depositors. This occurs either from an excessive increase in debt relative to equity, placing the bank in a higher risk position, or from borrowing at high rates of interest relative to lending rates, which results in net losses, or both. Thus, the manner in which liquidity is managed has an important role in the bank's overall profitability and stature with regulatory agencies, shareholders, and depositors.

In the final analysis, while it is important to have adequate liquidity, it is also important to diversify sources of liquidity to avoid undue leveraging of the banks' capital position.

Time Horizon

The time horizon for banks is obviously short term. Although some loans, particularly mortgages, are made over longer terms, the high volatility of interest rates over the past several years has changed even the pattern of this type of lending. Variable rate mortgages, short-term renewable mortgages with long-term amortization schedules, floating rate notes, and other creative types of instruments have helped to match up and shorten the maturities of assets and liabilities to reduce the interest rate risk.

Regulatory and Legal Considerations

As banks made the transition from passive management of assets to far more sophisticated matching of assets and liabilities, one regulatory aspect created considerable difficulty. This was Regulation Q, which fixed the interest rates banks could pay on many of their liabilities. As interest rates rose rapidly in the 1970s and 1980s and savings depositors became more aware of alternative, higher yielding investment opportunities, the whole complexion of liability management changed drastically. By the same token, usury laws in many states restricted the interest rates banks could charge on assets and also impacted on lending policies. Regulation eventually did provide for certificates of deposit, tied to Treasury bill rates, with maturities of six months or two and one-half years. To some extent, this enabled banks to compete for deposits that were being lured away from low-rate passbook savings accounts. The advent of money market funds provided further competition. Smaller low-rate passbook savings accounts were reduced or closed, to be replaced by large denomination, high yielding CDs issued by the banks and bought by the money market funds. (In part this was a recycling of funds, since many former passbook holders became money market fund holders.) Regulation Q is being phased out and investment policies will be modified accordingly. And if the Glass-Steagall Act is modified or repealed, bank customers will be able to buy money market funds from their bank. In the meantime, some banks are allowing proprietary money market funds for which they are an investment advisor or subadvisor to solicit certain of their customers.

Unique Needs, Circumstances, and Preferences

The difference in unique needs, circumstances, and preferences will probably revolve around the size of banks, their locality, the mix of their uncontrollable liabilities (core deposits), and the individual skills of each bank in matching assets and liabilities in the most productive way. Small community banks, for example, may well have significant core deposits of relatively unsophisticated individual depositors that will stay with them; by the same token, they will likely be denied opportunities to purchase liabilities available to large money center banks.

Determination of Portfolio Policies

The success of a bank in increasing or maintaining profitability will depend on its ability to manage its assets and liabilities in an environment of widely fluctuating interest rates. Portfolio policies will directly reflect this central fact. Scenario forecasting, for example, has become an important tool, with bank economists developing several different interest rate scenarios based on forecasts of the economy and other factors bearing on interest rates and then assigning varying probabilities to these different scenarios. These scenarios then bear directly upon the investment policies established in terms of sensitivity ratios and the gaps between assets and liabilities at different maturity levels. It is desirable, where possible, to fix the spread between the cost of funds borrowed and the return on loans, so as to increase the stability or predictability of earnings from this spread.

INVESTMENT COMPANIES

Investment companies, or mutual funds as they are more commonly known, are important institutional investors that should be mentioned. However, because they are regarded more as conduits for investment funds—and thus more like investment vehicles—rather than as institutional investment entities, they are discussed only briefly here.

There are more than 600 mutual funds in the United States. Each has its own statement of objectives and policies. These may range all the way from short-term liquidity, as in the case of money market funds, to aggressive growth, utilizing leverage, options, and other more aggressive investment techniques (see Table 4-8 on page 120). Investors, whether individuals or

TABLE 4-8. Classification of Mutual Funds by Size and Type (as of December 31, 1980)

Size of Fund	No. of Funds	Combined Assets (000)	Percent of Total	Type of Fund	No. of Funds	Combined Assets (000)	Percent of Total
Over $1 billion	30	$ 66,148,100	47.6%	Common stock			
$500 million–$1 billion	36	24,575,900	17.7	Maximum capital gain	98	$ 8,252,700	6.0%
$300 million–$500 million	33	12,580,400	9.1	Growth	139	19,110,100	13.5
$100 million–$300 million	128	22,066,400	16.0	Growth and income	85	16,994,300	12.2
$50 million–$100 million	98	6,961,400	5.1	Specialized	19	2,045,400	1.5
$10 million–$50 million	205	5,423,300	4.0	Balanced	26	3,502,300	2.6
$1 million–$10 million	117	571,400	0.5	Income	128	9,875,300	7.2
Under $1 million	12	6,200	0.0	Bond and preferred stock	11	1,454,400	1.1
				Money market	101	71,992,900	52.1
				Tax-exempt municipal bond	43	3,269,100	2.4
				Tax-free money market	9	1,836,600	1.4
Total	659	$138,333,100	100.0%	Total	659	$138,333,100	100.0%

institutions, may use mutual funds in various combinations to develop investment programs designed specifically to meet their own particular investment goals and objectives. By doing so, they are able to obtain diversification and professional management at a reasonable cost. Whether one's objectives require the use of equities, real estate, or fixed income securities, appropriate mutual fund vehicles are available.

The development of the money market fund will certainly go down as one of the great investment innovations of the 1970s, and perhaps even of the twentieth century. By mid-1982, these funds exceeded $220 billion in total assets and were sponsored by a wide variety of investment counseling organizations, banks, and brokerage firms. They allow investors to pool their resources and, at modest cost, participate in high yielding, short-term investment instruments that previously would have been available only to large individual or institutional portfolios. So important have these funds become as an investment intermediary for short-term money that round lots in CDs and commercial paper, once customarily $1 million (or even lower under certain circumstances), quickly became $5 million or more as borrowers preferred to deal directly in large amounts with these institutions.

In short, mutual funds, like portfolios of individual securities, can be used by individual and institutional investors to accommodate risk-return tradeoffs, time horizon, liquidity needs, diversification, and tax requirements.

SUMMARY

This chapter has focused on the investment objectives, constraints, and policies of institutional investors, the initial steps in the portfolio management process. Using the traditional building block analogy, this stage of the process can be characterized as the foundation. It begins with the establishment of objectives (the risk-return tradeoff), and then considers the various investment constraints, including liquidity requirements, time horizon, taxes, regulatory and legal considerations, the unique needs, circumstances, and preferences of each investor, and how these constraints affect or modify the risk-return relationship. This foundation is completed with the establishment of investment policies designed to meet each investor's objectives as modified by the constraints.

In discussing the broad variety of institutional investors, distinctions have been drawn between those where the asset/liability relationships are rather clear and quantifiable, such as defined benefit pension plans, insurance companies, and banks, and those where these distinctions are far less clear and easily identifiable, such as defined contribution retirement plans, endowments, and investment companies. Chapter 5, using the same basic approach, will take up the objectives, constraints, and policies of individual investors.

FURTHER READING

When the ICFA's Portfolio Management Review Subcommittee reviewed the extant materials on portfolio management with a view toward modifying these materials for the entire CFA exam program, the whole area of investor objectives, constraints, and policies, the subject of Chapters 4 and 5 of this book, provided a relative dearth of good material. While there were many good examples dealing with specific, narrow subjects, the Committee found no single source material that "brought it all together." As a first effort in rectifying this, the Committee itself wrote *Determinants of Investment Portfolio Policy* to rectify this problem for the 1982 exam program. This chapter and the next represent a second and more comprehensive effort.

An enduring textbook on the subject of portfolio management, with particularly good material on investor objectives, constraints, and policies, is Sauvain [1973]. Another important text, which has served as a major study material for the CFA program, is Cohen, Zinbarg, and Zeikel [1982].

Material about retirement funds generally tends to focus on a single subject such as ERISA regulation, actuarial funding methods, and the like. Prior to the writing of this chapter, one area that seemed to be almost totally lacking in coverage was profit-sharing (defined contribution) plans. Particularly useful in the preparation of this chapter were Ezra [1979], Gray [1981], Kent [1979], and Murphy [1976].

The rather rapid evolution in the management of endowment funds referred to in this chapter seems to have left the written material behind. Although there are occasional articles and chapters from texts available, this author drew largely on his own experience in managing this type of fund. For good background material, Ford Foundation [1972] and Williamson and Sanger [1980] are recommended.

If there has been a rapid evolution in the management of endowment funds, we are very much in the middle of what can only be characterized as a revolution in the management of insurance company assets. As one might expect, primary source materials are in the form of articles in journal or newspaper publications. Particularly useful in describing the new techniques are Brenner [1981] and Noble [1981]. For background material on insurance companies, see Maginn [1981].

Banks also are in a rapidly developing stage of asset and liability management so periodicals again proved to be a useful source. This author, starting with relatively limited knowledge of the subject, found writing this section of the chapter was facilitated by Binder [1980] and Miller [1980].

BIBLIOGRAPHY

Best's Insurance Management Reports, Oldwick, N.J.: A. M. Best Company, August 24, 1981a and October 12, 1981b.

Binder, Barrett F., "Asset/Liability Management," *The Magazine of Bank Administration,* November 1980.

Brenner, Lynn, "Can the Life Insurance Industry Survive?" *Institutional Investor,* September 1981.

"Changing Life Insurers, The," *Business Week,* September 14, 1981

Cohen, Jerome B., Edward D. Zinbarg, and Arthur Zeikel, *Investment Analysis and Portfolio Management,* Homewood, Ill.: Richard D. Irwin, 1982.

Ezra, D. Don, *Understanding Pension Fund Finance and Investment,* Toronto: The Pagurian Corporation Ltd., 1979.

Fitzgerald, T. H., Jr., *Ed., Money Market Directory,* Charlottesville, Va.: Money Market Directories, 1982.

Ford Foundation Advisory Committee on Endowment Management, *Managing Educational Endowments,* 2nd ed., 1972.

Gray, William S., III, "Pension Funds," in *Determinants of Investment Portfolio Policy,* Charlottesville, Va.: The Institute of Chartered Financial Analysts, 1981.

Investment Companies, Boston: Arthur Wiesenberger Companies Services, 1981.

Kent, Glenn H., "Team Management of Pension Money," *Harvard Business Review,* May/June 1979.

Life Insurance Fact Book, Washington, D.C.: American Council of Life Insurance, 1982.

Maginn, John L., "Insurance Companies," in *Determinants of Investment Portfolio Policy,* Charlottesville, Va.: The Institute of Chartered Financial Analysts, 1981.

Miller, Donald C., "New Opportunities in Liquidity Management," presented at a symposium on Future Sources of Loanable Funds for Agricultural Banks, Kansas City, Missouri, December 9, 1980.

Murphy, Robert W., "Interpreting the New Prudent Man's Standard Introduced by ERISA," Proceedings of a Seminar on ERISA, January, 1976, appearing in *CFA Readings in Portfolio Management,* Charlottesville, Va.: The Institute of Chartered Financial Analysts, 1980.

Noble, Kenneth B., "Insurer's Shift on Investments," *New York Times,* December 19, 1981.

Sauvain, Harry C., *Investment Management,* 4th ed., Englewood Cliffs, N.J.: Prentice-Hall, 1973.

Vawter, Jay, "Endowment Funds," in *Determinants of Investment Portfolio Policy.* Charlottesville, Va.: The Institute of Chartered Financial Analysts, 1981.

Williamson, J. Peter, and Hazel A. D. Sanger, "Educational Endowment Funds," in Sumner N. Levine, Ed., *The Investment Manager's Handbook,* Homewood, Ill.: Dow Jones-Irwin, 1980.

Determination Of Portfolio Policies: Individual Investors

Robert D. Milne, C.F.A.

Management of portfolios of individuals, whether done directly by the individual or indirectly via an agent or trustee, offers the most diverse of investment situations. There is literally a different set of portfolio management circumstances, needs, and opportunities for every individual investor.

Although the considerations that shape and modify investment objectives and strategies for individuals are extremely wide, there are enough commonalities to allow us to draw some generalizations that apply to the bulk of individual investor situations. This chapter seeks to identify and enumerate those commonalities and generalizations. It also attempts to provide the principal contrast between direct investing by individuals, which is almost totally unconstrained given some minimum wealth or income position, and indirect investing via mutual fund, investment counsel, or other agency accounts, or via trust accounts.

THE INDIVIDUAL INVESTOR

The individual investor covers the widest possible range of investor characteristics, needs, desires, and abilities. The one universal commonality is risk aversion. All rational investors, regardless of circumstances, are risk averse. That is, in risk and return terms, an investor will be willing to take additional investment risk only if there is the likelihood of obtaining additional return relative to his current situation. Otherwise, individual investors are a heterogeneous lot, differing in age, family circumstances, source and amount of

TABLE 5-1. **The Consumer Balance Sheet, Third Quarter 1981 Data (billions of dollars)**

	Amount		Percent of Total
Cash and liquid assets		$1,965	35%
Residences	$2,699		
Mortgage debt	992		
Net equity in real estate		1,707	30
Stocks		1,034	18
Bonds		440	8
Pension funds, life insurance and others		1,079	19
Total net assets		$6,225	110%
Consumer credit outstanding		586	10
Net worth		$5,639	100%

SOURCE: *Pocket Chartroom* [1982].

income, wealth position, location of residence, insurance coverage, and tax situation.

In the aggregate, as shown in Table 5-1, securities comprise only about 26 percent of the net worth of individuals. Real estate (net of mortgage debt) accounts for 30 percent, and cash and liquid assets (certificates of deposit, money market funds, savings accounts, and the like) represent about 35 percent of net worth. Only a minority of individuals, approximately 20 percent according to a 1980 New York Stock Exchange survey, invest in securities. Nevertheless, individuals have long used common stocks as a viable investment alternative.

Individuals can invest directly via institutions such as commercial banks and brokerage houses or indirectly via agents. The most common types of agency vehicles are mutual funds, investment counsel arrangements, and nontrusteed accounts at commercial bank trust departments. Mutual funds represent pools of funds obtained from many individual investors and invested in one or more types of financial or real assets. They offer better diversification, more professional money management, and smaller trading

TABLE 5-2. **Estimated Ownership of Stocks Listed on the NYSE**

	1950	1960	1970	1980
Individuals				
Direct	65.4%	60.9%	54.2%	48.4%
Trusts	21.9	20.4	18.2	16.2
Total	87.3%	81.3%	72.4%	64.6%
Institutions	12.7	18.7	27.6	35.4
Total ownership	100.0%	100.0%	100.0%	100.0%

SOURCE: *NYSE Fact Book 1980* [1980] and estimates by author.

TABLE 5-3. Distribution of Largest Wealthholders in the United States in 1980

Wealthholder Category	Number of Wealthholders
$100,000–$500,000	2,059,000
$500,000–$1,000,000	425,000
Over $1,000,000	218,000

SOURCE: Internal Revenue Service, U.S. Department of the Treasury.

costs than are typically available to the smaller and less sophisticated investor acting alone. In terms of ownership of New York Stock Exchange-listed stocks in 1980, despite the increase in institutional stock ownership in the post-World War II period, individuals still owned directly, or through trusts, almost 65 percent of the stocks listed thereon. (See Table 5-2).

Wealthier or higher income investors may want to employ the services of an investment counselor, either on (1) a fully discretionary basis where the counselor completely controls the investment process, (2) a partially discretionary basis where the investment decision making is shared between the counselor and client, or (3) an advice-only basis where the client retains full control.[1] Equally attractive alternatives for indirect investing are trust departments or asset management groups typically in commercial banks, where accounts of all three types are handled on an agency or nontrust basis. The author estimates that for every ten investors with sufficient assets to warrant professional assistance, only three of the ten utilize a trust department and only one employs the services of an investment counselor. Table 5-3 provides information on the population of investors with liquid assets of sufficient size to warrant outside investment advice and/or management through a vehicle other than mutual funds. Only those with investment assets in excess of $500,000 will be actively sought by investment counselors and trust departments.

PERSONAL TRUSTS

In contrast to individual investment, a bank, a savings and loan association, an attorney, an investment professional, or other qualified institution or individual may act as a trustee for individuals by establishing a personal trust relationship. Here the trustee acts as a fiduciary, and investment of the account is subject to state trust laws, prudent man rules, and court interpretations.

[1] Wealth among individuals in the United States tends to be highly concentrated. One study reports that the 1 percent of American households with the largest income owned 51 percent of the market value of common stock owned by all families, while the 10 percent with the highest income owned 74 percent of the market value.

Commercial banks, savings and loans, and other institutional trust groups are chartered either by the individual states under the supervision of state regulatory commissioners or the federal government under the jurisdiction of federal regulatory bodies. Larger trust departments offer a variety of services, including investment, custodial, real estate, closely held business, estate probate, and guardianship management. Investment counselors or other qualified parties frequently serve as trustees or cotrustees; the latter arrangement is frequently desirable to ensure that the individual's best interests are adequately protected.

Trusts are established when an individual (the *trustor* or *grantor*) confers legal title to property to another person or institution (the *trustee*) who agrees to manage that property for one or more other individuals (the *beneficiaries*). Beneficiaries are customarily divided into *income beneficiaries*, who typically receive the income from the trust during their lifetimes, and *remaindermen*, who receive the corpus or principal of the trust when the income beneficiary dies and the trust is dissolved.

Types of Trusts

The two principal types of trusts are *testamentary trusts*, created under the will of an individual, and *living trusts*, established during an individual's lifetime. There are two kinds of living trusts: *revocable* and *irrevocable*. A revocable living trust is established during the trustor's lifetime according to terms and conditions that the trustor can change at any time prior to death. An irrevocable trust's terms and conditions, however, cannot be changed once the trust is established. In exchange for this inflexibility, the irrevocable trust can achieve substantial tax savings under certain circumstances. The living trust also can be a convenience for retired individuals, since the mechanics of collecting interest and dividends and other chores are taken care of by the trustee. In addition, the trustee can provide security in handling the individual's affairs in the event age results in physical or mental incapacity.

Organization of Trust Departments

In terms of organization, a typical institutional trust department is divided into a trust administration unit that handles all the legal and administrative functions and a trust investment unit that is responsible for portfolio management, security analysis, and securities trading activities. The key interaction comes between the trust administrator who knows the risk and return preferences of clients and the portfolio manager who, based largely on inputs from security analysts and traders, knows the risk and return opportunities in the marketplace.

In order to facilitate professional management of personal trust funds, especially smaller trusts, at minimum cost, many trust departments have created common trust funds that allow them to pool accounts and concen-

TABLE 5-4. Types of Accounts and Kinds of Assets in Trust Departments, 1980

Types of Accounts	Percent of Dollar Total	Kinds of Assets	Percent of Dollar Total
Trusts and estates			
Employee benefit	30.7%	Common stock	48.1%
Personal trust	36.9	U.S. government and agency	
Estates	3.2	obligations	13.1
		State, county, and municipal	
		obligations	5.1
Agencies		Other short-term obligations	10.4
Employee benefit	9.4	Other notes and bonds	10.5
All others	19.8	Real estate	4.1
		Real estate mortgages	1.2
		Deposits at own bank	1.8
		Deposits at other banks	3.4
		Preferred stock	0.7
		Miscellaneous	1.6
Total	100.0%	Total	100.0%

SOURCE: Board of Governors of the Federal Reserve System et al. [1981].

trate investment management expertise. Trust departments utilizing the common fund approach will have a series of mutual fund-type pools of money, each one invested in a specific category of asset and each one managed by a portfolio manager specializing in that particular asset (e.g., government bonds, corporate bonds, high yield common stocks, high growth common stocks, and so on).

Table 5-4 provides a breakdown of types of accounts in trust departments as of 1980. It shows personal trusts accounting for almost 37 percent of all trust assets. It also shows common stocks accounting for about 48 percent of the dollar value of all trust assets, down from just over 62 percent at the beginning of the decade, with the decline largely being accounted for by increases in high interest bearing short-term debt obligations.

Table 5-5 (page 130) illustrates the size of bank-managed trust assets and their concentration at the largest trust institutions. At half a trillion dollars in 1980, trust assets were 74.9 percent larger than six years earlier. And these assets were still highly concentrated, with $100 billion-plus trust departments holding 74 percent of their dollar value. Actually, asset control was even more concentrated than these numbers would suggest. For example, the ten largest trust departments, five of them in New York, held over $155 billion in assets at the end of 1980, about 27 percent of the total.

INVESTMENT OBJECTIVES

The investment objectives of individual investors and personal trust accounts can be expressed in terms of return and risk. The following is a brief recap of the extensive discussion of risk and return in Chapter 3. Return is

TABLE 5-5. Distribution of Assets in Trust Institutions in 1980

Size of Trust Assets	Number of Trust Depts.	Number as Percent of Total	Assets Held ($ millions)	Percent of Total Assets Held	Percent of Total Trust Dept. Accounts	Average Size of Account ($ thousands)
Under $10 million	2,506	61.8%	$ 5,629	1.0%	7.0%	$ 57.4
$10 to $25 million	501	12.4	8,181	1.4	6.2	94.3
$25 to $100 million	568	14.0	28,895	5.1	14.9	138.4
$100 to $500 million	326	8.0	69,591	12.2	26.3	188.5
$500 million to $1 billion	53	1.3	36,229	6.3	8.5	303.5
$1 billion and over	100	2.5	422,668	74.0	37.1	813.4
Total	4,054	100.0%	$571,193	100.0%	100.0%	$407.5

SOURCE: Board of Governors of the Federal Reserve System et al. [1981].

defined as total return. It consists of an income component equal to current yield (coupon divided by price) or dividend yield (dividend divided by price), plus a capital change component equal to the percentage change in price (ending price minus beginning price divided by beginning price). Risk is either total risk, represented by a quantitative measure of return variability over time (e.g., standard deviation), or systematic risk. Systematic risk is that part of total risk accounted for by the comovement of securities returns and which cannot be eliminated by diversifying a portfolio across a spectrum of securities.

Individuals

As indicated previously, the return and risk possibilities are virtually unconstrained for individuals, a unique investing situation. Why? Because, assuming a minimum wealth or income position, essentially all possible asset categories and all investment strategies are open to the individual investing directly for his or her own account. This is in contrast to the legal and/or regulatory constraints that characterize institutional investors as described in Chapter 4.

To elaborate, the individual has available the entire risk spectrum of investment assets, ranging from essentially risk-free assets such as short-term government fixed income securities to the riskiest assets such as common stock option contracts and commodities futures contracts.

In addition, the individual can choose from among the entire spectrum of investment strategies. Unlike other investors, he or she can establish either long or short positions in securities, and can opt for a variety of different leverage positions. That is, the individual can invest all of his or her net worth in a portfolio of risky assets or part of net worth in risky assets and part in safe assets, or all in risky assets plus borrowing on margin and investing that borrowed money in risky assets. The end result is the ability of the individual, by choice of portfolio assets and investment strategies, to position himself or herself anywhere along the upward-sloping line in Figure 5-1 (page 132), plotting higher expected returns for higher risk.[2] The investment advisor (whatever the title) can assist in determining the risk tolerance of individuals by asking questions to identify the hopes and fears of the investor. It is even possible to simulate portfolio results from historic data to acquaint the investor with the range of volatility that has been experienced with various portfolios in the recent past.

Life Cycle Approach. Individuals' risk and return preferences are often portrayed in terms of stages of their *life cycle*. That is, individuals are described by the stage of their lifetime or career where they are currently located.

[2] While it is true that the individual investor is unconstrained with respect to assets and strategies, he or she should consider the same kinds of factors (wealth, income requirements, time horizon, and so on) as an institutional manager dealing with the same situation.

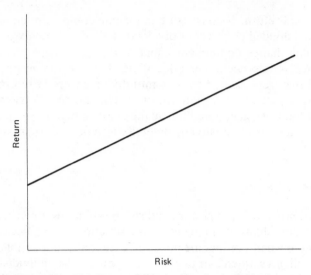

Figure 5-1. Risk-Return Opportunities for Individual Investors.

The first stage is the early career situation. Assets are small relative to liabilities, especially when the latter include a large house mortgage and other debts from credit purchases. The individual's assets are typically non-diversified, with house equity the largest asset held, and inaccessible, in the form of employer pension contributions. Priorities include savings for liquidity purposes, life insurance for death protection, and—only third—investments. But because the individual has a very long time horizon with a potentially growing stream of discretionary income, he or she can undertake high return, high risk, capital gain oriented investments. Point *A* of Figure 5-2 is the approximate risk-return tradeoff for the early career person.

The middle stage is the mid-career individual. Assets equal or exceed liabilities, savings and life insurance programs are well underway, a basic investment program has been established, and home equity and potential pension benefits are substantial. At the same time, while the time horizon is still relatively long (≥20 years), it is not so long that capital preservation is unimportant. The investor can continue to undertake high risk, high return investments and reap the growth and capital gain benefits therefrom, but may wish to reduce the overall risk exposure involved. The individual is located at point *B* in Figure 5-2.

The final phase is late career or brink of retirement, where the individual's time horizon has diminished and income needs—in terms of size and stability—have risen. Assets significantly exceed liabilities; savings, pension, and life insurance programs are complete; and the house mortgage has been repaid. Income is reduced to investment returns, Social Security, and other pension payments. The investor's portfolio is typically shifted to significantly lower return, lower risk assets with large dividend or interest payment components and relatively secure asset values. Inflationary economic

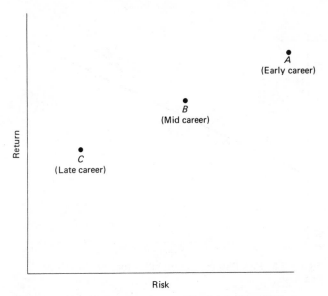

Figure 5-2. Risk-Return Positions of Individuals at Various Life Cycle Stages.

conditions may require the sale of assets to make up income shortfall. The investor moves to point *C* in Figure 5-2.

A concluding caveat is appropriate at this point. Exactly where each investor fixes his or her risk-return tradeoff at various life cycle stages depends on individual circumstances and individual risk-taking attitudes. Given two mid-career individuals, for example, the extremely cautious investor might be significantly to the left of point *B*, whereas a more aggressive individual might be substantially to the right.[3]

In effect, an individual's risk tolerance is unique and subject to changes influenced by the investor's wealth position, health, family situation, age, and temperament. As discussed in Chapter 13, the portfolio manager must be alert to changes in the investor's objectives and be prepared to rebalance the portfolio accordingly.

Personal Trusts

As compared with the scope available to individuals who invest directly, the world of personal trust investing is much more limited. Because of their fiduciary nature, personal trust and investment counsel accounts would have truncated risk exposure. Instead of the situation portrayed in Figure

---

[3] Practitioners have observed that some investors do *not* appear to become more averse to risk as they grow older. But this may be because of "hidden" assets, such as pension account accumulations, that do not explicitly appear in their portfolios. Or because, with experience, their "gambles" are actually less risky (i.e., have a higher probability of success) even though they do not *appear* to be less risky on the surface.

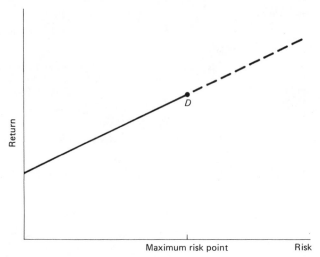

Figure 5-3. Risk-Return Opportunities for Personal Trust Accounts.

5-1, personal trust opportunities would look more like Figure 5-3, with high risk assets such as stock options and futures contracts and high risk strategies such as short positioning and stock buying on margin—points to the right of point *D*—being eliminated from consideration.

INVESTMENT CONSTRAINTS

Liquidity

Just as for investment objectives, the constraints imposed on individual investors are subject to wide variance. Certainly that is true of liquidity. Liquidity needs are highly personal and, hence, highly variable from individual to individual.

Some individuals use their investment accounts as combination checking and savings accounts. For these individuals, an "adequate" amount of funds should be kept in a liquidity reserve as large as the largest cash drain net of cash inflows that is budgeted. This reserve is usually easy to program. It should be invested in exceptionally high quality, short maturity debt issues, such as a money market fund or the types of issues—Treasury bills, commercial paper, certificates of deposit, and bankers acceptances—in which these funds are invested.[4]

---

[4] An alternative way of providing for liquidity, especially large, unanticipated, and temporary needs, is to arrange a loan with a commercial bank or other financial institution using portfolio securities in the trust as the collateral. Depending on availability and cost of borrowed funds, such an arrangement may be made on terms ranging from satisfactory to unsatisfactory.

Furthermore, if the assets held have poor marketability, such as residential real estate or stock in a closely held business, liquidity needs should be especially carefully estimated and generously funded.

In practice, few individuals, or management organizations acting in their behalf, actually hold a liquidity reserve. Rather, they hold less of a reserve than they might, selling assets as necessary to meet shortfalls. One liquid way of holding these assets is in a cash management account that offers the combination of an interest-bearing checking account and a residual mutual fund invested in money market instruments with attractive returns that are passed through to the investor.

Time Horizon

Almost as important as risk and return in investment decision making is time horizon, defined as the investment planning period for individuals and personal trusts. It, too, is highly variable from individual to individual.

As indicated in the discussion of life cycles, individuals who are early in their life cycle have a long horizon, one that can absorb and smooth out the ups and downs of risky combinations of assets like common stock portfolios. These individuals can build portfolios of riskier assets and can use more risky investment strategies.

Individuals who are later in their lifetimes have a much shorter horizon. They should, therefore, tend toward less volatile portfolios, typically consisting of more bonds than stocks, with the former of higher quality and shorter duration (maturity/coupon combination) and the latter of higher quality and lower volatility.

With personal trusts the time horizon is ambiguous when there are a late stage income beneficiary and earlier stage remaindermen. The income beneficiary is exposed only to income variation; this usually is not large because the trust will typically be invested in assets with dependable income expectations. The remaindermen, however, will be exposed to asset value variation. For this reason, personal trust accounts may concentrate in stocks having only moderate capital appreciation or depreciation possibilities.[5]

Regulatory and Legal Considerations

Legal considerations play a large role in the personal trust area in contrast to the situation with individual investors. And, unlike pension trusts, the law is state rather than federal. State law is often common law, with the law being made and modified in the courts as the result of decisions in cases typically brought by remaindermen plaintiffs against trust department defendants.

---

[5] While not stated in trust terminology, this same ambiguity exists in most individuals' family situations. In both cases, a life expectancy assumption is used—usually that of the youngest income beneficiary in the case of a personal trust.

Some states have codified the law into prudent man statutes outlining the role and duties of personal trustees, a typical example of which appears in Appendix A to this chapter.

Prudent Man Rule. As noted in Chapter 4, with the advent of the Employee Retirement Income Security Act (ERISA) in 1974, the federal pension trust law has recognized the need for considering assets in a portfolio— not each individual asset—context, and the need for adequate portfolio diversification. At the same time, pension plan sponsors are asked to set limits for systematic or portfolio risk, risk that remains after diversifying across and within asset categories.

The same is not yet true for personal trusts. The prudent man concept in personal trusts has not yet moved away from asset-by-asset, case-by-case consideration of appropriateness, thus foreclosing the consideration of higher risk assets even when their riskiness is reduced by other portfolio assets with relatively uncorrelated returns patterns. Actions have been brought by beneficiaries when one or two securities in a portfolio performed unsatisfactorily. At least one recent case of this type was decided for the defendant trustee. The court found that an investment should be evaluated in terms of its intended contribution to the entire portfolio and not solely in terms of its own characteristics.[6]

Income Beneficiaries vs. Remaindermen. Another area where legal considerations play a major role is situations involving both life (or other limited period) income beneficiaries and remaindermen beneficiaries. This is because trust law perpetuates the dichotomization of total return into dividend or interest income and capital gain (net of loss) income. The former goes to the income beneficiary, whereas the latter accumulates to the benefit of the remainderman, as do unrealized gains net of losses.

This situation presents the trustee with an inherent conflict between the interests of the two sets of beneficiaries. Often the conflict is resolved almost totally in favor of the income beneficiary, with portfolio investments favoring income, especially tax-sheltered income from assets such as municipal bonds, to the almost complete exclusion of consideration of the remainderman. This lack of impartiality between income beneficiaries and remaindermen has been the source, if not the basis, for numerous remaindermen lawsuits.

Hence, only if the income beneficiary has limited need for income is the trust focused on long-term growth. For the typical case where the life benefi-

[6] This case, *Chase vs. Pevear,* decided by the Massachusetts Supreme Judicial Court in April 1981, involved an interpretation of the Massachusetts prudent man rule with respect to seven different investments that had been purchased by a Massachusetts trustee upon the recommendation of an investment counsel firm. The Massachusetts Probate Court had concluded that all seven investments were imprudent on the basis of a fixed list of investment criteria, including Moody's and Standard & Poor's ratings, a defined seasoning period (five to six years), and line-of-business labels. The decision was reversed by the higher Massachusetts court.

ciary has substantial needs for income, there is pressure on the trustee to invest heavily in fixed income securities or high dividend yielding, no-growth preferred or common stocks, such as stocks of public utilities. In prolonged inflationary times, this may result in a reduction of the real value of the trust. A better approach would be to invest in a portfolio of securities that provides the largest after-tax expected total return for the level of risk desired and take advantage of the limited or unlimited ability to pay out trust principal to life beneficiaries included in most recently drawn agreements.

Revocable vs. Irrevocable Trusts. A third legal area is the distinction between a *revocable* trust where the grantor is still living and an *irrevocable* trust with income and remainder interests. This distinction is a key one for many trustees. Whether the trustor is alive or dead is not really important. Whether the trust is created via a will or a trust agreement is not of real significance. What often has a major effect on investment policy is whether the trust is revocable or irrevocable.

If the grantor of a revocable trust is still living and is competent, he or she is really in a position to control the investments. If the grantor directs the trustee in writing to make investment decisions that are at variance with investment policies, strategies, or approved working lists of investment assets and even, for some trustees, the prudent man rule, the trustee would comply with the direction for at least two reasons: (1) legally, the grantor is the only person who has an interest in the trust and, therefore, he is the only one who could maintain an action against the trustee for a breach of the prudent man rule; because that grantor directed the breach of the rule, he cannot criticize the trustee; and (2) as a practical matter, the trustee knows that the grantor will, in all likelihood, revoke the trust if the trustee does not go along with the grantor's direction, thereby forcing the trustee to comply if it wishes to keep the business. These comments are not necessarily aimed at grantors who direct the trustee to invest in exotic, imprudent investments. Rather, this situation arises most frequently when a grantor directs the trustee to invest 100 percent of the trust assets in fixed income securities, either because the low-bracket grantor seeks to maximize income or the high-bracket grantor desires a tax-free return. While it usually is not prudent for a trustee to invest 100 percent of the trust assets in either bonds or stocks, the trustee of a revocable trust will, most likely, comply with that written direction from a competent grantor.

If, on the other hand, the trustee is dealing with an irrevocable trust with income and remainder interests, a different set of rules governs. Under those circumstances there is no beneficiary who could exonerate the trustee from liability for a breach of the prudent man rule; therefore, the trustee must make investment decisions with regard to the interests of both sets of beneficiaries. As indicated above, while the income beneficiaries wish the trustee to maximize income, a prudent trustee cannot invest 100 percent of the portfolio in bonds and ignore the remaindermen's desire for appreciation; the opposite, of course, is equally true. Typical personal trust investment policy grants discretion to portfolio managers to arrive at the best possible tradeoffs while dictating that no more than 70 percent of the portfolio be invested in either fixed income securities or equities.[7]

The differing treatment of the trustee's investment options in the case of an irrevocable trust extends to the competing investment needs of multiple income beneficiaries. The trustee may be dealing with two income beneficiaries, where, for example, one of them may (because of other sources of income) be in a high income tax bracket and the other in a low tax bracket. It is not prudent for the trustee to comply completely with the wishes of either beneficiary, investing the bond portion of the portfolio totally in tax frees or in taxables. Rather, some form of compromise is sought, perhaps by splitting the fixed income portion of the portfolio between tax frees and taxables. While the income tax laws require each beneficiary to report a pro-rata share of the taxable income (it cannot be said that the tax-free income went to one beneficiary and the taxable income went to the other), such a division of the bond portfolio gives in a little bit to the wishes and needs of each income beneficiary.

Tax Considerations

Since individuals have the opportunity to select from the widest range of asset types and investment strategies, and since different individuals, depending on their incomes, are subjected to the widest range of marginal tax rates, tax considerations are among the most important portfolio strategy modifiers for individuals.

The importance of these considerations stems from the differing tax treatment of (1) returns from different kinds of assets (tax-sheltered or not) and (2) different components of total return (dividends or interest income versus capital gains).

Investors in high marginal tax brackets should consider investing the fixed income part of their portfolio in a diversified group of tax-exempt municipal issues if their taxable equivalent expected return exceeds the expected return on taxable issues in the same risk category. The same rule should apply to all tax-sheltered investments, although the risk categories of some assets are difficult to ascertain, especially among tax shelter exposures. High tax bracket investors are interested in investments that are designed to avoid paying federal, state, and/or local taxes, to postpone a tax, or to reduce a tax.

Investors in high marginal tax brackets should consider investing the equity part of their portfolio in a diversified group of stocks with large capital gain components relative to dividend income for any given level of risk,

---

[7] While this 70 percent figure is reasonable as a typical maximum, trust departments use guidelines for investing personal trusts that provide for maximum equity ratios as high as 90 percent and minimum equity ratios as low as 10 percent. They even grant special approval to invest such accounts 100 percent in equities or 100 percent in fixed income securities, usually on the basis that such positions are justified when viewed in combination with other assets available to the parties involved.

assuming, of course, that the after-tax result is favorable as compared with high (dividend) yielding stocks. Investors in low marginal tax brackets should make the opposite comparison.

Several financial advisory services provide stock recommendations that include tax considerations for high marginal tax bracket investors. One investment advisory service, for example, provides dividend yield/total expected return tradeoffs for stocks based on investor marginal tax brackets.

Personal Trusts. Tax considerations are particularly vexing for personal trusts. In a personal trust a situation frequently arises where common stocks having a low cost basis are evaluated as being currently overpriced. For example, stocks of large capitalization, solid, blue-chip companies that have had outstanding past records may still possess excellent prospects for the long run future. However, because of institutional buying support or other reasons, they may be fully priced or even overpriced relative to current intrinsic value and should be sold.

If these securities were sold now, however, a large capital gain would be realized and a sizeable income tax liability would be created. This liability would have to be paid out of the corpus of the trust, thereby reducing its size. This, in turn, would cause consternation to income beneficiaries because a smaller principal would likely produce less income at the same time that it reduced the value of the remainderman's interest.

The key, of course, is what might have happened to the stock's price had the sale *not* occurred and, more importantly, what was done with the net proceeds of the sale. If the proceeds were used to broaden diversification, invest in similar-risk assets producing a higher return, or otherwise strengthen and improve the portfolio relative to beneficiary needs, the action would be clearly meritorious.

Tax laws are subject to change and sometimes those changes can be revolutionary rather than evolutionary. The Economic Recovery Tax Act of 1981 represents the most sweeping change in the tax law in decades and has caused portfolio managers to reassess income and estate tax constraints and, in many cases, rebalance portfolios to reflect these changes.

Appendixes B, C, and D of this chapter briefly discuss the individual investor's tax considerations in terms of Individual Retirement Accounts, tax shelter types of investments, and capital gain and estate tax planning.

Unique Needs, Circumstances, and Preferences

One of the special circumstances associated with personal trusts is the receipt of a single-asset (or nearly so) nondiversified equity portfolio into a personal trust or investment advisory account.

In principle, a systematic program of diversification should be initiated upon receipt of such a portfolio. Such programs can be problematic, however, especially for revocable trusts. The decision might be an emotional one where the single asset is the stock of a family or long-time employer corporation. Getting a sale approved may be difficult. Also, it may be difficult to find a buyer willing to buy except for a large price concession.

Other problems are tax related. For example, the cost basis for such securities is frequently low, resulting in large capital gain taxes. Often the move toward diversification is governed by the amount of taxes the account beneficiaries can tolerate paying.

Another tax-related situation involves a revocable living trust with an elderly person as the income beneficiary. Rather than selling the single asset and diversifying now, it might be more advantageous to wait until the death of the income beneficiary when a new, higher cost basis for the trust asset would be established. A sale of the stock shortly thereafter would incur little or no capital gain tax liability.

Still another tax-related situation has to do with the exclusion of a certain amount of income-producing assets, such as bonds, from an elderly parent's living trust, particularly if the remaindermen are in high marginal income tax brackets. Why? Because at the income beneficiary parent's death, income from a living trust automatically starts going to the remaindermen beneficiaries and is taxable at rates of up to 50 percent. But if some bonds are kept out of the trust, they could pass under the parent's will to those same beneficiaries; the interest on the bonds received by the executor would be taxed as estate income at a rate that is potentially significantly lower. The after-tax estate income could later be distributed to the estate beneficiaries when the estate administration is terminated. If because of the existence of the trust no other assets in the estate were subject to probate, the costs incurred under this approach frequently would be nominal as compared to the saving in taxes.

Other special circumstances of personal trusts involve the holding and operation of nonmarketable assets such as closely held corporations, partnerships, and proprietorships. The trust department is called upon to collect receipts and make disbursements to keep these businesses operating until a buyer can be found or some other resolution is arranged.

Another circumstance unique to personal trusts is the ability, through terms of the trust agreement, to relieve the trustee of fiduciary responsibility on specified assets. Such exculpatory provisions are not, for example, permitted in pension trust agreements. Furthermore, the terms of personal trust agreements can be used to truncate the spectrum of asset categories and investment strategies more drastically than called for under prudent man rules, or to enlarge them.

DETERMINATION OF PORTFOLIO POLICY

The diversity of individual investors results in a unique set of circumstances and needs for each. This in part explains why explicit investment policy statements, which are an integral part of institutional portfolio management, have been the exception rather than the rule for individual investors.

TABLE 5-6. Description of the Trust Account Investment Process

Customer	Account Manager	Portfolio Manager
A. Has assets, needs, constraints, and preferences	B. Determines needs and wants (checklists)	
	C. Establishes realistic, mutually understood, and acceptable goal with customer covering overriding constraints, priorities, trade offs, preferences, and time horizon	
	D. Prepares statement of goal	
		E. Accepts attainable goal statements, reviews assets, and prepares a statement of expected results and, if needed, an investment plan
	F. Reviews and approves statement of expected results and investment plan	
G. Reviews and approves goal statement and, if required, the investment plan		H. With an accepted investment plan, moves on an ongoing basis to establish appropriate portfolio in terms of asset mix, sector weighting, and security selection, utilizing the appropriate fund vehicles and/or benchmark portfolios
	I. Reviews performance against established goal and periodically communicates status of portfolio to customer and alerts customer to significant changes in expected results	
J. Receives results and evaluation of performance relative to goal and updates goal relative to assets, needs, constraints, preferences, and outlook	K. Updates statement of goal (then back to step E)	

SOURCE: The Connecticut Bank and Trust Company.

TABLE 5-7. **Personal Trust Account Investment Objectives and Guideline Asset Mixes**

Profile Code	Primary Objective	Secondary Objective	Asset Mix	Comments
S-1	Stability of principal Stability of principal Stability of principal	Current income Growth of income Appreciation	Short-term debt portfolio Unacceptable goal Unacceptable goal	Similar to short-term investment fund
C-1	Current income	Stability of principal	Fixed income portfolio	Minimum maturities necessary to achieve required income flow.
C-2	Current income	Growth of income	40–60% debt 40–60% equities	Stability of principal third. Within the debt portfolio the portion invested short term will depend on the need for stability of principal relative to stability of income.
C-3	Current income	Growth of income	50–65% equities 35–50% debt	Appreciation third. Fixed income is to secure needed level and stability of income. Maturity of debt is not constrained by a need for stability of principal.
C-4	Current income	Growth of income	100% equities	For where an account can and wants to achieve needed income from an all equity portfolio.
C-5	Current income	Appreciation	Open	Infrequent goal. Tailored solution, similar to Employee Benefit Fixed Income Fund.
G-1	Growth of income Growth of income	Stability of principal Current income	Unacceptable goal 60–100% equities 0–40% debt	Note: Appreciation should be coded third and debt portion could be tax-exempt issues. Stability is fourth goal.
G-2	Growth of income	Appreciation	75–100% equities 0–25% debt	Note: Current income should be coded third; stability is fourth goal.
A-4 A-3	Appreciation Appreciation	Stability of principal Current income	Infrequent goal Infrequent goal	Tailored solution, such as discount bond portfolio. Tailored solution—probably balanced with aggressive equity holdings mixed with tax-free issues.
A-1	Appreciation	Growth of income	0–10% debt 90–100% equities	
A-2	Appreciation	Growth of income	85–100% equities 0–15% debt	Aggressive equity portfolio. Similar to Supplemental Fund.

SOURCE: The Connecticut Bank and Trust Company.

TABLE 5-8. Guideline Ranges for Maturity, Quality Rating, Issuer Type, and Coupon Level for Four Personal Trust Common Funds

	Taxable Fixed Income Fund: C-1 (taxable)	Tax-Exempt Fixed Income Fund: C-1 (tax-exempt)	Employee Benefit Fixed Income Fund: C-5	Employee Benefit Short-Term Investment Fund: S-1
Maturity Distribution				
Short (under 1 year)	5–30% residual	nominal–20% residual	5–50% residual	100% 0–29 days: 10–80% 30–179 days: residual
Intermediate				
Long (over 15 years)	30–60%	50–75%	20–85%	180–365 days: 0–80%
Quality Structure				
Aaa	high	high	high	highest
Aa				
A	Investment Grade: Moody's Aaa to Baa inclusive			
Baa	≤15%	≤15%	≤25%	
Issuer Type*				
U.S. Treasury	all	all major issues over $25MM	all	yes
Federal Agency				yes
Corporates				yes
Foreign/"Yankee"	≤15%		≤15%	no
Other				repurchase agreements
Coupon Level	all	all	all	current

SOURCE: The Connecticut Bank and Trust Company.
* Subject to individual issuer concentrations of less than 10%.

TABLE 5-9. **Expected Appreciation, Stability, Yield, Income Growth, and Total Return to Each Personal Trust Portfolio Type**

Profile Code	Asset Mix	Mean Appreciation (%)	Market Value Stability (%)	Yield (%)	Mean Growth of Income (%)	Total Percent Return (Appr. and Yield) (%)
	100% equities	8	8 ± 22.5 (−14.5 to +30.5)	5.5	8	13.5
	100% debt	0	0 ± 7.0	9.5	0	9.5
C-2	40% market equities 60% debt	40 × 8 = 3.2 60 × 0 = 0 3.2	40 × 22.5 = 9.0 60 × 7 = 4.2 3.2 ±13.2 (−10.0 to +16.4)	40 × 5.5 = 2.2 60 × 9.5 = 5.7 7.9	28 × 8 = 2.2 72 × 0 = 0 2.2	11
C-3	60% market equities 40% debt	60 × 8 = 4.8 40 × 0 = 0 4.8	60 × 22.5 = 13.5 40 × 7 = 2.8 4.8 ±16.3 (−11.5 to +21.1)	60 × 5.5 = 3.3 40 × 9.5 = 3.8 7.1	46 × 8 = 3.7 54 × 0 = 0 3.7	12
C-4	100% income equities	6.5	6.5 ± 21 (−14.5 to +27.5)	6.5	6.5	13
G-1	80% equities growth of income 20% debt	80 × 9 = 7.2 20 × 0 = 0 7.2	80 × 23 = 18.4 20 × 7 = 1.4 8 ±19.8 (−11.8 to +27.8)	80 × 5 = 4.0 20 × 9.5 = 1.9 5.9	68 × 9 = 6.1 32 × 0 = 0 6.1	13
G-2	100% equities growth of income	9	9 ± 24 (−15 to +33)	5	9	14
A-1	100% equities	10.5	10.5 ± 25 (−14.5 to +35.5) (−10.5 to +40.5 total return)	4	10.5	14.5
A-2	100% equities (supplemental fund)	12.5	12.5 ± 26 (−13.5 to +38.5)	2.5	12.5	15

SOURCE: The Connecticut Bank and Trust Company.

Note: Returns are longer term normalized returns assuming a 6% base rate of inflation and well-diversified, actively managed portfolios. The above represents the best judgment of the Bank but the results expected cannot be guaranteed.

Books on individual investing speak of investment plans and caution investors to know why they are making an investment. Some suggest that the investor write down the reasons for making each investment and review those notes periodically in light of the investor's actual experience.

Bank trust departments and investment counselors, for example, compile information on their clients. In general, however, it has not been their practice to develop an explicit policy statement that incorporates the objectives, constraints, and unique preferences for each client. Although investment managers are required to know their client and be aware of changes in the client's circumstances, their procedures for doing so are quite often informal and unwritten.

A 1982 ruling of the Comptroller of the Currency requires explicit documentation of investment policy updated at regular intervals for each bank-administered trust account. This is expected to bring about more systematic and formalized policy-setting procedures for individual investors whose accounts are managed by bank trust departments. It is possible that counselors and individual investors themselves will appreciate the benefits accruing from preparing and updating explicit policy statements and will adopt similar procedures.

Although examples are limited, Tables 5-6 to 5-9 provide an illustration of investment policies, strategies, and expected outcomes for personal trust accounts developed by a large commercial bank trust department. Table 5-6 gives a description of the trust account investment process. Table 5-7 provides the primary and secondary objectives and the asset mix of each of the portfolios managed; note that three portfolios have no profile code because their primary and secondary objectives are mutually inconsistent. Table 5-8 shows the guideline ranges of maturity, quality rating, issuer type, and coupon level for each of the fixed income portfolios. Finally, Table 5-9 lists, for each portfolio type, the expected mean appreciation, stability, yield, income growth, and total return.

SUMMARY

This chapter has reviewed the investment objectives and constraints for the management of portfolios of individuals. Investing directly, individuals were portrayed as having the most flexibility and the most diverse set of objectives and constraints. When investing indirectly, however, especially via an agreement that creates a trusteed relationship, the picture was considerably more complicated, constrained, and cloudy. Particularly interesting were regulatory and legal considerations and tax issues as they affect personal trust investment, especially the divergence between the common-law environment of personal trusts and the ERISA-determined habitat of pension trusts.

FURTHER READING

There is one classic text that is an outstanding presentation of case studies and principles governing individual investors' objectives and constraints, Professor Harry Sauvain's *Investment Management,* published first in 1953 and revised most recently in 1973.

Cohen, Zinbarg, and Zeikel [1982] is the best of current investment texts in covering the needs of the individual investor. Tuttle [1982] effectively summarizes the major topics in the field. Most recent texts give the topic only cursory attention. Some thoughtful authors who have addressed the subject are listed in the Bibliography.

BIBLIOGRAPHY

Bauman, W. Scott, *Performance Objectives of Investors,* Charlottesville, Va: Financial Analysts Research Foundation, 1975.

Beman, Lewis, "How to Think About Those New IRAs," *Fortune,* November 16, 1981.

Black, Fischer, "The Investment Policy Spectrum: Individuals, Endowment Funds and Pension Funds," *Financial Analysts Journal,* January/February 1976.

Board of Governors of the Federal Reserve System, Federal Deposit Insurance Corporation, and Office of the Comptroller of the Currency, *Trust Assets of Banks and Trust Companies—1980,* Washington: Federal Financial Institutions Examination Council, 1981.

Cohen, Jerome B., Edward D. Zinbarg, and Arthur Zeikel, *Investment Analysis and Portfolio Management,* 4th ed., Homewood, Ill.: Richard D. Irwin, 1982.

Milne, Robert D., "What Are Responsible Investment Objectives?" in *Evolving Concepts of Prudence,* Charlottesville, Va.: Financial Analysts Research Foundation, 1976.

NYSE Fact Book, 1980, New York: New York Stock Exchange, 1980.

Pocket Chartroom, Economic Research, Goldman Sachs & Co., March 1982.

Sauvain, Harry, *Investment Management,* 4th ed., Englewood Cliffs, N.J.: Prentice-Hall, 1973.

Tuttle, Donald L., "Individual and Personal Trusts," in *Determinants of Investment Portfolio Policy,* Charlottesville, Va.: The Institute of Chartered Financial Analysts, 1982.

APPENDIX A

Sample Codification of Personal Trust Prudent Man Rule

Shown below is the codification of the prudent man rule under the Indiana Trust Code, I.C. §30-4-3-3(c). The wording is representative of the common-law status of the rule.

In acquiring, investing, reinvesting, exchanging, retaining, selling and managing property for any trust heretofore or hereafter created, the trustee thereof shall exercise the judgment and care under the circumstances then prevailing which men of prudence, discretion and intelligence exercise in the management of their own affairs, not in regard to speculation but in regard to the permanent disposition of their funds, considering the probable income as well as the probable safety of their capital. Within the limitations of the foregoing standard, the trustee is authorized to acquire and retain every kind of property, real, personal or mixed, and every kind of investment, including specifically, but without in any way limiting the generality of the foregoing, bonds, debentures and other corporate obligations, stocks, preferred or common, and real estate mortgages, which men of prudence, discretion and intelligence acquire or retain for their own account, and within the limitations of the foregoing standard, the trustee is authorized to retain property properly acquired, without limitation as to time and without regard to its suitability for original purchase.

APPENDIX B

Individual Retirement Accounts

The number of individuals who are potential candidates for professional investment management services is expected to increase as a result of changes in the eligibility requirements for Individual Retirement Accounts (IRAs). The original IRAs were created by the Employee Retirement Income Security Act of 1974 (ERISA) to assist individuals not participating in an employer-sponsored pension plan. The Economic Recovery Tax Act of 1981 broadened the eligibility to all employed persons, regardless of any employer-sponsored pension plan participation. It is estimated that approximately 50 million Americans are eligible to deduct $2,000 of earned income annually from their tax return and put it aside in an IRA. Employed spouses are also entitled to put aside $2,000 of earned income. Even if the spouse does not work, a couple can deduct another $250, or a total of $2,250 annually. In Canada, Registered Retirement Savings Plans (RRSPs) are designed to accomplish the same purpose as the IRAs, although the amounts and regulations are different. In both cases, a major requirement is that the investments be segregated with a custodian or trustee. With-

TABLE 5B-1. Potential Value of an Individual Retirement Account at Age 65 Under Various Percentage Return Assumptions Based on a $2,000 Annual Contribution

Age at Start of IRA	ASSUMED PERCENTAGE RETURN		
	5%	10%	15%
25	$241,600	$885,195	$3,571,514
35	132,878	328,992	869,490
45	66,132	114,552	204,887
55	24,556	31,875	40,607

TABLE 5B-2. Where the Biggest IRA Bonuses Are: Gain on $2,000 Investment Over 10 Years

	Newly Issued Bond 15% COUPON, DUE 1992 CURRENT PRICE $1000		Income Stock 3% ANNUAL GROWTH 9% YIELD		Discount Bond 6% COUPON, DUE 1992 CURRENT PRICE $580		Growth Stock 15% ANNUAL GROWTH NO YIELD	
	In IRA	*Not in IRA*	*In IRA*	*Not in IRA*	*In IRA*	*Not in IRA*	*In IRA*	*Not in IRA*
After-tax income	$4,781	$1,887	$3,213	$1,282	$3,187	$1,258	—	—
After-tax capital gain	—	—	$687	$549	$1,448	$1,159	$6,091	$4,873
Total proceeds	$4,781	$1,887	$3,900	$1,831	$4,635	$2,417	$6,091	$4,873
Net proceeds (after 50% tax on IRA funds withdrawn)	$2,391	$1,887	$1,950	$1,831	$2,317	$2,417	$3,046	$4,873
IRA bonus (penalty)	$504		$119		($100)		($1,827)	

SOURCE: Beman [1981]. Table by FORTUNE Art Department, © 1981 by Time, Inc.

drawal is not permitted (except at a penalty) sooner than age $59\frac{1}{2}$ and, for an IRA, must be started no later than age $70\frac{1}{2}$.

From an investment policy standpoint, the ability to compound on a tax deferred basis over a definable time horizon requires selection of the appropriate investment alternatives (collectibles are not eligible investments). For the individual there is the opportunity for significant accumulations of wealth (as indicated in Table 5B-1 on page 147) to provide a supplemental retirement income.

The selection of the appropriate investment alternatives is deserving of further comment and illustration because of the tax characteristics involved. As a rule of thumb, investments that are noted for their tax savings features—tax-exempt bonds, depreciable property, and so on—should be avoided in an IRA account. Since all withdrawals from an IRA account are taxed at ordinary income rates, investments from which a major portion of the expected return is in the form of capital gains— real estate, discount bonds, and common stocks, particularly growth stocks—may be more appropriately held by an individual outside of the IRA.

Table 5B-2 opposite illustrates the comparative after-tax returns for four investment alternatives, depending upon whether they are held in an IRA or not. For purposes of illustration, income is assumed to be reinvested at 10 percent and the individual is assumed to be in the 50 percent tax bracket throughout the ten-year time horizon. The tax advantage of being able to deduct the IRA contribution was ignored in this illustration because the comparable amount invested outside the IRA would have been only $1,000 per year. Although not explicitly included in the illustration below, zero coupon bonds, which have recently become popular, would be of less interest than discount bonds for most IRA participants. The exception would be IRA investors approaching retirement age; for these individuals, the lack of reinvestment rate risk (because there is no coupon income to reinvest) and the guaranteed rate of return to maturity—matched by the number of years to retirement—would be extremely appealing.

The impact of the individual's tax rate at the time of withdrawal is further illustrated in Table 5B-3, which repeats the 50 percent tax bracket line from Table 5B-2, but also includes comparative figures assuming tax rates of 45 percent and 38 percent at the time of withdrawal. Since, for many individuals, IRA withdrawals will supplement taxable income from pensions, deferred compensation, and investments, it is possible that tax rates for such individuals will not decrease materially after retirement. However, the flexibility of the timing and rate of withdrawals from an IRA account lends itself to tax planning even after retirement.

TABLE 5B-3. **How Tax Rates at Retirement Affect IRA Results: Gain on $2,000 Investment Over 10 Years**

	Newly Issued Bond	Income Stock	Discount Bond	Growth Stock
Not in IRA	$1,887	$1,831	$2,417	$4,873
In IRA (Tax bracket at time of withdrawal)				
50% (Taxable income: $215,000+)	$2,391	$1,950	$2,317	$3,046
45% ($85,600 to $109,400)	$2,630	$2,145	$2,549	$3,350
38% ($45,800 to $60,000)	$2,964	$2,418	$2,874	$3,777

SOURCE: Beman [1981]. Table by FORTUNE Art Department, © 1981 by Time, Inc.

APPENDIX C

Tax Shelters for Individuals

The topic of tax shelter investments typically involves the concept of deferring or postponing taxes, as well as changing fully taxable ordinary income into an investment return taxed at a lower rate. For example, oil and gas drilling partnerships often provide a tax deduction in the first year equal to 75 percent or more of the amount invested. If the venture is successful, income will result in future years and the depletion allowance will ease the tax burden. Table 5C-1 illustrates the tax aspects as they influence the potential return from a natural gas drilling partnership in the short-lived Ohio gas fields.

Tax shelters such as this one are promoted on the basis of the immediate tax savings plus the fact that "you get your money back in five years and then it's all profit that also has tax benefits."

The project would have provided a 5.5 percent after-tax return for a taxpayer in the top tax bracket if there were no special tax features. By matching the total net investment with the present value (using an 8% discount rate) of net after-tax distributions, Table 5C-1 shows that the return has been boosted to 8 percent after tax because of the tax shelter characteristics. In other words, the tax shelter in this case added only modestly to the true economic return for the project, perhaps too little to more than outweigh the risk of total loss of net investment for such a venture.

Real estate tax shelters may provide even greater tax writeoffs in the early years and can be analyzed in the same general manner. With real estate, the buildup in the value of the equity (as contrasted with the depletion of oil and gas properties) becomes a more important element. However, the lower ordinary income tax brackets incorporated in the Economic Recovery Tax Act of 1981 have reduced the attractiveness of tax shelters in general.

TABLE 5C-1. **Potential Returns From Drilling Partnerships**

Investment	$10,000	
First year tax savings	3,500	
Net Investment	$ 6,500	

Year	Estimated Distribution	Net After Taxes	Discounted at 8%
1	$ 1,800	$1,125	$1,042
2	1,800	1,125	964
3	1,800	1,125	893
4	1,800	1,125	827
5	1,800	1,125	766
6	1,800	1,125	709
7	1,800	1,125	656
8	1,800	1,125	607
	$14,400	$9,000	$6,464

APPENDIX D

Capital Gains and Estate Taxes*

Over the past several decades, taxes have had an increasingly greater impact on Americans generally, and investors have certainly been no exception. Other than retirement funds and some endowment funds, investors must take account of the tax implications of their actions. Even portfolio managers who deal in tax-exempt funds should be aware of tax laws because of the effect of taxes on market liquidity, turnover, and security selection.

Capital Gains Taxes

The rules of U.S. capital gains taxes for individuals are relatively simple. Any security sold in one year or less from date of purchase is treated as a short-term transaction, whereas a security sold after one year is a long-term transaction. To calculate the tax, an investor offsets short-term losses against short-term gains, then offsets long-term losses against long-term gains. Finally the net results of those two calculations are offset against each other. Under the Revenue Act of 1978 (reaffirmed by the Economic Recovery Tax Act of 1981), 40 percent of the net long-term gain is taxable at one's ordinary income tax rates. One hundred percent of net short-term gains are also taxed as ordinary income. The following is a straightforward capital gain and loss example.

Assume an investor's top income tax bracket is 40 percent with the following gains and losses: long-term capital gains of $10,000, long-term capital losses of $3,000, and short-term capital losses of $4,000.

Looking first at the short-term, there was a loss of $4,000 but no gains, leaving a net short-term loss of $4,000. Offsetting the long-term capital losses of $3,000 against long-term capital gains of $10,000 leaves a net long-term gain of $7,000. This is reduced by the net short-term loss; a taxable long-term gain of $3,000 remains. Only 40 percent of this, $1,200, is taxable. When we apply this investor's top tax bracket of 40 percent against the taxable gain, the tax is $480.

The above example resulted in a net gain. What if the investor has net losses for the year? Because only 50 percent of long-term gains were taxable under the previous capital gains tax laws, only 50 percent of net long-term losses could be used to reduce ordinary income for tax purposes. Furthermore, under the Tax Reform Act of 1976, a new and higher limit was placed on the amount of such losses that could be used to offset ordinary income. Up to $6,000 of long-term losses can be used each year to generate a $3,000 reduction of ordinary income (the 50-percent rule). One hundred percent of short-term losses can be so used up to the limit of $3,000 each year. If an investor has both net long-term and short-term losses, the short-term losses are used first; then, to the extent needed, the long-term losses. Interestingly, the Revenue Act of 1978, which reduced the taxable portion of capital gains from 50

* This appendix was originally written by Jay Vawter, C.F.A., for the C.F.A. candidate program. Its purpose was to provide a basic understanding of the taxes that might have an impact on the investment decision-making process. Financial analysts should have a minimum working knowledge of taxation as it applies to investments and, at the very least, know when to refer problems to an attorney or an accountant.

percent to 40 percent, did not modify the 50-percent rule with regard to net long-term losses. This means that a long-term loss standing on its own is worth somewhat more in tax savings to the investor than the same loss applied against long-term gains, which suggests a strategy of realizing $6,000 of net long-term losses each year where it makes sense from an investment standpoint. Any amount of losses, either long-term or short-term, that exceeds these limits can be carried forward to future tax years indefinitely to offset future capital gains, if any, or ordinary income if no gains exist to offset. Any losses carried forward retain their character as to holding period—a short-term loss is carried forward as a short-term loss and a long-term loss is carried forward as a long-term loss. The following example illustrates the carry-forward principle:

Consider the same investor as in the problem above, but with the following gains and losses: long-term capital gains of $4,000, long-term capital losses of $11,000.

In this case, offsetting long-term gains and losses leaves a net long-term loss of $7,000. Only $6,000 of this, however, can be used in determining the amount by which ordinary income may be reduced before taxes. The remaining $1,000 may be used to offset gains the following year, if any, or to reduce ordinary income if there are no gains. As to the tax calculations, $3,000 (50%) of the $6,000 is used to reduce ordinary income before tax. The tax saving on a $3,000 deduction is $1,200 to our investor in a 40-percent bracket. Had this $7,000 loss been all short-term, $3,000 could have been used to reduce ordinary income with the balance, $4,000 carried forward. The following example illustrates this point where the net loss is short term.

Again take our same investor: short-term capital gains $2,000, short-term capital losses $4,000.

In this case the investor has a net short-term capital loss of $2,000. Because this is less than the $3,000 limit, all of it may be used to offset ordinary income, resulting in an $800 tax saving to the investor in a 40-percent bracket.

As indicated, taxes often play an important role in investment decisions. However, all too often taxes take too important a role and, frequently, bad investment decisions are made because of tax considerations. However, the decision on whether or not to realize a capital gain should take into account the tax cost of that decision and thus consider the future potential of the securities to be sold versus other opportunities. A simple calculation of the tax liability will give the portfolio manager a fairly good idea of how well the replacement stock must do to make up this tax cost and subsequently to provide a greater return over time. If it appears that the stock to be sold has pretty well run its course and there are other more attractive opportunities, it generally pays to take the gain, pay the tax, and switch to the other investment. Regrettably, many investors choose to hold an unattractive stock because they do not want to pay the capital gains tax and, therefore, miss other, more attractive alternatives, or watch the profit disappear as the stock subsequently declines. Certainly the reduction of the maximum capital gain tax from nearly 50 percent prior to the 1978 law to 20 percent in the 1981 law should reduce the reluctance to sell stocks at gains.

There are times when gains or losses can be used successfully to improve the position of a portfolio. This is especially true now in an era of discounted commissions, where the transaction costs need not significantly reduce the advantage of making tax-motivated switches. If a particular security has failed to live up to expectations and shows a loss, it may very well be desirable to sell it at a loss, either to offset other gains already realized or to reduce ordinary income up to the limits discussed earlier.

The timing of realization of tax losses is also important. Many investors wait until the end of the year. It may be assumed that if you have a loss in a stock, many others do also; stocks that have done unusually poorly in the last year or two will often be sold in heavy volume toward the end of the year, depressing the price still further. (Managers of tax-exempt funds take note!) It is generally desirable, therefore, to complete tax loss selling well before the year's last month or two. Failing this, one should keep in mind that a loss can be realized on a stock right up to the last few days of the year, but a gain can be realized only if it will be *settled* by the end of the year. This means either selling the security at least five business days prior to the end of the year (don't forget Christmas is not counted as a business day), or delivering the stock for a cash settlement by the end of the year if the trade is made less than five business days before the end of the year.

Another technique is useful in tax selling. Under the present law, a security sold at a loss and repurchased in less than 31 days becomes a wash sale and the tax loss is negated. The investor has two ways to avoid this problem. The first involves purchasing a number of shares equal to those to be sold, thus doubling up the holding, and then selling the loss shares 31 days later. This establishes the desired tax loss and maintains the original position. The doubling up must be done at least 31 days before year-end or the loss would be realized in the following year. The risk, of course, is that if the stock continues to fall during the 31-day period the investor would have been better off selling the original shares outright without doubling up.

This suggests an alternative method—selling stock, realizing the loss, then buying it back 31 days later. The risk of this is that if the stock goes up in the interim the investor must pay more to reestablish his position. The sale and buy-back technique may work best toward the end of the year when additional tax loss selling may push the stock lower and provide an opportunity to repurchase it at a cheaper price. Perhaps the safest way to deal with this problem is to sell the stock at a loss and buy a similar stock at the same time. Wash-sale rules do not apply to gains—you can sell a stock for a gain and buy it back at once.

Tax-Exempt Securities

Certain types of securities produce income that is exempt from federal, and in some cases, state income taxes. The most prevalent are tax-exempt bonds issued by states, counties, and municipalities. For individuals in high tax brackets who need fixed income, tax-exempt bonds offer a useful and valuable alternative to taxable securities such as federal government obligations and corporate issues. In order to determine whether or not it is advantageous to use tax-exempt bonds, a simple calculation can be made. One can simply apply one's highest or marginal tax bracket to a taxable yield, such as that available on AAA telephone bonds. If the net yield remaining is below the tax-free yield of municipal bonds of comparable quality, it will pay to use municipals. Another way of looking at this is to see what the taxable equivalent yield of a tax-free obligation is (in other words, what you have to get on taxable bonds before taxes to be equivalent to your tax-free income). A simple formula makes this calculation possible: tax-exempt yield divided by 1 minus marginal tax bracket. For example, if taxable yields are 16 percent, tax-exempt yields are 12 percent, and the investor's tax bracket is 40 percent, the calculation is:

$$12\% \div (1 - 0.4) =$$
$$12\% \div 0.6 = 20\%.$$

Because this figure is higher than the actual taxable yield of 16 percent, it is clearly advantageous to buy tax-exempt bonds.

The decision to buy taxable bonds or tax exempts is not quite so simple, however. Tax-exempt bonds tend to be considerably less liquid in most cases than corporate or government bonds. Thus, the yield differentials that one might expect may or may not prove to be the case in the actual marketplace.

Also, while it might pay to buy a certain amount of tax-exempt bonds, too much tax-exempt interest could pull the taxpayer into such a low bracket that further purchases would be disadvantageous relative to taxable bonds. In addition, one must keep in mind potential changes in the investor's tax bracket due to retirement, change of job, or other reasons. The purchase of tax-exempt securities must also take into account state taxes payable. While it is desirable to own issues in one's own state to get the benefit of further tax exemption (most states tax the interest of other states' tax-free issues), the principle of geographical diversification that suggests spreading risk among issues from other states will usually be an overriding consideration.

Finally, with the maximum tax on unearned income reduced from 70 percent to 50 percent on January 1, 1982, the tax benefit of municipal bonds becomes less for high bracket investors. The effects of income tax reduction through 1983 must also be monitored carefully in determining the desirability of tax-exempt bonds.

Another form of tax-exempt income applies only to corporations. Since 85 percent of all dividend income is tax exempt to corporations, preferred stocks, high yielding common stocks, and convertible preferreds are particularly useful to casualty insurance companies, personal holding companies, and other corporations. Because preferred stocks are a relatively scarce security relative to the demand for them by corporations, it is not unusual for preferred stock yields to be as low as, or in some cases lower than, the bonds or debentures of the same issuer. Corporations also are frequent purchasers of utility common stocks, which provide relatively high dividends that are 85 percent tax exempt.

U.S. Estate Taxes

The Economic Recovery Tax Act of 1981 has had a sweeping impact on estate tax rules and regulations and, therefore, on estate planning. The net impact of this law is the elimination of most estates from any estate taxation whatsoever over the next few years. The purpose here is to discuss broad principles, recognizing that individual circumstances may well dictate different approaches. Legal counsel in these matters is essential.

There are several aspects to estate tax law that may have a direct impact on the investment decision-making process. These have to do with lifetime gifts, the stepped-up cost basis on assets at death, the Unified Tax Credit, and, finally, the marital deduction. The first, lifetime gifts, has been changed significantly by the 1981 legislation. Under the old law, gifts of up to $3,000 per donor could be made to each of an unlimited number of donees. With the consent of a spouse, thus, gifts of up to $6,000 annually could be made by a couple to their children, grandchildren, and others.

The Economic Recovery Tax Act of 1981 increased the amount of these gifts from $3,000 to $10,000 annually. Thus, under the new rules, a couple could give up to $20,000 to each child, grandchild, or other person. Furthermore, gifts made for school tuitions or medical expenses are no longer treated as a gift as they were under the old rules.

(These limits do not apply to charitable donations, before or after the 1981 legislation. Deductible charitable donations are determined by federal income tax laws, rather than estate and gift tax laws, and may be well in excess of these limits, depending on the donor's income level.)

Certain strategies can be applied to making gifts of $10,000 to individuals or making charitable gifts (not limited to $10,000) to colleges, foundations, and so on. In the case of gifts to one's family, it might be desirable to give away stocks having very low cost bases to members in low tax brackets who could sell these securities with little or no capital gains tax impact, especially given the reduction of capital gains taxes starting in 1981. On the other hand, if the donee is in a high tax bracket, this approach would clearly reduce the value of the gift, so cash or higher cost securities might be more appropriate. In the case of charitable gifts, it is by far best to give away securities with low cost bases rather than selling the securities yourself, paying capital gains tax, and then making the gift in cash. The recipient can sell free of capital gains tax. In making large charitable gifts, however, one must be mindful that the deduction limits under federal income tax law are lower for gifts of appreciated property than for gifts of cash.

Another change concerning gifts has to do with the old *contemplation of death* rule. Under this rule all gifts made within three years of death were regarded as having been made in contemplation of death and were added back into the estate for tax purposes. The new law eliminates this rule. All gifts, no matter when made, are excluded from the taxable estate to the extent that they meet the annual exclusion rules discussed above. As will be discussed later, gifts exceeding the $10,000 annual exclusion rules ($20,000 for couples) are treated under the Unified Tax Credit rules.

Another aspect of estate taxation that has an extremely important impact on investing is the provision that the cost basis of all property—whether securities, real estate, or other assets—will be stepped up, either to the value on the date of death or six months later at the option of the executors. This rule has not been changed by the 1981 legislation, although Congress did try unsuccessfully to eliminate the benefit in the Tax Reform Act of 1976. The decision as to which valuation to use depends on the amount of estate tax calculated on each date; executors generally elect the lower valuation to minimize taxes.

The stepped-up basis rule gives us some insight into the interplay between capital gains taxes and estate planning. Frequently, older investors own stocks purchased many years earlier, which are on the books at extremely low cost. Because the cost basis will be stepped up at death to the date-of-death valuation, a real deterrent exists to taking these gains and paying a sizable capital gains tax. The problem discussed earlier of imposing a tax judgment on top of an investment judgment is even more acutely felt in the case of older investors, simply because the potential time horizon for recovering the tax in other, more attractive investments is potentially much shorter than for younger persons. In many cases, however, investors have lived beyond normal expectations and judicious sales for investment reasons might well have been made had it not been for the tax constraint. This surely has had some impact on the overall liquidity of our financial markets, since a considerable amount of securities no doubt are frozen because of it. The recent trend toward lower capital gains tax rates may significantly mitigate this problem.

The Tax Reform Act of 1976 introduced a new concept to estate and gift taxation, the Unified Tax Credit. Prior to this legislation estates enjoyed a $60,000 exemption from estate tax, with the balance being taxed according to estate tax tables. Gifts could be made during one's lifetime in excess of the then $3,000 annual exclusion and

TABLE 5D-1. U.S. Estate and Gift Tax Rate Schedule

TAXABLE ESTATE		TAX EQUALS		
From	To	Amount in This Column	+ %	Of Excess Over
$ 0	$ 10,000	$ 0	18	$ 0
10,000	20,000	1,800	20	10,000
20,000	40,000	3,800	22	20,000
40,000	60,000	8,200	24	40,000
60,000	80,000	13,000	26	60,000
80,000	100,000	18,200	28	80,000
100,000	150,000	23,800	30	100,000
150,000	250,000	38,800	32	150,000
250,000	500,000	70,800	34	250,000
500,000	750,000	155,800	37	500,000
750,000	1,000,000	248,300	39	750,000
1,000,000	1,250,000	345,800	41	1,000,000
1,250,000	1,500,000	448,300	43	1,250,000
1,500,000	2,000,000	555,800	45	1,500,000
2,000,000	2,500,000	780,800	49	2,000,000
2,500,000	3,000,000	1,025,800	53	2,500,000
3,000,000	3,500,000	1,290,800	57	3,000,000
3,500,000	4,000,000	1,575,800	61	3,500,000
4,000,000	4,500,000	1,880,800	65	4,000,000
4,500,000	5,000,000	2,205,800	69	4,500,000
5,000,000	—	2,550,800	70	5,000,000

were subject to a tax equal to 75 percent of the estate tax rates. The 1976 act eliminated the $60,000 exemption and the 75-percent gift tax rule, combining estates and gifts and making available to them a Unified Tax Credit. Under this rule, the value of an estate is calculated at the time of death, including any gifts made over and above the annual exclusion. The tax table shown in Table 5D-1 is then applied. From the resulting tax a credit is taken, which under the 1976 law rose to $47,000 in 1981. The practical effect of this credit was to eliminate all tax on estates up to $175,625— the amount of an estate which would have generated a tax of $47,000. The Economic Recovery Tax Act of 1981 merely extends the principle of the Unified Tax Credit by increasing the credit as follows:

Year	Unified Tax Credit	Amount of Estate Exempted from Tax
1982	$ 62,800	$225,000
1983	$ 79,300	$275,000
1984	$ 96,300	$325,000
1985	$121,800	$400,000
1986	$155,800	$500,000
1987	$192,800	$600,000

Thus, by 1987 all estates of $600,000 or less will be exempt from any estate tax whatever. Not only did the 1981 act increase the amount of the Unified Tax Credit over a five-year period ending in 1987, it also has reduced the maximum tax on

TABLE 5D-2. Projected Maximum Estate Tax Rates: 1982–85

	ESTATE TAX BRACKETS			
Taxable Estate	1982	1983	1984	1985
$4,000,000 and over	65%	—	—	—
3,500,000 and over	61	60%	—	—
3,000,000 and over	57	57	55%	—
2,500,000 and over	53	53	53	50%

estates from 70 percent to 50 percent over a four-year period from 1982 to 1985. Table 5D-2 shows the maximum rates effective from 1982 through 1985.

Perhaps the most significant change of the Economic Recovery Tax Act of 1981 was the major revision in the marital deduction rules. Prior to the Tax Reform Act of 1976, one-half of any estate could be left outright to a surviving spouse free of estate tax. The portion left as a marital deduction passed to the surviving spouse either outright, without restriction, or in trust, with the surviving spouse having a general power of appointment (meaning that he or she could leave the assets to anyone he or she chose). The Tax Reform Act of 1976 changed these rules slightly. Under that act one-half of an estate or $250,000, whichever was larger, could be left to a surviving spouse under the marital deduction. Again, the surviving spouse was required to have at least a general power of appointment over the assets.

The 1981 legislation permits a marital deduction of up to 100 percent of the estate, meaning that an entire estate can be left outright to a surviving spouse without any estate tax. Also, under the 1981 legislation the decedent's estate could be left in such a way that the surviving spouse did not necessarily have a general power of appointment over the assets received under the marital deduction. This is known as a *qualified terminable interest property* trust, or a Q-TIP trust. Under a Q-TIP, the decedent can assure that assets left to a surviving spouse pass upon that spouse's death to whomever the original decedent chose, perhaps his or her own children. Under the old rules, where the surviving spouse had a general power of appointment, the surviving spouse might well have remarried and left the entire estate to children of the second marriage, totally disinheriting the children of the first spouse.

By now the astute reader would have seen a potential flaw in the 1981 legislation. That is, if one's spouse became terminally ill, the other, possessing low cost basis stocks, might well make a gift of those stocks to the dying spouse. The gift would have no estate or gift tax implications since unlimited gifts can be made between spouses. Upon the death of the spouse receiving the gift, the cost of the assets would be stepped up to date-of-death valuation and passed back to the donor spouse. However, anticipating this possibility, the 1981 tax act prohibits the stepped-up basis on such assets (between spouses) within one year of the time such gifts are made. Thus, if the terminally ill spouse did, in fact, die in less than one year, the assets would be left to the surviving spouse at their original, low cost basis.

Simply because the new law allows an entire estate to be left to a surviving spouse without tax does not necessarily mean that it should be. If the estate is of sufficient size, the entire estate could be subject to considerable taxation upon the death of the surviving spouse.

The primary objective of estate planning is usually to minimize both the estate tax of the first person to die and the estate tax of the surviving spouse upon his or her eventual death. However, the need of the surviving spouse for flexibility must be balanced against this objective. Often a compromise is required.

There are three levels of estate value that must be considered in determining the best overall estate planning strategy. In this discussion we will use the amount that would be exempt from tax in 1987, $600,000, but the reader should be careful to substitute the appropriate amount actually exempt for each of the years between 1982 through 1987. Thus, if the date of death were 1985, a figure of $400,000 would be substituted.

The first of these levels are estates up to $600,000. In this case the surviving spouse could inherit the entire amount of the estate tax free. Upon his or her death, the whole estate would be passed on to his or her heirs tax free under the Unified Tax Credit rules. This, of course, assumes that no growth occurs in the estate and, thus, suggests that perhaps even here the entire amount should not be left outright to the surviving spouse—particularly if there were a significant age difference between the two spouses. For example, if the first spouse to die were 70 and the surviving spouse were only 55, it could be assumed that an estate of, say, $500,000 could well exceed $600,000 by the time the surviving spouse dies. It might therefore be desirable to leave at least part of this estate outside of the marital deduction, in trust for the couple's children with the wife retaining a life income benefit in the trust. Such a trust is usually referred to as an exemption equivalent trust and the assets escape taxes in the estates of both spouses.

The second level would be estates ranging from $600,000 up to $1.2 million. It is possible by careful planning to take advantage of two Unified Tax Credit exemptions. Take, for example, an estate of $1 million. It would be possible to leave $600,000 outright to the surviving spouse, recognizing that he or she in turn could leave this estate at death, taking advantage of yet another $600,000 exemption. The remaining $400,000 could be put in trust for their children, with the surviving spouse receiving income from the trust for life. However, as in the examples cited for estates up to $600,000, it can be assumed that the value of the marital portion of the estate would grow over time. If there were a significant age difference between the decedent and the surviving spouse, it might well pay to reverse the amount of these bequests, leaving $400,000 to the surviving spouse and putting $600,000 into a trust with their children as remaindermen.

Finally, the last level of estates to be considered are those of $1.2 million or more. In a case where the life expectancy of the surviving spouse is relatively short or health is poor, suggesting the probability of death soon after the first spouse, it would pay to split this estate into two equal portions. The first $600,000 in each would be tax free upon the death of each respective spouse and the balance, given the progressive nature of the tax tables, would be taxed at the lower brackets. Thus, the combined tax paid on these two estates would be less than if only $600,000 were left outright to the surviving spouse, with the balance going into trust. However, if the life expectancy of the surviving spouse is relatively long, it would probably pay to leave the tax-exempt portion of the first estate, $600,000, in trust outside of the marital deduction to take advantage of the Unified Tax Credit, with the balance of the estate left to the surviving spouse outright. Although this would result in a higher tax when the surviving spouse passes on, the time value of money would probably more than offset the additional tax if the surviving spouse, in fact, lived for many years following the death of the first spouse.

Consistent with our earlier comment on estate taxes suggesting that individual circumstances may dictate a different outcome than covered by broad principles, it is useful to give the executor of an estate broad discretion to choose the *best* approach after the death of an individual, adjusting to conditions that may be different than at the time a will is drawn.

Let us illustrate these principles with the following examples:

1. A widower dies in 1984, leaving his entire estate of $300,000 to his son. Using the tax amounts and rates in Table 5D-1 we find that the tax from an estate of this size would be $87,800. However, the Unified Tax Credit for 1984 is $96,300, an amount exceeding the tax due. Thus, this estate would have no tax.

2. A widower dies in 1985, leaving his estate of $500,000 to his sister. Two years earlier he had made a gift to her of $60,000, the only gift he has ever made to anyone. Under the Unified Tax Credit rule we must add back part of the gift to the estate of $500,000. Of the gift made two years earlier, $10,000 would have been exempt from any taxation under the annual exclusion rules. Thus, $50,000 of that gift must be added back into the estate for tax purposes, leaving a taxable estate of $550,000. Using Table 5D-1, we find the tax to be $174,300. In 1985 the Unified Tax Credit is $121,800, leaving a total tax due to the federal government of $52,500.

3. In 1987 a man dies, leaving an estate of $1.1 million. His wife is 35 years of age and they have three children. Although there are several possibilities here, the conditions of the situation suggest that $600,000, equal to the amount of estate exempt from all tax, be left outside the marital deduction in an exemption equivalent trust. The widow would receive income from this trust for her life, with the corpus passing on to her children upon her death. The remaining $500,000 might well be left in a second trust under the marital deduction, also with the children as remaindermen, but with the widow receiving income for life (a Q-TIP trust). The smaller amount is left to her because she is quite young and it can be expected that the growth of her portion over time will put the value of her estate well above the $600,000 exemption.

Also, because of her age it is not unlikely that she will remarry and could even have children of her own. By setting up the marital portion in a trust for the benefit of the couple's children, she would be prohibited from leaving her share of the estate to the children of a new marriage, something that might be against the wishes of her first husband. Even if she were older, such that she would not be expected to have children of her own from a second marriage, this approach might still be appropriate in order to ensure that upon her death the estate would go to the children of the first marriage. Prior to the 1981 legislation this would not have been possible—she would have been required to have a general power of appointment over the marital portion.

4. A woman dies in 1989, leaving an estate of $3 million. Her husband is 87 years of age and suffers from chronic heart problems. Given the advanced age and poor health of the surviving spouse in this case, it would probably pay to split the estate into two equal portions, one marital and one nonmarital. The nonmarital portion would go into a trust, with the couple's children, if any, as remaindermen. Of this portion of the estate, $600,000 would pass without estate tax under the Unified Tax Credit rules. The estate tax on $1,500,000 would be $363,000 ($555,800 from the tax tables minus the Unified Tax Credit of $192,800). Assuming the husband passed away fairly soon, his estate also would have a $600,000 exemption and an additional tax of $363,000, making a total tax on the two estates of $726,000. Had only $600,000 been put into a trust for the children, with the balance, $2.4 million, passing to the husband under the marital deduction, who died soon thereafter, the total tax would have been $784,000 ($976,800 on $2,400,000, less a Unified Tax Credit of $192,800).

Had the surviving husband been much healthier and younger, it probably would have paid to leave only $600,000 outside the marital deduction, with the balance outright to the surviving spouse. Given a long life expectancy, additional earnings on the amount of tax saved at the time ($363,000) would more than offset the reduced amount of tax paid by splitting the estates as described in our example. It seems likely that in most instances leaving the estate, after the $600,000 nonmarital portion, outright to the survivors will be preferred.

Another way to save estate tax is through the use of *flower bonds*. Certain U.S. Treasury obligations issued many years ago carry a right to pay estate taxes using the bond at par value rather than cost. Issued when interest rates were significantly lower than now, these low coupon bonds sell at substantial discounts. Thus, for example, one can buy an issue at 75¢ on the dollar and use it to pay estate taxes at 100¢ on the dollar, with the advantage to the estate of 25¢ (which is included in the taxable estate). Estate planning for an elderly investor might well include flower bonds. One drawback, however, is that yields on these bonds tend to be well below comparable yields on nonflower issues of the U.S. Treasury or corporations, thus reducing the income flow during the investor's remaining lifetime. Under certain circumstances, when the cost of borrowing is not too high relative to the interest earned on flower bonds, it may well pay to borrow, using the flower bonds as collateral. (This has not been practical for many years, except on a near-deathbed basis.) Thus it is not necessary to liquidate other assets, perhaps with substantial capital gains, in order to buy flower bonds.

The bonds must have been purchased and provision made for payment prior to death by someone legally competent to do it, either the investor personally or confirmed by the investor if done by an agent.

In many states deathbed purchases of flower bonds may not be valid if the dying individual is not competent at the time of purchase. In these states the laws automatically revoke powers of attorney when the grantor becomes incompetent. Thus, if the grantor of a power of attorney is in a coma or otherwise insufficiently competent to legally ratify a purchase, it is important to check state law before making the purchase.

We have reviewed here only a few of the more typical tax implications of investment management. Many other aspects must be considered in estate planning, and this should be done only with the advice of competent legal counsel. The investment manager should at least have a basic understanding of these principles in order to direct clients to legal counsel where called for and to understand the investment implications of the advice received from legal counsel. Each situation is different and offers the investment manager considerable opportunity to enhance the value of his or her services in working with the client.

Part III

Expectational Factors

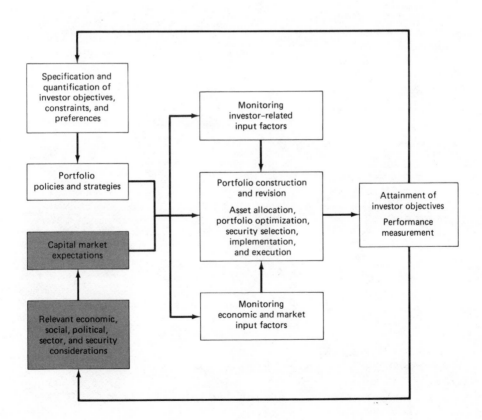

CHAPTER 6

Capital Market Expectations: The Macro Factors

Peter L. Bernstein

EXPECTATIONS RIGHT AND WRONG

The owner of any security that has a maturity date beyond the next five minutes—and equities are perpetuities—cannot escape from making a bet on the future. That is just the beginning of his difficulties, however. He must also continuously make judgments about the forecasts of other investors, for it is the consensus of their views that determines the prices at which he will trade in the marketplace. He should trade only when his expectations differ from theirs.

The main thesis of this chapter is that the investor's forecast by itself is worthless without an accurate analysis of whether the market shares that forecast. The most important lesson that history can teach us is that major changes in asset prices occur only in response to *unexpected* events. Therefore, the essence of the analytical process in investing is to distinguish the expected from the unexpected.

The discussion that follows will explore some of the complexities of this task, but we shall also develop methods for dealing with them. We shall find that the trick is in defining the whole range of possibilities that the future might hold, rather than in just setting our course toward what appears to be the most likely outcome.

We begin with a brief overview of some of the unexpected events of the past and their impact on security prices, but we shall also speculate about what might have happened in the capital markets if matters had in fact turned out as investors thought they were going to turn out. We go on from there to an analysis of the most cataclysmic and disruptive economic event of recent history—inflation—to see what generalizations we can draw from that distressing experience. Finally, we take a look at the future and attempt to appraise what it is that the market expects to happen and how far off the mark these consensus views might be.

Improving the Market's Forecast

Uncertainty is an essential element in any decision that involves the future. Human beings usually try to reduce uncertainty by predicting that the future will look a lot like the past. While this is in fact frequently the case, such an approach fails to detect change that may be evolving right around us. In other words, a careful study of the *present* may be much more rewarding than yielding to the habit of extrapolating the past into the future.

Take 1929 as an example. The preceding seven or eight years had indeed been an exciting period for investors. Led by the dynamic growth of the automobile and the electric power industries, dividends on the Dow Jones Industrials had risen by 55 percent between 1921 and 1927 and then proceeded to double between 1927 and 1929.

Nevertheless, worms were eating at the core of this superficially brilliant environment, and its ability to survive shocks was steadily diminishing. Indeed, no tree grows to the sky, but that was what most investors were apparently convinced was going to happen on this occasion. Furthermore, housing had peaked out in 1925 and languished thereafter; agriculture had never recovered from the food price bust after World War I and failures among banks in rural areas were steadily increasing; ominous trade and financial tensions in the international arena were building up to a crisis situation.[1]

In 1949, on the other hand, investors were haunted by the idea that World War II had only interrupted rather than ended the Great Depression. Everyone "knew" that a depression was in any case the inevitable consequence of war. This led them to ignore some overwhelmingly positive facts about the present.

Holdings of cash, bank deposits, and liquid U.S. government securities in 1949 were double the size of private debts. The stock market had shriveled in size from 52 percent of GNP in 1929 to only 26 percent of GNP, from 157 percent of deposits at thrift institutions to only 95 percent, and from 203 percent of the money supply to only 61 percent. Thus, the economy was well cushioned against economic adversity and, even if such adversity occurred, there was almost no likelihood that it would bring on a major stock market crash of the magnitude that so many people feared.

Seen in this light, we can only wonder why investors valued the Dow Jones Industrials at 19.9 times earnings in 1929 and at 6.9 times in 1949; logic

---

[1] See especially Milton and Rose Friedman [1979], but also the entire Fall 1979 issue of *The Journal of Portfolio Management* relates to the causes and consequences of the Great Crash.

would have dictated precisely the opposite. It is fair to ask, therefore, what would have happened to investors if they had correctly valued the stock market in 1929 in anticipation of the greatest depression in history and if they had correctly valued it in 1949 in anticipation of the greatest business boom in history.

If investors had paid more attention to the bad news than the good news in 1929 and had valued the Dow at 6.9 times earnings—but everything else had transpired in exactly the same fashion—the average would have fallen 79 percent from 1929 to 1932 against the actual drop of 89 percent, so it would still have been a terrifying experience. Nevertheless, in this terrible depression, the investor who bought at the very top would have been even or ahead of the game by 1935 (20 years earlier than what really happened), not counting dividends or the increased purchasing power of his stocks as a result of the broad decline in the cost of living. In fact, in terms of the more broadly diversified S&P 500 Composite Index, the theoretical decline would have been only 28 percent from 1929 to 1932, as against an actual drop of 72 percent, largely because average earnings on the 500 S&P stocks held up much better than on the 30 Dow Jones industrial stocks.

On the other hand, suppose that investors in 1949 had paid more attention to the good news in the present than to their fears of bad news in the future and had, therefore, been willing to pay 19.9 times earnings for the Dow Jones Industrials instead of 6.9 times earnings. This improved foresight would have significantly blunted the great bull market that crested some 15 years later in the area of 1000, for the Dow would have sold at 469—nearly 100 points above the 1929 high—at its 1949 low instead of at 162; it would only have doubled by 1965 instead of more than sextupling.

But what would have happened if the fearful investors had been right and an exact replay of the 1930s lay just ahead? Since the dividend on the Dow Jones Industrials was $12.75 in 1929 and $12.79 in 1949, this makes for a ready comparison. In the ten years that followed 1929, dividends on the Dow averaged $6.27 a year, touching a low of $3.40 in 1933. Consequently, investors buying the Dow at its 1949 average level of 180 would have earned an average annual yield of 3.5 percent on their investment over the next ten years, a full percentage point (or 40%) more than they could have earned if they had bought the highest grade bonds instead and held them for ten years. Furthermore, the yield on the bonds would already have been so low that they would probably have shown no price appreciation in a replay of the Great Depression. This is in sharp contrast to what happened during the ten years after 1929, when dividends provided an average yield of only 1 percent a year on the 1929 purchase price, while bonds paid three or four times as much and appreciated in value at the same time.

These are obviously vivid examples, but it is in giant moves of this type that fortunes are made and lost and in which portfolio decisions are most critical. Their very drama serves to remind us that expected events will move markets very little and that primary bull and bear markets are the consequence of outcomes that few people ever expected to occur.

Same Environment = Same Market?

The examples above were cases in which stocks declined during a depression and rose during a boom. In fact, however, things do not always work out in such logical fashion.

Theory may define for us what the relationship between security prices and economic fundamentals should be, particularly when the underlying trends in the economic fundamentals have persisted long enough to shape expectations, but generalizations about how security prices will react to a change in the environment—or to a continuation of a given environment—are nevertheless as likely to be wrong as right. The influence of the collective memories of investors at any point in time and the position of the market relative to its previous movements frequently dominate the economic fundamentals in the determination of security prices. The result is that we can find many cases when stocks and bonds failed to move in a manner that would have been consistent with the way they "should" have moved in terms of theory or logic.

The History of Stocks and Inflation. For example, are stocks a hedge against inflation, as tradition would have it? Or are they a disastrous holding, as the experience of the 1970s would suggest? History supports both propositions.

Figure 6-1 shows the major movements in the Consumer Price Index and in stock prices from 1871 to 1981, as well as the corresponding path of real stock prices—the stock index divided by the Consumer Price Index. A trend line has been drawn through the latter to help in analyzing the sequence of events.

As further help, Table 6-1, based on Steven Leuthold's [1980] invaluable compilation and sorting of the data, shows 106 years of experience by groups of years in descending order of the rate of price increase, compared with the mean and standard deviation of stock price changes for each group of years

TABLE 6-1. Inflation and Stock Prices, Annually, 1872–1979[a]

Years in Which Inflation Was:	Stock Market Mean Price Change	Percentage Change Std. Deviation	Number of Years in Which Stock Prices Rose
+8% thru +18%	+0.28	18.69	8 out of 18
+4% thru +7%	−4.58	15.37	11 out of 20
+2% thru +3%	+8.08	14.97	13 out of 20
−1% thru +1%	+9.13	15.65	21 out of 30
−2% thru −4%	+9.81	21.33	9 out of 13
−5% thru −11%	−2.65	26.09	4 out of 10

SOURCE: Leuthold [1980]. Reprinted with permission of Crain Books Division of Crain Communications Inc., copyright © 1980 by Steven C. Leuthold.
[a] Based on Cowles All-Stock Index to 1936, Dow Jones Industrial Average 1937–79, and Consumer Price Index.

Figure 6-1. Common Stocks and Consumer Prices, 1871–1981. (SOURCE: *Long Term Economic Growth: 1860–1970* [1973] and *Economic Report of the President* [1982])

plus a tabulation of the number of years in the group in which stock prices rose.

Both the chart and the table show that stock price performance is frequently excellent in years of moderate price change in either direction and frequently poor when price changes are large in either direction. "Frequently," however, is not the same thing as "always." Note that the standard deviations shown in Table 6-1 are large relative to the means for all six groups of years. In addition, there was no uniformity of direction to the movement of stock prices in any of the outlying groups.

Is it possible that inflation played only a partial or symptomatic rather than a determining role in the behavior of stock prices?

Note that stock prices declined in 19 of the years in which inflation was 4 percent or more. Eight of these declines, however—1903, 1907, 1937, 1946, 1957, 1969, 1973, and 1977—occurred either late in bull markets or at least followed steep increases in stock prices. In addition, three of these years— 1937, 1969, and 1973—were typical business cycle peaks leading up to recessions; stock prices have traditionally declined in those kinds of conditions. Here, then, are ten out of fifteen cases where the probabilities would favor the conclusion that stock prices were vulnerable to bad news in any case and would probably have declined even if inflation had been milder.

This hypothesis is even more appealing when we look at the seven years in which the stock market *rose* by at least 10 percent in the face of inflation of 4 percent a year or more: 1880, 1918, 1919, 1943, 1951, 1975, and 1976. All of these years began with stock prices well below previous bull market highs. A look at Figure 6-1 suggests, in fact, that the improvement in stock prices during 1978–80 may have been due as much to the deeply depressed valuations prevailing during 1977 and much of 1978 as to any change in investor perceptions of the underlying realities. We shall explore this possibility in more detail below.

Finally, we can also see in Table 6-1 that stock prices went up in 13 out of 23 years in which consumer prices *fell* at rates of 2 percent a year or more. Four of these were years in which deflation was the most severe and averaged 7 percent a year—1878, 1921, 1922, and 1933; as the chart shows, each of these was a year that was at the end of an extremely intense bear market episode.

If Not Stocks, Surely Bonds. If the evidence tells us that we are on shaky ground in making generalizations about stock market performance in differing types of economic environments, most people would still expect interest rates and inflation to show a consistent set of relationships. Yet even here, generalizations appear to be dangerous despite the relatively close correlation between interest rates and inflation since 1953.

A recent study by Levine and Kaplan [1981] going back to 1892 offers some surprising facts about long-term interest rates and inflation. He models inflationary expectations by means of a weighted moving average based on inflation during the two years preceding, the current year, and—on the assumption that the rate one year out is known "within reasonable limits"— during the year ahead. Table 6-2 shows his results for various time periods.

On the basis of simultaneous data—no leads or lags of either time series—inflation appears to explain only 6 percent of the variation in corporate bond yields over the period from 1892 to 1979! Furthermore, a change of one percentage point in inflation tends to make bond yields move by only 0.10 percentage points. Levine's data for commercial paper provide similar types of results. Thus, the relatively high correlation for the years since 1954 looks like an historical accident compared with the relationships that prevailed during the preceding 62 years.

For example, even though wholesale prices in 1930 were 44 percent lower than in 1920 and consumer prices had fallen 20 percent over the same period, long-term yields in 1930, at about 4 percent, were only 100 basis points lower than they had been 10 years earlier.

On the other hand, anxiety about moving from deflation to inflation developed only very slowly among bond investors in the 1890s, in view of the

TABLE 6-2. Corporate Bonds and Inflation Expectations

Time Period	Average Inflation Expectations	Average Interest Rate	Coefficient of Determination (ρ^2)	Slope
1892–1979	2.81%	4.43%	.06	.10
1892–1939	1.47%	3.91%	[a]	[a]
1940–1953	5.33	2.82	(.10)[b]	−.03
1954–1979	3.94	6.27	.91	.94
1954–1965	1.97%	4.20%	.01	.04
1946–1965	3.41	3.70	(.32)[b]	−.15
1946–1979	4.32	5.49	.14	.33

SOURCE: Levine and Kaplan [1981].
[a] Less than 0.005.
[b] Parentheses indicate years in which the underlying coefficient of correlation was negative.

rich real returns they had enjoyed during the long deflation of the 1870s and 1880s. The economy swung sharply away from that deflation after the large gold discoveries at the turn of the century; prices rose a total of 11 percent from 1895 to 1900, with more than half of that in 1899. Yet bond yields continued their long drift downward and were about 50 basis points lower in 1900 than they had been in 1890.

A similar pattern is apparent during the depression of the 1930s when bonds gained great popularity as a safe haven for money and stocks fell into disrepute. From late 1932 to the end of 1941 bond yields fell from 4.2 to 2.6 percent, even though consumer prices had risen at an annual rate of more than 2 percent from 1933 to 1937 and then held steady for the next four years. As we shall see later in the chapter, this type of reluctance to face the bad news reappears in the more recent history of the bond market, and for similar types of reasons.

All of this finds further confirmation in an intensely detailed analysis by Lawrence Summers [1981b], whose conclusions warrant two lengthy quotations:

The results suggest that prior to World War II inflation had only a negligible impact on interest rates. While there is evidence of a significant response of interest rates to inflation during the post-war period, there is no evidence that they have risen by as much as theory would predict in the presence of high marginal tax rates. Furthermore, almost all of the significant association between interest rates and inflation during the post-war period can be traced to the 1965–71 period. Sample periods excluding this interval reveal only quite small effects of inflation on interest rates. [p. 3]

Over the long term less than one eighth of changes in the rate of inflation are incorporated into interest rates. Changes in the decadal rates of inflation explain none of the variance in observed interest rates. . . . The variance of the real return far exceeds that of the nominal return. If nominal rates incorporated inflation, they should vary while real rates should remain fairly constant. [p. 16]

In short, even in the market, where the relationship between the fundamentals and security valuation is reputed to be the closest, investors have often deviated from textbook behavior.

The Moral of the Story

After looking at this jumble of historical facts, the analyst is tempted to throw up his hands and to confess that cranking expectations into portfolio decisions is a hopeless task. This would be a mistake on two grounds. First, difficult as it may be, it is an unavoidable task, since capital markets are nothing more than an arena in which investors price their expectations of future streams of income. Second, the historical jumble does lend itself to some broad and significant generalizations.

The first of these is a negative admonition: Do not make a forecast of the economic environment and then bet that the market will move up or down in accordance with the future you foresee. For one thing, your forecast stands an excellent chance of being wrong. Perhaps more important, your forecast may be correct, but the market may have seen what was coming sooner than you were able to recognize it. Under those conditions, the arrival of the events you expect will have little or no impact on the market.

Second, you have no choice but to examine with great care the whole range of possible outcomes, not just your own. This means that you will have to analyze the consequences for the capital markets of events that you believe unlikely but that you can nevertheless visualize as having even some small probability of occurring.

Third, fundamentals do ultimately win out in determining market valuations, but other investors may be maddeningly slow to recognize what is actually happening. These are the most fruitful opportunities for the investor who is willing to bet on this ultimate outcome. On the other hand, taking risks of that nature requires substantial staying power, not only in the financial resources that will make it possible to hold on until the market turns in the expected direction, but also in the psychological resources to withstanding being "wrong" for an extended period of time.

UNLOCKING THE INFLATION PUZZLE

The experience from about 1965 to the end of the 1970s is one of the most dramatic, tantalizing, and significant examples of how investors have struggled to come to grips with their memories of the past, their understanding of the present, and their expectations for the future. It is, therefore, important for us to examine this period in some detail, not just because of its relevance to what may happen in the 1980s but also as an illustration of how expectations and market movements interrelate.

The whole history of this period would be less interesting if it had been less devastating. Yet, in many ways, the performance of long-term financial assets over those fifteen years was as dismal as any period of comparable length in history, including the record of the Great Depression. An investor who simply rolled over 91-day Treasury bills from the end of 1965 through to the end of 1980 would have earned a compound annual rate of 6.3 percent; if instead he had taken the substantially greater risk of buying and holding the S&P 500, his total return would have been only 0.4 percent a year more than on the bills; if he had been so unfortunate as to have put all his money into long-term bonds, his return would have been a pitiful 3.2 percent—only half the return on bills.

While billholders should obviously do well in an inflationary period, and bondholders should obviously do poorly, the case is not so simple when it comes to equities. Indeed, we shall see shortly that logic would suggest that equities—even in the case of *unexpected* inflation—should have kept pace with or have outrun the rise in the price level. Why, then, were equity returns so disappointing during this period?

The problem falls into two parts, in line with the discussion at the outset of this chapter. First, what effect did inflation have on the fundamental variables that concern equity investors? Second, why did investors respond to the changes in those variables as they did instead of in a different fashion?

The Trouble with Inflation

One point is worth making before we move more deeply into the complexities of the matter. Inflation is almost always going to be a matter of concern to investors, unless they have precisely and completely anticipated it, because the accounting conventions and tax rules under which we have traditionally done business in the United States are inappropriate for periods when the price level is unstable. Once prices begin to swing persistently upward or downward, we no longer have a clear idea of precisely what our assets are worth, of how much we are really earning, and of what a consistent and equitable rate of taxation should be. Furthermore, by diminishing the present value of future dollars, inflation leads companies and households to favor long-term liabilities but to reject long-term assets.

In short, inflation confuses and obscures the most critical decision variables that corporate managements, investors, and policymakers have to consider. In addition, since rising prices can bail out bad decisions and can reduce the real cost of borrowing money, inflation encourages the more aggressive risk-takers in society.

But that is not all. Investors learn from experience, and postwar experience taught them that an accelerating pace of inflation tended to precede or accompany a recession or slowdown in real business activity and in corporate profits. Usually, this was a consequence of monetary policy decisions and steeply rising interest rates, as in 1957, 1960, 1966, 1973, and 1980, but it is also worth noting that the coefficient of correlation between the rate of change in real GNP and the rate of change in the GNP price deflator from 1965 to 1980 was -0.66. In other words, higher rates of inflation were associated with lower rates of real growth and vice versa.[2]

This explanation of the inverse relationship between stock returns and expected inflation is consistent with the clear tendency of stock prices to move in advance of changes in output and employment. Thus, quite aside from all of the intricate relationships that may exist between inflation and equity valuation, these real relationships among stock prices, output, and inflation may be sufficient to discourage investors when they anticipate a higher rate of inflation and to regenerate enthusiasm in the stock market at signs of lower rates of inflation.

Finally, it is worth noting that all these adverse influences of inflation on the general economic environment first became visible during the late 1960s, which was a time when the security markets may have been unusually vulnerable. We have already recognized this possibility in the discussion above, and we shall consider it in more detail shortly. Suffice it to say here that inflation broke out at a time of buoyant optimism and strong convictions about the ability of policymakers to overcome economic instability. No wonder, then, that markets collapsed during these years when inflation was most intense and recovered only as it subsided. It was unexpected, unfamiliar, poorly understood, and, at least at first, widely believed to be temporary.

This suggests an important conclusion. As investors understand inflation better, as they cease to believe that it is a temporary aberration, and as our tax and accounting rules are redesigned to deal with the distortions it causes, the impact of inflation on security prices in the future will be different from what it was in the past. But this is just another example of the basic thesis of this chapter.

Inflation and Profits

In theory, inflation should be a neutral variable in the equity valuation process. Inflation is a persistent and pervasive increase in the *general* price level, so businessmen should be able to raise their selling prices as rapidly as their costs rise. Profits, in the real sense of the word, would be unaffected under those conditions. Even higher interest rates should have no negative implications for equity investors, since the growth in nominal profits should match the inflation premium incorporated into the nominal rate of interest.

If businessmen fail to understand what is actually going on, however, or if they believe that the inflationary episode is going to be transitory rather

---

[2] For an authoritative and detailed analysis of this aspect of the matter, see Fama [1981].

than persistent, they may fail to raise their prices fast enough to keep pace with their soaring costs. That is in fact what happened during the first phase of inflation from 1966 to 1970: An index of the ratio of selling prices to unit labor costs in the nonfarm business sector, which had ranged between 100 and 104 (1977 = 100) from 1961 to 1966 and had averaged about 102, plummeted from 102 in 1966 to 97 in 1970. The evidence does suggest, however, that businessmen have improved their ability to deal with this aspect of the matter since the early 1970s; for this ratio—although never regaining the heights of the mid-1960s—stopped falling and moved essentially sideways in a range of 96–100 throughout the decade of the 1970s. We shall study these patterns in more detail below.

For the first five years or so of inflation, therefore, investors were primarily concerned about management's inability to sustain corporate earning power; subsequently, their concerns shifted to the distortions that developed because of inappropriate accounting conventions and tax rules.

The accounting conventions cause problems, because all fixed assets and most inventory are kept on the corporate books at original cost. This understates true cost, however, because the corporation will ultimately have to use some of its *reported* profits to replace those assets at higher prices than they cost originally. Thus, if the corporation were to distribute to its stockholders all of its reported profits, it would in fact be depleting its capital rather than maintaining its net assets at a constant value.

While this factor alone would justify a reduction in price/earnings ratios when inflation exceeds expectations—since reported earnings overstate the true condition of the corporation—a more serious consequence follows. The tax rules have required corporations to pay taxes on their reported earnings based on original cost, not on replacement cost. Table 6-3 on page 174 shows the path of nonfinancial corporate profits from 1954 to 1980, with and without these adjustments and before and after taxes.

We can see that these adjustments have become increasingly significant since 1972. In 1979, for example, taxes were equal to only 36 percent of unadjusted profits as reported; the same tax liability was equal to 51 percent of profits after these adjustments.

As a result of all these forces, adjusted profits after taxes averaged only 6 percent and never exceeded 8 percent of total corporate domestic income during the 1970s, as compared with an average of better than 10 percent and a minimum of 8 percent during the 1960s.[3]

Inflation and Interest

This is not the whole story, however. Stockholders provide only part of the corporation's capital; lenders contribute the rest. Interest payments to those

---

[3] A strong case could be made that inflation is the consequence rather than the cause of inadequate rates of profit and that inflation is lowest when true profits are highest. See especially Bernstein [1976], Kurz [1979], and Moscowitz [1976].

TABLE 6-3. **Profits of Nonfinancial Corporations, Before and After Adjustments for Original Cost Accounting and for Tax Liabilities, Annually, 1954–80 (in billions of dollars)**

Year	Unadjusted Total Profit	Inventory Valuation Adjustment	Capital Consumption Adjustment	Tax Liability	Net Adjusted Profit
1954	$ 32.1	$-0.3	$ -3.2	$15.6	$13.0
1955	42.0	-1.7	-2.0	20.2	18.1
1956	41.8	-2.7	-3.2	20.1	15.8
1957	39.8	-1.5	-3.4	19.1	15.8
1958	33.7	-0.3	-3.2	16.2	14.0
1959	43.1	-0.3	-2.7	20.7	19.4
1960	39.7	-0.2	-2.1	19.2	18.2
1961	39.5	+0.3	-1.5	19.5	18.8
1962	44.2	0.0	+1.4	20.6	25.0
1963	48.9	+0.1	+2.3	22.8	28.6
1964	55.4	+0.5	+2.9	24.0	34.8
1965	65.2	-1.2	+3.7	27.2	40.5
1966	70.3	-2.1	+3.9	29.5	42.6
1967	66.3	-1.6	+4.0	27.7	41.0
1968	72.9	-3.7	+4.0	33.4	31.8
1969	69.4	-5.9	+4.0	33.1	34.4
1970	56.8	-6.6	+2.4	27.0	25.6
1971	65.4	-4.6	+1.3	29.8	32.3
1972	76.6	-6.6	+2.7	33.6	39.1
1973	96.0	-20.0	+2.6	40.0	38.6
1974	105.3	-40.0	-1.8	42.0	21.5
1975	107.3	-11.6	-9.7	41.2	44.8
1976	135.0	-14.7	-13.0	52.6	54.7
1977	153.5	-15.8	-11.4	59.4	66.9
1978	174.3	-24.3	-12.4	67.3	70.3
1979	193.4	-42.6	-14.1	69.7	67.0
1980	183.8	-45.7	-14.4	63.1	60.6

SOURCE: *Economic Report of the President* [1982].

lenders are therefore part of the return earned by the total capital of the corporation. This can provide some favorable consequences for the stockholders, even if the interest payments appear to squeeze profits on a nominal basis.

Table 6-4 shows the share of total corporate income accounted for by profits (as calculated in the last column of Table 6-3) plus net interest paid to creditors, from 1954 to 1980. Although the superior results of the 1960s are still apparent, the share of capital income looks much better here than the pattern suggested by the discussion above on profits alone.

But the story continues further. Lenders receive a bonus from borrowers to compensate them for the reduction in the purchasing power of their claims as a result of expected inflation. This bonus conventionally takes the form of an increase in the interest rate rather than of a repayment of principal larger than the original amount borrowed. Nevertheless, the inflation premium in

TABLE 6-4. Nonfinancial Corporations: Profits After Taxes and Inflation Adjustments Plus Net Interest as a Percent of Total Corporate Domestic Income, Annually, 1954–80

Year	Percent of Domestic Income	Year	Percent of Domestic Income
1954	9.3%	1968	10.3
1955	11.0	1969	10.8
1956	9.3	1970	9.5
1957	9.2	1971	10.4
1958	8.8	1972	10.8
1959	8.5	1973	10.1
1960	9.8	1974	7.9
1961	10.0	1975	10.8
1962	11.8	1976	10.6
1963	12.5	1977	11.1
1964	13.9	1978	10.5
1965	14.6	1979	9.9
1966	14.2	1980	9.6
1967	13.5		

SOURCE: *Economic Report of the President* [1982].

the interest payments comes to the same thing as repaying more than the original principal amount borrowed, except that it comes on the installment plan.

The curious aspect of this matter is that this repayment of principal on the installment plan is included in operating expenses under current accounting conventions. Hence, it understates true profits. In addition, however, it also means that the corporation reports a deductible expense and saves taxes on something that in reality is a repayment of principal rather than a deduction from profits.

This means that the corporation is paying taxes on phantom profits resulting from original cost accounting on the one hand, and, on the other, is simultaneously saving taxes on phantom expenses that are really a return of principal to lenders. Modigliani and Cohn [1979] have put it aptly in observing that "the tax system in effect taxes what should not be taxed and does not tax what should be taxed."

Careful efforts to quantify all of these influences on profits have resulted in a voluminous literature on the subject. We have not even considered the additional tax burden on individual stockholder and bondholder returns that results from swollen nominal rather than real receipts during an inflationary period. Nor have we considered the untaxed capital gain that accrues to corporations when the interest rate they pay turns out to be less than the actual rate of inflation they experience.

Most available studies tend to agree with Lawrence Summers's finding [1981a] that tax savings on nominal interest payments are far exceeded by the tax effects of original cost accounting, to say nothing of the distortions that inflation introduces into personal income tax returns. The tax reform measures enacted in 1981 diminish but by no means eliminate these influences.

When all is said and done, however, accurate measurement of profits in an inflationary era may be an impossible task. A study by Bulow and Shoven [1981], for example, sets up nine different methods for measuring total profits of nonfinancial corporations, including the accounting systems required by the Financial Accounting Standards Board and by the Securities and Exchange Commission, as well as the system used to report profits in the National Income and Profits Accounts. For 1979, which is by no means atypical of other years, the range of results is from $89 billion to $318 billion, with a mean of $150 billion and a standard deviation of $69 billion!

Inflation and Stock Valuation

If controversy rages over the impact of inflation on earning power, it is even more intense on the subject of whether stockholders have judged that impact correctly or incorrectly.

Modigliani and Cohn, for example, argue that stockholders have not only failed to recognize the beneficial effect of the inflation premium in interest payments but also confuse real and nominal elements in calculating the present value of future income streams. These authors accuse investors of using an inflation-bloated nominal rate to discount future streams into present values and then estimating those future streams in real terms. This leads to a calculation that the S&P 500 at the end of 1977 was equal to only 46 percent of what their own valuation technique suggested as its true worth on that date.

Similar but smaller discrepancies were discovered by Cohn and Lessard [1981] for seven other major countries. Jones [1980] finds that investors act precisely as Modigliani and Cohn predict they would act if they were committing those kinds of valuation errors under inflationary conditions. Summers [1981] agrees with Modigliani and Cohn and demonstrates that, at least until 1978, investors appeared to have been fooled by nominal interest rates that seemed high because they were historically high; this led to overvaluation of bonds and undervaluation of stocks in relation to underlying trends in inflation.

On the other hand, one could argue that Modigliani and Cohn are conceptually gilding the lily. Adjustment of reported earnings for accounting conventions in an inflationary environment is not the same thing as adjusting them into a *real* mode. This would require deflating the adjusted earnings by the rate of change in the general price index. In other words, even if we correct for original cost accounting and the inflation premium in interest rates, the result is still a nominal figure. In that case, nominal rates in the discount or capitalization rate calculations are appropriate. This view would conclude that investors have not confused real and nominal elements but have in fact been correct in using nominal rates for valuation purposes.[4]

[4] I am grateful to William S. Gray, III for this insight.

TABLE 6-5. Dividend Growth Versus Inflation, Business Cycle Peaks, 1957–79, Percent Per Annum

Years	Dividend Growth S&P 500	Business Inflation Rate[a]
1957–66	5.4%	1.2%
1966–74	2.9	4.5
1974–79	9.4	7.0
1957–79	5.4	3.7
1966–79	5.4	5.5

SOURCE: *Security Price Index Record* [1981] and *Economic Report of the President* [1982].
[a] Deflator for gross domestic product of nonfinancial corporations.

Yet, many observers remain puzzled by market behavior that contradicts conventional valuation analysis. Marcelle Arak [1980–81], for example, concludes that "there is no single factor that can plausibly explain the substantial fall in real stock values over the past ten years." At the end of their comprehensively detailed analysis, involving seven different models for studying the intrinsic values of common stocks and the spreads between market values and those intrinsic values, Brainard, Shoven, and Weiss [1980] finally admit that much mystery remains:

> Perhaps even our most pessimistic earnings projections have not reflected the fears of the market. What does seem clear is that measurable characteristics of firms and conventional methods of projecting future earnings are not likely to explain the declines in market values that have occurred during the 1970's.

Inflation and Dividends.[5] If earnings analysis is ultimately a source of confusion, perhaps we can explain more of what happened to stock prices by turning to the trend of dividends. Dividends are hard information—unlike earnings, their measurement involves no interpretation. Furthermore, they are the best information that we have as to management's view of the long-run value of the corporation, since dividend policies are typically designed to be sustainable even in the face of unexpected adversities. To use Cohn and Lessard's expression, dividends are a proxy for "noise-free" earnings.

Table 6-5 shows the growth rate of dividends versus the price deflator for the gross product of nonfinancial corporations from business cycle peak to business cycle peak over the period from 1957 to 1979. The contrast between the periods before and after 1966 is striking: After having run far ahead of the business inflation rate before 1966, dividends fell far behind between 1966 and 1974. Some of this lag in dividend payments was, of course, associated with the restraints imposed during the price/wage regime of 1971–73. On the

---

[5] For a detailed analysis of the impact of inflation on dividends and, via dividends, on stock prices, see Moore [1980]. Baily [1981] considers the deterioration in equity valuation to be a confirmation, rather than a consequence, of the declining productivity of the capital stock.

other hand, intense cash binds did develop as a result of burgeoning replacement costs for inventories and fixed assets, together with the taxation of profits swollen by the distortions of original cost accounting.

Coming on top of the accelerated pace of debt issuance by corporations during the latter half of the 1960s, the slowdown in dividend growth is convincing evidence of a major deterioration in managements' views of the outlook for the long-term earning power of their assets, at least until 1976. Of course, managements could have made the same types of Modigliani-Cohn errors that investors made and thus failed to understand that they could in fact have afforded to pay out more in dividends. Yet, as the trend of dividend payments was the only hard information that stockholders could use to estimate their management's view of the value of the corporation, they would have had little reason to bet against it.

Profitability: A Brief Digression. The poor performance of corporate profitability during the 1970s has received an enormous amount of attention in recent years, with most of the blame attached to many forms of policy errors in Washington, plus an assist from OPEC. The corporate sector itself appears as an innocent bystander in these types of analyses.

Yet these critics fail to give sufficient weight to what may well have been unsustainably high rates of return on corporate assets in the mid-1960s and the inevitability that such high returns would have led to management errors in the form of overoptimism and overexpansion. To the extent that expansion was both too rapid and misguided during the 1960s, disappointing rates of return in the 1970s would probably have occurred even without the associated errors made in Washington.

Table 6-6 shows how sharply the growth in the capital stock accelerated after 1964 under the stimulus of tax cuts and dramatically improving rates of

TABLE 6-6. **Profitability and Growth in the Capital Stock, Averages for Five-Year Periods, 1955–80**

Five-Year Periods	Growth in the Capital Stock[a] (percent per annum)	Rate of Return on Depreciable Assets[b] (percent per annum)	Rate of Return on Stockholders' Equity[c] (percent per annum)
1955–59	3.1%	11.9%	5.1%
1960–64	2.8	12.7	5.9
1965–69	4.7	14.4	8.3
1970–74	4.1	9.8	6.9
1975–79	3.6	9.5	6.3

SOURCE: Musgrave [1981] and *Economic Report of the President* [1982].
[a] Gross stocks of business capital of nonfinancial corporations.
[b] Profits before taxes plus capital consumption adjustment and inventory valuation adjustment plus net interest paid divided by the stock of depreciable assets valued at current replacement cost.
[c] After-tax profits corrected for inflation effects divided by net worth (physical capital component valued at current replacement cost).

profitability (that were in turn the consequence of a slowly growing capital stock and low rates of return in the preceding years). As the history of our free enterprise system has demonstrated over and over, such ebullient episodes have always been unsustainable and are the root cause of the subsiding profitability patterns that follow them. It is worth noting, furthermore, that, despite the turbulence in the economic and financial environment during the second half of the 1970s, the record of that period still compares favorably with the ten years ending in 1965.

Hence, the practice of ascribing the decline in profitability to the heavy hand of government and to inflation may have become unquestioned conventional wisdom, but it is nevertheless a gross oversimplification of the facts—and naively ignores the oscillating manner in which our type of economic system inherently makes progress. Of course, unfortunate policy decisions and the ravages of inflation contributed to the poor performance of the corporate sector in the past decade, but they were by no means the only determining elements. The corporate sector itself, where management succumbed to overoptimism during the 1960s and paid too little regard to risk as a result, certainly deserves a fair share of the blame for the expensive retrenchments and the depressed profit ratios that inevitably followed.

This means, in short, that inflation may have been the most vivid and disruptive feature of the environment of the 1970s but that it was not the only force at work. To the extent that managements have been able to wipe the slate clean from earlier errors, therefore, the outlook for corporate profitability in the 1980s is likely to be substantially better than it has been.[6]

INFLATION PLUS BOND, STOCK, AND REAL ESTATE PRICES

Up to this point our observations about interest rates have been peripheral. We have seen that long-term rates may not follow inflation expectations as neatly as theory would predict. We have also noted Modigliani and Cohn's concern about the correct rate of interest to use in discounting expected streams of income and about proper accounting for the inflation premium. Finally, we have recognized that inflation frequently leads to restrictive monetary policies with higher interest rates that precede business recessions.

Now, however, we must turn to a more systematic analysis of the exact nature of the relationship between interest rates and equity valuation. This is no simple task, because this relationship has been far from stable over the past hundred years or so.

History does suggest that, despite the irregularities, some kind of relationship *does* prevail for much of the time. Generally speaking, stocks are

---

[6] For an illuminating discussion of why the decline in profitability was not directly caused by inflation, see Baily [1981]. For further authoritative evidence on this whole controversy, see Bernstein [1976 and 1979], Fraumeni and Jorgenson [1980], Holland and Myers [1977], and Lovell [1978].

insensitive to modest changes in interest rates, even if sustained, but are highly sensitive to sharp rises in interest rates, even if brief. Since interest rates in turn are in part the consequence of the actions of the Federal Reserve and the Treasury, monetary and fiscal policy also have an impact on stock prices.

These factors were unquestionably involved in contributing to the Great Depression and again to the 50 percent drop in stock prices that occurred in 1937. It is perhaps no coincidence that the long bull market from 1942 to 1946 was marked by stable (and controlled) interest rates and that the 25 percent drop that ended the bull market in September 1946 was associated with debate over the decontrol of the Treasury bill rate; this became an accomplished fact in 1947. In 1951, the entire interest structure was unpegged and interest rate volatility increased as a result. The bear markets of 1953, 1957, 1960, 1966, 1970, and 1973–74 were all associated with money crunches and steep increases in interest rates. Some observers believe that the shift in Federal Reserve targets in late 1979 from interest rates to monetary aggregates has led to even greater interest rate volatility that has kept price/earnings ratios at historically depressed levels.

The following discussion attempts to tackle this problem of stock/bond relationships with a novel approach that has not yet reached general acceptance in the analytical fraternity. Some of its features are admittedly controversial. Yet it does provide a logical and consistent explanation for the instability in the bond/stock relationship. Indeed, its central theoretical thesis is that *no* systematic linkage need exist; to the extent that we observe synchronous movements in the real world, they are frequently the consequence of imperfections in the system. This approach does have the attraction of providing fresh insights to a familiar problem and of identifying critical variables that may have received insufficient attention in the past.[7]

Yields and Yields. Lenders will refuse to lend money unless they expect the total stream of payments they contract for to match the purchasing power of the money turned over to the borrower plus an additional sum that will add to their wealth. Conventionally, loan contracts in the United States provide for this by promising repayment of the original sum lent plus an interest payment that will take care of both the anticipated inflation premium and the real return.[8]

This is not the only way to do it, however. No logical reason exists why the borrower should not pay the lender only the real return via the interest

---

[7] I am especially indebted to the insights of Keran [1976 and 1981] on this matter. The concept of the dividend yield as a proxy for the real rate of interest finds impressive support in Summers [1981a]. Keran [1981] and Estep and Hanson [1980] are most explicit on the relationship between the inflation pass-through and the independence of stock valuation from interest rates and inflation. In addition, Fama [1981] argues at length that equity valuation is more sensitive to events in the real economy than to inflation as such or to financial influences.

[8] The basic concept of the nominal rate of interest as the total of a real rate plus expected inflation was originally developed by Irving Fisher [1907] early in the twentieth century.

payments and then agree to make the final principal payment equal to the original amount plus some increment that would compensate the lender for the rate of inflation across the life of the loan. When we look at the matter from this viewpoint, we can see that the inflation premium that Americans conventionally include in the interest payment is not an interest payment at all. It is a repayment of principal, but is made on the installment plan instead of in a lump sum at the maturity of the loan.

We do have some instruments that are hybrids by providing for a variable nominal return to the lender. Variable rate notes index only the interest payment, not the principal, to inflation; the same is true of real estate mortgages that include a claim on the gross revenues of the underlying property. Convertible bonds, on the other hand, provide for a fixed interest payment but give the lender a claim on the changing value of the underlying assets.

The important point is that all of these hybrids carry lower current yields than pure credit instruments of comparable risk and marketability. The more completely we can index the borrower against a loss of purchasing power, in other words, the closer his interest payment is likely to be to his real rate of return.

None of the examples cited so far is in fact a fully indexed security. To meet that requirement, the borrower would have to promise to raise his interest payment each year in step with the increase in the lender's cost of living and, in addition, to repay the principal amount at maturity in dollars equivalent in purchasing power to the original advance. Under those conditions, the originally stipulated fixed interest payment would be the negotiated real return to the lender, or the addition to his real wealth in return for making his savings available to the borrower for the term of the contract; everything else would simply preserve the lender's purchasing power.

COMMON STOCKS AS INDEXED SECURITIES. While no one in the United States has borrowed or lent money under precisely those conditions, we do have one class of securities that has the *potential* of fulfilling them: common stocks. Even if a corporation achieves no real growth at all, its common stock could still function as a fully indexed security just as long as the corporation is able to index its after-tax earnings stream to the increase in the cost of living. Then its dividend could regularly rise right along with the inflation rate. In addition, since the estimated growth rate of the dividend would be equal to the rate of inflation, the price of the stock—or the present value of the future stream of payments—would also rise along with the rate of inflation. With both principal and current income thus linked to the rise in living cost, we could use common stocks as our fully indexed securities.

This ideal instrument would consequently have a current yield equal to the real rate of return that the corporation provides to its owners. In other words, as long as the increase in the dividend payments and the expected value of the future payments march along with inflation, the yield of that stock need contain no inflation premium in the sense that the yield of a fixed income security like a bond must contain an inflation premium.

We shall explore the empirical evidence in this area just below, but it is worth mentioning here that the dividend yield shown by equities over the past 100 years has in fact tended to settle down in the 3 to 4 percent area during the most prosperous and optimistic periods—and that that is precisely the level that most people believe defines the real rate of interest.[9]

In practice, the yield on common stocks will deviate from this theoretically ideal level for three reasons. First, most companies do achieve real growth, which means that their yields can in fact fall below, say, 3 percent, because their future payments may be expected to rise more rapidly than the rate of increase in the price level. Second, equities are riskier than bonds in the sense that their returns are more uncertain; therefore, their yields may (and should) contain a risk premium even if they do not contain an inflation premium. Finally, corporate profits may fail to keep pace with inflation; the greater the lag between the growth in dividend payments and the rate of inflation, the more equities will resemble fixed income securities and will ape their performance.[10]

LINK BETWEEN YIELDS MISSING. The crucial point, however, is that no systematic link need exist between dividend yields (or price/earnings ratios) and bond yields, even in an inflationary period, and most assuredly no link need exist when corporate earnings are expected to grow as fast as or faster than the price level is expected to increase. Consequently, the only conditions under which equities will act like fixed income securities and contain an inflation premium in their dividend yields will be when corporate managements are unable to index profits to inflation. Equities will be "interest sensitive" when they have fixed income characteristics, but not otherwise.

This conclusion suggests another intriguing possibility. We have just hypothesized that dividend yields can serve as a proxy for the real rate of interest when corporate earnings are fully indexed, because dividend yields would then require no inflation premium. Under those conditions the spread between stock yields (that is, the real rate of interest) and bond yields (the nominal rate of interest) will be a proxy for inflation expectations! We usually think of that spread as a reflection of how investors feel about owning the riskier asset in contrast to the less risky asset, but our analysis reveals that this interpretation is an oversimplification of the ingredients that go into the determination of that spread.

Of course, conditions are seldom ideal. To the extent that corporate earnings are not fully indexed, dividend yields would contain an inflation premium and the spread between bond and stock yields would be less than inflation expectations. To the extent that investors add a premium to dividend yields simply because they are concerned about risks to the corporate sector—too much debt, political factors, low profit margins, and so forth—

---

[9] This was the case from 1895 to 1913, in the late 1920s, and from 1959 to 1972. See Molodovsky [1974].

[10] See Buffett [1977] for a strongly worded demonstration of how this can happen.

the spread between bond and stock yields may still be an accurate reflection of inflation expectations, but bond yields may be higher than they would be if perceptions of risk were lower. This means that stock yields can push bond yields upward under certain conditions, which is the precise opposite of the way most people view the process. Yet, it stands to reason that bond yields would be higher in a risk-prone economy, because they are, after all, the price of debt, and uncertainties about debt repayment or the variability of interest rates are a function of the degree of risk in the economy.

How Does It Work?

Figure 6-2 shows the path of the current yield on the S&P 500 from 1954 to 1981, plotted against the yield on Aaa corporate bonds. It is a striking illustration of the thesis presented here. Where the thesis fails to hold up, the lesson is equally instructive.

Note, first of all, that the current yield on stocks may have wobbled with the business cycle from 1964 to 1973, but that it was essentially trendless around 3 percent. Furthermore, until after 1973 the current yield shows no positive correlation whatsoever with the long-term bond yield. This would suggest that the increase in expected inflation reflected by the upward trend in the long-term bond yield after 1965 had no significance for owners of equities. They must have believed that they were holding a fully indexed security.

What about the period from 1952 to 1958, when bond yields were lower than stock yields? Two factors would explain this. First, the stock yield obviously incorporates a premium for risk, even if it theoretically contains no inflation premium. Investors during those years were concerned about

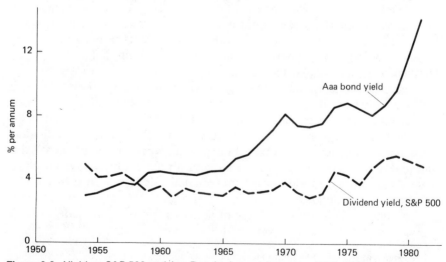

Figure 6-2. Yield on S&P 500 and Aaa Bonds, Annual Averages, 1952–81. Source: *Economic Report of the President* [1982])

the imminent arrival of a postwar depression in which dividends would be cut sharply. Second, much of this concern related to *deflationary* expectations, in which case bonds would gain in purchasing power and stocks would lose. Hence, the lower yields on bonds was rational in that expectation set.

After 1970, and more dramatically after 1973, we can see that stock yields mimicked bond yields until 1978. Indeed, stock yields went up even faster than bond yields in those years, so the spread between them narrowed. Aside from the observations above about the inevitable arrival of disappointing stock performances after the tremendous bull market of the 1950s and 1960s, can we find a rational reason for this change in behavior? Why did stock yields totally ignore interest rate trends for 30 years, then lock into the interest rate pattern for nearly ten years, and then start going their own way once again after 1978?

Figure 6-3 provides a rough picture of the likely answer. It shows the ratio of selling prices to labor cost per unit of output for the nonfarm business sector from 1954 to 1981, taking the 1977 relationship as 100, plotted against the yield on the S&P 500. The latter is inverted to facilitate the comparison with the price/unit labor cost ratio.

The price/unit labor cost ratio is a handy measure of inflation pass-through—of the degree to which businessmen are able to pass along rising costs to their customers. We can see the extended rise in profitability in the 1960s, followed by the deterioration at the end of the decade, to which reference was made earlier. Substantial improvement took place after the 1974 recession, but the business slowdown of 1979 and recession of 1980 held the ratio at deeply depressed levels.[11]

The association is not perfect—the deviation of the ratio from its mean level "explains" about 45 percent of the dividend yield—but it is close enough to be suggestive of the kind of relationship hypothesized above, in which yields will be low under conditions in which corporations function as fully indexed units. As we would expect, yields will not only rise when indexing is incomplete—they will echo the movements of bond yields; that is, stocks become more interest sensitive as they acquire bond-type characteristics at the expense of their unique equity-type characteristics.

Figure 6-3 contains additional significant information. For example, in 1971–72, investors tended to ignore the failure of the price/unit labor cost ratio to return to peak levels, doubtless ascribing this failure to the impact of wage and price controls.[12] Yet, we saw earlier that the developing difficulties were more fundamental than that. In any case, when disappointment set in and reality had to be faced, investors overdid it the other way; yields remained high after 1973 and were at exceptionally high levels in 1978 and 1979 despite vigorous dividend growth in the interim.

The unusually pessimistic view of stocks as an inflation hedge and the conviction that they were a very high risk asset during the 1977–79 period

[11] Estep and Hanson [1980] have an elegant description of this process.

[12] Of course, all 1971–72 data are also distorted by restrictions on dividend payments in those years, but these restrictions are insufficient to explain the wide discrepancy that appears in Figure 6-3.

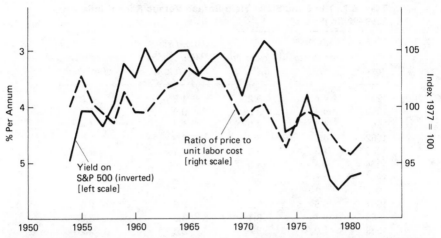

Figure 6-3. Yield on S&P 500 (Inverted) vs. Ratio of Price to Unit Labor Cost, Nonfarm Business Sector, Annually, 1954–81. (SOURCE: *Economic Report of the President* [1982])

was subsequently corrected by a decline in dividend yields after 1979 in the face of deteriorating economic conditions. This is not only a perfect demonstration of how stock prices can move in the opposite direction from what we might expect in terms of the fundamentals when matters turn out to be different from those expectations. It is an important story in itself worth a more detailed examination.

Another Look at 1978–81

Between November 1979 and the end of 1980, the yield on the S&P 500 dropped from 5.9 percent—an historically high level—to 4.5 percent. Over the same period of time, however, the yield on Aaa corporate bonds rose from 11 to 13 percent. Thus, the spread between bond and stock yields jumped from about 500 to nearly 900 basis points. This widening process continued on into 1981, even though stock yields were rising: By late summer, stocks were yielding 5.2 percent, but bond yields had surged upward even faster and had broken through the 15 percent level, stretching the spread between the two to 1000 basis points in favor of bonds.

Why did the spread widen so dramatically? If the dividend yield is a proxy for the real rate of interest, did this widening spread mean that inflation expectations were rising? That seems odd in retrospect: While the unfortunate blow-up in inflation during 1980 was probably unexpected, one could hardly argue that expectations of future inflation had accelerated to that degree.

What, then, was really going on?

Let us step back a bit before answering. A glance at Table 6-7 on the next page will show that the spread between bond yields and stock yields from the late 1950s to at least 1972 was approximately equal to recent past inflationary

TABLE 6-7. The Bond/Stock Yield Spread Versus Recent Inflation, 1959–80 (in percent)

Year	Aaa Bond Yield	Yield on S&P 500	Bond Yield Minus Stock Yield	Moving Average of Inflation[a]
1959	4.4%	3.2%	1.2%	1.9%
1960	4.4	3.5	0.9	2.1
1961	4.4	3.0	1.4	1.4
1962	4.3	3.4	0.9	1.1
1963	4.3	3.2	1.1	1.2
1964	4.4	3.0	1.4	1.2
1965	4.5	3.0	1.5	1.4
1966	5.1	3.4	1.7	2.0
1967	5.5	3.2	2.3	2.3
1968	6.7	3.1	3.6	3.2
1969	7.0	3.2	3.8	4.2
1970	8.0	3.8	4.2	4.9
1971	7.4	3.1	4.3	4.8
1972	7.2	2.8	4.4	4.4
1973	7.4	3.1	4.3	5.2
1974	8.6	4.5	4.1	7.2
1975	8.8	4.3	4.5	7.7
1976	8.4	3.8	4.6	7.6
1977	8.0	4.6	3.4	7.8
1978	8.7	5.3	3.4	7.4
1979	9.6	5.5	4.1	8.5
1980	11.9	5.3	6.6	10.5
1981	14.2	5.2	9.0	10.7

SOURCE: *Economic Report of the President* [1982].
[a] "Recent inflation" is a four-year moving average of the percentage change in the Consumer Price Index, with the fourth year weighted double.

experience and therefore fitted our hypothesis. The spread did fail to rise after 1972 despite accelerating inflation, but we should remember that most people continued to believe that what was happening was not a permanent state of affairs and, even after the oil price crisis in 1973, that it was still susceptible to properly applied medicine. The financial crunch of 1974 and the deep recession of 1974–75 were in fact followed, as expected, by rapidly improving inflation figures in 1976.

The odd occurrence was in what happened after 1976. The spread between bond and stock yields narrowed from about 450 basis points in 1976 to 340 basis points in 1977–78, even as investors became increasingly discouraged about the outlook for inflation and bond yields began moving upward.

The more we look at the four years 1977–80, the more curious they become. As we shall see shortly, however, the uncharacteristic behavior that the capital markets displayed during that period is unusually helpful to us in understanding what makes them tick.

Stock valuations dropped (P/E ratios fell and yields rose) during 1977–78, despite clearly improving fundamentals, including an acceleration in dividend payments that brought them in 1978 to a level 60 percent higher than they had been in 1973 and comfortably ahead of the rise in the Consumer Price Index over the preceding 13 years. Corporate bond yields, on the other hand, held steady at around 8 percent in 1977 and moved up only gradually during 1978, despite an uninterrupted speedup in inflation after mid-1977, a steep and persistent rise in the interest rate on federal funds, and deepening trouble for the dollar on the foreign exchange markets.

The answer to this riddle lies in the irresistible habit that leads investors to shun securities on which they have lost money and to accumulate securities that have treated them relatively well. Table 6-8 shows how the vivid memories of the swings in stock and bond prices during 1973–74 led investors to shun the risks of equity ownership despite improving earnings and dividends and to turn to the apparently safer haven of bonds despite intensifying inflationary pressures and rising short-term interest rates.

Now the events of 1979–80 will be much clearer. After 1978, stock prices rose in the face of falling bond prices simply because the markets were finally adjusting to increasingly visible present realities and were breaking away from the tenacious hold of past experiences. In other words, the doubling of the spread between stock yields and bond yields from 500 to 1000 basis points during 1979–80 and on into 1981 apparently was not a reflection of an upward jump in inflation expectations. Rather, it was a return to more rational valuation levels than had prevailed during the preceding couple of years.

Thus, as suggested earlier, while inflation is a powerful influence on security valuation—negative or positive, as the case may be—and while the bond/stock yield spread in many instances will reflect the general level of expected inflation, inflation was by no means the *only* influence on the markets nor was it always the most dominant one. Shifting risk premiums that reflect both happy and unhappy experiences with one asset or another tend to distort relationships that we might otherwise define with cold econometric models but that will frequently fall wide of the mark. Rational valuation techniques may tell us where asset prices *should*, and ultimately *will*, move, but we must recognize that investors will wander away from such valuations for extended periods of time—sometimes quite far.

TABLE 6-8. **Institutional Investor Demand for Bonds and Equities, 1965–73 and 1974–79**

	1965–73	1974–79
Bonds purchased	$ 81.6 bil.	$160.3 bil.
Equities purchased	93.5	70.9
Total bonds plus equities	$175.1 bil.	$231.2 bil.
Bonds as percent of total	47%	69%
Real return on bonds	3.30%	1.50%

SOURCE: Paulus [1980].

Thus, the end of the 1970s was notable for the dramatic shift in yield relationships between equities and fixed income securities, but it was also notable because of increased interest in new types of assets designed to provide better hedges against inflation. These included money market funds, funds concentrating in commodities and option contracts, GNMA pass-through securities, and equity positions in real estate. With the exception of the last, these assets were variations on old themes in the arena of market-able securities; money market funds, in particular, exceeded $220 billion by mid-1982 and were equal to 10 percent of M2 (which includes the $150+ billion of MMF assets held by individuals directly) and even exceeded 15 percent of the equity market.

Real Estate

Real estate was different in the sense that it was a diversion of money away from the conventional channels feeding the markets for tradable securities. Even in the institutional area, it was much less liquid; large transaction units complicated the diversification process and it required different structures for portfolio management and management compensation. For individual investors, however, it became the prime asset on their balance sheets.

The reason for this, of course, was the vastly superior performance of real estate as compared with the returns on marketable securities or the rate of inflation from about 1965 onward. One study (Ibbotson and Fall [1979]) shows a 17 percent compound annual rate of return on farm real estate and about 9 percent on residential real estate from 1965 to 1978. Another study (Webb and Sirmans [1980]) shows returns averaging 8 to 10 percent a year on multifamily buildings and a wide variety of nonresidential properties for the period 1966–77. The real estate portfolio construction chapter elsewhere in this book indicates that industrial real estate in an equally weighted portfolio returned about 8 percent a year during 1973–78, while a value-weighted portfolio of the same properties returned about 13 percent a year.

These estimates are in contrast to an inflation rate of about 6 percent a year from the mid-1960s to the late 1970s, when the annual compound total return on stocks was about 5 percent and Treasury bills provided 6 to 8 percent. The chapter also demonstrates, however, that, contrary to the evidence of other researchers, accurate measures of variability suggest that real estate returns were at least as great as the variability in stock returns and far above the variability of fixed income security returns.

FRAMING THE FORECAST

We are now ready to take all of the observations, hypotheses, and history set forth in the preceding pages and apply them to a long-range forecast of what the future might look like and how the capital markets might respond to it.

Our focus here, however, is not on the fine points. Rather, our primary objective is to demonstrate how to relate the patterns of investor expectations to the patterns of fundamental economic forces.

Of course, long-term forecasts are grist for the mills of scorn. When placed in print, with a pretense to some degree of permanence, they are even more vulnerable to hilarious second-guessing.

What follows, therefore, is not a long-term forecast, even though we shall contemplate the foreseeable future with some care. Rather, it is a demonstration of a technique for dealing with uncertainty. The aim is to stress the method rather than the particulars of the projections; the particulars, after all, will inevitably change as security prices vary and the future shifts along with the passage of time.

The most important element in this technique is to be sure that we include outcomes that may seem unfamiliar, extreme, or unlikely. This is the only way we know to minimize the disastrous surprises that have assailed the excessively aggressive bulls and the excessively timorous bears on so many occasions in the past.[13]

Even so, however, we would do well to recognize that the probabilities of our range of outcomes may sum to less than 100 percent. In other words, we are frequently incapable of conceiving the *entire* possible range of outcomes and should not fool ourselves into thinking that a process like this can be more than a rough estimate of what future returns from securities might look like.

John Maynard Keynes, who was a brilliant mathematician and author of *A Treatise on Probability* as well as a famous economist, was particularly skeptical about "pretty, polite techniques made for a well-paneled board room" but inappropriate for a turbulent world. As he put it [1937],

> By "uncertain" knowledge . . . I do not mean merely to distinguish what is known for certain from what is only probable. The game of roulette is not subject, in this sense to uncertainty. . . . About [some] matters, there is no scientific basis on which to form any calculable probabilities whatever. *We simply do not know.* [Emphasis added]

Yet, he admits that "the necessity for action and for decision compels us as practical men to do our best to overlook this awkward fact" and to consider the prospective outcomes "each multiplied by its appropriate probability waiting to be summed."

We shall begin with a specification of the valuation parameters for our major assets that would appear to be appropriate to the range of possibilities as they appear at this writing. We shall then define in more detail the range of outcomes we might expect over the three years or so from early 1982 to mid-1985. Finally, we shall apply the valuation parameters to the various out-

---

[13] A good analysis of the scenario forecasting process is in Carman [1981], Gray [1979], and Edesess and Hambrecht [1980].

comes and study their impact on holding period or total returns for each of the asset classes.

Valuation Parameters

Equities. The analysis above emphasized the superior quality of the information embodied in dividends in contrast to earnings data. As a result of the inflation that began in the mid-1960s, no one has an accurate method for measuring earnings; we rely on what are essentially rough estimates with a wide margin of error. Dividends, on the other hand, are not manufactured by accountants but are declared by managements and received by stockholders and should therefore be a more precise and a more meaningful benchmark for equity valuation.

The specification of valuation parameters for equities through the dividend, therefore, must go in two steps. First, we must find a good method for projecting what the dividend payment itself would be under different types of environments. Second, we must then find a good method for projecting dividend yields, or the capitalization rates that the market will apply to those dividend payments under varying conditions.

Figure 6-4 provides a helpful set of relationships for studying dividend behavior. It shows the dividend on the S&P 500 (multiplied by 100) compared with net interest payments by nonfinancial corporations, both as a percentage of GNP. The net interest/GNP ratio has been inverted so that the two lines move up and down together—but the relationship is obviously inverse.

The intimacy of this relationship is striking: a correlation analysis reveals a ρ-squared of 0.92 and a standard error of only 0.02 percent. The persistent substitution of debt for equity in the capital structure of these companies has increased the share of total capital income going to creditors and has reduced the share available to stockholders.

Perhaps the most striking feature of the chart, however, is the clear change in the patterns after 1975. Even though interest payments more than doubled from 1975 to 1981, we can see that their ratio to GNP moved essentially sideways. Thanks to inflation flow-through, in other words, the interest *burden* ceased to grow. The rapidly growing dollar volume of business, in fact, not only helped to cover the explosion in interest payments but also made it possible for dividends—after lagging far behind for about a decade— to grow to just about the same pace as interest payments.

While this analysis of the corporate interest burden has the attraction of capturing in one number the whole quality of the economic environment in which managements must make their decisions, Figure 6-4 does show that the relationship between dividend payments and interest payments is not perfect. For example, dividends held up well during 1960–65 as the interest burden grew heavier, but then dividend payments fell far behind from 1970 to 1975 even though the interest burden was growing more slowly.

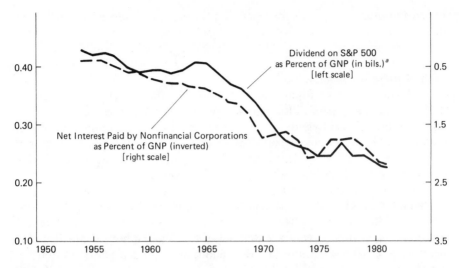

[a] GNP divided by $1 million.

Figure 6-4. Dividends vs. the Interest Burden, Annually, 1954–80. (SOURCE: *Security Price Index Record* [1981] and *Economic Report of the President* [1982]).

These differences reflect a complex set of forces. The most helpful element to explain the ratio of dividends to GNP other than the interest burden appears to be variations in real growth. The introduction of a four-year moving average of the rate of change in real GNP to the regression of dividends and interest payments as a percent of GNP for the period 1960–81 raises ρ-squared by 0.05. More important, it shows that the change in real GNP is a statistically significant variable that eliminates the tendency of the calculated line to run above or below the actual line for a number of years in a row.[14] In short, this means that, all other things being equal, corporate directors tend to lean on the generous side when real growth in the economy has been strong for a while but to shift to a more stingy dividend policy when the economy is soft.

Having found a reliable set of relationships to assist us in projecting the future level of dividend payments, we must now seek variables we can use to project dividend *yields*—the value that investors will place on those dividend payments—under different types of economic environments.

Let us turn back to Figure 6-3, which showed the path of the dividend yield on the S&P 500 and the ratio of price to unit labor cost in the nonfarm business economy. Although the relationship is variable, the trends in the price/cost ratio do appear to exert a powerful influence on dividend yields. The yield may wander and wiggle away from the price/cost ratio, but it does not defy the ratio for long, nor, having wandered away, does it fail to return.

[14] Without the GNP variable, the regression has a Durbin-Watson statistic of 0.885; with real GNP, the Durbin-Watson rises to 1.624, or no evidence of serial correlation.

Furthermore, since the price/cost ratio is a sensitive indicator of the health and vigor of the corporate sector, we should be able to make reasonable projections of its level under different economic environments, thus deriving a good approximation of what dividend yields are likely to be under each of these environments.

Unfortunately, as with all such relationships, the correlation is less than perfect. This means that although the price/cost ratio may be a dominant influence on dividend yields, it is not the only one. An examination of the patterns in Figure 6-3 suggests that once again the sheer weight of memories of past experiences will occasionally drive valuation levels away from where coldly rational calculations would otherwise place them.

Thus, anxieties about an imminent return of the Great Depression necessitated a long period of superior performance by the price/cost ratio during the late 1940s and the 1950s (only partially visible on the chart) before investors were willing to believe that better times might have some degree of permanence. After 1968, on the other hand, an extended period of deteriorating profitability was necessary before investors were willing to acknowledge that better times were not permanent and to shift the parameters by which they valued earnings and dividends to much more conservative levels than those prevailing during the previous ten years.

These tendencies for investors to wait until change is strongly visible before radically revising capitalization rates is important for our task of projecting the parameters for different types of environments. If the history of the past 25 years is any guide, yields will vary from year to year by only about 50 basis points on average. Even over three-year time spans, the mean change is only 67 basis points and it is less than 120 basis points 83 percent of the time. Projections of radical changes in capitalization rates—say, more than 100 basis points or so in yields over a time period of three years—would therefore be justified only if the economic environment is also *significantly* different from what it was during the latter years of the 1970s.

Figure 6-3 does show that yields tend to be about 5 percent when the price/cost ratio is around 95 (1977 = 100), about 4 percent when the ratio is around 100, and about 3 percent when the ratio is around 105. This is a useful set of rules of thumb for projecting future yield levels. On the other hand, before we could project 3 percent yields for 1985, for example, even if we believe that the ratio might be up to 105 by then, we would also have to specify an environment in which investors would be completely convinced of the viability of that environment; otherwise, yields would probably be somewhat higher than 3 percent, even under such favorable conditions in that particular year.

Bonds. Conventional wisdom tells us that bond yields are a function of a relatively constant real rate of return and a premium to compensate the lender for expected inflation.[15] We noted earlier, however, that nominal

---

[15] The most complete review and analysis of the controversies over the existence and stability of the real rate of interest are in Mishkin [1981] and Summers [1981a], but see also Friedman [1980], Fisher [1907], Leuthold [1980], and Levine [1981].

interest rates fail to fit this formulation as neatly as we would like, both because of varying tax rates and, perhaps even more important, because long-term lenders change their view of the future more slowly than shorter term trends might warrant. In recent years, furthermore, inflation has taken such unexpected leaps and has made bond prices so volatile, that some kind of implicit risk premium has also entered into long-term bond valuation procedures.

Hence, although we should expect bond yields to rise and fall as expectations of inflation rise and fall, nothing like a one-to-one relationship is likely. On the contrary, the patterns of many decades of history provide consistent evidence to show that long-term interest rates move upward and downward with more modest amplitudes than the upward and downward movements of inflation. Indeed, the lags are so long that we occasionally find interest rates still moving in one direction when inflation rates have reversed their trends.

The disasters that befell the bond market after 1977, and most particularly during the precipitous declines in bond prices in early 1980 and during the summer of 1981, are a warning that the relationship with inflation may be asymmetrical during the first half of the 1980s. In other words, long-term interest rates will be inclined to fall more slowly than inflation if inflation improves but to climb almost as rapidly as inflation if the situation deteriorates.

Short-term Instruments. Most short-term interest rates move together, with close turning points at peaks and troughs, although with differing variability. We shall focus here on the rate on 91-day U.S. Treasury bills, as this is the rate that calls the tune for the others to follow.

Over the long run the return on U.S. Treasury bills has tended to come close to the rate of inflation. Over the great time span from 1926 to 1981, for example, the inflation rate as measured by the Consumer Price Index was 3.0 percent a year; on Treasury bills, the annual compound return was 3.0 percent.

In shorter periods of time, however, the relationship is much less neat. The annual standard deviation of the inflation rate has actually been more than twice as large as the annual standard deviation of Treasury bill returns. During all but one of the six years from the end of 1972 to the end of 1978, in fact, the return on Treasury bills fell short of the inflation rate by more than one percentage point; this was in part the consequence of a relatively easy money policy that kept short-term interest rates well below long-term rates. From 1978 to the end of 1981, on the other hand, as monetary policy shifted to a more aggressive approach to restraining money supply growth, bill rates were well into double digits, except briefly in 1980, and exceeded inflation by some five percentage points or more in 1981 and early 1982.

Historical experience with the spreads between short-term and long-term yields suggests that the spread will be negative (long yields below short yields) in the late stages of a boom, particularly under the conditions of high and unstable inflation rates that usually prevail at such times. It tends to be about even under conditions of more stable inflation rates, and positive in the early stages of business recovery and/or when inflation is diminishing in intensity.

If we use this approach in projecting bill yields for 1985 and assume that they move smoothly from their early 1982 levels to the designated 1985 levels, we will make a more realistic estimate of probable returns from short-term paper than if we simply assume them equal to the rate of inflation. Our analysis would have to stretch out over a much longer period of time before that assumption would be appropriate.

Real Estate. Data on real estate returns are so sketchy that the available estimates of the past provide only a tenuous basis for projections into the future. Furthermore, "real estate" is a catch-all for a widely diversified package of assets whose covariance is less clearly defined than it is for stocks and bonds. Nevertheless, some rough guesses are possible.

One view would be to argue that real estate was seriously overvalued by 1980, since, as we saw earlier, real estate prices and returns had outrun inflation and the returns on conventional marketable securities by such a wide margin over the preceding 15 years. From this standpoint, we might expect real estate returns to lag behind inflation, except under those environments where the inflation rate was substantially in excess of consensus expectations.

This argument is not so easy to support, however. In the first place, real estate outran inflation during the 15 years prior to 1965 as well, even though it did fail to perform as well as common stocks during those years. Hence, real estate may tend to provide real rates of return under most types of conditions except, perhaps, deflation; the more complicated question would be how it would perform relative to other types of assets.

Furthermore, inflation is not necessarily the only guideline to consider with respect to real estate. If the returns on real estate averaged 8 to 10 percent a year from 1965 to 1980, as indicated earlier, those rates are almost identical to the growth rate of nominal GNP, nominal reported profits, and rental income of persons over the same period. It was slightly above the growth in average hourly earnings, which was 7 percent a year.

Nevertheless, inflation would appear to be the dominant influence on real estate. The Ibbotson-Fall study shows that the years of biggest returns on residential housing—1951, 1970, 1974–75, and 1977–78—were all associated with suddenly elevated inflationary expectations. This study also shows that a regression of housing returns against inflation for the period 1947–78 showed a ρ-squared of 0.671, which was far higher than for any financial asset. The regression's alpha and beta coefficients were highly significant at 3.82 and 0.84, respectively. For 1965–78, the alpha was over 4 percent, the beta was 0.81; the ρ-squared was down to 0.545, but still was higher than on stocks and bonds.

These data suggest that we should continue to expect real estate to outperform inflation, even in the face of high real interest rates, although it may not outperform financial assets during periods of lower inflation. On the other hand, real estate has been so clearly identified as a prime inflation hedge that it would be likely to turn in a disappointing performance if inflation is going to be unexpectedly low or even turns over into deflation.

A Set of Scenarios—And Their Consequences

What kinds of outcomes are possible—including those that are unlikely—in the years ahead? Any answers that we can provide to this question as these words are written will appear obsolete by the time they are read. Nevertheless, rational decisions are impossible without some sense of the range of possibilities. Thus, we have no choice but to proceed with the task of defining them, in full recognition that we shall make fuzzy oversimplifications and may fail to consider new environments that are as yet totally unimaginable.

While all kinds of random outcomes are conceivable, the most systematic way to approach this problem is to rank the possibilities in terms of the success or lack of success of the new directions to economic policy provided by the Reagan administration. What will happen to the capital markets if the administration achieves its stated objectives of rising output and employment combined with diminishing inflation rates? What forces would block the achievement of those goals, and in which directions would they drive the economy? At the worst, how bad can things get?

This analytical method explicitly excludes problems of war and peace, of renewed energy crises prompted by OPEC, of a new wave of trade protectionism, and of other types of international complications. On the other hand, disturbances from outside our borders will largely depend on the state of affairs within them. If the administration is successful in its objectives, even if less than perfectly so, international problems are much more likely to fall into line than if we persist in displaying the volatile and discontinuous patterns that have characterized our economy and financial system over the past fifteen years.

The Reagan administration aims to achieve higher output and lower inflation in three ways. It seeks to reduce the scope of government, so that the private sector can play a more dominant role. It depends upon monetary policy to provide a steady rate of growth in the money supply, which it hopes will suppress inflationary expectations and will alter price- and wage-setting behavior. Tax reform, deregulation, easier environmental requirements, a more determined defense posture, and a strong hand in labor negotiations should encourage businessmen to invest for higher productivity and greater capacity and should induce households to save in the expectation of higher real after-tax returns.

Yet, by the first quarter of President Reagan's second year in office, the behavior of the capital markets signaled the skepticism of investors about the probability that all of these pieces would fit together. On the other hand, one needs little imagination to foresee the tremendously positive impact that success would have on the valuation of both stocks and bonds. A significant improvement in the ratio of price to unit labor cost, the centerpiece of the whole program, would enhance the attractiveness of stocks; in addition, higher levels of profitability would reduce cost-push pressures on the price level and would add to corporate cash flows and dividend growth, thereby contributing to lower interest rates.

Success in the form of higher real growth and lower inflation by 1985, however, does require each of the separate pieces of the program to fit compatibly with one another. If the tax cuts and defense expenditures provide too much stimulus, inflation will pick up again, perhaps more stubbornly and more intensely than in the past. If monetary policy is too restrictive or savings incentives cut too deeply into consumer demand, economic growth will falter. Rearmament may put government spending beyond control. State and local governments may have no choice but to raise taxes enough to offset the salutary impact of federal tax reductions. To these concerns, one should add the precarious state of the Social Security system, the delicate balance of political and military forces outside the United States, and the inability of our major trading partners to solve the same kinds of problems that have plagued the U.S. economy for so long.

Therefore, while success in achieving the administration's joint objectives is surely one possibility for the future, it is not the most likely outcome. We can define five other states that would describe the varying directions that the economy might take if the program does not succeed.

The first is that the administration succeeds in generating a relatively high rate of real growth in the economy but fails to achieve its inflation objectives. In this case, growth might come close to administration expectations but inflation would linger around the levels of recent years. Powerful inertia in inflationary forces does exist, especially in the wage area, and productivity improvement from new capital investments will take time; on the other hand, our projections start from the relatively depressed level of output in early 1982. Hence, high real growth combined with a high but stable rate of inflation is by no means a dismal projection and may well be a likely one.

The second alternative, which is probably the consensus view at this writing, is that inflation will be higher and real growth will be lower than the administration expects; this would be an environment roughly comparable to, say, 1977–81.

The third possibility would be a situation in which slow money growth and the persistence of high real interest rates gradually suppress inflation but simultaneously repress profitability to a point where real growth is also restrained; this would be comparable to 1958–62.

The two remaining possibilities are cases in which the administration's program not only falls short of expectations in one area or another, but does so to a catastrophic degree. If impatience builds up with slow growth and high interest rates, or with the painful consequences of efforts to balance the budget, political pressures can break the resolve of the Federal Reserve and the administration to a point where growth may revive but where inflation accelerates to new highs.

The final case would be the opposite, where excessive zeal in the execution of conservative monetary and fiscal policies collides with the fragility of the worldwide financial and debt structure, so that we topple over into a deflationary smash reminiscent of the 1930s.[16]

MODELING THE OUTLOOK

A Look at the Data

We must now select mid-1985 capital market values for stocks, long-term bonds, Treasury bills, and real estate for each of these six environments. Table 6-9 shows the underlying economic assumptions and the assumptions for each asset class; in Table 6-10 we can see the rates of return that would be generated from early 1982 to mid-1985 as a result of the movement in values implied by the underlying assumptions.[17]

The most meaningful view of the results appears in Tables 6-11, 6-12, and 6-13. Table 6-11 shows probability-weighted returns—or, more properly, the "expected" return—for each asset class as well as for real growth and inflation from three different viewpoints. Table 6-12 shows the uncertainty that would surround those expectations. The first viewpoint, equal-weighted, would reflect the position taken by an investor who frankly believes that the future is unpredictable and that anything can happen. The second reflects the attitude of an investor who is doubtful that extreme outcomes are likely and believes that disinflationary forces may be stronger than inflationary forces. The third shows the expectations of an investor who thinks continued high inflation is the most likely environment.

Table 6-13 shows correlations between the asset classes, as well as between each of the assets and the major economic variables. These numbers show the likelihood that each will vary in the same or opposite direction from the others and the degree to which their movements will tend to be correlated.

In setting the assumptions for the equity valuations, some simplifying steps were necessary. We saw earlier that dividend payout ratios are probably sensitive to the general level of the stock market itself as well as to the internal financial condition of the firm. We also saw that dividend yields are

[16] The reader should be aware that the scenarios and projections discussed here were formulated in early 1982 and therefore may fail to reflect unexpected but significant events affecting the future, such as tax increases and spending cuts enacted in September 1982.

[17] Note the positive correlation between high returns on bonds and stocks under the administration outcome in Table 6-10. For persuasive discussion of the causal inverse relationship between profits and interest rates, see Moscowitz [1976].

TABLE 6-9. **Projections of Capital Market Assumptions Under Different Environments, Early 1982 to Mid-1985**

GNP Assumptions

	PERCENT CHANGE PER ANNUM[a]			Nominal GNP in 1985 (billions of dollars)
Environment	Real GNP	GNP Deflator	Nominal GNP	
Administration	4.0%	+ 5.4%	+ 9.6%	$4212
Higher inflation, high growth	4.0	+ 9.0	+13.4	4829
Higher inflation, lower growth	3.0	+ 9.0	+12.3	4644
Lower inflation, lower growth	2.5	+ 6.5	+ 9.2	4152
Accelerating inflation	3.0	+11.0	+14.3	5178
Deflation	− 4.0	− 3.3	− 7.2	2166

Dividend Yield Assumptions

Environment	Ratio of Dividends to GNP	1985 Dividends	Yield	S&P 500
Administration	.234	$ 9.86	3.50%	282
Higher inflation, high growth	.222	10.72	4.00	268
Higher inflation lower growth	.192	8.92	4.25	210
Lower inflation, lower growth	.197	8.18	5.00	164
Accelerating inflation	.191	9.89	5.75	172
Deflation	.140	3.03	4.00	76

Interest Rate Assumptions

Environment	Inflation Expectation Assumed	Assumed 1985 Yield	Bond Price[b]	1985 T-bill Yield
Administration	5.0%	9.0%	110	6.8%
Higher inflation, high growth	11.0	14.5	70	16.5
Higher inflation, lower growth	9.5	14.0	72	13.0
Lower inflation, lower growth	5.0	9.0	110	6.0
Accelerating inflation	15.0	18.0	56	20.0
Deflation	2.0	9.0	110	2.0

Real Estate Assumptions

Environment	Returns Will Exceed Inflation by
Administration	1.0%
Higher inflation, high growth	3.5
Higher inflation, lower growth	3.5
Lower inflation, lower growth	0.5
Accelerating inflation	5.0
Deflation	−3.0

[a] Calculated from estimated levels for 1982 to 1985. Administration projection generally conforms with the projections in the President's Budget Message of January 1982. Deflation projection roughly based on 1929–32 experience.

[b] Based on 10 percent bond due in 2011, Aaa, callable at 110, purchased at 65 to yield 15.5 percent to maturity. It would probably have been called before 1985 under the deflation outcome.

sensitive to the yield level that has prevailed during the recent past. Thus, the exogenous variables of market valuation have strong endogenous content. This meant that the data in Table 6-9 required shading in one direction or the other from the levels that would have been appropriate without these all too human characteristics of the capital markets.

One further assumption requires some comment, because it is a controversial one. In selecting the levels of the ratio of price to unit labor cost for each outcome, we have to consider how that ratio would behave in high or

TABLE 6-10. Total Returns to Investors Under Assumptions in Table 6-9, Early 1982 to Mid-1985 (percent per annum)

Environment	Stocks[a]	Bonds[b]	Real Estate	Treasury Bills[c]
Administration	+32.8%	+25.8%	+ 6.4%	+ 8.9%
Higher inflation, high growth	+31.2	+14.7	+12.5	+15.3
Higher inflation, lower growth	+22.9	+15.3	+12.5	+13.0
Lower inflation, lower growth	+15.3	+25.8	+ 7.0	+ 8.3
Accelerating inflation	+17.2	+10.1	+16.0	+17.7
Deflation	− 5.7	+25.8	− 6.3	+ 5.7

[a] Assumes purchase in early 1982 at 115. Dividends in 1982 assumed unchanged from $6.60 for 1981. Thereafter, growth is smooth to amount shown in Table 6-9 for 1985, but only one-half the 1985 dividend is included.

[b] Assumes seven coupons of $5/$1000, not reinvested.

[c] Assumes smooth movement from 13.0 percent in early 1982 to amount in 1985 shown in Table 6-9.

TABLE 6-11. Probabilities for Various Environments Under
Differing Assumptions

	PROBABILITY		
Environment	Equal-Weighted	Disinflationary Emphasis	Inflationary Emphasis
Administration	.167	.15	.10
Higher inflation, high growth	.167	.21	.30
Higher inflation lower growth	.167	.22	.40
Lower inflation, lower growth	.167	.22	.10
Accelerating inflation	.167	.05	.06
Deflation	.167	.15	.04

TABLE 6-12. Expected Returns and Standard Deviations Under Differing Probability
Assumptions (percent per annum)

	EQUAL-WEIGHTED	
Asset	Expected Return	Standard Deviation
Stocks	19.0%	14.0%
Bonds	19.6	7.0
Treasury bills	11.5	7.9
Real estate	8.0	7.2
Inflation	6.3	5.1
Real growth	2.1	3.0

	DISINFLATIONARY EMPHASIS	
	Expected Return	Standard Deviation
Stocks	19.9%	12.6%
Bonds	20.4	5.8
Treasury bills	11.0	3.7
Real estate	7.0	6.6
Inflation	6.2	4.3
Real growth	2.2	2.7

	INFLATIONARY EMPHASIS	
	Expected Return	Standard Deviation
Stocks	24.1%	8.3%
Bonds	17.3	5.8
Treasury bills	12.8	3.0
Real estate	11.1	4.3
Inflation	8.1	2.7
Real growth	3.1	1.5

TABLE 6-13. Correlations Among Asset Class Returns

	Stocks	Bonds	T-Bills	Real Estate	Inflation
Stocks	1.00	—	—	—	—
Bonds	−0.30	1.00	—	—	—
Treasury bills	0.50	−0.96	1.00	—	—
Real estate	0.71	−0.80	0.90	1.00	—
Inflation	0.69	−0.77	0.88	0.99	1.00
Real growth	0.94	−0.42	0.62	0.86	0.87

higher inflation environments. In the analysis here, the assumption is that prices would rise faster than unit labor costs and that, as a result, the ratio would be higher, perhaps a lot higher, than in 1981.

While this is contrary to historical experience, as we can see by looking at the experience shown in Figure 6-3 for 1969–70, 1973–74, and 1979–81, these earlier episodes may not be comparable to the current outlook. All three were strongly influenced by cost explosions, the first as President Johnson abandoned wage guidelines to buy labor support for the Vietnam war, and the other two as a consequence of the two surges in oil prices (to say nothing of the end of wage controls in 1973 and the push to higher minimum wages after 1977). Barring a repetition of those elements in the picture and substituting instead strong demand-pull forces in our assumptions, we would in all likelihood see a widening rather than a repression of profit margins under inflationary environments.

On the other hand, a careful examination of the projections will show that real growth may turn out to be a more dominant influence than inflation on the final results. For example, the two lower growth environments have lower price/labor cost ratios and higher ratios of interest payments to GNP than the high growth cases—which in turn imply slower rates of growth in dividend payments.

Analyzing the Results

Four aspects of the tables are worthy of note.

First, under the first three outcomes (which exclude the grinding disinflation outcome and the two extreme outcomes of accelerating inflation and deflation), stocks, bonds, and real estate all provide positive nominal returns that exceed the rate of inflation, but only stocks outperform real estate and paper in the two high inflation outcomes. In the case of lower inflation and lower growth, however, the margin for stocks over real estate and Treasury bills is so small as to be statistically insignificant; only bonds do really well. All the assets are obviously sensitive to the extreme outcomes, although both stocks and bonds are likely to perform better under accelerating inflation than they did during similar conditions over the past 15 years.

Second, the negative correlation between equities and bonds and the positive correlation between equities and bills are especially important. Conventional wisdom in early 1982 holds that high interest rates are a primary depressant on stock prices and that a lower rate of inflation is automatically bullish. The results here, and the discussion above, lead to the opposite conclusion: equities are now hedged against inflation to a much greater degree than they were in the past in terms of both their valuation level and the ability of corporations to index their profits to inflation. On the other hand, as a result of the difficulties disinflation or deflation may create for profitability, they are likely to have a negative influence on stock returns, except under the highly favorable assumptions of full achievement of the administration's goals.

Third, because of the inclusion of extreme outcomes in these calculations, the range of possible returns is very wide indeed. An investor who places high probabilities on the extreme outcomes, and especially if he believes accelerating inflation is more likely than deflation, should eschew long-term assets altogether.

Indeed, when we look at the expected returns under each outcome in relation to the uncertainty of those expected returns (whether measured by the range or by the standard deviations shown in Table 6-12), the more conservative assets—bonds and bills—do appear to be more attractive than equities or real estate. The reason, of course, is that bonds already reflect deep pessimism (and are therefore well hedged against inflation) and would outperform all other assets by an enormous margin in the extreme deflationary outcome; bills provide modest but more certain returns than any of the long-term assets. The variability of real estate returns appears to be the lowest among the long-term assets, but its absolute expected returns are clearly higher than on stocks and bonds in only limited cases.

Finally, the most curious aspect of the matter is that the markets do not appear to be in equilibrium. In other words, it is difficult to set credible probability distributions in which stocks, the asset with highest risk, have expected returns that are comfortably above the expected returns on bonds, the less risky asset, unless one is deeply convinced about the inability of this country to make any inroads at all under any circumstances in the struggle to overcome inflation. Yet, theory tells us that investors will tend to price the risky asset so that it will provide higher expected returns than the less risky asset except under outcomes with very small probabilities.

Of course, we may have misspecified our assumptions. Perhaps corporate managements will be less successful than we have indicated here in raising their prices relative to the increase in their unit labor costs under inflationary conditions. We may also have overstated dividend yield levels in some outcomes by placing too much weight on historical yield levels, especially in the administration outcome. Finally, we may have underestimated the risk premium that could linger on in the level of bond yields, so that bond returns will work out to be less than suggested here.

On the other hand, we do have to face the possibility that, at this writing, bond investors may be overly pessimistic and shell-shocked from their disastrous experiences in recent years while stock investors may be too optimistic as a result of the vigorous growth in dividends since 1975 and the probusiness attitudes of the Reagan administration. In that event, the markets are *not* in equilibrium and bonds will provide as high or higher returns than equities under almost all conditions.

A Final Word

Perhaps the most pertinent finding that emerges from this analysis is that disinflation in itself is not necessarily bullish for equities, unless it is accompanied by major tax reforms that promote productivity and by improved methods of wage negotiation that hold costs in check. If managements are unable to raise prices as rapidly as costs increase, returns on equities will be disappointing absolutely and also relative to the potential gains that can accrue to bond investors under those conditions.

Indeed, the implications for bondholders are also significant. This asset, which is most unpopular in early 1982 because it has treated its owners in such shocking fashion for so long, turns out to have an extraordinarily favorable set of risk-return tradeoffs over the whole range of outcomes analyzed above.

The outlook for equities, is, therefore, more controversial. It is the less attractive asset under conditions of disinflation and perhaps insufficiently attractive under conditions of high inflation. Equity investors, therefore, appear to be hoping for good luck in achieving the administration's goals but are betting on an acceleration in inflation rather than a further diminution to lower, single digit rates of price increases.

Thus, our analysis has come full circle. The market, as a proxy for the consensus expectations of investors, is performing as it usually does. It is placing a bigger bet on an environment similar to the environment of the past five years than on a significantly different environment.

Yet nothing in history can promise us that the next five to ten years will look much like the past five to ten years, especially when the volatile and disruptive character of the past decade has torn apart so many traditional political, social, and economic relationships both at home and internationally. The future is more likely to be much better or much worse than to be more of the same. The investor who can accept that proposition can expect to lose less and win more than the investor who chooses to ignore the forces of change that are at work.

FURTHER READING

Source material

The four best sources of data on security prices, security returns, and inflation, in addition to the basic sources such as *The Economic Report of the President* [1982],

The Dow Jones Investor's Handbook [1982], and *Security Price Index Record* [1982] are: Fisher and Lorie [1977], Ibbotson and Fall [1979], Ibbotson and Sinquefield [1982], and Leuthold [1980].

Financial history

The best and most comprehensive description of the process of change and development in American financial markets since World War II is in Friedman [1980].

Interest rates and stock prices

Some of the material on this subject obviously spills over into the work on inflation and stock prices, but especially important are: Fama [1981], Fama and Schwert [1977], Keran [1981, 1976, and 1975], Leuthold [1980], Modigliani and Cohn [1979], Moscowitz and Harben [1978], and Summers [1981b].

Inflation and stock prices

One could read endlessly on this subject, but the seminal work in the area consists of: Bodie [1976], Fama [1981], Lintner [1975 and 1973], Modigliani and Cohn [1979], and Reilly [1975]. Further insights and commentary may be found in: Arak [1980–81], Brainard, Shoven, and Weiss [1980], Buffett [1977], Cagan [1974], Cohn and Lessard [1981], Connolly [1981], Estep and Hanson [1980], Feldstein [1979], Fuller and Petry [1981], Jones [1980], Keran [1981 and 1976], and Moore [1980].

Inflation and corporate earnings

Good reviews of the research in this area are available in: Arak [1980–81], Bulow and Shoven [1981], Cagan and Lipsey [1979], Fraumeni and Jorgenson [1980], Holland and Myers [1977], Lovell [1978], Rippe [1980], and Summers [1981b].

Inflation and interest rates

The basic work on this subject is Fisher [1907], but the following are also strongly recommended: Fama [1981], Friedman [1980], Leuthold [1980], Levine [1981], Mishkin [1981], and Summers [1981b].

Forecasting

Needless to say, no limits exist to the literature on this subject, but the following were particularly helpful in the preparation of this chapter: Carman [1981], Brainard, Shoven, and Weiss [1980], Estep and Hanson [1980], Gray [1979], Keran [1981], Mishkin [1981], Moore [1980], and Shiller [1981].

BIBLIOGRAPHY

Arak, Marcelle, "Inflation and Stock Values: Is Our Tax Structure the Villain?" *Quarterly Review,* Winter 1980–81, Federal Reserve Bank of New York.

Baily, Martin Neil, "Productivity and the Services of Capital and Labor," *Brookings Papers on Economic Activity* 1:1981.

Bernstein, Peter L., "The Wedge Theory: Pie In the Sky?" *Financial Analysts Journal,* March/April 1979.

———, "Hate: The New Force In the Stock Market," *Institutional Investor,* November 1977.

————, "Profits, Inflation, and Flag-Waving," *The Morgan Guaranty Survey,* November 1976.

Bodie, Zvi, "An Innovation for stable real retirement income," *The Journal of Portfolio Management,* Fall 1980.

————, "Common Stocks As a Hedge Against Inflation," *The Journal of Finance,* May 1976.

Brainard, William C., John B. Shoven, and Laurence Weiss, "The Financial Valuation of the Return to Capital," *Brookings Papers on Economic Activity* 2:1980.

Buffett, Warren, "How Inflation Swindles the Equity Investor," *Fortune,* May 1977.

Bulow, Jeremy I., and John B. Shoven, "Inflation, Corporate Profits, and the Rate of Return to Capital," National Bureau of Economic Research, Conference Paper No. 107, March 1981.

Cagan, Phillip, "Common Stock Values and Inflation—The Historical Record of Many Countries," National Bureau of Economic Research, Report Supplement, 1974.

————, **and Robert E. Lipsey,** "The Financial Effects of Inflation," National Bureau of Economic Research, 1979.

Carman, Peter, "The Trouble With Asset Allocation," *The Journal of Portfolio Management,* Fall 1981.

Cohn, Richard A., and Donald R. Lessard, "The Effect of Inflation on Stock Prices: International Evidence," *The Journal of Finance,* May 1981.

Connolly, John D., "Corporate and Investor Returns: A Guide to Strategy," *The Journal of Portfolio Management,* Summer 1981.

Dow Jones Investor's Handbook, The, Princeton, N.J.: Dow Jones Books, 1982.

Economic Report of the President, Washington, D.C.: U.S. Government Printing Office, 1982.

Edesses, Michael, and George A. Hambrecht, "Scenario forecasting: Necessity, not choice," *The Journal of Portfolio Management,* Spring 1980.

Estep, Tony, and Nick Hanson, "The Valuation of Financial Assets in Inflation," New York: Salomon Brothers, May 9, 1980.

Fama, Eugene F., "Stock Returns, Real Activity, Inflation, and Money," *American Economic Review,* September 1981.

————, **and G. W. Schwert,** "Asset Returns and Inflation," *Journal of Financial Economics,* November 1977.

Feldstein, Martin, "Inflation, Tax Rates, and the Stock Market," National Bureau of Economic Research, Working Paper No. 403, November 1979.

Fellner, William, "American Household Wealth in an Inflationary Period," in *Contemporary Economic Problems, 1979,* William Fellner, Ed., Washington, D.C.: American Enterprise Institute, 1979.

Fisher, Irving, *The Rate of Interest: Its Nature, Determination, and Relation to Economic Phenomena,* New York: Macmillan, 1907.

Fisher, Lawrence, and James Lorie, *A Half Century of Return on Stocks and Bonds,* Chicago: University of Chicago, 1977.

Fraumeni, Barbara M., and Dale W. Jorgenson, "Rates of Return by Industrial Sector in the United States, 1948–76," *American Economic Review,* May 1980.

Friedman, Benjamin M., "Postwar Changes in the American Financial Markets," in *The American Economy in Transition,* Martin Feldstein, Ed., Cambridge, Mass: National Bureau of Economic Research, 1980; also as NBER Reprint No 150.

————, "Price Inflation, Portfolio Choice, and Nominal Interest Rates," *The American Economic Review,* March 1980.

Friedman, Milton and Rose D., "The Anatomy of Crisis," *The Journal of Portfolio Management,* Fall 1979.

Fuller, Russell J., and Glenn H. Petry, "Inflation Return on Equity, and Stock Prices," *The Journal of Portfolio Management,* Summer 1981.

Gray, William S., III, "Developing a Long-Term Outlook for the U.S. Economy and Stock Market," *Financial Analysts Journal,* July/August 1979.

Holland, Daniel, and Stewart Myers, "Trends in Corporate Profitability and Capital Costs," Working paper, Sloan School of Management, Massachusetts Institute of Technology, October 1977.

Ibbotson, Roger G., and Carol Fall, "The United States Market Wealth Portfolio," *The Journal of Portfolio Management,* Fall 1979.

——, **and Rex A. Sinquefield,** *Stocks, Bonds, Bills and Inflation: The Past and the Future,* Charlottesville, Va.: Financial Analysts Research Foundation, 1982.

Jones, David S., "Expected Inflation and Equity Prices: A Structural Econometric Approach," National Bureau of Economic Research, Working Paper No. 542, September 1980.

Keran, Michael W., "Bond Market in Turmoil," *Weekly Letter,* Federal Reserve Bank of San Francisco, June 5, 1981.

——, "Inflation, Regulation, and Utility Stock Prices," *The Bell Journal of Economics* 7, Spring 1976.

——, "Forecasting Stock Prices," *The Journal of Portfolio Management,* Winter 1975.

Keynes, John Maynard, "The General Theory of Employment," *Quarterly Journal of Economics* 51, February 1937.

Kurz, Mordecai, "A Strategic Theory of Inflation," National Bureau of Economic Research, Working Paper No. 379, August 1979.

Leuthold, Steven C., *The Myths of Inflation and Investing,* Chicago: Crain Books, 1980.

Levine, David A., and Neal Kaplan, *Interest Rates and Inflation,* New York: Sanford C. Bernstein & Co., Inc., 1981.

Linter, John, "Inflation and Security Returns," *The Journal of Finance,* May 1975.

——, "Inflation and Common Stock Prices in a Cyclical Context," in *Annual Report,* Cambridge, Mass.: National Bureau of Economic Research, 1973.

Long Term Economic Growth: 1860–1970, Washington, D.C.: U.S. Department of Commerce, 1973.

Lovell, Michael, "The Profit Picture: Trends and Cycles," *Brookings Papers on Economic Activity,* 3:1978.

Mishkin, Frederic S., "The Real Interest Rate: An Empirical Investigation," National Bureau of Economic Research, Working Paper No. 622, January 1981.

Modigliani, Franco, and Richard A. Cohn, "Inflation, Rational Valuation, and the Market," *Financial Analysts Journal,* March/April 1979.

Molodovsky, Nicholas, *Investment Values in a Dynamic World,* Robert D. Milne, Ed., Homewood, Ill.: Richard D. Irwin, Inc., 1974.

Moore, Basil, "Equity Values and Inflation: The Importance of Dividends," *Lloyds Bank Review,* July 1980.

Moscowitz, Arnold, "Beyond the Monetarist Mind-Set: 'Keep Profits,' " *The Journal of Portfolio Management,* Winter 1976.

——, **and George A. Harben,** "Keep Profits: The True Discount Factor," *The Journal of Portfolio Management,* Summer 1978.

Musgrave, John C., "Fixed Capital Stock in the United States: Revised Estimates," *Survey of Current Business,* January 1981.

Paulus, John D., "Have Bond Rates Overshot?" *Financial Market Perspectives,* New York: Goldman Sachs & Co., March 1980.

Reilly, Frank K., "How to Use Common Stocks as an Inflation Hedge," *The Journal of Portfolio Management,* Summer 1975.

———, **and Edward A. Dyl,** "Inflation and Portfolio Management: Be Nimble!" *The Journal of Portfolio Management,* Spring 1976.

Rippe, Richard D., "Corporate Profitability in the United States: Some Perspectives," New York: Dean Witter Reynolds, December 1980.

Roulac, Stephen E., and Donald A. King, Jr., "Institutional Strategies for Real Estate Investment," *The Journal of Portfolio Management,* Summer 1977.

Security Price Index Record, New York: Standard & Poor's Corp., annually.

Shiller, Robert J., "The Use of Volatility Measures in Assessing Market Efficiency," *The Journal of Finance,* 1981.

Summers, Lawrence H., "Taxation and Corporate Investment: A q-Theory Approach," *Brookings Papers on Economic Activity,* 1:1981a.

———, "The Non-Adjustment of Nominal Interest Rates: A Study of the Fisher Effect," Paper presented to Arthur Okun Memorial Conference, Columbia University, New York, September 25, 1981b.

Webb, James R., and C. F. Sirmans, "Yields and Risk Measures for Real Estate, 1966–77," *The Journal of Portfolio Management,* Fall 1980.

CHAPTER 7

Sector and Individual Asset Expectations: The Micro Factors

William A. Cornish, C.F.A.

In Chapter 6 Peter Bernstein developed the thesis that asset values change only in response to unexpected events. Further, he submits that expectations built into current market prices can be quantified, and he sets forth six ways to measure this. From the vantage point of micro analysis, it is critical to make explicit the key assumptions behind current expectations indicated by relative values, test the assumptions as to their validity, and monitor events for changes that have the potential of impacting the assumptions. The application of this process, utilizing proper disciplines and systems, offers (though it does not guarantee) the opportunity for above-average portfolio performance.

The purpose of this chapter is to provide an analytical framework to identify the interrelated influences of political, social, and economic dynamics on the capital markets in general and individual sectors and securities in particular. The objective is to focus on how these forces have caused changes in the past and may cause changes in the future. Forecasts in this chapter may differ from those in Chapter 6, but such differences of opinion are characteristic of the market and add realism for the reader. The inescapable fact is that the purchase, retention, or sale of even a single security implies a judgment of the future; and the current market price usually reflects a consensus view. The latter is the major underpinning of the efficient

The author wishes to acknowledge the invaluable assistance of Donald Hahn, C.F.A., Donald Guy, C.F.A., and Robert Marks. Don Hahn provided invaluable insights as to historical market, political, and economic trends. Don Guy provided general counsel as well as critical support, and Robert Marks provided economic counseling.

market theory. Even before the theory's evolution, investment professionals recognized the inherent difficulties of outguessing the market. Nevertheless, there is a strong belief that certain individual investors can outperform the market through superior timing and, more importantly, security selection, both by shifting proportions between stocks and bonds and by choosing individual securities. This is felt to be true particularly with respect to smaller portfolios.

Finally, although the approach taken in this chapter is an analysis of the more micro economic, political, and social factors that influence the securities markets, it is made from the perspective of the portfolio manager attempting to build efficient portfolios. That is, while any number of other books on security analysis that have the perspective of the investment analyst can be consulted, the intention here is to examine the view of micro factors taken by the portfolio manager.

EXPECTATIONAL ANALYSIS

Expectational analysis is built on the presumption that market price relationships can be "used" and thus become the starting point to achieve above-average returns given some desired level of risk. The theory is that the current price of any security reflects *conventional wisdom,* or what the average participant in the marketplace feels is the correct forecast. The purpose of expectational analysis is to judge whether conventional wisdom is reasonable, both on an absolute and a relative basis. All valuations are assumed to be linked together.

One way to measure the relationship between the bond and stock markets is to calculate the difference between U.S. Treasury bond yields and "the rate of return implicit in equities" (dividend yield plus the *internal growth rate,* which is equal to the retention rate times the return on equity).[1] Significantly, in most time frames the relationship provides critical insights. One question to be resolved is whether the spread is too large, just about right, or too small in view of the future as perceived by the individual portfolio manager. An additional question is which of the asset classes is out of line (i.e., either over- or under-valued).

The primary tools of expectational measurement for equities are relative price/earnings ratios and yields that lead to judgments about expected returns, standard deviations, and coefficients of correlation. These provide a way to judge whether conventional wisdom is reasonable in light of ensuing independent forecasts of expected returns and risks.

While the absolute value of variables such as price/earnings ratios is, of

---

[1] This is a key measure of earnings growth for equities, since the more earnings are retained—rather than paid out in dividends—and the higher the rate earned on those retentions, the stronger the rate at which earnings will compound into the future. It should be noted that there are times at both peaks and troughs of business cycles when these relationships become distorted and adjustments must be made.

course, important, the primary emphasis in this chapter will be on the *relative values* of such variables. The reason: only when the analyst considers price/earnings ratios (P/Es) relative to some benchmark do they really become meaningful. This relative analysis can be done in two basic ways. One is a time series analysis where the P/E on a stock is compared to its average P/E over some relevant past period. The other, and more frequently encountered way, is a cross-sectional analysis where the stock's P/E is compared to P/Es on other stocks in the same industry or economic sector or to the P/E on a stock market benchmark or reference portfolio such as the Standard & Poor's 500 Stock Composite Index.

This chapter begins with a discussion of expectational analysis as it has applied historically to equities. Then, the framework for expectational analysis is developed for both equities and fixed income securities.

An Historical Perspective

The massaging of the post–World War II capital market history indicates that relative valuations are premised upon some widely held perceptions. Inevitably, the consensus on which these valuations are built breaks down due to significant change either at the macro, sector, industry, or company level followed by the emergence of a new consensus.

Further, analytical techniques are frequently perfected in relationship to the past consensus much as generals seem to be preparing for the last war. For example, the popularity of tables "proving" that the higher the growth rate of earnings and/or dividends the greater the appreciation potential of the equity increased during the 1950s and early 1960s. The sophistication of these tables—initially rather simple—increased and the number of approaches based on the theory grew as multiples soared. The theory is mathematically indisputable provided there are either no changes or only increases in price/earnings multiples from year to year.

In taking a look at history, clearly the 1950s and early 1960s were a period of rising valuations, one in which selling equities—because multiples became too high—often turned out to be a mistake. The conclusion was frequently reached that a stock selling at 40 times earnings with no dividend but a 20 percent growth rate was a more attractive investment than one selling under 10 times earnings, yielding over 5 percent but with only a 10 percent growth rate.

Unfortunately for the believers, this approach failed to provide consolation when growth rates declined and, along with it, the multiples which investors were willing to pay. That is, this approach provided no help when investor attitudes changed toward the general level of the market and the premium to be paid for growth stocks disappeared. What was last year's bargain became this year's overpriced stock.[2]

---

[2] Actually, even if investors' growth expectations had been valid, future returns on these stocks likely would not have been superior because growth was fully impounded in their current price.

APPROACH TO HISTORICAL EXAMPLES

This section illustrates how economic, social, and political factors caused major differences in relative equity valuation levels during selected postwar periods and how the consensus unraveled with subsequent shifts in relative valuations. The periods selected were chosen to show how and why changes have occurred, not to provide a complete history of postwar capital markets. The intent has been to recreate how the average or consensus market participant viewed the market.

One should also keep in mind that summarizing leads to broad generalizations and tends to ignore exceptions. Thus, other observers may see these periods in a somewhat different light and may not agree with this author's conclusions. This should in fact be the case, because not all investors should be snared by the same spider's web of consensus. With this caveat, the author intends to show that expectational forces can be identified, are subject to change, and are the most dynamic set of forces operating in the portfolio decision-making process.

Expectational Changes in Selected Postwar Periods

For the periods selected, the economic conditions, political and social attitudes, market postures, and relative valuations are summarized, as well as the factors that changed the consensus. For purposes of this discussion, sectors will be defined as follows.

Economic Sectors. Included here are such familiar categories as consumer nondurables, consumer durables, intermediate goods, industrial expendables, capital goods, services, defense products and specific industry groupings such as energy, electronics, paper, and so forth.

Conceptual Sectors. This approach links together established growth stocks, emerging growth stocks, large capitalization companies, newly public companies, basic or cyclical industry groups (consisting of autos, steel, and the like), and stable or defensive industries such as foods, utilities, and so on. Other conceptual schemes involve classification by "investment" quality or risk, such as beta or systematic risk groupings. These are often terms that catch the portfolio manager's fancy, and we would expect new ones to be invented in future years.

Over time, the popularity of sectors shifts, and often the change is dramatic. The time periods selected by the author were chosen in part to dramatize such change. To provide a frame of reference, Table 7-1 (see pages 214 and 215) provides a history of the Standard & Poor's 500 Stock Composite Index for the period 1929–81.

The 1958–61 Period

Economic Conditions. These years were ones of general prosperity following a decade of recovery and expansion after World War II. The period began with a recovery from a mild recession (officially beginning in 1957 and ending in 1958). Proper and prompt applications of fiscal and monetary policy were given credit for the snap back, and there was confidence that the United States could control its economic destiny. Inflation was low, averaging $1\frac{1}{2}$ percent, and viewed as not much of a problem. Nevertheless, the overall rate of growth was moderate, with real Gross National Product increasing at an average rate of $2\frac{1}{2}$ percent. Expansion of corporate profits was also moderate, averaging 6 percent annually. The sluggishness of the recovery was regarded in some quarters as a problem caused in part by restrictive monetary policy.[3]

Political and Social Attitudes. The Eisenhower years were characterized by tranquility at home and recognition abroad that the United States was the dominant world power. While there were stirrings of labor unrest and racial problems were on the rise, most citizens were busy enjoying prosperity. Confidence was strong in government and other institutions and, most importantly, in the future economic prospects of the United States.

Market Attitudes. Economic prosperity and favorable political climate led to a growing belief in equity investments. At the beginning of the postwar period, there was great concern over the possibility of another deep depression, but confidence increased as each test of the economy's resilience was passed. Further, those who had purchased equities found them to be a quite profitable investment. From 1946 through 1961 the S&P 500 rose 312 percent, and from 1957 through 1961 the increase was 53 percent. Institutional investors began to increase their equity exposure, initially to obtain income (in 1946, stocks, as measured by the S&P 500, yielded $4\frac{1}{2}$ percent and U.S. Treasury bonds 1 percent) but later to obtain appreciation. There was growing talk of a "shortage of stocks" as the rising level of institutional interest was recognized and investors became aware of the growth of pension funds.

Relative Values. All of these factors had a major impact on stock market valuations—both absolute and relative. The price/earnings ratio on the S&P 500 rose from a mean of 9.5 times ($9.5\times$) earnings in 1947 to $17\times$ earnings in 1959. More impressive was the wide spread between P/E ratios of stocks perceived by investors to be growth stocks and those in other categories. As to economic sectors, noncyclicals commanded a premium over cyclicals. Consequently, by 1961 such companies as Xerox and Control Data sold at over $100\times$ current earnings or more than five times the average market

---

[3] Because of a desire to minimize the complexities of monetary policy and its influences, elaboration in this area will be foreshortened.

TABLE 7-1. Standard & Poor's 500 Stock Composite Index

Year	MARKET				Earnings	Dividend	YIELD			P/E MULTIPLE		
	High	Low	Close	Yearly Change			High	Low	Close	High	Low	Close
1929	31.92	17.66	21.45	-11.9%	$ 1.61	$ .97	4.90%	2.88%	4.56%	19.8×	11.0×	13.3×
1930	25.92	14.44	15.34	-28.5	.97	.98	5.78	3.69	5.69	26.7	14.9	15.8
1931	18.17	7.72	8.12	-47.1	.61	.82	9.17	4.87	8.86	29.8	12.7	13.3
1932	9.31	4.40	6.89	-15.1	.41	.50	11.21	4.45	7.43	22.7	10.7	16.8
1933	12.20	5.53	10.10	46.6	.44	.44	6.67	2.83	3.66	27.7	12.6	23.0
1934	11.82	8.36	9.50	-5.9	.49	.45	4.33	3.03	4.33	24.1	17.1	19.4
1935	13.46	8.06	13.43	41.4	.76	.47	4.59	3.20	3.37	17.7	10.6	17.7
1936	17.69	13.40	17.18	27.9	1.02	.72	4.41	3.06	4.40	17.3	13.1	16.8
1937	18.68	10.17	10.55	-38.6	1.13	.80	8.45	3.36	8.45	16.5	9.0	9.3
1938	13.79	8.50	13.21	25.2	.64	.51	8.19	3.45	3.45	21.5	13.3	20.6
1939	13.23	10.18	12.49	-5.5	.90	.62	4.60	3.32	4.60	14.7	11.3	13.8
1940	12.77	8.99	10.58	-15.3	1.05	.67	6.56	4.43	6.37	12.2	8.6	10.1
1941	10.86	8.37	8.69	-17.9	1.16	.71	8.53	6.24	8.12	9.4	7.2	7.5
1942	9.77	7.47	9.77	12.4	1.03	.59	8.69	5.70	5.70	9.5	7.3	9.5
1943	12.64	9.84	11.67	19.4	.94	.61	5.63	4.45	5.06	13.4	10.5	12.4
1944	13.29	11.56	13.28	29.5	.93	.64	5.11	4.61	4.79	14.3	12.4	14.3
1945	17.68	13.21	17.36	30.7	.96	.66	4.69	3.69	3.69	18.4	13.8	18.1
1946	19.25	14.12	15.30	-11.9	1.06	.71	4.64	3.39	4.45	18.2	13.3	14.4
1947	16.20	13.71	15.30	—	1.61	.84	5.62	4.26	5.52	10.1	8.5	9.5
1948	17.06	13.84	15.20	-0.7	2.29	.93	6.27	4.85	6.22	7.4	6.0	6.6
1949	16.79	13.55	16.76	10.3	2.32	1.14	7.15	6.14	6.73	7.2	5.8	7.2
1950	20.43	16.65	20.41	21.8	2.84	1.47	7.35	6.03	7.11	7.2	5.9	7.2
1951	23.85	20.69	23.77	16.5	2.44	1.41	6.46	5.68	5.97	9.8	8.5	9.7
1952	26.59	23.09	26.57	11.8	2.40	1.41	6.13	5.37	5.37	11.1	9.6	11.1
1953	26.66	22.71	24.81	6.6	2.51	1.45	6.23	5.41	5.86	10.6	9.0	9.9

1954	35.98	24.80	35.98	45.0	2.77	1.54	5.78	4.32	4.32	13.0	9.0	13.0
1955	46.41	34.58	45.48	26.4	3.62	1.64	4.44	3.64	4.13	12.8	9.6	12.6
1956	49.74	43.11	46.67	2.6	3.41	1.74	4.41	3.83	4.20	14.6	12.6	13.7
1957	49.13	38.98	39.99	−14.3	3.37	1.79	4.75	3.91	4.66	14.6	11.6	11.9
1958	55.21	40.33	55.21	38.1	2.89	1.75	4.52	3.24	3.24	19.1	14.0	19.1
1959	60.71	53.58	59.89	8.5	3.39	1.83	3.35	3.07	3.16	17.9	15.8	17.7
1960	60.39	52.30	58.11	−3.0	3.27	1.95	3.69	3.15	3.35	18.5	15.6	17.8
1961	72.64	57.57	71.55	23.1	3.19	2.02	3.33	2.81	2.86	22.8	18.0	22.4
1962	71.13	52.32	63.10	−11.8	3.67	2.13	3.97	2.88	3.38	19.4	14.3	17.2
1963	75.02	62.69	75.02	18.9	4.02	2.28	3.41	3.02	3.11	18.7	15.6	18.7
1964	86.28	75.43	84.75	13.0	4.55	2.50	3.08	2.94	3.03	19.0	16.6	18.6
1965	92.63	81.60	92.43	9.1	5.19	2.72	3.11	2.88	3.04	17.8	15.7	17.8
1966	94.06	73.20	80.33	−13.1	5.55	2.87	3.89	3.01	3.64	16.9	13.2	14.5
1967	97.59	80.38	96.47	20.1	5.33	2.92	3.65	3.03	3.06	18.3	15.1	18.1
1968	108.40	87.72	103.86	7.7	5.76	3.07	3.36	2.87	2.99	18.8	15.2	18.0
1969	106.20	89.20	92.06	−11.4	5.78	3.16	3.59	2.98	3.48	18.4	15.4	15.9
1970	93.46	69.29	92.15	0.1	5.13	3.14	4.35	3.36	3.36	18.2	13.5	18.0
1971	104.80	90.16	102.09	10.8	5.70	3.07	3.39	2.95	2.99	18.4	15.8	17.9
1972	119.10	101.70	118.05	15.6	6.42	3.15	2.99	2.67	2.71	18.6	15.8	18.4
1973	120.20	92.16	97.55	−17.4	8.16	3.38	3.77	2.65	3.64	14.7	11.3	12.0
1974	99.80	62.28	68.56	−29.7	8.89	3.60	5.87	3.56	5.37	11.2	7.0	7.7
1975	95.61	70.04	90.19	31.5	7.96	3.68	5.25	3.92	4.08	12.0	8.8	10.1
1976	107.80	90.90	107.46	19.1	9.91	4.05	4.12	3.57	3.87	10.9	9.2	10.8
1977	107.00	90.71	95.10	−11.5	10.89	4.67	5.17	3.93	5.08	9.8	8.3	8.7
1978	106.99	86.90	96.11	1.1	12.33	5.07	5.83	4.74	5.28	8.7	7.0	7.8
1979	111.27	96.13	107.94	12.3	14.86	5.65	5.88	5.08	5.23	7.5	6.5	7.3
1980	140.52	98.22	135.76	25.8	14.82	6.16	6.27	4.38	4.54	9.5	6.6	9.2
1981	138.12	112.77	122.55	−9.7	15.26	6.63	5.88	4.80	5.41	9.0	7.4	8.0

SOURCE: Duff & Phelps, Inc.; data provided by Standard & Poor's Corporation.

multiple of about 18.5×, which itself represented a postwar peak. Certain "growth" utilities, such as Texas Utilities, had multiples of almost 30×, while cyclicals such as U.S. Steel commanded a market multiple of approximately 20× earnings. Clearly, there was confidence in the future, confidence in the concept of growth, and confidence in higher quality companies.

Consensus Breaker. Frequently a single event will set in motion a change in relative market valuations that by hindsight was overdue. Such an event causes the investment community to refocus its analysis and a new consensus emerges.

In the fall of 1960 that event occurred: John Kennedy defeated Richard Nixon by a slim margin and was inaugurated as President in January 1961. His principal campaign pledges were "To get America moving again," and "To close the missile gap." By the spring of 1961, the new President and the steel industry had had a bitter confrontation over steel price increases, precipitating a sharp decline in stock market prices. The S&P 500 fell 21 percent from its high of 72.64 to its low of 57.57 for the year. This forced a major reappraisal by investors of the government's attitude toward business in general and toward various industries in particular. The end result with respect to relative valuation of the growth stocks, as shown in Table 7-2, was startling.

As the table shows, there was a sharp narrowing of the sizable gap between selected examples of high growth, stable low growth, and basic industries stocks. Thus IBM, the classic growth stock, saw its relative multiple decline from three times the market multiple at the 1960 peak to two times at year-end 1962, and Xerox from six times to 2½ times. U.S. Steel's relative multiple showed only a moderate decline from the 1960 peak to 1962 year-end. This revaluation seemingly corresponded to economic reality. That is, in the 1958–61 period the expansion of corporate profits was slow and companies experiencing earnings gains sold at a premium.

More importantly, despite the concern about Kennedy's attitude toward business, the fact was that the new administration embarked on stimulative fiscal and monetary policies that benefited basic industries. The result was a rapid expansion of profits. From 1960 through the year 1966, the peak prior to the next recession, earnings growth for the S&P 500 averaged 9½ percent annually compared with only 3 percent in the 1958–60 period. In sum, concern with dividend yields, balance sheets, and book values diminished and growth of earnings and dividends became the primary justification for owning equity securities. Real growth translated into nominal growth and made equities a highly attractive investment vehicle.

The 1966–69 Period

Economic Conditions. Similar to the 1958–61 time span, this was a period of moderate growth in economic activity. However, some of the growth

TABLE 7-2. **Changes in P/E Ratios for Selected Stocks**

Conceptual Classification	P/E Peak 1960	P/E Low 1961	P/E 1962 Year-End	P/E 1963 Year-End
High Growth				
IBM				
Actual	54×	42×	35.5×	39×
Relative to S&P 500	2.92	2.33	2.06	2.09
Xerox				
Actual	115×	50×	44×	75×
Relative to S&P 500	6.22	2.78	2.56	4.01
Stable Low Growth				
General Foods				
Actual	28×	24×	25×	27×
Relative to S&P 500	1.51	1.33	1.45	1.44
Texas Utilities				
Actual	28×	27.5×	28×	28×
Relative to S&P 500	1.51	1.53	1.63	1.50
Basic Industries				
U.S. Steel				
Actual	20×	25×	17×	16×
Relative to S&P 500	1.08	1.39	0.99	0.86
Whirlpool				
Actual	14×	13×	10.5×	13.5×
Relative to S&P 500	0.76	0.72	0.61	0.72

SOURCE: Duff & Phelps, Inc.

was stimulated by the Vietnam war, as the Johnson administration persisted with a policy of "guns and butter." Negatively, both inflation and interest rates began to rise noticeably. Specifically, the GNP deflator rose an average of 5 percent annually from 1966 to 1969, while the yield to maturity on long U.S. Treasury bonds increased from $4\frac{1}{2}$ percent to 6 percent.

More significantly, the advance in corporate profits slowed dramatically. For example, earnings on the S&P 500 between 1966 and 1969 rose by an average of only $1\frac{1}{2}$ percent annually. By contrast, the average annual growth of S&P 500 earnings from 1962 through 1966 was 11 percent. As a result, business became increasingly concerned about its ability to sustain profitability.

Political and Social Attitudes. Social tensions, caused by the pressures of the Vietnam war, racial problems, and the maturation of post–World War II babies, began to rise. The result was increasing skepticism in many quarters about the ability of our institutions to cope with changing circumstances and with a growing division in society, such as the "generation gap," which was receiving much popular attention.

Market Attitudes. The stock market mirrored the change in economic conditions and attitudes. There was a serious questioning of the old approaches to value; many blue-chip stocks faltered as earnings growth became hard to achieve.

By contrast, the new and exciting dominated the scene as speculative "story" stocks—stocks whose issuers had a semiunique story to tell about their products and services—such as Kentucky Fried Chicken and Polaroid's instant photography became popular. Recommenders pointed to sizable (and neverending) projections of high earnings growth. Fundamentals, including attention to conservative accounting, were often ignored. In fact, a breed of portfolio managers called "gunslingers" appeared on Wall Street. These portfolio managers vigorously condemned what they termed outmoded fundamentals. These super stars purchased the story stocks and conveyed the belief that a new era of unending appreciation for these stocks had arrived.

By contrast, the rest of the market was considered dull and unrewarding. In fact, the general market averages showed little progress from the 1966 to the 1968–69 peak. For example, the high of 995.15 for the Dow Jones Industrial Average in 1966 was not topped by the 1968 high of 985.21. The more broadly based S&P 500 did reach a new high of 108.40 in 1968, but this was only modestly above its 1966 high of 94.06. Clearly this was an era when the concepts dominated the fundamentals.

Relative Values. Price/earnings ratios for the market averages remained in a relatively narrow band, with the annual high P/E on the S&P 500 in a 17–18× range and the low ranging between 13× and 15×. As to market favorites, growth stocks such as office equipment, drugs, and electronics improved their relative valuations from the 1965–66 period, but the spread between P/Es was narrower than in 1958–59. The most spectacular changes were in the smaller companies and the fledgling conglomerates that pyramided their earnings through acquisition. Further, the franchise stocks, like Holiday Inns and McDonald's, and newer computer companies, such as Memorex and Telex, had a meteoric increase in market value. At its peak in 1969 Memorex sold at 94× earnings and Telex at 167×.

Consensus Breakers. Even before the 1969 downturn, chinks appeared in the seemingly invincible armor of story conglomerates.

Litton Industries' announcement of a decline in quarterly earnings in mid-1967 was a harbinger of coming developments. Earnings weakness developed in many of the speculative favorites, and the accounting practices of some were discredited. Some selected graphic examples of the change in market valuation are shown in Table 7-3.

TABLE 7-3. The Collapse of the Story Stocks

	1968–69 Market Price High	1969–70 Market Price Low	Peak 1968–69 P/E Ratio	Percent Change in Price 1968–69 High to 1969–70 Low	Percent Change Net Per Share 1968–69 Earnings Peak to 1970–71 Low
Story Stocks					
National Student Marketing	$ 71½	$ 1	94×	−99%	−87%
Telex	112	9	164	−92	−70
Four Seasons Nursing Centers of America	102	½	170	−99	a
Memorex	174	44½	94	−74	a
Viatron Computer Systems	58½	1	b	−98	b
Equity Funding	81½	13	62	−84	+58
Litton Industries	105	15	57	−86	−20
University Computing	187	13	119	−93	a
Blue Chip Growth Companies					
International Business Machines	375	219	49	−42	+16
Hewlett-Packard	57	19½	57	−66	+8
Merck & Company	115	73½	40	−36	+11

SOURCE: Duff & Phelps, Inc.
a Extremely large percentage number.
b Calculation not meaningful due to deficit earnings.

One result of the discrediting of the story stocks was a change in the leadership of the next market advance in 1971–72. Large capitalization companies with strong finances, conservative accounting, and excellent management became the "one decision" stocks of the early 1970s (those that you bought once and never sold), and the leaders of this group were the so-called "nifty fifty." This phenomenon clearly was a reaction to the story stocks but, as with the latter, was carried to excess with a subsequent painful decline in prices of the "nifty fifty" from vastly overvalued levels.

The Period from 1974 to the Present (1982)

Economic Conditions. The recent period has been one of massive readjustment caused by increased energy costs and expanding concern about the possible limitations of U.S. economic growth. From early 1975, economic activity grew steadily until 1978, plateaued between 1978 and 1980, and only in early 1980 did a recession commence. However, higher energy costs and stimulative fiscal and monetary policies resulted in rapidly accelerating inflation and interest rates, with both reaching record double-digit levels. One result was that real (inflation-adjusted) personal income made only marginal progress at best after 1978, halting a relatively steady pattern (except during recessions) of postwar wealth expansion. In general, consumers moderated their expectations and lifestyles to cope with these adverse economic trends.

For the most part, U.S. business displayed an increasing ability to pass inflation through the income statement. At the outset of this period, many business managers were slow to react to inflation because their previous experience had been in periods when price adjustments were difficult to make and maintain. Indeed, certain industries continued to suffer, especially those with low unit growth and limited pricing flexibility due to excess capacity (for example, the tire industry). Nevertheless, strategic adjustments were made by business in general, and the period proved to be one of strong nominal earnings growth. From 1974 (the previous cyclical peak) through 1980, earnings on the S&P 500 experienced a $9\frac{1}{2}$ percent average annual growth rate.

Political and Social Attitudes. These were turbulent years with not only a weakening of the U.S. position internationally, but a degree of internal political instability as well. In the seven years 1975–82, there were four different Presidents. One President was forced from office; two failed to win reelection. The current incumbent, President Reagan, seems dedicated to fiscal and monetary policies aimed at reversing trends set in motion during the New Deal in the 1930s. Clearly, there was concern in 1982 about the effectiveness of the U.S. political system and a lingering uncertainty about the future.

Market Attitudes. During these years market attention shifted as the environment was perceived to change. Emerging from the 1974 recession, the favorites proved to be the "shortage stocks." This conceptual category was identified as the cyclically sensitive steels, copper, and paper, where sizable commodity shortages led to price increases which in turn led to large earnings increases. Subsequently, attention turned to the so-called Bet Against America issues, namely energy and aerospace. Energy issue earnings benefited from a second round of extraordinary energy price increases in 1979, at the expense of causing price inflation in every other sector (often in spite of declining unit production). Aerospace issues benefited from the perceived need to strengthen our weak defenses. The year 1980 proved to be particularly challenging for investment managers as relative performance was directly related to the proportion of energy and aerospace equities in their portfolios. Most other groups lagged the market averages.

In addition, time horizons were shortened as confidence waned. In contrast with the buy-and-hold strategies of the late 1950s, and the one-decision stocks of the early 1970s, investors moved rapidly to capitalize on both shifts in attitudes and valuation levels. Long term was defined as the time to the next quarterly earnings report.

Relative Values. Following the economy's recovery from the sharp decline in 1973–74, the general market averages remained in a narrow trading range through early 1982. For example, for the period 1976–80 the S&P 500 traded between a high of 140.52 (1980) and a low of 86.90 (1978), reflecting a sharp contraction in absolute price/earnings ratios. The S&P 500 P/E which had been in a 16–18× range in the early 1970s, declined to 7× in 1974, reached a nadir of 6.5× in 1979, and had only a moderate recovery in 1980.

In addition, the gap between the relative valuation of large, high quality growth companies and the rest of the market narrowed. Whereas in the early 1970s certain of the popular growth companies traded at 2 to 4 times the S&P 500 multiple (and were regarded as cheap at that price), by 1980 it was rare to see such stocks selling at as much as 2 times the market multiple. This narrowing of P/E spreads appeared to reflect: (1) a broad expansion of corporate profits, making earnings gains a common characteristic (rather than the exception as had been the case in the late 1960s); (2) a shortening of time horizons (or, alternatively, a raising of the discount rate and its effect on distantly future profits); and (3) increasingly sophisticated market participants making use of analytical tools such as valuation models. Certainly, the increasing emphasis by institutional investors on controlling risk has had a major influence.

Consensus Breakers. In the author's opinion the major consensus elements during this period were skepticism and a lack of confidence in the future. The goal of the Reagan administration's economic policies was to break the back of inflation by restraining fiscal and monetary growth and encouraging private sector savings and investment. Nevertheless, a key question in mid-1982 was whether the electorate, particularly their representatives in Congress, would accept the short-term consequences of rising unemployment and other problems as these new economic policies attempt to change the course of the massive and complex American economy. The market, in mid-1982, was undecided as to whether the investment environment would get much better (because of recession-caused lower inflation in the short run) or much worse (because of deficit-spending-caused higher inflation in the longer run).

ANALYSIS OF EXPECTATIONAL FACTORS FOR EQUITIES

Over the postwar period, both absolute and relative security valuations have shifted dramatically, and these massive changes have resulted from fundamental adjustments in the political, social, and economic climates. It is certain that these climates will change again. The question is how to develop an analytical framework that takes into account the assumptions behind current valuation levels, and how to monitor for distortions and change so that timely portfolio adjustments can be made through the purchase and sale of individual securities.

The nature of the investment process involves forecasting future rates of return and risk for classes of securities in general, particular industry groups or sectors, or the specific securities of individual companies. There are many ways to do this forecasting, but there is no one formula or series of formulas that assures success. The analyst and portfolio manager must integrate creativity and intuition with tools of the trade such as knowledge of financial analysis, accounting, economics, statistics, and modern portfolio theory.

Indeed, much work has been done on an eclectic basis with flashes of intuitively brilliant conceptual understanding. Certain investors seem more in tune with certain climates than others. This is one reason why some portfolio managers or portfolio management styles do extraordinarily well for a period (often several years) and then seem to lose touch with the marketplace.

But in fact, it has been the author's experience that much that parades as insight is merely reporting the views of others. How often have portfolio managers merely repeated to their clients what their favorite Wall Street seer was saying? How many analysts merely extrapolate past trends indefinitely into the future? This approach is easily marketed but exposes the investor to risks associated with inadequate information and analysis and the instability that characterizes the follow-the-crowd or stay-in-style approach.

The development and utilization of a systematic, organized process of developing and quantifying expectations requires expense, discipline, and diligence, but it offers the promise of continuity and the opportunity to evaluate the consensus rather than being swept along by it.

Top-down vs. Bottom-up Approach

There is much discussion among forecasters as to whether a bottom-up (micro-first) analysis, beginning with the company and then moving to the industry, sector, and the economy, is better than a top-down (or macro-first) analysis that goes from the economy to the sector to the industry and then to the company. The macro-first approach is more widely used for several reasons, not the least of which is efficiency. If the sectors or industries that are likely to do well are identified through macro analysis, then the analytical effort devoted to security selection can be concentrated in those areas.

However, the top-down approach does have two potential shortcomings. First, macro analysis relies heavily on standard government statistics and economic indicators. The quality and interpretation of such data is often suspect, however, particularly at turning points. For example, in early to mid-1973, analysts at one large investment advisory organization began to report that their field work had identified conflicting economic trends that were not evident in current official government statistics. Analysts following the consumer sector reported a slowing in demand, with retailers indicating an overinventoried position. By contrast, field reports from intermediate goods producers such as chemicals reported a boom in progress with earnings estimates moving upward. Clearly, an imbalance that contained the seeds of a future recession was developing, and the firm was able to indicate this to its clients. This was the result of listening to the information being fed back and having greater confidence in timely, personally developed field reports than in what was being reflected in lagged, macro, official government statistics. In this case, the bottom-up approach yielded much more reliable data for the portfolio manager.

Second, there are numerous situations when micro conditions clearly dominate. This is particularly true with respect to innovative companies, where new markets are being created almost without regard for what is happening to the general economy. Genetic engineering companies in 1982 were examples where management skills to cope with the very new technology and find major new markets for their research are the key elements rather than overall business conditions.

Both approaches, top-down and bottom-up, have validity and certainly are not mutually exclusive. Each can and should be used as a cross check upon the other. Nevertheless, it is recognized that much of the total investment environment is governed by macro conditions. Further, the portfolio management process requires macro asset allocation decisions between bonds, stocks, and real estate to construct a portfolio. Thus, the discussion of developing expectations for sectors, industries, and specific equity and bond investments will follow the top-down format. This approach recognizes that investment decision-making processes are varied and time horizons can differ materially. It also recognizes that security price peaks and troughs typically (but not invariably) have preceded turning points in general business activity.

Portfolio managers and analysts can and should develop an analytical framework to measure events, making the necessary adjustments as required by actual or potential changes in the economy and the capital markets. Judgments should be reduced to quantitative terms, thereby allowing cross comparisons. Further, the basic assumptions should be made explicit as outlined below. A specific example of a macro market forecast used by one leading investment firm that specifically employs a dividend discount model approach is shown in the appendix to this chapter.

Macroeconomic Forecast

The first step is a macroeconomic forecast incorporating the long-term outlook, and including the amplitude and timing of cyclical turning points. Preferably, the macroeconomic forecast should be multiscenario with the most probable outcome identified. The forecast should incorporate such usual measures as real GNP growth, the inflation rate, and assumptions about fiscal and monetary policy. The objective is to provide a consistent framework within which to project interest rates as well as earnings and dividend growth for individual companies on a secular basis, with careful attention to the degree of sensitivity to cyclical changes. The major output from the macro projection is the expected average rate of profit and dividend growth for the economy, which then sets the stage for sectoral, industry, and company profit and dividend growth.

Table 7-4 (pages 226 and 227) represents an example of the macro approach, recognizing that others may be more complex or include other indicators found to be more useful. The most recent five-year history has been included for comparative purposes to highlight differences between the two five-year time frames. Among other things, the differences between the past and future expectations reflect changes in the shape of the economy that may impact the economic sectors, the industries therein, and specific companies, thus suggesting a shift in investment perceptions.

The quantification process should provide the projection maker with greater insights as to what the critical variables are. These should be identified and carefully monitored for change. Using the most likely scenario in the projection shown in Table 7-4, the critical variables are (1) a continuation of the recent relatively consistent monetary policies and fiscal policies, including some success in restraining the growth in government spending, and (2) ample supplies of energy over the period or, in general, the absence of serious negative exogenous factors. Both are vital to the quantitative projections of reduced inflation rates (indicated by the GNP deflator) and lower interest rates that should lead to sustained real earnings and dividend growth. These are the elements that should be monitored intensely to transform the projection process into a dynamic, useful tool as opposed to a oneshot exercise. Specifically, if political pressures cause further uncapping of the federal government's purse strings, then these basic quantifications would have to change and the result would be adjustments in interest rates as well as earnings and dividend growth expectations and consequently valuation levels.

Relating the Macro Forecast to Broad Economic Sectors

The second step is to relate the macro forecast to broad economic sectors, using the national income accounts that break down into personal consumption expenditures, gross private domestic investment, net exports, and government purchases of goods and services. The emphasis here should be on estimating the relative outlook for each sector. A major factor to analyze is the difference in the future period compared with the most recent historical period. For example, under the Reagan administration, the intent is to reduce federal government spending as a percent of GNP while increasing nonresidential gross private domestic investment. However, the assumption behind this is that consumers will increase their savings rate rather than increase spending. If consumer spending is increased, then investment may not immediately increase as expected. A critical variable to be monitored has been identified.

Relating Broad Sector Forecast to Specific Industries

The third step is to relate the broad sector forecast to specific industries recognizing that the individual characteristics of the industry will modify the previous macro conclusion. For example, the sectoral analysis may indicate incentives for consumer savings. However, the pent-up consumer demand created during the 1974–82 stagflation may override these incentives, suggesting an above-average but cyclical outlook for consumer durables. The question then becomes one of identifying the relative prospects of specific consumer durable industries on a supply/demand basis. For example, one might conclude that the outlook for the U.S. passenger car industry was restricted by the supply and competitiveness of foreign cars, the implications of high gasoline prices, and continued government regulation. All these factors might adversely impact unit demand and limit price increases to a percentage amount equal to or less than the average of the inflation rate despite the favorable pent-up replacement demand. By contrast, the consumer appliance industry outlook might seem more favorable due to major new products such as energy-efficient washers and a stable replacement cycle for washers and dryers.

Effect of Inflation. In mid-1982 one of the most critical aspects was assessing how an industry responds to varying levels of inflation or possibly even a prolonged period of disinflation. Analysis might result in the conclusion that the passenger car industry, because of excess capacity, could not raise prices as fast as the general inflation rate without restricting aggregate demand and widening the opportunity for imports. Further, reduced demand adversely impacts unit costs since indirect costs are spread over fewer units produced and sold. On the other hand, under conditions of disinflation, unit

TABLE 7-4. Example of a Macroeconomic Forecast (percent change—previous year)

	ACTUAL					FORECAST				
	1977	1978	1979	1980	1981	1982	1983	1984	1985	1986
Gross National Product										
Constant Dollars (Real Growth)										
High						0.0%	3.5%	4.0%	2.5%	4.0%
Most likely	5.5%	4.8%	3.2%	-0.2%	2.0%	-1.2	2.1	2.9	1.1	2.8
Low						-2.5	0.5	1.5	0.0	1.5
GNP Deflator										
High						8.8	8.0	8.5	9.0	7.5
Most likely	5.8	7.3	8.5	9.0	9.2	8.3	6.9	5.6	5.5	5.2
Low						7.5	4.5	4.0	3.5	3.5
Nominal Dollar GNP										
High						8.8	11.8	12.8	11.7	11.8
Most likely	11.6	12.4	12.0	8.8	11.4	6.9	9.1	8.6	6.7	8.1
Low						4.8	6.5	6.1	4.0	5.1
Selected Components of GNP										
Personal Consumption Expenditures										
High						1.3	2.7	3.2	3.4	3.1
Most likely	4.9	4.7	2.9	0.5	2.5	0.5	1.9	2.3	1.7	2.2
Low						-0.5	0.1	1.2	0.4	0.8
Durable Goods										
High						-1.7	6.6	7.9	6.0	5.1
Most likely	9.3	5.7	0.2	-7.4	2.7	-3.9	3.7	5.8	1.4	4.7
Low						-7.5	-0.8	3.1	-0.8	0.8
Nondurable Goods										
High						1.3	1.9	2.1	2.6	2.5
Most likely	3.6	3.5	2.6	1.1	2.4	0.8	1.4	1.6	1.6	1.6
Low						0.2	0	0.8	0.5	0.8
Services										
High						2.1	2.2	2.5	3.1	2.8
Most likely	4.5	5.4	4.1	2.6	2.6	1.7	1.7	1.9	1.9	1.9
Low						1.0	0.4	0.9	0.6	0.9
Gross Private Domestic Investment										
High						-4.7	10.7	9.7	-1.2	8.9
Most likely	15.7	7.6	1.3	-12.5	5.6	-7.9	6.8	7.3	-3.3	6.2
Low						-10.7	4.2	4.5	-4.8	0.5

Nonresidential Fixed										
High						−0.1	4.3	4.7	2.3	3.9
Most likely	11.9	9.1	6.5	−3.0	2.4	−2.3	2.5	3.4	1.5	2.6
Low						−4.4	1.0	1.6	0	1.3
Residential										
High						−9.3	17.1	18.8	0	12.3
Most likely	18.4	3.0	−5.3	−18.6	−6.0	−12.6	8.9	14.0	−4.1	6.4
Low						−15.9	6.6	8.6	−9.1	4.9
Government Purchases	2.1	2.0	1.4	2.9	0.6	0.9	1.2	2.0	1.6	1.9
Corporate Profits: After Tax										
High						1.1	14.0	19.0	12.7	13.8
Most likely	17.1	16.4	19.6	−2.7	−4.8	−2.1	9.9	13.8	2.1	11.9
Low						−8.6	2.1	9.0	−3.2	9.8
Dividends										
High						11.3	11.4	16.0	17.2	8.9
Most likely	6.7	11.8	12.6	11.6	12.7	7.8	7.4	11.0	6.2	7.0
Low						2.2	0	4.3	0.7	5.0
Other Selected Indicators										
Industrial Production Index										
High						−2.5	6.0	6.0	4.0	6.0
Most likely	5.9	5.7	4.4	−3.6	2.7	−3.0	4.1	4.2	−0.6	4.1
Low						−5.5	2.0	1.0	−3.0	2.0
Housing Starts										
High						3.5	33.3	26.7	5.3	22.5
Most likely	29.2	1.7	−13.6	−26.0	−15.9	−1.6	26.2	22.2	−12.1	17.2
Low						−12.5	15.8	13.6	−20.0	12.5
Money Supply (M-2)										
High						9.9	10.0	10.0	9.0	9.0
Most likely	10.9	8.3	8.6	9.5	10.3	9.4	8.7	8.2	7.0	7.5
Low						8.8	7.5	6.5	5.0	6.0
Federal Deficit (billions of dollars)										
High						$100	$130	$145	$150	$150
Most likely	$45	$49	$28	$60	$58	90	100	100	85	60
Low						80	80	80	60	30
Interest Rates (average for year)										
Long Treasury bond yield	7.67%	8.49%	9.29%	11.30%	13.44%	13.25%	12.90%	11.80%	11.60%	10.30%
Profits and Dividends (percent change)										
S&P 500 net per share	9.9%	13.2%	20.5%	−0.3%	3.0%	−4.2%	8.2%	12.3%	−2.0%	9.9%
S&P 500 dividend	15.3	8.6	11.4	9.0	7.6	4.1	5.1	8.3	3.8	4.3

SOURCE: Duff & Phelps, Inc.; data provided by Robert Marks of Siff, Oakley & Marks, Inc.

costs might moderate providing an opportunity to stimulate unit demand and ultimately profits.

By contrast, under favorable conditions an industry such as aluminum, with restrained expansion plans resulting in little excess capacity, might benefit from high inflation rates by being able to raise product prices at a rate in excess of the inflation rate. In a disinflationary environment, competition on a price basis from such substitutable materials as steel or plastics might restrict the ability of the aluminum industry to maintain price and profit levels.

The examples above indicate the importance of considering price elasticity of demand—namely the relationship between price and supply/demand conditions. In an inflationary environment, the most important consideration is the industry's or company's ability to pass through cost increases as higher product prices.[4] Another consideration is the ability and willingness of an industry or company management to adapt to a shift in demand. An immediate reaction to a short-term decline in demand is to consider cost savings through layoffs of employees; on a longer term basis, plant closings, relocations, and modernizations might result. For example, from 1976 to 1981 the tire industry reduced effective capacity by some 20 percent by plant closings. Likewise, as demand dropped, effective steel and auto capacity were shrunk because of plant obsolescence and lack of efficiency. By contrast, higher energy prices—and thus above-average and increasing rates of return on investment—resulted in rapid expansion for the energy exploration and service industries during the same period.

Management Responsiveness. In short, changing economic conditions require responsiveness on the part of the management of an industry. The portfolio manager must be alert to both the change in economic conditions and the responsiveness of corporate management.

The acceleration of inflation has caused numerous changes in outlook and management approaches over the past decade. Different responses will be required if a prolonged period of disinflation occurs. Corporate managers will have to change from demand-oriented price pass-through strategies to a more supply-oriented strategy. From the viewpoint of expectational analysis the task is to develop sets of reasonable assumptions and then test them against future events.

Relating Industry Forecast to Company Analysis

The fourth step in the top-down process is applying the industry assumptions to individual companies. At the outset we recognize that since most companies are diversified both as to products and markets, this complicates the application of sectoral analysis. For illustrative purposes we presume

---

[4] An extensive investigation of these relationships can be found in Estep and Hanson [1981].

that the company can be identified closely enough with an industry so that unit growth relative to real GNP and price improvement relative to the inflation rate can be estimated. This frame of reference identifies an environment for the company that can be further refined by answering a two-part question.

First, is the environment for that company likely to be favorable or unfavorable? If favorable, then even the marginal producers may benefit and may perhaps even show the fastest growth in profits. There is a mathematical reason for this. Assume that the industry conditions permit net margins to improve by two percentage points. The company starting with 2 percent margins and no other source of earnings improvement will double its profits under this assumption; one starting with 8 percent margins will show only a 25 percent gain. Conversely, if the environment is expected to be unfavorable, the competitive strengths of the more profitable company should show forth. In this case the marginal company will most likely disappoint the investor.

The next question concerns the individual company factors that will cause its business to do better or worse than the industry. An excellent discussion of both industry and company factors is contained in the book *Competitive Strategy* by Michael Porter [1980]. Rising market share, more efficient plant, or a cheaper source of raw materials could all result in better-than-average performance. All such factors should be quantified in the form of projections to facilitate cross company comparisons.

The Maytag Example. For illustrative purposes Table 7-5 (pages 230 and 231) outlines elements that should be incorporated in such a forecast for the Maytag Company in early 1982. First, note the inclusion of the record of the past five years for comparative purposes with actual results placed in the most likely category. This is to highlight differences from one five-year period to the next.

Next, for all key variables except the tax rate, the projections are multi-level, including high, most likely, and low. Although the table calls for the identification of unit growth and price change, it is recognized that such information on an historic basis often is not obtainable. Even where it is available the price change number may be influenced by a future change in product mix. If the rate of growth of products with higher unit values is faster than those with lower unit values, then the company's sales growth will exceed its unit growth. Despite the imperfection of the data, the analyst still has the obligation to seek whatever clues are available.

Maytag is an excellent case in point because the company does not disclose unit prices, unit sales, or its market share in washing machines, dryers, or dishwashers. Thus, the analyst must utilize industry data for unit shipments and unit price changes and make adjustments for differences between Maytag's product line and the industry in general. Another important variable, estimates of Maytag's market share, can be obtained from trade sources. In short, the historical figures as to unit shipments and price

TABLE 7-5. Example of Company Projections: The Maytag Company

	ACTUAL					FORECAST				
	1977	1978	1979	1980	1981	1982	1983	1984	1985	1986
Sales Components (percent change)										
Washers										
Unit change										
High	19%	2%	12%	-9%	9%	3%	8%	3%	-4%	8%
Most likely						1	6	2	-6	10
Low						-2	4	1	10	4
Price change										
High	4	-3	1	5	4	1	10	7	0	5
Most likely						0	7	5	-2	4
Low						-2	3	1	-4	2
Dryers (electric/gas combined)										
Unit change										
High	22	-1	14	2	1	6	5	5	-3	6
Most likely						4	3	3	-7	4
Low						-1	1	1	-9	2
Price change										
High	5	-9	5	-4	7	4	8	7	0	6
Most likely						3	6	5	-3	5
Low						-1	4	2	-5	3
Dishwashers										
Unit change										
High	7	6	-2	-28	1	4	14	10	-5	15
Most likely						2	10	8	-10	10
Low						-2	8	6	-12	6
Price change										
High	9	3	7	8	7	8	10	7	4	8
Most likely						6	8	5	2	6
Low						4	5	3	0	4

Revenues										
High	$299.4	$325.0	$369.1	$349.2	$408.6	$440	$515	$580	$560	$660
Most likely						425	470	515	480	505
Low						400	430	445	390	435
Pretax Margins (percent)										
High	21.8%	21.8%	22.6%	18.6%	16.7%	18.0%	19.0%	22.0%	18.0%	22.5%
Most likely						17.5	18.0	21.0	17.0	19.0
Low						16.0	17.0	18.0	16.0	18.0
Effective Tax Rate (percent)	47%	48%	46%	45%	45%	45%	45%	45%	45%	45%
Net Income (millions)										
High	$34.6	$36.8	$45.1	$35.7	$37.5	$43.6	$53.8	$70.2	$55.4	$81.7
Most likely						40.9	46.5	59.5	44.9	52.8
Low						35.2	40.1	44.0	34.3	43.1
Dividends (millions)										
High	$23.4	$24.5	$28.1	$28.0	$28.0	$28.0	$35.0	$45.5	$36.3	$53.0
Most likely						28.0	30.4	39.0	31.7	37.0
Low						28.0	28.0	31.0	31.0	30.4
Retained Earnings (millions)										
High	$11.2	$12.3	$17.0	$7.7	$9.5	$15.6	$18.8	$24.7	$19.1	$28.7
Most likely						12.9	16.1	20.5	13.2	15.8
Low						7.2	12.1	13.0	3.3	12.7
Retained Earnings as Percent of Average Common Equity										
High	8.6%	8.6%	10.9%	4.3%	4.7%	7.2%	8.2%	9.8%	7.1%	9.6%
Most likely						6.1	7.2	8.5	5.2	5.7
Low						3.5	5.5	5.7	1.5	5.2
Average Common Shares Outstanding (millions)										
High	13.4	13.4	13.4	13.3	13.3	13.3	13.2	13.2	13.2	13.2
Per Common Share										
Net Earnings										
High	$2.58	$2.75	$3.37	$2.68	$2.82	$3.30	$4.10	$5.30	$4.20	$6.20
Most likely						3.10	3.50	4.50	3.40	4.00
Low						2.65	3.05	3.35	2.60	3.25
Dividends										
High	$1.75	$1.83	$2.10	$2.10	$2.10	$2.10	$2.65	$3.45	$2.75	$4.00
Most likely						2.10	2.30	2.95	2.40	2.80
Low						2.10	2.10	2.35	2.35	2.30

SOURCE: Duff & Phelps, Inc.

change are estimates based on the best information available and the analyst's interpretation of those data.

Typical of the real world, Maytag presents other complications. First, Maytag acquired the Hardwick Stove Company, with this manufacturer of gas and electric ranges and microwave ovens being included in Maytag's statements on a purchase accounting basis beginning in 1981. Thus, the forward projections include Hardwick. The Maytag analyst built into the projections the potential for ranges and microwave ovens as well as Hardwick's position therein. (These were not set forth separately in the example.) Also, allowance was made for Hardwick's lower margins as compared with Maytag. A second consideration was with respect to internal factors. In 1980 Maytag introduced a new line of washers and dryers—amazingly the first since 1966. The immediate impact was a reduction in profitability due to the costs of such an introduction and the close-out of the old lines at discounted prices. The assumption was that the new line would be successful, resulting in a moderate increase in market share over the next five years. This discussion serves to illustrate the fact that the analyst had to consider both external and internal factors in developing his projections.

Sustainable Internal Growth. Critical insights can be obtained by comparing the expected rate of revenue (or sales) growth to the company's return on equity after deducting dividends (in other words, earnings minus dividends as a percent of average invested capital). As discussed earlier, this measure is called the sustainable internal growth rate, or the rate of earnings plowback. If the revenue growth rate exceeds the plowback, this means any of a combination of three possible developments: (1) the need for additional outside funds which, if they are borrowed funds, will result in greater leverage, (2) better management of internal resources by improving profit margins and asset turnover (and thereby raising profitability measures), and (3) reducing the dividend payout ratio. If the analyst determines that the intent is to hold balance sheet and payout ratios constant, this may point to the sale of additional shares of common stock, which would dilute earnings growth for existing shareholders. In sum, the company's financial needs are also critical to the valuation process.

Spelling Out Assumptions. Obviously, multiindustry companies—companies involved in several widely disparate lines of business—require separate projections for each product category and then a consolidated projection. It is vital that the critical assumptions behind the projections be spelled out and that these be continually monitored, challenged, and changed as necessary. Specifically, for Maytag, the major relevant macro assumptions underlying Table 7-5 are the relative strengths of personal income and spending on consumer durables. Next would be that the importance of laundry equipment to the American public would remain relatively stable. Nevertheless, it is possible that a change in housing patterns or attitudes toward cleanliness or different types of garments might result in more or less usage of the washing machine. Third in importance would be competitive conditions within the industry; a shift here could impact Maytag's market share or pricing policies. The assumption for Maytag is that market share will gradually increase, with most of the increase occurring toward the peak of the appliance cycle (when unit growth begins to slow) and in the downturn. Critical to this assessment is the assumption that Maytag's reputation for superior quality will remain unblemished. This should permit its marketing strength to show forth when industry conditions become difficult. The list of assumptions should contain other relevant items of input to develop comprehensive expectations for the company being analyzed.

VALUATION OF INDIVIDUAL STOCKS

Expectations for sectors, industries, and companies ultimately require a valuation judgment that can be simply stated: Does the current market price properly reflect the forecasted profit expectations and the risk of error in that forecast? This is the most important and frustrating part of the analyst's job because these judgments influence the portfolio manager's asset allocation decisions and ultimately the construction of the investor's portfolio.

While analysts and portfolio managers have their preferences for valuation measures, the two most commonly used techniques are the classic dividend discount approach to valuation and the more pragmatic approaches using price/earnings ratios and asset book values. Inflation has distorted the results of the latter approaches; thus, in recent years the discounted dividend approach has received increased attention. Actually, it is no easier to determine fair values with P/E analysis than with the discounted dividend analysis. Therefore, the two approaches should be viewed as complementary rather than as alternatives. This chapter will focus on P/E ratio-oriented valuation techniques; the chapter appendix and Chapter 10 will discuss dividend discount models.

Continuing through the top-down approach, the analyst is now prepared to utilize the comprehensive set of expectations that have been developed in order to arrive at valuation conclusions for the portfolio managers. Sequentially, the analyst develops his conclusions:

1. By estimating the price/earnings ratios of the universe, the market's relative expectations for each company can be determined. The higher the estimated market P/E, assuming normal earnings levels (i.e., eliminating distorting nonrecurring factors or cyclical peaks and troughs), the better the expected business prospects and the higher the expected return for individual stocks. Other elements are the volatility expectations for earnings and the confidence factors in the projections.
2. The relationship between past growth, volatility of earnings and dividends, and current valuations can be determined. For most

companies there is a positive, though not perfect, relationship between past performance and future earnings expectations. This observation ties into the efficient market hypothesis. Nevertheless, the past is not necessarily prologue to the future, and it is important to note that the market heavily discounts the obvious at any given point in time.

3. Next, the differences between future growth and volatility expectations and past results may be determined. Where major change is properly anticipated, there frequently is opportunity for better-than-average returns, particularly if market valuations are more reflective of the past.

Analysis of Conceptual Sectors

At this point, the problem of dealing with the conceptual sector must be broached. This is a very difficult problem, although certain clichés that have heavily influenced past markets are widely accepted. A definite need exists to contrast the existing level of a stock's valuation expectations (as revealed by relative P/E ratios and other measures) with expected levels of earnings and dividends as developed by the analyst.

Two recent examples pertain to individual stocks. The first is the conceptual analysis of Squibb's potential from a breakthrough drug called Capoten. Glowing institutional research reports, many describing in great detail (including a host of polysyllabic words) how the drug worked, supported this analysis. The result was that Squibb sold at a premium relative to earnings, reaching a peak relationship of 2 times the S&P 500 P/E average in 1979 versus an average of 1.3 times over the four preceding years. Nevertheless, earnings failed to expand. Squibb's earnings per share reached an all-time high of $2.60 in 1978, remained in that area in 1979–80, and then in 1981 declined to $1.83 before unusual items.[5] The price of the stock fell dramatically; by early 1982 it was some 40 percent under the 1979 high. While in 1982 the new drug was still regarded as having good potential, the concept clearly had outrun the realized earnings for a number of years. Further, questions continue to be raised about the potential of Squibb's core product line.

A second recent example of shifting conceptual views is that of the aerospace industry in general and General Dynamics in particular. In the mid-1970s, government policy was implemented to reduce funding for defense as a percent of Gross National Product. Beyond that negative factor, General Dynamics had specific problems, including a dispute with the U.S. Navy concerning its participation in the nuclear submarine program and a large potential liability with its participation in the liquid natural gas (LNG) tanker shipbuilding program. New management was brought into General

[5] Earnings figures used in these examples are adjusted figures based on Duff & Phelps analyses.

Dynamics and earnings began to improve beginning in 1975. Nevertheless, the stock remained in a \$9–\$13 share price trading range through 1977. The conceptual climate changed as the Navy made adjustments with respect to the submarine program and General Dynamics's LNG tanker exposure began to resolve itself. Finally, the aerospace common stock group came into favor with investors. The result was that General Dynamics common, at \$9 by 1977 year-end, rose 75 percent in 1978 and by 1980 reached a high of \$45 or five times the 1977 close. The combination of sharply improving earnings and a changing conceptual environment was the cause. Earnings per share about doubled from 1977 through 1980 and the P/E ratio relative to the market increased from 0.6 times in 1977 to 1.3 times in 1980.

These examples show that it is difficult to put the analyst or portfolio manager in a room completely devoid of the conceptual environment for his or her decision making. That is, quantitative projections are often influenced by very qualitative and imprecise common wisdom rampant in the marketplace. Nevertheless, the discipline of contrasting levels of valuation expectations with levels of earnings expectations provides valuable insights despite its being performed in a less than ideal environment. Distortions become readily apparent in both positive and negative directions and provide opportunities for those with good insight and superior forecasts to have their judgments subsequently incorporated into common wisdom via market fulfillment of their expectations. However, even if the analysis proves correct, time lag remains a major problem.

Correcting Consensus Errors

The recognition and correction of value distortions (consensus errors) can be a long, often frustrating task. The critical aspect of this problem is to make explicit the quantitative projections, assumptions, and conceptual background on which expectations are based.

One of the reasons for the discouraging outlook for passenger cars in early 1982 was that it was expected that gasoline prices would increase faster than the inflation rate and that the auto industry would continue to have difficulty in raising prices under conditions of higher inflation. However, if oil price increases continued to moderate or if a price decline were to set in, the general inflation rate also would be reduced and this would be twice beneficial to the auto industry.

The positive attitude toward capital goods in early 1982 reflected the Reaganomic assumption that the tax cut program would encourage savings and thus investment. However, if consumers spent their tax savings rather than saved them, the expectations for capital goods markets would be adversely affected.

Internal developments can be critical. The drive toward efficiency can be hampered by poor planning. A classic example was the pulp mill constructed in Quebec by ITT Rayonier Incorporated. At one time, Rayonier was con-

TABLE 7-6. Common Stock Evaluation Factors

| | Average Annual Growth Rate | | | | |
| | NET PER SHARE | | DIVIDENDS PER SHARE | | |
	(1) 1976–80 Actual	(2) 1981–85 Projected[a]	(3) 1976–80 Actual	(4) 1981–85 Projected[a]	(5) Anticipated Cyclical Decline[b]
S&P 500	13.2%	11.0%	10.9%	10.0%	−10.0%
Atlantic Richfield	34.0	13.0	23.4	11.0	−15.0
Beatrice Foods	9.6	10.0	11.9	10.0	+3.0
Caterpillar Tractor	7.0	15.0	13.6	15.0	−10.0
Digital Equipment	33.6	30.0	—	—	−5.0
Dow Chemical	4.5	10.0	17.0	9.0	−20.0
Ingersoll Rand	5.4	15.0	6.0	6.0	−12.0
Maytag	6.6	4.8	8.5	3.4	−8.0
Motorola	32.2	13.0	15.7	13.0	−25.0
Polaroid	6.3	6.0	26.0	6.0	−30.0
SmithKline	34.2	16.0	28.2	16.0	+10.0
Texas Utilities	9.5	6.0	7.3	6.0	+3.0
Timken	8.5	18.0	9.0	18.0	−20.0

SOURCE: Duff & Phelps, Inc.
[a] Based on most likely projections.
[b] Estimated decline in net per share in next economic downturn assumed to be in 1985.

sidered the brightest jewel in the ITT picture, and the pulp mill was expected to be a major contributor to earnings. However, a number of problems occurred during the construction of the mill, including difficulties with the project's engineering design, an ill-trained, small pool of labor with a bad attitude, and a location in a remote area of Quebec. In short, poor execution caused failure of what might have been good business strategy. In 1979 ITT took a $320 million writedown to close down this mill. Recently it has offered to sell Rayonier. As of mid-1982, the sale had not been consummated.

Summarizing the Key Variables

For illustrative purposes, Table 7-6 provides a summary as of 1981 of key financial variables that allows the investor to "read the market." Quantification of data in this format also permits the portfolio manager to evaluate and monitor the basis for the analyst's recommendations. The elements of the table are discussed below:

RISK FACTORS			CURRENT MARKET DATA			
(6) Confidence Factor[c]	(7) Beta[d]	(8) Credit Ratings[e]	(9) Price	(10) P/E on 1981 Earnings	(11) Yield on Current Dividends	(12) Projected Total Return
3.0%	1.00	NA	$111.59	7.3×	6.0%	16.0%
5.0	1.18	4/Aaa/AA+	36	5.4	6.7	17.7
2.0	0.87	1/Aaa/AAA	18	5.5	7.0	17.0
3.0	0.98	2/Aa/AA	48	7.5	5.6	20.6
10.0	1.24	1/Aa/AAA	82	12.2	—	—
7.0	1.31	5/A/A+	21	8.1	8.6	17.6
6.0	0.93	5/A/A	52	5.6	6.8	12.8
6.0	0.81	f	24	8.5	8.8	12.2
7.0	1.18	3/Aa/AA	54	9.6	3.0	16.0
8.0	1.22	5/A/A+	19	13.1	2.1	8.1
4.0	1.02	1/Aa/AA	67	12.1	3.5	19.5
1.0	0.76	1/Aaa/AAA	21	6.0	9.7	15.7
4.0	0.82	f	53	5.9	6.4	24.4

[c] Estimated deviation from projected growth rate. Thus, the most likely net per share growth rate for the S&P 500 is 11 percent, with the low 8 percent and the high 14 percent.
[d] As calculated by Duff & Phelps.
[e] Senior debt rating with Duff & Phelps rating first followed by Moody's and Standard & Poor's. The Duff & Phelps 1 is the equivalent of a Triple A, 2–4 Double A, and 5–7 Single A.
[f] Not rated, but company has exceptional financial strength the equivalent of 1/Aaa/AAA.

1. The first two columns, (1) and (2), compare actual net per share growth for the past five years with that projected in the future. This allows quick scanning for areas of change.

2. Columns (3) and (4) focus on past and potential dividend growth rates. There is evidence that dividend growth is a better proxy for the underlying strength of the company than earnings gains. There are two distortions in reported earnings. The first has to do with accounting conventions. Despite much improvement in the direction of standardizing accounts in recent years, companies are still allowed to use different expensing practices (for example, longer or shorter depreciation lives) resulting in earnings statements that may not be comparable. Next is the impact of inflation. Any company has to reinvest to maintain itself, and often the replacement cost of new equipment is substantially in excess of that in use. Also, inflationary price boosts increase the amount of working capital, as measured in current dollars, necessary to support the same historical level of unit shipments (nominal versus real sales growth). Thus, a larger portion of earnings has to

be reinvested just to stay even. Consequently, only the remainder is available for distribution as dividends. The result is that the ability to increase dividends is regarded as a more meaningful measure of distributable cash flow than earnings alone.[6]

Again, while the approach being discussed in this chapter stresses relative price/earnings ratios (i.e., the P/E ratio relative to other stocks' P/E ratio), many investors build valuation systems based on dividends and dividend growth rate expectations. In the author's view, both have validity and both depend on the analytical skills emphasized in this chapter—namely, an ability to understand what is behind current market valuation levels, to develop an independent forecast of the future that will detect differences between market valuation levels and the analyst's expectations, and to continually monitor for change. Critically, if the initial analysis proves wide of the mark and/or significant change is not detected, then the results from any model will be randomly erroneous despite the model's firm theoretical underpinnings. This is the now infamous computer model phenomenon of GIGO (garbage in, garbage out).

3. The fifth column shows the magnitude of the expected percentage earnings decline in the next business cycle. For purposes of this projection, the assumption is that a cyclical decline will occur in 1985 and that 1986 will be an on-trend-line earnings year.

4. Columns (6), (7), and (8) address themselves to the question of risk, which is generally defined as the chance that the expected return on securities will not be realized. From a practical viewpoint, especially the client's, the risk is that the securities under consideration may decline in price.

From the standpoint of the analyst making projections, the key is what can be termed the confidence factor—namely, an assessment of how likely the forward projections are apt to be realized. Thus, column (6) measures the differential in the annual projected growth rate between the most likely and either the high or the low. The presumption is the wider the spread and the higher the number, the lower the confidence in the forward projections. Conversely, the narrower the range, the more confidence the analyst has in the projection. This could also be termed the business risk, as this is a way of indicating the probabilities that a company will realize an unexpected earnings or dividend per share growth over a specific time horizon. Clearly, it says nothing about price change that is a function of (1) the general market price change and (2) the change in price of the security under consideration relative to the market's price change, which together consist of the security's systematic risk.

Column (7) shows the stock's beta as calculated by Duff & Phelps. This is a measure of the stock's systematic risk or price change (or total return) sensitivity to the general market's price movements. Portfolio managers use

---

[6] At least a partial offset to these negative effects of inflation is the positive effect inflation has on companies that are heavy net monetary debtors. This argument is explored in depth in Chapter 6.

this measure to adjust or tilt their portfolios in the direction of their market forecast; that is, they move into higher beta stocks when a bullish market is expected and into lower beta stocks when a bearish market is forecast. However, calculations of beta by different advisory services can differ materially depending on the methods used. Further, betas change over time even when the same methodology is used. In short, beta is a tool and, like all such devices, it should be used only with recognition of its limitations.

Column (8) is a measure of the element of financial risk—namely, the chance that financial strains will prevent the achievement of the most likely earnings and dividend growth path. Excess use of leverage (borrowings) in itself can cause earnings shortfalls, particularly in an environment of high and volatile interest rates and especially if the company is one that, at critical points, finds it impossible to obtain funds at any price. The earnings shortfall can result in dividend growth targets not being met and force reduction in the dividend rate, even to the extent of dividend omission. Severe financial strain, of course, can even cause bankruptcy. As a measure of financial risk, we use bond ratings as provided by Duff & Phelps, Moody's, and Standard & Poor's in column (8). (Note that the Duff & Phelps 1 is equivalent to a Moody's triple A; Duff & Phelps 2 through 4, to gradations of double A; and Duff & Phelps 5 through 7, to gradations of single A.)

5. Columns (9), (10), and (11) relate to current market valuation factors, showing the most recent price and the P/E and yield based on the current price. The P/E and yield on individual stocks relative to those for the S&P 500 indicate the market's relative valuation of the common stock—i.e., the consensus viewpoint.

6. Column (12) indicates the analyst's expectations of future return. The comparison of the analyst's expectations to those implicit in the market forecast should lead to investment recommendations. Clearly, if the projected rate of return is low, the P/E high, the cyclicality factor high, and the confidence factor low, the stock would be unattractive. If the resulting return expectation relative to systematic risk or beta is considered unfavorable, this could lead to a sell decision if the stock is held in a portfolio under management or to a decision not to purchase it. For example, Table 7-6 would single out Polaroid as a candidate for sale due to its low projected total return, relatively high P/E, high projected cyclical sensitivity, and low confidence factor. Contrarily, a buy decision would likely occur if the P/E were low, the projected rate of return high, the cyclicality factor low, and the confidence factor high (once again, after adjusting for beta risk). Again, Table 7-6 would point to Timken as an undervalued security. An acceleration in the growth rate is projected, the P/E is below the market P/E average, and the yield is above the S&P 500 yield. Timken's only shortcoming is its poor cyclicality factor.

Obviously, the quality or accuracy of the analyst's projection compared with the market's consensus is the vital ingredient. If the analyst's projection is correct, but the market's conceptual view of the company is high for an otherwise overpriced stock or low for an underpriced security, the expected return may not materialize in the coming holding period—a frustrating experience. The two examples cited are classic examples of concept stocks. Polaroid at one time was viewed as a glamour stock and apparently some of this luster remains. Timken's position as a manufacturer of bearings and steel has never been associated with pizzazz. As a result, the length of time for the market price to adjust to an appropriate level for Timken or Polaroid could be considerable.

The point is that investment organizations should have a disciplined approach that contrasts the expectations implied by the market with the expectations of the organization's analytical staff. Most of the time the market's expectations and those of the staff analysts will be reasonably close. The areas of difference offer the potential of above-average performance—provided the analyst's perceptions prove closer to the mark.

Clearly, this should be a continuous process, since both market consensus and analyst's expectations will constantly change. These changes in turn will lead to new differences of opinion as to relative attractiveness. Thus, the assumptions and analyses at all levels—market, sector, industry, and company—need continual review. The organization that identifies change most promptly should produce superior recommendations for portfolio managers.

EXPECTATIONAL FACTORS: FIXED INCOME SECURITIES

The purpose of this section is to briefly discuss changes in investor expectations toward fixed income securities during the post–World War II period and the forces that caused those changes. Then, a frame of reference will be provided that incorporates factors that may cause future change. This discussion will be extended to consider such factors as maturity differences, sector differentials (i.e., governments, municipals, industrials, and so forth), and quality differentials.

Postwar Changes in Expectations

Following World War II, the relationship between stock and bond yields was classical in the sense that the dividend yield on stocks was significantly larger than the yield to maturity on fixed income securities. Observers at that time felt that the relationship—which focused only on the income portion of the return—was appropriate, due to the greater inherent risk in equities. This risk appraisal differential was reinforced by the then most recent applicable past experience—the depression years of the 1930s—even though that experience had been uncharacteristic of longer run experience. While there was recurrent talk about inflation, this had little influence on the fixed income buyer. Most trust accounts were heavily weighted toward bonds and, in fact, often equities were used only as a means of providing sufficient income to the beneficiaries. Bond yields were in the 2–4 percent range and

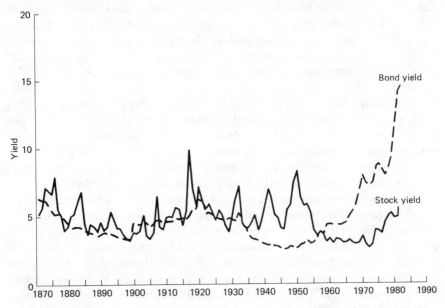

Figure 7-1. Stock Yield vs. Bond Yield. (Source: The First Boston Corporation)

equity yields ranged from 4 to 7 percent. The concept of equities as a source of growth in market value and dividend payments was muted by fears of a future depression.

In terms of price changes and total returns, the bond market and the stock market were generally independent of each other in the immediate postwar period. In fact, as Ibbotson and Sinquefield [1982] showed, there was almost no correlation between bond and stock returns in the 50 years from 1926 to 1981, and there was negative correlation between common stocks and bills. Of course, the use of such a long time frame obscures interim periods. However, by the 1970s a dependent relationship between the two markets became increasingly apparent, as indicated by the bond and stock yields plotted in Figure 7-1.

As a consequence of the strong advance in stock prices and a gradual upward drift in interest rates during the 1950s, the plot of yield on stocks intersected that on fixed income securities in 1956 and then fell below it in 1957, where it has remained ever since. At that time the rationale for the change in relationship was attributed to the superiority of equities as price appreciation vehicles, rather than to a changed attitude toward bonds. Put another way, there was a perceived decline in the risk premium with respect to equities as investors reappraised their expected earnings and dividend growth potential. For a perspective on what created this change, consider that from year-end 1947 to year-end 1957 the S&P 500 average rose over $2\frac{1}{2}$ times; in 1958 alone, the year of the largest postwar gain, the index rose 38 percent.

Further, until the mid-1960s, the bond market was characterized by general price stability compared with the volatility of the stock market. In short, despite the gradual secular advance in interest rates (and thus price declines, especially for the lower coupon issues), the perceived function of bonds as anchors to the windward—offsetting the vicissitudes of the market for stocks—was being realized, particularly since bonds generally were held to maturity.

In the mid-1960s, rising and volatile inflation expectations began to have their impact in terms of increased volatility in bond prices. During this period some of the now-popular bond swapping techniques were developed—in part as a consequence of increased bond price volatility. However, during this period institutional investors continued to increase the equity proportion of assets in portfolios under management and cited the poor total return performance of bonds (i.e., return inclusive of change in market price). Exacerbating bonds' plight was a flood of lower quality bonds entering the market and a declining dollar in the foreign exchange markets. The popularization of this view culminated with an *Institutional Investor* article entitled "Can the Bond Market Survive?" [1969]. Others referred to bonds as "certificates of guaranteed confiscation." Intriguingly, in the years immediately thereafter (1971–72), bonds regained some favor, although the stock market's decline in 1969–70 was a factor in moderating the disenchantment with bonds.[7]

The decade of the 1970s saw major changes in the way fixed income securities were being regarded and the manner in which fixed income portfolios were being managed. These changes were in response to ever-higher levels of inflation and more volatile bond markets, as well as to increasing sophistication on the part of fixed income managers. Active bond management and bond swapping techniques became much more widely utilized. These are discussed in Chapter 9. Further, the fixed income market began increasingly to move in synchronization with the equity market as inflation dominated both markets. A related factor was the ever-higher level and increased volatility of interest rates, both long and short term, and the recognition that there was competition for the investor's money between bonds and stocks.

A major development during this period was the growth of performance measurement—first being applied to equities and then to the fixed income portfolio. This measurement, typically made quarterly or annually, is based on total return—namely, price change and income earned during the measuring period.

To the extent that this approach to bond performance measurement is accepted, then investors during the postwar period have completely reversed their view of fixed income securities. At the start, the vast majority of portfolio managers regarded fixed income securities as a way to obtain timely payment of interest and principal at maturity yet one that insulated

---

[7] A rule of thumb in the investment business is that the easier it is to popularize a concept, the more likely it is to change.

them from market risk. The newer and growing view is that fixed income securities are like any other marketable asset, subject to volatile price movements leading to significant total return volatility. This view, in turn, has encouraged active bond management, as opportunities for large returns in some periods and small returns in other periods have grown.

As part of this concern with volatility, many investors are shortening the maturity of fixed income investments in their portfolios. The intent is to "see the green" (roll bonds into cash) more often. This is affecting the nature and volume of new offerings, with five-, seven-, and ten-year notes becoming more popular than the traditional 20- to 30-year maturities. In Canada, put options are provided for bond investors as an incentive to purchase longer term issues. Thus, as with equities, there have been major shifts in the way investors have regarded and have in fact utilized fixed income securities to achieve investment objectives.

Analysis of Expectational Factors

Interest Rates. Obviously, the dominant factor in bond portfolio management has become the magnitude of changes in the general level of interest rates. The linkage between inflation and interest rates and the deterioration in the liquidity and financial positions of issuers are additional and related factors. Even so, this relationship has in no way been constant as can be seen in Figure 7-2 on page 244, which compares long-term U.S. Treasury bond yields with the GNP deflator. As the figure shows, during the post–World War II years, up to about 1970, there was a fairly constant 400-basis-point difference between the two series. Since the early 1970s, there has been a general tendency for the spread between these two series to be in the area of 250 to 300 basis points; this spread represents the *real* or inflation-adjusted rate of interest.[8] However, the spread relationship has been volatile and there have even been several periods of negative spread where the yield was less than the inflation rate, most recently in 1979. That year was characterized by accelerating inflation rates that subsequently cooled. The negative spread seems to have anticipated the subsequent cooling of inflation.

As was the case with equities, the market's perception can be read. For example, long Treasuries in early 1982 were yielding 14 percent. If you assume that a 300-basis-point spread over the GNP deflator is normal, then the inflation rate anticipated by the market was 11 percent. However, the most common forecast in early 1982 was for an 8 percent inflation rate in the 1982–84 period, with a range from 7 to 10 percent. Thus, the market's view—even utilizing a top-of-the-range 10-percent assumption—and that of the forecast were seriously at variance. One way to capitalize on this variance—but only if you think the explicit forecast of inflation is correct and the

---

[8] This is, of course, the relationship developed originally by Fisher [1930] and estimated by a number of authors, including Yohe and Karnosky [1969] and Burger [1976], most frequently in terms of interest rates on short-term U.S. government securities and consumer prices.

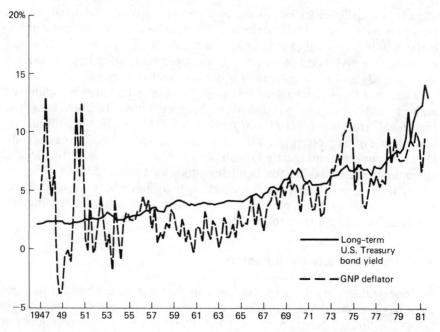

Figure 7-2. GNP Deflator vs. Yield on Long-Term U.S. Treasuries. (SOURCE: Duff & Phelps, Inc.)

forecast implicit in long-term interest rates is incorrect—is to purchase long Treasuries.

As a note of caution, the record of most predictors of inflation and interest rates has been notoriously poor, particularly over the last several years. The theory can be more easily stated ex post than strategized in terms of ex ante expected returns. Thus, the analyst and portfolio manager should practice the discipline of articulating critical assumptions, subjecting them to review, making those adjustments that are required by unforeseen events, and measuring their significance as to future outcomes.

Fixed Income vs. Equity Returns. A task that is equally, if not more, difficult for analysts and portfolio managers is determining whether the valuation relationship between fixed income securities and equities is appropriate or whether an imbalance exists.

This complex subject may be approached in many ways, no single one of which is universally accepted or acceptable. The difficulty is not in assembling the statistics but in applying them. The elements are (1) developing a way to compare equity returns with fixed income returns and (2) developing a method to judge whether the spread relationships developed in the comparisons are sufficient for the different risks involved, with one investment vehicle offering a greater risk-adjusted return than the other.

One method of comparing returns and developing expectations is relating

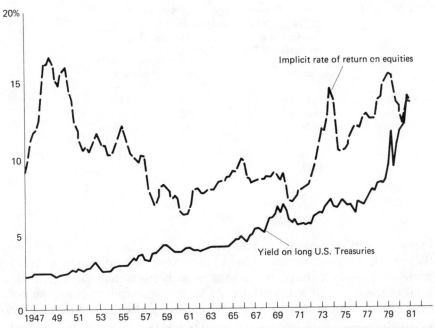

Figure 7-3. Yield on Long-Term U.S. Treasuries vs. Implicit Rate of Return on Stocks. (SOURCE: Duff & Phelps, Inc.)

the historical yield on long U.S. Treasuries to what is termed the implicit return on stocks, utilizing the S&P 500. The latter is admittedly an imperfect calculation, for it combines dividend yield with internal growth rate. As indicated earlier, the internal growth rate, or plowback, is defined as the earnings retention rate times the return on equity or as retained earnings as a percent of average common equity.[9] Presumably, this is the rate of growth a company can sustain without affecting its balance sheet ratios. This approach assumes a stable P/E ratio and further assumes that the combination of dividends received plus the internal growth rate is a proxy for or indicator of the likely future return.

Although there is no empirical evidence to support the validity of this comparative valuation methodology, it is cited frequently in trade material and is used by some portfolio managers as at least one indicator of the relative value position of the two markets. Figure 7-3 is a graphic illustration of the relationship between yields on long U.S. Treasuries and the implicit return on stocks for the period 1947–81. The spread between the two is considered to be an indicator of the investor's perception of the relative risk of owning stocks vs. owning bonds. The wider the spread, the greater the

[9] This algebraic equivalency is straightforward.

$$\text{Internal growth rates} = \frac{\text{retained earnings}}{\text{earnings}} \times \frac{\text{earnings}}{\text{equity}} = \frac{\text{retained earnings}}{\text{equity}}$$

Table 7-7. Percentage Point Spread Between Yield on Long-Term U.S. Treasuries and Implicit Return on Stocks[a] for Selected Time Periods

Period	High	Low	Average[b]
1962–64	4.64	2.92	4.09
1966–68	5.54	3.38	4.26
1974–76	7.87	3.41	5.30
1977–79	7.98	5.09	6.14
1980	5.55	1.94	4.03
1981	1.28	−.28	.60

SOURCE: Duff & Phelps, Inc.
[a] Standard & Poor's 500 Stock Composite Index.
[b] Average of monthly basis point spreads.

implied risk of owning stocks relative to bonds. Conversely, the narrower the spread, the lower the implied risk. Since there are no empirically tested guidelines, it is up to the portfolio manager to interpret the valuation implications of these spread relationships. As with any spread analysis, the portfolio manager attempting to determine and support expected returns must determine which of the two factors is out of line or, more specifically, which of the two is under- or over-valued relative to the other. It is also important to note that major economic events, such as recessions, can cause distortions; thus, Table 7-7 covers four nonrecession intervals from 1962 up to 1978.

Peter Bernstein in Chapter 6 provided an alternative approach to the relative valuation of bonds vs. equities. The reader may want to contrast the two approaches because different perspectives can provide different conclusions, and that is the reality of the marketplace.

Maturities. From the standpoint of fixed income portfolio strategy, the selection of maturities, or durations, doubtless is the most important decision insofar as relative performance is concerned. If interest rates are expected to decline substantially across the maturity spectrum, then the portfolio's maturity or duration should be lengthened, and reduced if higher rates are expected. In the past 30 years, the yield curve usually has been positively sloping—that is, the longer the maturity, the greater the yield. However, at certain times, and particularly near interest and inflation rate peaks, the slope is negative. At that time expectations are that short rates (typically much more volatile than long) will decline and those staying short will sacrifice the opportunity both for market appreciation and to lock in high yields. Again, the market's expectations can be read and the analyst's task is to decide whether those expectations do or do not match those of the forecast. Figure 7-4 provides an illustration of positively and negatively sloping yield curves.

From a technical viewpoint, there are three areas of note. First, in a period of rapidly rising and volatile interest rates, there is a trend toward the

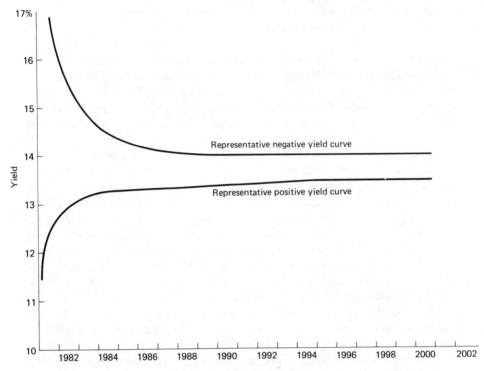

Figure 7-4. Representative Yield Curves. (SOURCE: Duff & Phelps, Inc.)

issuance of more intermediate-term issues (5 to 10 years). The issuer finds this desirable as he does not wish to be locked into a high coupon for 20 to 30 years. His implicit forecast is that rates will decline by the time refunding is necessary. Conversely, the buyer does not wish to go long but for a different reason. The buyer does not want to take the risk of trend-extrapolating, spectacularly rising interest rates and/or the interim, downside price volatility associated therewith.

The second area is call protection. Those bond buyers who want to lock away returns for a long period, 20 years or more, typically concentrate on Treasuries that are noncallable. For industrials and utilities, however, call features (and sinking fund provisions) must be analyzed carefully and appropriate strategies developed. Presumably under conditions of lower interest rates, the company will exercise the call option and refund the debt at a lower interest cost. The company can hedge against lower rates, but the investor is not similarly protected in the United States. (Extendibles, such as those issued in Canada, provide the necessary protection for the investor.)

To counter this, a new vehicle called the original issue deep discount (OID) bond had achieved fairly broad acceptance by early 1982 with tax-exempt investors such as pension funds. The OIDs are not as attractive for taxable accounts. For example, this type of bond with a 20- to 25-year maturity may have a 7 percent coupon and sell at 50 ($500 for a $1,000 face value bond). If it were a conventional issue, the coupon would probably be around

15 percent and sell at par. Assuming the bond is not traded, a sizable portion of the dollar return would be realized by accretion of the discount over the years to maturity since the intervening coupons are so small. An OID characteristically has no call protection, but if called the owner would receive the full par or face value of the bond. The high cost to the company of calling the issue is believed to be an effective barrier to early call. There seem to be two classes of buyers for these bonds, both sophisticated but with different objectives. The first class is bond portfolio managers who specialize in market timing. Believing that interest rates will decline, the attraction of this type of bond is the greater price volatility (and thus appreciation potential on the upside) associated with the deep discount. The second group is some very large fixed income funds whose managers feel interest rates are high, want to lock in the high total return, and plan to hold the bond to maturity. The advantage of deep discounts is that a large portion of the yield to maturity is in the difference between purchase price and par. This eliminates one of the major risks of actually achieving promised yield, namely, the need to reinvest coupon income at the yield rate in order to achieve the promised yield to maturity. Clearly, expectations have influenced both classes of buyers but each has a different time horizon. The issuer is attracted by the reduced cash outlays in early years and somewhat lower effective yields; the investor is willing to sacrifice some yield to achieve protection from reinvestment rate risk.

The concept involved in OIDs has been extended to so-called zero coupon bonds—a debt instrument with no coupon and priced at an even larger discount from par. In early 1982 these bonds typically carried a maturity of 10 years and sold for about 25 ($250).

Sectors. By tradition the fixed income market is divided into broad economic sectors categorized by issuer—namely, U.S. or Canadian government and federal agencies, industrials, utilities, financial companies, and municipals. Spread differentials between these groups reflect supply/demand factors and tax considerations. For example, municipal bond prices fared much worse than other bond prices in 1981. First, there had been an anticipated change (followed by the actual change) in individual tax rates. Along with a general reduction in U.S. federal income tax rates this reduced the maximum tax rate on unearned income from 70 to 50 percent. This has affected tax-equivalent-basis comparisons, increasing the yield required to make municipals competitive with taxable fixed income securities.

The second influencing factor was the widening of underwriting losses by property and casualty insurance companies. As pointed out in Chapter 4, when insurance companies are in a profitable (and hence taxable) position, municipals are attractive as portfolio investments for these companies. Conversely, they typically sell tax exempts when underwriting losses are likely (as in 1981), switching instead to higher yielding corporates. The market tends to anticipate this change by shifting yield relationships in anticipation of the event. In sum, structural factors cause the shift in spreads between tax-free municipals and taxables, and these probable shifts can be exploited for higher portfolio return if correctly analyzed. For example, if the property and casualty underwriting profitability were to be restored, this would undoubtedly have a favorable influence in favor of municipal bond prices.

Supply/demand considerations influence spread relationships in other sectors. In recent years, long Treasuries and long triple A industrials (Duff & Phelps 1 rating) have occasionally sold on approximately the same yield basis (and on a couple of occasions the industrials actually have yielded less) despite the higher credit quality and superior call protection of the Treasuries. The reason has been the relative scarcity of long triple A industrial obligations, as contrasted with the expanding supply of long Treasuries being issued to finance the federal deficit.

By contrast, utilities typically sell on a higher yield basis than either industrials or long Treasuries. While there has been some concern about the credit quality of utilities compared with other categories of issuers, the major relevant fact is the abundance of supply, with approximately 60 percent of all corporate debt outstanding falling in this category. The critical variable to watch here is projected utility capital spending programs. Also, the limited deferral of call protection (typically five years from issuance until call provisions can be invoked) contributes to the spread.

Credit Quality. There are two aspects to credit-quality expectational analysis—namely, changes in spread relationships between quality grades, and changes in credit quality for an individual company or issue.

The deterioration in quality within an industry sector, namely, electric utilities, is dramatically illustrated in Table 7-8. In 1970 only 4 percent of the senior debt of electric utilities was rated below Standard & Poor's quality grade A. However, a decade of rising fuel and construction costs, regulatory rate increase delays, and consumer electricity conservation eroded the financial position of the electric utilities to the point where one-third were rated below A in late 1981.

As can be seen in Figure 7-5 on page 252, the cyclical influence is readily apparent by comparing spreads between Moody's Aaa and A issues. That is, the spread expands during periods of economic downturns and contracts

Table 7-8. Electric Utilities—Senior Debt Ratings by Issuers

	AAA	AA	A	BBB	BB	B
1970	8%	52%	36%	4%	—%	—%
1974	4	31	53	11	1	—
1980	2	28	40	29	1	—
11/1/81	3	22	42	30	2	1

SOURCE: Standard & Poor's Corp.

TABLE 7.9. Caterpillar Tractor Co. (dollars in millions)

	1980A	1981A	1982E	1983E	1984E	1985E
Income Statement						
Revenues	$8,598	$9,155	$ 8,500	$ 9,500	$12,500	$15,000
Pretax Margin	9.0%	8.6%	3.1%	5.0%	9.0%	10%
Pretax Income	$ 770	$ 786	$ 265	$ 475	$ 1,125	$ 1,500
Tax Rate	30%	29%	30%	35%	37%	37%
Net Income Before Subsidiary Earnings	$ 539	$ 562	$ 185	$ 309	$ 709	$ 945
Subsidiary Earnings (equity basis)	$ 26	$ 17	$ 15	$ 21	$ 21	$ 25
Net Income	$ 565	$ 579	$ 200	$ 330	$ 730	$ 970
Fixed Charges	$ 188	$ 244	$ 320	$ 300	$ 280	$ 260
Sources of Funds						
Net Income	$ 565	$ 579	$ 200	$ 330	$ 730	$ 970
Dividends	201	209	240	240	240	280
Retained Earnings	364	370	(40)	90	490	690
Depreciation	370	448	500	525	550	600
Deferred Taxes	47	75	50	50	50	50
Payables/Accruals	342	257	20	100	200	200
Total Sources	$1,123	$1,150	$ 530	$ 765	$ 1,290	$ 1,540
Uses of Funds						
Acquisitions/Investments	$ —	$ 292	$ —	$ —	$ —	$ —
Plant/Equipment	749	713	600	625	800	1,000
Receivables/Inventories	299	546	75	—	400	400
Other	—	—	50	50	50	50
Total Uses	$1,048	$1,551	$ 725	$ 675	$ 1,250	$ 1,450

Financing

Short-Term Debt	$ (16)	$ 400	$ (405)	$ (190)	$ (40)	$ (90)
Long-Term Debt	(21)	29	600	100	—	—
Equity Issues	3	55	—	—	—	—
Conversion of Debentures	—	—				
Total Financing	$ (34)	$ 484	$ 210	$ (90)	$ (40)	$ (90)
Change in Cash & Equivalent	$ 41	$ 83	$ 0	$ 0	$ 0	$ 0

Balance Sheet

Cash & Equivalent	$ 104	$ 81	$ 81	$ 81	$ 81
Receivables/Inventories	2,662	3,283	3,283	3,283	4,083
Current Assets	$2,766	$3,364	$3,364	$3,683	$4,164
Net Property	3,009	3,496	3,596	3,846	4,246
Other	324	650	700	750	800
Total	$6,099	$ 7,510	$ 7,660	$ 8,360	$ 9,210
Short-Term Debt	$ 447	$ 442	$ 252	$ 212	$ 122
Payables/Accruals	1,265	1,542	1,642	1,842	2,042
Current Liabilities	$1,712	$1,984	$1,894	$2,054	$2,164
Long-Term Debt	932	1,561	1,661	1,661	1,661
Deferred Taxes	23	148	198	248	298
Total Equity	3,432	3,817	3,907	4,397	5,087
Total	$6,099	$ 7,510	$ 7,660	$ 8,360	$ 9,210

Key Ratios

Fixed Obligations as % Invested Capital	29%	34%	33%	30%	26%
Fixed Charge Coverage	5.15×	1.9×	2.6×	5.0×	6.8×
Debt/Internal Funds	1.8 yrs.	3.9 yrs.	2.9 yrs.	1.7 yrs.	1.3 yrs.
Return on Average Equity	17.4%	5.1%	8.5%	17.5%	20.2%

SOURCE: Duff & Phelps, Inc.
A = actual; E = estimated

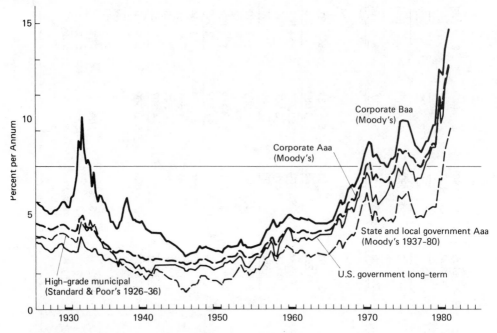

Figure 7-5. Long-Term Bond Yields by Sector and Quality Grade, 1926–80 (quarterly averages). (SOURCE: *1981 Historical Chart Book* [1981])

during periods of prosperity. Clearly, the ebb and flow of confidence in business generally is the major ingredient.

Concerning changes in credit quality for industrial issues, the techniques utilized for fundamental equity analysis apply. Thus, the past is reviewed for clues to the future, and then projections are made to see what changes are likely and how these compare across a broad universe of companies. The emphasis is on earning power and cash flow, the variability of those factors, and the confidence level in the future projections. The quantitative measures used include fixed charge coverage and the fixed obligation debt/equity ratio, as well as measures of liquidity. An example of forward projections made by Duff & Phelps for Caterpillar Tractor in early 1982 is shown in Table 7-9 (preceding pages). Though only a one-scenario forecast is reproduced in the table, others are considered internally and specific assumptions are spelled out in the company's credit report. Changes in perceptions of credit quality do cause shifts in spread relationships. Thus they play an important role in fixed income investing and are deserving of analysts' and portfolio managers' attention.

SUMMARY

Expectational analysis is built on the presumption that market price relationships can be used to achieve above-average returns. The theory is that the current price of any security reflects conventional wisdom, or what the average participant in the marketplace feels is the correct appraisal of return and risk. The analyst or portfolio manager then should decide whether conventional wisdom is reasonable on both an absolute and relative basis. By seeking exceptions, portfolios can be constructed of individual securities that offer the prospect of above-average return relative to risk. A related task is to develop a systematic, disciplined approach to monitoring events to determine whether any change in the political, social, or economic climate is sufficient to cause a shift in the underlying assumptions and, consequently, conventional wisdom and attendant market valuation levels.

FURTHER READING

The most comprehensive record of returns, risk, and correlations on various categories of assets over the period 1926–81 can be found in Ibbotson and Sinquefield [1982].

One practitioner-developed approach to making above-average returns on common stock industry groupings under conditions of rapidly increasing or rapidly decelerating rates of inflation can be found in Estep and Hanson [1980].

A truly outstanding guide through the key characteristics of various industry and company groupings and why they are profitable or unprofitable is provided by Porter [1980]. The specific examples illustrating critical points sparkle. It is *must* reading for any financial analyst.

An excellent discussion of the implication of growth patterns, industry analysis, and equity valuations appears in Cohen, Zinbarg, and Zeikel [1982].

An excellent discussion relating macroeconomic factors to an appraisal of the outlook for stocks can be found in Gray [1979].

For a colorful discussion of the valuation levels during the days of the gunslingers, please read Malkiel [1981].

The importance to bond portfolio management of forecasting interest rates is set forth in detail in Meyer [1977].

While there have been several systems to outline the methodology of projecting future earnings and dividend streams, one that is designed to share the relationships between the many financial measures, including the income statement and the balance sheet, is The Bisect System developed by H. C. Wainwright Company in the early 1970s and still maintained by Goldman Sachs & Company.

A dramatic graphic presentation of the sources of earnings growth is a chart prepared by Wertheim & Company, Inc., entitled "Critical Investment Variables Are Often Found Among Sources of Earnings Growth."

BIBLIOGRAPHY

Burger, Albert E., "An Explanation of Movements in Short-Term Interest Rates," St. Louis Federal Reserve Bank *Review*, July 1976.

"Can the Bond Market Survive?" *Institutional Investor*, 1969.

Cohen, Jerome B., Edward D. Zinbarg, and Arthur Zeikel, *Investment Analysis and Portfolio Management*, 4th Ed., Homewood, Ill.: Richard D. Irwin, 1982.

Estep, Tony, and Nick Hanson, "The Valuation of Financial Assets in Inflation," New York: Salomon Brothers, May 9, 1980.

Fisher, Irving, *The Theory of Interest,* New York: Macmillan, 1930.

Gray, William S., III, "Developing a Long-Term Outlook for the U.S. Economy and Stock Market," *Financial Analysts Journal,* July/August 1979.

Ibbotson, Roger G., and Rex A. Sinquefield, *Stocks, Bonds, Bills and Inflation: The Past and the Future,* Charlottesville, Va.: The Financial Analysts Research Foundation, 1982.

Malkiel, Burton G., "Risk and Return: A New Look," Working Paper No. 700, National Bureau of Economic Research, 1981.

Meyer, Kenneth R., *Forecasting Interest Rates: Key to Active Bond Management,* A paper presented at the 1977 Financial Analysts Federation Conference.

1981 Historical Chart Book, Washington, D.C.: Board of Governors of the Federal Reserve System, 1981.

Porter, Michael, *Competitive Strategy,* New York: Macmillan, 1980.

Yohe, William P., and Denis S. Karnosky, "Interest Rates and Price Level Changes, 1952–1969," St. Louis Federal Reserve Bank *Review,* December 1969.

APPENDIX

Dividend Capitalization Approach to Common Stock Valuation*

General Comment on Table 7A-1

The valuation approach detailed utilizes as key determinants of the justifiable price-earnings ratio (line 11) the long-term bond rate (a measure of alternative return) and the profitability of industry (ROE). Our basic premise is that a security's market value consists of two components: the contribution to value from the current dividend, capitalized by the investor's required rate of return, and the contribution to value deriving from the profitable retention of earnings that will generate future dividend payments. This contribution is enhanced to the extent ROE (the return industry can earn on funds) exceeds the market's required rate of return (a proxy for what investors can earn on funds). Over the past decade improvement in ROE has not kept pace with advances in the required rate of return, i.e., profitability has not kept pace with inflation. This, coupled with supply side constraints to economic growth, leads us to believe that ROE will move upward, and we have assumed this in our model.

Current Comment on Table 7A-1

Based on August month-end prices, the S&P 400 had an estimated annual return of 15.5 percent compared with a required return (discount rate) of 14.5 percent. The 14.5 percent discount rate consists of the yield on 5-year government bonds and a 2 percent equity risk premium. The current 1 percent excess return suggests a slightly undervalued equity market—priced to provide a return about equal to the yield to maturity of a 5-year bond and a 2 percent risk premium. Prior to this equity market advance, the excess return was 3.0 percent. The principal message of this evaluation framework is that the equity market has squeezed out just about all that is likely from

* Appendix material courtesy of Goldman Sachs and Company.

TABLE 7A-1. **Valuation Analysis for the Average Common Stock, September 1982**

Assumptions:

	Low	*High*
1. Five-year government bond rate	11.5%	13.5%
2. Required risk premium to buy common stock	2.0	2.0
3. Total required return	13.5%	15.5%

	DJIA	*S&P 400*
4. Assumed (3–5 yr.) sustainable return on equity (ROE)	13.0%	15.0%
5. Rate of earnings retention	55.0	58.0
6. Payout ratio	45.0	42.0
7. Internally financeable earnings per share growth (ROE times retention rate)	7.0%	9.0%
8. Estimated 1986 trend earnings per share	$170.00	$26.00
9. Estimated 1986 trend dividends per share	$69.00	$11.00
10. Justifiable price range (1986)[c]	1290–1000	213–174
11. Justifiable multiple on estimated trend earnings[c]	7.6×–5.9×	8.2×–6.7×
12. Indicated annual rate of return (1982–1986)[c]	17.0–10.0%	18.0–13.5%
13. Current multiple on estimated 1982 earnings[a]	9.5×	9.0×
14. Current multiple based on 1982 trend earnings[b]	6.9×	7.2×

Valuation model: $P = \dfrac{D}{R} + \dfrac{\dfrac{ROE}{R} \cdot (RE)}{R/(1+g)}$

Where:

P = justifiable price for the DJIA and S&P 400
D = estimated trend dividends per share (line 9)
R = total required return for equity investment (line 3)
ROE = sustainable return on equity (line 4)
RE = estimated trend retained earnings per share (line 8 minus line 9)
g = sustainable earnings growth (line 7)

SOURCE: Goldman Sachs & Co.
[a] Based on the following data: DJIA: 901; Earnings: $95.00
       S&P 400: 134; Earnings: $14.90
[b] 1982 trend earnings: DJIA: $130.00; S&P 400: $18.25
[c] Based on total required return of 13.5%–15.5%.

the already large decline in bond rates. Further sustained gains in the (equity) market require lower interest rates—to provide less bond competition and allow for an earnings underpinning to share prices.

Two other points. First, we have lowered our trend earnings growth rate (S&P 400) estimate to 9 percent (sustainable ROE of 15 percent) from 10 percent (ROE of

TABLE 7A-2. Cost vs. Return on Capital, September 1982 (Based on the S&P 400)

	1962–65	1965–69	1970–72	1973
Assumptions				
Sustainable return on equity	11.5%	12.5%	12.0%	13.5%
Sustainable dividend payout ratio	52.0	52.0	50.0	45.0
Earnings retention rate	48.0	48.0	50.0	58.0
Earnings growth	5.5	6.0	6.0	7.4
Opportunity cost (S&P AAA utility rate)	4.5%	6.0%	7.7%	8.0%
Assumed risk premium	3.0	3.0	3.0	3.0
Total return required to own equities	7.5%	9.0%	10.7%	11.0%
Theoretical justified multiple	17.3×	13.7×	10.3×	11.0×
Actual multiple range	19–15×	18–15×	19–16×	15–12×

17 percent). Certainly the current and anticipated wage/price data suggest some deceleration in nominal earnings growth. Second, a point we have made before, every one percentage point decline in bond rates allows for a 0.7 percentage point advance in the S&P 400's P/E within the confines of our dividend discount model. The market's P/E is currently 8.5× on latest 12-month earnings. Valuation considerations would permit a P/E of 9.5× based on a 125 basis point decline in long-term interest rates (our expectation by the middle of next year).

General Comment on Table 7A-2

The valuation approach taken in Table 7A-1 is checked against the last 19 years of market valuation. As can be seen, the model suggests overvaluation of equities in the 1966–72 period. In these years, we believe it was more apparent than real, due to the extreme overvaluation of growth stocks. In the 1962–66 period, P/E's were bid up as institutional investors began restructuring portfolios toward increased representation in equities.

Current Comment on Table 7A-2

From the early 1960s through 1978, the estimated sustainable growth rate for the S&P 400 equalled or exceeded long-term interest rates. In 1979, bond rates importantly exceeded the trend earnings growth rate. And this remains the case. Currently, assuming a 9 percent trend EPS growth rate and a 5.5 percent dividend yield, the total return on equities (excluding P/E change) is 14.5 percent—not far above the presently available 12.5 percent return on 5-year government bonds. Based on trend earnings, a bull market (where stocks importantly outperform bonds) requires P/E expansion. This requirement was not necessary for most of the last two decades. The reason: Some disinflation has crept into trend ROE and earnings growth expectations but very little of a disinflation mentality has reflected itself in bond interest rates. From another perspective, given the current inconsistency between monetary and fiscal policies, a sluggish (year-term) earnings recovery makes near certain that continuation of the recent market advance should be P/E-fueled, not earnings-fueled.

1974	1975	1976	1977	1978	1979	1980	1981	1982
13.5%	13.5%	13.5%	13.5%	13.5%	15.5%	17.0%	17.0%	15.0%
42.0	42.0	42.0	42.0	42.0	42.0	42.0	42.0	42.0
58.0	58.0	58.0	58.0	58.0	58.0	58.0	58.0	58.0
7.8	7.8	7.8	7.8	7.8	9.0	10.0	10.0	9.0
8.5%	8.5%	8.5%	8.1%	8.8%	10.6%	11.8%	14.1%	14.5%[a]
3.0	3.0	3.0	3.0	3.0	3.5	2.5	2.5	2.0
11.5%	11.5%	11.5%	11.1%	11.8%	14.1%	14.3%	16.6%	16.5%
10.0×	9.7×	10.1×	10.7×	9.0×	8.4×	7.8×	7.0×	6.5×
11–7×	13–9×	12–10×	10–8×	9–7×	8–7×	10–7×	9.5–7.6×	9.2–7.7×[b]

SOURCE: Goldman Sachs & Co.
[a] Average through August.
[b] Based on 1982 earnings estimate and price range through August.

Part IV

Integration of Portfolio Policies and Expectational Factors

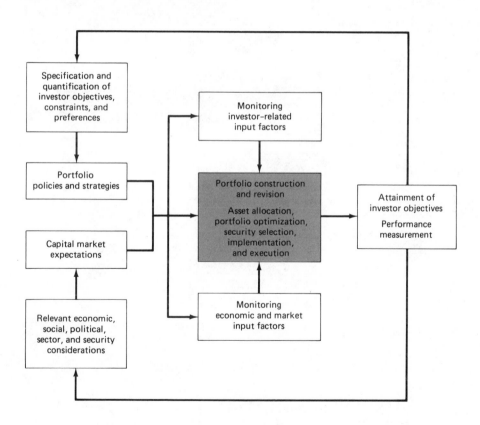

CHAPTER 8

Portfolio Construction: Asset Allocation

_____ *Kathleen A. Condon, C.F.A.*

One of the most important decisions that any investor must make is the selection of an appropriate asset mix for his portfolio. Previous chapters have dealt with the issues of establishing investment policies and ascertaining capital market expectations, and these are precisely the input needed for making an intelligent asset mix allocation, the first of several key investment strategy decisions.

In recent years increased attention has been focused on this topic and, as a result, a number of new approaches have been developed. In this chapter we will review these approaches as well as the related areas of selecting managers and structuring the portfolio.

IMPORTANCE OF THE ASSET MIX DECISION

Why is so much attention focused on setting asset mix? One answer is that for most portfolios the asset mix is the single most important determinant of performance. Large institutional portfolios such as pension funds tend to be well diversified within the asset components utilized. Therefore, although most equity managers focus on stock selection, specific stocks held will not have nearly as much impact on total performance as will the overall level of equity commitment. The same observation holds for the other asset components of well-diversified funds.

Historically, the asset mix decision has tended to be unstructured, without reference to a quantitative, analytical framework. New methodologies emphasize explicit assumptions and forecasts. Although there are a number of distinct approaches currently being used, the necessary data are straight-forward and common to all:

1. Some statement of the investor's objectives and constraints that will be used to select the appropriate mix. Constraints include time horizon, liquidity needs, and tax and regulatory issues.
2. Forecasts of return for each asset class.
3. Estimates of risk for each asset class.
4. Estimates of correlation among asset class return patterns.

WHO SHOULD MAKE THE ASSET MIX DECISION

Since investor objectives and constraints are such key considerations, the investor must provide input to the decision. For pension funds, for example, this duty usually falls to the plan sponsor. A consultant or portfolio manager can do much of the analysis, but only the investor truly can set objectives and determine risk tolerance.

The common practice at one time was for the portfolio manager to select the asset mix. When a portfolio manager is responsible for all of an inves-tor's assets, this is possible although not optimal. Today, however, many large institutional portfolios are split among a number of managers. Often these managers are specialty managers, focusing on one type of asset or style of management. In such a situation the investor must take responsibil-ity for setting the asset mix and allocating funds among managers.

As this responsibility has come to be more widely recognized, investors or agents acting on behalf of investors, most frequently pension plan spon-sors, have begun to monitor their abilities in this area, just as they monitor managers' investment performance. An example of a framework for doing this was provided by Myron D. Stolte [1981]. Stolte isolated four distinct decisions to be evaluated:

I. Selecting asset classes.
II. Allocating funds among asset classes.
III. Selecting money managers.
IV. Allocating funds among money managers.

The first decision, selecting asset classes, is evaluated by calculating the dollar impact on fund results of investing in a "normal mix" of various assets as opposed to naively putting the entire portfolio in a single "risk-free" asset, Treasury bills. In Table 8-1, the normal asset mix is assumed to be 60 percent common stocks and 40 percent bonds. That is, funds are assumed invested 60 percent in a broad stock market index (such as the Standard & Poor's 500 Stock Composite Index) and the remaining 40 per-cent in a broad bond market index (such as the Lehman Brothers Kuhn

TABLE 8-1. Fund Impact Analysis

Decision Level	Decision Made	Impact (in thousands)
I	**Asset class selection**	
	Result (60–40 central policy allocation)	$49,705
	Less benchmark (Treasury bill base return)	55,088
	Value added	$ (5,383)
II	**Asset class allocation strategy**	
	Result (deviation to 50–50 mix)	$50,101
	Less benchmark (60–40 central policy allocation)	49,705
	Value added	$ 396
III	**Fund manager selection**	
	Result (equal allocations within classes)	$52,327
	Less benchmark (deviation to 50–50 mix)	50,101
	Value added	$ 2,226
IV	**Fund manager allocation strategy**	
	Result (deviation from equal allocations)	$51,652
	Less benchmark (equal allocations within classes)	52,327
	Value added	$ (675)

SOURCE: Courtesy of Myron D. Stolte, President, Asset Allocation Incorporated, Minneapolis, Minn. [1981]. Reprinted by permission of the *Harvard Business Review*. Copyright © 1981 by The President and Fellows of Harvard College; all rights reserved.

Loeb Corporate Bond Index). The return on the portfolio so generated is compared with the return on a portfolio invested entirely in Treasury bills. Assuming a beginning portfolio of $50 million, the normal mix (60–40 in this example) portfolio over the period monitored produced a terminal market value $5,383,000 lower than the value that would have been produced by a 100 percent commitment to Treasury bills.

The second decision involves the decision to consciously deviate from the assumed normal asset mix and therefore the decision to actively, rather than passively, allocate funds among asset classes. The impact of the decision is calculated by determining the market value of a fund invested at the actively determined asset mix (assumed to be 50–50) and comparing it to results for the normal mix. That is, the return on a 50-percent stock index/50-percent bond index portfolio is compared with the return on a 60-percent stock index/40-percent bond index portfolio. In Stolte's example, the 50–50 portfolio did better than the 60–40 portfolio and the differential return was applied to the starting dollar amount. The value added was $396,000.

Decision III involves fund manager selection but not the dollar allocation among the managers. It compares percentage return performance of the managers selected versus percentage return of index funds, both assuming a 50–50 asset allocation. The result shows the differential returns for a group of active managers versus passively managed money.

The last decision examines the impact of the specific allocation of assets among the managers. In most instances, each manager does not manage an equal portion of the assets within asset categories, as was assumed in monitoring decision III. Rather, different amounts of money have generally been channeled to each manager. The impact of this decision is captured by examining the actual performance. In our example, whereas $2,226,000 was added by manager selection, $675,000 was lost by a suboptimal allocation of assets among those managers.

Although Stolte addressed his article to pension plan sponsors, sponsors of other large investment portfolios would find the approach useful. As all parties increasingly come to recognize their responsibilities for setting asset mix objectives, approaches of this sort to monitoring value added will become increasingly popular.

CONSIDERATIONS IN SETTING ASSET MIX

Investor Objectives and Constraints

As previously mentioned, there are a variety of approaches currently being used to set asset mix; however, certain basic input is common to all. First and foremost, one needs a statement of investor objectives and constraints.

Different types of portfolios will have very different objectives and constraints. A number of the key issues in this area for individual investors were covered in Chapter 5. For example, a young person with funds to invest may be primarily interested in long-term growth and capital appreciation. Dividends and other income taxed at normal rates may not be of interest. Conversely, a retired person may be primarily concerned with stability of principal and income. The retiree's tax bracket has dropped and the income may be necessary to maintain an accustomed lifestyle. Often the manager of a personal trust fund must trade off the desire for capital appreciation with the desire for high income, since the income may be going to one generation of beneficiaries upon whose deaths the principal will be distributed to the next generation.

As discussed in Chapter 4, various types of institutional portfolios will also have very different objectives and concerns. For some, taxes are a major consideration; others have legal restrictions. At first glance, pension funds might seem to be fairly homogeneous and uniquely free of these types of constraints. They are tax exempt and, for the most part, can be invested in a wide array of asset classes. There are wide differences even here, however.

States and municipalities tend to place more restrictions on their pension funds investments than do private pension funds. Often there is a ceiling on common stock investments of 25–50 percent with the remainder allocated to bonds and real estate. Also, since funding for these plans comes largely from taxpayers' money, there is likely to be considerable interest in and concern for social investing. Two broad issues are frequently debated.

The first is the desirability of avoiding investments in companies that are perceived to discriminate (companies with operations in South Africa, EEO violators, and so on) or in companies engaged in activities that people may find offensive (tobacco and liquor companies, companies perceived to pollute the environment, and so on).

A second issue is the desirability of making investments that will benefit a given state or municipality. A good example would be the investment of pension assets in mortgages to stimulate the local housing industry during a period of tight money. A similar example was New York City's desire to have its municipal pension funds invest in city securities at a time when the city was short on cash and having trouble placing the securities elsewhere, despite the inability of the funds to take advantage of the securities' tax-exempt features. There continues to be a lively debate as to whether social concerns should be allowed to impact pension investment decisions.[1] Suffice to say at this point that the debate is far from over.

Probably because private pension funds are so large and represent such a significant expense to corporations, much more attention has been focused on their management in recent years. Most of the more innovative asset mix work has been geared toward the pension fund market. For this reason much of the discussion in this chapter centers on pension funds; however, the techniques cited can be readily adapted for use with other types of portfolios.

Selecting Asset Classes

When undertaking an asset mix study it is important to incorporate all assets in which the investor might have an interest. As recently as a few years ago most formal analyses were confined to common stocks, bonds, and sometimes cash equivalents. Now other types of investments are being incorporated. Among the more popular are:

Real Estate. Investing in real estate has long been attractive to individuals because of tax considerations. More recently, pension funds have become active investors because of a perception that real estate provides both a hedge against high inflation and enhanced overall portfolio diversification.

---

[1] Critics of the concept cite ERISA's mandate that pension assets be invested for the sole benefit of plan participants. Secretary of Labor Raymond J. Donovan, in a statement before the Senate Subcommittee on Labor [1982], noted: "I want to also emphasize that we intend to enforce vigorously the mandate of the law that the fiduciaries of funds act solely in the interests of the participants and beneficiaries. We will not allow increased risk or decreased returns by so-called social investments—even those which may have the noblest of purposes. Plan assets must be protected fully." Public pension funds, however, are not subject to ERISA, so the issue is less clear cut. It has been argued by Baldwin et al. [1980] that one can invest in a socially responsible manner without sacrificing return or significantly increasing risk.

The inclusion of real estate in asset mix models poses some unique problems. Historical data are scarce and, when available, usually cover only the 1970s, a period of rapidly rising inflation and even more rapidly rising real estate prices. It can be argued that extrapolation from this recent period does not provide a realistic perspective on the relative attractiveness of real estate versus other asset classes, and further that results for open-end real estate mutual funds tend to understate the volatility of real estate investments since market values are estimated by appraisal rather than from actual transactions. These issues are covered in detail in Chapter 11. At this point it is sufficient to note that they exist and should be considered when estimating return, risk, and correlations for real estate.

International Equities. Common stocks from markets outside U.S. or Canadian have generated interest because of studies showing that, at least during some historical time periods, they have yielded higher returns than have domestic equities while enhancing portfolio diversification. Over the 20-year period 1960–79, Capital International's EAFE (Europe and the Far East) index returned 8.6 percent per year, with a standard deviation of 14.7 percent, while the Standard & Poor's 500 compounded at 6.4 percent with a standard deviation of 16.2 percent. Over the 10-year period 1970–79, the return spread was even more dramatic, with the EAFE compounding at 9.4 percent versus 4.6 percent for the S&P 500. All of these calculations are adjusted for currency fluctuations. Further, since the correlation between the two indexes has tended to range between +0.5 and +0.7, including some international securities in a portfolio would have enhanced overall portfolio diversification.

Guaranteed Investment Contracts (GICs). GICs are investments with insurance companies that generate a guaranteed return over a specified period. An attraction of this type of investment is that current regulations permit them to be valued at cost rather than market, providing stability to valuations of the portfolio. Some pension funds have made substantial investments in GICs so that their actuaries, being assured of a given return, will increase the earnings assumptions on the funds, thus lowering the required corporate contributions. A drawback to this type of investment is that severe return penalties are imposed for withdrawing funds prior to the contract's expiration.

Other financial assets being considered and used include options, financial futures, and venture capital. The more robust models can handle any asset classes for which expectations can be formulated. They can also be extended to include other investment strategies such as leveraged equity investment (buying stocks on margin).

Forming Expectations

As has been made abundantly clear in Chapters 6 and 7, forecasting returns for assets is no simple task. Numerous factors influence returns, and it is a frustrating fact that the most carefully thought out forecasts may prove to be in error because of events impossible to anticipate. Nonetheless, even imperfect forecasts can add value to an investment process.

In working with an asset mix model, estimates of return and risk must be made for each asset class. Correlations among assets must also be projected. Investors have developed a variety of approaches toward making these forecasts. Three of the more popular are discussed here.

Extrapolating from History. This probably has been the most widely used approach. The premise is that historic relationships between asset class returns, as well as historic risk levels, will persist in the future. An investor using this approach begins by examining a series of historic returns. Without doubt the most widely used such series was developed by Roger G. Ibbotson and Rex A. Sinquefield [1982]. Included in the data are returns for common stocks, long-term bonds (both government and corporate), and Treasury bills, dating back to 1926. From these data one can calculate returns and standard deviations over various time periods. Since a series on inflation is included, one can also determine the real returns available from each asset class.

This work has been updated periodically. Returns for the 56-year period 1926–81 shown earlier in Chapter 3 are repeated as Table 8-2. In making forecasts for an asset mix study, an investor will usually begin with a forecast of inflation. Forecasts of returns are then made for the different asset classes, relying heavily on historic relationships; i.e., since common stocks have returned 9.1 percent per year over a period when inflation averaged 3.0 percent, a reasonable projection in a 7 percent inflation environment might be 13.1 percent, maintaining a constant 6.1 percent inflation premium. Investors using this approach frequently assume that historic standard deviations and correlations will persist.

One question that must be addressed is the time period to use as a base. Should one use a long period of history such as the last 50 years or should one focus only on the most recent 5 or 10 years? Differences can be quite significant, depending upon the period selected. Long-term corporate bonds, for example, compounded at 3.6 percent over the 56-year period 1926–81; however, over the 11-year period 1970–81, they compounded at 5.3 percent; while for the 5 years ending 1981 they compounded at −1.3 percent (see

TABLE 8-2. Investment Total Annual Returns, 1926–81

Series	Geometric Mean	Arithmetic Mean	Standard Deviation
Common stocks	9.1%	11.4%	21.8%
Long-term corporate bonds	3.6	3.7	5.6
Long-term government bonds	3.0	3.1	5.6
U.S. Treasury bills	3.0	3.1	3.1
CPI	3.0	3.1	5.0

SOURCE: Ibbotson and Sinquefield [1982].

Table 8-3. Compound Annual Rates of Return and Rankings for Selected Asset Categories Over Three Time Periods Ended June 1, 1982

Asset Category	10 Years	Rank	5 Years	Rank	1 Year	Rank
Oil	29.9%	1	21.2%	4	6.3%	3
U.S. coins	22.5	2	21.4	3	−27.8	13
U.S. stamps	21.9	3	26.6	1	−3.0	9
Oriental rugs	19.1	4	17.1	6	−16.2	11
Gold	18.6	5	17.3	5	−34.0	14
Chinese ceramics	15.3	6	23.7	2	−0.5	6
Farmland	13.7	7	10.7	9	−0.9	7
Silver	13.6	8	5.5	13	−44.5	15
Diamonds	13.3	9	13.7	7	0.0	5
Housing	9.9	10	10.0	10	3.4	4
Old masters	9.0	11	13.7	8	−22.0	12
CPI	8.6	12	9.6	11	6.6	2
Stocks	3.9	13	7.7	12	−10.5	10
Foreign exchange	3.6	14	1.6	14	−1.9	8
Bonds	3.6	15	0.6	15	11.4	1

Source: Salomon [1982].

Ibbotson and Sinquefield [1982]). Which of these periods is the appropriate basis for extrapolation? Since there is no obvious answer, some practitioners have taken the approach of trying to isolate specific periods in the past that replicate the economic environment being forecast. This is probably the better approach, despite the fact that no past period can truly replicate today's situation.

Another comparison among a larger number of asset categories over three different assumed holding periods is shown in Table 8-3. Here, compound annual rates of return and their rankings are shown for 10-year, 5-year, and 1-year periods prior to June 1982 for 15 asset categories. All categories exhibited positive—though widely different—returns over the preceding 10 and 5 years, although not the preceding year. Note the widening *range* of returns, from 26.3 percent to 55.9 percent, as the holding period diminishes from 10 years to 1 year. The wide differences that can occur from one annual period to the next in 1-year returns and their rankings is shown in Table 8-4.

Another issue is how to model assets for which little historic data are available, such as options. International equities have developed different return and risk characteristics since floating exchange rates were introduced in 1974. Also, no generally accepted index of real estate returns was available in 1982, and, in such a diverse market, no single index may ever be widely used. However, as indicated in Chapter 11, some initial progress has been made. Other approaches must be taken to estimate the risk and return characteristics of these asset classes.

Multiple-Scenario Forecasting Approach. This methodology for forecasting return and risk has gained popularity in recent years, undoubtedly

TABLE 8-4. Compound Annual Rates of Return and Rankings for Selected Asset Categories Over Two 1-Year Time Periods

Asset Category	PERIOD ENDED 6/1/82		PERIOD ENDED 6/1/81	
	Return	Rank	Return	Rank
Bonds	11.4%	1	−9.6%	12
CPI	6.6	2	10.0	6
Oil	6.3	3	14.3	5
Housing	3.4	4	8.1	8
Diamonds	0.0	5	0.0	9
Chinese ceramics	−0.5	6	36.5	1
Farmland	−0.9	7	9.7	7
Foreign exchange	−1.9	8	−17.3	14
U.S. stamps	−3.0	9	18.0	4
Stocks	−10.5	10	25.3	2
Oriental rugs	−16.2	11	−0.2	10
Old masters	−22.0	12	22.9	3
U.S. coins	−27.8	13	−8.0	11
Gold	−34.0	14	−13.9	13
Silver	−44.5	15	−26.6	15

SOURCE: Salomon [1982].

because of its intuitive appeal to money managers and economists. The premise underlying this approach is that one can add value by attempting to explicitly forecast the economic and capital market environment. As a practical matter, those using this approach tend to focus on a shorter time frame, such as three to five years, since to forecast the economy for much longer than this would be of questionable value, unless forecast errors tend to cancel each other in longer periods (e.g., 20 years).

The usual approach is to forecast an array of independent economic scenarios. Any environment that has a reasonable chance of occurring is modelled. For each, very explicit forecasts of GNP, inflation, corporate profits, and so forth are made. Given these forecasts as a framework, returns for each asset class are projected within each scenario. Probabilities of occurrence are assigned to the different scenarios and the overall expected return for each asset class is simply the weighted average of the forecasts within each scenario.

This was the approach illustrated in Chapter 6. Six economic scenarios were portrayed and equal or unequal weight was assigned to each. Table 6-10 (see page 199) listed return forecasts within scenarios for each of four assets: stocks, bonds, real estate, and Treasury bills. In the simplest case, where each scenario was assumed to have an equal probability of occurrence, the expected return for any asset was the average of the scenario returns. Stocks, for example, had an expected return of 19.0 percent in the equal-weighted environment.

The array of forecasts across scenarios can also be used to derive the expected standard deviation of returns for each asset (see Tables 6-11 and 6-12 on page 200). It is therefore extremely important to postulate enough scenarios. If one thinks that a very negative environment could develop—even though it may not be likely—it should be included. Otherwise the risk being forecast will be understated. A reasonable criticism sometimes leveled at scenario forecasting is that it can lead to truncated distributions. Care must be taken to avoid this. It is interesting to speculate whether someone detailing scenarios in December 1972 would have included one along the lines of what really happened in 1973–74.

An argument in favor of scenario forecasting is that it encourages the investor to take a prospective view toward asset mix. Since most professional investors do some sort of economic forecasting, it is a logical extension of processes already in place. Since multiple scenarios are used, the framework lends itself to input from a variety of sources: money managers, economists, or consultants. Finally, it encourages the investor to be consistent; if corporate planning is based on a series of economic projections, these can be included as a scenario in the asset mix analysis.

In reality, most investors using a multiple-scenario approach temper their forecasts with some historic perspective. If their forecasts are radically different from history, an explanation is sought. They may well be comfortable with the forecasts; on the other hand, some factor could have been overlooked.

Market Consensus Approach. A somewhat different approach has been taken by one large investment advisory firm. They feel that the best source of expected returns comes from the market consensus. For bonds they use yield to maturity and for common stocks they use the required return generated from a dividend discount model. These returns are prospective, but they do not rely on the forecasting ability of the person doing the analysis; rather, they are consensus estimates of participants in the various markets. Likewise, return estimates for other asset classes are prospective and based on the discounting of estimated cash flow. Estimates of standard deviations and correlations are historical numbers adjusted judgmentally.

Taxes and Transaction Costs. Regardless of how returns are forecast, they should be modified for two factors: tax status and transaction costs. As discussed previously, tax considerations can have a major impact on asset mix. Municipal bonds, for example, may be attractive to the wealthy individual or the casualty insurance company, but they are unlikely to be appropriate for tax-exempt pension funds. Likewise, real estate has tax advantages for individual and certain institutional investors but not for endowment and pension funds. Expected returns can differ widely because of the tax impact and these adjustments should be factored into the forecasts if the results are to have any validity. Incorporating taxes also tends to lower standard deviations and can affect correlation coefficients.

Transaction costs also will have an impact on expected return. In trading most types of assets, some costs are incurred: commissions, taxes, dealer spread, market impact. Research undertaken by the author (Condon [1981]) found that common stock transaction costs for a given six-month period approximated 1 percent each way. Thus, a portfolio that moves from 20 percent to 60 percent in common stocks will incur costs that will substantially lower the overall expected return as compared with a portfolio with a constant 60 percent investment. Again, these adjustments should be factored into the model explicitly. More will be said on this subject in Chapter 12.

SELECTING THE OPTIMAL MIX

Given forecasts of return and risk for an array of asset classes, how does one go about selecting the appropriate asset mix? Numerous approaches are taken, some of which we will discuss here.

Beginning with the simplest approach, there is the technique known as following the herd. In other words, do what other investors are doing and, it is hypothesized, you can't go too far wrong. With this approach one need not have explicit forecasts; nor are specific objectives factored in. One assumes that the consensus, however arrived at, is adequate for the portfolio in question. Although many more investors are undertaking formal asset mix studies today, some of the follow-the-herd instinct remains. The great increase in interest in real estate investment on the part of pension funds probably stems from this type of thinking. If a plan sponsor sees many other plan sponsors putting 5–10 percent of their assets in real estate, there is some inclination to do likewise.

Another somewhat more sophisticated approach is to structure the portfolio so as to meet certain income objectives. If a certain amount of income is needed annually, a portfolio mix that is highly likely to yield that amount can be determined. This approach is common with portfolios for individuals and for institutions such as endowment funds (as discussed in Chapter 4). These sorts of objectives are similar to those underlying dedicated bond portfolios. A dedicated bond portfolio is simply a portfolio constructed so as to have the cash flow from coupon income plus cash from maturing securities total a certain prespecified amount each year. More will be said about this in Chapter 9.

Before discussing the final three approaches it is important to review the concept, introduced in Chapter 2, of an efficient frontier. Given an array of return, standard deviation, and correlation forecasts, there exists a series of asset mixes, each of which offers maximum expected return for a given level of risk or standard deviation. This array of portfolios is known as the efficient frontier. It is reasoned that a rational investor would always opt for a portfolio on the efficient frontier since to do otherwise would be a suboptimal strategy.

Figure 8-1 depicts an efficient frontier for three asset classes: common stocks, bonds, and cash equivalents reading from top to bottom at each of

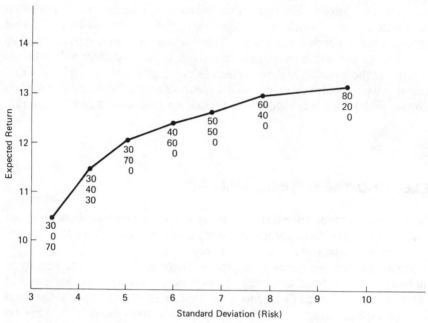

Figure 8-1. Efficient Frontier—Three Asset Class Portfolios. (SOURCE: Bankers Trust Company)

the data points. In general, as one moves from left to right, one can expect to receive higher returns although at increasing levels of risk. The task then becomes to determine the desired risk-reward tradeoff for a given investor. The following discussion focuses on three approaches currently being used.

Avoiding Performance Shortfalls

One approach frequently taken is to set return objectives and then seek to minimize the probability of falling below them over a specified number of years. An example, shown in Figure 8-2, covers a 10-year period. Portfolios hold common stocks and long-term bonds, in combinations ranging from 100 percent bonds on the left to 100 percent stocks on the right. The top curve represents the probability of not achieving a return goal of 11 percent per annum at various mixes of stocks and bonds. Since there is a sizable probability of each mix returning less than 11 percent, one is next interested in the probability of falling below return goals that are lower. Here we examine the probabilities of failing to meet return objectives of 8, 7, and 6 percent. One can examine these curves and infer what range of asset mixes might be appropriate.

Since, in this example, common stocks have an expected return of 12.0 percent versus 8.5 percent for bonds, it is easy to understand why portfolios with a higher equity exposure have a lower probability of returning less than

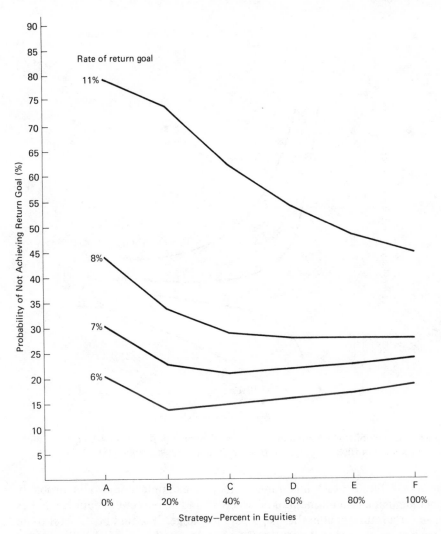

Figure 8-2. Investment Projections—10 Years: Probability of Failing to Meet Selected Rate of Return Goals for Various Portfolio Mixes of Stocks and Bonds. (SOURCE: Bankers Trust Company)

11 percent. For lower return objectives such as 8, 7, and 6 percent, however, the curves have a different shape. Some equity exposure increases the probability of meeting these objectives, but equity exposure in excess of about 60 percent lowers the probability of meeting them. This is because common stocks are assumed to be much riskier, with a standard deviation of 21.9 percent versus 9.7 percent for bonds. At high equity levels this higher standard deviation results in raising the probability of failing to meet these objectives.

One problem with this type of approach is that the curves tend to be fairly

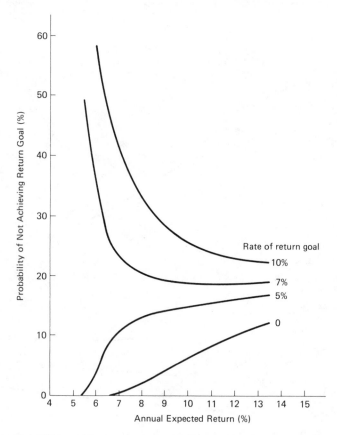

Figure 8-3. Risk-of-Nonachievement Analysis: Probability of Not Achieving the Return Goal for Minimum Risk Portfolios, 1-Year Projection. (Source: Fong [1980])

flat across broad asset mix ranges. In this example one would probably conclude that a commitment of between 40 and 60 percent in equities makes sense for a return goal in the 7 to 8 percent range. It would be difficult to be more precise than that, however. One should also be aware that the curves are heavily influenced by the time horizon selected. The longer the time horizon, the lower the probability of failing to meet a given return. As pointed out by Fong [1980], although return compounds over time, risk grows with the square root of time. Therefore, it is often argued that if one can take a long-term perspective (and ignore short-term market fluctuations), one should invest more heavily in common stocks or other high return–high risk assets. The impact of a changing time horizon on this type of analysis is graphically illustrated in Figures 8-3 and 8-4. Figure 8-3 shows projections for a one-year period while Figure 8-4 covers a 5-year period. Note the dramatic shift downward in probability of not achieving the return goal for various levels of expected return when one shifts to a 5-year horizon.

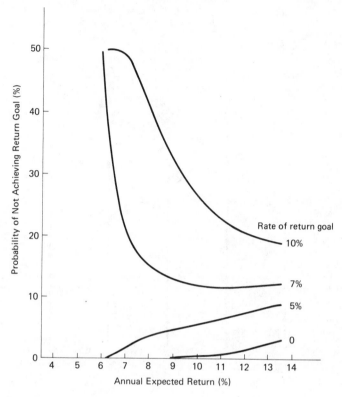

Figure 8-4. Risk-of-Nonachievement Analysis: Probability of Not Achieving the Return Goal for Minimum Risk Portfolios, 5-Year Projection. (SOURCE: Fong [1980])

Liability Simulation Models

Many pension plan sponsors now analyze the impact of alternative asset mixes on future plan contributions, reasoning that their objectives and risk tolerances can only become clear by simulating the impact of investment experience on the "bottom line," or contributions. To facilitate this type of analysis, a number of consulting firms now offer sophisticated liability simulation models that allow the plan sponsor to work through a series of actuarial valuations, projecting fund liabilities, market values, contributions, benefit payments, and so on.[2] The range of possible values for each of these variables, given different asset mixes, can be studied, providing the sponsor

[2] The more sophisticated liability simulation models use Monte Carlo simulations to generate a range of possible outcomes. Expected returns, standard deviations, and correlation coefficients are specified for each asset class as well as for inflation. The process begins with a "draw" from the pool of possible inflation rates (consistent with the prespecified expected inflation value and standard deviation). This, in turn, influences salary projections and future plan liabilities, as well as investment return. At the end of the year an actuarial valuation is superimposed on this hypothetical real world environment. This process is repeated each year

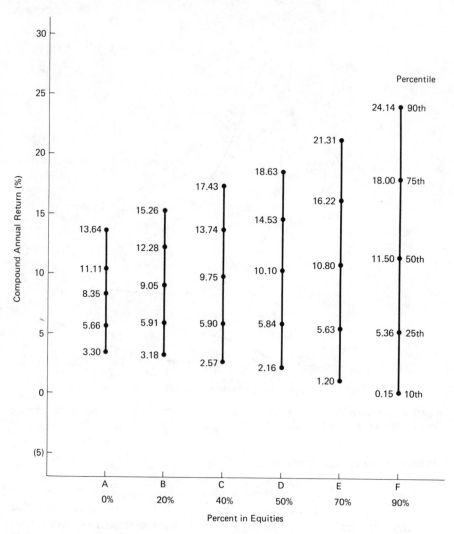

Figure 8-5. Distributions of 5-Year Percentage Rates of Return for Various Bond/Stock Asset Mixes. (Source: Bankers Trust Company)

with insight into the potential impact of both good and bad investment environments. This type of simulation is invaluable in trying to assess the risk-reward tradeoff of various investment strategies.

Sample output from one such model is included in Figures 8-5 through 8-7. Figure 8-5 shows a range of projected investment returns for six selected

for up to 20 years. The result is a simulation of a series of possible events and the impact on future pension values and contributions.

In doing the typical analysis, the full 20-year simulation will be repeated several hundred times. The resulting data provide insight not only on expected values but also on the range of possible outcomes.

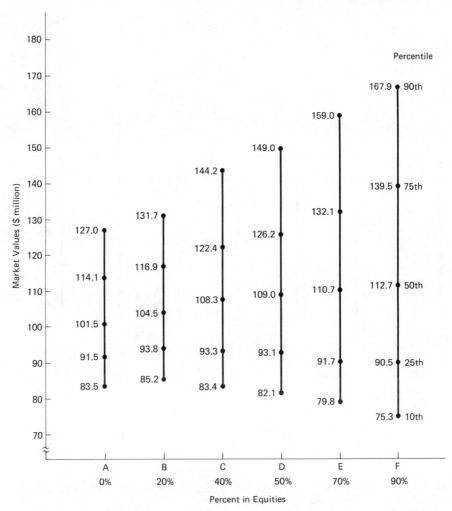

Figure 8-6. Distributions of Fifth-Year Market Values (in $ million) for Various Bond/Stock Asset Mixes. (SOURCE: Bankers Trust Company)

asset mixes over a 5-year period. As can readily be seen, as the percentage invested in common stocks is increased, the expected return and the range of possible outcomes also increase. Figure 8-6 translates these returns into market values that can be compared with plan liabilities. The sponsor can then judge whether, for a particular asset mix, the market value that could be realized in a bad market is one the company can tolerate.

Finally, Figure 8-7 translates these returns into their impact on future plan contributions. Here a range of possible contributions in year 5 is shown for each asset mix. (The vertical axis is inverted to make the figure comparable to the two preceding figures, since smaller contributions are preferred to larger.)

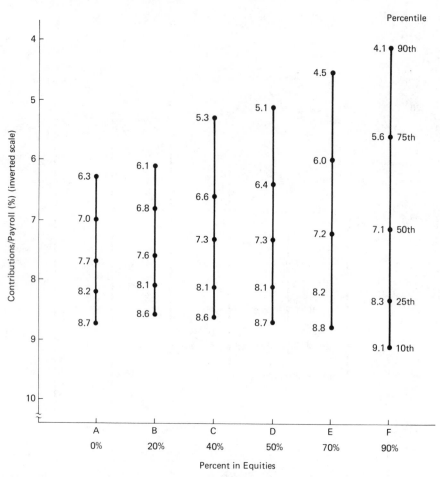

Figure 8-7. Distributions of Contributions as a Percent of Payroll for Various Bond/Stock Asset Mixes. (SOURCE: Bankers Trust Company)

Portfolio A with 100 percent in bonds leads to an expected contribution rate of 7.7 percent of payroll in five years. There is a 10 percent chance that contributions will exceed 8.7 percent and, conversely, if performance is good, a 10 percent chance that contributions will decline below 6.3 percent. Portfolio F, with 90 percent in equities, could result in a higher contribution, but in a good environment for stocks has the potential to lower costs significantly. This type of information can be helpful to the plan sponsor in assessing the attractiveness of different asset mixes, since contribution levels are a key decision variable for the sponsor.

Investor Preference Approach

Even with all of the information from a liability simulation model, it can be difficult to select an asset mix. How does the sponsor make the tradeoff

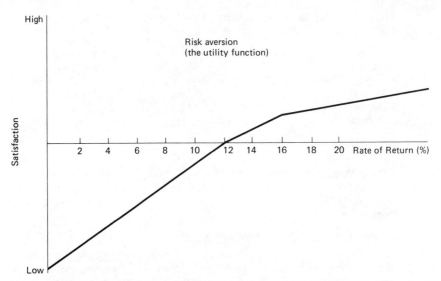

Figure 8-8. Risk Averse Investor's Utility Function. (SOURCE: Wells Fargo Investment Advisors)

between risk and return? Working with a utility function is one technique currently gaining popularity. Different approaches can be taken to soliciting information from the plan sponsor, but ultimately what one is after is a statement of objectives for the fund and a quantification of how important various objectives are and how much risk one can take in pursuing them.

One large investment advisor uses a utility function that requires the investor to specify three key variables: two threshold returns that represent levels at which the attitude toward return changes, and a risk ratio that specifies the marginal utility of returns below the lower threshold (numerator) to returns above the upper threshold (denominator). Together these three variables shape the utility function.

Figure 8-8 depicts one investor's function. The threshold returns are 12 and 16 percent. The risk ratio is 5 to 1. That is, each unit of return below 12 percent is assumed to be five times as valuable as a unit of return above 16 percent. For this investor, as for most, utility increases as return increases but at a declining rate. This makes sense intuitively. A less risk averse investor would have a lower risk ratio; a more risk averse investor would have a higher one. Once the utility function is defined, asset mixes are ranked based on their contribution to utility.

Table 8-5 on page 280 details the results for portfolios of common stocks and bonds ranging from 100 percent stocks to 100 percent bonds with a different set of threshold returns. The optimal mix, given these assumptions, is 40 percent common stocks and 60 percent bonds. It is interesting to note that had one focused simply on maximizing the probability of earning 15 percent (the lower threshold), the mix selected would have been quite different, probably 80 percent common stocks. This points up a value of the utility

TABLE 8-5. Utility Values for Selected Asset Mixes, 5-Year Time Horizon

Assumptions	Return	Standard Deviation
Stocks	18.2%	18.0%
Bonds	15.0	8.0
Correlation	+0.5	

Utility function
Lower threshold: 15%
Upper threshold: 18.2%
Risk ratio: 5/1

Results

Asset Mix

Stocks	Bonds	Mean Return	Standard Deviation	Utility Ranking	Probability of Earning 15%
100%	0%	18.2%	7.9%	11%	59.48%
90	10	17.9	7.3	9	59.48
80	20	17.6	6.8	8	59.48
70	30	17.2	6.2	6	59.10
60	40	16.9	5.6	5	58.71
50	50	16.6	5.1	3	57.93
40	60	16.3	4.7	1	57.14
30	70	16.0	4.2	2	55.17
20	80	15.6	3.9	4	53.19
10	90	15.3	3.7	7	50.00
0	100	15.0	3.6	10	46.81

SOURCE: Wells Fargo Investment Advisors.

function approach: It allows the investor to factor several objectives and tradeoffs simultaneously into a decision.

RECONCILING THE DIFFERENT MODELS

Obviously, there are many ways of selecting an asset mix and valid reasons why different investors with identical market outlooks will have different mixes. Going back to the concept of an efficient frontier, each mix on the frontier offers maximum expected return for some level of risk; i.e., each mix is optimal for some investor. All of the techniques discussed in this chapter—risk (of not achieving a specified return) curves, liability simulation models, utility functions—are designed to help an investor assess what point on the frontier is appropriate for his or her portfolio.

A question frequently asked is why different asset mix models yield different results. Since differing expectations for asset class returns and risks can obviously be a factor, we will assume these forecasts are constant across models. What else impacts results?

A factor not to be overlooked is that some models incorporate transaction costs while others do not. Depending upon the size of assumed transaction costs and the spread among projected asset class returns, the impact of incorporating these costs can be significant. An issue to consider is the appropriate time period over which to amortize transaction costs. Turnover levels in the portfolio can provide insight on this.

By far the most significant reason why different models yield different results is that they encourage investors to assess the risk-reward tradeoff in different ways. As was demonstrated in Table 8-5, focusing only on the probability of failing to achieve a return objective may lead to a different conclusion than would be derived by employing a more fully developed utility function.

For a pension fund, framing objectives in terms of lowering contributions to a target percentage of payroll will often lead to still a different solution. In one asset mix study involving the development of a utility function, the pension plan sponsor originally framed objectives in terms of investment return, i.e., striving to earn at least the assumed actuarial rate of return. Given these goals, an optimal mix was determined. Later the sponsor became involved in some liability simulation work and decided that the real objective was to keep costs at or below competitive levels while still maintaining a well-funded plan. Since his original return objectives could not produce this result, the optimal asset mix had to change. This case is reviewed in detail in the appendix to this chapter.

In the final analysis, the function of an asset mix model is to systematize and quantify basically subjective judgments on return and risk. As we have seen, this can be done in different ways.

IMPLICATIONS OF THE TAX ARBITRAGE THEORY

No discussion of asset mix determination would be complete without some mention of the theory, espoused by Fischer Black [1980] and others, of tax arbitrage. The concept is that pension assets and liabilities should be considered as assets and liabilities of the corporation. Therefore, a firm should incorporate pension assets into any analysis of its total financial position. A typical pension plan will have holdings of both stocks and bonds. Likewise, the sponsoring corporation will have both equity and debt on its balance sheet. However, since income from pension assets is tax free and interest expense for a corporation is tax deductible, the case is made that all of the pension assets should be placed in bonds with an equal amount of debt issued by the firm. Proceeds from the debt sale would then be used to buy back the firm's stock. This series of transactions would not change the firm's overall capital structure or risk exposure. It would, however, result in substantial tax savings.

Obviously, this is a radically different way to view the management of a pension fund and, while the theory has generated widespread interest, few if any companies had implemented it in 1982. Since tax implications are what make the idea attractive, it is an open question as to what the Internal Revenue Service's response might be if this type of arbitrage became general practice. More important, since the prescribed activity would not be for the exclusive benefit of pension beneficiaries (a requirement under ERISA), it might attract adverse action by the Department of Labor.

ADJUSTING THE ANALYSIS FOR ACTIVE MANAGEMENT

Return and risk forecasts incorporated in asset mix models frequently assume the use of passive market indexes such as the S&P 500. Since the majority of portfolios are not passively managed, using passive bogies in an asset mix model may fail to capture adequately the characteristics of the actual investment. Assume, for example, that an investor decides on a mix with 60 percent in common stocks, based on risk and return estimates for the S&P 500. The equity portfolio, however, is invested largely in very small growth companies with considerably more risk. A 60 percent commitment to this type of investment may well be too risky for this investor. Conversely, an investor who hires an equity manager with the optimistic expectation that the manager will deliver a positive alpha—excess return for undertaking unsystematic risk—might well decide to place more money in equities than would be the case if the equity option were an index fund. Active management, by changing the expected risk-reward characteristics of an asset class, can affect the asset mix decision. Therefore, it is important to model the impact of active management correctly.

Investors have debated for years whether or not active money management can add value. It is certainly true that historically the S&P 500 has outperformed the vast majority of actively managed equity portfolios over any extended period. Those who believe that active money managers cannot add value argue that the averages are derived from the performance of professional managers, most of whom are bright, rational, and have access to reasonable research. To outperform this field consistently, a manager would have to have an edge of some sort, such as unique insight on some class of investments. Performance will be further diluted by transaction costs and management fees. This has led some to characterize active money management as a losing proposition.

Others, notably Keith Ambachtsheer and James Farrell [1979], reason that it is not a lack of research ability or investment insight that leads to submarket performance; rather it is an inability to translate this information appropriately into a portfolio. Studies have shown that research departments often have some ability to rank stocks by relative attractiveness. Ambachtsheer and Farrell argue that even a little ability can be used to advantage in a portfolio context. The key is to know one's predictive ability (*information coefficient* or "I.C.") and adjust the size of one's bets accordingly. Their studies have shown that alphas of 1–2 percent are attainable given reasonable forecasting ability and optimal translation of these forecasts into portfolio positions. This concept is explored more fully in Chapter 10.

These arguments notwithstanding, most organizations hire active money managers in the belief that they will outperform passive indexes. Most take incremental risk, some a considerable amount. Forecasts used in an asset mix model should be adjusted upward to reflect this added risk. The expected return may also be adjusted upward but should be kept within reasonable limits. Large alphas in actively managed portfolios are very uncommon and if used in an asset mix model can lead to erroneous conclusions.

STRUCTURING THE MIX OF MANAGERS

Once an investor has formulated investment objectives and determined the appropriate asset mix, he or she has the further task of developing a portfolio structure to reflect this chosen mix. The options are varied, especially for large institutional funds. The money can be run in-house or external managers can be hired. One manager can run the entire fund or several can be used. These managers can run balanced portfolios or specialty accounts concentrating on just one asset class or investment strategy. Some or all of the money can be run passively. There are pros and cons to each strategy.

Use of Multiple Managers

Hiring multiple managers for large funds has become common practice in recent years. At one time most large portfolios were run by one manager, either a bank or an insurance company. With the growth of independent investment advisors in the 1960s, plan sponsors began splitting their funds. Probably most funds were split in an attempt to diversify risk across managers.

More recently, plan sponsors have come to realize that they need not split funds to diversify risk. Rather, the reason to split funds is to take advantage of the expertise of various managers who the sponsor thinks can add value.

Although it is by no means assured that multiple managers will add more value than a single manager, it is assured that having multiple managers will complicate life for the plan sponsor, who will have to monitor and evaluate each individual portfolio as well as the aggregate. Further, the sponsor must check periodically to ensure that the aggregate portfolio reflects the chosen risk-reward posture and that each manager's contribution to the aggregate is in line with the sponsor's objective in hiring him. Too often, sponsors focus on the individual portfolios and lose sight of the aggregate.

Master Trust Arrangements

The advent of *master trusts* has made it simpler for the pension plan sponsor to utilize multiple managers. Many large corporations have serveral pension plans; separate plans for hourly and salaried employees are common as are separate plans for various subsidiaries. With a master trust a corporation can consolidate these plans for investment purposes while keeping them separate in every other respect. This allows the plan sponsor to hire a variety of money managers and invest assets of each plan in each portfolio. In this way even very small plans can be invested in an array of portfolios.

Figure 8-9 depicts a typical master trust arrangement. Five separate plans are invested across nine investment portfolios. Although each plan could have the same percentage of its total assets invested in each portfolio, this is not necessary. Plan I could elect to place most of its funds with the active equity managers, while plan IV could be wholly insured assets (GICs). Any combination is possible. Since each plan need not have individually managed portfolios, there is a savings in fees. Management reports are provided by plan, by portfolio, and in aggregate. The reporting package can include portfolio analysis and performance measurement reports.

Managers as Advisors

A unique approach to utilizing multiple managers adopted by a few plan sponsors is to have the managers team together and formally serve as advisors on the overall structure of the pension fund. Probably the best-known example of this is at Honeywell as described by Kent [1979]. Each manager,

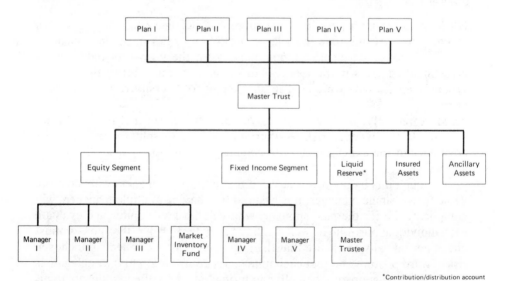

*Contribution/distribution account

Figure 8-9. Typical Master Trust Organization. (SOURCE: Bankers Trust Company)

in addition to being responsible for running his own portfolio, participates with the other managers in recommending how assets should be deployed. To ensure that the manager will not take a parochial view, his compensation is based on his original dollar allocation and on total fund performance. This should, for example, encourage an equity manager to recommend more fixed income investments if his outlook for that area is positive (and vice versa).

In-House Management

On another topic, some companies have elected to run some or all of their pension money in-house. Because of the set-up costs involved, most industry sources believe this makes sense only for very large companies. Various reasons advanced for in-house management include the following:

1. It saves on management fees. This argument is frequently advanced by those considering running index funds in-house.
2. Running money in-house keeps the plan sponsor closer to the capital markets and gives him a better perspective on evaluating his managers.
3. An in-house fund can be structured to offset gaps created by the selection of specialized managers that do not cover the full spectrum of securities. This is the rationale behind the *completeness fund* concept at Standard Oil Company (Indiana). This concept is discussed in more detail in Chapter 10.

Passive Management

Another question is: Should money be run actively or passively? The answer to this question depends on several factors. Using passively managed fixed income and equity portfolios as a reference point, the following must be considered:

1. The objectives and risk tolerance of an investor.
2. Whether an investor feels active managers can add substantial value, and, if so,
3. Whether he is confident that he can pick successful managers.

Some large funds index a portion of assets as a core portfolio and also hire active managers. This is an approach similar to that suggested by Rosenberg [1981]. A few who have done this have structured the index fund as a *market inventory fund* (MIF) through which the active managers can trade (for example, see Figure 8-9). The premise underlying an MIF is that it can track an index fairly closely while still absorbing trades initiated by the active managers, thereby avoiding market trading via brokers and thus lowering transaction costs. It should be noted, however, that this kind of situation is feasible only with fairly large pools of money.

Criteria for Evaluation

Whatever the ultimate structure, the investor must select the money manager or managers. What criteria should be used to evaluate prospective managers? Some frequently cited criteria are:

1. A defined investment style
2. Specific investment objectives and a process for delivering on those objectives
3. A style and objectives consistent with the investor's goals
4. Personnel with whom the investor is comfortable
5. Low turnover of personnel

Past investment performance will invariably be a factor but, since it is usually not indicative of future performance, its value is limited. In any event, the issues raised here are but the tip of the iceberg of managing and evaluating money managers. Much more will be said on this topic in Chapters 14 and 15.

SUMMARY

Selecting the appropriate asset mix for a portfolio is the single most important decision any investor must make. As many investors have come to recognize this fact, analytical approaches have been developed to facilitate the decision. The minimal input needed to work with these models is expected returns, standard deviations, and correlations for an array of assets, together with a statement of investor objectives and constraints.

In this chapter we have reviewed various models and approaches currently being used. Although the differences are obvious, the similarities are striking. All encourage the investor to make explicit forecasts of asset return and risk. Also, all encourage the investor to examine various asset mixes against specific investment objectives. The details are different for each model, but this general framework is consistent.

Many times investors frame their forecasts for risk and return by using market indexes such as the S&P 500. If the funds are actively managed, this approach can be somewhat misleading. It is important, therefore, to take the specific characteristics of portfolio style into consideration in any asset mix analysis.

In the next three chapters, the management of bonds, equities, and real estate will be discussed in detail. Insight on different management techniques and their potential risk and reward attributes will be provided. The objective in working with an asset mix model should be to capture these attributes precisely. This makes the output far more meaningful.

FURTHER READING

Textbooks that deal with the issue of asset mix include Cottle [1980] and Sharpe [1981].

The following general articles on asset mix may be of interest to the reader: Brinson [1978] and Fong [1980].

In addition, three papers presented at the Financial Analysts Federation Annual Conference and available for $3 the set from The Institute of Chartered Financial Analysts, P.O. Box 3668, Charlottesville, Va., 22903, are of interest: Condon [1980], Fouse [1980], and Kritzman [1980].

A good reference for historical asset class returns is Ibbotson and Sinquefield [1982].

The discussion on utility functions appears in the Wells Fargo Investment Advisors Institutional Counsel Service *Newsletter*, published in November 1981.

Discussions on incorporating international equities into a portfolio appear in Ammerman [1982] and Swanson [1980].

A framework for plan sponsors to use in monitoring their value added was provided by Stolte [1981].

For discussion of social investing and a review of practices in California, see Baldwin et al. [1980]. For the Labor Department's position on social investing, see Donovan [1982].

Analyses of equity transaction costs are detailed in two papers: Beebower and Priest [1980] and Condon [1981].

The tax arbitrage theory is developed in Black [1980].

To review the pros and cons of active money management, see Ambachtsheer and Farrell [1979], Ellis [1975], and Rosenberg, [1981].

Finally, for a discussion of the Honeywell pension framework, see Kent [1979].

BIBLIOGRAPHY

Ambachtsheer, Keith P., and James L. Farrell, Jr., "Can Active Management Add Value?" *Financial Analysts Journal*, November/December 1979.

Ammerman, Robert C., "International Investment Management: Questions the Pension Plan Sponsor Should Ask," *Pension World*, May 1982.

Baldwin, Stuart A., et al., *Pension Funds and Ethical Investment,* New York: Council on Economic Priorities, 1980.

Beebower, Gilbert, and William Priest, "The Tricks of the Trade," *The Journal of Portfolio Management,* Winter 1980.

Black, Fischer, "The Tax Consequences of Long-Run Pension Policy," *Financial Analysts Journal*, Winter 1980.

Brinson, Gary P., "The Applications of Investment Theory to the Asset Allocation Process," Paper presented at the Financial Analysts Federation Annual Conference, New York, N.Y., May 1978.

Condon, Kathleen A., "Asset Mix Model," Paper presented at the Financial Analysts Federation Annual Conference, Houston, Texas, April 1980, in *Asset Allocation Decisions in Portfolio Management,* Charlottesville, Va.: Institute of Chartered Financial Analysts, 1982.

————, "Measuring Equity Transaction Costs," *Financial Analysts Journal,* September/October 1981.

Cottle, Sidney, et al., *Pension Asset Management: The Corporate Decisions,* New York: Financial Executives Research Foundation, 1980.

Donovan, Raymond J., Secretary of Labor, Testimony before the Subcommittee on Labor, Committee on Labor and Human Resources, United States Senate, January 26, 1982.

Ellis, Charles D., "The Loser's Game," *Financial Analysts Journal,* July/August 1975.

Fong, Gifford, "An Asset Allocation Framework," *The Journal of Portfolio Management,* Winter 1980.

Fouse, William L., "Asset Allocation," Paper presented at the Financial Analysts Federation Annual Conference, Houston, Texas, April 1980, in *Asset Allocation Decisions in Portfolio Management,* Charlottesville, Va.: Institute of Chartered Financial Analysts, 1982.

Ibbotson, Roger G., and Rex A. Sinquefield, *Stocks, Bonds, Bills and Inflation: The Past and the Future,* Charlottesville, Va.: The Financial Analysts Research Foundation, 1982

Kent, Glenn H., "Team Management of Pension Money," *Harvard Business Review,* May/June 1979.

Kritzman, Mark P., "A Fundamental Approach to Asset Allocation Analysis," Paper presented at the Financial Analysts Federation Annual Conference, Houston, Texas, April 1980, in *Asset Allocation Decisions in Portfolio Management,* Charlottesville, Va.: Institute of Chartered Financial Analysts, 1982.

Rosenberg, Barr, "Capital Asset Pricing Model and the Market Mode," *The Journal of Portfolio Management,* Winter 1981.

Salomon, Robert S., Jr., "Bonds May Still Be the Only Bargains Left," *Investment Policy, Stock Research,* Salomon Brothers Inc., June 8, 1982.

Sharpe, William F., *Investments,* 2nd Ed., Englewood Cliffs, N.J.: Prentice-Hall, 1981.

Stolte, Myron D., "Pension Plan Sponsors: Monitor Yourselves," *Harvard Business Review,* March/April 1981.

Swanson, Joel R., "Investing Internationally to Reduce Risk and Enhance Return," Morgan Guaranty Trust Company, New York, 1980.

APPENDIX

Asset Mix Analysis: XYZ Corporation Pension Fund

A study was undertaken by a large commercial bank pension consulting group to determine the appropriate asset mix for the XYZ Corporation pension plan. This was a well-funded plan with costs, as a percentage of payroll, of 8.3 percent. The primary objective of the plan sponsor was to have costs of no more than 8.0 percent in the future. Asset classes considered were domestic common stocks, international

TABLE 8A-1. Average Annual Expected Returns, Standard Deviations, and Correlations for Selected Asset Classes over the Succeeding 4-Year Period

Asset Class	Expected Return	Standard Deviation	Correlation Matrix			
Domestic equities	16.08%	15.53%	1.00			
International equities	18.78	13.04	0.80	1.00		
Equities 90% domestic 10% international	16.21	15.04	1.00			
Options	14.28	9.22	0.80	1.00		
Intermediate bonds	13.53	4.50	0.58	0.58	1.00	
Cash equivalents	10.89	2.46	−0.48	−0.48	−0.96	1.00

equities, options, intermediate bonds, and cash equivalents. In addition, constraints were imposed as follows: (1) no more than 2 percent of the total fund in covered call options, and (2) no more than 10 percent of the equity portfolio in international equities.

Parameter Forecasts

Returns, standard deviations, and correlations were forecast for a period covering the subsequent four years. Adjustments were made to reflect the styles of the plan's money managers. These forecasted figures are shown in Table 8A-1.

TABLE 8A-2. Current Asset Mix, Assumed Transactions Costs, and Efficient Frontier Portfolio Asset Mixes for XYZ Pension Fund

Asset Class	XYZ Pension Fund Current Mix	Transaction Costs (each way)
Equities	52%	1.0%
Options	2	1.2
Intermediate bonds	29	0.25
Cash equivalents	17	0.0

EFFICIENT FRONTIER
PORTFOLIO CHARACTERISTICS

Asset Class	1	2	3	4
Equities	98%	24%	0%	0%
Options	2	2	2	0
Intermediate bonds	0	74	39	35
Cash equivalents	0	0	59	65
Expected return	15.64%	13.81%	11.45%	11.26%
Standard deviation	14.89	6.36	0.68	0.45

TABLE 8A-3. **Comparison of Optimal with Current Asset Mix of XYZ Pension Fund**

Asset Class	Optimal	Current	Change
Common stock	47%	51%	−4%
International equities	5	1	+4
Options	2	2	—
Intermediate bonds	46	29	+17
Cash equivalents	0	17	−17

Since international equities were projected to have a higher expected return as well as a lower standard deviation than domestic equities, it was readily apparent that the portfolio should hold the full 10 percent amount allowed. Therefore, an asset class labeled simply equities, with a 90 percent domestic/10 percent international split, was set up to be incorporated in the analysis.

Efficient Frontier Formation

An efficient frontier was derived, incorporating both constraints and transactions costs. Four points on that frontier, along with the plan's current asset mix and assumed transactions costs, are shown in Table 8A-2.

Selecting the Mix

Since the sponsor's objective was to control costs as a percentage of payroll, it was necessary to integrate these return forecasts with a liability simulation model. The primary objective was to have payroll costs of no more than 8 percent; costs above 8 percent were viewed negatively, while costs above 9.4 percent were regarded as extremely undesirable. A utility function was set up to reflect these objectives. Results of the analysis appear in Table 8A-3.

Conclusions

It turned out that to have costs of 8.0 percent or lower, one needed a return of at least 13.7 percent per year. A return of 10.0 percent was necessary to keep costs from escalating above 9.4 percent. The sponsor had originally articulated an objective of earning the assumed actuarial interest rate (7 percent) or better, so the addition of a liability simulation model and the switch in emphasis to controlling costs in the form of pension expense as a percent of payroll resulted in a fairly dramatic change in plan objectives and asset mix to meet those objectives.

CHAPTER 9

Portfolio Construction: Fixed Income

H. Gifford Fong

$\mathbf{T}$he role of fixed income portfolio construction logically follows the previous chapters. Establishing the investor's objectives and constraints (Chapters 4 and 5) provides the basic policy framework by which the portfolio management process will operate; stated another way, it provides the basic "trip plan" as to the general course and destination. The macro and micro expectations for return and risk (Chapters 6 and 7) can be thought of as the market environment through which the journey will be made. The vagaries of the weather, road conditions, traffic patterns, and fuel costs may be thought of as corollaries to the analysis of return and risk. Asset allocation (Chapter 8) is akin to the final selection of the mode(s) of travel that is the result of integrating the findings of all of the previous analysis.

The next problem becomes the process of selecting specific portfolios of the asset classes chosen. The emphasis is on identifying, measuring, and controlling the return and risk characteristics of the alternative portfolios available. These then can be most effectively matched to best serve the needs of the previously defined objectives of the investor. In a general sense this is what modern portfolio management is concerned with.

Fixed income portfolio management can be considered unique in that it represents an investment asset class falling between cash equivalents and stocks in terms of return and risk. This permits a continuum of choice and also a potential synergistic blending of type—a dual dimension that makes the role of portfolio management both rewarding and challenging.

This chapter begins with a review of the types of fixed income securities and their respective roles in a portfolio. Included is a discussion of return

291

and risk characteristics. Portfolio strategies are then identified; these include passive or buy-and-hold strategies, immunization strategies, and active strategies, together with variants on these approaches. Fixed income portfolio constraints are discussed, including liquidity needs, tax considerations, time horizon, regulatory or legal considerations and, finally, considerations unique to the particular investor.

ROLE OF THE FIXED INCOME PORTFOLIO

Fixed income securities are one of a number of asset categories that may be part of the total portfolio. Whether they belong in the portfolio, and in what proportion, is related to the investment objectives of the investor and investment policies commensurate with those objectives. That is, the return and risk characteristics of fixed income securities should be directly related to the objectives and constraints of the investor. The problem from a bond portfolio construction standpoint is to select fixed income assets such that total return is the highest for a desired level of risk; or, alternatively, a specified return is achieved with the lowest level of risk.

Asset Class Alternatives

Among the most common asset types (stocks, bonds, and Treasury bills), fixed income securities cover the middle range of both risk and return. As a reminder of data provided in Chapter 3, Table 9-1 provides an indication of their relative return and risk characteristics for the 56 years ending December 31, 1981. Stocks rank the highest on both risk and return, followed by bonds and then Treasury bills. As one proceeds from stocks to bonds to bills, it can be seen from the coefficient of variation that there is a lower risk per unit of return. This can be interpreted as an incentive to seek only those levels of return that fit the needs of the investor, since for a given increment of expected return there is increasing associated risk.

While the figures in Table 9-1 represent averages over an extended historical time period, they are representative of a basic structure. The character-

TABLE 9-1. Common Stocks and Bonds Return and Risk Comparison, 1926–81

	Geometric Mean Return	Arithmetic Mean Return	Risk (Standard Deviation)	Coefficient of Variation[a]
Common stock	9.1%	11.4%	21.9%	1.9
Long-term bonds	3.6	3.7	5.6	1.5
Treasury bills	3.0	3.1	3.1	1.0

SOURCE: Ibbotson and Sinquefield [1982].
[a] Coefficient of variation is risk divided by arithmetic mean return.

istics of each asset class tend to perpetuate their return and risk relationships on a relative basis. Over long time horizons, stocks should have both greater return and risk than bonds, given their residual position in the capital structure of a corporation and the growth opportunities associated with that position. For example, bonds have a defined promised cash flow while stocks do not; bonds have a specific maturity while stocks do not. These features contribute to a greater confidence in future cash flows for bonds and hence less associated risk or uncertainty of returns for bonds. On the other hand, bonds have a specified interest payment while stocks have the potential for increases in dividends, suggesting a potential lower return for bonds.

Recently, the increase in uncertainty associated with higher and more volatile interest rate levels has led to an increase in the volatility of returns of long bonds, a point that will be discussed and illustrated in Table 9-4 later in the chapter. That is, bonds clearly became more risky in the 1970s and early 1980s as measured by their standard deviation of returns. Over longer time horizons, higher returns must be achieved to justify the higher risk. However, because of the features of bonds, the more likely expectation is that this markedly higher volatility of bonds is a temporary phenomenon, and that the long-term historical relationship of bonds providing both lower return and risk will again prevail.

Whatever the appropriate average historical values and relative relationships, there will likely be wide variation of return experience among various asset classes. It is the existence of this dispersion, both in terms of the level and the relative ranking of return and risk of various asset groups, that provides the opportunity for profitable management. While one can easily measure what has been the historical level and relative rank of asset classes, the much more difficult managerial challenge is to provide expectations of what these will be over the future planning horizons.

Alternatives Within Fixed Income Asset Class

Within the fixed income asset class there can also be found a range of return and risk characteristics. In fact, a case can be made that under some circumstances the entire return and risk range can be covered by bonds. For example, very short bonds can be considered cash equivalents and some convertible bonds have the same characteristics as their underlying stocks. And they can be leveraged to even higher risk levels by buying them on margin. However, the illiquidity of individual bond issues and the large number of noncomparable issues available are just two examples of bond characteristics that make it difficult to cover the asset risk spectrum with only fixed income securities.

In more general terms, fixed income securities may be identified by characteristics such as maturity, i.e., short-, intermediate-, and long-maturity classes. While no specific definition applies, maturities up to three years are generally considered to be short, from three to 12 years are intermediate, and more than 12 years are long. Other things being equal, Homer and Leibowitz [1972] have demonstrated that for a given basis point (one basis point equals 1/100 of a percent) change in yield, there generally is more bond price volatility the longer the maturity and the lower the coupon (interest paid on the bond). These are just two examples of how interrelationships of bond terms act to determine its price and, therefore, its return and risk characteristics.

The emphasis in this chapter is on the fixed income securities and portfolios that make up the middle range of return and risk between equity portfolios and money market portfolios. If one assumes a one-period planning horizon of one year or less, then a zero coupon default-free security maturing at the end of the horizon could qualify as a money market alternative, i.e., a security not subject to much, if any, change in price from interest rate change. This special case is an obvious one. Of more interest is the management of portfolios with extended horizons and a broad range of terms that offer alternative return and risk combinations.

Such a fixed asset portfolio represents a tradeoff or balance between high return-high risk equity portfolios and low return-low risk money market portfolios. By properly blending the available return-risk characteristics, a virtual continuum of alternatives becomes available.

In the next section, the characteristics of fixed income securities and portfolios will be summarized. Identifying these characteristics provides the basis for understanding how and why individual securities can be selected and combined in portfolios to meet return-risk characteristics specified by the asset allocation decision.

CHARACTERISTICS OF FIXED INCOME SECURITIES AND PORTFOLIOS

A review of the characteristics of fixed income securities that affect their return and risk parameters is useful as background for the portfolio analysis to follow. The range of alternatives is wide. The intent here is not to describe in detail all possible types, but rather to identify the main features. For more detailed treatment, please see any standard text such as Sharpe [1981].

Fixed income assets are generally divided into three broad classifications: bonds, mortgages, and preferred stocks. Within each category, they may be further classified by certain characteristics, a selected number of which are summarized in Table 9-2 on pages 296 and 297. By the proper selection of the appropriate features, the basic ingredients for alternative portfolio strategies are determined.

Return Characteristics of Fixed Income Securities

The most distinguishing features differentiating fixed income securities from equities are the priority of lien position and, generally, the size and certainty of cash flows. Fixed income securities have specified, contractually guaranteed interest payments during the period to maturity that are typically larger, in percentage (yield) terms, than the dividends paid on stocks. They also have a defined maturity date as opposed to stocks, which have a perpetual existence. Finally, fixed income securities have relatively large assured cash flows permitting the accommodation of particular investment objectives, as will be discussed.

Sources of Return. There are three principal sources of fixed income security return. These are coupon or interest payments and capital changes—the usual components of total return—plus reinvestment returns for portfolios where coupon instruments are rolled over or invested in succeeding coupon instruments when the original instruments mature or are sold. Depending on the length of the planning horizon, the dominant source of return actually realized over that time period will vary.

Over horizons of greater than two or three years, the reinvestment rate becomes the chief determinant of return for accounts that are able to reinvest interest coupons. For example, if we held a 5-year, 9-percent par bond over a 5-year horizon, the realized yield would be 8.66 percent at a 7-percent coupon reinvestment rate, 9.00 percent at a 9-percent coupon reinvestment rate, and 9.35 percent at an 11-percent coupon reinvestment rate. As a consequence, the yield to maturity or promised yield is a valid measure of the prospective return to maturity only if future coupons are reinvested at the indicated yield to maturity. If the reinvestment rate should change, up or down, there will be a direct impact on the realized return. For zero coupon or deep discount low coupon bonds, the effects of reinvestment are minimized because the indicated yield to maturity is dominated by the bond's accretion of discount and gradual price appreciation rather than by its coupon. Therefore, the exposure to reinvestment risk is dampened or, in the case of a zero coupon bond, eliminated. This influence on the total realized return to maturity, which dominates the other sources of return for longer time horizons, is illustrated in Table 9-3 on page 298. Note that as the reinvestment rate is increased, larger percentages of total return are accounted for by the reinvestment effect.

For investment management horizons where time frames are measured in months instead of years, the greatest marginal impact on return is due to price changes, which are caused chiefly by changes in interest rates. If rates rise, then the price of the outstanding bond will fall to reflect the new available yield; conversely, if rates decline, the price of the outstanding bond will increase. This would occur when bonds are held with a maturity different from the managerial planning horizon.

Yield Curves. A popular indicator of changes in interest rates is the yield curve for government securities where the percentage yield is plotted as a function of maturity. Any change in rates across the maturity spectrum will be reflected by comparing the position and shape of the curve at different points in time.

TABLE 9-2. Selected Characteristics of Fixed Income Securities

	Bonds	Preferred Stocks	Real Estate Mortgages

Issuers	Federal government
	Federal agencies
	Corporations
	  Industrial
	  Financial
	  Railroads
	  Utilities
	States (Provinces)
	Municipalities
	Municipal agencies
	Foreign governments
	Foreign corporations
		Corporations
		(typically utilities)
			Corporations
			Partnerships
			Individuals

Security	First mortgage Mortgage-backed pools Collateral trust Equipment trust Debentures Subordinated debentures Income bonds	Unsecured	First mortgage Second mortgage
Income	Fixed coupon rate Variable rate Zero coupon	Fixed dividend rate Variable rate	Fixed interest rate Variable rate

	(Bonds)	(Preferred Stocks)	(Real Estate Mortgages)
Maturity	Fixed date for final principal payment; for mortgage-backed or sinking fund issues, the average life is more important to portfolio managers than the final maturity because of periodic principal repayments	Perpetual (no maturity)	Fixed date for final principal payment, but average life is more important to portfolio managers due to periodic principal repayments
Sinking fund	Retirement of principal on a specified basis with significance dependent on issuer; typically significant for industrials but not for utilities	Some issues have sinking funds	Most mortgage payments include interest and amortization of principal on a monthly, quarterly, or annual basis
Call and/or refunding provision	Utility issuers have the option to retire part or all of the issue after five years; industrial issues—typically ten years; government issues—typically noncallable	Issuer has option to retire part or all of the issue prior to maturity	Mortgagor has option to refinance or pay down the loan after a stipulated period, often five years
Conversion feature	Some corporate issues can be converted into the common stock of the issuer	Some corporate issues can be converted into the common stock of the issuer	Not applicable
Maturity/put option	Many Canadian issues—federal government, provincial, and corporate—provide the holders the option to *retract* the original maturity to an earlier date or *extend* the original maturity to a later date. Some recent U.S. tax-exempt bond issues allow the holder to retract the original maturity to an earlier date. Allowing a holder to retract a bond's maturity date effectively adds a put option to the issue since the holder can redeem or put the bond to the issuer at its par or face value.	Not applicable	Not applicable

TABLE 9-3. Effect of Reinvestment Rate on Total Realized Return on an 8 Percent Noncallable 20-Year Bond Bought at 100 to Yield 8 Percent

Reinvestment Rate	% of Return	Amount	Coupon Income	Discount	Total Return	Total Realized Compound Yield
5%	41%	$1,096	$1,600	0	$2,696	6.64%
6	47	1,416	1,600	0	3,016	7.07
7	53	1,782	1,600	0	3,382	7.53
8	58	2,201	1,600	0	3,801	8.00
9	63	2,681	1,600	0	4,281	8.50
10	67	3,232	1,600	0	4,832	9.01

SOURCE: Homer and Leibowitz [1972].

A brief analysis of a simple change in position (level) and shape (slope) of the yield curve is illustrated in Figure 9-1. From this basic illustration, the following three sources of return impact can be identified:

1. The impact of time as the bond moves closer to maturity from point A_1 to point B_3. That is, if there is no change in either the slope or level of the market yield curve—represented by curve 1—or in the bond's valuation relative to the market, this bond will "ride the yield curve" from A_1 to B_3.

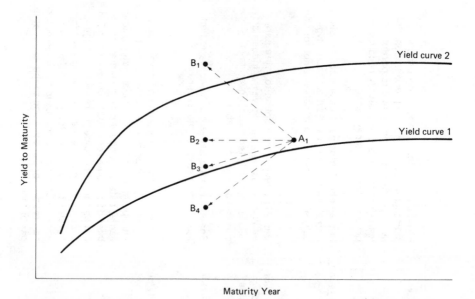

Figure 9-1. Yield Curve Analytical Framework.

2. The impact of changes in market valuation that can be based on the characteristics of the bond itself. This is illustrated by the movement from A_1 to B_4, as the yield to maturity changes from a premium relative to the market—again represented by curve 1—to a discount with the consequent increase in market value relative to the market. A widening of the yield premium and the consequent lower valuation relative to the market are reflected in the movement from A_1 to B_2.
3. The impact of changes in the slope and/or level of interest rates, such as from curve 1 to curve 2. This is illustrated by the movement from A_1 to B_1.

Figure 9-2 further illustrates a current and projected yield curve as of June 30, 1981. Both the capital changes and the reinvestment return of fixed income assets will be directly affected by changes in interest rate levels. Interest rate changes can be characterized by various yield curve shifts, as shown in Figure 9-3. Parallel changes are those having equal basis point

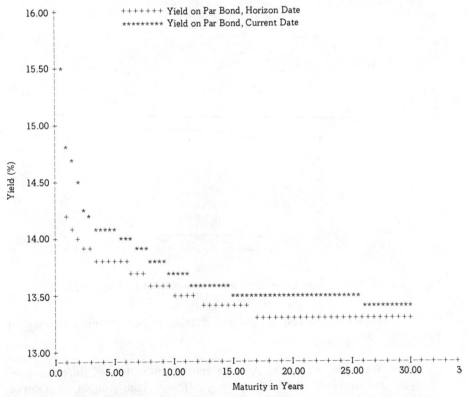

Figure 9-2. Current (6/30/81) and Projected (12/30/81) Yield Curves, U.S. Treasury Issues. (SOURCE: Gifford Fong Associates)

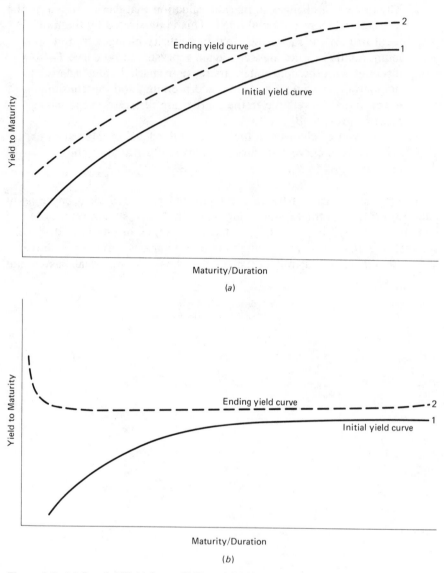

Figure 9-3. (a) Parallel Yield Curve Shift and (b) Nonparallel Yield Curve Shift.

moves across all maturities; nonparallel changes are exemplified by unequal basis point shifts.

Term Structure Analysis. An alternative indicator of interest rate change, term structure analysis, which is different from straight yield curve analysis, may be used as described by Fong and Vasicek [1982]. The term structure may be defined as the spot rate or yield on a pure discount or zero coupon security for each maturity for a homogeneous universe of bonds. In its most fundamental form the universe would be made up of default-free U.S. Treasury issues. The resulting term structure would consist of a series of spot rates representing the yield on a pure discount or zero coupon default-free security for each maturity in the structure. That is, yields on U.S. Treasuries at any given point in time are adjusted to remove the coupon or tax effect (the effect resulting from different sources of total return—capital change versus coupon income—and their resulting differential tax treatment) and the residual spread between same-maturity Treasury yields that remains even after the coupon/tax effect has been adjusted for. Thus a market-equilibrium, default-free, pure-discount yield curve is, in effect, created.

As shown in Fong and Vasicek [1982], each of the theoretically pure spot rates located on this pure-discount yield curve can be mathematically converted into a set of one-period spot and forward rates based on the *pure expectations theory*. That is, every multiperiod spot rate in the term structure is equal to the compound average (*n*th root) of the current one-period spot rate times all the successive one-period forward rates mathematically implied into the future to the maturity of the multiperiod spot rate. For example, the five-year maturity spot rate would be equal to the compound average (geometric mean) of the current one-year spot rate and each of the four succeeding one-year forward rates, or the 5th root of the product of these five rates.

In effect, each of the spot rates, and, taken together, all of the spot rates in the total term structure, implies a continuum of one-period future reinvestment rates that are expected at each future maturity date *if* the term structure created is assumed to remain constant. When compounded together, this continuum of forward rates or returns on pure discount zero coupon bonds provides the bond investor with a basic market-implicit return *regardless of maturity*—that is, it is the equilibrium-expected compound rate of return for the entire term structure such that no maturities or payment schedules are *ex ante* (before the fact) preferred to any others. Why? Because it encompasses all that the market is currently requiring in the way of return across the entire spectrum of future maturities.

The question then remains of how the market-implicit rate so derived can be most effectively used. Like any other forecast of future interest rates, it has not been an accurate estimator of future rates in an absolute sense. In a relative sense, however, the approach has been shown to be a better prognosticator than recent forecasts by two highly regarded econometric models in a 1982 proprietary study. The prime benefit of market-implicit returns is to provide a most-likely forecast in a probabilistic decision-making framework. This forecast is then bracketed by less probable optimistic and pessimistic rate forecasts to produce a probability distribution of returns. The approach can also be used in simulations where sensitivity analysis is done and the effect of "what if" changes in assumed rates are measured. Hence, this use of the term structure should provide a more comprehensive perspective of potential rate changes and can serve as a basic building block for much further analysis, such as for bond performance analysis as discussed in Fong, Pearson, and Vasicek [1981].

Risk Characteristics

Inextricably, return cannot be discussed without also discussing the dimension of risk. In general, unsystematic risk is attributable to those factors that are due to the individual characteristics of the security. Systematic risk arises from the influence of overall changes in interest rates, affecting both capital changes as well as reinvestment return. Because a change in interest rates can affect returns on all bonds, systematic risk is a pervasive characteristic of bond investing. While stocks are also exposed to systematic risk, the effects of overall market conditions are less pervasive because they are far more heterogeneous than bonds. Thus stocks have much more risk specific to the individual security.

Specific or Unsystematic Risk. If interest rates do not change and the security is held to maturity, then the only source of risk in nominal terms is that of default. In this sense, then, the importance of unsystematic risk vis-à-vis systematic risk is much less for fixed income securities than for stocks. Through diversification of issuers and classes of fixed income securities, unsystematic risk can be minimized.

Another manifestation of this risk source is in the yield spread relationship that may exist between securities. For example, a corporate bond that appears to be similar in all respects to another corporate bond but is selling at a higher yield reflects an issuing sector difference of some kind—typically in quality grade—that has gone undetected by the rating agencies. The variation in yield spread resulting from quality grade adjustments is an additional source of unsystematic risk.

By staying with high quality securities, the risk of default or unsystematic risk can be essentially eliminated under all but the most dire economic circumstances. For example, Treasury securities can be considered default-free. A portfolio of Treasury securities can therefore be thought of as having only systematic risk and subject only to price and return variation due to change in interest rates.

Market or Systematic Risk. A central issue is how one controls market or systematic risk, which is the dominant influence on marginal return, positive or negative, that is implied by a bond's current yield to maturity. Traditionally, systematic risk has been controlled by varying the effective maturity (more accurately, duration or weighted average maturity—explained later in this chapter) over time. In effect, diversifying maturities provides one way to control systematic risk. Maximum systematic risk exposure as measured in terms of standard deviation of return, given a specified interest rate change, is achieved with the longest maturity (duration) portfolio. Conversely, the minimum exposure to systematic risk is achieved by a short maturity (duration) portfolio. This holds assuming there is an equal basis point move across all maturities, i.e., a parallel shift in the yield curve. If there is a nonparallel change in rates, then a closer evaluation of return and risk impact is necessary. Return simulation analysis, described in a subsequent section, is a useful tool for this.

Alternatively, systematic risk may be controlled by investment strategies that seek to match maturity or duration of the securities (assets) with the investment need (liabilities) of the portfolio. By virtue of the size and certainty of cash flows, it is possible to minimize the adverse effects of systematic risk. This topic will be discussed later in this chapter in the section on bond portfolio *immunization* strategies. To summarize, since the investor who is very concerned with systematic risk can effectively immunize his bond portfolio, the only risk that remains is unsystematic risk, which can be essentially eliminated by diversifying the portfolio across a spectrum of high quality bond issues.

Measures of Risk. For asset allocation purposes, suitable risk measures are standard deviation and covariance of returns. In the context of fixed income securities these are directly related to the volatility of interest rates. As the magnitude of interest rate change increases, this will directly increase the standard deviation of fixed income returns. Since systematic risk is attributable to changes in interest rates, this implies a need to evaluate the standard deviation of interest rate change.

Tables 9-4 and 9-5 (following pages) reflect the total returns and standard deviations of a high grade corporate bond index's monthly returns for holding periods ranging from one year to twenty years over the two-decade-plus period 1960–81. Table 9-6 (pages 306 and 307) reflects the correlation of monthly total returns between bonds and stocks (represented by the S&P 500 Stock Composite Index) for similar combinations of holding periods.

Specifically, in Table 9-4, the numbers down the diagonal are the geometric mean (compound average) returns of the monthly total returns on the bond index from January to December of each year. As such, they represent the annual wealth increments of the index. The numbers in each column below the first number (the diagonal element defined in the previous sentence) are the geometric means of the corresponding numbers down the diagonal. For example, the 1963 value of 6.0 in the 1960 column is equal to $[(1.091 \times 1.048 \times 1.079 \times 1.022)^{1/4} - 1] \times 100$.

By contrast, in Table 9-5, the numbers down the diagonal are the standard deviations of the 12 monthly returns in each year, and the numbers in each column below the diagonal element are the standard deviations of the monthly returns from January of the column-heading year to December of the row-heading year. Hence, in the 1960 column the number 2.8 in the 1963 row is the standard deviation of the 48 monthly returns from January 1960 to December 1963.

TABLE 9-4. Composite Total Annual Returns (in percent). Based on Monthly Returns from Jan. 1 to Dec. 31 of Years Shown for a High Grade Corporate Bond Index

From	1960	1961	1962	1963	1964	1965	1966	1967	1968	1969	1970
1960	9.1										
1961	6.9	4.8									
1962	7.3	6.4	7.9								
1963	6.0	5.0	5.0	2.2							
1964	5.7	4.9	4.9	3.5	4.8						
1965	4.7	3.8	3.6	2.1	2.1	−0.5					
1966	4.0	3.2	2.9	1.7	1.5	−0.1	0.2				
1967	2.9	2.0	1.5	0.3	−0.2	−1.9	−2.4	−5.0			
1968	2.8	2.1	1.7	0.7	0.4	−0.7	−0.8	−1.3	2.6		
1969	1.7	0.9	0.4	−0.6	−1.1	−2.2	−2.7	−3.6	−2.9	−8.1	
1970	3.1	2.5	2.3	1.6	1.5	0.9	1.2	1.5	3.7	4.3	18.4
1971	3.7	3.3	3.1	2.6	2.6	2.3	2.8	3.3	5.5	6.5	14.6
1972	4.0	3.6	3.5	3.0	3.1	2.9	3.4	4.0	5.8	6.7	12.1
1973	3.8	3.4	3.3	2.9	2.9	2.7	3.1	3.6	5.0	5.6	9.3
1974	3.3	2.9	2.8	2.4	2.4	2.1	2.4	2.7	3.9	4.1	6.7
1975	4.0	3.7	3.6	3.3	3.3	3.2	3.6	4.0	5.1	5.5	8.0
1976	4.8	4.5	4.5	4.3	4.4	4.4	4.9	5.4	6.6	7.1	9.4
1977	4.6	4.4	4.3	4.1	4.2	4.2	4.6	5.0	6.1	6.5	8.4
1978	4.4	4.1	4.1	3.8	4.0	3.9	4.2	4.6	5.5	5.8	7.5
1979	3.9	3.7	3.6	3.4	3.4	3.3	3.6	3.9	4.7	4.9	6.2
1980	3.6	3.3	3.3	3.0	3.1	3.0	3.2	3.4	4.1	4.2	5.4
1981	3.4	3.2	3.1	2.8	2.9	2.9	3.0	3.2	3.8	3.9	4.9

TABLE 9-5. Annual Standard Deviations (in percent). Calculated from Composite Total Returns Based on Monthly Returns from Jan. 1 to Dec. 31 of Years Shown for a High Grade Corporate Bond Index

From	1960	1961	1962	1963	1964	1965	1966	1967	1968	1969	1970
1960	3.5										
1961	3.4	3.3									
1962	3.1	2.8	2.0								
1963	2.8	2.4	1.8	1.2							
1964	2.6	2.2	1.7	1.3	1.3						
1965	2.5	2.2	1.9	1.6	1.8	1.9					
1966	3.0	2.8	2.7	2.7	3.0	3.5	4.6				
1967	3.9	3.9	3.9	4.1	4.6	5.1	6.2	7.3			
1968	4.3	4.4	4.5	4.7	5.1	5.7	6.4	7.2	6.9		
1969	4.8	4.8	5.0	5.2	5.6	6.1	6.7	7.2	7.2	7.1	
1970	5.5	5.6	5.8	6.1	6.5	7.0	7.6	8.2	8.4	9.0	9.2
1971	6.0	6.1	6.3	6.6	7.0	7.5	8.1	8.6	8.7	9.3	9.5
1972	5.8	5.9	6.1	6.4	6.7	7.1	7.5	7.9	7.9	8.2	8.0
1973	5.9	6.0	6.2	6.5	6.8	7.1	7.5	7.8	7.8	8.0	7.9
1974	6.4	6.6	6.7	7.0	7.3	7.6	8.0	8.3	8.4	8.6	8.7
1975	6.7	6.9	7.0	7.3	7.6	7.9	8.2	8.6	8.6	8.9	8.9
1976	6.6	6.8	7.0	7.2	7.4	7.7	8.0	8.3	8.3	8.5	8.5
1977	6.5	6.7	6.8	7.0	7.3	7.5	7.8	8.0	8.0	8.1	8.1
1978	6.4	6.6	6.7	6.9	7.1	7.4	7.6	7.8	7.8	7.9	7.8
1979	6.7	6.8	7.0	7.2	7.4	7.6	7.8	8.0	8.1	8.2	8.2
1980	7.9	8.0	8.2	8.4	8.6	8.9	9.2	9.4	9.5	9.7	9.8
1981	8.6	8.8	9.0	9.2	9.4	9.7	10.0	10.2	10.4	10.6	10.8

1971	1972	1973	1974	1975	1976	1977	1978	1979	1980	1981
11.0										
9.1	7.3									
6.4	4.2	1.1								
3.9	1.7	−1.0	−3.1							
6.0	4.8	4.0	5.4	14.6						
8.0	7.4	7.5	9.7	16.6	18.6					
7.1	6.4	6.3	7.6	11.4	9.9	1.7				
6.2	5.5	5.2	6.0	8.4	6.4	0.8	−0.1			
5.0	4.2	3.8	4.3	5.8	3.7	−0.8	−2.1	−4.1		
4.2	3.5	3.0	3.3	4.3	2.4	−1.3	−2.3	−3.4	−2.7	
3.8	3.1	2.6	2.8	3.7	2.0	−1.1	−1.8	−2.3	−1.4	−0.2

SOURCE: Gifford Fong Associates.

1971	1972	1973	1974	1975	1976	1977	1978	1979	1980	1981
9.6										
7.1	2.9									
7.2	5.5	7.1								
8.5	7.9	9.4	11.2							
8.8	8.5	9.7	10.7	9.6						
8.3	8.0	8.8	9.2	7.5	4.3					
7.9	7.5	8.1	8.3	6.9	4.8	4.3				
7.5	7.2	7.7	7.7	6.5	4.8	4.3	4.3			
7.9	7.7	8.1	8.3	7.5	6.8	6.9	7.9	10.3		
9.8	9.8	10.4	10.8	10.7	10.8	11.6	13.2	15.9	19.9	
10.9	11.0	11.5	11.9	12.0	12.3	13.2	14.6	16.6	19.0	18.1

SOURCE: Gifford Fong Associates.

TABLE 9-6. Correlations (in percent) of Monthly Total Returns on Standard & Poor's 500 Stock Composite Index with Returns on a High Grade Corporate Bond Index

From	1960	1961	1962	1963	1964	1965	1966	1967	1968	1969	1970
1960	−7.0										
1961	6.0	41.3									
1962	3.5	10.2	2.5								
1963	−0.0	5.8	−9.9	−1.2							
1964	−0.0	5.8	−8.1	−1.4	9.0						
1965	1.6	7.8	−3.2	11.8	19.4	21.3					
1966	18.7	26.8	23.9	45.1	55.3	56.3	76.3				
1967	28.3	35.4	34.2	52.9	59.1	60.2	66.0	79.7			
1968	17.3	21.5	19.3	28.4	30.6	30.5	31.8	23.0	−27.9		
1969	20.9	24.5	22.7	30.6	32.1	31.6	32.4	27.3	5.5	28.3	
1970	33.2	36.5	36.2	43.2	45.2	45.3	46.8	44.2	40.5	61.1	79.0
1971	33.0	35.8	35.6	41.4	43.2	43.4	44.7	42.3	39.4	53.3	58.2
1972	34.0	36.8	36.7	42.4	44.3	44.5	45.7	43.4	40.5	53.8	57.6
1973	28.6	30.8	30.5	34.6	36.0	36.1	37.0	34.4	31.1	40.6	41.4
1974	34.1	35.8	35.7	38.7	39.7	39.8	40.5	38.9	37.6	43.9	45.7
1975	37.2	38.8	38.8	41.7	42.7	42.8	43.4	42.1	41.2	46.7	47.9
1976	37.8	39.3	39.4	42.1	43.1	43.2	43.9	42.5	41.7	47.0	47.9
1977	38.4	39.9	40.0	42.6	43.6	43.7	44.4	43.1	42.5	47.6	48.7
1978	38.5	40.0	40.0	42.5	43.4	43.5	44.1	42.9	42.2	46.9	47.9
1979	39.8	41.2	41.3	43.8	44.5	44.6	45.1	44.1	43.4	47.6	48.4
1980	32.2	33.3	33.2	35.1	35.6	35.7	36.0	35.0	33.8	36.6	36.3
1981	33.9	34.9	34.9	36.7	37.2	37.3	37.6	36.8	35.9	38.4	38.3

SOURCE: Gifford Fong Associates.

Finally, in Table 9-6, the diagonal numbers are the coefficients of correlation (in percentage terms) of the 12 monthly returns on stocks and bonds from January to December of each year. The numbers in each column below the diagonal element are the correlation coefficients of the monthly paired stock and bond returns from January of the column-heading year to December of the row-heading year. For example, in the 1960 column, 1966 row, the number 18.7 indicates there was 0.187 correlation between the paired monthly returns on a stock and bond index over the period January 1960 to December 1966.

Looking down the diagonal of each of the tables, it can be seen that bond returns have varied on a yearly basis from −8.1 to 18.6 percent; the standard deviation from 1.2 to 19.9 percent; and the correlation from −.279 to .797. The compound or geometric average return for the entire period was 3.4 percent. Average and standard deviation numbers such as those generated in these tables usually provide the basis for forecasting expectations of future return and risk. But in the case of these distributions of returns, the range of the numbers shown is so wide that the average is not really representative or descriptive of the underlying distribution. It is important to keep in mind that it is the underlying economic process that is important for providing a credible basis for forecasting purposes. Identification of clear and unambiguous

1971	1972	1973	1974	1975	1976	1977	1978	1979	1980	1981
34.8										
39.0	75.8									
17.2	−2.8	−26.5								
36.1	36.2	32.5	49.5							
41.6	43.4	42.4	54.1	55.8						
42.2	44.3	43.7	53.6	49.6	41.3					
43.4	45.4	44.8	54.5	55.5	56.2	59.7				
43.0	44.9	44.2	52.9	52.9	50.2	49.2	49.2			
44.4	45.9	45.3	52.7	54.3	51.8	53.2	55.6	71.6		
32.3	32.0	31.4	35.4	31.6	25.4	23.8	23.3	23.1	4.7	
35.1	35.1	34.6	38.1	37.1	33.7	33.3	33.3	35.1	27.8	69.6

trends in the data—not present here—can be helpful in better understanding the process.

The recent increase in the standard deviation of bond returns reflects a sharp change in the riskiness of fixed income securities. If this represents secular rather than cyclical change in the risk characteristics of these securities, investors will have to reassess the role of bonds within the risk spectrum of all investable assets. The traditional role of bonds as a "safe" asset, with low price volatility and predictable cash flow, has been clouded by recent experience. Such abrupt changes in the characteristics of a class of securities like bonds are difficult to forecast with implicit or explicit models. But even though return and risk are not static phenomena, it is of some comfort to know that time has a way of smoothing out the peaks and valleys in bond market prices and returns. Risk, in particular, has a tendency to increase at a slower rate than return increases as the investor's time horizon is extended. Hence for investors with relatively long future time horizons, portfolio strategies allow and even encourage the inclusion of higher-return, higher-risk assets such as long maturity bonds.

Understanding the return and risk characteristics leads to the consideration of alternative strategies making use of these features. In the next section, a discussion of strategy implementation is pursued.

PORTFOLIO STRATEGIES

Passive or Buy-and-Hold Strategy

A buy-and-hold strategy essentially means purchasing and holding a security to maturity or redemption (e.g., by the issuer via a call provision) and then reinvesting cash proceeds in similar securities. Ongoing cash inflows, as well as outflows, are generally present via coupon income being received and reinvested. The emphasis is on minimizing the expectational inputs, i.e., the assumptions about the future level and direction of interest rates. By holding securities to maturity, any capital change resulting from interest rate change is neutralized or ignored (by holding to maturity, the par amount of the bond will be received). Portfolio return, therefore, is controlled by coupon payments and reinvestment proceeds. While interest rate forecasting is largely ignored, analysis is important to minimize the risk of default on the securities held.

Income-Maximizing Investors. The passive or buy-and-hold strategy is used primarily by income-maximizing investors who are interested in the largest coupon income over a desired horizon. These types of investors include endowment funds, bond mutual funds, insurance companies that are seeking the maximum yield over an extended period of time, or other large pools of money where the size of the fund and large cash inflow make portfolio turnover difficult because of possible market impact. The buy-and-hold strategy was justifiable for many investors because fixed income securities were traditionally characterized as safe assets with predictable cash flows and low price volatility. By assuming a long-term perspective, a return in excess of inflation with interest rate risk minimized is the objective. This is a classic example of seeking less than maximum return to avoid the inherent risk associated with the highest return strategy, and, in turn, is dictated by the investment objectives, constraints, and attendant policies as discussed in Chapters 4 and 5.

Techniques and Vehicles. One technique for a passive strategy is an index fund. Index funds basically provide diversification along with minimum transaction costs. This is certainly a tractable notion for equities as exemplified by S&P 500-type and other funds as discussed in Chapter 10. For bonds, index funds take on new meaning.

The fixed income market is much larger than the equity market in terms of both the dollar amount and number of issues outstanding. Because of this fragmentation, replication of a significant percentage of the total market capitalization can be considered a problem. However, indexes can be selected on the basis of maturity, coupon, issuing sector, quality, or combination thereof. Table 9-7 (pages 310 and 311) lists 65 bond market sectors, each of which is a potential ingredient for indexing. From the variation in return for various market cycles, it can be seen that the correct selection of sector to index for a particular time period can make a sizable difference. However, broad replication of the market is not difficult. While more diverse than the stock market in types and number of issues, the dominance of the systematic risk component for institutional-grade fixed income securities provides a fairly homogeneous universe from a return-risk standpoint.

Once the desired index or *bogey* is chosen, the next task is forming a representative portfolio. One of the key considerations in forming such a portfolio is how many bonds it takes to obtain adequate diversification. McEnally and Boardman [1979] have shown how diversification of bonds varies with portfolio size. It appears that the effect of portfolio size parallels closely the relationship found in common stock portfolios. This suggests that once an index is selected, it can be replicated with a manageable number of securities, probably fewer than 40. Table 9-8 on page 312 provides the relationship between portfolio size and the mean and standard deviation of returns, both empirically observed as well as theoretically expected.

Semiactive Management: Immunization

Immunization, a hybrid strategy having both active and passive elements, is a strategy that was originally formulated a number of years ago by Macaulay [1938] and Reddington [1952]. A number of advances extending their analysis will be discussed.

Accumulation-Maximizing Investors. Accumulation-maximizing investors, who require a high degree of assurance of compound return over the time horizon, use this semiactive bond management approach. By accepting a more modest return than the highest that can be expected, they achieve a greater likelihood of realizing the desired return. This is another example of the classic tradeoff between return and risk. More recent work has extended the concept of immunization to explicit risk measures and multiperiod analysis (see, for example, Fong and Vasicek [1980]).

Techniques and Vehicles. Classical immunization can be defined as the process by which a fixed income portfolio is created having an assured return for a specified time horizon irrespective of interest rate change. In a more concise form, the following are the important characteristics:

1. Specified time horizon.
2. Assured rate of return during holding period to a fixed horizon date.
3. Insulation from the effects of potential adverse interest rate change on portfolio value at the horizon date.

Potential users include life insurance companies, some pension funds, and some banks for their own investment portfolios. Life insurance compa-

TABLE 9-7. Sector Trend—Absolute Total Return

	Sector Name	Bear Cycle (12/72–8/74)	Rank	Bull Cycle (8/74–12/76)	Rank	Full Cycle (12/72–12/76)	Rank	Bear Cycle (12/76–6/30/81)	Rank
1	LBKL Index	-10.93%	40	49.42%	21	33.09%	44	-0.36%	37
2	Government/Agency Index	1.75	3	31.47	58	33.77	32	18.12	9
3	Government/Corporate Index	-4.80	20	39.68	46	32.98	46	10.63	22
4	GNMA Index	-4.64	19	44.75	35	38.07	4	0.29	36
5	Yankee Index	N/A		N/A		N/A		18.69	8
6	Eurobond Index	N/A		N/A		N/A		N/A	
7	Intermediate LBKL Index	-2.65	13	40.18	45	36.47	14	17.54	11
8	Intermediate Government/Agency Index	2.82	1	30.24	59	33.91	28	22.78	3
9	Intermediate Government/Corporate Index	1.78	2	32.20	57	34.55	22	21.88	4
10	Intermediate Yankee Index	N/A		N/A		N/A		24.80	2
11	Intermediate Eurobond Index	N/A		N/A		N/A		insuff. data	
12	Long-Term LBKL Index	-12.94	49	52.63	13	32.88	47	-6.89	52
13	Long-Term Government/Agency Index	-6.31	22	42.58	41	33.58	35	-6.69	51
14	Long-Term Government/Corporate Index	-12.14	46	51.23	16	32.87	48	-6.67	50
15	Long-Term Yankee Index	N/A		N/A		N/A		insuff. data	
16	Long-Term Eurobond Index	N/A		N/A		N/A		N/A	
17	Industrials	-7.90	25	44.88	34	33.43	38	0.47	34
18	Utilities	-12.69	48	52.62	14	33.25	42	-2.91	41
19	Finance	-8.23	28	45.83	31	33.83	31	5.93	25
20	AAA Rated	-8.91	31	46.94	27	33.85	30	-3.38	42
21	AA Rated	-10.24	39	47.15	26	32.08	51	-0.55	39
22	A Rated	-11.39	44	48.30	24	31.41	54	0.78	38
23	BAA Rated	-17.42	57	64.24	3	35.63	17	3.26	29
24	AAA Industrials	-6.54	23	42.70	40	33.37	39	-2.22	40
25	AA Industrials	-7.11	24	43.66	39	33.45	37	0.42	35
26	A Industrials	-8.28	29	45.14	33	33.12	43	1.04	32
27	BAA Industrials	-9.83	35	53.03	12	37.99	5	4.39	28
28	AAA Utilities	-9.98	36	49.26	22	34.36	24	-7.23	54
29	AA Utilities	-11.72	45	49.46	20	31.94	52	-4.15	45
30	A Utilities	-13.54	51	51.05	18	30.60	56	-1.34	38

31	BAA Utilities	-23.65	58	70.57	2	30.23	58	2.73	30
32	AAA Finance	-5.92	21	42.17	42	33.75	33	4.52	27
33	AA Finance	-8.11	27	46.15	30	34.30	26	5.03	26
34	A Finance	-10.04	37	47.70	25	32.87	49	8.35	23
35	BAA Finance	-11.29	42	55.64	7	38.07	3	5.97	24
36	Intermediate Industrials	-0.83	5	38.17	51	37.02	10	16.77	16
37	Intermediate Utilities	-3.22	16	41.81	43	37.24	7	20.08	7
38	Intermediate Finance	-2.82	14	39.16	48	35.24	20	15.57	18
39	Intermediate AAA Industrials	-0.83	6	36.63	56	35.50	19	17.15	12
40	Intermediate AA Industrials	-0.10	4	36.76	55	36.62	13	15.98	17
41	Intermediate A Industrials	-1.28	11	38.94	50	37.16	9	17.07	13
42	Intermediate BAA Industrials	-0.92	7	44.67	36	43.34	1	20.19	6
43	Intermediate AAA Utilities	-1.38	10	38.10	52	36.19	15	16.88	15
44	Intermediate AA Utilities	-1.88	12	39.25	47	36.63	12	17.07	14
45	Intermediate A Utilities	-3.38	17	39.73	49	35.01	21	20.52	5
46	Intermediate BAA Utilities	-9.72	34	50.31	19	37.20	8	24.82	1
47	Intermediate AAA Finance	-3.20	15	37.72	53	33.31	41	15.28	19
48	Intermediate AA Finance	-1.18	9	37.53	54	35.91	16	14.21	20
49	Intermediate A Finance	-4.02	18	41.19	44	35.51	18	17.81	10
50	Intermediate BAA Finance	-1.05	8	44.00	38	42.49	2	11.66	21
51	Long-Term Industrials	-9.08	32	46.80	29	33.47	36	-5.09	46
52	Long-Term Utilities	-14.43	53	55.43	8	33.00	45	-7.99	58
53	Long-Term Finance	-13.12	50	53.88	6	33.69	34	-6.28	48
54	Long-Term AAA Industrials	-8.42	30	44.66	37	32.48	50	-7.60	56
55	Long-Term AA Industrials	-8.02	26	45.73	32	34.04	27	-6.41	49
56	Long-Term A Industrials	-9.19	33	46.81	28	33.32	40	-3.79	43
57	Long-Term BAA Industrials	-11.33	43	55.31	9	37.71	6	-1.43	39
58	Long-Term AAA Utilities	-11.17	41	51.22	17	34.33	25	-10.02	61
59	Long-Term AA Utilities	-13.73	52	51.98	15	31.11	55	-8.38	59
60	Long-Term A Utilities	-15.34	55	54.19	10	30.54	57	-7.04	53
61	Long-Term BAA Utilities	-28.19	59	80.03	1	29.28	59	-5.56	47
62	Long-Term AAA Finance	-10.17	38	49.05	23	33.89	29	-8.65	60
63	Long-Term AA Finance	-12.24	47	53.20	11	34.45	23	-7.58	55
64	Long-Term A Finance	-16.72	56	58.31	5	31.84	53	-3.91	44
65	Long-Term BAA Finance	-15.32	54	61.49	4	36.75	11	2.32	31

SOURCE: Lehman Brothers Kuhn Loeb Inc., Fixed Income Research Department, August 19, 1981.

TABLE 9-8. Return Variance of Randomly Generated Portfolios of Corporate Bonds of All Quality Classes, January 1973 to June 1976 ($\times 10^4$)

Number of Bonds in Portfolio	Mean[a] (Standard Deviation) of V_{Pn}	Theoretical[a] V_{Pn}
1	9.367 (7.471)	9.257
2	7.469 (3.972)	7.148
4	6.004 (2.102)	6.094
6	5.782 (1.701)	5.742
8	5.591 (1.469)	5.566
10	5.376 (1.327)	5.461
12	5.401 (1.220)	5.391
14	5.341 (1.098)	5.340
16	5.299 (1.035)	5.303
18	5.266 (0.973)	5.273
20	5.274 (0.902)	5.250
40	5.155 (0.633)	5.144

SOURCE: McEnally and Boardman [1979].
[a] Variable V_{Pn} is the expected value of the variance of returns of portfolios constructed by investing $1/n$ of the portfolio in each of n randomly selected securities.

nies can use immunization to invest the proceeds from their guaranteed investment contracts (GICs) and fixed annuities. GICs provide for a lump sum payment at a prespecified time in the future at some rate of return guaranteed by the insurance company. Annuities provide for a series of payments for a predetermined time frame (sometimes to death). In both contracts the specific terms are important, especially the premature redemption and reinvestment terms. These are investment vehicles that have a specified required payment at some defined future date. The difference between the promised return on the contract or annuity and the realized return would be revenue available for expenses and profit. It is the ability to fund specified liabilities on a timely basis that makes immunization attractive. Pension funds seeking to fund the retired lives liability or seeking an alternative to a GIC vehicle for the funding of such liabilities have also used immunization strategies. This latter application represents an asset alternative that can fill an investment need customized for the fund sponsor. Use among banks and other savings institutions involves structuring the assets of the investment portfolio to match the liabilities of the balance sheet. Multiperiod immunization provides the basis for the analysis that follows.

The fundamental mechanism underlying immunization is a portfolio structure that balances the portfolio capital changes (from interest rate change) with the return from reinvestment of portfolio cash flows (coupon payments and maturing securities). In other words, if rates rise, the higher reinvestment return will offset the decrease in portfolio value caused by such a rise; conversely, as rates decline, the increase in portfolio value will offset a lower reinvestment return. To accomplish this balancing requires the use of the concept of duration, the mechanics of which are explained in Table 9-9.

TABLE 9-9. The Computation of Duration

Duration is generally defined as the average time required for a bond to generate the present value of all future payments to the bond holder. Thus it may be thought of (and calculated) as the average time to all payments weighted by the principal value or each, or

$$D = \frac{1}{P} \sum_{i=1}^{N} t_i c \left(1 + \frac{y}{2}\right)^{-2t} i + \frac{1}{P} t_N A \left(1 + \frac{y}{2}\right)^{-2t} N \tag{1}$$

for semiannual interest payments, where the t_i is the length of time (in years) to the ith payment and t_N is the length of time to maturity or effective maturity of the bond, c is the amount of the semiannual coupon payments, y is the yield to maturity, and A the amount of the payment at redemption. The current calculated value, P, of the bond is the present value of all future payments:

$$P = \sum_{i=1}^{N} c \left(1 + \frac{y}{2}\right)^{-2t} i + A \left(1 + \frac{y}{2}\right)^{-2t} N \tag{2}$$

As an example of these calculations, consider a simple case of a single 6% bond with no call provisions maturing in exactly one year. Suppose that this bond is priced to yield 8% to maturity. Then

$N = 2$ $c = \$30$
$t_1 = 0.5$ year $A = \$1000$
$t_2 = 1.0$ year $y = 0.08$

so that

$$P = \frac{30}{1.04} + \frac{30}{(1.04)^2} + \frac{1000}{(1.04)^2} = \$981.14$$

and

$$D = \frac{1}{981.14}\left(\frac{\frac{1}{2}(30)}{1.04} + \frac{1(30)}{(1.04)^2} + \frac{1(1000)}{(1.04)^2}\right) = 0.9853 \text{ year}$$

SOURCE: Fong [1980].

DURATION. *Duration* can be defined as a measure of the average life of a security or, more precisely, the average time (in years) necessary to receive the present value of all future payments (coupon plus principal repayment), where each cash flow is discounted by the security's yield to maturity. This has been called Macaulay's duration to distinguish it from a number of alternative measures such as those described in Bierwag, et al. [1980]. For our discussion this is the measure most commonly used and tested for immunization purposes (see, for example, Fisher and Weil [1971] for concurrence with this belief). By setting the duration of the portfolio equal to the desired portfolio time horizon, the balancing of positive and negative incremental return sources can be assured. This is a necessary condition for effectively immunized portfolios.

Based upon the beginning of the time horizon term structure of interest rates or yield curve, the assured rate of return can be determined. It is the total return of the portfolio assuming no change in the term structure. This will always differ from the portfolio's present yield to maturity unless the term structure is described by a flat line, since by virtue of the passage of time there will be a return effect as the portfolio moves (matures) along the yield curve. That is, for upward-sloping yield curves such as curve 1 in the nonparallel situation in Figure 9-3, the present yield on a long maturity bond would be quite different from its assured rate of return, whereas for essentially flat curve 2, yield would roughly approximate the assured return.

The limiting factor is the ability to match the investor's desired time horizon with the weighted average duration of the portfolio. In principle, duration matching is straightforward: Portfolio duration is equal to a weighted average of the individual security durations. Yet under 1982 market conditions, it was difficult to find securities with durations beyond ten years or so. Given double-digit interest rates, which significantly increase the upper limit of the denominators of the duration formula, ten years generally had become the upper limit of achievable duration of a portfolio. However, in 1982 a limited number of zero coupon, long maturity/duration bonds began to appear. The most typical immunized time horizon is five years; it is a common planning period for GICs and it allows flexibility in security selection since there is a fairly large population of eligible securities. In addition, the type of security in the portfolio should be limited to high quality, very liquid instruments since portfolio rebalancing is required to keep the portfolio duration synchronized with the horizon date.

Perhaps the most critical assumption of classical immunization techniques concerns the type of interest rate change anticipated. Specifically, the yield curve is assumed always to move in a one-time parallel fashion during the portfolio time horizon, i.e., interest rates either move up or move down by the same amount for all maturities. This would appear to be an unrealistic assumption, since such behavior is rarely, if ever, experienced in reality. According to the theory, if there is a change in interest rates that does not correspond to this *shape preserving shift,* matching the duration of the in-

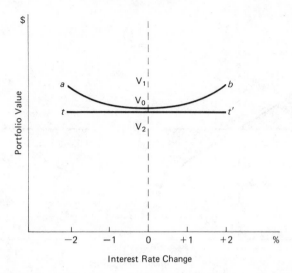

Figure 9-4. Changes in Portfolio Value Caused by Parallel Interest Rate Changes for an Immunized Portfolio.

vestor's desired time horizon no longer assures immunization. For a more complete discussion of these issues, see Cox, Ingersol, and Ross [1979].

Figure 9-4 illustrates the nature of portfolio value given an immunized portfolio and parallel shifts in rates. The curve ab represents the behavior of the portfolio value for various changes in rates, ranging from a decline to an increase as shown on the horizontal axis. Point V_0 (or line tt') is the level of portfolio value assuming no change in rates. It can be seen that an immunized portfolio subjected to parallel shifts in the yield curve will actually provide a greater portfolio value than the assured target value, which therefore becomes the portfolio's minimum value.

Figure 9-5 (page 316) illustrates the relationship when interest rates do not shift in a parallel fashion and indicates the possibility of a portfolio value less than the target. Depending upon the shape of the nonparallel shift, either the (a) or the (b) relationship will occur. The important point is that merely matching the duration of the portfolio with the portfolio time horizon as the condition for immunization may not prevent significant deviations from the target rate of return.

MATURITY VARIANCE. To handle this problem, the concept of *maturity variance* has been introduced by Fong and Vasicek [1980]. The greater the dispersion of cash flows about the liabilities being funded, the greater the risk. Risk is defined as the potential dispersion of return (standard deviation) around the target return. In the special case of choosing from a universe of pure discount securities, holding securities with the same maturities as the liabilities would result in no immunization risk. At the other extreme, high

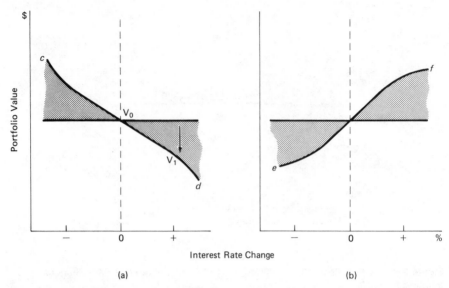

Figure 9-5. Two Patterns of Changes in Portfolio Value Caused by Nonparallel Interest Rate Shifts for an Immunized Portfolio.

coupon securities that are "laddered" over the portfolio time horizon would result in very high immunization risk. A laddered portfolio is one constructed with securities having regularly spaced maturities (the steps of the ladder being each maturity). This type of portfolio would have a part of the portfolio regularly maturing and subject to reinvestment. But because of the representation of many maturities and frequent principal reinvestment requirements, there is high exposure to reinvestment risk and, therefore, high immunization risk exposure. Such a portfolio would have high sensitivity to nonparallel (as well as parallel) changes in rates. Therefore, for a single period liability, such as one represented by a GIC, the best minimum risk portfolio would be one holding securities that best resembles a portfolio of pure discount securities.

Semiactive Management: Dedicated Portfolios

Where there are a number of liabilities to fund, a dedicated portfolio approach may be appropriate. This is a portfolio with a structure designed to fund a schedule of liabilities from portfolio return and asset value, with the portfolio's value diminishing to zero after payment of the last liability. Two approaches to a dedicated portfolio are available.

Immunization Approach. The first uses an immunization approach. For a multiperiod situation, where there is a series of liabilities over the portfolio time horizon, the following two conditions must exist: (1) the (composite) duration of the portfolio assets equals the (composite) duration of the liabilities and (2) the distribution of durations of individual portfolio assets has a wider range than the distribution of durations of the liabilities.

The first condition is straightforward; the second requires that the portfolio payments received be more dispersed in time than the liabilities. That is, there must be an asset with a duration equal to or less than the duration of the shortest duration liability in order to have funds to pay the liability when it is due. And there must be an asset with a duration equal to or greater than the longest duration liability in order to avoid the reinvestment rate risk that might jeopardize payment of the longest duration liability were the longest duration asset of shorter duration. This *bracketing* of shortest and longest duration liabilities with even shorter and longer duration assets ensures the balancing of changes in portfolio value with changes in reinvestment return. If both of these conditions are met, then the portfolio can be structured to generate the necessary cash flows on a timely basis at minimum immunization risk. For a more complete discussion of these sophisticated immunization techniques, see Fong and Vasicek [1980].

Cash Flow Matching. A procedure called *cash flow matching* is an alternative to multiple period (liability) immunization. This method can be described as follows. A bond is selected with a maturity that matches the last liability. An amount of principal equal to the amount of the last liability is then invested in this bond. The remaining elements of the liability stream are then reduced by the coupon payments on this bond, and another bond is chosen for the new, reduced amount of the next-to-last liability. Going backward in time, this is continued until all liabilities have been matched by the payments on the securities in the portfolio.

Table 9-10 (page 318) displays a portfolio chosen to match a sequence of liability payments shown in the second-to-last column of Table 9-11 (page 319). Table 9-10 also includes a number of descriptive statistics of the individual securities held and the portfolio as a whole. Table 9-11 provides a cash flow analysis of sources and applications of funds. The last column in the table shows the excess funds remaining at each time period that are reinvested at the assumed 6 percent reinvestment rate supplied by the user.

To the extent such matching is possible, it would indeed produce a portfolio similar to an immunized portfolio, since interest rate changes would not affect a portfolio whose payments match exactly in timing and amount the liabilities to be paid. However, given typical liability schedules and bonds available for cash flow matching, perfect matching is unlikely. Under such conditions a minimum immunization risk approach would, at worst, be equal to cash flow matching and would probably be better, since an immunization strategy would require less money to fund liabilities. This is due to the higher reinvestment risk of cash flow matching as discussed in Gifford Fong Associates [1981]. That is, even with the use of sophisticated linear programming techniques, cash flow matching may be technically inferior to immunization. Using cost of the initial portfolio as an evaluation measure, the author has found that cash-flow-matched portfolios cost from 3 to 7 percent more, in

TABLE 9-10. Characteristics of a Sample Universe for Cash Flow Matching (Evaluation Date 12-31-81)

Bond No.	Par Value ($)	% of Total	CUSIP	Issuer Name	Coupon %	Effective Maturity Date	Price ($)	YTM (%)	Duration (yr.)
				Price Scan					
15	$ 517	2.2%	888888AA	Cash	0.000%	1/ 1/82	$100.000	0.00%	0.00
14	233	0.9	313388FB	Federal Home Ln. Bks.	7.850	8/27/84	86.000	14.36	2.36
13	1199	4.6	912827KT	United States Treas. Nts.	9.625	8/15/85	88.125	13.89	2.99
12	1215	3.8	812404AD	Sears Roebuck Accep. Corp.	8.375	12/31/86	75.500	15.61	4.04
11	2353	7.6	901178BY	Twelve Fed. Ld. Bks.	7.600	4/20/87	75.625	14.30	4.23
10	2474	10.0	667332AF	Northwest Bancorporation	15.350	5/ 1/89	94.750	16.60	4.46
9	4080	18.1	313311FX	Federal Farm Cr. Bks.	14.700	7/22/91	100.000	14.69	5.10
8	1382	4.5	912810CJ	United States Treas. Bds.	10.125	11/15/94	77.438	13.94	6.63
7	6021	21.7	912810CR	United States Treas. Bds.	11.500	11/15/95	84.938	13.98	6.61
6	1402	3.7	149123AK	Caterpillar Tractor Co.	8.750	11/ 1/99	61.125	15.08	7.02
5	1357	3.7	302292AC	Exxon Pipeline Co.	8.875	10/15/00	63.750	14.55	7.17
4	1294	5.4	912810CW	United States Treas. Bds.	13.375	8/15/01	95.344	14.07	6.77
3	2649	6.7	880370AK	Tenneco Inc.	8.375	4/ 1/02	58.500	14.91	7.12
2	1206	3.2	370424BW	General Mtrs. Accep. Corp.	9.400	7/15/04	59.875	16.04	6.41
1	1228	4.0	749285AF	RCA Corp.	12.250	5/ 1/05	76.000	16.24	6.46

Portfolio Totals

Average Duration (years)	5.563
Average Yield (%)	14.440
Duration Weighted Average Yield (%)	14.715
Average Effective Maturity	1–5–94
Total Par Value ($000)	28610.000
Total Market Value ($000)	24001.990
Number of Issues	15

SOURCE: Gifford Fong Associates.

TABLE 9-11. Cash Flow Analysis of a Sample Universe for Cash Flow Matching: Reinvestment Rate—6% (Evaluation Date 12-31-81)

				Cash Flow Analysis			
Date	Prev. Cash Balance ($) +	Interest on Balance ($) +	Principal Payments ($) +	Coupon Payments ($) +	Reinvestment of Payments ($) −	Liability Due ($) =	New Cash Balance ($)
12-31-82	$ 0	$ 0	$ 517	$3128	$125	$3770	$ 0
12-31-83	0	0	0	3128	93	3104	117
12-31-84	117	7	233	3128	98	3584	0
12-31-85	0	0	1199	3110	120	4428	0
12-31-86	0	0	1215	2994	88	4298	0
12-31-87	0	0	2353	2803	185	4170	1171
12-31-88	1171	71	0	2714	82	4038	0
12-31-89	0	0	2474	2524	180	3900	1278
12-31-90	1278	78	0	2334	72	3762	0
12-31-91	0	0	4080	2334	181	3624	2971
12-31-92	2971	181	0	1734	47	3474	1460
12-31-93	1460	89	0	1734	47	3330	0
12-31-94	0	0	1382	1734	57	3174	0
12-31-95	0	0	6021	1594	89	3012	4692
12-31-96	4692	286	0	902	28	2850	3059
12-31-97	3059	186	0	902	28	2682	1493
12-31-98	1493	91	0	902	28	2514	0
12-31-99	0	0	1402	902	42	2346	0
12-31-00	0	0	1357	779	42	2178	0
12-31-01	0	0	1294	659	51	2004	0
12-31-02	0	0	2649	375	134	1836	1321
12-31-03	1321	80	0	264	9	1674	0
12-31-04	0	0	1206	264	42	1512	0
12-31-05	0	0	1228	75	53	1356	0

SOURCE: Gifford Fong Associates.

dollars, than immunized portfolios. However, cash flow matching is easier to understand, and this has occasionally led to its suboptimal selection over an immunization strategy for multiperiod problems.

Active Strategies

Total Return-Maximizing Investors. For those seeking the highest return for a given level of risk, active strategies offer the greatest opportunity. These are used primarily by total return-maximizing investors, either in single or multiple holding period frameworks. The objective is to maximize return, whether it be from capital changes or income or a combination thereof.

Most pension funds and some closed-end mutual funds embrace this approach. Since it requires making assumptions about the future, the greater the accuracy of those assumptions the greater the return for a given level of risk. Active strategies, which are dominated by interest rate anticipation and sector/security strategies, actually span a fairly wide range of possibilities. Indeed, the increased volatility of the bond market has stimulated the development of active management techniques.

Techniques and Vehicles. The philosophy in rate anticipation is to take advantage of the return implication of expected interest rate change through bond portfolio management. As has been discussed, interest rate change is the dominant source of marginal total return—return relative to that if no rate change occurred. As long as there is volatility in rates, this will exist. If one is to pursue an active management strategy, there must be an explicit recognition of its effect.

Interest Rate Anticipation Strategies. As an active management technique, interest rate anticipation should be concerned with three dimensions: direction of the change in rates; magnitude of the change across maturities; and the timing of the change. If interest rates drop, the price of the bond will rise to reflect the new yield level. Conversely, if rates increase, the price of the bond will decline. The increase or decrease will be directly related to the security's duration. Therefore, the maturity should be lengthened and coupon decreased—or, equivalently, duration should be increased—when rates are expected to drop, and the opposite action taken when rates are expected to rise. Where along the maturity spectrum to position the portfolio should be guided by the shape of the expected yield curve change. Finally, the timing of the expected rate change will be important in evaluating the relative importance of rate change, coupon return, and reinvestment return. This subject will be discussed in more detail later in this chapter.

Interest rate anticipation strategies seek to recognize and assess the role of interest rate changes on the total return of a portfolio over a specified time horizon. For purposes of discussion the generation of the required interest

TABLE 9-12. Return Simulation Example of Bond Portfolio Analysis

PORTFOLIO: Model Portfolio—High Coupon U.S. Treasury

INTEREST RATE PROJECTION: 6-30-81 to 6-30-82

SCENARIO 1 (33.33% Probability): Falling Rates, 29-Year Historical Volatility Basis (5-52 to 6-81); Reinvestment Rate Is Calculated for Each Bond.

SCENARIO 2 (33.33% Probability): Market Implicit Forecast; Reinvestment Rate Is Calculated for Each Bond.

SCENARIO 3 (33.33% Probability): Rising Rates, 29-Year Historical Volatility Basis (5-52 to 6-81); Reinvestment Rate Is Calculated for Each Bond.

Interest Rate Projection

		FORECAST YIELD (PERCENT)		
Maturity	Present YTM		Scenario	
(Yrs.)	(%)	1	2	3
0.250	15.738%	9.734%	14.387%	24.524%
0.500	15.502	10.907	14.411	20.879
1.000	14.786	9.467	14.106	22.340
2.000	14.469	9.802	13.836	20.296
3.000	14.195	10.269	13.796	18.737
4.000	14.094	10.723	13.776	17.948
5.000	14.034	11.062	13.732	17.491
10.000	13.723	11.957	13.461	16.046
20.000	13.452	12.110	13.249	15.463
30.000	13.419	12.156	13.181	15.417
30.999	13.419	12.156	13.181	15.417

SOURCE: Gifford Fong Associates.

rate forecast itself will not be covered (see Chapter 6). Rather, the emphasis will be on harnessing the forecasts once determined. To assess the impact and implications of interest rate change, it is useful to apply the forecasts of interest rate change to a portfolio (see, for example, Fong [1980]).

Table 9-12 summarizes inputs suitable for simulating the effect of interest rate change. A time frame of one year has been chosen, but this would vary according to one's own expectations and desires. Three scenarios of interest rate change are shown. These have been derived from historical interest rate change tendencies over the last 29 years. There is a bullish scenario, a market-implicit forecast, and a bearish scenario. Multiscenario approaches recognize the uncertainty associated with interest rate forecasting and, accordingly, they allow a form of sensitivity analysis. In the example these forecasts take the form of the most-likely (market implicit), optimistic (declining rates), and pessimistic (rising rates) cases. The manager's own forecast would be, of course, an alternative. Each scenario is described along with specified probability. Figures in Table 9-12 reflect the forecast yield for each scenario, as well as the present yield to maturity for each maturity period shown.

TABLE 9-13. **Bond Portfolio Analysis of High Coupon U.S. Treasury Bonds: Three Scenario Interest Rate Forecast (Current Date: 6-30-81; Projection Date: 6-30-82)**

Face Value ($000)	Bond Description		Price ($0)	Yield to Effective Maturity (%)	
	1 888888AA				
$0	Cash Equivalents	Curr:	$ 98.536	15.10%	MAT
	0.0% 8- 6-81 G AAA	Scen 1:	100.000	0.0	MAT
		Scen 2:	100.000	0.0	MAT
		Scen 3:	100.000	0.0	MAT
		Comp:	100.000	0.0	
	2 888888AB				
$46723	1.0–2.0 Yr U.S. Treasuries	Curr:	98.047	14.69	MAT
	13.2430% 1-19-83 G AAA	Scen 1:	101.890	9.67	MAT
		Scen 2:	99.447	14.31	MAT
		Scen 3:	94.980	23.39	MAT
		Comp:	98.772	15.79	
	3 888888AC				
$16931	2.0–3.0 Yr U.S. Treasuries	Curr:	97.567	14.25	MAT
	13.1090% 2-15-84 G AAA	Scen 1:	105.129	9.63	MAT
		Scen 2:	98.895	13.89	MAT
		Scen 3:	89.555	21.01	MAT
		Comp:	97.859	14.84	
	4 888888AD				
$19759	3.0–4.0 Yr U.S. Treasuries	Curr:	96.476	14.33	MAT
	13.0140% 1- 3-85 G AAA	Scen 1:	106.049	10.22	MAT
		Scen 2:	97.974	14.00	MAT
		Scen 3:	87.264	19.68	MAT
		Comp:	97.096	14.63	
	5 888888AE				
$9456	4.0–5.0 Yr U.S. Treasuries	Curr:	95.924	14.26	MAT
	13.0300% 2-15-86 G AAA	Scen 1:	106.671	10.76	MAT
		Scen 2:	97.338	13.99	MAT
		Scen 3:	86.111	18.45	MAT
		Comp:	96.707	14.40	

SOURCE: Gifford Fong Associates.

Table 9-13 exemplifies the result of translating interest rate change into expected rates of return for individual securities. In this example a hypothetical Treasury bond portfolio is analyzed. The columns are largely self-explanatory, but those of particular importance are described below:

- Yield curve   = return due to changes in the nominal yield curve.
- Time   = return assuming the initial yield curve remains constant over the projection horizon.
- Spread change = return attributable to spread change and volatility effects that are assumed to be zero for Treasury issues.
- Earned interest = interest accrued over the projection period.

		COMPONENTS OF RETURN (%)				Total Return (%)	Effective Maturity Date	Dura-tion (yrs.)	Note
Yield Curve	Time	Spread Change	Earned Interest	Maturity Call	Reinv.				
							8- 6-81	0.10	
0.0%	0.0%	0.0%	0.0%	1.5%	11.0%	12.5%	8- 6-81	0.00	Matured
0.0	0.0	0.0	0.0	1.5	13.5	14.9	8- 6-81	0.00	Matured
0.0	0.0	0.0	0.0	1.5	18.9	20.4	8- 6-81	0.00	Matured
0.0	0.0	0.0	0.0	1.5	14.4	15.9	8- 6-81	0.00	
							1-19-83	1.45	
3.0	0.9	0.0	13.5	0.0	0.4	17.8	1-19-83	0.55	
0.5	0.9	0.0	13.5	0.0	0.5	15.4	1-19-83	0.55	
−4.0	0.9	0.0	13.5	0.0	0.6	11.0	1-19-83	0.55	
−0.2	0.9	0.0	13.5	0.0	0.5	14.8	1-19-83	0.55	
							2-15-84	2.30	
7.3	0.4	0.0	13.4	0.0	0.4	21.6	2-15-84	1.52	
0.9	0.4	0.0	13.4	0.0	0.5	15.3	2-15-84	1.52	
−8.6	0.4	0.0	13.4	0.0	0.6	5.8	2-15-84	1.51	
−0.1	0.4	0.0	13.4	0.0	0.5	14.2	2-15-84	1.52	
							1- 3-85	2.92	
9.4	0.5	0.0	13.5	0.0	0.4	23.8	1- 3-85	2.23	
1.1	0.5	0.0	13.5	0.0	0.5	15.5	1- 3-85	2.22	
−10.0	0.5	0.0	13.5	0.0	0.6	4.5	1- 3-85	2.20	
0.2	0.5	0.0	13.5	0.0	0.5	14.6	1- 3-85	2.22	
							2-15-86	3.59	
10.7	0.5	0.0	13.6	0.0	0.4	25.2	2-15-86	3.03	
1.0	0.5	0.0	13.6	0.0	0.5	15.5	2-15-86	3.00	
−10.7	0.5	0.0	13.6	0.0	0.5	3.9	2-15-86	2.95	
0.3	0.5	0.0	13.6	0.0	0.5	14.9	2-15-86	2.99	

- Maturity/call   = change in principal value for securities projected to be called or to mature.
- Reinvestment   = interest on interest earned over the projection period.
- Total return   = the sum of all components of return.
- Duration   = first figure in column is current duration; remaining figures are the duration at the *end* of the assumed holding period for the particular scenario.

The foregoing analysis can be extremely helpful in executing an effective active management strategy. Analytical insights are achieved by partitioning

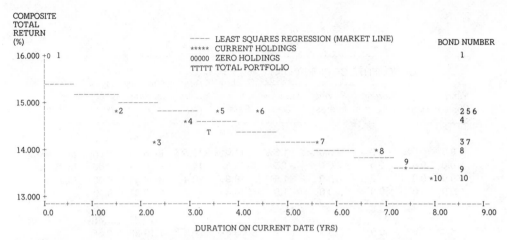

Figure 9-6. Relative Return Valuation Analysis. Three Scenario Interest Rate Forecast: Model Portfolio—High Coupon U.S. Treasury (6-30-81 to 6-30-82). (Source: Gifford Fong Associates)

a set of expected interest rate changes into implied rates of return. This provides an important dimension for evaluating rate anticipation strategies.

Relative Return Value Analysis. An example of the possible analytical insight that can be derived from the return simulation process is illustrated in Figure 9-6. Duration is on the horizontal axis and on the vertical axis is the composite expected return, which is the probability-weighted average of each of the three scenario returns. Within the diagram is a regression line (downward-sloping dashed lines), individual security representation (asterisks), portfolio average return/duration (letter T) and bond identification number (far righthand margin). The regression line represents the average relationship between return and duration exhibited by the individual securities making up the portfolio. Bonds above the line are those with greater expected return per unit of duration than the average relationship; bonds below the line have less return per unit of duration. For example, the best bond for the total expected return and duration optimizer appears to be bond 6, which has a duration of about 4.4 years and a composite return of about 14.9 percent. The worst bond appears to be bond 3, with a duration of about 2.3 years and a composite return of about 14.2 percent. Referring back to Table 9-12 the return components of security 3 can be evaluated. The biggest negative impact on return can be seen to be due to the security's sensitivity to the adverse interest rate change of scenario 3.

Strategic Frontier Analysis. Figure 9-7 illustrates another display useful for analytical insight. The total return of the best case (scenario 1) is measured along the vertical axis; the total return of the worst case (scenario 3) is measured along the horizontal axis. Each security is represented within the diagram (asterisks) and identified by bond number (righthand margin). Cash

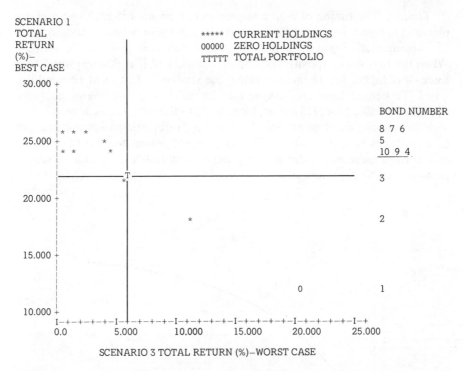

Figure 9-7. Strategic Frontier Analysis. Three Scenario Interest Rate Forecast: Model Portfolio—High Coupon U.S. Treasury (6-30-81 to 6-30-82). (SOURCE: Gifford Fong Associates)

(equivalents) is identified by the number 0. The portfolio average (letter T) is at the origin, or center, of the quadrants. The upper lefthand quadrant represents securities having aggressive qualities. That is, if the best case scenario (rate decline) materializes, they will achieve high returns but if the worst case scenario (rate rise) occurs then they will do relatively poorly. Securities 8, 7, 6, 5, 10, 9, and 4 have these return characteristics. Securities in the upper righthand quadrant are superior securities because, regardless of the scenario outcome, the portfolio average return (letter T) will be enhanced. There are no securities in this quadrant, but if there were, these would be the purchase candidates regardless of scenario expectation. The lower right quadrant has securities with defensive characteristics; if the worst case materializes they will do well, but if the best case occurs they will do relatively poorly. Bonds 1 and 2 are defensive. The lower left quadrant (where security 3 is found) would be those securities that are inferior because, regardless of scenario outcome, they would pull down the return of the portfolio.

Both of the analyses just described provide examples of extensions to the return simulation process. Using a multiscenario approach, the return and risk characteristics of individual bonds as well as the portfolio can be evaluated.

Timing. The timing of active strategies can be important. Over a given planning horizon, judgment is necessary to determine when a strategy is to be implemented. Figure 9-8 illustrates two common yield curve shapes. When the first curve (positively sloped) exists, and if it is interpreted as a forecast of higher future interest rates, the strategy taken must be carefully timed. To benefit from an ensuing rate increase, a shortening of maturity (duration) is called for. However, by moving to the left of the curve, a lower yield to maturity must be accepted. Premature rate anticipation under these circumstances would result in a lower realized return for the time frame before rates increase; if the increase never materializes, significant return give-up may be experienced.

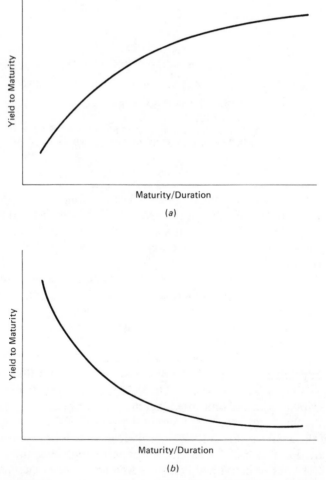

Figure 9-8. (*a*) Positive or Upward Sloping Yield Curve; (*b*) Negative or Downward Sloping Yield Curve.

Conversely, if the second curve (negatively sloped) prevails and rates are expected to decrease, again timing is important since a premature lengthening of maturity results in a lower yield to maturity with much riskier longer maturity (duration) portfolios. The conclusion is that effective timing of rate anticipation is a necessary and important consideration. (See Appendix A to this chapter for historical data on yield spreads and slopes of yield curves.)

Moreover, rate anticipation should not be considered complete after the initial timing issue is resolved. When to reverse or modify the strategy must be continually considered. The return component interactions originally estimated will be constantly in flux, and the manager must continually balance anticipated capital changes against current yield and reinvestment return effects. This makes the "round-trip" character of successful rate anticipation apparent. That is, the rate anticipation efforts of the manager cannot be judged to be successful until the move taken in anticipation of any given rate increase (decrease) is reversed with a timely opposite move when rates are expected to decrease (increase). It should be pointed out, however, that the manager's performance is most appropriately judged over an entire interest rate cycle and in the context of the entire portfolio rather than on individual transactions.

In addition, other terms of a security should be analyzed, such as the effects of refunding terms. For example, suppose that in a scenario of rising rates the prepayment experience of GNMA securities (Ginnie Maes) is expected to decline as mortgage holders tend to want to hold on to lower interest rate mortgages. Conversely, if rates decline, there is an incentive to refinance; hence, higher refunding and shorter-lived Ginnie Maes can be expected. Forearmed with knowledge of the anticipated average life of a GNMA security under various interest rate scenarios, the manager can decide whether he or she wants to embrace or avoid these securities with their potentially altered average maturity.

As another example, the call feature of bonds tends to be unused by issuers if rates rise because the issuer will not want to retire or refinance bonds issued at rates lower than current rates. As a result, callability is not of concern to the manager when scenarios call for rising rates. Just the opposite is true when rates are expected to fall. In such case, the issuer will have an incentive to retire callable bonds and refinance at lower rates.

Fortunately, all considerations can be integrated into the return simulation analysis described. This allows the manager to focus attention on the most important dimensions of direction, shape, and timing of interest rate change.

Interest rate forecasting in Canada and the United States may be thought of as a good example of an activity associated with a highly efficient market. That is, wide distribution of information, low transaction costs, and many intelligent participants contribute to the difficulty of consistently and correctly forecasting the direction of rate changes. This does not say that some people cannot do it well, but it does suggest success will be extremely difficult to achieve on a consistent basis. However, the rewards of being right are great, not only in terms of realized returns, but in the amount of investment management business one can accrue. Unfortunately the converse is also true.

Sector/Security Strategies. Beyond rate anticipation, there is the possibility of enhancing returns relative to risk by evaluating individual securities and subgroups of securities. This takes three basic forms: credit analysis, spread analysis, and bond valuation.

CREDIT ANALYSIS. Credit analysis is concerned with the assessment of default risk—the probability that the issuer will be unable to meet all contractual obligations fully and in a timely manner. Default risk is important for two reasons. The first is the chance of loss due to actual acts of default. The second is the likelihood of adverse bond price changes that are precipitated by the increased probability of default, typically via downgrading of a bond's quality by the rating agencies, even though no act of default actually takes place.

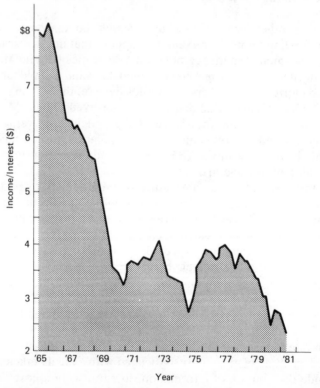

Figure 9-9. Corporate Pretax Income Available for Each Dollar of Interest Paid by U.S. Corporations. (SOURCE: Foldessy [1981])

Default risk has both systematic and unsystematic elements. For a variety of reasons, individual bond issuers may experience difficulty in meeting their obligations from time to time. If these are isolated acts of default, they may be diversified away or be eliminated by effective credit analysis. More worrisome is the possibility of adverse general business conditions, such as occurred during the 1930s, the mid-1970s, and in the early 1980s, which are associated with significant increases in the frequency of acts of default and widespread price declines due to concern over credit quality. This event requires more macro-oriented analysis such as found in Chapter 6. Default was a real concern in 1981–82, as depicted in Figure 9-9, which reflects the steady deterioration in the coverage of interest charges by corporate earnings over the preceding decade.

As indicated previously, risk of default is often quantified by quality ratings provided by Duff & Phelps, Moody's, and Standard & Poor's. Historically, such ratings have proved to be valid, but they are not foolproof indicators of risk. They also appear to be closely related to other traditional measures of credit quality, such as relative debt burden, interest or fixed charges expense coverage (by earnings before deduction of interest and tax expenses), and variability in earnings streams. However, many fixed income investors do not rely exclusively on the rating agencies; they also engage in their own credit analysis (see Chapter 7). There are two reasons for this activity, both of which are based on the assumption that yields in the marketplace are closely correlated to agency ratings, *ceteris paribus*.

1. The analyst's assessment of credit quality may be more accurate and/or timely than those of the rating agencies. In this case the portfolio manager can achieve added yield at relatively small cost in terms of credit risk exposure, or can avoid paying in terms of reduced yield for nonexistent incremental quality.
2. Agency ratings for a bond are revised upward or downward only as it is clear that the issuer's financial circumstances have changed. With astute credit analysis it may be possible to anticipate such upgrades or downgrades and profit from the yield and price changes which ensue.

SPREAD ANALYSIS. Spread analysis involves sectoral relationships. It may be possible to identify subclasses of fixed income securities that tend to behave in a highly similar manner. For example, prices and yields on lower investment-grade bonds tend to move together, as do yields on utility bonds. Such identifiable classes of securities are referred to as sectors. (In this sense maturity ranges are also sectors, but the influence of maturity on total return is so dramatic that yield/maturity analysis is usually treated separately.) Relative prices or yields among sectors may change due to (1) altered perceptions of the creditworthiness of a sector or of the market's sensitivity to default risk; (2) changes in the market's valuation of some attribute or characteristic of the securities in the sector, such as a zero coupon feature; (3) changes in supply and demand conditions.

Analysis of relative sectoral relationships coupled with appropriate management response can be rewarding in fixed income portfolio management. The objective, obviously, is to be heavily invested in the sector or sectors that will display the strongest relative price movements. In monitoring such sectoral relationships, it is customary to concentrate on spreads—i.e., the difference, usually measured in basis points, in yield between two sectors— among yield series that are broadly representative of the securities in the sector. A number of brokerage firms maintain such yield series on an historical basis so that abnormal differences can be identified. These firms are usually able to conduct specialized analyses for clients, such as measurement of the historical average, maximum, and minimum spread among sectors. Such analysis plus consideration of other relevant factors leads to what is, in effect, a relative valuation of a sector's worth. If the relative values are enough out of line, the results will be arbitragelike sector swapping so as to obtain the largest gain or smallest loss as sector yields return to more normal relationships.

In both credit analysis and spread analysis the potential for return enhancement, while dominated by gains from proper rate anticipation, still holds the promise of a significant contribution to portfolio objectives. The drawbacks may include the need to do many trades for the contribution to be meaningful, and the danger that overall changes in interest rates will dwarf these efforts.

VALUATION ANALYSIS. Bond valuation is a relatively recent approach to active management. From the estimated term structure of pure-discount zero coupon bonds discussed earlier, the value of default-free securities such as U.S. Treasuries can be estimated. This has the effect of holding the maturity constant. Using such a forecast as a basis, other characteristics of the bond can be valued by using a form of least squares regression. Holding maturity constant, "dummy variables" on bonds with certain characteristics are regressed against the actual yields in excess of the default-free yields. This regression analysis allows one to determine the relative role, holding maturity constant, attributable to the quality rating of the bond, size of coupon, industry classification of the issuer, call provision, and sinking fund features of the issue in the determination of the premium over the risk-free rate of that issue. Once the current market valuation of the various bond attributes has been estimated, the value of any given bond can be determined by adding the yield premium for each of the bond's characteristics to the appropriate default-free yield. The valuation model can be used for a number of purposes including:

1. *Yield component analysis.* By identifying the components of yield, the model can contribute to an understanding of risk-return relationships in the bond market.

2. *Identification of mispriced securities.* The price fitted by the model can be compared to the actual price to show the extent to which the given security deviates from the pricing, either relative to the aggregate of bonds in the market or to those in a particular issuer sector or maturity range.
3. *Pricing of private placements.* The fitted price can be used as a price estimate in the valuation of issues for which market values are not readily available, such as inactive securities or private placements.
4. *Performance measurement.* Prices fitted by the model can be used in historical valuation of securities and portfolios, a necessary step in performance measurement when infrequently traded bonds are in the portfolio.
5. *Active bond management.* Knowing the response of other, primarily corporate, bond yields to the structure of default-free interest rates allows the portfolio manager to concentrate on forecasting Treasury yield changes.

For an example of the type of output that can be generated, refer to Table 9-14 on pages 332 and 333.

Active Portfolio Optimization

Variance/Covariance Approach. The objective of portfolio optimization is to maximize expected return at a given level of risk or to minimize risk at a given level of expected return. Two alternative methods of optimization can be identified. The difference between the two is in the treatment of risk. How to measure the *ex ante* risk of a bond portfolio is an elusive problem.

In most equity optimization approaches, the standard deviation or variance of portfolio returns has been used as the risk objective to be minimized. The process for equities involves creating a covariance matrix that, along with expectations of stock returns, is then optimized by a quadratic optimization program. Including such things as turnover, concentration, and dividend yield constraints, a minimum risk portfolio for a given level of return is produced. The problem is tractable since the creation of the covariance matrix can always resort to an estimate based upon historical return experience.

In bond analysis, however, no such convention is available. Because of the finite life of a fixed income security, its covariance characteristic with other bonds changes with time, if for no other reason than just because the maturity of each bond becomes shorter with time. Moreover, with a given rate change, there can be yield curve shape changes as well as direction changes. The latter can alter, and in some cases reverse, the covariance relationship between securities. The problem thus becomes one of estimation. Indeed, if a covariance matrix could be created, then the optimization process could parallel the analysis for stock.

TABLE 9-14. Bond Valuation Computer Program Output

BOND DESCRIPTION		Default-Free	Issuing Sector	Quality	Current Yield	Call Effect	Fitted Value	Actual Value	Residual
1 027321AG American Mail Line Ltd. 7.900% 1-1-87 AG A	Price ($)	80.015	-1.107	0.0	-2.000	0.0	76.908	77.969	1.061
	Yield (%)	13.040	0.331	0.0	0.613	0.0	13.984	13.656	-0.328
2 029105AU American President Lines Ltd. 4.800% 11-1-91 AG A	Price ($)	55.543	-1.267	0.0	-1.975	-0.036	52.264	52.781	0.517
	Yield (%)	12.565	0.331	0.0	0.536	0.010	13.442	13.299	-0.143
3 313586GJ Federal Natl. Mtg. Assn. 8.200% 7-10-02 AG A	Price ($)	68.323	-1.742	0.0	-3.655	-1.385	61.541	61.000	-0.541
	Yield (%)	12.484	0.331	0.0	0.745	0.302	13.862	13.983	0.121
4 370334AB General Mills 8.875% 10-15-95 E1 D	Price ($)	75.870	-4.022	0.0	-3.444	-0.913	67.491	68.000	0.509
	Yield (%)	12.533	0.783	0.0	0.726	0.202	14.244	14.131	-0.113
5 842400BL Southern Calif. Edison Co. 7.250% 7-1-84 E2 B	Price ($)	84.770	-1.719	-0.661	-1.130	-0.002	81.258	81.188	-0.070
	Yield (%)	13.424	0.783	0.307	0.53	0.001	15.045	15.078	0.033
6 186108AF Cleveland Elec. Illum. Co. 7.125% 1-15-90 E2 D	Price ($)	71.172	-3.129	-1.176	-2.302	-0.096	64.469	64.781	0.312
	Yield (%)	12.719	0.783	0.307	0.621	0.026	14.456	14.370	-0.086

7 842400BH Southern Calif. Edison Co. 8.875% 3- 1-00 E2 B	Price ($) Yield (%)	73.963 12.498	-4.197 0.783	-1.537 0.307	-3.504 0.745	-1.220 0.276	63.505 14.607	62.625 14.812	-0.880 0.205
8 040555AP Arizona Pub. Svc. Co. 12.125% 10-15-09 E4 D	Price ($) Yield (%)	97.074 12.498	-5.589 0.783	-9.594 1.575	-4.051 0.775	-4.278 0.908	73.562 16.539	76.281 15.951	-2.719 -0.588
9 319279AB First Bank Systems Inc. 8.750% 6-30-83 F1 B	Price ($) Yield (%)	90.969 13.867	-1.492 0.910	0.0 0.0	-0.961 0.597	-0.003 0.002	88.512 15.376	87.500 16.014	-1.012 0.638
10 894180AA Travelers Corp. 8.700% 8- 1-95 F1 A	Price ($) Yield (%)	74.839 12.534	-4.580 0.910	0.0 0.0	-3.333 0.721	-0.819 0.186	66.107 14.351	65.500 14.491	-0.607 0.140
11 02518AD American Express Credit Corp. 8.500% 12-15-85 F2 B	Price ($) Yield (%)	84.389 13.169	-2.680 0.910	-0.879 0.307	-1.755 0.625	-0.045 0.016	79.029 15.027	80.000 14.679	0.971 -0.348
12 637432AA National Rural Utils. Coop. F. 7.400% 12- 1-07 F2 B	Price ($) Yield (%)	60.962 12.475	-4.237 0.910	-1.307 0.307	-2.983 0.753	0.0 0.0	52.437 14.445	53.969 14.048	1.532 -0.397
13 893502AB Transamerica Financial Corp. 7.875% 11- 1-91 F3 D	Price ($) Yield (%)	72.871 12.623	-4.019 0.910	-3.296 0.803	-2.584 0.671	0.0 0.0	62.972 15.007	63.000 15.000	0.028 -0.007

SOURCE: Gifford Fong Associates.

Worst Case Approach. An alternative approach defines risk as the worst case interest rate scenario or the outcome with the most adverse change (increase) in interest rates. The objective becomes maximizing bond portfolio expected return with risk, defined as the level of return under the worst case interest rate scenario, constrained to some minimum level. Risk is specified in terms of minimally acceptable return levels that in turn are a direct result of the interest rate scenario expectations. Because the analytical procedure is linear, it allows a computationally more efficient algorithm via a linear programming optimization. A detailed example is illustrated in Appendix B to this chapter.

Other Active Strategies or Tactics

In addition to the active strategies already discussed, a number of other approaches may be identified. While their potential impact on total portfolio return may not be as great, they still may make a significant contribution and for many managers represent a chosen expertise.

Total Realized Yield. As intimated in the earlier discussion of immunization, implicit in the yield to maturity of a fixed income security is the ability to reinvest coupon payments at the same rate. If the reinvestment rate is different, then the actual realized return will diverge considerably from promised yield. In maximizing the total return, the management of cash flow is therefore important, and increasingly so the longer the time horizon. Part of the problem is the ability to reinvest what may be relatively small amounts of funds, since transaction costs and available investment alternatives may be unfavorable. Return simulation analysis, discussed earlier, can be a useful tool for determining the optimal strategy for reinvesting bond portfolio cash flow; it requires expectations of the direction, shape, and timing of interest rate (yield curve) changes.

Pure Yield Pickup Trade or Exchange. Switching to a security having a higher yield is called a pure yield trade or exchange (sometimes referred to by other writers as swaps). The transaction may be made to achieve either a higher coupon yield or a larger yield to maturity. It would appear that such transactions would always be done as long as there is no significant shift in risk level (or liquidity). However, accounting rules or regulatory mandates constrain some investors from yield pickup trades that create a loss, usually unless offset by a gain elsewhere in the portfolio, even though a portfolio benefit would result.

Substitution Trade or Exchange. This transaction involves substituting one security for another that has a higher yield to maturity but is otherwise identical in terms of maturity, coupon, and quality. This type of trade depends on a capital market imperfection. As such, the portfolio manager expects the yields to maturity on the two securities to reestablish a normal yield spread relationship, usually resulting in a price increase and hence capital appreciation for the holder of the higher yielding issue. The workout period (time for the expected realignment in yields to occur) can be critical, since the sooner it occurs the greater the return on an annualized basis; if the security must be held to maturity, the realized annual return may be marginal.

Intermarket or Sector Spread Trade or Exchange. Based on the expected normal yield relationship between two different sectors of the bond market, trades may be made when there is a perceived misalignment. This may involve switching to the higher yielding security when the yield spread is too wide and is expected to narrow, and to the lower yielding security when the spread is too narrow and is expected to widen. The risk, especially of the latter switch, is that the anticipated adjustment will not be made, resulting in a reduced portfolio yield.

Maturity-Spacing Strategies. Alternative portfolio maturity structures may be used. These include a balanced maturity schedule with equal spacing of maturities held; an all-short or all-long maturity strategy; or a *barbell* structure, where bond holdings are concentrated in short maturities and long maturities, with the intermediates of lesser or no importance. The rationale for an equal-maturity portfolio is to provide the portfolio with some reinvestment risk protection, spreading out reinvestment over the full interest rate cycle. That is, there will be a relatively continuous cash flow over time from maturity *laddering*, and these funds can be reinvested at the then current rates. The effects of overall interest rate change will tend to be averaged and the extremes of return and risk will be truncated. An all-short or all-long maturity portfolio strategy is frequently a temporary strategy adopted as a result of rate (change) anticipation, but it is a strategy of potentially large reinvestment rate risk. For those who stay with an all-short portfolio there is usually either a preference for high liquidity or an extreme aversion to principal risk. A barbell approach anticipates that the best return-risk reward is achieved by balancing the defensive qualities of short-term securities with the aggressive qualities of long-term securities and avoiding the intermediates.

There is no assurance, from empirical testing of these various strategies, that any one has been consistently superior over time (see, for example, Fogler, Groves, and Richardson [1976] and Fogler and Groves [1976]).

Consistency of Style. As a general observation, consistency of management style is important. Given the range of strategies and expertise required, it is important to identify the style that is compatible with the investment policy established for the portfolio or is most effective for the portfolio management organization. Pursuing this style with emphasis should provide the best results. This is not to say that other strategies should be neglected.

In some cases there should be attempts at insulating the portfolio from the effects of interest rate change or quality effects; in other cases there might be some attempts at, say, substitution trading. The point is that consistency of management style, assuming the rationale for that style has been carefully thought through, should provide the best results over time and therefore should be stressed.

Measuring Bond Performance. To provide a standard by which both short- as well as long-term performance of active strategies may be evaluated, the concept of a *baseline portfolio* has been suggested by Leibowitz [1979]. This is a normative portfolio that is structured to reflect the minimum portfolio risk that will also fulfill the investment return objectives of the client over the long term. The performance of the actual portfolio can be compared to the baseline portfolio results over time, with the latter portfolio serving as a benchmark standard of comparison.

The manager then has an objective standard by which he can be evaluated and which can serve to guide his future management activity. Structural deviations from the benchmark may be evaluated in terms of their return-risk experience compared to the baseline portfolio. Since there is a high covariability of most fixed income returns, this can be a useful approach.

The primary problem in the use of a baseline evaluative approach arises in properly defining the objectives of the client and translating these objectives into a representative portfolio structure.

Combination Strategies

A number of basic portfolio strategies have already been reviewed. It should be kept in mind, however, that the range of portfolio strategies is really a continuum. At various phases during an interest rate cycle, particular strategies may be most appropriate, but more often than not a blending of alternatives is best for part or all of the cycle. The determination of what is optimal may be made by the investor or pension plan sponsor or, alternatively, the portfolio manager. Under conditions of high conviction, a one-strategy approach may be optimal; in the more customary situation of large uncertainty, strategy combinations may be the best in a return-risk tradeoff sense. This might result, for example, in a portion of the portfolio return and risk being tied to some baseline portfolio, the performance of which over the long term should provide satisfactory results, with the remaining portion being actively managed. By retaining an active component, the opportunity for superior performance is retained. How best to determine the proportion to be allocated to each strategy could follow the same general procedure for asset allocation discussed in Chapter 8. This, in effect, would be an allocation among strategies within the fixed income asset category.

Active/Passive Combination. Two of the most popular strategies are an active/passive or an active/immunization combination. An active/passive combination consists of a core component of the portfolio allocated to a passive strategy, with the balance allocated to an active component. The passive strategy would consist of some form of replicating an index or some sector of the market. The active portion would be free to pursue a return maximization (for some given level of risk) strategy.

Active/Immunization Combination. Similarly, an active/immunization combination consists of two components. The immunization component could be either one-period or multiperiod immunized. In the one-period situation an assured return would be established and would serve to stabilize the total portfolio return over the planning horizon. In the multiperiod situation (such as for the retired lives of a pension fund or any other schedule of liabilities subject to estimation), the subportfolio could be immunized now, with new requirements taken care of through reimmunization as they become known. This would be an adaptive strategy in that the immunization component would be established based on an initial set of liabilities and modified over time to take care of new retired lives or other new liabilities. The active portion would continue to be free to maximize expected return given some acceptable risk level.

CONTINGENT IMMUNIZATION. Two specific forms of active/immunization combinations have been suggested. Leibowitz and Weinberger [1981] have called one version *contingent immunization*. This consists of identifying both the available immunization target return and some lower safety net return with which the investor would be minimally satisfied. The manager can continue to pursue an active strategy until an adverse investment experience drives the then available, combined active (from actual past experience) and immunized (from expected future experience) return down to the safety net level; at such time, the manager would be obligated to completely immunize the portfolio and lock in the safety net level return. As long as this safety net is not violated, the manager can continue to actively manage the portfolio. The key considerations include establishing accurate immunized initial and ongoing available target returns, identifying a suitable and immunizable safety net, and implementing an effective monitoring procedure to ensure the safety net is not violated. An example of a monitoring analysis is shown in Tables 9-15 through 9-17.

Table 9-15 provides a summary description of the contingently managed portfolio and the return status of the portfolio relative to the inception date, present date, and horizon date. In the return analysis section of that table, the return to date is the return actually achieved by active management since the inception date. The present immunization target return is the return that could be earned between the present and horizon dates from immunization of the portfolio only, i.e., not including the active management component. The return achievable with immunization strategy is the combined return from active management between the inception and present dates and from immunization between the present and horizon dates. Finally, the required

TABLE 9-15. **Summary Description of a Contingently Immunized Portfolio**

Performance Monitoring

		Actual Asset Values ($000)	Required Asset Values ($000)
Inception Date	12- 1-77	$12000	
Present Date	12- 1-81	16483	$15766
Horizon Date	7- 1-91		54802
Time to Horizon	9.58 yr.		
Actual Portfolio Duration	5.68 yr.		

Asset Value Analysis

Present Actual Asset Value	$16483	Achievable Terminal Asset Value	$57296
Present Required Asset Value	15766	Required Terminal Asset Value	54802
Present Excess Asset Value	$ 718	Achievable Excess Terminal Asset Value	$ 2494

Return Analysis

Return to Date	8.10%/yr.	12- 1-77 to 12- 1-81
Present Immunization Target Return	13.43%/yr.	12- 1-81 to 7- 1-91
Return Achievable with Immunization Strategy	11.85%/yr.	12- 1-77 to 7- 1-91
Required Return on Assets	11.50%/yr.	12- 1-77 to 7- 1-91
Achievable Excess Return (Cushion)	0.35%/yr.	12- 1-77 to 7- 1-91

SOURCE: Gifford Fong Associates.

return on assets is the safety net return. The "achievable excess return" is the difference or cushion between these last two returns.

Table 9-16 evaluates the current portfolio for interest rate change sensitivity. The various scenarios of interest rate change are shown in the bottom panel of the page. In the upper panel, under sensitivity relative to asset value analysis, the column titled Actual Asset Value shows the actual market value of the bond portfolio under each interest rate assumed, diminishing (from actual) with higher rates and increasing with lower rates. The column titled Required Asset Value provides the amounts needed (as of the present date for each interest rate assumed) that, if immunized, would result in the achievement of the safety net return. The third column in this group indicates the excess of column 1 over column 2 for each interest rate. Note that, under the 200 basis point increase, there is a negative excess asset value. This would mean that the safety net return could not be achieved, which is also indicated by the − 0.25 percent achievable excess return (last column to the right) for this same interest rate change assumption. Finally, Table 9-17 (page 340) summarizes the characteristics of the optimal portfolio.

An accurate immunization target is critical in determining not only the basis for the initial problem set-up (e.g., the safety net will usually be a

TABLE 9-16. Sensitivity Analysis of a Contingently Immunized Portfolio

Sensitivity of Achievable Portfolio Performance to Present Interest Rates

Interest Rate Scenario	Assumes Parallel Shift	ASSET VALUE ANALYSIS				RETURN ANALYSIS			
		Actual Asset Value ($000)	Required Asset Value ($000)	Excess Asset Value ($000)	Scenario Modified Return to Date (%/yr.)	Estimated Immunization Target Return[a] (%/yr.)	Return Achievable with Immunization Strategy (%/yr.)	Required Return (%/yr.)	Achievable Excess Return (%/yr.)
Actual	—	$16483	$15766	$ 718	8.10%	13.43%	11.85%	11.50%	0.35%
2	200 B.P. Up	14895	13201	1694	5.48	15.42	12.44	11.50	0.94
3	100 B.P. Up	15650	14424	1226	6.75	14.43	12.14	11.50	0.64
4	100 B.P. Down	17405	17253	152	9.52	12.43	11.57	11.50	0.07
5	200 B.P. Down	18430	19040	−609	11.02	11.34	11.25	11.50	−0.25

SOURCE: Gifford Fong Associates.
[a] Average yield of immunized portfolio

TABLE 9-17. Characteristics of Optimal Portfolio Under Contingent Immunization

Selection Criterion: Risk Minimization

Portfolio	No. of Issues	Par Value ($000)	Market Value ($000)	–	Accrued Interest ($000)	=	Principal Value ($000)	YIELD TO MATURITY (%) Mkt. Val. Weighted	YIELD TO MATURITY (%) Duration Weighted	Average Coupon (%)	Average Quality Rating	Average Duration (yr.)
Current	49	$20010	$16483		$372		$16111	13.776%	13.824%	10.472%	AA	5.677
Optimal	20	19700	16442		476		15966	13.431	13.376	10.206	AAA	5.916
Transaction Summary												
Bought	5	11090	9215		333		8882	13.081	13.045	9.653	AAA	5.933
Sold	32	11415	9271		229		9042	13.693	13.843	10.112	AA	5.498
Held	19	8610	7227		143		7084	13.877	13.801	10.912	AA	5.896

Estimated standard deviation of terminal value ($000): $112

Estimated standard deviation of target return: 2 B.P./yr.

Estimated return at confidence level of:

90% = 13.35%

95 = 13.34

99 = 13.32

SOURCE: Gifford Fong Associates.

certain basis point difference from the target over a specified time period), but also in determining what immunization levels are available during the management horizon. A safety net too close to the initial target return makes triggering the immunization process highly likely, while too low a safety net defeats the purpose of the process since the very low satisfactory minimum return would probably never trigger immunization. Finally, without an adequate monitoring procedure, the benefits of the strategy may be lost because of the inability to know when action is appropriate.

Figure 9-10 graphically illustrates the potential rewards and risks involved with contingent immunization as of a single point in time. The figure assumes an active manager has purchased a 30-year portfolio that can be classically immunized to produce a 12-percent return. Instead, the manager hopes to achieve a larger return than 12 percent, principally via a fall in long-term interest rates. If this in fact occurs, the portfolio return will move up as yields fall in the left half of the figure. But if rates trend up instead of down, the manager wants to earn no less than 11 percent, which is the trigger point for immunization in the right half of the diagram.

By contrast, Figure 9-11 (page 342) shows the pattern of potential returns for successful and unsuccessful active management, with the latter involving immunization when the 11-percent safety net return is reached.

COMBINATION BY FORMULA. Another example of a combination strategy where active and immunization approaches are combined has been described by Gifford Fong Associates [1981]. In contrast to contingent immuni-

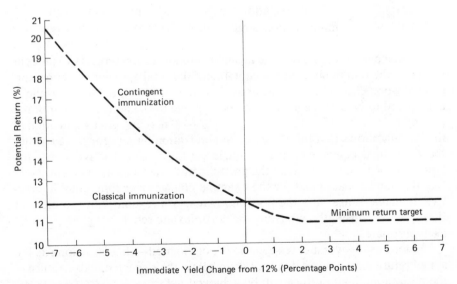

Figure 9-10. Potential Returns on a 30-Year Bond Portfolio Under 12-Percent Classical Immunization and 11-Percent Contingent Immunization for Various Yield Change Assumptions. (SOURCE: Salomon Brothers)

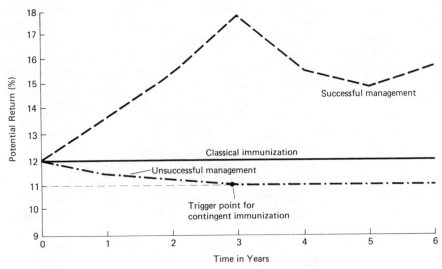

Figure 9-11. Potential Returns Over Time on a Successfully and an Unsuccessfully Actively Managed 30-Year Bond Portfolio with Contingent Immunization. (SOURCE: Salomon Brothers)

zation, this procedure allocates a portion of the initial portfolio to active management, with the balance being immunized according to the following relationship, which assumes that the immunization target return is greater than either the minimum or expected worst case active returns:

$$\frac{\text{Active}}{\text{component}} = \frac{\text{immunization target return} - \text{minimum return}}{\text{immunization target return} - \text{worst case active return}}$$

As an example, assuming that the available immunization target is 15 percent per year, the minimum return acceptable to the fund sponsor is 10 percent, and the worst case return for the actively managed portion of the portfolio is anticipated to be 5 percent, then the percentage in the active portion of the portfolio would be $(15 - 10)/(15 - 5) = 5/10 = 50$ percent. An examination of the formula shows that for any given immunization target return the smaller the minimum acceptable return and the larger the expected active return, the larger will be the percentage of the portfolio under active management. Note that the numbers assumed for the example change over time in an interactive, dynamic sense; it is the portfolio manager's responsibility to monitor these factors constantly, adjusting the portfolio and rebalancing the portfolio as appropriate.

As long as the worst case scenario is not violated—that is, as long as the actual return experienced does not drop below the expected active return—the desired minimum return will be achieved.

While managers may have a preference for having the entire fund actively managed at the outset, this is somewhat mitigated by portfolio constraints that are commonly associated with contingent immunization (e.g., permissible duration range). The approach described here permits the manager to pursue active management without additional portfolio constraint.

Fixed Income Portfolio Return and Risk Modifiers

Aside from the strategies that have been discussed, a number of types of securities with special characteristics provide opportunities for bond portfolio return and risk modification.

Convertible Bonds. Convertible bonds are fixed income securities that provide the holder with the option of converting the bond to the issuer's common stock. A dual pricing structure exists so that if the bond is selling close to the conversion value then it will have similar return and risk characteristics to the stock; if not, it will behave like a bond. There may be a call provision that, at the option of the issuer, may force conversion. The call would be exercised only if the selling price of the bond exceeded the call price.

Bonds with Puts. Bonds with put options allow the purchaser an option to redeem the bonds at specified terms. This permits the purchaser to hedge against a possible increase in interest rates. Canadian "retractable" bonds, in effect, give the bond purchaser a put option since they are redeemable at par prior to the stated maturity date of the bond. Furthermore, Canadian extendible issues give the holder the option of extending the maturity of the bond for an additional five to ten years. This permits the holder to hedge against a possible decline in interest rates.

Interest Rate Futures. Interest rate futures provide the opportunity to increase as well as decrease the return-risk opportunities. Buying or selling interest rate futures is a highly leveraged and speculative use of rate anticipation. For a modest margin requirement or downpayment various futures contracts can be purchased or sold (short), including contracts to receive or deliver Treasury bills, long-term Treasury bonds, GNMA pass-through securities and certificates of deposit.

Alternatively, and importantly for most bond portfolio managers, futures can be used to hedge a portfolio. If, for example, there are loss constraints for securities owned in the portfolio, futures contracts can be bought or sold to guard against loss from pursuing a rate anticipation portfolio strategy. The assumption is that the interest rate effect on the futures, whether positive or negative, will largely if not completely offset those same effects on the portfolio holdings. How complete a hedge strategy is depends on whether the *basis*, the difference between the current or cash price of a bond and the futures price of that bond, moves in your direction (favorable) or against you (unfavorable) during the life of the futures contract. An example of a complete futures policy statement for the Federal Home Loan Bank system in use in 1982, including several hedging examples, is included in Appendix C to this chapter.

To summarize, in the case of special terms such as those found in convertibles or bonds with put options, the advantage to the bondholder is usually offset by a lower yield to maturity associated with the security. In the case of the use of interest rate futures, significant risk is assumed in the case of speculative buying or selling of futures as a result of the high leverage. In futures hedging the risk is less-than-perfect negative correlation of the bond portfolio returns with the returns of the futures contracts.

Interest Options. Interest options are a new investment vehicle which, at this writing, are not being traded but should be in the near future. They resemble stock options in form. For a specified price, called the *premium*, a right either to purchase or to sell a bond with specified characteristics for a specified time horizon is acquired. Compared to the financial futures contract there is limited investment exposure; i.e., the interest option limits the loss to the holder to the premium paid. Financial futures have no premium (exclusive of transaction costs), but they also have no limitation on the potential loss if the price of the underlying fixed income security changes adversely and the futures contract is not closed out. The most important feature to the investor of interest options is the need to pay a specific, fixed fee in return for limiting the potential loss. Note that basis risk, which either adds to or reduces the potential loss of financial futures contracts, is subsumed in the interest option premium.

From an institutional standpoint, the limit on the potential loss can be compelling. Fiduciary concerns and regulatory restrictions have limited widespread use of financial futures by institutions primarily because of exposure to unlimited loss. For a financial option, since the loss is limited to the premium paid, a form of insurance is created that can serve the same hedging or speculative role as financial futures. A remaining issue is under what circumstances the insurance premium required by financial options justifies their use as a substitute for financial futures. This should be apparent once trading in these securities commences.

One other problem with financial futures has been the inability to construct complete hedges because contracts have been available only on a very limited number of underlying securities relative to the population of securities and coupon/maturity combinations available in the marketplace. This paucity of coverage may be alleviated if interest options become a more popular hedging and speculative vehicle than have interest futures.

FIXED INCOME PORTFOLIO CONSTRAINTS

The return objectives and risk tolerance of investors is further modified by investor constraints, some of which are characteristic of a class of investors while others may be unique to a particular institutional or individual investor. Chapters 4 and 5 have covered these constraints for various types of investors. The comments below briefly relate the characteristics of fixed income securities and fixed income markets to these investor constraints.

Liquidity Needs

Fixed income securities are looked upon primarily as providing a secure cash flow stream and a fixed maturity. Thus, they are well suited to meeting an investor's need for continuous or periodic cash flow from income and/or maturing principal. Endowment funds, casualty insurance companies, and widows or retirees are classic examples of investors who typically modify their return objective and risk tolerance because of a basic need for an assured schedule of cash flow from their investment portfolio.

A liquidity reserve may be derived from the cash flow from coupons and maturing fixed income instruments or created and maintained by holding money market instruments, such as Treasury bills and commercial paper. Furthermore, liquidity may be derived from a spaced schedule of maturing obligations over a few months or a few years.

Liquidity can also be achieved by emphasizing or limiting portfolio investments to the most readily marketable and liquid types of bonds; that is, those issues that could be sold quickly with little or no price concession from currently quoted prices.

High credit quality and short maturity are the most dominant characteristics of readily marketable bonds. It should also be noted that round lot holdings—typically $500,000 par value of a corporate issue—are more marketable than odd lots—less than $500,000 par. The marketability of round lots is reflected in the narrower dealer spreads between bid and ask prices than occur for odd lots. Odd lot long bonds typically have wide spreads. On the other hand, Treasury bills and certain other money market instruments can be purchased in odd lots with little or no yield penalty.

Actively managed bond portfolios develop periodic liquidity needs in the form of reserves held in anticipation of a change in yields and bond prices. Minimum market risk is sought with the least sacrifice in interest income.

Liquidity characteristics are determined by:

1. Amount outstanding (dollar amount of the issue of bonds outstanding)—the more the better.
2. Amount closely held (dollar amount of issue)—the less the better.
3. Coupon level—the closer to the current coupon level the better because there is an investor preference for current coupon securities to avoid the accounting and tax implications of discounts or premiums.
4. Age of issue—recently issued securities tend to be more actively traded.
5. Quality—the higher the better.
6. Terms (such as callability or sinking fund provisions)—tend to re-

duce liquidity but if a bond is redeemed by being called, the call feature provides a potential liquidity source.

7. Maturity (duration)—fixed income securities with a maturity or duration of less than one year tend to be more liquid than any longer maturity/duration securities for any given issue.

Tax Considerations

Individual investors and financial institutions such as banks and insurance companies are subject to income and capital gains taxes. Thus, these investors seek the highest after-tax return in their fixed income investments. In the United States, income from municipal bonds is exempt from federal income tax. State income tax laws and regulations vary by state, with most states exempting domestic issues (issuers domiciled in that state) and some states exempting all interest from municipal bonds regardless of the domicile of the issuer. All states exempt interest on U.S. government securities from state income taxes. Accretion of the discount in bonds purchased in the secondary market at a price below par is normally not taxed until the security is sold or matures. However, original issue discount (OID) bonds are treated differently. Taxable investors are required to treat accretion of discount on an OID bond as ordinary income for tax purposes. As mentioned earlier, this type of bond is attractive only to tax-exempt investors such as pension funds, endowment funds, and, more recently, IRA accounts.

Finally, it is the *marginal* tax rate of the investor—whether it be zero percent for a pension fund or the full corporate income tax rate of 46 percent and corporate capital gains rate of 28 percent or the maximum income tax rate of 50 percent and capital gains rate of 20 percent for individuals—that must be applied to determine the after-tax return of an investment under consideration. These tax considerations constrain the investment alternatives for investors.

Time Horizon

Each investor has a specified time horizon or period over which the return objectives are intended to be satisfied. The life cycle of the individual investor or the pension fund or the operating cycle of a financial institution or endowment fund largely determines the portfolio time horizon. Fixed income securities have a definite investment life or maturity that can be matched or related to the investor's time horizon. In fact, this certainty of term to maturity provides the portfolio manager with a base for fitting expected returns with investor return objectives. Preferred and common stocks, which have a perpetual life, provide no similar certainty or structure.

The essence of fixed income management is to take advantage of this structure. In its most basic form quality analysis ensures against experiencing default, while more active forms of management seek to exploit cyclical or temporary return opportunities. Time horizon tradeoffs, where the relatively certain returns of holding a security to maturity are balanced against a more active trading strategy, must be a continual consideration. For example, if you begin to actively manage a portfolio that has employed a buy-and-hold approach, you may jeopardize the high cash flows that had been expected from buying and holding. Similarly, if you decide to actively manage a previously immunized portfolio where coupon reinvestment risk has been balanced against discount accretion, you may jeopardize the original objective sought via immunization. It can be seen from these examples that both the decision to change strategy—and to begin to actively manage—*and* the timing of that decision can be critical to the attainment of fixed income portfolio objectives.

Active strategies are concerned with planning horizons within the portfolio time horizon; hence, the manager is faced with a sequence of decision horizons. Logically, each of these would be concurrently, rather than sequentially, optimized, so that the decision-making process would span multiple horizons instead of one period at a time. However, because of the uncertainty of expectations, considerations beyond the next planning period become very complicated. For example, a three-scenario forecast leads to a nine-scenario projection if two periods are considered at once, since each period-one scenario can lead to three possible period-two scenarios. This would continue to increase by a factor of three with each additional time period. Providing the inputs to and understanding the outputs from such a process would be beyond the capacity of most managers. The solution has been to retain the one-period framework, to continuously monitor the analysis, and to be open to adjustments with the passage of time—especially whenever a change in expectations takes place. A moving window of a desired planning horizon emerges within the overall portfolio time horizon.

Regulatory or Legal Considerations

The environment in which fixed income management must operate includes a number of exogenous constraints.

Taking Losses. Because bonds eventually mature at par value, investors, even those who are not legally constrained, are often loath or at least reluctant to sell a bond at a price below the cost of the bond and realize a capital loss. This preoccupation with book loss (the difference between cost and market) or even par value loss (the difference between par and market) may appear prudent on the surface. However, for an income-oriented investor in particular, such concerns ignore the opportunity costs involved.

These opportunity costs represent the loss of increase in investment income that could be realized from the sale of a bond and reinvestment of the proceeds in another suitable and higher yielding bond. Such higher yielding opportunities often arise if the investor is willing to lengthen maturity (assuming a positively sloped yield curve) or reduce quality. Less frequently, market inefficiencies provide the observant investor with the opportunity to reinvest at a higher yield without extending or downgrading. For example, sinking-fund bids for industrial bonds frequently provide the opportunity to sell older issues at a premium over current market prices on similar bonds except for sinking-fund purchasing activity.

Most importantly, the opportunity cost must be sufficiently great or, in other words, the yield advantage must be sufficiently large to allow the investor to recover the loss (book or par) out of the additional interest income at or prior to the maturity of the bond sold. Because tax regulation allows the offset of gains and losses, some taxable investors might adjust the realized loss by the amount of the capital gains tax that could be saved. Table 9-18 is an example that illustrates that taking losses can be both prudent and profitable when market inefficiencies provide such opportunities.

TABLE 9-18. Example of Loss Makeup on a Corporate Bond Sold

Sold: American Telephone and Telegraph Company
2⅝% Debentures due 7-1-86
Price: 73½   YTM: 10.66%

Purchased: U.S. Treasury
12¾% Notes due 2-15-87
Price: 96.469   YTM: 13.76%

Investment Results

	Including Capital Gains Tax Savings	Excluding Capital Gains Tax Savings
I. CAPITAL LOSS		
Tax basis of bonds sold	$208,000	$208,000
Less proceeds	152,880	152,880
Gross loss	$ 55,120	$ 55,120
II. INCOME RESULTS		
Proceeds	$152,880	$152,880
Add prospective capital gains tax savings @ 28% corporate rate	15,434	—
Total reinvested	$168,314	$152,880
New annual income @ 13.76%	$ 23,160	$ 21,036
Less previous income	5,460	5,460
Annual increase	$ 17,700	$ 15,576
Percent increase	324%	260%
III. LOSS MAKEUP TIME		
Time required to recover gross loss	3.1 years	3.3 years
Time to maturity of sold bonds	4.2	4.2
Maturity of Treasury bond purchased	4.8	4.8

GIC Valuation.   Another example of this type of constraint is the special treatment afforded guaranteed investment contracts (GICs) by actuaries who will accept valuation of GICs at book. Immunized portfolios on the other hand are usually valued at market. This makes GICs appear more attractive because of their resulting lack of principal volatility. There does not appear to be any movement toward having immunized portfolios treated similarly.

The point to be made in this discussion is that fixed income strategies cannot be considered in the abstract. Realistically, depending on the type of investor and the jurisdiction(s) that may be controlling, theoretical optimality may be modified via regulator constraints.

Unique Considerations of the Investor

Portfolio construction would be sterile without provision for the special requirements of each investor. Some of these have already been covered in the other sections on fixed income portfolio constraints. Beyond these, institutional investors may be concerned with such things as social responsibility issues that may preclude investing in firms that make objectionable products or do business in certain countries; predefined portfolio structures where the quality and/or maturity range of the portfolio holdings may be restricted; and special strategy arrangements, as described by Black and Dewhurst [1981] and discussed in Chapter 8, that suggest an all-bond portfolio for pension funds because of tax arbitrage reasons. For the individual investor, the status of his or her estate, retirement objectives, and cash flow needs should be taken into account.

The important point is to recognize that the portfolio construction process does not proceed in a vacuum. Optimal return-risk tradeoffs may have to be compromised to adhere to the investor's preferences. In the final analysis, however, it is the client's portfolio and if an effective relationship is to be maintained, the portfolio manager and the client will have to come to a meeting of the minds on these issues.

SUMMARY

Two dominant themes may be identified in this chapter. The first involves the investment characteristics of fixed income securities, and the second, the procedures for harnessing these characteristics in a portfolio.

The range of investment return-risk combinations is wide for fixed income securities, wider than ever before in the history of money and capital markets. Because fixed income securities have an assured cash flow including a specified maturity, a number of policy and strategy objectives are made possible. In response to high levels as well as increased volatility of rates, additional security types have been introduced. Variable rate securities, original issue discount securities, and financial futures contracts are just three examples that add to the already formidable arsenal of alternative vehicles. The result is not only a robust set of investment types but also an organic asset responsive to changing circumstances. By taking advantage of these characteristics, a number of investment policies and objectives can be achieved.

Based upon the range and variety of the individual security characteristics, the policy and strategy options follow. These can span the return-risk spectrum from cash equivalents to common stock portfolios by the proper selection and blending of the individual securities. More exclusive strategies include immunization approaches, where a predefined return can be assured over a wide range of time horizons and schedules of liabilities may be systematically funded.

In the pursuit of these strategies a number of tools drawing from recent advances in investment technology may be identified. As an example, return simulation allows an overview as well as a detailed analysis of a portfolio for insights into prospective return sensitivity. This leads to effective portfolio monitoring and revision and contributes to more effective portfolio management as well as promoting more effective policy and strategy communication.

Finally, the reality of portfolio construction requires a discussion of some of the constraints that must be taken into account. Optimality in the abstract has limited relevance to the investor. The most important constraints are reviewed.

In the next two chapters two other important asset alternatives will be covered. While each asset alternative has its own role in the overall asset allocation framework discussed in Chapter 8, the interrelationships among all of the alternatives should be kept in mind.

FURTHER READING

A description of duration and a theoretical discussion of its uses and limitations is included in Cox, Ingersoll, and Ross [1979]. For a review of alternative measures of duration and empirical results of immunization as a fixed percentage income strategy, see Bierwag et al. [1980].

A number of articles describe the earliest theoretical derivation of the immunization concept. See Macaulay [1938] and Reddington [1952]. Another extension of classical immunization strategy, including the provision for active management, is described in Leibowitz and Weinberger [1981]. A more recent theoretical treatment of immunization, including extensions of the classical approaches described above to include all types of interest rate changes, an explicit risk measure, and multiperiod capability can be found in Fong and Vasicek [1980]. For a review of the relative merits of immunization and cash flow matching from the standpoint of the funding requirements of the respective strategies, see Gifford Fong Associates [1981].

An overview of fixed income portfolio management, including a review of important concepts and definitions, may be found in Sharpe [1981]. A more detailed treatment of fixed income strategies for the practitioner is included in Homer and Leibowitz [1972], Leibowitz [1979], and Fong [1980]. Two studies that report on the effectiveness of various spaced-maturity bond portfolio management strategies are Fogler, Groves, and Richardson [1976] and Fogler and Groves [1976]. For an interesting rationale for the use of bonds for pension funds to make use of attractive current tax treatment see Black and Dewhurst [1981].

A use of financial ratios for quality analysis of issuing firms is described in Murphy and Osborne [1979]. The relationship of portfolio size to the diversification of fixed income portfolios is described along with empirical results in McEnally and Boardman [1979].

A detailed decomposition of realized returns is described for the portfolio as well as for individual securities in Fong, Pearson, and Vasicek [1981].

The theory and analysis appropriate for determining the term structure of interest rates is contained in Fong and Vasicek [1982].

BIBLIOGRAPHY

Bierwag, G. O., G. G. Kaufman, R. Schweitzer, and A. Toevs, "Risk and Return for Active and Passive Bond Portfolio Management: Theory and Evidence," Unpublished paper, Center for Capital Market Research, University of Oregon, October 1980.

Black, Fischer, and Morey P. Dewhurst, "A New Investment Strategy for Pension Funds," *The Journal of Portfolio Management,* Summer 1981.

Cox, John C., John E. Ingersoll, Jr., and Stephen A. Ross, "Duration and the Measurement of Basis Risk," *Journal of Business,* 1979.

Fisher, Lawrence, and R. Weil, "Coping with Risk of Interest Rate Fluctuations: Returns to Bondholders from Naive and Optimal Strategies," *Journal of Business,* October 1971.

Fogler, H. Russell, and William A. Groves. "How Much Can Active Bond Management Raise Returns?" *The Journal of Portfolio Management,* Fall 1976.

———, **William A. Groves, and James G. Richardson.** "Managing Bonds: Are 'Dumbbells' Smart?" *The Journal of Portfolio Management,* Winter 1976.

Foldessy, Edward P., "Companies Facing Severe Problems Because of Rising Short-Term Debt," *Wall Street Journal,* October 26, 1981.

Fong, H. Gifford, *Bond Portfolio Analysis,* Monograph No. 11., Charlottesville, Va.: The Financial Analysts Research Foundation, 1980.

———, **Charles J. Pearson, and Oldrich A. Vasicek,** "Bond Performance Analysis," New York: Institute for Quantitative Research in Finance, 1981.

———, **and Oldrich A. Vasicek,** "A Risk Minimizing Strategy for Multiple Liability Immunization," New York: Institute for Quantitative Research in Finance, 1980.

——— and ———, "Term Structure Modeling Using Third Order Exponential Splines," *The Journal of Finance,* May 1982.

Gifford Fong Associates, "The Costs of Cashflow Matching," 1981.

Homer, Sidney, and Martin L. Leibowitz, *Inside the Yield Book: New Tools for Bond Market Strategy,* Englewood Cliffs, N.J.: Prentice-Hall, 1972.

Ibbotson, Roger G., and Rex A. Sinquefield, *Stocks, Bonds, Bills and Inflation: The Past and the Future,* Charlottesville, Va.: The Financial Analysts Research Foundation, 1982.

Kaufman, Henry, "The Many Faces and Implications of the Yield Curve," Speech at the 32nd Annual Investment Seminar, New York State Bankers Association, November 30, 1981 and published by Salomon Brothers, Inc., 1981.

Leibowitz, Martin L., "Trends in Bond Portfolio Management," *CFA Study Guide III,* Charlottesville, Va.: The Institute of Chartered Financial Analysts, 1979.

————, **and Alfred Weinberger,** "The Uses of Contingent Immunization," *The Journal of Portfolio Management,* Fall 1981.

Macaulay, Fredrick R., *Some Theoretical Problems Suggested by the Movement of Interest Rates, Bond Yields and Stock Prices in the United States Since 1856,* New York: National Bureau of Economic Research, 1938.

McEnally, Richard W., and Calvin M. Boardman, "Aspects of Corporate Bond Portfolio Diversification," *The Journal of Financial Research,* Spring 1979.

Murphy, Joseph E., Jr., and M. F. M. Osborne, "Games of Chance and the Probability of Corporate Profit or Loss," *Financial Management,* Summer 1979.

Reddington, F. M., "Review of the Principle of Life Office Valuations," *Journal of the Institute of Actuaries* 18:1952.

Sharpe, William F., *Investments,* 2nd Ed., Englewood Cliffs, N.J.: Prentice-Hall, 1981.

APPENDIX A

History of Yields, Yield Differentials, and Yield Curves on Selected Money and Capital Market Instruments*

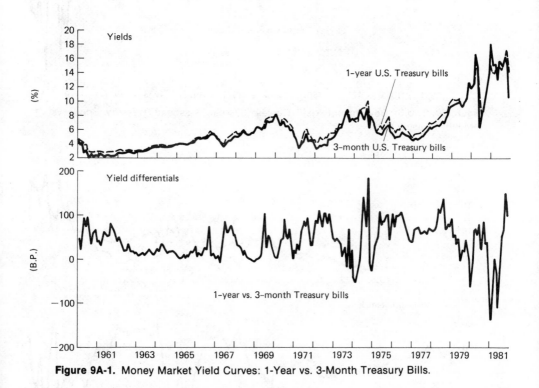

Figure 9A-1. Money Market Yield Curves: 1-Year vs. 3-Month Treasury Bills.

* The source for all of the figures in this appendix is Kaufman [1981].

Figure 9A-2. U.S. Government Yield Curves: 30-Year Seasoned Treasury Bonds vs. 3-Month Treasury Bills.

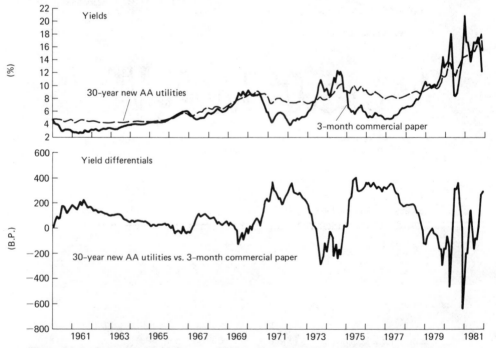

Figure 9A-3. Corporate Yield Curves: 30-Year New AA Utilities (Salomon Brothers Estimates) vs. 3-Month Commercial Paper.

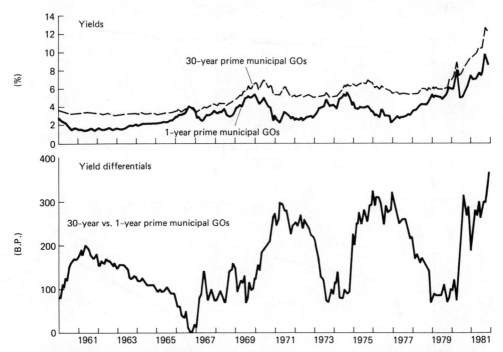

Figure 9A-4. Municipal Yield Curves: 30-Year vs. 1-Year New Prime General Obligations (Salomon Brothers Estimates).

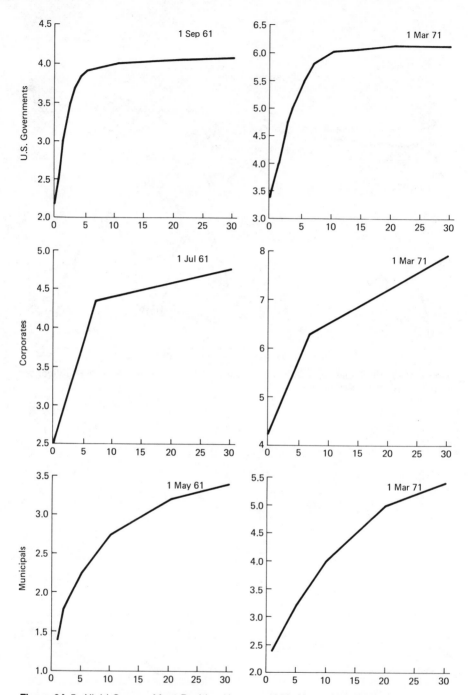

Figure 9A-5. Yield Curves: Most Positive (January 1960–November 1981).

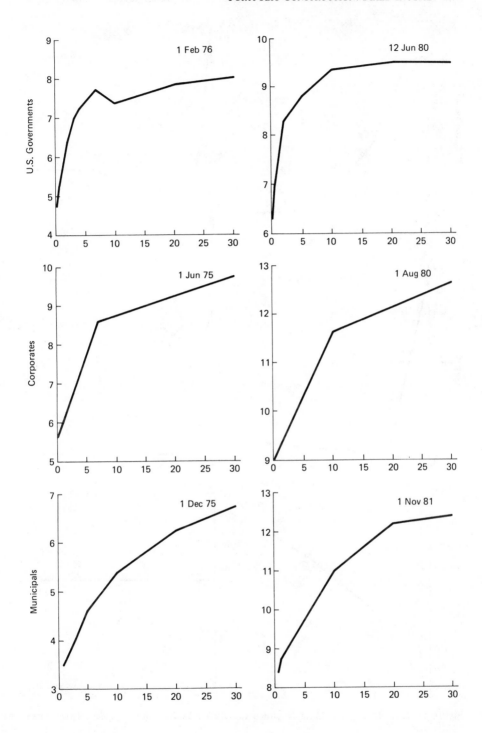

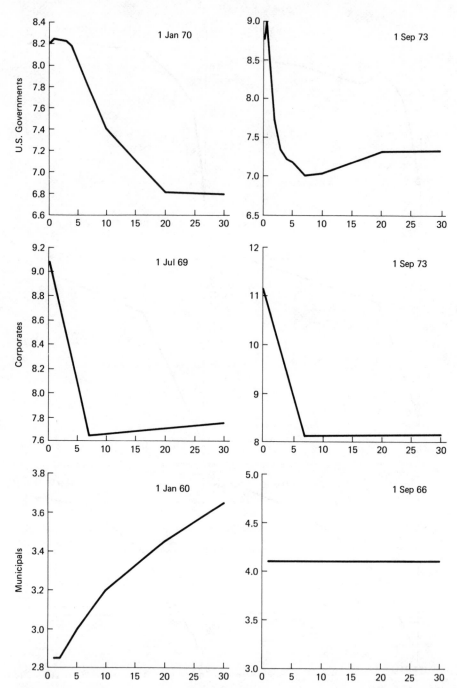

Figure 9A-6. Yield Curves: Most Negative or Least Positive (January 1960–November 1981).

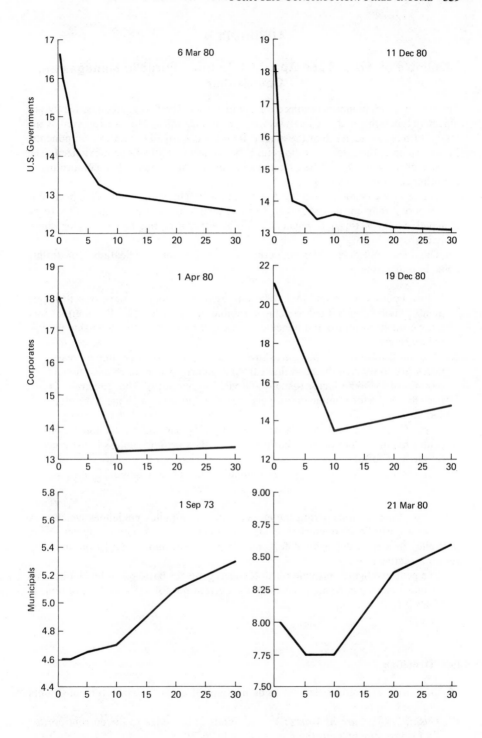

APPENDIX B

Example of Worst Case Approach to Bond Portfolio Management Optimization

There are four main inputs required for optimization. The first is an objective [66] or objective function which the analysis will seek to maximize. This is expressed as the total return of any scenario or the composite return or any of the return components. In the example, the total portfolio return for scenario 2 [70] will be maximized. The essence of the analysis will be to maximize this return element while conforming to the other three input classes.

The second category of input is the cash flow [67] to be invested at the beginning of the period (current date 4/26/79). In the example there are no cash flows to be included; however, this option can be useful in either investing new money or generating cash.

The third input category is concerned with constraint specification. Constraints come in four forms:

1. Return Policy Constraints [68]: Where individual or combinations of return elements may be constrained to achieve minimum return levels. This in effect sets a lower limit on return and hence controls risk by limiting the downside potential on return.
2. Portfolio Duration [75]: Measures the value-weighted average time in years necessary to receive the cash flows from a security where each cash flow is discounted by some factor (usually the yield to maturity). This constraint is especially useful for immunization purposes and can serve as a measure of average life.
3. Upper Concentration Limit on Any Security [76]: This allows a blanket concentration maximum on all securities held in the portfolio (unless constrained by the next form).
4. Individual Security Limits [77]: Individual securities may be constrained so a range or particular level of concentration is specified.

These constraint options permit the implementation of policy guidelines which seek to control portfolio characteristics. One frequent use is in monitoring the many portfolios in a trust department for uniformity of portfolio construction and risk-return objectives.

The next two figures provide portfolio aggregates for basic portfolio characteristics. Comparisons can be made between the current portfolio [80] and the optimized portfolio [81].

Item Definition

66. *Objective.* The return element to be maximized consistent with the constraints imposed.
67. *Cash Flow to Current Market Value.* Funds to be added to the current portfolio for investment as of the current date (4/26/79).

68. *Return Policy Constraints.* Permits specifying limits on the level of return elements. This is a form of risk control in that minimum return levels can be specified for one or a number of return elements in the optimization process.
69. *Portfolio Return Component.* Specifies one or a combination of return elements which will be constrained. In the first specification the total return of scenario 3 is constrained and in the second specification the combination of earned interest, plus interest on interest, and plus interest on redemptions of scenario 1 is constrained.
70. *Scenario.* Identification of which scenario is being constrained for return level.
71. *Relationship.* Description of the nature of the return constraint.
72. *Return Requirement.* Level of return specification.
73. *Optimized Portfolio.* Level of return expected from the optimized portfolio.
74. *Impact.* Marginal cost (shadow price) to the specified objective function of changing a binding constraint. In the first constraint, relaxing the 3.0% return requirement by 1.0% (to 4%) would result in a .37 basis point reduction in the objective [66]. Conversely, tightening this constraint by 1.0% (to 2%) would result in a .37 increase in the return objective. This provides a sensitivity measure of the effect of constraints which are binding (constraints at their specified value) on the optimized solution.
75. *Limits on Portfolio Duration.* A range or target on portfolio duration available along with a measure of the impact [74].
76. *Upper Concentration Limit on any Security.* A blanket constraint on all securities held in the optimized portfolio. This specification will be operative unless an individual security is constrained.
77. *Individual Security Limits.* Allows the turnover and concentration of individual securities to be constrained. The last column providing Net Impact measures the cumulative effects on that security from the Individual Security Limits (if binding).
80. *Projected Portfolio Performance—Current Portfolio.* For each scenario (numbered 1 to 3) and the probability-weighted composite scenario (C), the statistics are given for the current portfolio (i.e., before optimization). Each scenario represents an expected shift in the U.S. Treasury yield curve over the investor's desired time horizon. Under Scenario 1, for example, the reinvestment interest amounts to $9,401,000 and the return from yield change impact is 8.05 percent.
81. *Projected Portfolio Performance—Optimized Portfolio.* After the current portfolio is optimized to maximize the desired return component [66], the statistics are shown for the modified portfolio. For example, the optimized portfolio would have a reinvestment interest of $28,163,000 and a return from yield change impact of 10.21 percent for Scenario 1. This would result if the current portfolio were subjected to the specified changes due to purchases [90] and sales [91].
83. *Current Par Value.* Par value of current holding in thousands of dollars.
84. *Optimal Par Value.* Par value as the result of the optimization process in thousands of dollars.
85. *Change in Par Value.* Difference between [84] and [83].

(*continues on page 364*)

TABLE 9B-1. Constraint Data for Sample Optimization Problem

Portfolio: Sample Profit Sharing Plan—CURRENT CALLS
Constraints: Sample Optimization Problem

Current Date: 4-26-79
Projection Date: 12-31-79

66 OBJECTIVE: MAXIMIZE TOTAL PORTFOLIO RETURN FOR SCENARIO 2
67 CASH FLOW TO CURRENT MARKET VALUE OF TOTAL PORTFOLIO:$0.

68 RETURN POLICY CONSTRAINTS

69 Portfolio Return Component	70 Scenario	71 Relationship	72 Return Requirement	73 Optimized Portfolio	74 Impact (%/%)
Total (Unadjusted)	3	Greater Than Or Equal To	3.00%	3.00%	−0.37
Earned Interest = Interest On Interest = Interest On Redemptions	1	Greater Than Or Equal To	5.00%	5.91%	0.0
Earned Interest = Interest On Interest = Interest On Redemptions	2	Greater Than Or Equal To	6.00%	6.07%	0.0

Earned Interest	3	Greater Than Or Equal To	6.00%	6.27%
= Interest On Interest				
= Interest On Redemptions				0.0

75 LIMITS ON PORTFOLIO DURATION (YRS)

Minimum	Maximum	Optimized Portfolio	Impact (%/Yr)
3.0	9.0	6.4	0.0

76 UPPER CONCENTRATION LIMIT ON ANY SECURITY: 15.0000% OF TOTAL PORTFOLIO MARKET VALUE
(UNLESS INDIVIDUAL LIMIT IS SPECIFIED)

77 INDIVIDUAL SECURITY LIMITS (% OF MARKET VALUE)

Security Number	TRANSACTIONS (%)		CONCENTRATION (%)			Net Impact of All Individual Security Limits (%/%)
	Allowed	Required To Optimize	Minimum	Maximum	Required To Optimize	
1			5.00	25.00	17.83	8.0

86. *Change in Market Value*. Difference between optimized market value subtracted from current market value.
87. *Description of Security*. Name, coupon, maturity, price and quality rating of security to be changed.
88. *Expected Return*. The return for the security under the scenario defined as the Objective Component as well as the Total Return for the Composite Scenario. Constraint Impact conforms to [74].
89. *Transaction Cost*. Cost of making the security change expressed as a negative return from the expected return of the security. The last column gives the return of the security under the composite scenario net of the transaction cost.
90. *Purchases*. Security additions required by the optimization process.
91. *Sales*. Security subtractions required by the optimization process.

TABLE 9B-2. Projected Portfolio Performance for Sample Optimization Problem

Portfolio: Sample Profit Sharing Plan—CURRENT CALLS
Constraints: Sample Optimization Problem

Current Date: 4-26-79
Projection Date: 12-31-79

66 OBJECTIVE: MAXIMIZE TOTAL PORTFOLIO RETURN FOR SCENARIO 2

	MATURED BONDS		CALLED BONDS			PORTFOLIO RETURN ON BEGINNING MARKET VALUE (%)								
	Face Value ($000)	Reinvstmt. Interest ($000)	Face Value ($000)	Redmptn. Value ($000)	Reinvstmt. Interest ($000)	Yield Change Impact	Time (Roll) Impact	Spread Change Impact	Earned Intrst.	Coupon Reinvstmt.	Matured/ Called	Mat/Call- Reinvstmt.	Total	Annual Total
80 Current Portfolio														
1[a]	$204	$ 9.401	$0	$0.0	$0.0	8.05%	0.19%	-1.15%	5.91%	0.07%	0.02%	0.28%	13.35%	19.59%
2[a]	204	11.156	0	0.0	0.0	1.94	0.19	-0.54	5.91	0.07	0.02	0.33	7.92	11.61
3[a]	204	13.385	0	0.0	0.0	-3.65	0.19	-0.42	5.91	0.08	0.02	0.40	2.52	3.69
C[b]	204	11.561	0	0.0	0.0	1.18	0.19	-0.60	5.91	0.07	0.02	0.34	7.11	10.43
81 Optimized Portfolio														
1[a]	$610	$23.163	$0	$0.0	$0.0	10.21%	0.42%	-0.33%	4.98%	0.09%	0.03%	0.83%	16.25%	23.83%
2[a]	610	33.439	0	0.0	0.0	2.17	0.42	-0.10	4.98	0.09	0.03	0.99	8.59	12.61
3[a]	610	40.139	0	0.0	0.0	-3.79	0.42	0.07	4.98	0.10	0.03	1.19	3.00	4.40
C[b]	610	34.658	0	0.0	0.0	1.59	0.42	-0.08	4.98	0.03	0.03	1.03	8.06	11.83

SOURCE: Gifford Fong Associates.
[a] Scenario number
[b] Probability-weighted composite scenario

TABLE 9B-3. Changes Required to Optimize Sample Optimization Problem

Portfolio: Sample Profit Sharing Plan—Current Calls
Constraints: Sample Optimization Problem

Current Date: 4-26-79
Projection Date: 12-31-79

66 OBJECTIVE: MAXIMIZE TOTAL PORTFOLIO RETURN FOR SCENARIO 2

83 Current Par Value ($000)	84 Optimal Par Value ($000)	85 Change In Par Value ($000)	86 Change In Mkt Value ($000)	87 Description Of Security	88 EXPECTED RETURN			89 TRANSACTION COST	
					Objective Component (%)	Total Composite (%)	Constraint Impact On Portfolio (BP/Bond)	As Return Component (%)	Composite Return (%)
90 Purchases In Order Of Decreasing Change In Market Value—									
$ 0.0	$566.4	$566.4	$506.5	United States Treas. Bds. 7.8750% 2-15-93 89.438 16 912810CA	9.3%	8.6%	‚ 0.010	−0.250%	8.3%
0.0	816.2	816.2	506.5	Southwestern Bell Tel. Co. 4.6250% 8-1-95 62.063 AAA 17 845335AD	9.7	9.0	0.010	−0.250	8.8

					#					
200.0	602.1	402.1	402.1	Cash Equivalents 9.9500% 6-1-79 100.000	1	6.7	6.9	0.0	-0.167	6.7
250.0	567.0	317.0	283.2	025195AZ American Commercial Lines 7.8000% 8-15-92 89.344	7	9.3	8.5	0.010	-0.140	8.4
278.0	537.9	259.9	223.5	GNMA 7.5000% 12-15-98 86.000	8	8.7	7.9	0.0	-0.121	7.8

91 Sales In Order Of Decreasing Change In Market Value—

					#					
$500.0	$0.0	$-500.0	$-496.9	040555AL Arizona Pub Svc. Co. 9.5000% 2-15-82 99.375 A	3	7.3%	6.1%	0.021	0.0%	0.0%
500.0	0.0	-500.0	-485.0	665500BD Northern Nat. Gas. Co. 90000% 5-1-85 97.000 A	4	7.6	6.6	0.021	0.0	0.0
500.0	0.0	-500.0	-480.0	302292AA Exxon Pipeline Co. 9.0000% 10-15-04 96.000 AAA	10	7.9	7.1	0.031	0.0	0.0

SOURCE: Gifford Fong Associates.

APPENDIX C

Futures Policy of the Federal Home Loan Bank System, March 1982

Purpose of Futures Policy

The primary purpose of the Bank System's Futures Policy is to provide a number of flexible, efficient tools to reduce the interest rate risk of the Banks and the Bank System as a whole. Tools for asset/liability management in the cash market are already basically developed. Proper use of financial futures by the Bank System should allow the separation of the liquidity decision for the Bank System and the profitability impact on individual Banks.

Objectives of this Futures Policy are to:

1. Establish the Federal Home Loan Bank Board policy regarding the use of financial futures contracts for bona fide hedging transactions or positions. Hedging is the voluntary assumption of one risk to offset another risk which occurs in the normal course of business.*
2. Delegate the responsibility for implementation, execution and administration of this futures policy.

Futures Policy Guidelines

1. Positions in financial futures contracts are justified if they reduce the interest rate risk exposure to which the Federal Home Loan Banks are subjected in their normal course of business. Net interest rate risk exposure can be defined as the volatility in earnings resulting from the mismatch of asset and liability maturities and commitments for advances to members. Speculation in the futures market is not permitted.
2. The board of directors of each Bank must adopt written policies and establish internal control procedures for the use of futures contracts. The board of directors and senior management of each Bank must authorize hedge strategies and be informed of futures transactions and positions including unrealized gains and losses on a routine and timely basis.
3. Hedges must be specific. That is, a financial futures contract must be identified with a specific asset (or group of assets), liability (or group), or commitment (or group) at the time the futures contract is executed.
4. The purpose of the hedge must be explicitly stated at the time of execution and a written record of purchases and sales of contracts maintained.
5. If a hedge is against an anticipated rather than an existing cash transaction (e.g., issuance of a future liability, purchase of a security, funding of an advance, making a commitment for an advance), the cash transaction must reasonably be expected to occur.
6. A bank may take delivery of a security specified by a futures contract provided it is an eligible investment.
7. When a hedged cash position is closed the corresponding futures position must be closed on the same trade day.

---

* Regulation 1.3 of the Commodity Futures Trading Commission defines bona fide hedging transactions and positions to mean transactions or positions in a contract for future delivery on any contract market, where such transactions or positions normally represent a substitute for transactions to be made or positions to be taken at a later time in a physical marketing channel, and where they are economically appropriate to the reduction of risks in the conduct and management of a commercial enterprise.

Authorized Hedges

A Bank's futures strategy must be part of its overall asset/liability strategy. The sum of its futures position must be reviewed regularly in this context. Permissible transactions are long and short positions which fall under these general categories:

1. Reducing financing risks associated with the allocation of consolidated bonds and discount notes and with the issuance of terms deposits;
2. Enabling a Bank to transfer the risk involved in making commitments for advances from the Bank to the futures market;
3. Effectively altering the maturity of advances or the maturity of the supporting liabilities including the structuring of synthetic fixed rate loans;
4. Only shortening the maturity of the Bank's investment portfolio but to not less than zero days. Hedging securities in the investment portfolio with long futures positions is not permitted.

Examples of hedges are appended to this Policy.

Eligible Futures Contracts

On the basis of two criteria, sufficient liquidity and relatively high price correlation with the cash instruments of the Federal Home Loan Banks, use of the following contracts is permitted:

1. The three-month Treasury bill contract traded on the International Monetary Market (IMM);
2. The Treasury bond contract traded on the Chicago Board of Trade (CBT); and
3. The Certificate of Deposit (CD) contract traded on the IMM.

If other contracts which are highly correlated with Bank System assets and liabilities develop sufficient liquidity, this Policy will be amended.

Limitations

The net position of the 12 Banks in any futures contract in a given contract month must not exceed 25% of the total open interest in that contract month. The total System participation in each contract and month will be monitored and reported on by the Office of Finance.

Accounting

In the absence of a Financial Accounting Standards Board (FASB) ruling and Generally Accepted Accounting Principles on accounting for futures, the recommendations of the American Institute of Certified Public Accountants (AICPA) Task Force generally will be followed. According to the Task Force, hedge or deferral accounting best reflects the economic effects of hedging transactions for futures positions satisfying three criteria:

1. When the futures position is initiated, the hedge must be clearly identified with specific assets or liabilities.
2. A high positive correlation must exist between price movements of the futures and cash instruments.
3. The cash market transaction underlying an anticipatory hedge must be expected to occur.

Gains or losses on futures transactions should be deferred and applied to carrying value of hedged liabilities or assets accounted for on a cost basis. The following standards proposed by the Task Force will apply to the FHL Banks until the accounting profession adopts formal standards:

1. Any deferred gain or loss accruing from a hedge should be realized immediately if the related asset is sold or the hedged liability honored.
2. The purchase or sale of a futures strip (a series of successive futures contracts) should be treated as a composite transaction. For accounting purposes, a strip is equivalent to a single security with a price and yield equal to the average of those on the component contracts.
3. Anticipatory hedges should be placed in contracts that extend at least as far into the future as the expected date of the cash transaction. If no single contract satisfies this criterion, a hedge may be initiated in one delivery month and moved forward into others. However, the intention to roll a hedge must be declared when the first futures position is assumed. Otherwise, each extension should be regarded as a separate transaction on which profit or loss should be recognized currently.
4. Gain or loss on an anticipatory hedge that is terminated before the related cash market transaction is completed should nevertheless be deferred and incorporated in the carrying value of the asset purchased for the liability incurred.
5. If it becomes clear that the cash market transaction underlying an anticipatory hedge will not occur, any gain or loss should be recognized immediately.

Implementation

1. The board of directors of each Bank must establish a written policy for the use of futures contracts within the confines of this Policy.
2. Each Bank must authorize a limited number of individuals to trade futures and must establish internal control systems and internal auditing programs. Duties and responsibilities must be divided between trading, accounting, and internal auditing functions of the Bank.
3. Each Bank must choose specific commodities futures merchants which are members of the appropriate exchange from firms approved by the Office of Finance.
4. Each Bank will report information concerning its position daily to the Office of Finance. The Office of Finance and the Banks will produce reports and periodic summaries of each Bank's position and the position of the System. Each futures transaction will be subject to examination for conformity to this Policy by the Director, Office of Finance. The board of directors of each Bank will review its futures activity at each regular board meeting.
5. The Director, Office of Finance, will be responsible to the Bank Board for the implementation and administration of this Futures Policy.
6. This Policy is effective March 15, 1982 and will be reviewed at a Bank's request.

HEDGING EXAMPLES

FHLB Long Bond Hedge

Objective: To buy futures as a temporary substitute for advances to be funded with a new bond issue.

Date	Cash Market	Futures Market
2/17	Receive Allocation: $20 million 7-year bonds @ 15.25%; 7-year advance rate is 15.75%	Buy: 300 June T-bond contracts @ $58^{31}/_{32}$ = 14.24%
4/25	Lend: $20 million to a member @ 13.75%	Sell: 300 June T-bond contracts @ $68^{19}/_{32}$ = 12.24%

Results

Opportunity loss/year = 2% × $20 million = $400,000	Price change = $^{308}/_{32}$
Annual interest on	Gain/contract = $31.25 × 308 = $9,625
13.75% advance $2,750,000.00	Gain on 300 contracts = $2,887,500
Plus ⅟₇ futures gain 410,785.71	Less transaction costs* of $12,000 =
Total income $3,160,785.71	$2,875,500 net gain
Effective annual yield on $20 million advance = 15.80%	Amortization of gain (7 years) = $412,500

Hedge coverage (410,785.71/400,000) = 103%

   * Assumes $40/contract transaction cost

FHLB Deposit Hedge

Objective: To lock in the interest cost on a 6-month deposit for a 1-year period.

Date	Cash Market	Futures Market
3/82	Issue: $1 million 6-month term deposits @ 14%	Sell: Two Sept. 82 C.D. contracts @ 88.02
9/82	Reissue: $1 million 6-month term deposit @ 15%	Buy: Two Sept. 82 C.D. contracts @ 87.20

Results

Interest on 14% deposit = $70,000
Interest on 15% deposit = $75,000
Increased cost of 15% deposit
= $5,000
Gain on futures = $4,020

Effective interest cost of 15%
deposit = $75,000 − $4,020 =
$70,980
Effective interest rate on 15%
deposit = 14.20%

Price change = 82 basis points
Gain/contract = 82 × $25 = $2,050
Gain on two contracts = $4,100
Less transaction costs of $80
= $4,020 net gain

Hedge coverage (4020/5000) = 80%

FHLB Deposit Hedge
Protecting Two Rollover Periods

Objective: To fix the cost of 6-month deposits for $1\frac{1}{2}$ years.

Date	Cash Market	Futures Market
5/80	Issue: $2 million 6-month term deposits @ 8.00%	Sell: 4 Dec. 80 T-bill contracts @ 92.39 (to hedge first rollover) Sell: 4 June 81 T-bill contracts @ 91.99 (to hedge second rollover)
11/80	Reissue: $2 million 6-month term deposits @ 14.80%	Buy: 4 Dec. 81 T-bill contracts @ 86.19
5/81	Reissue: $2 million 6-month term deposits @ 15.93%	Buy: 4 June 81 T-bill contracts @ 83.92

Results

Interest on $2 million @ 8.00% = $80,000

Interest on $2 million @ 14.80% = $148,000

Increased cost of first rollover = $68,000

Effective interest on first rollover = $148,000 − $61,840 = $86,160

Price change on Dec. contracts = 620 basis points

Gain/Dec. contract = $15,500

Gain on four Dec. contracts = $62,000

Less transaction costs of $160 = $61,840 net gain

Interest on $2 million @ 15.93% = $159,300

Increased cost over 5/80 deposit = $79,300

Effective interest on second rollover = $159,300 − $80,540 = $78,760

Effective rate on second rollover = 7.88%

Price change on June contracts = 807 basis points

Gain/June contract = $20,175

Gain on four June contracts = $80,700

Less transaction costs of $160 = $80,540 net gain

Effective rate on total rollovers = 8.25%

Hedge coverage: First rollover (61,840/68,000) = 91%
Second rollover (80,540/79,300) = 102%
Total (142,380/147,300) = 97%

FHLB Discount Note Rollover

Objective: To stabilize the cost of 6-month discount notes for 1 year.

Date	Cash Market	Futures Market
3/82	Issue: $2 million 6-month discount notes @ 14.30% (15.40% coupon equivalent)	Sell: Four Sept. 82 T-bill contracts @ 87.67 (12.33% implied discount)
8/82	Issue: $2 million 6-month discount notes @ 15.85% (17.21% C.E.)	Buy: Four Sept. 82 T-bill contracts @ 84.61 (15.39% implied discount)

Results

Interest on 14.30% notes =
$154,000
Interest on 15.85% notes =
$172,100
Increased cost of 15.85% notes =
$18,100
Gain on futures = $30,440

Price change = 306 basis points
Gain/contract = 306 × $25 =
$7,650
Gain on four contracts = $30,600
Less transaction costs of $160 =
$30,440 net gain

Effective cost of 15.85% notes =
$172,100 − $30,440 = $141,660
Effective interest rate on rollover =
14.17%

Hedge coverage (30,440/18,100) = 168%

Rate Guaranteed Commitment

Objective: To provide members with a guaranteed rate on future advances while
protecting the Bank from a possible rise in interest rates.

Date	Cash Market	Futures Market
4/4/82	Issue: $1 million commitment for 30 days @ 15% for 1-year advance	Sell: Two June 82 T-bill contracts @ 86.50
5/4/82	Issue: $1 million 1-year advance @ 15%; current 1-year advance rate is 16%	Buy: Two June 82 T-bill contracts @ 85.00

Results

Interest income on 15% advance =
$150,000
Interest income on 16% advance =
$160,000
Opportunity loss = $10,000

Price change = 150 basis points
Gain/contract = 150 × $25 =
$3,750
Gain on two contracts = $7,500
Less transaction costs of $80 =
$7,420 net gain

Effective interest on advance =
$150,000 + $7,420 = $157,420
Effective rate on advance = 15.74%

Hedge coverage (7,420/10,000) = 74%

Asset Maturity Imbalance

Objective: To protect against loss of earnings if advances are rolled over at interest rates below those on the longer-term fixed rate liabilities which finance them.

Date	Cash Market	Futures Market
8/82	$40 million in 12% advances mature in 90 days. The bonds which finance them mature in $1\frac{1}{4}$ years	Buy: 160 Dec. T-bill contracts @ 89.10
11/82	$40 million in advances mature; $40 million new advances made @ 11%	Sell: 160 Dec. T-bill contracts @ 90.10

Results

Interest on $40 million @ 12% = $4,800,000	Price change = 100 basis points
Interest on $40 million @ 11% = $4,400,000	Gain/contract = 100 × $25 = $2,500
Loss over year on 11% advances compared with 12% advances = $400,000	Gain on 160 contracts = $400,000
	Less transaction costs of $6,400 = $393,600 net gain

Effective interest on 11%
  advances = $4,400,000 +
  $393,600 = $4,793,600
Effective yield on 11% advances =
  11.98%

Hedge coverage (393,600/400,000) = 98%

Liability Maturity Imbalance

Objective: To protect against loss of earnings if liabilities are rolled over at interest rate above the yields on longer-term fixed rate advances which they fund.

Date	Cash Market	Futures Market
8/82	$10 million in bonds @ 11% mature in 90 days. The advances they finance mature in $1\frac{1}{4}$ years	Sell: 40 Dec. T-bill contracts @ 90.0
11/82	$10 million new 1-year bonds issued @ 12%	Buy: 40 Dec. T-bill contracts @ 89.0

Results

Interest on $10 million @ 11% = $1,100,000

Interest on $10 million @ 12% = $1,200,000

Increased financing cost on roll-over = $100,000

Price change = 100 basis points

Gain/contract = 100 × $25 = $2,500

Gain on 40 contracts = $100,000

Less transaction costs of $1,600 = $98,400 net gain

Effective interest rate on 12% bonds = $1,200,000 − $98,400 = $1,101,600

Effective interest rate on $10 million bonds = 11.01%

Hedge coverage (98,400/100,000) = 98%

CHAPTER **10**

Portfolio Construction: Equity

_____ **William S. Gray, III, C.F.A.**

Construction of an equity portfolio, or any other type of portfolio, must be preceded by a determination of objectives: What important purposes are to be served? Knowledge of any applicable constraints is also required: What legal considerations, contractual provisions, or client preferences must be observed?

Like an engineer designing a bridge, the portfolio manager must consider objectives in terms of materials available and their likely behavior in alternative configurations and under a variety of conditions (for the engineer, temperatures, wind velocities, and so forth) that may arise. Of course, the materials of the equity portfolio manager are mostly common stocks. The configurations take the form of the weights or portfolio proportions invested in the chosen issues, and the conditions are reflected in ever-changing political, economic, and financial market developments.

It is generally desirable to deal with these many factors in a systematic way. Figure 10-1 on page 378 indicates how uncertain market factors and known investor factors come together in a balanced portfolio, each set impacting the asset class (e.g., stocks, bonds, and so on) proportions to the degree appropriate for the particular circumstances.

If an equity portfolio is part of a multiple-manager fund or some other larger portfolio, the investor factors may not involve extensive evaluation by the investment manager. The consideration of objectives is quite likely to be in the hands of the investor or, perhaps, an investment consultant. Specifications for the equity portfolio manager are expressed in terms of its specialized role (presumably as it fits into the larger whole).

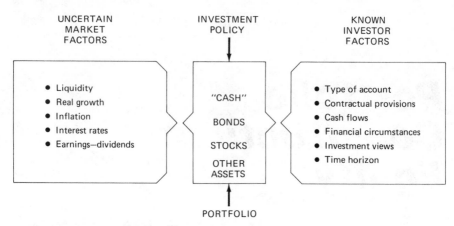

Figure 10-1. The Two-Way Investment Process Interface.

Risk and Return Basics

Most investors are judged to be risk averse. This does not necessarily mean that they will choose to avoid risk, but it does mean they will want to be compensated for taking risk. Generally speaking, the greater the amount of risk exposure, the more an investor will expect in rate of return. In cases where taxes are applicable to all, or any part, of the return, the expectations will be evaluated on an after-tax basis.

Risk is usually considered in terms of the probability of loss *or* the likelihood of failure to achieve an expected level of return. Such risk is usually caused by unexpected adverse developments. Such developments may affect all common stocks, just a group of stocks, or a single issue. Some issues will be greatly impacted by sweeping developments; others will be less vulnerable. Stock prices are likely to behave in a way that is very sensitive to these kinds of differences in risk exposure. Thus, relative price volatility and, therefore, variability in total return are believed to be suitable risk measures.

If all common stocks went up and down together in perfect lockstep, very little would be gained through diversification. Because they do not, it is essential to have some notion of how their behavior is likely to differ. (For more complete discussion of some important concepts about risk as it relates to the investment process, see Chapter 2. For more specific discussion of variability, covariability, systematic risk, and unsystematic risk, see Chapter 3. For a detailed review of quantitative methods pertaining to portfolio management—key formulas, sample calculations, and so on—Reilly [1982] provides a clear exposition.)

Portfolio Management Concepts

Since it is seldom, if ever, desirable to invest an entire portfolio in a single security, it is essential to have some notion of how the risk exposures of two or more issues (hence, divergent price behavior) come together in a particular portfolio. An individual security's total risk (return variability) is not of prime importance, only its contribution to the total risk of a portfolio.

Subject to other particular objectives—one is current income—rational investors will seek *efficient portfolios,* which implies maximum expected return for a given degree of risk or, equivalently, minimum risk for a given expected return. Markowitz [1952] showed how identifying such portfolios is theoretically possible by proper analysis of the expected return and the variance of return for each security, and also by the covariance relationship between the return for each security and that for every other security. As shown by Lorie and Hamilton [1973] this can be done on a computer, but it involves mind-boggling calculations. Nevertheless, it permits the identification of the efficient frontier of portfolios as shown in Figure 10-2.

Since the expected return on a given security depends on its sensitivity to price changes in the overall market, Sharpe [1963] showed how an enormous reduction in the number of estimates can be achieved as compared with the Markowitz approach. Eliminated are the estimated relationships between the return of each security and that for every other security. Instead, only the relationship of each security's returns with a pervasive financial data series, such as the returns on an equity market portfolio, is needed. The efficient portfolios from this simplified process are not significantly different from those resulting from the much more complex Markowitz process. (For a discussion of this, see Lorie and Hamilton [1973].)

The capital asset pricing model (CAPM) describes the way in which expected returns and, therefore, market prices are related to risk, if investors behave in the manner prescribed by portfolio theory. (Refer to Chapter 3 for a more detailed discussion of the CAPM and empirical tests of its credibility.) Briefly, the CAPM implies that an investor will not be rewarded for any unsystematic risk exposure, because this risk component can be diversified away.

Unsystematic risk need not be present in an equity portfolio beyond the

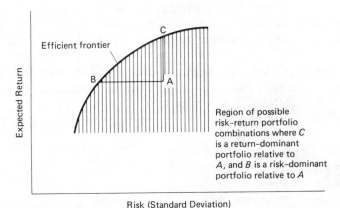

Figure 10-2. The Efficient Frontier of All-Equity Portfolios.

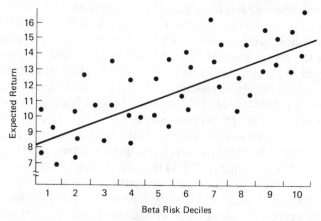

Figure 10-3. Diagram of a Security Market Line.

amount that the manager and/or the investor determine(s) to be appropriate. Whatever the amount (if any), it should be justified by some reasonable expectation that it will be accompanied by some unique return, e.g., an increment of return beyond what the level of systematic risk (beta) of a portfolio (or a stock) would explain. Such unique return is probably the most sought after, and most elusive, ingredient in the investment management process, assuming other basic objectives are satisfied.

The security market line (SML) provides a method for determining whether the expected returns, generated by any given investor or manager, for individual securities are in equilibrium, i.e., perfectly related to their respective systematic risk (beta) exposures. It is derived by running a regression line through a set of points (representing any fairly diverse group of stocks) in which the position of each stock is determined by coordinates representing the expected return and the beta of each issue (see Figure 10-3). Many of the issues are likely to be at least a little out of equilibrium. This approach identifies which issues are undervalued (dots above the line) and which are overvalued (dots below the line) and by how much.

Whether investment management is conducted in a traditional way or with the benefit of some of the newer quantitative tools, these important ideas about portfolio and capital market theory should be helpful.

This review of investor objectives, basic risk and return relationships, and some of the more fundamental portfolio management concepts should help set the stage for a more complete discussion of equity portfolio construction, which will be separated into the following principal parts:

- Role of equity portfolio management
- Characteristics of equity securities
- Equity management styles
- Use of information

- Equity portfolio management strategies
- Equity portfolio management constraints

Greatest emphasis will be given to portfolio strategies, covering both passive and active management strategies and, also, the way in which these strategies can be combined. Considerable attention will be given to equity management styles, pointing out important differences among nondiversified, diversified, and rotational approaches.

ROLE OF EQUITY PORTFOLIO MANAGEMENT

In the broadest sense the role of equity portfolio management is to achieve or exceed objectives at the lowest possible cost. In each case the effort involved should be related to the particular investor or fund objectives. As more fully developed in Chapters 4 and 5, these objectives may be related to current income return, income growth to keep pace with the cost of living, the most favorable rate of total return, and the like. Total return is not the most important objective for many investors. Furthermore, once the decision on active versus passive management has been made, cost (within reasonable limits) does not represent a very important consideration if the portfolio experience is successful and objectives are met.

Within the Total Portfolio

An equity portfolio may stand by itself as the only investment exposure of a particular investor or, in the case of commingled equity funds (including mutual funds), it may exist as an isolated entity with many participants. However, most equity portfolios represent a portion of a larger investment fund. For example, there is normally an equity component in every balanced fund portfolio, and there are likely to be two or more equity portfolios included in the entire portfolio of a multiple-manager arrangement for many larger institutional and some very large individual investors.

In these predominant cases, it is necessary for the equity portfolio manager to relate to investor objectives in a somewhat different way than when such a portfolio stands by itself. One way or another, the amount and the characteristics of investments held or managed elsewhere must be taken into account. As pointed out in Chapters 2 through 5, this can be done by an equity portfolio manager who gathers (or is provided) such information, along with other pertinent data relating to investor circumstances. Alternatively, it can be done by the investor or an investment consultant, in which case the equity portfolio manager may simply receive instructions as to the objectives for his or her particular component.

The important point to emphasize is that having direct investment responsibility for only a portion of the assets of a particular investor does not diminish the significance of the client's overall objectives. An equity portfolio should fit into the larger whole in such a way that the total portfolio has characteristics that are suitable and appropriate, i.e., compatible with the investment objectives.

In cases where an equity portfolio manager has fiduciary responsibilities, failure to determine whether an equity portfolio fulfills such a role within the total portfolio could create some liability exposure. At the least, any such failure would deserve a label of irresponsible investment management practice. The only notable exception would be commingled funds (including mutual funds), in which case the portfolio manager must adhere to objectives established by the fund sponsor. In those cases a trust account manager (or the mutual fund salesperson) must shoulder responsibility for determining whether the fund is appropriate for the particular investor.

Dealing with Particulars

The investment characteristics of an equity portfolio will be determined by the particular common stocks that are held. Since these investment characteristics will largely determine the portfolio's compatibility with investment objectives, the equity portfolio manager must do a skillful job of selecting particular issues *and* weighting them in the most advantageous manner. Both issue selection and the proportions represented in each will determine the risk, including liquidity, characteristics of the portfolio and the extent to which the relationship between its total risk and expected return is optimal.

It is the manner in which an equity portfolio manager deals with these particulars, especially issue selection, that primarily affects perceptions of value added. Unique return is the proverbial pot of gold.

CHARACTERISTICS OF EQUITY SECURITIES

Within the spectrum of investment alternatives, equities are generally considered to be fairly high risk. From the standpoint of tangible reward, they stand last in line vis-à-vis senior ranking securities. Interest payments on fixed income securities represent an obligation of the corporation. Both interest and federal income taxes come ahead of any dividend payments. In most cases preferred stock dividends come before any payments to common stockholders.

Given this residual position with respect to any income payments, a common stockholder may do very poorly or very well. When business conditions deteriorate, earnings may diminish or disappear and this will affect the ability to pay dividends, even while interest charges are being paid. When business improves, the pendulum should swing the other way. Earnings recover and provide the funds to pay dividends with greater ease and/or at higher levels.

This relative uncertainty about the timing and amount of future dividend payments largely explains the perception of high risk, but it does not fully account for the volatile price behavior of common stocks. Also important is the competition from alternative investment media. For example, change in the level of interest rates is likely to have a significant effect on stock prices, although at times with a lag.

Risk and Return

As clearly implied in the foregoing comments, the relatively high risk characteristics of common stocks are reflected in relatively high volatility in their total rates of return. This is especially true when focusing on time intervals out to one year or so. Consistent with investment theory, high volatility in total return is accompanied by high rates of total return, at least over longer periods of time. (This was discussed and illustrated in Chapter 3.)

Nevertheless, there have been periods of five to ten years in which the rates of return from common stocks did not exceed those from fixed income securities, including some periods during which the returns from common stocks were negative. However, it should be noted that there has been a strong tendency for periods of poor stock returns to be followed by periods of especially good stock returns, as indicated in Table 10-1.

Whatever the experience of the stock market as a whole, there is always a wide dispersion of price movement between individual common stocks. As Fisher and Lorie [1970] showed, during a year in which "the market" is up 20 percent there will be more than a few issues that are up more than 70 percent and down more than 30 percent. Generally, these differences will reflect both the variability of or changes in systematic risk and the variability of or changes in nonsystematic risk to be found within a broad array of stock issues.

There are some other financial instruments, not all of which are necessarily securities in a technical sense, that are very closely related to common

TABLE 10-1. **Common Stock Returns After 5-Year Periods of Negative Returns**

5-YEAR PERIODS SHOWING NEGATIVE TOTAL RETURNS		TOTAL RETURNS IN SUBSEQUENT 5-YEAR PERIODS	
Ended 12/31	Compound Annual Rate of Return	Ended 12/31	Compound Annual Rate of Return
1931	− 5.1%	1936	+22.5%
1932	−12.5	1937	+14.3
1933	−11.2	1938	+10.7
1934	− 9.9	1939	+10.9
1941	− 7.5	1946	+17.9
1974	− 2.4	1979	+14.8

SOURCE: Ibbotson and Sinquefield [1982].

stocks. Convertible securities, stock warrants, and stock options (puts and calls) are the most important. These instruments represent either a magnified or diminished risk exposure compared with the related common stock itself, or they may be used in ways to achieve such telescoped effects. Expected returns will be higher or lower than for the related common stock issues, but because of their unique terms, specialized knowledge and tools are necessary to participate on a sound basis.

Voting Rights and Responsibilities

In most cases common stock ownership involves voting rights. At least once a year, but sometimes more often, there will be a stockholders' meeting. Various matters will be presented, such as the election of directors or the selection of auditors. Most stockholders vote, usually by proxy.

During the past decade the responsible exercise of voting rights has become much more involved. Social responsibility issues have proliferated due to minority shareholder initiatives. Such matters cannot be ignored by investment managers with fiduciary responsibilities.

EQUITY MANAGEMENT STYLES

There may be several dimensions to a particular equity investment style; however, much of the attention has focused on the extent of the diversification of common stock portfolios and the manner in which that diversification is managed. These style traits presumably reflect important business decisions that have been made by each equity portfolio management organization. Such decisions have to do with the choice of an investment philosophy, the client market(s) to be served, the magnitude of resources to be committed to the activity, and perceptions as to the possession of particular skills that may provide some relative advantage vis-à-vis other investment managers.

Within the equity management arena there are three major categories of style: diversified, nondiversified, and rotational. No precise boundaries separate one style from another. However, through the application of quantitative analytical tools, some progress has been made in the systematic classification of particular equity managers, although some managers may fall into gray areas between two of the described categories.

Some useful insights are to be derived from the effort to classify managers in this way. It points up some cases in which a manager does not remain consistent with respect to style, and it sometimes reveals that a manager is not demonstrating a style in keeping with its self-description, e.g., through marketing presentations and promotional literature. These are matters a client—existing or prospective—should want to know.

Since style has become such an important consideration, especially within the market for institutional investment services, each of the three categories will be discussed separately.

Nondiversified Equity Management

This category covers all those equity managers who have a heavy emphasis, i.e., concentration, on a chosen sector of the market. These managers are often referred to as *specialist managers*. As discussed in Chapter 8, within the institutional market, especially employee benefit funds, a strong preference has developed for such specialty managers in cases where the pension sponsor has chosen to take a multiple-manager approach. It is a more costly approach to the management of such funds. So far, sponsors appear satisfied that there are or will be more than offsetting benefits. However, there is very little documented evidence concerning the cost-benefit relationships.

Any specialized equity management worthy of the name will create and sustain portfolios that generate returns that *do not* correlate very closely with those of the general market. This is not an objective, but instead a by-product of the decision to specialize. These portfolios may underperform or overperform the market for extended periods (even several years). This is a form of unsystematic risk exposure; to compensate for it, a specialty manager should be able to generate some unique return (alpha) for the investor. If this unique return is achieved, it is most likely to come during periods when a particular style is in phase relative to the general market.

Growth Stock Management. This is one of the most popular forms of specialization. It stems from the philosophy that above-average earnings growth over time will produce above-average returns. The idea has much appeal. However, the realization of such returns is complicated by two problems: picking stocks that will have (or continue to have) above-average earnings growth and avoiding the payment of an excessive price.

During the late 1960s and early 1970s there was enormous interest in large capitalization growth stocks, which were doing very well at that time. A number of leading firms were prominently identified with the phenomenon, along with many other equity managers. As noted in Chapter 7, these kinds of stocks became known as *one-decision issues,* suggesting that they could be bought and put away for the long term. Unfortunately, the group became so popular that they became overpriced. Also, slower earnings growth companies seemed to benefit relatively more from accelerating inflation. The large capital growth stocks substantially underperformed the general market between mid-1973 and year-end 1981, as reflected in Table 10-2, especially by their decline in value relative to all stocks in the S&P 500.

Of course, growth stocks come in all sizes. In fact, smaller growth stocks far outnumber larger ones. Thus, there are probably more specialty managers who are focusing on small- and medium-sized companies than concentrating on the larger ones. This may be especially true since the larger growth

TABLE 10-2. The 25 Largest Growth Stocks
Represented in the S&P 500 Stock Index in
October 1973

Date	Percent of S&P 500[a]	WEIGHTED AVERAGE	
		P/E Ratio	Yield
6-30-73	33.95%	33.9x	1.22%
10-11-73	31.22	28.5	1.27
1-25-74	31.23	24.1	1.56
3-29-74	30.67	22.8	1.72
6-28-74	31.91	21.4	1.90
9-27-74	28.42	13.0	2.94
12-31-74	28.29	15.2	2.82
3-28-75	28.89	19.2	2.29
6-27-75	27.89	21.3	2.17
9-26-75	26.74	17.9	2.61
12-31-75	27.13	16.3	2.37
3-26-76	26.72	17.9	2.18
6-25-76	24.27	17.1	2.28
9-24-76	24.47	17.7	2.45
12-31-76	23.14	14.8	2.56
3-31-77	22.51	13.3	3.08
6-24-77	21.39	12.9	3.34
9-30-77	22.11	13.2	3.36
12-31-77	21.92	11.8	3.64
3-31-78	20.66	10.2	4.30
6-30-78	21.80	11.6	3.87
9-30-78	21.53	12.3	3.73
12-31-78	22.64	11.0	4.03
3-30-79	21.71	11.0	4.15
6-30-79	20.68	10.7	4.35
9-30-79	19.32	10.1	4.42
12-31-79	18.92	10.0	4.60
3-31-80	18.47	9.2	5.20
6-30-80	17.53	10.0	4.86
9-30-80	17.40	9.8	4.52
12-31-80	16.72	10.6	4.37
3-31-81	16.90	10.4	4.36
6-30-81	16.67	10.1	4.62
9-30-81	16.50	9.2	5.26
12-31-81	16.30	8.4	5.12

SOURCE: Harris Trust & Savings Bank.
[a] S&P 500 was 104.26 on June 30, 1973 and 122.54 as of December 31, 1981.

stocks in 1982 had done quite poorly for so long. Also, there was an extraordinary number of relatively young, high technology stocks that had attracted a great deal of investor interest.

As a general rule, portfolios that are heavily concentrated in smaller growth stocks will tend to have a fairly high amount of systematic risk exposure (beta). Thus, returns should tend to be above average in rising markets. In addition, unsystematic risk is likely to be very high. In cases where unique return has been achieved by managers of smaller growth stocks in recent years, it may very well indicate good managerial skills. On the other hand, it may simply reflect some development of excessive prices, based on a gradual build-up of unrealistic expectations for such issues. Similar stocks did become overvalued back in 1968 and their returns suffered for some time thereafter. Figure 10-4, which shows the P/E ratio of New Horizons Fund (which has concentrated on smaller growth stocks) relative to the S&P 500, illustrates the ever-changing assessment of such characteristics by the marketplace.

Undervalued Stock Management. The standards normally used to determine whether a stock is undervalued are high dividend yields, low price/earnings ratios, and low market-to-book value ratios. *High yield manager* is perhaps the most common label for this specialty. Like other sectors of the market, this one enjoys periodic popularity. For example, increased economic uncertainty has sometimes caused a preference for more current income. This, in turn, will cause a shift in holdings from low yield to high yield issues with corollary impact on their respective price behavior.

Depending on the pattern of pricing in the market at a given time, undervalued stocks can be positioned anywhere in the spectrum of systematic risk exposure. Turnover is likely to be somewhat higher than in the case of growth stock management. Even with much statistical evidence, such as that provided by Bidwell [1979 and 1981], this form of specialization has

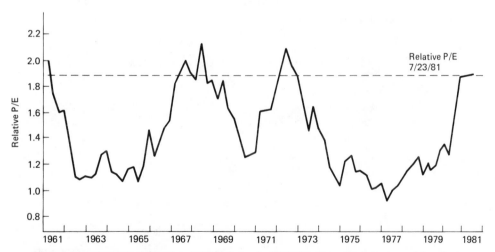

Figure 10-4. New Horizons Fund P/E Relative to S&P 500. Note: Market prices of the stocks are as of each quarter end, with earnings per share estimates issued by the Fund's investment advisor for 12 months ahead from each quarter end. (SOURCE: Morgan Stanley & Co., Inc., courtesy of Dennis G. Sherva)

been less popular than growth stock management. Low P/E ratios convey an impression that something must be wrong. Furthermore, practitioners find it difficult to accept the idea that a simple yardstick of value (such as low P/E ratio or high yield) can beat an exhaustive consideration of all relevant factors.

Small Capitalization Stock Management. This form of specialized management has been developing a great deal of momentum in recent years. There have been several historical studies showing that smaller companies have better returns than, and lower correlations with, the broad stock market. Table 10-3 provides strong support on this point.

This is consistent with the fact that as a group smaller companies have somewhat above-average systematic risk. Furthermore, they did especially well between the mid-1970s and the early 1980s. Figure 10-5, which compares the equal-weighted experience of the S&P 500 with that of its market-weighted experience, demonstrates this quite clearly.

The experience of the 1975–81 period may have been affected by the broader diversification that was encouraged by ERISA, the movement to various kinds of index funds, and growing pressures to improve investment results. All of these have resulted in the movement of some institutional funds away from the traditional, large, blue-chip stocks. The smaller issues in the S&P 500 and non-S&P 500 issues have become an investment alternative for some of these institutional funds.

Diversified Equity Management

This category covers all of those equity managers who do not particularly concentrate on a chosen sector of the market, but maintain a fairly broad

TABLE 10-3. Company Size and Rates of Return (NYSE Listing)

Size Decile	1947–76 Compound Annual Rate of Return	Coefficient of Variation (ρ^2) with Total NYSE
1	10.6%	0.947
2	11.8	0.882
3	11.3	0.844
4	12.5	0.801
5	11.4	0.731
6	12.4	0.676
7	12.5	0.624
8	13.0	0.528
9	13.0	0.487
10	14.7	0.328

SOURCE: College Retirement Equities Fund.

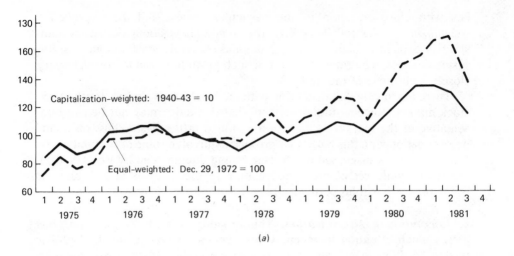

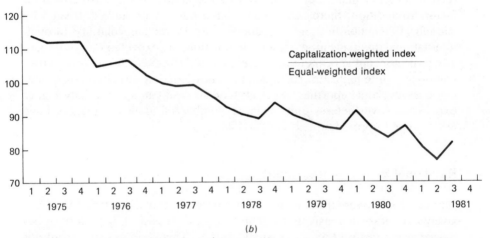

Figure 10-5. (a) Capitalization-weighted and Equal-weighted S&P 500 Indexes, 1975–81, (b) Ratio of Capitalization-weighted Index to Equal-weighted Index. (SOURCE: Harris Trust & Savings Bank)

exposure to all or most sectors of the market at all times. Although more likely to serve the entire equity management needs of a particular client than any single specialty manager, they have suffered some loss in popularity. Some of them are referred to with disdain as closet indexers because their portfolios approximate index fund characteristics.

Domestic Diversification. Until recently, diversified equity management has been thought of in the context of the U.S. stock market, with the S&P 500 used as a proxy. The issues represented in the S&P 500 account for about 65 percent of the market value of all U.S. common stocks ($1.36 trillion at the end of 1980). Many diversified managers construct their portfolios with close attention to the particular issues, and their respective weights, in the S&P 500. Therefore, they tend to have about average systematic risk exposure (betas close to 1.00) and relatively small amounts of unsystematic risk. The rates of return of such portfolios tend to correlate very closely with those of the S&P 500.

There is growing dissatisfaction with the S&P 500 as a proxy for the U.S. stock market. Recent studies indicate that this index may not be as representative of the market as had been assumed in the past. Thus, an undue preoccupation with this particular proxy may involve some opportunity loss. Furthermore, as discussed in Chapter 14 and documented by Roll [1978], it creates a whole set of problems relating to the analysis of risk and the evaluation of portfolio performance.

International Diversification. This broader form of diversification has gotten much attention in recent years. The weakness of the U.S. dollar relative to other major currencies during the middle 1970s was certainly a factor. In addition, there have been a large number of studies, treated by Ehrlich [1981], pointing out the opportunity to reduce volatility through international diversification without diminishing the expected rate of return. The basic concept appears to have great merit. However, the costs of participation are quite high. Efforts to acquire knowledge, transaction costs, special custody, and reporting needs all tend to result in substantially higher expenses. Nevertheless, quite a large number of money managers have taken steps to provide this broadened coverage.

Rotational Equity Management

This category covers those equity managers who regularly attempt to offensively exploit, or defensively insulate from, the ever-shifting pattern of behavior of various sectors of the stock market. This style has some, but not all, of the characteristics of both nondiversified and diversified equity managers. At any given moment the rotator will have some fairly heavy concentrations in the types of issues that are expected to do relatively well, at least for the time being. As a corollary, the issues that are expected to do poorly will be very much downplayed, if not avoided entirely. On the other hand, during the course of a market cycle (historically, three to five years) most significant areas of the stock market, e.g., sectors, will be included in the portfolio at one time or another.

Market Timer. This describes a particular kind of rotator, namely, one who attempts to exploit, or insulate from, the general movement of the stock market as a whole. To be successful, a market timer must be very close to fully invested in common stocks when the stock market is rising and, contrariwise, have fairly significant cash reserves as a portion of the portfolio during periods when the market is going down. While market timers may have somewhat different objectives, many simply seek to attain a total rate of return over a full cycle that is better than the S&P 500.

This kind of market timing effort would normally be used as an adjunct of a diversified equity portfolio. However, there is no reason why it could not be used by a nondiversified equity manager. During the course of a market cycle, a market timing effort would result in some changes in systematic risk exposure by increasing or reducing the proportion or relative weight held in cash equivalents. If used in fairly normal proportions, e.g., varying holdings of cash equivalents from zero up to 30 percent or so of a given equity portfolio, market timing is not likely to affect the unsystematic risk exposure to any large extent.

In referring to the normal range of cash equivalents and, therefore, market timing, it is important to understand that many equity managers do not attempt to apply this technique at all. However, for those who do, it is recognized that it would be unwise to carry such a technique to an extreme. The opportunity loss associated with a large cash position during a rising market could be very substantial. In any event, it is unnecessary to reposition the portfolio in extreme amounts in order to outperform the S&P 500 over a complete cycle.

One of the problems of a market timer is to clearly identify what part of the investment return is due to the timing effort. In many cases the impact, whether good or bad, becomes lost in a blur of the overall result on the portfolio to which it is applied. Some newer statistical methods are helping to overcome this problem.[1] However, an alternative is to literally isolate the market timing activity within a separate portfolio. For example, an equity manager could set up two separate accounts, one for the permanent equity holdings and the other for the timing effort. The latter would be managed to have cash reserves representing anywhere from zero to 100 percent, depending on the overall market outlook, with the balance usually invested in a broadly diversified list of stocks.

DIFFICULTY OF TIMING. There is a broadly held belief that market timing is more difficult than issue selection. It requires an understanding of a more complex set of factors than is the case in identifying an undervalued stock. Furthermore, it is recognized that many equity mutual funds tend to hold larger cash reserves at market bottoms than they do at market peaks. This has been interpreted to mean that market timing is usually counterproductive.

Studies which maintain that market timing can be done successfully, especially if the effort is conducted within a disciplined framework, are

---

[1] An example of one such methodology is the BARRA Perfam-Perfat Performance Analysis Program that decomposes the total rate of return of a portfolio in a way that reveals the source of each component.

offset by studies, such as the one by Sharpe [1975], which show that it has not been worthwhile after allowing for transaction costs.[2] Certainly, unwavering success is not possible, but moderate success should not be impossible. In any event, there has been a developing client market for a good solid market timing effort.

As a concluding observation, it is important to note the difference between portfolio adjustments that reflect market timing judgments and those that are due to asset allocation decisions. The former are motivated by some sense of opportunity with respect to near-term or intermediate-term prospects for the stock market. The latter come about as a result of changes in client objectives and/or a sense that basic longer term value relationships between broad classes of investments warrant such repositioning. The distinction is not always clear because either may involve movement of funds from stocks to cash, or vice versa.

Group Rotators. This describes the most common type of rotational management. It derives from the perception that the equity market is made up of various groupings of relatively homogeneous issues. Each set of groupings involves the classification of individual issues, usually according to a particular criterion. For example, issues may be classified by industry group, economic sector, level of systematic risk, or source of return, i.e., dividends versus capital gains. The issues within any such group tend to be somewhat homogeneous; that is, they have some important risk exposures in common.

Several years ago, Farrell [1975] completed a noteworthy study on stock price behavior that was designed to identify truly homogeneous groups. It was found that the best grouping resulted in four categories: consumer, cyclical, growth, and oil. Nevertheless, most equity managers have their own approach to the classification of issues. Some managers use several different classifications concurrently. Figure 10-6 provides a graphic representation of the stock market based on three cross-sectional views, developed by Robert F. Marchesi of DeMarche Associates.

At least two criteria determine the probable usefulness of a particular group classification system. The issues within a single group should be fairly well correlated in their respective price movements. The greater the price dispersion within a single group, the more likely that a good judgment on the relative prospects for such a group will be diluted by the unfortunate selection of particular issues. In addition, the weighted average price behavior of a given group should relate to one or more series of economic or financial market data in a way that provides some forecasting possibilities.

A group rotator's portfolio will tend to have a fairly high level of unsystematic risk exposure at all times. The amount of systematic risk will vary

---

[2] Sharpe's study, however, is not without its shortcomings. Sharpe looked at market timing in terms of calendar year performance, defining up-market years as years with a positive return and down-market years as those with negative returns, regardless of the amount of return. This is quite different from testing timing over the up and down phases of a (multiyear) market cycle.

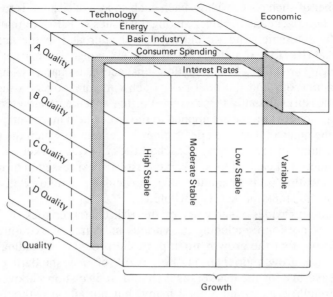

Figure 10-6. Common Stock Sectors Cube. (SOURCE: DeMarche Associates [1978])

substantially during the course of a cycle. Because there is substantial move-ment from one group to another, transactions costs will tend to be fairly high. In order to compensate for the relatively high level of unsystematic risk and the fairly high transactions costs, it is necessary for the manager to have a strong unique return (alpha) generating potential.

Whether or not an equity manager is really a rotator, it is usually neces-sary to express views on the outlook for different sectors of the market. Clients are curious about such matters and expect their managers to have some of the answers on which groups are most attractive. As a general observation, there is more talk than action on this subject. Because of trans-action costs, it is probably preferable to limit actions to those instances in which it is believed that especially good information or unusual depth of insight is in hand.

Evaluation of Equity Management Styles

In the earlier discussion of various equity management styles, the nature of both systematic and unsystematic exposures was indicated. However, there are more powerful tools available to make a more definite assessment of a given manager's style. These tools involve a more penetrating analysis of the unsystematic risk exposure. Of the two parts of this unnecessary risk, dis-cussed in Chapters 2 and 3, one is of particular interest: extra-market.

Extra-market Risk. *Extra-market risk* refers to those sources of risk that are not common to all common stock issues, but that are common to a fairly large number of such issues. Thus, each such source of risk tends to produce somewhat homogeneous behavior among the issues sensitive to that particular risk characteristic. The Rosenberg [1974] approach to the analysis of extra-market risk, for example, is based upon six categories: market variability, earnings variability, low valuation–unsuccess, immaturity–smallness, growth orientation, and financial risk. Each category covers a number of different measures (usually three to five) of the specified characteristic.

Measures of covariance are applied to the issues held in a given portfolio. In effect, the analytical process determines the extent to which the portfolio is high, medium, or low in terms of each of the six extra-market risk categories. The amount of each of these characteristics is expressed in terms of the standard deviation (plus or minus) for a particular portfolio relative to the average for the stock market as a whole.

Table 10-4 provides a summary of the risk characteristics of a typical growth stock portfolio, including the various measures of extra-market covariance. Note that the growth stock portfolio produces a reading of well-above-average growth orientation, i.e., 0.701 of one standard deviation above the average for the market, as it should. It also shows above-average market variability, as would a good many, but not all, growth stock portfolios.

The portfolios of a growth stock manager should reflect well-above-average growth orientation consistently over time. Likewise, the portfolios of a small capitalization stock manager should consistently reflect well-above-average immaturity–smallness. A diversified manager's portfolios should reflect exposures that are consistently close to average in all six risk categories. By contrast, a group rotator's portfolios should reflect both well-above- and well-below-average exposures at a given time for particular risks,

TABLE 10-4. Diagnostic Analysis of a Typical Growth Fund

Predicted beta (3 months)		1.16
Predicted beta (5 years)		1.13
Decomposition of variance:		
Market		588.2
Nonmarket		
Extra-market[a]	37.4	
Specific	10.8	48.2
Total variance		636.4

SOURCE: FRS Associates [1980a].
Note: One standard deviation is used to describe the width of the distribution of probable outcomes.
[a] Sources of extra-market covariance (zero represents average exposure):

Market variability	.546
Earnings variability	−.032
Low valuation, unsuccess	−.383
Immaturity, smallness	−.772
Growth orientation	.701
Financial risk	−.353

but with some definite changes in the categories that are either high or low during the course of a market cycle.

The S&P 500 Index is a suitable standard of performance for a diversified manager throughout a cycle, and it is probably suitable for a rotator, but only for a complete cycle. For the standard to be viable longer term for a given type of specialty manager, it is necessary to produce results that are favorable compared to the S&P 500 over the course of two or three cycles. However, the S&P 500 Index is a very unsuitable standard to apply to a specialty manager for shorter periods of time. Instead, an index of the sector of the market on which the manager is specializing is needed. Sometimes this will take the form of a hypothetical *benchmark portfolio* that captures the specialty sector of the particular manager. However sound this approach might be from a theoretical standpoint, the proper selection and use of benchmark portfolios involve a number of thorny implementation problems. (For a more complete discussion, see Chapter 14.)

Commingled Funds

Commingled funds, often called *pooled funds,* are portfolios in which two or more investment clients have a participating interest. This interest takes the form of *units of participation.* These units are similar to shares in a mutual fund. Trust companies and insurance companies are the principal users of such funds. The law has constrained other applications.

The early use of commingled funds was almost entirely for the purpose of handling the investments of small clients. However, this has been in the process of changing during the past ten or fifteen years. At the outset, many of the original commingled funds were balanced, i.e., held both stocks and bonds, but there has been a strong movement toward specialized funds for many years. As specialized commingled funds developed and some of their unique advantages were recognized, they were created for and used to serve larger clients as well. While not really an investment style at all, specialized commingled funds have become closely identified with certain styles, e.g., special equities, venture capital, and so on. In addition, they are often used by institutions where a wide range of investment alternatives, each supported by a group of investment specialists within the organization, is offered. This modular approach is now an important element of organizational philosophy for many larger investment managers.

There is a large number of clients who do not wish to have their investments handled through commingled funds because they believe that investment results will not be as good. If that were true, it would be undesirable to use such vehicles unless there were no other practical alternatives. But the truth of the matter is rather elusive. Over the past ten or fifteen years a great deal of information has been assembled on the performance of commingled funds. There is nothing even closely comparable on the experience of individually managed accounts. Even the performance evaluation services, such

TABLE 10-5. Commingled vs. Noncommingled Equity
Accounts Average Annualized Total Returns Before
Expenses (cumulative periods ended December 31, 1977)

Length of Period Examined	Becker Commingled Accounts	Becker Noncommingled Accounts	Difference[a]
1 year	− 5.9%	− 5.2%	−0.7%
3 years	11.9	11.8	0.1
5 years	− 2.7	− 2.7	0.0
7 years	2.8	2.7	0.1
9 years	1.0	0.7	0.3
10 years	2.3	1.9	0.4

SOURCE: Bogle and Twardowski [1980] and Becker Securities Corporation.
[a] None of the differences is statistically significant at the 95 percent level of confidence.

as A. G. Becker's Funds Evaluation Service, only cover a portion of the individually managed employee benefit accounts. Furthermore, the rate of return figures are not weighted by the market value of assets represented. Nevertheless, some comparative data have been presented by Bogle and Twardowski [1980] that may be of some help (see Table 10-5).

These data indicate that commingled funds have marginally outperformed the noncommingled funds in their sample. As footnoted, the differences were not statistically significant.

USE OF INFORMATION

It is quite possible to select investments for purchase or sale without any information. Indeed, some academicians have argued that an investor (at least the typical investor) would do just as well, or possibly better, if stock selections were determined by throwing darts at the page on which stock prices are quoted in the *Wall Street Journal*. The innuendo is that stock recommendations (on average) and various other kinds of market information are not likely to be very helpful. This view is a derivative of the *efficient market hypothesis* (EMH).

Efficient Market Hypothesis

In general terms, the efficient market hypothesis recognizes that there is a lot of information that may have some bearing on the perceived value and, therefore, prices of publicly traded securities. Furthermore, it recognizes that much of the information that is likely to be important is disseminated and broadcast promptly, properly taken into account by market participants, and immediately reflected in the prices of securities. This is perceived to happen so quickly that there is very little practical opportunity for anyone, except specialists on the stock exchange or other market makers, to derive any advantage from such information. It appears that most practitioners and most investment clients do not believe that the market is all that efficient— or at least they are not behaving as though they believe it.

This widespread tendency to ignore the EMH may be justified. Now that investment professionals understand that the market is at least relatively efficient, they have started to deal with the investment management process in different and better ways. They concentrate on the development of unique insights, utilize computer screening methods to identify issues that may have interesting potential, and, in general, approach the task in a more disciplined way. Out of this could come greater instances of success. On the other hand, it may lead to even more efficient markets, thereby compounding the problem of attaining unique positive return.

An often-cited work by Ambachtsheer and Farrell [1979] provides some basis for hope. They used two sets of valuation judgments (from Wells Fargo and Value Line) and found that both delivered predictive power in a reasonably consistent fashion. They found mean correlation coefficients between *forecast* security return rankings and *actual* security return rankings in the 0.05 to 0.20 range. Brealey and Hodges [1973] had found that a correlation coefficient of 0.05 was sufficient to "add value" relative to buy-and-hold strategy.

Given that there is some predictive ability in security return rankings, why is this not reflecting itself more clearly in portfolio performance? The answer seems to lie in the method of translating forecasts into portfolio changes. Security analysts are often not explicit or consistent in communicating their judgments. Even in those cases where they are, portfolio managers will not necessarily use these judgments sufficiently or in a timely way in constructing or rebalancing portfolios.

These findings underscore the importance of determining who has some predictive ability, establish that not a great deal is needed to be successful, and suggest that there are two types of risk in portfolio management. The first is the uncertainty of actual portfolio return, given an assumed level of accuracy associated with the security return predictions. The second is that the assumed level of predictive accuracy is wrong. It may be essential, or at least helpful, to deal with each explicitly in the portfolio management process, if value added is expected to include some unique return.

Types of Information

Although information can be classified in many ways, it is important to be especially aware of the distinction between inside information and public information.

Inside Information. This phrase refers to all corporate information that is not available to the public, i.e., information that has not been disseminated and is of a *material* nature. Information is material if it would be likely to have a large and immediate effect on the price of the securities of a company affected by the information. Simply stated, it is illegal to *use* such information. Because of the potential damage to career, investment practitioners must develop a high degree of sensitivity to the issues involved. Gillis [1980] has written extensively in the *Financial Analysts Journal* and elsewhere in an effort to guide professional investment managers through this difficult subject.

Public Information. This covers all of the information contained in corporate disclosure documents or otherwise broadly disseminated by the issuers of securities. It also covers a lot more: investment publications, the news media, government publications, trade journals, academic literature, most public and private studies, and the like. The quality and usefulness of such information is extremely varied, although the latter is often a matter of judgment. Inflation has greatly complicated the problem of providing good information. Leuthold [1980], among others, has called attention to the flaws in the Consumer Price Index (CPI), and Norby [1981] has updated his writing on inflation accounting.

Methods of Using Information

With all of the information that is available, it is generally considered necessary to try to deal with it in some organized or systematic way. Since the ultimate objective is to select issues that are suitable (within a portfolio) for the client and that, hopefully, may experience some unique return, information should be gathered and analyzed in ways that will contribute to this purpose. The way in which this is done varies a great deal. Nevertheless, a meaningful example is suggested by Figure 10-7.

The particulars of this chart are based on the assumption that three principal variables determine common stock prices: (1) current dividend payments, (2) the growth rate expected of such payments in the future, and (3) the rate at which such future payments are to be discounted. The peripheral factors impacting the three principal variables represent the kinds of things that an investor might consider in trying to gauge the stock market as a whole. If the focus were on a particular common stock instead, the peripheral factors would be expressed more in terms of unit growth, the particular company's product pricing, competitive position, and financial leverage, for example.

Such models of price behavior are being used increasingly by professional investors. Wright [1981] has suggested that these and other quantitative methods are especially helpful in trying to identify where more intensive fundamental research and analysis might be worthwhile. The advent of the computer and the collection of large amounts of data have made this possible.

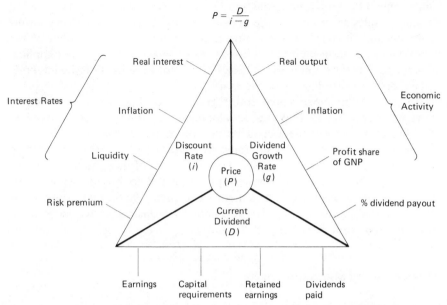

$$P = \frac{D}{i - g}$$

Figure 10-7. Market Valuation Factors. (SOURCE: Harris Trust & Savings Bank)

Once an investor or investment manager has narrowed down the field of possible issues to some manageable level, it is feasible to apply some of the more fundamental techniques. This is where the most creative and innovative talents are likely to make the greatest difference. There is always a potential opportunity to come up with a perspective that may lead to capturing some unique return. However, unlike some fields of endeavor, despite the application of considerable intelligence and much effort, the manager will come up empty-handed on many occasions. Market efficiency is a constant beneficiary of these endeavors, but personal benefit is certain to be sporadic.

EQUITY PORTFOLIO MANAGEMENT STRATEGIES

As discussed earlier, the principal focus of equity portfolio management should be on the investment objectives of each client. An equity portfolio should be designed to match such investment objectives as nearly as possible. However, whatever the objectives may be, there is an underlying desire to achieve the best possible investment results consistent with the objectives. The measurement of such investment results will usually include total return (income plus appreciation) over some reasonable period of time.

For most entities, such as employee benefit funds that have no particular current income requirement, total return is the primary objective. Elaborate performance measurement systems have been devised to measure results in this particular way. Since these performance measurement tools are more highly refined than any that relate to other objectives, they tend to be used to evaluate results regardless of the investment objectives. This is very unfortunate because it simply is not appropriate in many instances. Other objectives (such as current income) cannot be emphasized without some implications for total return potentials. These implications are likely to be adverse, at least during some phases of the market.

Because of the enormous attention given to total return, a great deal of effort has been devoted to the development of strategies best suited to achieve that particular objective. This has been accompanied by an examination of investment results, after transaction costs and investment management fees. Out of this have come two basic schools of thought regarding the best strategic approaches. The newer approach, still not broadly accepted, is referred to as "passive" management. The more traditional approach is called "active" management. The terminology alone may have some influence on the greater popularity of the latter.

Passive Equity Management

Historically, there have been a number of investors who used a buy-and-hold approach. Since it involved very little activity beyond the purchases required to establish positions, it could be said to represent a "passive" approach. However, that style has nothing to do with the approach developed within the past ten to fifteen years, that has come to be called *passive equity management*.

Passive equity management had its genesis with the efficient market hypothesis, which assumes that if investors behave in a rational way, they will seek the best rates of return relative to the risks involved. Since unsystematic risk can be eliminated through diversification, securities prices should form in such a way that expected returns are related to systematic risk only. As noted by Sharpe [1981], among others, it was not a terribly large leap from there to the notion that the portfolio with the best risk-return relationships would be the market portfolio or a proxy thereof.

Value-weighted Index Funds. Since the market portfolio covers the entire population of common stocks (thousands of different issues), it has seemed impractical to replicate in real life this theoretically ideal portfolio. Instead, the proxy that has emerged is a broadly diversified portfolio in which the amount of each issue held is in proportion to the respective market value of outstanding shares of the various issues included. The S&P 500 Index, which is a market value-weighted index, has become the most widely used standard for developing such proxy portfolios; hence, the designation *index fund.*

Wells Fargo was probably the first major investment organization to establish an index fund. It chose to replicate the S&P 500 except for a few issues that seemed to be in danger of bankruptcy. The latter were omitted out of some concern about liability exposure relating to the prudent man rule. However, since the adoption of ERISA in 1974 the total portfolio view of prudence has been strongly encouraged by this author [1977], among others, for employee benefit funds. Furthermore, the Department of Labor [1979] has issued regulations that provide some comfort to the idea that extensive knowledge about issues held in an index fund is not required.

Batterymarch and the American National Bank (Chicago) have also been prominently identified with index fund services. In fact, both used the approach in a way that gave them considerable market penetration in the investment management business. While they have each used the S&P 500 Index as a target, they have chosen to avoid quite a number of the smaller and/or riskier issues in that index. Instead, by holding 250 to 350 of the largest issues, they found it necessary to fine tune the normal market weightings in an attempt to make up, in part, for what is lost by not having the other issues. In spite of this fine tuning, their index funds have not tracked the S&P 500 Index quite as well. Whether the difference is really significant is a matter of personal judgment.

One of the major concerns about the avoidance of the smaller and/or riskier issues is that they may provide a better rate of return. Companies on the verge of bankruptcy are usually priced very low in the market. Those that survive and recover may experience extraordinary returns. Furthermore, smaller companies in general may provide better rates of return, either because they are riskier than average or possibly for other reasons. They may also provide some meaningful diversification because they do not necessarily correlate with the market as a whole.

Given the perception of an opportunity to reduce risk and elevate returns by using smaller issues, much of the recent activity with respect to index funds has been on using much larger numbers of issues. The New York Stock Exchange Index (covering over 1,600 issues) and the Wilshire 5000 Index represent alternative targets. Going to the extreme, it would be possible to develop an international index fund in which something like the Capital International Index might serve as the target.

Although index funds seek to avoid selection and timing problems (on the premise that such efforts are nonproductive), it should be understood that they cannot escape them entirely. The population of common stocks to be targeted clearly poses a selection problem. The reinvestment of dividend income presents both selection and timing problems. It is not practical to reinvest a single dividend payment over 500 issues, or even 250 issues. The problem becomes greater in contemplating index funds with 1,500 or 5,000 issues. It is necessary to utilize some kind of optimization program to minimize the distorted weightings that will result from the reinvestment of income.

In spite of their pedestrian characteristics most index funds have come very close to matching the index they were targeting, usually the S&P 500. While there is a tendency to slightly underperform, this will occur either because they have avoided some smaller issues or transaction costs have made a small dent. Therefore, as explained quite clearly by Bogle [1980], there are situations in which an index fund may be very appropriate. By contrast, the median experience of actively managed equity portfolios has been well below (1 to 2 percent) the S&P 500 in most years during the 1970s and early 1980s. Of course, an active approach creates the potential to beat an index fund as well.

Buy-and-Hold Funds. Perhaps the best example of this approach was the growth stock portfolios of the late 1960s and early 1970s. As previously noted, the IBMs and Eastman Kodaks were considered to be one-decision stocks by a fairly large number of institutional money managers. Equity portfolios comprised of such issues had exceptionally good results for many years. However, there did come a day of reckoning. The same outcome is almost inevitable for any such buy-and-hold approach.

At least in relative terms, a buy-and-hold approach is better suited for investors who must pay taxes on realized capital gains. The incidence of such taxes reduces the proceeds available for reinvestment. Investment returns may compound on a larger amount by avoiding such costs. Since individual investors may avoid such costs entirely by holding throughout their lifetimes and capitalizing on the new tax-cost basis that will apply at death, this may turn out to be the very best course. Nevertheless, it would seem very unwise to buy and hold with the thought of forgetting the investments and what may be happening to them. A decision to use this approach should be the result of a determination that it is likely to be in the best interest of the client, not the result of neglect.

Active Equity Management

Active equity management is based on the hope that it will produce better results than can be obtained from a passive approach, particularly an index fund. To create the potential to outperform an index fund, it is necessary to accept something less than complete diversification. In turn, this requires some unsystematic risk exposure. The problem is to decide what unsystematic risk exposures to establish. Such exposures can be harmful as well as beneficial.

The unsystematic risk decisions are reflected in portfolio positions that are either above or below the proportions that would be found in a market portfolio or, to be practical, an index fund. This can be done in a two-stage process that starts with the identification of attractive and unattractive sectors of the equity market. Alternatively, it can be a one-step process concentrating directly on the identification of undervalued and overvalued common stock issues. Implicit in the latter would be some notions about the prospects for various sectors.

The two-stage approach seems relatively popular, especially with clients, because it entails explicit discussion of the market outlook in terms that can be readily understood. Many people have a sense of the stronger and weaker areas of the economy. They tend to be comfortable with portfolio positions that emphasize the stronger areas of the economy. Unfortunately, this is likely to be either nonproductive or counterproductive, since the market would tend to discount what is readily apparent to the casual observer.

Although they are more difficult for the client to understand, there are other approaches to the identification of attractive sectors. For example, a potentially successful method would be to emphasize sectors that will become strong within the next six to twelve months. Usually, that requires emphasizing sectors that are weak (or neutral) at the present time. Such action is difficult for many clients to understand, in some cases because they are fearful that it is too early. And, of course, there is always a good chance that such an approach will prove to be premature.

Another problem with the two-stage approach is that enthusiasm about particular sectors may not be accompanied by enthusiasm about particular common stocks within that sector. Sector decisions may force issue decisions that are uncomfortable. This is likely to be more of a problem in larger investment organizations (than in smaller ones) where the input for sector decisions may come from persons different from those who provide the input for issue decisions. Thus, this approach may create a potential source of conflict within the organization.

Perhaps the most promising two-stage approach would limit the number of sectors that are significantly overweighted or underweighted to permit concentration on those sectors where there is strong conviction and/or unique insight. Such an approach would keep to a practical minimum the potential for conflict between sector decision makers and issue decision makers.

Selection of Issues. Any approach to active equity management involves the identification of the common stocks that are to be purchased or held. Similarly, the identification of common stocks that are to be sold or not bought cannot be avoided. In many cases, the major portion of the issues not to be purchased is determined by the equity manager's style. For example, a growth stock manager would automatically exclude nongrowth stocks. In other cases the issues never invested in are a by-product of an approved list, prescribed by the organization's portfolio managers, of issues that are suitable to hold.

Within the territory in which an equity manager operates, be it defined by sector, quality considerations, or whatever, it is necessary to identify both the relatively attractive and unattractive issues. This process is often reflected in the form of a buy list (if an issue is not on that list, it is not attractive) or a rating sheet. The latter provides a clear indication of the relative attractiveness of all the issues represented within the equity manager's population.

This effort to identify both attractive and unattractive issues may focus entirely on relative price appreciation prospects, relative total return (price appreciation plus dividend yield) prospects, or unique return prospects. As explained earlier, the latter attempts to identify issues whose total return prospects are favorable or unfavorable relative to their respective systematic risk exposures. This is the most appropriate focus according to current capital asset pricing theory. However, successful ranking of total return prospects (say, for the next twelve months) without regard to risk considerations, may be quite helpful in the issue selection process.

There are probably about as many ways to judge which securities are mispriced as there are persons who are trying to do it. Any effort to classify the methods is bound to be somewhat arbitrary. Nevertheless, it is interesting to consider various approaches in terms of the categories addressed by the efficient market hypothesis. These may be summarized as follows:

Form of EMH	Form of Analysis
1. Weak	Technical (supply–demand patterns)
2. Semistrong	Fundamental (public information-based)
3. Strong	Other methods (inside information-based)

As indicated in most discussions of the EMH, both technical analysis and information-based fundamental analysis are somewhat suspect as sources of value added. A rather large number of studies have concluded that they do not work; that is, they do not provide any meaningful chance of establishing any advantage over other participants in the process. The only significant exception would require the use of inside information—and that is illegal. These studies represent a large red flag with respect to either of these approaches, but it may be safe to proceed if great caution is exercised.

The strong form of EMH would also deny the usefulness of any method of fundamental analysis. However, the evidence is not as compelling; indeed, it tends to be more circumstantial. The fact that a majority of equity portfolios do not perform as well as the S&P 500 is taken to be consistent with the strong form version, but neither confirms nor denies it directly. It appears that the principal hope for successful issue selection must rest on other than public information-oriented fundamental analysis.

FUNDAMENTAL ANALYSIS APPROACHES. Approaches to substantive fundamental analysis range all the way from the classical top-down approach used by securities analysts to the valuation screens used by "quants" (persons who do a lot of securities numbers crunching with the help of computers). The top-down approach usually starts with a forecast of the economy and the sectors in which a particular company is represented. It moves through an analysis of the sales and earnings prospects for the company. It concludes with a judgment on the relative attraction of the particular company's common stock, given its price/earnings ratio, dividend yield, and so forth. (For a more extensive discussion of such methods, refer to Chapter 7.)

Affirmative evidence of the viability of such methods is largely lacking. However, in a study by Groth et al. [1978] it appeared that the more painstaking craftsmen, that is, those who spend more time on each recommendation, are the stronger performers. This would appear consistent with the notion that unique insights are required to win the game and that it takes hard work to obtain them. There are said to be experiences involving securities analysts who consistently achieve better than random results in ranking issues within their industry groups. This is consistent with the notion that some specialization of endeavor is likely to be helpful. However, translating any such skill into portfolio results is a major challenge.

CONTRARY OPINION APPROACH. In the aspect of the fundamental analysis approach dealing with the relative attraction of the issue, recognition of the divergent price behavior of individual common stocks is helpful. In the market for stocks, some issues will be doing relatively well as others are behaving rather poorly. In most cases, an issue that has been doing quite well for a while will then have a period of disappointing price action. Thus, there is a strong empirical basis for that form of skepticism called *contrary opinion*. It has been used alone as an approach to the selection of attractive common stocks, or it can be assimilated with other elements of fundamental analysis. The latter application can be particularly rewarding.

Since one of the important foci of fundamental analysis is estimated future earnings, there tends to develop a consensus as to what the earnings forecast for each company is most likely to be. It is presumed that the price of a given stock will reflect this consensus. If one can identify cases where the consensus is wrong—a form of contrary opinion—it is quite likely that price will ultimately adjust to reward such insights. In fact, Elton, Gruber, and Gultiken [1979] say that taking exception to the consensus forecast and being right is an almost certain way to achieve unique return. Williams [1980] has said that "the essence of successful stock market investing, as we define it, is early recognition of change." Of course, this comment was not limited to changes in earnings expectations.

VALUATION SCREENS. At the other extreme, the use of valuation screens has become practical because of the computer. However, it also recognizes that the enormous amount of data on each stock, times the number of issues to be followed, makes an almost impossible task for a human being. This in no way denigrates human talent. It merely distinguishes between those things that the mind does poorly from others that it does very well. Crunching numbers is definitely in the former category.

Dividend discount models provide one of the more popular valuation screening methods. Since these are forward-looking tools, it is necessary to input dividend payment forecasts for each common stock involved. There is a very significant role for securities analysts in providing such estimates. The end product of such models is expected rates of return for each issue. These expected returns are judged in relation to the historical systematic risk (adjusted as necessary) of each issue and expressed in terms of unique return expectations, i.e., relative mispricing. While this approach could include the opportunity to forecast the risk (beta) for each issue, that would be cutting new territory for most analysts.

There are many other types of valuation screens. A very simple one based on relative price/earnings ratios was previously mentioned. Some others that appear to have merit are based on earnings momentum (increasing or decreasing), stock price momentum, dividend momentum, and various indications of changing returns on book equity or reinvestment rate (retained earnings as a percent of book value).

Even in cases where particular valuation screens seem to work fairly well, they do not work all the time. One apparent exception is the valuation screen used by The Value Line Investment Survey. Eisenstadt [1979] has reported that the Value Line stock rankings have performed quite well over a considerable period of time. However, a study by Lee and Nachtmann [1981] questions whether the Value Line results reflect unique returns. They claim that for the average investor the market inefficiency picked up by the model is of no major economic significance once transaction costs of portfolio turnover are taken into consideration. If the Value Line screen is an exception, it is important to recognize that the value of most such screens will be enhanced if they are used selectively, e.g., when the factors they emphasize are particularly market sensitive. This is not easy to determine in advance.

The use of a fundamental approach or valuation screens need not be viewed as an either/or proposition. As a matter of fact, as has been suggested already, probably the two should be combined to achieve the most efficient use of resources and, therefore, the best chance for good results. The valuation screens may be used to identify many of the issues that seem most promising. Fundamental analysis may be used to determine whether the apparent mispricing indicated by the screen is merely a trap or whether it is real.

Weighting of Issues. As mentioned in the introductory comments of this section, the only way to create potential for better results than an index fund is to accept some unsystematic risk. If this is done in a *two-stage approach,* it will start with the identification of undervalued and overvalued sectors of the equity market. Sectors may be represented by industries, relative systematic risk (beta) categories, and so on. It will be completed by selecting particular common stock issues to represent each of the sectors.

To illustrate the particulars of the process, industry groups will be used as the basis of sector classification. Industries that appear undervalued will be weighted heavily relative to their respective proportions in the S&P 500. Table 10-6 summarizes the various industry weightings for the S&P 500 in early 1982, the percentage industry representation in a hypothetical portfolio, and the difference between these two distributions.

This general approach is used quite often by equity managers. However, it does have some fairly serious shortcomings which are not always recognized. Although it requires a specific decision process to weight the various

TABLE 10-6. **Hypothetical Strategic Industry Diversification**

Industry	Outlook for Industry Group	WEIGHTING (IN PERCENT) Portfolio	S&P 500	Difference
Electrical & Electronics	Good	7.0%	5.1%	1.9%
Machinery	Average	6.5	6.4	0.1
Office Equipment	Good	8.0	6.0	2.0
Autos & Parts	Poor	1.0	2.5	(1.5)
Food	Average	2.8	2.8	—
Health Care	Good	9.0	6.6	2.4
Chemicals	Poor	1.5	3.1	(1.6)
⋮	⋮	⋮	⋮	⋮
Total		100.0%	100.0%	0%

sectors, it does not remove the necessity to weight individual common stock issues as well. The latter requires a second set of decisions. After all of this, it is not at all clear just how much systematic and unsystematic risk are represented in the portfolio. Furthermore, it provides no indication of the efficiency of the portfolio, i.e., the expected return to risk relationships.

Quantitative tools are, however, available to measure the risk exposures of an equity portfolio constructed in this way. Such measurement involves a separate information processing procedure. If there are particular targets or ranges for risk exposure, a good deal of trial and error may be required to come out with an equity portfolio that reflects both the sector preferences and the desired risk characteristics. Clearly, this approach is rather cumbersome if both risk and return dimensions are to be carefully considered and controlled.

The disadvantages of this two-stage approach may be insignificant if an equity manager is quite successful using it. An investment client is likely to be quite pleased with a good result even though achieved in a cumbersome way.

The *one-step approach,* which avoids any explicit consideration of the sector weighting possibilities, can be accomplished in many ways. The simplest method is very closely related to the two-stage approach described above. The percentage holdings in each issue will be related to their respective market value of outstanding shares. Those issues perceived to be most attractive within each systematic risk class will be most heavily weighted in that context. Unfortunately, this method shares most of the disadvantages of the two-stage process. Again, if an equity manager is a good "stock picker," the disadvantages may be overlooked.

If a sense of the relatively attractive issues and knowledge of their respective capitalization weights can be combined with estimated betas for each issue, it is possible to construct equity portfolios with some attention to both risk and expected return considerations. However, the focus on risk is limited to the systematic portion. The beta of each common stock, multiplied

TABLE 10-7. **Hypothetical Equity Portfolio Diversification Using Stock Ratings**

	% of S&P 500	S&P Weighted % of Portfolio	Issue Rating	Portfolio Percentages	Beta
AT&T	5.5%	22.2%	3	18%	0.5
IBM	3.7	15.0	1	18	0.8
Exxon	3.2	12.9	3	10	0.7
Schlumberger	1.8	7.3	1	10	0.9
General Electric	1.6	6.5	2	6	0.9
Atlantic Richfield	1.3	5.3	2	5	1.0
Eastman Kodak	1.3	5.3	3	3	0.9
General Motors	1.3	5.3	1	8	1.2
Johnson & Johnson	0.8	3.2	2	3	0.8
Procter & Gamble	0.8	3.2	3	2	0.7
Phillip Morris	0.7	2.8	1	5	0.6
Merck	0.7	2.8	1	5	0.8
Minn. Mining	0.7	2.8	2	3	0.9
DuPont	0.7	2.8	3	1	0.9
American Home	0.6	2.6	2	3	0.7
Total	24.7%	100.0%		100%	0.78[a]

Ratings:
1. Very attractive
2. Moderately attractive
3. Average attraction

[a] Individual issue betas weighted by respective portfolio percentages.

by its percentage weight in the portfolio, will determine the level of systematic risk for the portfolio as a whole. Unfortunately, this approach does not provide any clear indication of the amount of unsystematic risk exposure. Table 10-7 provides an illustration of this particular method.

In cases where an equity manager identifies the relative attraction of common stocks on the basis of expected return calculations, the weighting of each issue in a portfolio may be influenced by the amount of unique return that is implied. Such unique return expectations may be derived from a security market line (SML) at that same time. The risk-return coordinates for each issue will have a certain position relative to the SML. The distance from the SML indicates the amount of unique return expected and whether it is positive or negative.

Some attention must be given to the slope of the SML at any given point in time. The slope does change quite a bit over time. When the SML has very little upward slope (from left to right), there is not much incremental reward expected for taking additional risk. When it is sloping upward rather sharply, it indicates that greater risk-taking is expected to be well rewarded. Although the patterns are not entirely consistent, a modestly sloping SML would be somewhat natural toward market peaks and a sharply sloping SML would be most likely toward market bottoms. Figure 10-8 illustrates the differences in slope at specific dates.

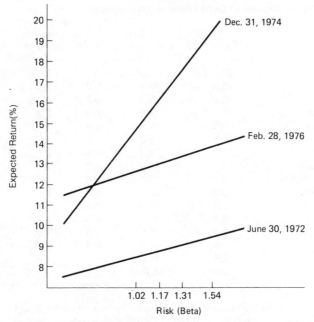

Figure 10-8. Security Market Line Slope on Selected Dates. (SOURCE: Wells Fargo Investment Advisors)

In general, if the SML has a slope that is normal, i.e, somewhere between very modest and sharply rising, the unique returns might be used directly to influence the holding of each issue relative to its market capitalization. However, if the SML is relatively flat, the higher beta issues should be largely ignored unless some have unusually high unique return expectations. Similarly, if the SML is sharply rising, the lower beta issues would receive less attention, except for those with unusually large unique return expectations. Table 10-8 (page 410) provides an example of equity portfolio weightings based on this general approach and assuming the SML has a normal slope.

The considerable use of modern concepts in this last example does not overcome some fundamental deficiencies. There is no direct indication of the position of this portfolio with respect to an efficient frontier. There is no indication of the amount of unsystematic risk for the total portfolio. There is no way of determining whether the amount of unique return expected is reasonable in relation to the amount of unsystematic risk. All these are matters of great concern within the framework of modern portfolio theory. They cannot be determined without a great deal of additional data processing.

As noted earlier, another problem with all these weighting approaches is that there are quite likely to be some people conflicts involved. This comes about when the attractive issues are identified by one person (or group) and the weightings in the portfolio are determined by another person (or group). Bad ideas of the former can destroy the efforts of the latter. Good

TABLE 10-8. Determination of Equity Portfolio Weightings

	S&P Weighted % of Portfolio[a]	Expected Returns	Beta	Unique Return[b]	Portfolio Percentages
AT&T	22.2%	12.5%	0.5	0	18%
IBM	15.0	16.0	0.8	2.0	18
Exxon	12.9	13.5	0.7	0	10
Schlumberger	7.3	16.5	0.9	2.0	10
General Electric	6.5	15.5	0.9	1.0	6
Atlantic Richfield	5.3	16.0	1.0	1.0	5
Eastman Kodak	5.3	14.5	0.9	0	3
General Motors	5.3	18.0	1.2	2.0	8
Johnson & Johnson	3.2	15.0	0.8	1.0	3
Procter & Gamble	3.2	13.5	0.7	0	2
Phillip Morris	2.8	15.0	0.6	2.0	5
Merck	2.8	16.0	0.8	2.0	5
Minn. Mining	2.8	15.5	0.9	1.0	3
DuPont	2.8	14.5	0.9	0	1
American Home	2.6	14.5	0.7	1.0	3
	100.0%	15.05%[c]	0.78[c]	1.12%[c]	100%

[a] Taken from Table 10-7.
[b] Assumes a risk-free return of 10 percent and an expected market return of 15 percent.
[c] Individual issue return/risk weighted by respective portfolio percentages.

ideas of the former can be washed out by the weightings of the latter. Ego involvement may accentuate inherent conflicts. Knowing that this can happen, the management organization must try to deal with it, lest the client suffer as a result. Nevertheless, the combination of issue selection and portfolio weightings offers the potential for much good.

Portfolio Optimizers. Computer programs have been developed to solve the portfolio weighting problem in an optimal way. Optimization involves the determination of the best tradeoff between the expected return and the risk of the portfolio given the various issues that may be included. Since each issue that is a candidate for a portfolio will have its own systematic (beta) and unsystematic risk characteristics as well as an expected return, it represents a very complicated problem of blending the ingredients to achieve the best finished product.

If the market for common stocks were entirely efficient, the price of each individual issue would be such that its expected return would relate directly and exclusively to its own systematic risk and the expected return for the market as a whole. There would be no opportunity to obtain any unique return in exchange for the assumption of unsystematic risk exposure. The optimal portfolio would be the market portfolio or a suitable proxy, e.g., an index fund. However, since the market is not entirely efficient, there are potentially better solutions. This section will discuss portfolio optimization within the context of a somewhat *in*efficient market.

The objective of portfolio optimization is to construct a portfolio with an appropriate level of systematic risk (given the client's objectives), along with an amount of expected unique return that is favorable relative to the unsystematic risk exposure. The importance of the latter relationship is simply based on the fact that the assumption of any unsystematic risk will increase the total risk of the portfolio. Any increase in the total risk should be compensated by some incremental return beyond that which would be indicated by the systematic risk exposure itself. Otherwise, it would be irrational to assume the extra risk.

All portfolio optimization programs that focus on equity portfolios use the market portfolio, or a suitable proxy for it, as a basic frame of reference. This is necessary to compare the risk and return characteristics of alternative common stock exposures. The risk is measured in terms of the standard deviation of total returns or the variance. (The latter is simply the standard deviation squared.) Using such calculations, it is possible to determine the impact on total risk that will result from any departures from the market portfolio.

USE OF A RISK MODEL. To make the necessary calculations, some sort of a risk model is required. The risk model will specify a method for dealing with the risk-return relationships, including the covariance relationships, between the various common stocks that might be included in the portfolio. The available methods seem to fall into three basic categories: (1) the Markowitz model that requires covariance assumptions or estimates for each possible pair of issues, (2) multi-index models that substantially remove the need for covariance assumptions, and (3) single-index models that entirely remove the need for covariance assumptions. The multi-index models represent a practical compromise, combining some degree of simplicity with some attention to group behavior based upon the amount of exposure to certain fundamental characteristics, e.g., growth, size, maturity, and the like.

In addition to the determination of the most favorable unique return relative to unsystematic risk (from the population of issues that might be used), portfolio optimization programs may allow for the specification of certain other constraints, such as yield level for the total portfolio, minimum number of issues, or maximum percentage in any single issue or industry group. Attention to such refinements add further to the complexity of the problem. For example, the expected returns for each issue are judgmental. There may be varying degrees of confidence in one estimate versus another. Therefore, the degree of skill ascribed to those who are providing such estimates can and should be included.

While it is almost impossible to verbalize the data processing that takes place within a portfolio optimization program, it may be helpful to illustrate some possible outcomes. Cohen, Zinbarg, and Zeikel [1982], with the help of Drexel Burnham Lambert, do that quite effectively using 63 common stock issues represented in a mutual fund portfolio managed by Merrill Lynch Asset Management. The particular issues involved, measures of their expected returns and risk, actual weightings in the original portfolio, and the weightings in four efficient model portfolios are shown in Table 10-9.

TABLE 10-9. Composition of Model Portfolios

	Expected Return[a]	Risk[b]	Original Portfolio	MIX PERCENT — EFFICIENT PORTFOLIOS A	B	C	D
1. Newmont Mining	26.0%	3.1	0.9%	5.0%	4.8%	—	—
2. Occidental Pet.	22.8	2.4	1.8	5.0	5.0	4.5%	—
3. Singer	22.5	3.0	1.2	5.0	3.5	—	—
4. NL Industries	22.2	2.1	3.2	5.0	5.0	2.1	—
5. Santa Fe Industries	22.1	2.7	0.8	5.0	5.0	3.1	—
6. Pullman	22.1	3.6	0.8	5.0	—	—	—
7. Heller, Walter E.	21.5	3.7	1.4	5.0	0.5	—	—
8. Reynolds Metals	21.0	2.2	1.0	5.0	3.2	0.1	—
9. Signal Companies	20.7	2.3	3.2	5.0	—	0.1	—
10. Hercules	20.4	2.3	1.2	5.0	1.7	—	—
11. Bucyrus Erie	20.1	2.3	1.0	5.0	3.2	0.9	—
12. UAL	19.7	3.1	1.1	5.0	—	—	—
13. Joy Manufacturing	19.7	2.3	1.8	5.0	—	—	—
14. Marshall Field	19.7	2.3	0.7	5.0	—	0.5	—
15. Chessie System	19.4	2.1	1.8	5.0	—	—	—
16. Crum & Forster	19.3	2.0	1.0	5.0	3.5	—	—
17. Xerox	19.2	1.7	1.5	5.0	1.4	4.7	—
18. Harcourt Brace	19.2	1.9	0.7	5.0	0.4	—	—
19. Greyhound	19.1	1.9	0.8	5.0	2.5	5.0	0.7%
20. Texaco	19.1	2.0	2.3	5.0	5.0	5.0	4.6
21. Int'l Tel. & Tel.	19.1	1.6	1.9	—	5.0	5.0	—
22. Barnett Bank FL	19.0	2.0	0.8	—	1.5	—	—
23. Mattel	19.0	2.6	1.9	—	2.3	—	—
24. Martin Marietta	18.9	2.0	4.7	—	5.0	3.2	—
25. Boise Cascade	18.9	2.0	1.6	—	—	—	—
26. Warner Lambert	18.8	1.8	1.7	—	—	—	—
27. Bendix	18.8	2.0	0.6	—	—	—	0.5
28. Westinghouse	18.7	1.9	1.1	—	4.5	1.4	—
29. Union Carbide	18.3	1.7	2.0	—	5.0	5.0	—
30. Esmark	18.3	2.8	2.9	—	0.7	0.1	—
31. National Distillers	18.2	1.8	2.4	—	1.1	—	—
32. Searle	18.1	2.2	2.1	—	—	2.4	—
— S&P 500 Composite	18.0	1.0	—	—	—	—	—
33. Mead	17.7	1.7	1.4	—	—	—	—
34. Great Northern Nekoosa	17.5	1.8	1.6	—	—	1.4	—
35. Champion Int'l	17.3	2.0	1.3	—	—	—	—
36. Exxon	17.3	1.4	3.1	—	5.0	5.0	5.0
37. Chase Manhattan	17.1	1.6	2.2	—	2.3	—	—
38. Ideal Basic	17.0	2.0	1.5	—	—	—	—
39. Riegel Textile	17.0	1.6	0.6	—	—	—	—
40. RCA	17.0	1.5	2.1	—	—	—	3.8
41. La. Land & Expl.	16.9	2.8	1.2	—	3.3	4.7	5.0
42. Federal Co.	16.7	2.0	1.7	—	2.2	3.2	3.3
43. Goodyear Tire & Rub.	16.5	1.6	1.7	—	—	0.1	0.2
44. J. C. Penney	16.5	1.9	0.9	—	4.4	4.0	4.3
45. Goodrich, B. F.	16.5	1.8	1.2	—	1.2	2.4	5.0

| | | | | MIX PERCENT | | | |
| | | | | EFFICIENT PORTFOLIOS | | | |
		Expected Return[a]	*Risk*[b]	*Original Portfolio*	A	B	C	D
46.	Sterling Drug	16.4	1.9	1.5	—	—	—	—
47.	Homestake Mining	16.1	3.0	3.3	—	—	4.2	2.8
48.	Inland Steel	16.0	1.2	1.5	—	—	0.2	5.0
49.	Fruehauf	15.7	1.3	1.1	—	—	—	5.0
50.	Fed'l Nat'l Mtge.	15.7	1.9	1.2	—	5.0	5.0	5.0
51.	DeBeers Cons. Mines	15.3	2.7	3.1	—	—	—	1.0
52.	Transway Int'l	15.3	1.5	0.9	—	—	—	5.0
53.	Armstrong World	15.1	1.7	1.0	—	1.9	1.1	3.0
54.	Eastman Kodak	15.1	1.3	1.1	—	5.0	5.0	5.0
55.	Colgate Palmolive	15.0	2.0	1.7	—	—	—	—
56.	Clark Equipment	15.0	1.5	1.1	—	—	—	5.0
57.	Deere	14.7	1.4	1.7	—	—	5.0	5.0
58.	Bell Telephone Canada	14.5	1.2	1.5	—	—	4.4	5.0
59.	Florida Power	14.2	1.3	1.6	—	—	1.1	5.0
60.	Pabst Brewing	14.1	3.1	1.4	—	—	—	0.9
61.	Lomas & Nettleton	13.8	1.7	0.9	—	—	—	5.0
62.	Southern Cal. Edison	13.2	1.4	1.3	—	—	5.0	5.0
63.	Sears	13.0	1.4	1.8	—	—	5.0	5.0

SOURCE: Drexel Burnham Lambert, Inc.
[a] Nominal annual rate.
[b] Relative standard deviation of periodic return; the market is equal to 1.0.

The risk and return characteristics of these four efficient portfolios are shown in relation to the calculated efficient frontier of portfolios that can be constructed from the issues represented in the original portfolio, with the constraint that no one holding may exceed 5 percent of the portfolio. Thus, every such portfolio must have at least 20 issues. The frontier and the individual portfolios are plotted in risk-return space in Figure 10-9 (page 414).

These four efficient portfolios cover the full spectrum of possible outcomes, given the 63 issues involved, their respective estimated returns and risk, and the 5 percent limit on any single holding. Portfolio A is the highest risk-return combination and Portfolio D is the lowest. More detailed statistics on the original portfolio, the S&P 500, and the four illustrative efficient portfolios are provided in Table 10-10.

Two interesting phenomena are apparent from an examination of these three tables and figures. Portfolios A and D, at the extreme ends of the return-risk spectrum, contain significantly fewer stocks and are substantially less correlated (ρ-squared values) with the market portfolio than portfolios B and C, which are closer, on the efficient frontier, to the market portfolio. The maximum return (A) and minimum risk (D) portfolios contain only a minimum or near-minimum number of companies and represent a limited

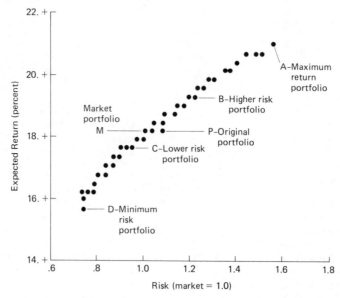

Figure 10-9. Calculated Efficient Frontier of Portfolio Stocks. (SOURCE: Drexel Burnham Lambert, Inc.)

spectrum of the United States and Canadian economies. Portfolios B and C, on the other hand, have their weightings spread over a larger number of companies with similar return-risk characteristics and in lines of business that are much more representative of these macroeconomies.

These are not the kind of problems that the mind is very well equipped to handle. Limited memory capacity and the inability to clearly perceive the

TABLE 10-10. Quantitative Characteristics of Alternative Efficient Stock Portfolios

	Original Portfolio P	S&P 500 Portfolio M	EFFICIENT PORTFOLIOS			
			A	B	C	D
Expected return (percent):						
Total	17.9	18.0	20.8	19.2	17.3	15.5
Alpha factor	0.46	0.00	− 0.01	0.55	0.40	0.19
Dividend	5.5	4.8	4.3	5.4	6.4	7.6
Expected risk (market = 1.00):						
Total	1.07	1.00	1.53	1.20	0.90	0.73
Beta	0.95	1.00	1.43	1.18	0.88	0.62
Residual	0.43	0.00	0.54	0.20	0.17	0.38
ρ-squared (percent)	83.49	100.00	87.43	97.16	96.58	72.31
Other:						
Issue count	63	500	20	31	33	26

SOURCE: Drexel Burnham Lambert, Inc.

implications of an extraordinary number of partially interrelated variables are both inherent weaknesses. Given these and other problems (discussed in the previous section on weighting) that may arise in trying to get good ideas represented in a portfolio, optimization programs would seem to represent a much needed technological breakthrough. Furthermore, their use would permit a greater concentration of human effort on the generation of good ideas. However, adoption of such programs is proceeding very slowly.

The lack of sufficient mathematical background among most portfolio managers is certainly a major deterrent. However, the Elton, Gruber, and Padberg [1978] proposal permitting highly simplified procedures (involving rank-ordering devices) to achieve similar optimization results has not produced a more enthusiastic response. This may reflect a considered judgment that such methods are not worthwhile. On the other hand, it could reflect merely another case of deep-seated resistance to change.

Combination of Active/Passive Management

The existence of both active and passive equity management approaches suggests the potential for some combined applications. Although a few investment managers have developed such applications, the major impetus for the combined use of both active and passive strategies has come from pension sponsors.

Since the larger pension sponsors have hundreds of millions (or even billions) of dollars to invest, there is some feeling that, because of sheer size, the equity portion is very likely to approximate the characteristics of an index fund. Even sponsors who have carefully selected active equity managers may not escape this outcome to any significant degree. Consolidating the multiple-manager accounts of a given sponsor is almost bound to reduce unsystematic risk exposures and, of course, produce a dollar-weighted average of their respective systematic risk positions.

If it is very difficult and/or quite expensive to avoid this outcome, it may be worthwhile to consider something other than 100 percent active management. For the most part, attempts to do this have involved a decision to take a portion of the equity portfolio and handle it in some passive mode. Two principal concepts have emerged thus far, the so-called *passive core* and the *completeness fund*.

Passive Core. This would be viewed as the primary source of broad diversification for the equity portion of the entire portfolio. It could involve any percentage of the equity portion, but has normally represented less than one-half and often less than one-quarter of the total common stock position. It is often invested as an index fund, thus assuring an experience that closely approximates the S&P 500—at a cost that is well below typical active management fees.

The index used as a target need not be the S&P 500. As more attention has been directed to the deficiencies of the S&P 500 as a proxy for the market portfolio, sponsors have been experimenting with broader groups of common stocks. The Wilshire 5000, the entire U.S. common stock market, and the Capital International Index are all viable alternatives, at least from a theoretical standpoint. All appear to offer somewhat better risk-return relationships than the S&P 500. However, as indicated in our earlier discussion of diversification, they do pose much larger practical problems of implementation and, possibly, some legal problems as well.

Whatever the specific make-up of the passive core, it serves as a base upon which the active component of the equity portfolio rests. Its existence normally permits more aggressive management of the active component than would otherwise be the case. Whatever the active management approach, the passive core tends to reduce the unsystematic risk of the total portfolio.

Completeness Fund. This idea has developed recently as a better way to handle an active/passive split within an equity portfolio. Rather than being viewed as a base for the equity portfolio, it tends to be thought of as a residual. After the pension sponsor has decided upon the particular set of active equity managers who are to be involved (or after such a set has been functioning for a while), the areas of the whole market not adequately represented should be quite clear. The completeness fund would be designed to fill any such gaps.

A very simple example would be a sponsor that decided upon a single active equity manager who concentrated on larger capitalization growth stocks. If the areas of the market covered by that manager accounted for 40 percent of the total market, the completeness fund might represent 60 percent of the total equity portfolio. On the other hand, if a pension sponsor had four specialty equity managers, each with a different specialty, who together covered about 60 percent of the total market, the completeness fund might account for about 40 percent of the total equity portfolio. Figure 10-10 provides a visual representation of this concept. For a simple example of how to actually construct a completeness fund, see the chapter appendix.

Although a completeness fund might be handled as an index fund to cover areas of the market not otherwise represented, it is likely to be structured in a more sophisticated manner. In either case, the main objective is to reasonably assure that the total equity portfolio does not suffer unduly as a result of an underweighting of certain characteristics that may be more in phase with the market than those covered by the active managers.

Equity Portfolio Modifiers

There are a variety of financial instruments, not securities per se, that may be used in combination with equity securities. The purpose of such instruments is to provide a different pattern of risk-return exposures. The desirability of using such devices in combination with equity securities

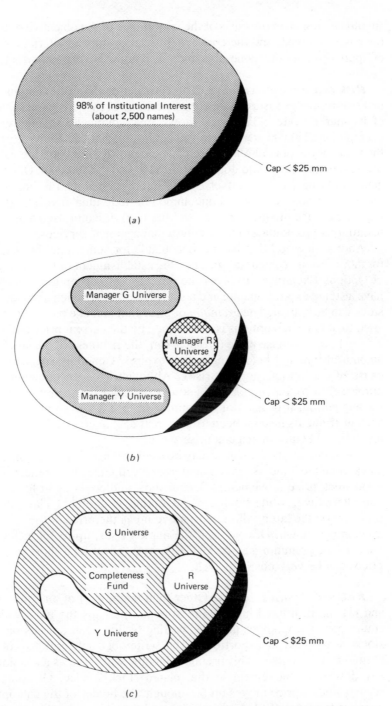

Figure 10-10. Completeness Fund. (a) Domestic Equity Market, (b) Institutional Domestic Equity Market Coverage Provided by Managers, (c) Institutional Domestic Equity Market Coverage Provided by Completeness Fund. (SOURCE: Standard Oil Company [Indiana])

should be judged on the basis of the importance of the objective to be served, the costs involved, and the cost-benefit relationships of alternative methods of approximating the same objective. The latter is very important.

Risk and Return Extenders. The classical method of extending the normal risk-return exposure of an equity portfolio is by borrowing some portion of its market value. This was shown diagramatically in Figure 2-3. For example, if $250,000 were borrowed against a $500,000 equity portfolio and the value of the portfolio increased 50 percent (to $750,000), the value of the ownership interest would double (from $250,000 to $500,000). Of course, this gain would be partially offset by the interest costs of the borrowing. Although such borrowing is not uncommon for individual investors (for financing the exercise of stock options and the like), it is not used a great deal by institutions providing ordinary equity management services.

Another method that has been available for some time, but has come in for more serious consideration since the establishment of the Chicago Board of Options Exchange, involves the purchase of call options. Such options have a stated expiration date and a specified price at which a named common stock can be bought. The *premium* or price that must be paid (plus a commission) to obtain such options is determined by the current price of the particular stock, the exercise price (*strike price*), the riskiness of the stock, and the amount of time left before the option expires. Generally speaking, the purchase of call options is very risky. Although it is not uncommon for the purchaser to double or more than double the value of the premium during the holding period, it is also not uncommon to lose it all. To date, purchase of such instruments has not been used a great deal in connection with standard institutional equity management services.

These two methods, which may be used to magnify the benefit of upward stock price movements, have counterpart techniques to capitalize on downward stock price movements. Selling short and covering at lower prices is one alternative, while buying a put option is another. The value of the premium on the latter will tend to move up as the price of the related stock issue moves down. Of course, if the market rises, up to 100 percent of the value of the premium may be lost. Likewise, covering a short sale at higher prices can be very costly as well.

Risk and Return Limiters. Other than taking part of an equity portfolio and placing it in fixed income investments, perhaps the most widely used equity portfolio modifier involves writing (selling) call options on common stock issues held in a portfolio. The writer of such options collects the premium at the outset. This premium income will serve as a cushion against any downward movement in the related stock's price. Of course, if the related stock's price moves up far enough, the holder of the call option may exercise the option at the strike price and the writer may be called upon to supply the necessary shares. This particular approach, called *covered call option writing* places an upper limit on opportunity.

Covered call option or *buy-write programs* writing has been used by a number of institutional investment managers. Because the device is inherently conservative, it was the first use of options that was approved by the Comptroller of the Currency [1979]. Its appeal has been somewhat related to the more volatile financial markets that have developed in recent years. In theory, the use of covered call options reduces the expected returns in line with the reduced risk exposure that is achieved. Some advocates have suggested something better, i.e., an improvement in the risk-return relationships. In any event, the costs of such programs (valuation models, staff time, and so on) are likely to be fairly significant if they are managed in a responsible way. Garbade and Kaicher [1978–79] have provided helpful material to understand the pricing of options, while Slivka [1980] discusses some applications.

EQUITY PORTFOLIO MANAGEMENT CONSTRAINTS

Beyond the desired risk-return characteristics of an equity portfolio, a variety of other considerations such as liquidity requirements, tax considerations, time horizons, and applicable legal provisions have a constraining influence. Each of these will be discussed briefly here. (Chapters 4 and 5 provide fairly extensive discussion of these topics.)

Liquidity Requirements

The need for liquidity may be related to obligations that must be met at specified future dates or to plans to expend funds for some particular purpose. The latter is not mandatory, but may be just as important as a formal liability. Thus, both need to be dealt with in a way that provides a very high degree of assurance that such needs can be met at the appropriate times.

If the income produced by an equity portfolio is not dedicated to some kind of ongoing needs, such as a current operating budget, it can be viewed as a source or partial source of funds to meet future obligations or plans. Such income should be accumulated in a form that assures it will be available when needed. Many times this would be cash equivalent investments, e.g., U.S. Treasury bills, high-grade commercial paper, and the like. In some particular instances it might take the form of somewhat longer term (one to three years) fixed income investments, still very high quality, with maturities closely matching the timing of the future obligations. Grieves [1982] addresses this general subject.

In cases where the income produced by an equity portfolio is dedicated to ongoing needs, it is appropriate to prepare to meet future obligations by liquidating longer term assets and using the proceeds to establish a reserve. Depending on the circumstances, the investment of such reserve funds should be in either of the two forms suggested above.

With the proliferation of lower quality short-term instruments in recent years, it becomes very tempting to consider using them as a cash equivalent. Generally, they provide somewhat better rates of return. Although there is certainly room to exercise judgment, it is probably unwise to compromise on quality, price stability, and so forth, for a small increment of additional return. The decision might tilt just a bit for greater return in cases where the reserves are related to future plans (where, for instance, there may be a little flexibility on timing) rather than fixed liabilities.

Liquidity as an Investment Strategy. It is very important to distinguish clearly between liquidity reserves of the kind just discussed and those related to the implementation of investment strategies. The latter would come about as a consequence of a decision to reduce common stock or longer term bond holdings, presumably awaiting a more favorable price level to reestablish such positions. The proceeds would normally be held in the form of cash equivalents until redeployed. (See the discussion of market timing earlier in this chapter.) To make certain that there is no confusion about which reserve is for which purpose, it may be desirable to establish a separate account for the reserve to meet future obligations.

If the income flows and liquidity reserves of an equity portfolio are sufficient to cover both ongoing and special needs, the marketability of common stocks held may not be critical. However, an active equity manager must be satisfied that the portfolio has sufficient marketability, that is, that it includes a sufficient number of stocks that can be sold with little delay and little, if any, market price concession. Furthermore, there may be a certain value in having some marketability to provide the potential for liquidating some holdings for unexpected needs or alternative investment opportunities.

Tax Considerations

There are two rather broad aspects of this subject: (1) How do the various tax laws, the tax status of particular securities, the distribution of securities ownership, and the tax position of the holders come together to impact the pricing of various securities? (2) Given the impact on securities prices and hence on expected pretax returns, what combination of securities is most appropriate to meet the objectives of the particular client?

With respect to the *general impact* on securities prices, it seems quite reasonable to assume that the tax status of specific securities and the tax positions of principal holders are very significant. The pricing of tax-exempt municipal and taxable corporate bonds provides a very clear example. Yields to maturity on the former tend to be lower than on the latter. However, the focus of this chapter is on common stocks. In this category of securities the major area of attention is on the difference in the tax treatment of dividend income and capital gains or losses.

Dividends vs. Capital Gains. Individual holders of common stocks, especially those in higher tax brackets, can keep a larger portion of any capital gains after taxes than of dividend income. The capital gains tax advantage is even greater since the passage of the Economic Recovery Tax Act of 1981. Thus, it has been argued that growth stocks will tend to be overpriced relative to (high) yield stocks, at least from the point of view of tax-exempt funds, e.g., pensions, endowment funds, and the like. This has led to the idea of a *yield tilt* equity portfolio emphasizing higher yield stocks for such tax-exempt funds. The theory is that the yield tilt will produce a better total return for such holders.

This idea has not worked particularly well in recent years. Changes in the tax laws, including more favorable treatment of capital gains, may be at least part of the reason. Miller and Scholes [1978] argue that many other factors are likely to confuse or neutralize the basic merit of the yield tilt idea. Corporate holders can exclude 85 percent of their dividend income, so dividends are likely to be more attractive than capital gains for them. It appears that more and more stock ownership is moving into pension funds, which are completely tax-exempt. Many individual holders are able to shelter otherwise taxable income by borrowing or in other ways. For all these reasons the normal tax exposure of dividends becomes irrelevant. The ebb and flow of risk tolerance, i.e., the market psychology of all investors, is likely to have an independent effect on the relative pricing of the expected appreciation and the expected income components of expected total return, further confounding the viability of the concept. (For a discussion of this contrary point of view, see Malkiel [1981].)

It appears that there is no simple solution to the problem of dealing with the impact of tax considerations upon securities prices. It seems likely that the impacts are very great, but there are so many subtleties involved (along with a multitude of nontax factors) that the net impact may be very hard to discern. In any event, it would seem unwise to view the impact of tax considerations simplistically.

Use of After-tax Discount Rates. With respect to *selection of particular issues* for a given equity portfolio, two steps are involved. First, the expected returns must be determined for each issue that might be used. These expectations would reflect all relevant factors, including the current and future price impact of tax factors. Second, it is necessary to consider the impact that the tax exposure of the particular client will have on the issue's after-tax returns. For this purpose it may be very useful to determine the discount rate implicit to the price of each issue, using only that portion of the income and ultimate selling price that can be kept after taxes as the stream of future payments. Vandell and Pontius [1981] have suggested methods for working with such individualized after-tax discount rates in combination with the riskiness of the individual issues.

The tax treatment of certain commingled funds must be recognized as a special problem. Capital gains and losses resulting from transactions within common trust funds and investment trusts are passed along to shareholders or unit holders. These gains may very well have arisen before a particular holder became involved. Thus, such funds may result in some inequities and/ or some less-than-optimal timing of gains and losses from a particular holder's point of view. Such passed-along gains and losses may be used to adjust the cost basis of units purchased in common trust funds. These tax treatments must be taken into account by managers of equity portfolios holding such funds. They must be taken into account by the client representative as well.

Time Horizon

The time horizon is quite important because of the volatility of return experienced by most equity securities. Thus, in the short to intermediate term, a particular common stock or an entire group of common stocks may experience a return that falls well short of any original expectation. This possibility must be recognized in determining the suitability of common stocks in the first place. In the same vein, to avoid unnecessary realization of what are likely to be temporary losses, this volatility must be recognized as a possible reason to cause a delay in the liquidation of common stock positions.

Any given equity portfolio may have at least two different time horizons. The first would be related to the expected life of the account. The age of the client, the future timing of needed funds, and so on, would influence that time horizon and the basic asset allocation decision for the portfolio. The second would be more closely related to the amount of time needed to provide a good indication of satisfactory achievement of investment results. For the latter, the investment style and strategies of the equity manager should be considered, as well as the interim needs and preferences of the client.

As demonstrated by Lloyd and Haney [1980], the longer the time horizon (whichever kind), the less concerned an equity manager needs to be in considering the riskiness of common stocks. Table 10-11 illustrates how the standard deviation of returns from common stocks and various stock/bond combinations diminishes, the longer the holding period.

This particular indication of the volatility of common stock returns was based on the actual behavior of financial markets between 1926 and 1976. Any different time interval would probably show a somewhat different experience. The 25-year period from 1926 to 1951 (encompassing the Great Depression) was characterized by greater market volatility than the 25-year period from 1951 to 1976. Within the more recent 25-year period, the decade from 1966 through 1976 witnessed greater market volatility than the prior 15 years.

Volatility in Different Situations. The fact that the degree of volatility is constantly changing underscores the importance of judgment in attempting

TABLE 10-11. Actual Rates and Minimum Likely Rates of Return over Various Planning Periods for Various Portfolio Mixes (1926–76)

	100/0%	90/10%	80/20%	70/30%	60/40%	50/50%	40/60%	30/70%	20/80%	10/90%	0/100%
						DEBT/EQUITY MIX					
						Actual Average Annual Rates of Return					
Mean Rate of Return:	4.07%	4.58%	5.10%	5.60%	6.11%	6.63%	7.14%	7.66%	8.19%	8.71%	9.23%
Mean Return Less Standard Deviation											
						Minimum Likely Average Annual Rates of Return					
1 Year	−1.36%	−1.15%	−1.65%	−2.60%	−3.77%	−5.06%	−6.41%	−7.81%	−9.20%	−10.60%	−11.99%
2 Years	0.20	0.49	0.28	−0.26	−0.98	−1.77	−2.63	−3.53	−4.42	− 5.32	− 6.24
3 Years	0.88	1.23	1.15	0.79	0.29	−0.28	−0.91	−1.56	−2.22	− 2.90	− 3.57
4 Years	1.32	1.67	1.66	1.42	1.05	0.61	0.23	−0.38	−0.89	− 1.42	− 1.95
5 Years	1.60	1.98	2.02	1.86	1.57	1.24	0.85	0.44	0.03	− 0.39	− 1.12
10 Years	2.33	2.74	2.91	2.93	2.88	2.79	2.65	2.51	2.36	2.19	2.02
15 Years	2.64	3.07	3.31	3.42	3.47	3.48	3.47	3.44	3.41	3.36	3.30
20 Years	2.83	3.27	3.55	3.71	3.82	3.89	3.95	3.99	4.03	4.06	4.08
25 Years	2.96	3.41	3.71	3.90	4.06	4.19	4.28	4.37	4.47	4.54	4.61

SOURCE: Vandell, Harrington, and Fisher [1977].

to deal with the implications of different time horizons. The future is very likely to differ in some respects from the past. Nevertheless, as a general proposition it seems reasonable to assume that common stocks will have more volatile returns than long-term bonds which, in turn, will produce more volatile returns than short-term fixed income obligations (unless we have an extended period of erratic, but high, inflation rates). Furthermore, whatever the differences, they will tend to be greater over shorter time spans and gradually less over longer time spans.

Given these general tendencies, an equity portfolio with a fairly long time horizon can reasonably emphasize issues that are somewhat riskier in nature than a portfolio with a significantly shorter time horizon. The more diversified the portfolio, the greater the comfort in relying on this general approach. The impact of a single issue whose volatility turns out to be all on the downside will be much less on a well-diversified portfolio.

Pension funds tend to have very long time horizons. All but the smaller ones may establish highly diversified positions. Together, these characteristics permit a large amount of volatility or risk exposure, unless the particular actuarial accounting methods are likely to cause unexpected changes in contribution requirements.[3] By contrast, individuals will have somewhat shorter time horizons. However, a person who is 45 years old is likely to have a much longer horizon than a person who is 70 years old.

Regulatory and Legal

An equity portfolio manager has many legal and regulatory constraints with which to contend. The particulars will vary depending upon the type of institution, e.g., trust company, insurance company, investment company, or investment counselor. They will also vary with the location of the activity (which state), the type of account (pension, individual, and so on), and whether or not the fund is commingled. Separate but sometimes overlapping rules and regulations pertain to each of these categories. An equity manager must become thoroughly acquainted with all the rules that apply to any particular account.

Fiduciary Responsibility. Many equity portfolio management situations are affected by statutory and case law pertaining to *fiduciary responsibility*, which prescribes the application of care, skill, prudence, and diligence in the performance of duties, the diversification of investments, and unwavering commitment to the interests of those parties being served. There may be certain prohibitions, such as the use of options, short sales, the use of foreign securities, and/or the use of margin accounts.

With the adoption of the Employee Retirement Income Security Act

---

[3] The Financial Executives Research Foundation has published a volume entitled *Pension Asset Management: The Corporate Decision*, prepared by FRS Associates [1980b], which provides useful insights into the factors that bear on the management of pension funds.

(ERISA) in 1974, there are significant differences between a fiduciary's view of pension funds and personal trusts. Federal law has preempted state law with respect to all employee benefit funds. State laws continue to govern personal trusts. The prudent man of ERISA is held to a standard that is based on what someone with similar responsibilities would do. The prudent man of state laws is held to a lesser standard, e.g., a man handling his own personal affairs. With respect to personal trusts, the focus of prudence is still largely on each individual security. With respect to employee benefit funds, the focus of prudence is much more heavily oriented toward the characteristics of the total portfolio.

Given the important differences between federal and state laws, pension funds have greater latitude to use high risk securities (including venture capital), non-dividend-paying stocks, and the like, as long as each such investment has a role within the total portfolio, and its characteristics are consistent with the objectives of the plan. Furthermore, the Department of Labor has issued regulations under ERISA that permit some movement away from the careful investigation of each investment when an index fund is involved.

There is also a vast "patch-quilt" of law that attempts to address the abuses that are quite likely to arise from conflicts of interest. Such conflicts exist when the personal interest of the equity manager might influence an action taken on behalf of an investment client and such interest might cause actions or omissions that would be contrary to the client's interest. In general, the equity manager must subordinate personal interests.

Commission Payments. Another important area of the law applies to the handling of commissions paid to securities brokers. Since the adoption of negotiated commissions by the New York Stock Exchange, there are numerous potential conflicts between the manager who handles the negotiation and the client whose funds are used to pay for items that the manager should pay out of pocket. In general, a portion of such commission payments may properly relate to research services that should be beneficial to the client, if the services are provided by the broker and if the amount of payment is reasonable in relation to the value of the research received. (See Section 28(e) of the Securities Exchange Act of 1934 and Securities and Exchange Commission [1976] for more perspective on this subject.)

Use of Information. In the earlier section on "Use of Information," an important distinction was made between inside information and public information. In general, it is illegal to use inside information. For further illumination on key aspects, reference to the earlier section is suggested.

Contractual Provisions. In addition to the aforementioned and many other similar areas of the law, there may be important contractual provisions, such as in a trust agreement or a somewhat less formal advisory agreement, that must be considered. These may be found in the various governing documents that relate to mutual funds, investment trusts, or common trust funds. The existence of such provisions creates a clear opportunity for legal recourse if there is any significant failure to comply.

Such contractual provisions are likely to specify maximum limits on the holding of particular issues or industry groups. They may very well prohibit the use of puts and calls, short sales, foreign securities, and the like. In trust agreements there will often be a requirement that each investment be income-producing. In some cases, there will be provisions with respect to liquidity and/or marketability thresholds. All must be respected.

Unique Considerations

This represents a catch-all that would cover any consideration of a rather unique nature, something that was important to a particular client.

Some examples of this would be a client's aversion to the payment of capital gains taxes, the use of securities of companies that are involved with products or engaged in activities that are opposed by the client, the purchase of non-dividend-paying issues, or the use of unlisted securities. From an objective point of view, such considerations may prevent some action that is deemed to be in the best interest of the client. However, unless there are compelling reasons to disregard such considerations, they should be observed. Failure to do so could result in the loss of the account. Beyond that, portfolio managers should always remember that the assets belong to the client, and that it is the client's objectives that are to be served.

SUMMARY

Equity portfolio management may stand alone in particular cases, but is usually related to other investment management endeavors within the context of a total portfolio. In any event, the process cannot take place in a meaningful way without a clear understanding of the investor's objectives, including annual income needs, avoidance of risk beyond specified levels, and/or some aspiration with respect to total rate of return.

The existence of an equity portfolio can be justified only if the characteristics of common stocks are deemed to be compatible with the investment objectives of the particular fund or client. Since common stocks tend to be somewhat risky, it is very important that the combination of such issues, along with other investments in the portfolio, be entirely suitable and appropriate for the specific situation.

The actual composition of a given equity portfolio, that is, the particular issues and their respective weightings, should reflect the integration of investment objectives, the characteristics of the common stocks involved, and the manager's expectations of the financial markets and specific companies. This blending of factors is absolutely essential to successful management of an equity portfolio. Because of the inevitable tradeoffs involved in this process, considerable knowledge and some very careful judgments are involved.

There are quite a number of equity management styles, but they tend to fall in one of three categories: (1) nondiversified, (2) diversified, and (3) rotational. The growth stock, undervalued stock, and other nondiversified equity managers are largely involved with the selection of issues from a particular sector of the market. They may represent the entire equity position of a given client, but are more likely to be part of a multiple-manager arrangement. The diversified managers select issues from across the entire market spectrum. The rotational managers are significantly involved with market timing, whether common stocks vis-à-vis cash equivalents or between sectors within the equity market.

Any approach to equity portfolio management involves considerable use of information. Due to the efficiency of the market, relevant information is normally reflected very promptly in common stock prices. There are many ways of trying to deal with this information, ranging from a top-down fundamental analysis of a given company to the use of quantitative screening devices to identify purchase or sale candidates from a broad list. In general, intensive fundamental analysis leading to unique insights or the early anticipation of change appear to have the greatest likelihood of success.

The availability of information, the resources and skills devoted to its interpretation, and the quantity of funds to be invested will all have some bearing on the portfolio strategy employed. Passive management through an index fund can assure a result that approximates the overall market at relatively low cost. Active management creates the potential for results that are better than the overall market, tends to be quite a bit more costly, and often fails to achieve results produced by an index fund. The combination of active/passive strategies is a growing phenomenon, especially among larger pension sponsors.

Whatever the basic style or strategy of a given manager, it is likely to be constrained in many cases by liquidity requirements, tax considerations, the time horizon of a given client, and a broad range of legal and regulatory provisions. Success in the management of an equity portfolio must be viewed in light of such constraints and any other client objectives. Performance evaluation is greatly complicated by the need to respect such special considerations. Simple comparisons with the experience of the S&P 500 are likely to be irrelevant in many cases.

FURTHER READING

For more in-depth treatment of many aspects of portfolio management, including the basic elements of risk and return, excellent references are provided by Lorie and Hamilton [1973] and Reilly [1982]. Some of the truly seminal work on portfolio management may be found in Markowitz [1952] and Sharpe [1963].

Characteristics of Equity Securities

There are a variety of factors that influence the characteristics of common stocks. Some of the legal, sociological, and political considerations are addressed by Molodovsky [1974] and Jensen [1978].

Some of the best data on the variability and the average level of rates of return experienced by common stocks are provided by Fisher and Lorie [1970] and Ibbotson and Sinquefield [1982]. The latter represents the third version of a publication that was originally printed in 1977.

The increased attention to a careful exercise of voting rights (by institutional investors) has been accompanied by the publication of informed analyses of issues ranging from the amendment of by-laws and the adoption of stock option plans to the construction of nuclear power facilities and the marketing of infant formulas in foreign countries. Two organizations that have been especially active in publishing such material are Daniels & Cartwright (brokerage firm), 32 Broadway, New York, N.Y. 10004 and the Investor Responsibility Research Center, Inc., 1522 K Street, N.W., Washington, D.C. 20005.

Equity Management Styles

Among the nondiversified equity management styles there is one version of undervalued stock management that has an unusual degree of empirical support, extending over a long period of years. This particular version is focused on low price/earnings multiples. Some very interesting recent verification of the significance of low P/E ratios has been done by Bidwell [1979, 1981].

For some additional insight into other popular forms of specialized equity management, knowledge of the primary characteristics of the homogeneous groups of equity securities to which this specialized management has been applied may be helpful. Two articles that cover such matters are Price [1979] and Reinganum [1981].

Diversified equity management is usually related to a proxy for the entire equity market, such as the S&P 500 population. Some of the problems arising from the use of various proxies for the market, especially in connection with performance measurement, are developed quite effectively by Roll [1978].

As thinking about diversification broadened to a global approach, there was some consideration given to U.S. multinational companies being a sufficient vehicle. However, the actual implementation of international diversification within U.S. pension funds has been through the use of foreign securities. The limitations of U.S. multinational companies as international diversification vehicles are treated quite clearly by Jacquillat and Solnik [1978]. A fairly recent review of international diversification by U.S. pension funds was performed by Ehrlich [1981].

With respect to market timing (as a form of rotational equity management), some of the distinctions between the theoretical potential and the likelihood of attaining incremental returns are treated quite well by Sharpe [1975] and Fuller [1978]. Equity management that emphasizes group rotation seems to have fewer skeptics than that which focuses on market timing. Nevertheless, it does require the identification of more or less homogeneous stock groups or the use of some of the newer quantitative methods that provide a clear indication of the particular risk factors being emphasized at particular times within the equity market. Some rather seminal work was done on each of the latter subjects, respectively, by Farrell [1975] and Rosenberg [1974].

Institutions that are permitted to use commingled funds will often reflect their management style(s) through such vehicles. However, there are some strongly negative feelings about such funds, due in part to a suspicion that the results will be not as good as they would be in an individual account handled by the same manager. Although it is not conclusive, some of the best comparative performance data were assembled and discussed by Bogle and Twardowski [1980].

Use of Information

Because information represents the lifeblood of the investment process, its use and perceived usefulness deserve much attention. One of the most constructive (and optimistic) treatments of what may be useful and to what extent is provided by Ambachtsheer and Farrell [1979]. In addition, strong encouragement for the combined use of quantitative screens and fundamental analysis is offered by many, including Wright [1981].

Of course, the quality of information available is terribly important and has many aspects. Good examples of the problems with quality of information in the area of government statistics and corporate financial statements are provided, respectively, by Leuthold [1980] and Norby [1981].

The law has encroached deeply into the disclosure and use of information. An unusually helpful summary of important legal considerations, from the user's point of view, was developed by Gillis [1980].

Equity Management Portfolio Strategies

The best material on this subject was assembled in a multiclient study that is not available to the general public. However, those who are employees of any of the sponsoring institutional investment firms and pension sponsors would have access to it. The producer was FRS Associates [1980a]. The basic strategies suggested in this multiclient study are passive, active, and a combination of passive-active.

During the past decade most of the attention devoted to passive management has been focused on market-matching or index funds. There were some important legal questions about the use of large numbers of issues, such as index funds normally use, without undertaking some reasonable investigation of each issue. The uncertainties that lingered on this matter at the time ERISA was adopted were later clarified by the federal government (see Gray [1977] and Department of Labor [1979]). Additional background material on the genesis of the index fund idea and an especially thoughtful analysis of when index funds should and should not be used may be found, respectively, in Sharpe [1981] and Bogle [1980].

A rather specialized application of the passive management approach is reflected in the inventory fund concept that is used to minimize transaction costs in otherwise actively managed multiple-manager portfolios. The benefits and problems of this specialized use are covered quite well by Ferguson [1978].

In spite of a multitude of empirical studies that lack any encouragement with respect to the cost-benefit relationships relating to active management, it was still the most popular strategy as of 1982. An important exception to the general pattern of empirical studies was one that related to the stock ratings published by *The Value Line Investment Survey*. The original encouraging findings and a rather recent challenge to those findings are provided by Eisenstadt [1979] and Lee and Nachtmann [1981].

There is much published material related to active equity portfolio management. Some particularly helpful articles on the generation and application of good ideas about individual issues may be found in Sanghvi and Dash [1978], Treynor and Black [1973], and Williams [1980]. Other interesting material on a variety of aspects of active management are provided by Blume [1978], Elton, Gruber, and Gultiken [1979], Financial Analysts Research Foundation [1978], Groth, Lewellen, Schlarbaum, and Lease [1978], and Rosenberg [1979].

At the frontier of investment technology is the array of portfolio optimization tools that are now available for those who are involved with active management situations. There are some very helpful discussions of the basic approach to portfolio optimization and a greatly simplified method of attaining the same kind of optimal weighting results in the work of Cohen, Zinbarg, and Zeikel [1982] and Elton, Gruber, and Padberg [1978], respectively.

The combination of active-passive management approaches provides an opportunity to derive some of the benefits of each approach, in proportions designed to be most appropriate for any given portfolio. The best material on the subject as a whole was produced by FRS Associates [1980a].

There are a variety of ways in which to modify the basic characteristics of an equity portfolio through the use of some of the newer financial instruments. Stock market index futures contracts in 1982 were just beginning to be available and will undoubtedly generate a volume of material on basic characteristics and possible applications. Of a much more established nature are puts and calls, which have been the subject of a considerable volume of literature. A seminal piece of work on the pricing of such options was reflected in Black and Scholes [1973]. Some additional reading that should be quite helpful to those who may be contemplating the use of options is provided by Comptroller of the Currency [1979], Garbade and Kaicher [1978–79], and Slivka [1980]. Given the volatility of the financial markets in recent years, there will probably be a further proliferation of instruments that permit some modification of the exposures that come about through the ownership of publicly traded securities.

Equity Portfolio Constraints

Generally speaking, these constraints arise from considerations that are likely to cause the use of different kinds of investments than those that would otherwise be considered most attractive and/or appropriate. Perhaps the most broadly relevant constraint to both individual and institutional portfolios is reflected in liquidity requirements. This subject is treated quite well in a recent publication of the Financial Analysts Research Foundation by Grieves [1982].

Tax considerations constitute a constraint in two important ways. They have some general impact on the pricing of different kinds of securities. Some very interesting (and sophisticated) empirical work on this aspect of tax considerations is provided by Miller and Scholes [1978] and Malkiel [1981]. The second aspect of tax considerations has to do with the selection of particular issues that are believed to be especially advantageous for a particular client portfolio. An interesting treatment of this aspect, which suggests how the output of a dividend discount model may be used for an investor with particular tax exposures, was published by Vandell and Pontius [1981].

With respect to the constraints imposed by the time horizon of a particular client or portfolio, some useful insights on the relationship between length of time and the range of possible outcomes, e.g., annual rates of return, are provided by Lloyd and Haney [1980] and Vandell, Harrington, and Fisher [1977].

Although the regulatory and legal considerations that pertain to various forms of investment management are enormous, it may be quite useful to start with a sense of the fiduciary responsibility that exists in so many situations where institutional investment managers are involved. Two publications that deal with this quite effectively are Financial Analysts Research Foundation [1976] and Marcus [1978].

Since the management of equity portfolios will involve some purchase and sale transactions (sooner or later), it is important to have a good understanding of the rules pertaining to the negotiation of stock commissions and the use of such commissions for research services. This is provided (in part) by Securities and Exchange Commission [1975, 1976].

BIBLIOGRAPHY

Ambachtsheer, Keith P., "Profit Potential in an 'Almost Efficient' Market," *Journal of Portfolio Management,* Fall 1974.

——, **and James L. Farrell, Jr.,** "Can Active Management Add Value?" *Financial Analysts Journal,* November/December 1979.

Bidwell, Clinton M., III, "A Test of Market Efficiency: SUE/PE," *Journal of Portfolio Management,* Summer 1979.

——, "SUE/PE Revista," *Journal of Portfolio Management,* Winter 1981.

Black, Fischer, and Myron Scholes, "The Pricing of Options and Corporate Liabilities," *Journal of Political Economy,* May/June 1973.

Blume, Marshall E., "Two Tiers—But How Many Decisions?" in *Security Selection and Active Portfolio Management,* New York: Institutional Investor, 1978.

Bogle, John C., "When to Index and When Not to Index," *Pension World,* April 1980 (Part I) and May 1980 (Part II).

——, **and Jan M. Twardowski,** "Institutional Investment Performance Compared: Banks, Investment Counselors, Insurance Companies and Mutual Funds," *Financial Analysts Journal,* January/February 1980.

Brealey, Richard A., and S. D. Hodges, "Portfolio Selection in a Dynamic and Uncertain World," *Financial Analysts Journal,* March/April 1973.

Cohen, Jerome B., Edward D. Zinbarg, and Arthur Zeikel, *Investment Analysis and Portfolio Management,* 4th Ed., Homewood, Ill.: Richard D. Irwin, 1982.

Comptroller of the Currency, "National Bank Trust Department Use of Exchange-Traded Put and Call Options," Trust Banking Circular No. 2 (Revised), December 19, 1979.

DeMarche Associates, "Stock Market Sector Statistics," October 1978.

Department of Labor, Section 2550.404a-1, "Investment Duties," *Federal Register,* 44 (no. 124), June 26, 1979 (and preamble thereto).

Ehrlich, Edna E., "International Diversification by United States Pension Funds," Federal Reserve Bank of New York, *Quarterly Review,* Autumn 1981.

Eisenstadt, Samuel, "Value Line Record Raises Questions on Validity of Efficient Market Theory," *Pensions & Investments Age,* June 18, 1979.

Elton, Edwin J., Martin J. Gruber, and Mustafa Gultiken, "Capital Market Efficiency and Expectational Data," New York: I/B/E/S (Institutional Brokers Estimate System), May 1979.

——, ——, **and Manfred W. Padberg,** "Optimal Portfolios from Simple Ranking Devices," *The Journal of Portfolio Management,* Spring 1979.

Farrell, James L., "Homogeneous Stock Groupings—Implications for Portfolio Management," *Financial Analysts Journal,* May/June 1975.

Ferguson, Robert, "Do Inventory Funds Make Sense?" *Financial Analysts Journal,* May/June 1978.

Financial Analysts Research Foundation, "Evolving Concepts of Prudence," The Proceedings of a Seminar (seven papers), New York, December 1976.

———, "Portfolio Management," The Proceedings of a Seminar (three papers), Bal Harbour, Florida, May 8, 1978.

Fisher, Lawrence, and James H. Lorie, "Some Studies of Variability of Returns on Investments in Common Stocks," *The Journal of Business,* April 1970.

FRS Associates, "Investment Management—The Active/Passive Decision," January 1980a.

———, *Pension Asset Management: The Corporate Decision.* New York: Financial Executives Research Foundation, 1980b.

Fuller, Russell J., "Timing vs. Selection: Which Holds the Key?" in *Security Selection and Active Portfolio Management,* New York: Institutional Investor, 1978.

Garbade, Kenneth D., and Monica M. Kaicher, "Exchange-Traded Options on Common Stock," Federal Reserve Bank of New York, *Quarterly Review,* Winter 1978–79.

Gillis, John G., "Inside Information Developments," *Financial Analysts Journal,* March/April 1980.

———, "The Supreme Court and Market Information," *Financial Analysts Journal,* November/December 1980.

Gray, William S., "The Major Shortfall of ERISA," *Financial Analysts Journal,* January/February 1977.

Grieves, Robin H., *Cash Management,* New York: Financial Analysts Research Foundation, 1982.

Groth, John C., Wilbur G. Lewellen, Gary G. Schlarbaum, and Ron C. Lease, "Security Analysts: Some Are More Equal," in *Security Selection and Active Portfolio Management,* New York: Institutional Investor, 1978.

Ibbotson, Roger G., and Rex A. Sinquefield, *Stocks, Bonds, Bills and Inflation: The Past and the Future,* Charlottesville, Va.: The Financial Analysts Research Foundation, 1982.

Jacquillat, Bertrand, and Bruno Solnik, "Multinationals Are Poor Tools for Diversification," in *Security Selection and Active Portfolio Management,* New York: Institutional Investor, 1978.

Jensen, Michael, "Can the Corporation Survive?" *Financial Analysts Journal,* January/February 1978.

Lee, Wayne Y., and Robert Nachtmann, "The Informational Content of Value Line Rankings: An Empirical Anomaly," Working Paper, Indiana University School of Business, October 1981.

Leuthold, Steven C., "Stop the Bleeding! Flaws in the CPI . . . ," *Pensions & Investment Age,* April 27, 1980.

Lloyd, William P., and Richard L. Haney, Jr., "Time Diversification: Surest Route to Lower Risk," *Journal of Portfolio Management,* Spring 1980.

Lorie, James H., and Mary T. Hamilton, *The Stock Market: Theories and Evidence,* Homewood, Ill.: Richard D. Irwin, 1973.

Malkiel, Burton G., "Risk and Return: A New Look," Working Paper No. 700, National Bureau of Economic Research, 1981.

Marcus, Bruce W., "The Prudent Man," *Pensions & Investments,* 1978.

Markowitz, Harry, "Portfolio Selection," *Journal of Finance,* March 1952.

McClay, Marvin, "The Penalties of Incurring Unsystematic Risk," *Journal of Portfolio Management,* Spring 1978.

Miller, Merton H., and Myron S. Scholes, "Dividends and Taxes," *Journal of Financial Economics,* December 1978.

Molodovsky, Nicholas, "The Business Corporation," in *Investment Values in a Dynamic World,* Homewood, Ill.: Richard D. Irwin, 1974.

Norby, William C., "Accounting for Financial Analysis: Inflation Accounting Revisited," *Financial Analysts Journal,* November/December 1981.

Price, Lee N., "Choosing Between Growth and Yield," *Financial Analysts Journal,* July/August 1979.

Reilly, Frank K., *Investments,* Hindsdale, Ill.: Dryden Press, 1982.

Reinganum, M. R., "Abnormal Returns in Small Firm Portfolios," *Financial Analysts Journal,* March/April 1981.

Roll, Richard, "Ambiguity When Performance Is Measured by the Securities Market Line," *Journal of Finance,* September 1978.

Rosenberg, Barr, "Extra-Market Components of Covariance in Security Markets," *Journal of Financial and Quantitative Analysis,* March 1974.

———, "How Active Should Your Portfolio Be?" *Financial Analysts Journal,* January/February 1979.

Sanghvi, Arun P., and Gordon H. Dash, "Core Securities: Widening the Decision Dimensions," in *Security Selection and Active Portfolio Management,* New York: Institutional Investor, 1978.

Securities and Exchange Commission, "Securities Exchange Act of 1934" (amended January 1, 1975), Section 28(e).

———, SEC Release No. 12251, March 24, 1976.

Sharpe, William F., "A Simplified Model for Portfolio Analysis," *Management Science,* January 1963.

———, "Likely Gains from Market Timing," *Financial Analysts Journal,* March/April 1975.

———, *Investments,* 2nd Ed. Englewood Cliffs, N.J.: Prentice-Hall, 1981.

Slivka, Ronald T., "Risk and Return for Option Investment Strategies," *Financial Analysts Journal,* September/October 1980.

Treynor, J. L., and Fischer Black, "How to Use Security Analysis to Improve Portfolio Selection," *Journal of Business,* January 1973.

Vandell, Robert F., Diana Harrington, and William Fisher, "Risk/Return Tradeoff in Pension Portfolio Policies: A Historic Perspective," Working Paper, Darden School, University of Virginia, 1977.

———, **and Marcia L. Pontius,** "The Impact of Tax Status on Stock Selection," *Journal of Portfolio Management,* Summer 1981.

Williams, Dave H., "Organizing for Superior Investment Returns," *Financial Analysts Journal,* September/October 1980.

Wright, John W., "MPT Is Imperfectly Applied," *Pensions & Investment Age,* October 12, 1981.

APPENDIX

How to Build a Completeness Fund

We show here a simple example of how to construct a completeness fund. The construction process is done on a stock-by-stock basis.

Shown in Table 10A-1 is the common stock of XYZ Corporation whose weight in the market index being used as the bogey or reference point is 6 percent. Assume there are three active equity managers with assets under management of $200 million, $50 million, and $150 million, respectively. In this example $100 million is assumed to have been allocated to the completeness fund (CF); another $400 million is assumed to be actively managed for a total equity portfolio of $500 million.

Manager 1 has a bogey weight of 7 percent in XYZ stock. This particular bogey weighting arises out of a careful study of Manager 1's universe of stocks and a negotiated determination between the corporate pension plan sponsor and Manager 1 of the appropriate bogey weight. A 7 percent bogey weight times the $200 million under management would place a $14 million investment in XYZ stock in the bogey portfolio for Manager 1. Since Manager 1's actual portfolio holds $16 million (8%) in XYZ stock, his holdings represent a $14 million passive position and $2 million active position in XYZ.

Manager 2's negotiated bogey weight is only 4 percent, in comparison to the 7 percent of Manager 1. Manager 2 also likes the stock and has allocated 10 percent ($5 million of $50 million) to XYZ. Manager 2, therefore, holds a $3 million active position in the stock in addition to a passive position of $2 million.

Manager 3 does not follow XYZ and, therefore, holds no opinion on it nor position in it. Manager 3's $150 million will be invested in other areas of the market.

Note that of the three managers, two follow XYZ and both hold overweighted positions in it. Yet in the aggregate actively managed portfolio of $400 million, only 5.25 percent or $21 million is invested in XYZ stock. Against a market weight of 6 percent, the 5.25 percent holding would represent an underweight, indicative of inferior investment potential even though the experts (the investment managers that follow the stock) are in total agreement that XYZ is an undervalued stock.

What's the problem? It is the composition of the aggregate actively managed bogey portfolio. In this case the aggregate bogey holds only 4 percent, or $16 million, in XYZ shares. If we want the aggregate bogey to have a market weight position of 6 percent, then we need $14 million more of XYZ in the completeness fund to reach an overall 6 percent position on the total of $500 million.

TABLE 10A-1. Completeness Fund Construction, Stock: XYZ; Market Weight: 6%

Manager	Portfolio Value ($MM)	Bogey Weight (%)	Bogey Value ($MM)	Actual Portfolio ($MM)	Active Position ($MM)
1	$200	7%	$14	$16	$2
2	50	4	2	5	3
3	150	—	—	—	—
Active	$400	4%	$16	$21	$5
CF	100	n.a.	14	14	—
Total	$500	6%	$30	$35	$5

The completeness fund, therefore, would buy $14 million of XYZ in its actual portfolio. The $14 million in the completeness fund plus the $21 million in the active manager accounts gives a total of $35 million in XYZ, which is a 7 percent overall weight representing a $5 million active position.

Looked at in this way, the completeness fund concept can be thought of as a *distributed core* concept. The core portfolio is a $30 million position in XYZ, distributed $14 million to Manager 1, $2 million to Manager 2, and $14 million retained in the passive completeness fund.

It should be noted that if allocations of the completeness fund are required in other parts of the actively managed equity portfolio in amounts similar to the amount required in this example, it is entirely possible that additional dollar amounts will be required for the fund.

CHAPTER 11

Portfolio Construction: Real Estate

Jeffrey D. Fisher*

Income-producing real estate is an asset that has received much attention in recent years as a complement to corporate equities and fixed income securities in individual and institutional portfolios. Because real estate has different investment characteristics than other assets, its performance in different economic environments tends to differ from that of other assets. For this reason alone, the attention has been warranted.

The purpose of this chapter is to explore real estate as an investment vehicle, with particular emphasis on its benefits in a portfolio. We will first discuss how real estate differs from other assets and examine the advantages and disadvantages of real estate as an investment. Second, the real estate investment universe will be identified in terms of the ways in which various real estate investments are made and in terms of the types of real estate investors who make them. Third, we will differentiate between evaluating real estate investment from the point of view of a particular individual or institution and determining the market value of a real estate investment. Fourth, the role of real estate in a portfolio will be explored in considerable detail.

This chapter represents the C.F.A. Institute's initial effort to broaden the body of knowledge for the Candidate Program to include real estate investment. Thus, this chapter has been elongated to provide the reader with a comprehensive range of information on this subject.

* George H. Lentz, research associate with the Foundation for Economic and Business Studies and doctoral candidate in the Indiana University Graduate School of Business, contributed significantly to the development and writing of this chapter.

REAL ESTATE AS AN INVESTMENT VEHICLE

Distinctive Qualities of Real Estate

There are several attributes of real estate that distinguish it from other assets. For example, real estate is fixed in location; thus, each parcel of real estate is essentially unique. Although different parcels of real estate may be substitutes for a particular use, no two parcels are perfectly alike. Each property has a different view, topography, and access. The spatial characteristic of real estate results in an interdependency between different properties. Most importantly, the value of one property depends on how adjacent and nearby properties are used. This makes what economists call the problem of externalities significant in the field of real estate. It also leads to a high degree of governmental regulation, such as zoning. The value of a property is also dependent on local and regional economic conditions. For example, an office building in an area of excess supply of office space cannot be moved to an area where there is excess demand.

Another important characteristic of real estate is that it is a durable good with a relatively long economic life. Once a building is constructed on a particular site, it will normally be there for many years. Thus, a builder or developer must attempt to determine not only what the best use of a site is today but also what the best use will be in the relatively distant future.

In addition to being relatively durable, real estate investments typically involve large economic units, often with a substantial amount of funds involved. Moreover, the units are not easily divisible.

The real estate market tends to be less efficient than the market for securities. First, for many properties, such as a large downtown office building, only a few buyers may be in the market. Because the market for real estate properties is not as active as that for many other investments, it is more difficult to establish a market price for such investments. Second, real estate is not traded in any kind of national market. Therefore, information on prices is more elusive. Because of these two factors, it typically takes much longer to sell a real estate investment than a security.

Return on investment from the use and ownership of real estate is dependent on the types of property rights that surround a particular transaction. A given parcel of real estate may involve many types of legal estates, each with its own set of rights, such as the rights of the lessee and lessor and the rights of the mortgagee and mortgagor. The ownership of a building may be different from that of the land under the building. For example, the owner of a building may lease the land on which the building is situated. In addition, usage of real estate can be restricted by zoning, building codes, deed restrictions, easements, and other types of regulatory and legal restrictions. Thus, the value of a property also depends on the nature of the legal factors surrounding ownership.

Another consideration in real estate ownership is the need to actively manage the property, either directly or through some type of property management arrangement. While ownership and management can be separated, there is usually more of a necessity to be aware of how well the property is being managed than is the case with many other types of investment. Institutional investors often look for a local partner when making a direct real estate equity investment in order to obtain management expertise familiar with the local market.

Due, in part, to the difficulty of obtaining information about real estate and the complicated legal factors often involved in real estate ownership, transactions costs for real estate tend to be higher than for many other types of assets.

Why Invest in Real Estate?

We have introduced some of the ways in which real estate differs from other assets, particularly financial assets. The obvious question is: Why invest in real estate? Several reasons can be identified. First, there is evidence that real estate is a good hedge against inflation. That is, real estate has performed better than most other investments in an inflationary environment.

Second, there is evidence that returns for real estate are not highly correlated with returns on corporate equities and bonds. In part, this may be due to differences in the way these assets respond to inflation. But there may also be other systematic factors that affect real estate returns differently from other assets. Thus, the inclusion of real estate in a portfolio may result in more efficient portfolios in the sense discussed in Chapter 10. In other words, the inclusion of real estate may improve the diversification of a portfolio and enhance its risk-return characteristics.

A third reason for investment in real estate stems from the tax benefits available to taxable investors relative to many other investments. The cost (less land) of real estate can be depreciated for tax purposes at a rate that generally far exceeds any actual decline in value of the property. In fact, the actual value of the property may increase, not decrease, over time. This "tax depreciation" usually leads both to deferral of taxes and conversion of income to a more favorable capital gains treatment. Furthermore, depreciation coupled with use of debt financing can lead to tax losses that can be used to shelter other income. Other tax benefits from real estate equity investment come in the form of tax credits and deductions. These tax benefits can obviously be used only by investors or institutions that are taxable. As discussed later, it is reasonable to assume that the price of real estate includes the value of the tax benefits, with the result that a real estate investment tends to have a lower before-tax return than would be expected for an otherwise equivalent (especially in terms of risk) taxable investment. Real estate investors should therefore be aware of the extent to which they are paying for tax benefits they may or may not be able to use.

THE REAL ESTATE INVESTMENT UNIVERSE

There are many ways in which investors can make real estate investments. They vary from direct equity ownership to indirect participation in real estate cash flows through security-type investments. The eight principal ways of investing in real estate are: (1) purchase properties outright, either individually or in conjunction with other investors through partnership and joint venture arrangements, (2) acquire a leasehold interest, (3) purchase interests in public limited partnerships, (4) purchase shares in real estate investment trusts (REITs), (5) participate in commingled real estate funds, (6) make a mortgage loan on a property, (7) purchase a mortgage, (8) purchase mortgage-backed securities.

This section begins with a brief overview of the real property opportunity set. Then the major institutional and individual investors involved in real estate are identified. Next, the different forms of real estate investment are examined, first discussing debt instruments, then hybrid debt-equity instruments and financing arrangements, and finally several forms of equity investment in real estate. Different vehicles for real estate investment are also examined, with emphasis given to ownership through the single proprietorship business form, partnerships (especially limited partnerships), commingled real estate funds, REITs, syndications, and the limited partnerships that typically involve institutional investors and real estate developers.

Types of Investment Property

Of the many types of property available for purchase, the major types sought by investors in recent years have been office buildings (especially in prime downtown and suburban locations), industrial buildings, shopping centers, apartment buildings, hotels, motels, and some types of specialty real estate such as restaurants. Institutional investors, who have now emerged as a dominant force on the real estate investment scene, have been primarily interested in office buildings, light industrial-type buildings, shopping centers, and some well-situated hotels. They have tended to shy away from apartments, specialty real estate, motels, and most hotels because of actual and potential regulatory controls, management-intensive characteristics, and higher business risk. Moreover, institutional investors have focused on the larger properties, leaving smaller properties, such as professional office buildings, strip shopping centers, and low-rise apartments to individual and smaller institutional investors. Table 11-1 shows the distribution by property type of the real property investments held in the 14 tax-exempt institutional (pension fund) portfolios that constitute the data base for the Frank Russell Company Property Index.

The property types most favored by institutional investors have shifted with changes in the economy and with demand/supply characteristics. For example, throughout much of the 1970s, shopping centers, especially large

TABLE 11-1. **Property Distribution by Type of Real Estate Properties in the Frank Russell Company Data Base, as of December 31, 1981 (all dollars in millions)**

	Market Value of Total Index	Market Value of Properties (%)	Number of Properties	Number of Properties (%)
Apartments	$ 97.4	2.9%	10	1.6%
Commercial	695.0	20.6	111	17.4
Hotels	123.5	3.7	5	0.8
Industrials	1,036.9	30.7	369	57.7
Offices	1,421.2	42.1	144	22.5
Total	$3,374.0	100.0%	639	100.0%

SOURCE: Frank Russell Company [1981].

regional centers, were the most sought-after type of property. But as the rate of increase in retail sales started to fall behind the pace of inflation with the advent of recessionary pressures in 1979, this type of investment began to fall out of favor. Shopping centers were then replaced by office buildings as the most favored property. In mid-1982, however, it was evident that office space had been overbuilt in many metropolitan markets. In short, income-producing property prices and returns tend to be highly cyclical, both nationally and regionally, pointing to the importance of timing in the purchase and sale of real estate.

Some real estate advisors are cautiously saying that apartments will become the darling of investors in the early to mid-1980s, since apartment vacancies reached an all-time low in 1982 in many markets. However, the possibility of regulatory controls, particularly rent control, is considered to be a deterrent to many would-be investors. Yet, the opportunities are present because, in the eyes of some experts, the shortage of rental apartments in some market areas has begun to outweigh the threat of rent control.

An important point to remember is that property types tend to go through periods of vogue or fashion, with investors tending to move *en masse* from one property type to another. At one time shopping centers may be in vogue, at another time office buildings, at still another industrial buildings—all depending on the environmental conditions and the supply and demand characteristics of the marketplace. A factor contributing to the fashionlike character of real estate investing is the herd psychology of institutional investors toward or away from certain asset categories for relatively long periods of time, as discussed in Chapter 6. This can be attributed, in part, to certain constraints and pressures relating to the fiduciary nature of institutional investors (discussed below). Thus, given the shifts that can occur in the real estate marketplace, it is not difficult to see the importance that investors must give to astute market analysis and appropriate diversification, especially in view of the long-term nature of real estate and the liquidity problems and costs associated with disposition of properties.

TYPES OF REAL ESTATE INVESTORS

In terms of types of real estate investors the universe can be divided into institutional and noninstitutional investors. The institutional category can be subdivided into taxable and nontaxable investors, with a view toward discussing the impact of taxes on investment behavior.

The major private sector institutional real estate investors are thrift institutions (principally savings and loan associations and mutual savings banks), commercial banks, insurance companies, and pension funds. The major noninstitutional investors are individuals and partnerships. Partnerships, along with REITs and other pooled funds, are really vehicles through which individuals and institutions can invest in real estate, and they will be treated as such in this chapter.

Institutional Real Estate Investors

Each type of institution has its own specific operating characteristics and liquidity needs, and each tends to have somewhat specialized investment policies. A general constraint on the investment behavior of institutions is that the type of revenue-earning assets acquired should be appropriately matched to the kind of liabilities the institution incurs and can expect to incur in the course of doing its business.

Moreover, all of the institutions listed above have to undertake investments within parameters established by certain standards of reasonable and responsible care, since they are all acting, at least to some degree, in a fiduciary capacity. That is, thrifts and banks have responsibilities for the safety and liquidity of the funds of their depositors, life insurance companies are responsible for fulfilling the contractual obligations that they have entered into with their policyholders, and pension funds are responsible for providing an adequate level of retirement benefits to their beneficiaries. Pursuant to their fiduciary trusts and responsibilities, all of these institutions must act in accordance with legal regulations that impose constraints on their investment behavior, as discussed earlier in Chapter 4. Banks, thrifts, and insurance companies must operate in accordance with federal and state laws and regulations. Private pension funds are required to operate in accordance with the rather strict rules set forth by the Employee Retirement Income Security Act (ERISA) and its associated regulations.

Thrifts and Commercial Banks. Thrifts and commercial banks are involved with real estate mainly as lending institutions. They do relatively little buying, selling, or developing of properties on their own, although these same institutions, through their trust departments, do administer real estate holdings for beneficiaries and commingled real estate funds for pension funds and other trust clients. Thrifts have traditionally invested in real estate principally by providing long-term mortgage loans to purchasers of residential real estate. Their largest share of mortgage loans has been for single-family homes, although they have also been the largest source of mortgage loans for multifamily residential housing units. By contrast, commercial banks are the dominant source of interim financing for real estate developers and investors. Some long-term mortgage financing is provided by mortgage banking subsidiaries of the bank holding companies.

Thus, the major real estate investments of thrifts and commercial banks are the loans they originate to purchasers, developers, and improvers of real property. For these financial institutions the real estate loans they originate and hold have been part of their total asset portfolio.

Life Insurance Companies. Traditionally, life insurance companies have been major investors in real estate and one of the most important sources of long-term real estate mortgage credit, especially for commercial properties. Since the late 1960s, in order to provide a hedge against inflation, life insurance companies have increasingly insisted on equity participation features as a condition for making mortgages. During the past few years they have become more aggressive in seeking direct equity positions in real estate and have developed a growing stake in direct ownership of properties. A major reason for this trend toward equity investment, with its potential for price appreciation, has undoubtedly been that the yields from long-term fixed rate bonds and mortgages could not be adjusted to keep up with inflation. Furthermore, as effective marginal tax rates for life insurance companies have increased (as discussed in Chapter 4), the favorable tax treatment of real estate has been an added motivation for its inclusion as a general account investment. It should be noted that insurance company accounting practices require equity real estate to be valued at depreciated cost; thus, it does not add to equity surplus until such time as the property is liquidated and a capital gain is realized.

Like other financial institutions, the investment objectives of life insurance companies are determined by the type of liabilities they incur in the general course of carrying on their business. The traditional actuarial liabilities of life insurance companies have been long-term and highly predictable, with the result that they have had little need for liquid assets. These characteristics of life insurance companies made them well-suited for real estate investing.

But events associated with the relatively high inflation and high market interest rates of the late 1970s and early 1980s have altered and, in effect, shortened the liability structure of life insurance companies (see Chapter 4 for a more detailed discussion). Also, life insurance companies have experienced increasing pressure to provide a more competitive rate of return to policyholders. This has led them to undertake more risky investments in an effort to achieve higher returns. The apparent willingness of life insurance companies to sacrifice some safety of principal in pursuit of higher overall returns can be seen in their shift from being involved in the real estate field primarily as lenders, concentrating on relatively safe long-term mortgage lending, to undertaking more risky lending activities, such as shared equity lending and construction lending, and to investing in equity real estate directly. The latter includes taking an increasingly active role in real estate development, often in joint ventures with proven real estate developers.

While there has been a willingness to sacrifice some safety of principal by more aggressively seeking higher returns, there is still great reluctance to significantly increase risk because of the high fiduciary standards placed on life insurance companies by public opinion and public policy. Thus, these companies have placed a great deal of emphasis on diversification in order to minimize the risks associated with their strategy of more aggressively pursuing higher returns. Moreover, to decrease risk as well as to increase potential return, life insurance companies have concentrated their interest in properties considered to be high quality investment-grade properties in prime locations.

Life insurance companies invest in real estate both for their own general account and for the separate accounts they administer for pension funds. The principal vehicle used by life insurance companies to invest the monies from the pension funds they manage is through separate accounts in real estate—the so-called *commingled real estate fund* (CREF) that will be discussed later in the chapter. The commingled real estate funds are only a small portion, less than 5 percent, of the total pension fund monies managed by life insurance companies, but they experienced rapid growth in the late 1970s and early 1980s.

Pension Funds

In recent years, because of their large and rapidly expanding pool of assets, pension funds have become recognized by the real estate industry as a potentially major force in real estate finance. But a pension fund represents a very different type of investor from that which has typically invested in real estate. Indeed, until the early 1980s the world of real estate seemed very different and even alien to pension fund sponsors, managers, and consultants. However, given the potentially large returns from real estate investments during periods of high price inflation, and the potentially beneficial portfolio diversification benefits, pension funds have increased their real estate investment activity. Innovative investment arrangements, vehicles, and instruments are being developed as the real estate industry attempts to fashion investments suitable to the needs and characteristics of pension funds.

Factors Inhibiting Real Estate Investments by Pension Funds. In the past, pension funds have shied away from investing in mortgages because of the costs and administrative burdens involved with originating and servicing them. Mortgages, in short, were seen as being too complicated relative to bonds, and had the added problem of illiquidity. As we will see, however, recent innovations in the mortgage market have made mortgage investments more attractive to pension funds.

In addition, there are a number of reasons why pension funds have been reluctant to become involved in real estate as equity investors. First, and perhaps most important, real estate investments have traditionally been structured to make maximum use of leverage and to provide sizable tax shelter benefits to taxpaying investors, with the amount of tax shelter benefits being directly proportional to the tax bracket of the investor. Since pension funds are tax-exempt and cannot take advantage of tax shelter benefits, real estate in the 1970s appeared overpriced to them because the price reflected the capitalized tax benefits that would accrue to taxable entities. That is, pension funds expected to be outbid by taxable investors who could use real estate tax benefits to increase their after-tax return. Moreover, pension funds have generally bought properties on an all-cash basis; thus, they have not been able to enjoy the return-magnifying effects of positive leverage (for reasons that will be explained later).

Second, real estate was perceived as a high risk investment area, ill-suited to the trustee-fiduciary character of pension funds. In other words, real estate was seen as an arena for entrepreneurs, where little regulation existed and where the principal approaches to investment seemed very different from those found in the traditional trustee-fiduciary setting in which pension fund managers were accustomed to operating.

Third, the demands involved in managing real properties have discouraged real estate investments by pension fund managers, who tend to be passive investors.

Fourth, and related to all of the above, the managers of and advisors to pension funds were trained in security (equities and fixed income) analysis and had little expertise in the intricacies of real estate investment, which appeared to be not only more risky but also more complex than the world of securities investing.

Finally, there are what can be called analytic reasons. The real estate market has been characterized by a lack of information of the type needed to perform adequate investment analysis. In other words, there has not been sufficient information from which to compile quantitative data that could be used to analyze and measure the expected return and risk of the various types of real estate assets in various market areas. Moreover, the characteristics of the real estate market were considered by many pension fund managers and advisors to be such that the gathering of reliable performance data over frequent time intervals was very difficult, at best. Without such data, quantitative tools developed to make optimal as well as prudent capital allocation decisions could not be used effectively, nor could performance be adequately measured.[1]

---

[1] It is worth noting that the prudence rules and guidelines established by ERISA, the Labor Department regulations, and the conventions of the pension fund investment management community do not require the use of currently accepted investment analysis and measurement technology. Nonetheless, pension fund managers and advisors who can justify their investment decisions by means of such technology are in a better position to guard against charges of being imprudent.

It is important to note that there are several reasons why pension funds have tended to avoid leveraged investments: First, they had plenty of cash; second, being very conservative and risk-averse investors, they feared the impact of negative leverage on portfolio performance; and third, until late 1980 they were subject to an unrelated business income tax on the income generated by leveraged investments (properties purchased using debt) under Section 514 of the Internal Revenue Code. With the 1980 tax law change, however, a disincentive for pension fund investors to use leverage in real estate purchases has been removed.

The Match Between Real Estate and Pension Funds. In the opinion of one real estate investment consultant, pension funds may well be the most matched pool of assets that has ever existed for the real estate industry (see "Consultant Says Pension Funds Are Still Misunderstood" [1982]). While this may be a stronger statement than is warranted, a few generalizations can be made about the characteristics that make pension funds well-matched to make real estate investments.

Many pension funds are cash rich, which puts them in a favored position to purchase real estate and to provide capital to developers of real estate projects during periods of high interest rates. This offsets, at least to some extent, the disadvantages they may face in competing against taxable entities. In fact, by selling the tax benefits to a taxable partner, pension funds can increase their return from real estate investments. In addition, except for mature funds with advanced-age characteristics, pension funds normally do not need a great deal of liquidity; their liabilities are generally long-term and actuarially highly predictable. In this respect pension funds resemble life insurance companies. They are also, of all the institutional investors discussed, probably the least subject to disintermediation. That is, during periods of high interest rates, pension fund contributions have continued to grow at the same time that people have tended to withdraw savings from thrifts and banks and to increase borrowings against their life insurance policies.

Objectives of Pension Fund Real Estate Investments. Since pension funds cannot take advantage of the ample tax benefits available from real estate, what are they looking for from real estate investments?

Essentially, pension funds are seeking real estate investments that would improve the risk-return profile of their overall investment portfolio and that would provide a fairly high, yet consistent, rate of return over a variety of economic scenarios. As the rate of inflation significantly increased during the 1970s, pension funds began looking to real estate as an inflation-hedged asset that would help their portfolio returns keep pace with the effect of inflation on their liabilities (i.e., from retirement benefit increases). In addition to the diversification benefits, there is some evidence that real estate returns have been less volatile than the returns from stocks (although these findings have been questioned on the basis of suspect underlying data). This evidence has led some to assume that adding real estate investments provides the opportunity to improve the stability of returns from the portfolio.

In other words, whereas common stock prices, and more recently bond prices, have experienced wide swings over fairly short time intervals, real estate prices (except perhaps residential real estate) have been considered to be fairly stable. How well real estate has performed with respect to the criteria of risk reduction, investment return increases, and moderation of returns volatility is discussed later in this chapter.

Extent of Current Real Estate Investment by Pension Funds. A survey of corporate pension fund sponsors by Ellis [1981] reported that 22 percent of the 1,800 largest plans now have real estate equity ownership investments, either directly or through commingled funds. Almost two-thirds of the responding corporate sponsors already investing in real estate as equity owners in 1981 indicated that they planned to increase their real estate equity investments, and 28 percent of plan sponsors not then investing in real estate indicated they would start to invest within the two years following. How accurately this survey of intentions is reflected in actual behavior depends, of course, on subsequent economic conditions. In mid-1982, one year after this survey was completed, there were signs that pension fund involvement in *new* equity real estate investments was decreasing, at least temporarily, in response to a cooling of inflation and a leveling off of or decline in real estate prices.

Even though the results of the Ellis survey found a great *breadth* of demand, this same survey also found that the *depth* of demand is still quite shallow, indicating that pension funds have been very cautious about increasing their real estate exposure. The survey estimated that only 1.6 percent of pension fund assets were invested in real estate in 1981.

However, a survey of the senior investment officers of the 1,200 largest corporate and government pension plans on their future intentions with respect to real estate investments completed in June 1981 by Money Market Directories, Inc. [1982] provided a breakdown of projected pension fund investment assets in 1995, as shown in Table 11-2 on page 448. Note that 12 percent of portfolio assets are intended to be invested in equity real estate, either directly or through commingled real estate funds. Another 5 percent of assets are invested in mortgages, giving a total of 17 percent of pension fund assets targeted for investment in real estate equity and debt. These figures are in line with other estimates that place the target for real estate equity investments as a percentage of pension fund portfolios at 5 to 15 percent (see "Consultant Says Pension Funds Are Still Misunderstood" [1982] and Hertzberg [1982].)

TYPES OF REAL ESTATE INVESTMENTS

As indicated earlier, there are many vehicles for investing in real estate. Some involve an ownership or equity interest in the property, others involve being a creditor. In some cases, the two are combined via a potential participation in the income or increase in the value of the property. In other words,

TABLE 11-2. Projected Composition of Pension Fund Assets in 1995

$ in Billions	Percent	
$1,225	49%	stocks
575	23	fixed income securities
150	6	international investments
150	6	real estate equities (direct)
150	6	real estate commingled funds
125	5	mortgages
50	2	venture capital investments
25	1	collectables and precious metals
50	2	other
$2,500	100%	

SOURCE: Money Market Directories, Inc. [1982].

real estate investments can be divided into two principal types: debt and equity.

Both debt and equity investments can be classified as either direct or indirect. With direct investments, the investor obtains all or part of the real estate asset. When making a direct investment, the investor may either actively manage the asset or delegate this responsibility to others for a fee and take a passive role. With indirect investments, the investor invests in real estate assets via the medium of an intermediary of some type. In the case of equity investments, such intermediaries would include, for example, equity REITs, commingled real estate funds, public limited partnerships, and syndicates. In the case of debt investments, indirect investments would include, for example, investing in mortgage REITs and mortgage-backed securities.

Mortgages

One way of investing in real estate is to provide debt capital in return for a claim on a portion of the income stream from the financed property or from the income of the owner of the property. Such a claim is normally secured by a lien on the same property. This lien is established by a debt instrument known as a mortgage. If the borrower (mortgagor) defaults on the payment of the debt, the lender (mortgagee) can have the property sold and the proceeds from the sale applied toward payment of the unpaid mortgage balance.

An Overview of the Mortgage Market. The mortgage market has normally been the largest user of credit in the United States. At the end of calendar year 1981, the outstanding mortgage debt on all types of property in the United States stood at $1.545 trillion, compared to $1.035 trillion for the outstanding debt of the federal government, the second largest user of credit in the Unites States. In the 11-year period 1971–81, as shown in Table 11-3 (page 450), funds raised via mortgages exceeded funds raised by any other instrument in all but three years. These three years were years of recession and therefore depressed real estate markets and mortgage activity, and they were also years of large federal government deficits resulting in greatly increased government borrowing activity.

Primary Mortgage Market. As in all credit markets, the mortgage market is divided into a primary market and a secondary market. The primary mortgage market, where mortgage loans are originated, is made up of mortgagors and the mortgage lenders who originate mortgage loans. The principal lending institutions that make up the lending side of this market tend to specialize in the kinds of mortgage loans they make. For example, the major long-term lenders in the residential sector are the thrifts, whereas the major long-term lenders in the nonresidential sector are the life insurance companies (both for their own general accounts and the separate accounts they maintain for pension fund clients). This specialization can be seen in the accompanying tables. Table 11-4 (page 451) provides a summary of primary mortgage originators for the private real estate market in 1980, and Table 11-5 (pages 452 and 453) summarizes the chief holders of the mortgage debt outstanding in the United States by property type during the period 1970–81.[2] Although not explicitly shown in the tables, the mortgage lending activity of commercial banks is concentrated in short-term construction loans.

Secondary Mortgage Market. The basic function of the secondary mortgage market is to provide a marketplace where mortgage originators can sell mortgages they do not want to hold in their portfolios. Unlike the secondary market for corporate securities where the principal participants are from the private sector securities industry, the principal participants in the secondary *residential* mortgage market are agencies of the federal government or federally sponsored corporations. Indeed, the role of these federal and federally sponsored institutions in the secondary residential mortgage market is so significant that this market, to a large extent, has become identified with them. On the other hand, the secondary market for *nonresidential* commercial mortgages is not an organized market, but rather involves direct transactions between the parties involved, usually on a one-on-one private placement basis.

Competitive pressures within the capital markets for investment funds, along with new financing programs the federal government developed in the late 1960s and early 1970s to aid the housing market, have been important factors in bringing about innovations in the secondary residential mortgage

---

[2] Note that while there is a fairly close association between the originators of mortgages and the holders of mortgages, such association is not necessary. For example, the mortgage companies (mortgage bankers and brokers) originated over 23 percent of mortgages on one- and four-family homes in 1980, but their share of mortgage holdings is insignificant.

TABLE 11-3. Funds Raised in U.S. Credit Markets, by Debt Instrument (billions of dollars)

Type of Instrument	1971	1972	1973	1974	1975	1976	1977	1978	1979	1980	1981
Mortgages	$52.5	$76.8	$79.9	$60.0	$59.0	$87.2	$132.3	$148.3	$155.9	$121.1	$96.5
U.S. government securities	30.7	23.7	28.3	34.5	98.0	84.6	79.9	90.5	85.7	122.3	130.6
State and local obligations	17.5	15.4	16.3	19.6	17.3	15.7	21.9	26.1	21.8	26.9	25.3
Corporate and foreign bonds	23.5	18.4	13.6	23.9	36.3	41.2	36.1	31.8	32.8	38.4	29.4
Consumer credit	11.6	18.6	21.7	9.8	8.5	25.4	40.2	47.6	46.3	2.3	26.4
Bank loans, not elsewhere classified	12.1	27.8	51.6	38.4	−14.4	6.2	29.5	59.0	51.0	48.4	62.1
Open market paper and repos	.9	4.1	15.2	17.8	.5	8.1	15.0	26.4	40.5	21.4	52.9
Other loans	4.2	8.0	18.5	22.5	8.7	17.8	27.4	41.5	41.9	36.7	54.8
Total	$153.1	$192.8	$245.2	$227.0	$214.0	$286.4	$382.3	$471.3	$475.8	$417.5	$478.0

Source: Board of Governors of the Federal Reserve System [1977, 1982].

TABLE 11-4. Total Mortgage Originations by Six Institutions in 1980

	Total	Mortgage Companies	Savings & Loans	Commercial Banks	Mutual Savings Banks	Life Insurance Companies	Federal Credit Agencies
Residential (dollars in millions)							
1–4 Unit residential	$130,251	$30,864	$61,095	$26,768	$5,435	$ 1,711	$4,378
FHA	14,308	11,823	1,265	899	136	185	0
VA	12,260	9,847	1,511	702	89	111	9
Conventional	103,683	9,194	58,319	25,167	5,210	1,415	4,378
Multiunit	11,748	2,468	3,100	1,278	543	1,427	2,932
FHA	3,536	1,278	108	72	96	1	1,981
Conventional	8,212	1,190	2,992	1,207	446	1,426	951
Total residential	141,999	33,332	64,195	28,046	5,978	3,138	7,310
Nonresidential	34,248	4,799	4,183	12,470	1,013	11,059	724
Total	$176,247	$38,131	$68,378	$40,516	$6,991	$14,197	$8,034
Residential (percentages)							
1–4 Unit residential	100.0%	23.7%	46.9%	20.5%	4.2%	1.3%	3.4%
FHA	100.0	82.6	8.8	6.3	1.0	1.3	0.0
VA	100.0	80.3	12.3	5.8	0.7	0.9	0.0
Conventional	100.0	8.0	56.2	24.3	5.0	1.4	4.2
Multiunit	100.0	21.0	26.4	10.9	4.6	12.1	25.0
FHA	100.0	36.1	3.1	2.0	2.7	—	56.0
Conventional	100.0	14.5	36.4	14.7	5.4	17.4	11.6
Total residential	100.0	23.5	45.2	19.8	4.2	2.2	5.1
Nonresidential	100.0	14.0	12.2	36.4	3.0	32.3	2.1
Total	100.0%	21.6%	38.8%	23.0%	4.0%	8.0%	4.6%

SOURCE: Mortgage Bankers Association of America [1981].

TABLE 11-5. Mortgage Loans Outstanding, by Type of Holder and Property Type (billions of dollars)

Year-End	S&Ls	Commercial Banks	Mutual Savings Banks	Life Insurance Companies	Federal & Federally Related Agencies[a]	Mortgage Pools and Trusts[b]	All Others[c]	Total, All Holders[d]
A. Total Mortgage Loans Outstanding, by Type of Holder								
1970	$150.33	$73.28	$57.95	$74.38	$33.58	$4.75	$79.92	$474.19
	(31.7%)	(15.4%)	(12.2%)	(15.7%)	(7.1%)	(1.0%)	(16.8%)	(100.0%)
1973	231.73	119.07	73.23	81.37	46.72	18.04	112.16	682.32
	(34.0)	(17.5)	(10.7)	(11.9)	(6.8)	(2.6)	(16.4)	(100.0)
1975	278.59	136.19	77.25	89.17	66.89	34.14	119.31	801.54
	(34.08)	(17.0)	(9.6)	(11.1)	(8.3)	(4.3)	(14.9)	(100.0)
1978	432.81	214.04	95.16	106.17	81.74	88.63	150.86	1,169.41
	(37.0)	(18.3)	(8.1)	(9.1)	(7.0)	(7.6)	(12.9)	(100.0)
1980	503.19	263.03	99.86	131.08	114.30	142.26	192.24	1,445.97
	(34.8)	(18.2)	(6.9)	(9.1)	(7.9)	(9.8)	(13.3)	(100.0)
1981	518.35	286.63	100.02	139.05	126.11	162.27	212.36	1,544.78
	(33.6)	(18.5)	(6.5)	(9.0)	(8.2)	(10.5)	(13.7)	(100.0)
B. Mortgage Loans Outstanding on One-to-Four-Family Homes, by Type of Holder								
1970	$124.97	$42.33	$42.15	$26.74	$21.77	$2.53	$37.64	$298.10
	(41.9%)	(14.2%)	(14.1%)	(9.0%)	(7.3%)	(1.0%)	(12.6%)	(100.0%)
1973	187.08	68.00	48.81	20.43	27.14	13.64	51.11	416.21
	(45.0)	(16.3)	(11.7)	(4.9)	(6.5)	(3.3)	(12.3)	(100.0)
1975	223.90	77.02	50.02	17.59	37.88	28.08	56.27	490.76
	(45.6)	(15.7)	(10.2)	(3.6)	(7.7)	(5.7)	(11.5)	(100.0)
1978	356.11	129.17	62.25	14.44	43.75	75.79	83.71	765.21
	(46.5)	(16.9)	(8.1)	(1.9)	(5.7)	(9.9)	(10.9)	(100.0)
1980	419.76	160.33	67.49	17.94	61.42	121.76	112.64	961.54
	(43.6)	(16.7)	(7.0)	(1.9)	(6.4)	(12.7)	(11.7)	(100.0)
1981	432.98	172.55	68.20	17.38	66.69	137.27	126.07	1,021.14
	(42.4)	(16.9)	(6.7)	(1.7)	(6.5)	(13.4)	(12.3)	(100.0)

C. Mortgage Loans Outstanding on Multifamily Residential, by Type of Holder[e]

Year								Total
1970	$ 13.83 (23.0%)	$ 3.31 (5.5%)	$ 7.79 (13.0%)	$ 15.97 (26.6%)	$ 3.41 (5.7%)	$ .06 (.1%)	$ 15.74 (26.2%)	$ 60.11 (100.0%)
1973	22.78 (24.5)	6.93 (7.4)	12.34 (13.3)	18.45 (19.8)	8.03 (8.6)	.62 (.7)	23.98 (25.7)	93.13 (100.0)
1975	25.55 (25.4)	5.91 (5.9)	13.79 (13.7)	19.63 (19.5)	12.32 (12.2)	1.26 (1.3)	22.14 (22.0)	100.60 (100.0)
1978	36.05 (29.8)	10.27 (8.5)	16.53 (13.6)	19.00 (15.7)	12.97 (10.7)	4.97 (4.1)	21.34 (17.6)	121.14 (100.0)
1980	38.14 (27.8)	12.92 (9.4)	16.06 (11.7)	19.51 (14.2)	14.88 (10.9)	8.27 (6.0)	27.16 (19.8)	136.95 (100.0)
1981	37.68 (26.7)	14.90 (10.5)	15.96 (11.3)	19.49 (13.8)	14.92 (10.6)	10.16 (7.2)	28.15 (19.9)	141.27 (100.0)

D. Mortgage Loans Outstanding on Nonresidential Properties, by Type of Holder

Year								Total
1970	$ 11.53 (13.5%)	$ 23.28 (27.2%)	$ 7.89 (9.2%)	$ 26.02 (30.4%)	$ .42 (.5%)	$ .50 (.6%)	$ 15.97 (18.6%)	$ 85.63 (100.0%)
1973	21.88 (16.6)	38.70 (29.4)	12.01 (9.1)	36.50 (27.7)	.22 (.2)	1.12 (.8)	21.30 (16.2)	131.73 (100.0)
1975	29.14 (18.3)	46.88 (29.4)	13.37 (8.4)	45.20 (28.4)	.19 (.1)	1.95 (1.2)	22.57 (14.2)	159.30 (100.0)
1978	40.64 (19.2)	66.12 (31.2)	16.32 (7.7)	62.23 (29.4)	.10	3.56 (1.7)	22.88 (10.8)	211.85 (100.0)
1980	45.29 (17.7)	81.08 (31.7)	16.28 (6.4)	80.67 (31.6)	.41	5.27 (2.1)	26.66 (10.4)	255.66 (100.0)
1981	47.69 (17.0)	90.72 (32.3)	15.81 (5.6)	89.09 (31.8)	.51 (.2)	6.16 (2.2)	30.59 (10.9)	280.57 (100.0)

SOURCE: Board of Governors of the Federal Reserve System [1981, 1982].

Note: Figures in parentheses underneath dollar amounts are percentages of row totals

[a] Includes mortgage holdings of Farmers Home Administration (FmHA), Federal Housing Administration (FHA), Government National Mortgage Association (GNMA), Veterans Administration (VA), Federal Home Loan Mortgage Corporation (FHLMC), Federal National Mortgage Association (FNMA), and Federal Land Banks.

[b] Outstanding principal balances of mortgages backing securities insured or guaranteed by GNMA, FHLMC, and FmHA; privately sponsored mortgage pools are not included.

[c] Includes individuals, mortgage companies, real estate investment trusts, pension funds, credit unions, and miscellaneous government agencies not included in the federal and federally related agencies category.

[d] Rounding errors may cause dollar amounts and percentages not to sum exactly.

[e] Residential structures of five or more units.

market.[3] A more recent factor inducing further innovation in this secondary market was, of course, the need of the thrifts to obtain greater liquidity for the mortgages they held so they could more readily undertake the portfolio readjustments required to cope with the effects of inflationary pressures.

INNOVATIONS IN THE SECONDARY MARKET. The innovations in the secondary residential mortgage market were intended to accomplish two major objectives. The first was to create an organized and actively supported secondary market for residential mortgages that could effectively provide liquidity for holders of mortgages. The second was to design new secondary market instruments that would appeal to investors—primarily large institutional investors like pension funds—who previously had not been significantly involved in the residential mortgage market, thereby attracting new sources of capital. By the early 1980s, these objectives were largely being accomplished.

The primary thrust for the development of the secondary residential mortgage market has come from the federal government, in particular from the activities of federal agencies and federally sponsored corporations. The Government National Mortgage Association (GNMA or Ginnie Mae), a federal agency, and two quasi-private corporations, the Federal National Mortgage Association (FNMA or Fannie Mae) and the Federal Home Loan

---

[3] From the Great Depression of the 1930s until the late 1970s, mortgage loans for the purchase of real estate were characteristically made for a fixed rate of interest. Such mortgage loans typically were also amortized, which meant that each payment consisted of both principal repayment and interest. In the case of a fully amortized mortgage, which was the basic form of mortgage instrument for financing single-family housing during this period, the loan was completely repaid with the last scheduled payment. Also, most mortgage loans involved a long-term commitment of funds (typically 25–30 years), with construction loans being the principal exception. However, the traditional ways of mortgage financing have been significantly altered in recent years by forces affecting the capital markets generally and the mortgage market in particular.

Two major sources of pressure have triggered significant developments in the area of real estate finance in recent years. One source of pressure has been the sustained periods of high and uncertain inflation, coupled with increasing interest rate volatility, during the decade of the 1970s and into the early 1980s. The impact of this experience on the balance sheets and psychology of major mortgage lenders has led to a virtual revolution in the instruments and methods of real estate finance. There have been far-reaching innovations in the design of mortgage instruments and in the structure of financing arrangements. Long-standing relationships between institutional lenders and real estate developers have been fundamentally altered. The emphasis of these lenders in the early 1980s was on equity and potential equity participations rather than on receiving a regular, fixed income return from loaned funds. At the core of these developments was the recognition that the long-term fixed rate mortgage, the chief instrument of real estate finance for most of the post–World War II period, was ill-suited to serve as the basic instrument of real estate finance in a period of rising and highly uncertain and variable inflation and interest rates. Consequently, the long-term fixed rate has been increasingly supplanted, and in some segments of the commercial real estate market nearly replaced, by other types of mortgage instruments, lending arrangements, and joint ventures.

The other source of pressure during this period was increasing competition within the capital markets for investment funds. Within the real estate market, the residential sector had been the most adversely affected by this competition by 1982.

Mortgage Corporation (FHLMC or Freddie Mac), were given specific powers by Congress to support the secondary residential mortage market Additionally, the Farmers Home Administration (FmHA) has been given expanded powers in several areas of mortgage financing for farm and rural nonfarm real estate. These agencies, especially GNMA, have also been the primary force behind the creation and growth of mortgage-backed securities, although by 1982 active private sector involvement in the issuing and marketing of such securities had also developed. Mortgage-backed securities, especially the GNMA modified pass-through security, have become very popular with investors, including nontraditional mortgage investors such as pension and other retirement funds. These securities are discussed further in a later section.

Types of Mortgage Risk. Like any other investment, investments in mortgages have certain risk and return characteristics. The basic types of risk associated with mortgage lending are default risk, spread or interest rate risk, and inflation (or purchasing power) risk.[4] These risks are common to fixed income securities and were discussed in Chapter 9.

---

[4] *Default risk* is the risk that the borrower will fail, due to lack of diligence, motivation, or ability, to make payments as scheduled. Default risk can be of two types. One type is *payment delinquency risk,* or the risk that the borrower will not make timely payments. Late payments have less time value than timely payments, thereby reducing the actual yield of the loan. Also, late payments can cause the lender to incur costs to induce the tardy borrower to pay, including legal costs involved in threatening foreclosure actions.

The other type of default risk is what is generally regarded as constituting default risk. It is the risk that the borrower will not pay the remainder of his debt obligation, thus necessitating foreclosure proceedings. Foreclosure is costly, and it often involves legal problems that can impede recovery of the full debt. This type of default can occur either because the borrower's ability to pay has been adversely affected by deteriorating economic or personal circumstances, or because the value of the underlying property has declined below the loan balance and the borrower decides that it is just not worth making any more payments. In such a circumstance the borrower, acting in a manner analogous to a holder of an option on a security when the market value of the security falls below the exercise price of the option, simply "walks away" from the mortgage obligation. Depending on state law, however, the borrower may be subject to a deficiency judgment allowing continued action on the note if a foreclosure sale does not satisfy the debt.

The function of the loan underwriting process is to ascertain the ability of the borrower to pay the proposed loan and to ascertain that the value of the property to be mortgaged is sufficient relative to the proposed loan. The latter determination is important, since it is primarily to the property that the lender must look for payment of the debt if the borrower should fail to pay. The risk of loss to the lender can be reduced by assuring that the property to be mortgaged will maintain sufficient value in excess of the loan value under the most adverse economic scenario and by loaning an amount that will produce a relatively low loan-to-value ratio. The lower the loan balance relative to the market value of the property, the less the risk that the borrower will not recover the value of its loan.

Spread or *interest rate risk* is the risk that the interest rate charged the borrower will fall below the cost of funds to the lending institution. When interest rates increase more than expected, the result is a negative spread between borrowing and lending rates. This type of risk was borne by mortgage lenders (especially residential mortgage lenders) during much of the 1970s, with a devastating impact on the balance sheets of the institutions that were the principal

The Pricing of Mortgages. The topic of risk leads to the topic of how loans are priced; that is, how the effective interest rate charged to borrowers is determined. Conceptually, one would start with the so-called real risk-free rate, the rate required to compensate lenders for the time value of money. To the real rate, which historically has averaged about 3 to 4 percent, is added a premium for *expected* inflation. Thus, if inflation were estimated to average 10 percent over the term of the loan, the nominal interest rate would be 13 to 14 percent. In recent years, a premium for uncertainty regarding future rates of inflation appears to have been reflected in nominal risk-free interest rates. To this inflation-adjusted nominal rate, an additional premium of one or more percentage points is added, primarily for default risk.

Alternative Mortgage Instruments. Because of the difficulties caused by long-term fixed rate mortgages, primarily for mortgage lenders but derivatively for borrowers, during periods of uncertain inflation and interest rates, a number of alternative mortgage instruments (AMIs) have been developed. The basic types of mortgage instruments currently in active use, or expected soon to be in use are the *variable rate mortgage* (VRM), the *renegotiable rate mortgage* (RRM), the *price-level adjusted mortgage* (PLAM), the *shared appreciation mortgage* (SAM), the *shared equity mortgage* (SEM), the *convertible mortgage,* the *graduated payment mortgage* (GPM), and the *growing equity mortgage* (GEM). Some of these instruments are at present used mostly in the residential market and others mostly in the commercial, nonresidential real estate market.

TRANSFERRING RISK TO BORROWERS. A principal feature of all these alternative mortgage instruments, with the exception of the GPM and GEM, is that *they transfer all or part of the burden of inflation and interest rate risk from the lender to the borrower.*[5] However, in return for assuming at least

---

residential mortgage lenders, savings and loan associations and mutual savings banks. The principal cause of the problem faced by thrifts in the early 1980s was their inability to adjust the rates on the existing, long-term fixed rate mortgages that comprised the bulk of their portfolios to match the cost of obtaining new funds, the vast majority of which had been borrowed short term. The problem was not nearly so severe for mortgage lenders who concentrated on commercial properties, since they were much freer to adapt their lending instruments and practices to the economic circumstances of the period than were the highly regulated thrifts.

Purchasing power or *inflation risk* is the risk that the *real* return expected when the loan was made will not be obtained due to inflation being greater than anticipated. The rates of inflation experienced during the 1970s were generally higher than anticipated, which meant that actual inflation was not completely compensated for by the interest rates charged borrowers. But, having been burned by interest rate fluctuations and inflation in the past, lenders in the early 1980s apparently were including large premiums for both purchasing power *and* interest rate risk in the nominal rates they were charging to borrowers.

[5] The GPM is designed to ameliorate the problem of the forward "tilt" in the real payments of the standard, fixed rate mortgage in order to enable primarily young borrowers with prospects of a growing income stream to qualify for a home purchase mortgage. The GPM, however, is a fixed rate mortgage and therefore does not relieve the lender of upside inflation and interest rate risk. The GEM is discussed later in this section.

some share of the inflation and interest rate risk, the lender is generally willing to give the borrower a lower (initial) interest rate than would be the case if the borrower obtained a comparable long-term fixed rate mortgage. It is important to note in this regard that the aggregate risk associated with using such mortgage instruments relative to conventional instruments is not reduced; rather, it is only transferred. Indeed, the total amount of risk associated with the loan may increase, since these AMIs often entail a potential increase in default risk in return for passing all or part of the inflation and interest rate risk to the borrower.

The transfer of inflation and interest rate risk from the lender to the borrower is accomplished primarily through adjustments to the payment pattern, either during or at the end of the loan term. There are at present three general ways in which the payment pattern is adjusted by these alternative mortgage instruments. The first is by indexing the mortgage payments to interest rate changes or to inflation, either by periodically adjusting the interest rate of the loan in accordance with some acceptable index of interest rates in the economy (as via the VRM) or by periodically adjusting the outstanding loan balance to some acceptable index of inflation (as via the PLAM). A second way is by considerably shortening the term (maturity) of an otherwise fixed rate mortgage (as via a renegotiable rate mortgage). The third way is by allowing the lender to benefit directly from any inflation-induced appreciation in the value of the property by giving the lender some sort of equity interest at the end of the loan term or at designated future dates. This equity interest can be contingent on the equity appreciation at the end of the loan term (as via the SAM); or it can include both a share of any appreciation and a share of the original equity in the property (as via the SEM); or it can be obtained at designated future dates through an option exercised at the lender's discretion (as via a convertible mortgage). The latter can be regarded as a type of joint venture arrangement between the lender and the borrower.

Apart from transferring risk through one of the various AMIs, an individual lending agreement can also incorporate one or more risk-transferring provisions. In the case of income-producing properties, lending agreements often give the lender some degree of participation in the income stream generated by the property beyond that provided by the debt service on the mortgage. The amount of such *participation* is normally expected to rise at or near the inflation rate, thus giving a lender an inflation hedge. In addition, the loan agreement may incorporate a call option that permits the lender, at its option, to call for payment of the entire mortgage debt at designated dates.

GROWING EQUITY MORTGAGE. Of these alternative instruments, the growing equity mortgage or GEM appears to be a compromise instrument designed to overcome borrower reluctance to accept the uncertain payments associated with an adjustable or variable rate mortgage and to provide the lender with some interest rate protection. The latter is accomplished by accelerating the cash flow received from the mortgage and by considerably shortening the loan term.

With the GEM, the interest rate is fixed but at a rate slightly below that for a traditional fixed rate mortgage. Like the GPM, the GEM has predetermined annual increases in mortgage payments. However, unlike the GPM, which has annual increases in mortgage payments only during the first few years and constant annual payments for the remainder of the loan term, the mortgage payments of the GEM increase at a fixed rate each year over the life of the mortgage. Four percent appears to be the annual rate of increase most commonly mentioned in connection with this type of mortgage. All of the annual increases in mortgage payments are applied to reduce the principal balance of the loan with the result that the loan is repaid within a much shorter period of time than the traditional fixed rate mortgage or the GPM.

In short, the payment pattern of the GEM is characterized by payments that increase annually at some predetermined fixed rate and by a fast paydown of the mortgage balance. Since the payment pattern is predetermined, the GEM is an attractive instrument to investors in the secondary market.

Risk Modification Techniques. Summarizing, there are four basic patterns currently in use in the real estate market to insulate (to the extent possible) lenders from inflation and interest rate risk.

1. *Indexation,* that is, tieing the interest rate of the loan or the outstanding loan balance to some public index at periodic intervals (annually, quarterly, monthly, perhaps even weekly).
2. *Shortened maturities,* through the use of some type of rollover mortgage instrument, the incorporation of a call option in the loan agreement, or accelerated payments.
3. A *claim to* some portion of the *equity* built up in the property, through a SAM, a SEM, or a convertible mortgage.
4. *Participation* in the income stream generated by the property over and above the payments on the mortgage (as provided for in the loan agreement).

The reader should not be left with the impression that the long-term fixed rate mortgage is dead or even obsolete. Such is not the case. However, in an economic environment with a potentially large amount of risk characterized by uncertain inflation and uncertain interest rates, this instrument will generally be available only at a price higher than alternatives that allow the borrower to avoid at least some of this risk.

On the other hand, if the economic picture concerning the long-term future course of inflation and interest rates should change substantially, then this instrument could well enjoy renewed popularity among lenders. Indeed, if the long-term prospect is for disinflation and falling interest rates, it would be advantageous for lenders to make loans with this instrument, along with provisions for large prepayment penalties.

Mortgage-backed Securities

The secondary residential mortgage market has experienced dramatic growth since 1970. One reason, mentioned earlier, has been the active commitment of the federal government to this market. Another major reason has been the innovative development of secondary market instruments, particularly the mortgage-backed securities. As Larkins [1982] notes, 46 percent of all home mortgages originated in the period 1979 through the third quarter of 1981 were sold in secondary markets, compared with only 36 percent in the 1976–78 period. In 1981, 10.5 percent of all mortgages outstanding were held by federal and federally related mortgage pools. It is the growth of the latter—the mortgage pools, as shown in Table 11-5—that has represented the most dramatic evidence of federal activity in the secondary market, and this directly reflects the growth of mortgage-backed securities.

Types of Mortgage-backed Securities. Mortgage-backed securities were designed to appeal to institutional investors, such as pension and other retirement funds, that had previously shied away from investing in residential mortgages. It was hoped that these investors would become the source of a large infusion of funds into the residential mortgage market. By the early 1980s, there was evidence that mortgage-backed securities had succeeded in attracting some additional funds into this market from these nontraditional mortgage investors. As Table 11-6 on page 460 shows, the Government National Mortgage Association estimates that 9.0 percent of GNMA securities outstanding were directly held by pension and other retirement funds at the end of 1981. It also estimates that one-third of the "nominee and others" category, which accounted for 48.4 percent of the amount of securities outstanding in 1981 (as compared with only 7.7 percent in 1971), represented indirect holdings by pension and other retirement funds, largely through life insurance accounts. Note how the percentage of holdings of thrift institutions (savings and loan associations and mutual savings banks) has diminished through the 1971–81 period.

The first and by far the most common type of mortgage-backed security is the GNMA pass-through security. Since the GNMA program began operation in 1970, a variety of mortgage-backed securities has been developed. The most important types developed to date are summarized in Table 11-7 on page 461. These are the GNMA pass-through security, the Federal Home Loan Mortgage Corporation (FHLMC) participation certificates (PCs), FHLMC guaranteed mortgage certificates (GMCs), privately insured pass-through securities, and tax-exempt mortgage revenue bonds.[6]

As reported by Olin [1982b], a new mortgage-backed security program for new conventional mortgages was inaugurated by the Federal National

---

[6] Tax-exempt mortgage revenue bonds are issued by state housing finance agencies and local governments; they are not similar to the other types of mortgage-backed securities. Though they have become a significant force in real estate finance, this type of mortgage-backed security will not be further discussed here.

TABLE 11-6. Percentage of GNMA Pass-through Certificates Outstanding, by Type of Holder, 1971–81

Year Ended	Total Amount Outstanding (billions of $)	All Holders	DEPOSITORY INSTITUTIONS				Credit Unions	Pension & Retirement Funds	Mortgage Companies & Investment Banks	Individuals	Nominees and Others
			Commercial Banks	THRIFTS							
				S&Ls	Mutual Savings Banks						
1971	$ 3.1	100%	4.0%	49.2%	19.2%		6.7%	5.1%	7.5%	1.0%	7.7%
1972	5.5	100	5.2	41.7	20.2		6.1	5.0	9.4	1.3	10.4
1973	7.9	100	5.7	33.3	21.6		5.1	7.1	10.1	1.9	13.3
1974	11.8	100	5.9	30.4	18.0		4.0	7.7	10.6	1.6	21.7
1975	18.3	100	4.8	27.3	14.7		3.2	7.9	18.9	1.2	22.0
1976	30.6	100	5.3	19.6	13.0		2.6	10.0	20.3	1.1	28.1
1977	44.9	100	6.0	14.7	11.7		2.6	11.4	17.3	1.2	35.0
1978	54.3	100	5.9	13.7	11.0		2.4	11.5	13.1	1.4	41.1
1979	76.4	100	5.9	15.3	9.8		2.1	9.8	6.6	1.6	48.9
1980	93.9	100	5.3	17.2	9.7		2.0	9.2	6.8	1.8	48.0
1981[a]	101.6	100	5.2	18.2	9.4		1.8	9.0	6.2	1.8	48.4

SOURCE: Government National Mortgage Association and Federal Reserve Board; compiled by *Survey of Current Business* [1982].
[a] July figures.

TABLE 11-7. Securities Backed by Mortgage Pools

Type	GNMA Pass-through	FHLMC Participation Mortgage Certificates	FHLMC Guaranteed Mortgage Certificate	Privately Insured Pass-through	Tax-exempt Mortgage Revenue Bond
Issued by	Private mortgage originators (more than 800 in 1981)	FHLMC	FHLMC	Private mortgage originators	State and local government agencies
Secured by	GNMA with "full faith and credit" of U.S. government	FHLMC	FHLMC	Private mortgage insurers	Not insured
First issue	1970	1971	1976	1977	1978
Amount outstanding July 1981	$101.6 billion	$21.6 billion[a]	$2.9 billion[a]	$12.6 billion	$37.0 billion[b]
Type of mortgage in pool	FHA/VA	Conventional	Conventional	FHA/VA and conventional	FHA/VA and conventional
Cash flow	Monthly pass-through of principal and interest whether collected by servicer or not	Same as GNMA pass-through	Semiannual interest payments, annual principal payments	Same as GNMA pass-through	Same as other tax-exempt revenue bonds
Comments	Active secondary market; traded in futures market since 1975		Designed to appeal to investors who prefer bond-type instruments; none sold since 1979.		

SOURCE: Government National Mortgage Association and Federal Reserve Board; compiled by Survey of Current Business [1982].
Note: GNMA: Government National Mortgage Association; FHLMC: Federal Home Loan Mortgage Corporation; FHA: Federal Housing Administration; VA: Veterans Administration
[a] Total sales through July 1981, outstanding amount of participation certificates and guaranteed mortgage certificates combined was $17.7 billion in July.
[b] Estimate

Mortgage Association (FNMA) in the first quarter of 1982. This new program is patterned after the GNMA program, with the difference that these securities are not given the full faith and credit guarantee of the federal government. Like the FHLMC participation certificates, these are backed by the lesser guarantee of the issuing agency, in this case FNMA.

Characteristics of Mortgage-backed Securities. Mortgage-backed securities allow investors to invest in mortgage assets without having to become involved in the administratively burdensome processes of mortgage origination and/or servicing. Indeed, the mortgage-backed securities have investment attributes similar in many respects to corporate and government bonds—marketability, administrative simplicity, reinvestment ease, and quality. Moreover, mortgage-backed securities have generally provided one of the highest yields available from high quality fixed income securities. Most also furnish monthly cash flows, a feature that is attractive to institutional investors that have obligations requiring continuous outflows (e.g., pension obligations).

In general, a mortgage-backed security represents a pro rata and undivided claim, generally evidenced by a certificate, to receive periodic payments consisting of interest and principal amortization from a pool of mortgages with very similar characteristics. The mortgages in the pool stand as collateral for this claim. The manner in which payments are made from the pool to the investor depends on the type of mortgage-backed security involved.

Risk-Return Attributes. The investor in mortgage-backed securities needs to be concerned with the following attributes to be able to fully appraise the risk and return characteristics of alternative mortgage-backed securities: (1) the safety of the issue with respect to risk of default and loss of payments, (2) the marketability of the issue, (3) the payment characteristics, (4) the method of determining the relative yield of the issue, (5) the denominations in which the security can be purchased, (6) the tax status of the issue, and (7) the expected maturity (loan life) of the issue.

There are two broad categories of mortgage-backed securities: (1) mortgage-backed bonds and (2) pass-through securities. The latter are by far the more commonly issued and purchased. Pass-through securities, as the name implies, pass through to the ultimate investor a fractional share of monthly payments received on the underlying mortgages in the pool, consisting of principal amortization and interest as these are received or scheduled to be received, including prepayments on those mortgages, less a small fee retained by the issuing entity for servicing.

A unique feature of pass-through securities is that the cash flow received each month by investors is uncertain due to the unpredictable nature of prepayments by the mortgagor. This cash flow uncertainty has been unattractive to some investors (although the monthly flow-through feature itself has been attractive to others).

Mortgage-backed bonds have payments that are structured so as to be similar to conventional bonds. The most common type of mortgage-backed bond was the guaranteed mortgage certificate (GMC) issued by the FHLMC. The GMC was designed to appeal to investors who preferred the payment pattern and cash flow certainty of a bond-type instrument. The principal characteristics of this security, outlined in considerable detail by Jacobe and Thygerson [1981], are: (1) semiannual payments of interest and annual repayment of principal, (2) minimum annual principal-reduction payments according to a predetermined schedule, (3) an unconditional guarantee by the Federal Home Loan Mortgage Corporation of interest payments (to the extent of the certificate rate) and of collection of principal, and (4) where principal payments (prepayments) exceed scheduled minimum amounts in a given year, a published notice, occurring not less than 25 days before principal payment date, of the amount of principal to be paid. As of mid-1982, GMCs had not been sold since the end of 1979, apparently due (in large part) to the complexity involved in restructuring the payments from the underlying mortgages into the above bondlike payment pattern.

GINNIE MAE PASS-THROUGHS. The prototype and most common pass-through security is the GNMA security. Many of the characteristics of GNMAs apply also to the FHLMC's participation certificates and to the privately insured pass-throughs, since they are established on essentially the same principles. The major differences revolve around the source and nature of the respective guarantees and the type of mortgages in the pools.[7] A detailed discussion of the characteristics of GNMA mortgage-backed securities appears below.[8]

---

[7] In addition, there are some slight differences in the way in which the mortgage payments received on the mortgages in the respective mortgage pools are remitted to investors. However, it is beyond the scope of this chapter to discuss the details of how monthly remittances from the respective pools are determined for each type of security.

[8] The purchaser of a GNMA pass-through security obtains a negotiable certificate, issued in registered form to the purchaser, representing a pro rata (fractional) undivided interest in a pool of mortgage loans. Each mortgage pool consists of mortgages that are nearly identical with respect to interest rate, term to maturity, and type of property secured by the mortgages. The vast majority of the GNMA mortgage pools consist of first mortgage loans on single-family homes. But pools also exist for multifamily residential projects and mobile homes.

GNMA mortgage pools must contain FHA, VA, or FmHA mortgages, although only the first two had been used in GNMA pools as of mid-1982. Mortgage pools are organized by private mortgage originators who, if approved by GNMA, become the actual issuers of the certificates. To qualify as a GNMA issuer, the private business entity must meet certain tests. For a list of tests see Wynn [1982]. The issuer is responsible for servicing the mortgage loans and for passing monthly payments of principal and interest to the certificate holders in accordance with their fractional share.

The key feature of the GNMA security is that the Government National Mortgage Association guarantees, backed by the full faith and credit of the United States government, that the investor will receive timely payments of principal and interest. The issuer passes through to the investor the principal and interest amounts scheduled to be paid every month, whether or not they have been collected from the mortgagor, plus any prepayments received. Thus, the investor receives a minimum of a fixed monthly payment at the same time each month (the 15th of

In addition to enjoying a degree of safety on a par with U.S. Treasury bills and bonds, GNMA securities also enjoy a high degree of marketability. A strong secondary market in these securities is provided by a large and active body of securities dealers, which is in turn made possible by the large volume of these securities available in the market due to their phenomenal growth since their inception in 1970.

YIELDS ON GINNIE MAES. The yields on GNMA securities, using the standard 12-year average life assumption, have generally exceeded that of any U.S. government security over the period 1971–81. Their yields have even exceeded those on high grade corporate bonds over much of this period. Since they pay interest and principal monthly rather than semiannually, as is normally the case with bonds, the effect of more frequent compounding boosts the effective rate of interest for Ginnie Maes to slightly higher levels than for bonds at the same nominal rate. See Table 11-8 for a comparison of yearly average interest rates on selected fixed income instruments.

A number of reasons have been cited for the relatively high yields on GNMAs and other pass-through securities. One reason cited is that investors seek a slight premium for the unevenness and unpredictability of cash flows due to uncertain prepayments. Another is that the cash flow pattern of

---

each month) plus a fractional share of any prepayments that are received on mortgages in the pool.

GNMAs carry a certificate, or coupon, rate that is 50 basis points below the ceiling interest rate on the mortgages in the pool; 44 basis points go to the issuer as a servicing fee and 6 go to GNMA as an insurance fee. Since the coupon rate is generally below the prevailing market rate of interest, the yield on GNMAs issued on a particular pool is brought up to the market rate by discounting the price by the appropriate amount below face value, in the same manner as pricing bonds. Thus, at any given time the price of a GNMA security will vary with current interest rates. However, estimating the yield on a GNMA security is not as clear-cut as it is for a bond. The reason is the uncertainty of prepayments.

Though FHA and VA mortgages on single-family homes have generally been written for a term of 30 years, the actual loan life is considerably less, since mortgagers usually prepay their loans for any of a variety of reasons. It is, of course, not possible to forecast the loan life of any particular mortgage or of any specific mortgage pool. But empirical data developed in 1980 by the Federal Housing Administration from prepayment experience place the national average life for FHA mortgages as 11.2 years. GNMA generally computes the yields it quotes based on a more conservative assumption of an average loan life of 12 years. When GNMAs are purchased at a discount, which is almost always the case, the true yield will be more than the quoted yield if the mortgages are paid off sooner than the loan life assumption used to compute the quoted yield; if the actual loan life turns out to be longer, then the true yield is less (see Peters [1980]).

To compute the after-tax yield on a GNMA security, five factors must be taken into account: (1) the price paid for the security, (2) the monthly interest payment, (3) the monthly scheduled principal amortization, (4) the assumed maturity of the mortgage pool, and (5) the receipt of unscheduled principal prepayments (commonly assumed to come at the end of the loan life as a lump sum payment). Since principal payments are considered a return of capital, they are tax-exempt. That is, only the interest portion of the monthly pass-through payment is taxable to the investor. Another characteristic of the tax status of GNMAs is that, unlike other direct obligations of the federal government, the interest income from these securities is not tax-exempt for purposes of state income tax.

TABLE 11-8. **Average Yearly Interest Rates on Selected Fixed Income Investments, 1971–81**

Year	GNMA Securities[a]	U.S. GOVERNMENT BONDS[b]		CORPORATE BONDS[c]		MORTGAGE RATES		Changes in CPI[f]
		5-Year	20-Year	Moody's Aaa	Moody's A	FHLBB Series[d]	Commercial Mortgages[e]	
1971	7.07%	5.99%	6.12%	7.39%	8.03%	7.74%	9.07%	3.4%
1972	6.97	5.98	6.01	7.21	7.66	7.60	8.57	3.4
1973	7.65	6.87	7.12	7.44	7.84	7.95	8.76	8.8
1974	8.70	7.80	8.05	8.57	9.20	8.92	9.47	12.1
1975	8.52	7.77	8.19	8.83	9.65	9.01	10.22	7.0
1976	8.17	7.18	7.86	8.43	9.09	8.99	9.83	4.8
1977	8.04	6.99	7.67	8.02	8.49	9.01	9.34	6.8
1978	8.98	8.32	8.48	8.73	9.12	9.54	9.59	9.0
1979	10.22	9.52	9.33	9.63	10.20	10.77	10.36	13.3
1980	12.55	11.48	11.39	11.94	12.89	12.65	12.53	12.4
1981	15.29	14.24	13.72	14.17	15.29	14.74	13.90	8.9

SOURCE: Board of Governors of the Federal Reserve System [1981, 1982], Council of Economic Advisors [1982], and American Council of Life Insurance [1982].
[a] Average net yields to investors, assuming prepayment in 12 years on pools of 30-year FHA/VA mortgages carrying the prevailing ceiling rate.
[b] Yields adjusted to constant maturities by the U.S. Treasury. That is, yields are read from a yield curve at fixed maturities. Based on recently issued securities.
[c] Seasoned issues, averages of daily figures from Moody's Investor Service. Based on yields to maturity.
[d] Average effective interest rates on conventional mortgage loans closed on new homes. Compiled by the Federal Home Loan Bank Board in cooperation with the Federal Deposit Insurance Corporation.
[e] Compiled from American Council of Life Insurance data for commitments of $100,000 and over. Note that the (lower) rate on commercial (relative to residential) mortgages does not reflect return features such as participations and joint venture arrangements frequently included in commercial mortgage contracts.
[f] Percent changes from December to December.

the GNMA is unfamiliar and forces investors to use an assumed average life rather than a fixed maturity date for determining yields. A third reason given is that the interest income from GNMA securities is not exempt from *state* income taxes. In a recent article, Clauretie [1982] claims to have established through an econometric study that this third reason is the most important of all in explaining the yield differential between GNMAs and other government securities. He argues that taxable investors, such as commercial banks and other financial institutions, require a before-tax yield spread between GNMAs and other government securities that are tax exempt to them at the state level to compensate for the state income tax they must pay. If this is indeed the major reason for the yield differential, then an implication is that the tax-exempt investor (e.g., a pension fund) can expect to receive a slight windfall as long as taxable investors remain a sufficiently important clientele for GNMAs to cause these securities to add such a tax premium to the before-tax yield.

FHLMC PARTICIPATION CERTIFICATES. The Federal Home Loan Mortgage Corporation (FHLMC) issues participation certificates (PCs) that are similar to the GNMA pass-through securities. There are, however, two main differences. First, the PCs are certificates secured by pools of *conventional* mortgages, whereas the GNMA pools consist of FHA and VA mortgages. Like the GNMA pools, however, the overwhelming majority of the mortgages in these pools are first mortgage loans on single-family homes. The other major difference is that the PCs are not backed by the full faith and credit of the U.S. government. Investors are guaranteed the timely payment of interest and principal by the Federal Home Loan Mortgage Corporation, representing a lesser guarantee. Although it is likely that the federal government would intervene on behalf of investors in a situation where the FHLMC is unable to cover its guarantee, payment would probably be delayed and could involve costly claim procedures.

Though the market for PCs is substantial, with $21.6 billion of these securities being in the hands of investors as of 1981, the volume of trading in PCs and the secondary market support for them are considerably less than for GNMAs. Because of the lesser guarantee and this poorer marketability, PCs have slightly higher yields than GNMAs. As reported by Rush and Bolger [1981], in recent years PCs have, on average, yielded about 20 basis points more than GNMAs.

PRIVATELY ISSUED PASS-THROUGH SECURITIES. Like the GNMA pass-through security and the FHLMC participation certificate, the privately issued pass-through security is a certificate representing an undivided pro rata ownership interest in a specific pool of mortgages with similar characteristics. These securities are issued by savings and loan associations, commercial banks, mortgage bankers and other mortgage companies, and private mortgage insurance companies on first mortgage loans that they either have originated or have purchased from the originator or a mortgage lender. While private pass-throughs provide no government guarantee, most private issues utilize mortgage pool insurance purchased from a private mortgage insurance company to insure against losses due to default by mortgagors. The typical mortgage pool insurance policy is written as a stop-loss policy for an amount up to 5 percent of the aggregate unpaid principal balance of the mortgage pool. In addition, individual mortgages in the pool might be covered by private mortgage insurance. In some cases investors may not demand mortgage pool insurance if the mortgages in the pool have low loan-to-value ratios or if the individual mortgages in the pool are adequately covered by private mortgage insurance.

Since private mortgage pool insurance covers only a small portion of the principal balance of a mortgage pool, the main protection for an investor in private pass-through securities comes from the underlying mortgages in the pool, which provide the collateral in case of default. The investor should be concerned with the following characteristics of the mortgage pool:

1. The quality of the mortgages in the pool as measured by the loan-to-value ratio and mortgage insurance coverage.

2. The number and size of the mortgages in the pool.
3. The location of the mortgaged properties and therefore their regional diversification.
4. The financial strength of the issuer or the ability of the issuer to stand behind the payment commitments of its mortgage pools.

Many private pass-through issues are rated by the rating services. The investor can use these ratings as an aid in evaluating alternative issues. As of mid-1982, Standard & Poors had given all of the issues it rates that utilize private mortgage pool insurance at least an AA rating, with a few having been given its highest AAA rating.

The market for private pass-through securities is still much thinner than that for GNMAs, with volume only about 2 percent of GNMA volume in 1981. One reason is that these securities are comparatively new; the first issue was in 1977. The amount of these securities outstanding had grown to $12.6 billion in 1981. Private sector pass-throughs are offered for sale publicly through underwriting channels or by private placement. Public offerings are more costly and therefore more limited. Private placements of these pass-throughs do not always become part of the public record; hence the exact volume of issues is not known. Because of their lower quality and lesser liquidity, private pass-through yields have averaged between 30 to 60 basis points higher than those for GNMAs (see Rush and Bolger [1981]).

Future Directions. The next logical step in the development of the mortgage-backed security would appear to be the development of mortgage pools containing adjustable rate and other alternative mortgages. However, the development of a secondary market for these instruments has been slowed by a lack of sufficient standardization of payments and lending terms and the difficulty in determining the worth of future payment streams.[9]

Recently there has been progress in developing standard types of adjustable rate mortgages (ARMs). Under the Federal Home Loan Bank Board definition, the term *adjustable rate mortgage* encompasses both VRMs and renegotiable rate mortgages. In July 1981, both the Federal National Mortgage Association (FNMA) and the Federal Home Loan Mortgage Corporation (FHLMC) began purchasing adjustable rate mortgages. The FHLMC

---

[9] The first of these problems, for example, has plagued the VRMs. The heterogeneity of the ways used to determine the adjustment of the mortgage interest rate and the variety of restrictions placed on the amount the interest rate would be allowed to vary has hindered the development of homogeneous pools of VRM mortgages.

The second problem has been particularly serious in the case of SAMs. Here the biggest difficulty has been that secondary market purchasers have little way to accurately estimate the probability that the appreciation in the value of the mortgaged property estimated by the makers of the mortgage loan will actually occur. Another difficulty is that the likelihood of appreciation varies with location—both regionally and within metropolitan areas—thus raising a host of appraisal-related problems. As a result, the market has had difficulty in pricing these instruments. As it is, the secondary market tends to discount these mortgages rather heavily because of the risk that the estimated appreciation will not occur.

purchases ARMs under two types of programs, called the "no cap" and the "2 percent cap" program, respectively. Under the no cap program, the FHLMC purchases ARMs that have no restrictions on the amount of annual interest rate adjustments.[10] The 2 percent cap program is for ARMs that limit the annual interest rate adjustment to plus or minus 2 percentage points.

The FNMA purchase program for ARMs establishes eight different loan designs. The FNMA loan designs have adjustment periods that range from six months to five years, whereas the two FHLMC loan designs call for annual adjustments. Four of the eight FNMA designs permit the use of negative amortization, whereas none of the FHLMC designs allows negative amortization. Table 11-9 summarizes the ARM loan designs approved by both FNMA and the FHLMC.[11]

In sum, innovative developments in the secondary mortgage market have been a response to the growing competition in the capital markets for funds. As a consequence of the development of mortgage instruments in the primary mortgage market that are designed to adjust the yields of lenders or investors in line with inflation and fluctuating interest rates, one can expect to see complementary innovations in the secondary mortgage markets. The development of inflation-adjustable mortgage instruments, in other words, should logically be followed by the development of inflation-adjustable mortgage pools and mortgage-backed securities. Inflation-hedged mortgages and mortgage-backed securities should help to attract new investors into the mortgage market, particularly if the prognosis is for continued inflation and interest rate volatility over the long term. If the economic scenario should change to that of very low rates of inflation, however, then adjustable mort-

---

[10] It should be noted that in April 1981 the Federal Home Loan Bank Board issued regulations permitting federally chartered savings and loan associations to make adjustable rate mortgages without any restrictions on the amount of adjustment of the interest rate, as long as the index used to peg the interest rate is readily verifiable by the borrower and beyond the control of the lender. In effect, the rules permit lenders to choose virtually any interest rate series as the basis for adjusting the interest rate on mortgage loans.

[11] The development of standardized types of SAMs suitable for secondary market trading might be a bit more difficult than the development of standard types of adjustable rate mortgages due to the pricing problems discussed above. In March 1982 the FHLMC announced that it intended to begin purchasing SAMs; however, details of this program were not known when this was written.

Once the two problems of lack of standardization and uncertainty of yield are overcome, there do not appear to be any insurmountable problems involved with issuing mortgage-backed securities on pools of inflation-adjustable mortgages. Remittances for any month, for example, could be based on the prior month's payments to the pool, much as monthly remittances on PCs are currently determined, with the result that there would be no need to guess interest rate or payment adjustments. In the case of pools of adjustable rate mortgages, where the rate is truly allowed to adjust freely to market rates, the certificates issued on such pools would always be priced at par, no matter when they are bought or sold, because the yield will continuously adjust to market rates through the flexible interest rate. When there is some stickiness in the adjustment, as, for example, when the interest rate could only be adjusted annually, there may be some interim price adjustments in order to approximate market yields at any one moment.

TABLE 11-9. Adjustable Mortgages in the Secondary Market in 1982

	Interest Rate Index[a]	Interest Rate Adjustment Period	Payment Adjustment Period	Maximum Interest Rate Adjustment (Percent)	Maximum Payment Adjustment (Percent)
Federal National Mortgage Association					
1[b]	6 months	6 months	6 months	—	7½%
2[b]	6 months	6 months	3 years	—	—
3[b]	1 year	1 year	1 year	—	7½
4[b]	3 years	2½ years	2½ years	—	18¾
5	3 years	2½ years	2½ years	5%	—
6	5 years	5 years	5 years	—	—
7	FHLB[c]	1 year	1 year	—	—
8	FHLB[c]	1 year	1 year	2	—
Federal Home Loan Mortgage Corporation					
1	FHLBC[c]	1 year	1 year	—	—
2	FHLBC[c]	1 year	1 year	2	—

SOURCE: Jones [1982].
[a] Treasury yields for Federal National Mortgage Association for plans 1 through 6; Federal Home Loan Bank Board conventional mortgage rate for others.
[b] Negative amortization permissible, so long as the loan balance does not exceed 125 percent of the original loan amount.
[c] FHLB average contract rate on existing homes.

gage investments would lose much of their attractiveness vis-à-vis fixed rate investments.

Equity Investments

Characteristics of Real Estate Equity Investments. One of the two types of real estate investments, mortgage debt, has already been discussed; the other, equity, will be explored presently. When people think of real estate investments, they usually have in mind equity investments. Just as there are a variety of real estate debt instruments, there are a variety of ways to invest as a real estate equity owner. Instruments such as the SAM, the SEM, and the convertible mortgage are hybrid investments, having both debt and equity characteristics.

MAJOR BENEFITS OF REAL ESTATE EQUITY INVESTMENTS. Before discussing several ways to invest in real estate as an equity owner, the reader should understand the principal types of potential benefits investors can obtain from real estate investments: (1) tax shelter, (2) cash flow (or the income component of total return), (3) price appreciation component (and attendant inflation protection), and (4) diversification. The first, tax shelter, is usually of most interest to high bracket taxpayers, since they can take maximum advantage of the tax shelter that can be generated by a properly structured real estate investment. Also, investors in higher tax brackets prefer appreciation eligible for long-term capital gain tax treatment to current cash flow in the form of taxable income. Diversification benefits are of most interest to investors seeking to reduce the risk of their overall portfolios. Thus, the value of tax shelter, cash flow, price appreciation, and diversification to a particular investor depends upon (1) the investor's overall tax and financial position, (2) the degree of the investor's risk aversion, (3) the composition of the investor's overall portfolio, and (4) what the investor is looking for from the real estate investment.

Real estate investments often can be structured so that investors can receive different proportions of tax shelter, cash flow, or price appreciation. In other words, these three components of return can, in effect, be packaged and sold, either individually or in various combinations. Furthermore, the relative amount of each component that an investor buys and holds will affect the overall diversification of his portfolio.

Classes of Real Estate Equity Investment. As discussed previously, real estate equity investment can be divided into two classes, *direct* and *indirect*. With respect to direct equity investments, a number of questions are applicable to all types of investors: (1) whether the investor should make the real estate investment and management decisions or hire a real estate expert to make them on his behalf, (2) what types of property and which individual properties to purchase, (3) how much property to purchase, (4) what equity/debt combination to use, (5) what type of benefits to seek (tax shelter, cash flow, appreciation, diversification, or elements of all four), (6) whether to use or develop the property himself or to lease it to others, (7) if leasing to others, what kinds of leasing arrangements and terms to use, and (8) what property disposition policy to adopt.

Equity Investment Vehicles Available to Individuals. Deciding to purchase a personal residence rather than rent an otherwise equivalent property is in part a real estate investment decision. Purchasing a home results in rent savings (implicit investment income that is not taxed) and a possible inflation hedge. Such a purchase produces large tax benefits because property taxes and interest on home financing are deductible for federal income tax purposes. Furthermore, any gain on the sale of a home may be tax-deferred in most cases. Thus, a home should be considered part of an individual's portfolio. Indeed, many individuals purchased homes during the 1970s in large part on the basis of investment value. During this period a home was one of the best investments available, especially for the smaller investor. The small investor's primary alternative, given government regulations, may have been limited to a low yield savings account, since relatively high minimum investments were required on investments such as Treasury bills. The benefits of housing as an investment were accentuated by long-term fixed rate mortgages at rates that were quite attractive when the inflation rate experienced turned out to be much higher than anticipated.

Because the value of houses rose during the 1970s, and because many individuals tended to overinvest in housing, real estate became the major component of many individuals' portfolios. This subjected the individual to more risk than if the portfolio were better diversified.

Whether housing will continue to be attractive relative to other investments is, of course, uncertain. As we have discussed, interest rates rose considerably during the 1970s and early 1980s, and long-term fixed rate mortgages were replaced by a myriad of alternative mortgage instruments. Thus, while housing will likely continue to be an important part of an individual's portfolio, it should be balanced with other assets, such as equity and fixed income securities, to allow the portfolio to be better diversified.

What investment vehicles are available to individuals who want to make direct equity investments other than their personal residences? If we assume that the individual is not a professional developer or builder, we can assume that when the real estate investment is sold, it will be treated as a capital asset and not taxed as ordinary business income.

SOLE PROPRIETORSHIP. Given the assumption that the individual investor is not a "dealer" of properties under the tax law, selecting a corporate form of business entity usually is not advantageous because it does not permit the pass-through of particular tax shelter items to the investor. For this reason, an individual would probably prefer to invest as a sole proprietor or in a partnership arrangement, since both forms allow the investor to take advantage of tax shelter items such as capital gains, pass-through of tax losses and/ or tax credits, and so on. Since the disadvantage of the proprietorship form of ownership is that the investor cannot avoid personal liability for debts (except nonrecourse debts) or torts incurred and that it is difficult to raise outside equity capital, the partnership form is much more common.

PARTNERSHIPS. An individual investor who does not have sufficient resources to acquire a property he or she wants will probably seek to enter into a partnership arrangement with other investors, either in the general or limited form. If the investor seeks to avoid personal liability for debts or torts and is content with being a passive investor (i.e., having no direct voice in the management of the partnership's real estate assets), then he or she can become a partner in a *limited partnership*. Limited partnerships generally enjoy the same tax treatment as general partnerships. In addition, they allow investors who do not care to take an active role in property management to enjoy the corporate attribute of limited liability. For these reasons, the limited partnership is the favored business entity among individual real estate investors.

The partnership itself is not a taxable entity; it files an information tax return only. Partners can be individuals, other partnerships, corporations, and trusts. The partners, not the partnership, pay all tax liabilities incurred by the partnership as a result of its activities. That is, each partner is taxed in accordance with the rules governing the particular type of taxpayer it is (e.g., individual or corporate). Since the partnership is not a taxpaying entity, there is no double taxation of partnership income. Some other characteristics of the partnership form that make it attractive to real estate investors are as follows:

1. Losses flow through to the partners. They then can use these to offset other taxable income with the carryback and carryforward provisions that are applicable at the individual taxpayer level.
2. The tax character of transactions at the partnership level also flows through to the partners, i.e., a capital gains transaction at the partnership level is taxable to the partners as a capital gain.
3. A partner's interest in the partnership is a capital asset. Thus, any gain (or loss) arising from the sale, exchange, or liquidation of a partnership interest is, in most cases, treated as a capital gain (or loss).[12]
4. The partnership form permits a great deal of flexibility with respect to how individual items of income, gain, loss, deductions, and credits are allocated to individual partners.[13]
5. Nonrecourse mortgage loans made to the partnership can be used to increase the tax basis of a partner's interest in partnership property to the extent he or she shares in partnership profits.

The ability to use nonrecourse mortgage debt for purposes of increasing a partner's share of depreciation and net operating loss deductions provides a big share of the tax shelter benefits from real estate investments. This characteristic of a partnership is of added significance to the real estate investor in light of the fact that a partner's loss deductions from real estate investments are specifically excluded from the *at-risk limitations* of Section 465 of the Internal Revenue Code. For limited partners to be able to add their share of the full amount of the mortgage debt to their partnership basis, however, no loans of the partnership can be of a recourse nature (i.e., no loans can involve the personal liability of any partner).

---

[12] The investors, however, need to be wary of transactions that fall within the coverage of Section 751 of the Internal Revenue Code (IRC), a very complex section that makes property in the form of "unrealized receivables" and "substantially appreciated inventory" taxable as ordinary income. Section 751 can apply both to partnership distributions and to the sale of a partnership interest. Partnership transactions involving real property can be ensnared by Section 751, since any portion of a distribution or any portion of consideration received that is attributable to depreciation recapture under either Section 1245 or Section 1250 of the Code may be an "unrealized receivable" for purposes of Section 751.

[13] In other words, the partners are given a great deal of flexibility to determine through the partnership agreement how items with respect to each of the three types of benefits obtainable from real estate equity investments—tax shelter, cash flow, and appreciation—are to be allocated among themselves, subject to the Internal Revenue Code requirement that the allocations must have "substantial economic effect."

SYNDICATES. A particular form of limited partnership that has become popular in recent years is the real estate syndicate. A real estate syndicate loosely refers to any group of investors who have contributed funds for the common purpose of carrying out a real estate project requiring a concentration of capital. Syndicates can take the business form of a corporation or a general partnership, but the limited partnership is the most common due to its combination of partnership tax characteristics and corporate limited liability for the limited partners.

There are two varieties of syndicates, public and private. The private syndicate is an arrangement among a number of investors to pool their money into one or more real estate projects. The public syndicate involves selling shares (or certificates of participation) to the public in what, in essence, is a real estate investment fund. Indeed, because they are deemed to be engaged in the public sale of securities, public syndicates come under the regulation of the Securities and Exchange Commission.

Equity Investment Vehicles Available to Institutions. There are several ways in which institutions, primarily pension funds, can make real estate equity investments. The two primary vehicles are direct equity investment and pooled funds.

DIRECT EQUITY INVESTMENT. In direct equity investment an institutional investor directly purchases ownership rights to a property for its own account. When a pension fund decides to make direct equity investments, it must then decide whether to set up its own in-house staff to make such real estate investment decisions and to manage the real estate assets it acquires or to employ the services of an independent real estate advisor to handle its investments.[14]

Only a fairly large pension fund has the resources to engage in direct real estate investments; and only the largest funds have the resources to develop an internal staff with the real estate expertise necessary to make investment decisions and to manage real estate assets. Selecting and managing real estate assets requires knowledge of and competency in a wide range of real estate matters: determining the quality of properties for possible purchase, real estate investment analysis, property performance measurement, obtaining an appropriate degree of risk diversification, property management, reporting techniques, appraisal procedures, and property disposition.

[14] The latter alternative typically involves employing an independent fee advisor who often can be appointed a trustee of the fund. The independent advisor makes recommendations for investment decisions and supervises the management of the fund's properties. A pension fund that employs the services of an independent advisor is nonetheless an active investor in real estate. Under ERISA's definition of a fiduciary, the investment advisor would assume liability for the reasonable care of the pension fund's assets, thus relieving the pension fund managers of some of the fiduciary burden involved in managing real estate investments. But even when it chooses the independent advisor alternative, the fund will still require someone in house who has real estate expertise to oversee the work of the advisor and who is able to make such final investment decisions as are required.

Moreover, larger funds may be willing to sacrifice direct control over the selection and disposition of real estate assets, and perhaps even a higher level of return obtainable via direct real estate investment, in return for the reduction of risk through investment in a well-diversified assortment of properties through the medium of pooled funds.

For these reasons, the most popular vehicle for real estate equity investment by pension funds is a commingled real estate fund. These funds provide both real estate expertise and a high degree of diversification.

COMMINGLED REAL ESTATE FUNDS. A commingled real estate fund (CREF) represents a pool of capital from a number of pension funds that has been assembled to invest in real estate properties. CREFs have been established primarily for pension fund clients by life insurance companies, commercial banks, and independent real estate investment companies. The first two types of institutions largely sponsor open-end commingled funds, whereas the latter sponsors primarily closed-end funds. A survey of the senior investment officers of the largest corporate and government pension funds by Money Market Directories, Inc. in 1981 indicated that pension fund money was distributed among the major sponsors of commingled funds as follows:

Type of Sponsor	Percent of Respondents Utilizing
Bank commingled funds	13%
Insurance company commingled funds	65
Other common trust funds	22

A somewhat different summary of commingled real estate fund sponsors in September of 1981 is provided by Frank Russell Company in Table 11-10. This breakdown of sponsors uses real estate investment companies as its third category of sponsor.

Commingled funds provide several advantages over direct equity investments for pension fund investors, such as professional management and, if

TABLE 11-10. Summary of Commingled Real Estate Funds, September 30, 1981 (in $ millions)

Type of Sponsor	Gross Assets of Commingled Real Estate Funds	Property Assets in Commingled Real Estate Funds
Insurance companies	$ 7,683	$6,751 (75%)
Commercial banks	1,317	1,092 (12%)
Real estate investment companies	1,530	1,139 (13%)
Total	$10,530	$8,982 (100%)

SOURCE: Eagle [1982].

they are large enough, geographic and property type diversification. In addition, open-end commingled funds can provide a greater degree of liquidity than do direct equity investments, although, as discussed below, even the open-end CREF, the most liquid type, may appear more liquid than it really is.

The commingled real estate fund is a relatively new investment vehicle. The first, the Wachovia Bank Fund, was established in 1968. Prudential Insurance Company of America followed with its open-end CREF, known as PRISA, in 1970. Over half the funds in existence today were established after 1974. The growth in CREF assets has been dramatic, although figures available on the industry differ. Piecing together figures from several sources, it can be *roughly* estimated that total assets of the largest open-end CREFs (both insurance company and commercial banks) increased from $750 million in 1974 to over $4 billion in 1979 to approximately $9 billion by September of 1981. Furthermore, Frank Russell Company estimates that pension funds invested between $12 and $14 billion in equity real estate in the 12-year period from the beginning of 1970 to the end of 1981. Of that amount, approximately 70 percent was estimated to have been invested in open-end CREFs.

The growth of PRISA, the largest of the CREFs in 1982, is illustrated in Table 11-11 (page 476). The 1975–81 performance of PRISA relative to other asset types and macroeconomic measures, in *constant* dollar total returns, is shown in Figure 11-1 (page 476).

OPEN-END COMMINGLED REAL ESTATE FUNDS. As with bond and common stock mutual fund vehicles, a major attraction of open-end CREFs is that they offer a potentially greater degree of liquidity than either direct real estate equity investments or closed-end CREFS. By retaining a small amount of assets in the form of cash and marketable securities, funds are available to buy out (or redeem) the units of participants who wish to leave the CREF. Such funds are obtained from current income earned on investments, sale of properties, or money provided by new participants (investors). Typically, however, this liquidity is far from being completely adequate for all situations that might arise, and redemption is usually subject to certain restrictions and conditions. These depend on the particular CREF's policy on redemptions as specified in the operating agreement established for its participants. Most importantly, virtually all open-end CREFs have provisions against permitting redemptions that would require forced liquidation of assets.[15]

Therefore, the appearance of liquidity offered by open-end CREFs may be an illusion when market forces are such as to cause many participants to want to redeem at the same time. Under such conditions, CREFs can obtain

---

[15] Advance notice to the CREF by the participant of its intention to withdraw is universally required (30 days is normally the minimum notice required). CREF units are normally redeemed at the end of calendar quarters. However, a waiting period that can be longer than 12 months may be required.

Table 11-11. Net Assets of PRISA for Fiscal Years 1970 Through 1981

Fiscal Year Ending September 30	Net Assets[a] ($ millions)
1970[b]	$ 5.0
1971	47.8
1972	119.0
1973	236.2
1974	479.0
1975	655.2
1976	681.0
1977	762.5
1978	855.5
1979	1,167.7
1980	2,130.1
1981	3,411.3[c]

SOURCE: *PRISA 1981 Annual Report* [1982].
[a] Net assets represent the equity of contract holders. The net asset figure is gross (or total) assets less liabilities.
[b] PRISA was established on July 31, 1970.
[c] Gross (or total) assets of PRISA as of September 30, 1981 were $3,926.7 million.

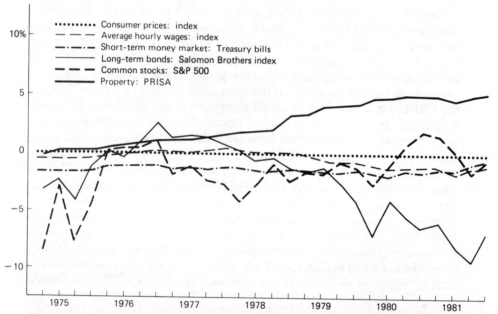

Figure 11-1. Effective Annual Rates of Total Investment Return Arising from Quarterly Investments of $1,000 Each in Various Economic and Financial Indexes, Measured from Results in Dollars of Constant Value, 1975–81. (SOURCE: MacKinnon [1982])

the funds to meet redemption requests only from selling properties. They thus become no more liquid than their underlying assets. In effect, the redemption capability of an open-end fund exists only as long as requests for liquidation do not exceed the liquid component of the real estate portfolio.

Prior to 1982, essentially all major open-end CREFs freely honored requests for withdrawals. In mid-1982, however, one of the largest of the CREFs did not have enough funds on hand to promptly honor all requests for redemption, as it had in the past. It notified clients requesting redemption that they might have to wait at least an additional quarter before redemption. In view of the downturn of the commercial real estate market, a senior investment officer of another major CREF reminded pension fund clients that investments in CREFs are still real estate investments, and as such must be viewed as long-term investments (see Hertzberg and Smith [1982]).

Apart from the possibility that open-end CREFs may be liquid in appearance only, open-end funds also have a problem with the valuation of their assets. Unlike mutual funds that are able to obtain daily market quotations to establish unit values, open-end real estate funds have properties that are not sold frequently enough to provide them with timely, market-determined pricing information. Consequently, they must rely largely on appraisals to establish a price for their participation units. Although substantial progress has been made toward developing a standardized body of procedures and techniques for deriving real estate value estimates and for measuring the performance of real estate assets, reaching the required estimates by means of the real estate appraisal process is a less than perfect way to solve the need for accurate market value data.

CREF real estate assets are appraised on a regular basis, normally quarterly but sometimes monthly, in order to establish the CREF's unit value. This appraised unit value serves as the current price for both entry and withdrawal. The general rule seems to be that at least one appraisal per year should be undertaken by an independent outside appraiser, with the remaining quarterly (or monthly) reports handled by the internal staff of the commingled fund.

CLOSED-END COMMINGLED REAL ESTATE FUNDS. The other type of commingled real estate fund is the closed-end fund. Four of the more prominent sponsors of these funds are: the Rosenberg Real Estate Equity Fund (RREEF) Corporation, LaSalle Partners, Inc., Corporate Property Investors (CPI), and Coldwell Banker Management Corporation. According to Frank Russell Company (see Eagle [1982]), the funds that these organizations sponsor managed approximately $2.4 billion of gross assets at the end of 1981, including properties already acquired as well as those on which they have forward commitments to purchase.

The closed-end fund provides a flexible vehicle for pension fund investors. For example, a closed-end fund can take a variety of organizational forms, such as group trusts, limited partnerships, and even REITs. The choice of a particular form used is governed in part by the investment objectives of the fund. What these funds have in common is that they are organized with a fixed capitalization to serve the investment needs of pension funds.

Closed-end CREFs differ from open-end CREFs in a number of ways. First, unlike the open-end CREF, the closed-end CREF typically does not accept money from new participants. Closed-end funds seek to initially raise a predetermined amount of money from investors, which they then commit to a predetermined real estate acquisition program. Once the fund has sold the number of units needed to raise the amount of money it seeks, usually no additional participants are accepted. Thus, the asset size of the fund remains more or less static, subject, of course, to underlying asset value changes.

Second, rather than buying into a closed-end fund at a value set by an appraisal, as with open-end funds, participants acquire a share of a pool of properties that were purchased at market prices, with the number of units they own being proportionate to the size of their investment in the fund. Thus, the value of each participant's investment in the fund, at least in the case of the original investors, is established by market prices. Since closed-end funds usually are closed to additional investors, there is no need for frequent appraisals. Generally, closed-end funds use annual appraisals to update the value of their asset holdings, but such valuations are strictly for information purposes.

Third, closed-end funds are generally established for a specific period of time (which varies from seven to fifteen years), at the end of which they are liquidated. The only way a participant can cash out of a closed-end fund is to find some would-be participant who is willing to buy those units. The sales price can be more or less than the selling participant's cost basis in the fund. In this respect participants in closed-end funds are analogous to investors in closed-end investment companies. Unlike the latter, however, there is no well-organized secondary market in which units of closed-end CREFs can be bought and sold.[16]

DISTRIBUTION OF CREF ASSETS. CREF assets, particularly those of the large open-end funds, typically are well diversified both by property type and geographic location. A study by Miles and Esty [1982] found that at the end of 1979 the distribution of assets of 20 of the largest insurance company and commercial bank commingled real estate funds by geographic region and property type were as shown in Tables 11-12 and 11-13.

John McMahan Associates [1981], using data from ten of the largest open-end funds, again from 1979, provide results that are similar to those reported by Miles and Esty. The McMahan diversification information is summarized in Figures 11-2 and 11-3 on page 480. Note that CREFs invest directly in all major types of income-producing property, although the three

---

[16] As a fourth, but less important, reason, closed-end funds are generally smaller than open-end funds and do not grow over time. Thus, participation in a closed-end fund may not be as well diversified among property types and geographic locations as open-end funds.

TABLE 11-12. Distribution of CREF Assets by Region (results weighted by size of the CREF)

Region	Mean Percent
South	32%
West	21
Midwest	25[a]
East	22
Sunbelt (the South and West combined)	53

SOURCE: Miles and Esty [1982].

[a] Miles and Esty place Colorado, Idaho, and Montana in the Midwest group rather than the West. Thus, from the point of view of more conventional classification schemes (which place these three states in the West), the West is somewhat under- and the Midwest somewhat overstated.

types that have predominated in recent years are office buildings, industrial facilities, and shopping centers.

TYPES OF INVESTMENTS BY CREFs AND PENSION FUNDS. CREFs and pension funds concentrate on institutional-grade properties, which are the premium investment-grade properties. These tend to be large (dollarwise) income properties that are well located, well maintained and serviced, and functionally up to date. Traditionally, CREFs and pension fund investors have been interested primarily (or exclusively) in properties that are already operating (as opposed to being under construction or in the preconstruction developmental stage), that are fully (or nearly so) leased, and whose tenants enjoy a high credit rating. Furthermore, in recent years CREFs and pension fund investors have desired properties with leases that have an inflation-adjustment capability so as to provide a potential inflation hedge for the property's income stream. Properties with these characteristics have a high probability of being able to increase in value along with inflation; indeed,

TABLE 11-13. Distribution of CREF Assets by Type of Asset (results weighted by size of CREF)

Asset Type	Mean Percent
Cash and marketable securities	6%
Hotel and resort	7
Industrial	22
Land	1
Office buildings	26
Residential	4
Retail	30
Other assets	4
Total	100%

SOURCE: Miles and Esty [1982].

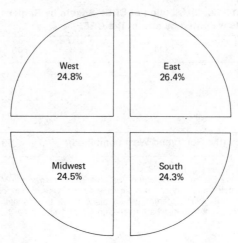

Figure 11-2. Geographic Mix of Ten Large Open-end Real Estate Funds in 1979. (SOURCE: McMahan [1981])

they even have a good chance of increasing fast enough in value to achieve real appreciation, especially if located in high demand areas.

Real Estate Investment Trusts

Real estate investment trusts (REITs) are both an investment vehicle and a form of financial intermediary that specializes in real estate investments. REITs are financial intermediaries in that they channel funds from financial markets to the real estate sector. They finance their activities in ways similar

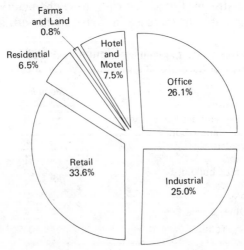

Figure 11-3. Types of Investments of Ten Large Open-end Real Estate Funds in 1979. (SOURCE: McMahan [1981])

to corporations. To raise the funds for investment in properties and/or mortgages, REITs issue shares of beneficial interest (analogous to common stock), borrow funds directly from other institutions such as banks and insurance companies, and issue a variety of debt instruments such as commercial paper, unsecured and mortgage notes, bonds, subordinated debentures, and convertible debentures.

As an investment vehicle, REITs are designed to provide small as well as large investors with an opportunity to invest in a professionally managed portfolio of diversified real estate assets. In a loose sense, they can be viewed as mutual funds that invest in real properties and/or mortgages instead of securities.[17]

[17] Organizationally, to qualify as an REIT under the tax laws, an organization must meet the following requirements: (1) it must be set up as a corporation, trust, or association, (2) it must be managed by one or more trustees or directors, with a trustee being defined as a person who holds legal title to the organization's property and who has the fiduciary duty to exercise continual authority over the management of the affairs of the organization, (3) it must have beneficial ownership evidenced by shares transferable by certificates, (4) it must have beneficial ownership by at least 100 persons, and (5) it must not have personal holding company status, which means that *not* more than 50 percent of its outstanding stock can be owned by five or fewer individuals during the last half of the organization's taxable year.

REIT tax legislation is designed to insure that REITs will be essentially *passive* investment vehicles specializing in real estate investments. Congress' intent that REITs should fulfill this role is evidenced by the following additional requirements that organizations must meet to qualify as REITs under the tax laws: (1) a distribution requirement that at least 95 percent of an REIT's taxable income be distributed to its shareholders; (2) an income derivation requirement that at least 75 percent of the gross income for a taxable year must be derived from real estate or real estate-related investments (e.g., mortgages); (3) a business activity restriction that REITs are not to engage in the active operation of a business such as land development, building homes for sale, or condominium conversion. As a general rule, REITs will lose their nontaxable status with respect to income received from the sale of properties developed, built, and/or held primarily for resale. However, the tax law has been modified to permit an REIT to sell off its investment property (primarily for purposes of portfolio restructuring) free of income taxation to the REIT if certain conditions are met, such conditions being restrictions on the kind of property and the manner in which properties can be sold; (4) a management activity restriction to ensure the passive nature of REITs such that the trustees, directors, or employees of an REIT are not actively engaged in managing or operating REIT property, in rendering services to tenants of REIT property, or in collecting rents from tenants; these functions are to be performed by an independent contractor. With regard to this latter set of restrictions, the trustees or directors of an REIT, in keeping with their fiduciary and management responsibilities for the affairs of the REIT, are permitted to make decisions with respect to the property of the REIT if such decisions are involved with the conduct of the affairs of the REIT itself. For example, they may establish rental terms, choose tenants, enter into and renew leases, deal with taxes, interest, and insurance, and make decisions about capital expenditures and even repairs, relating to REIT property.

Although REITs continue to be predominantly organized as trusts, federal law was modified in 1976 to permit REITs to incorporate. The primary reason REITs have remained largely organized as trusts is to remain exempt from state franchise and income taxes.

Many REITs were organized and/or sponsored by a financial institution, such as an insurance company, a commercial bank, or a mortgage banker. The sponsoring institution would also serve as an advisor to the REIT, either directly or through an affiliate. Responsibility was delegated to the advisor for managing the operations of the REIT, including management of the REIT's assets and liabilities. In the early 1980s, the use of advisors by REITs had become less common as REITs tended to become independent organizations.

The shares of most REITs are traded on a national stock exchange or the national or regional over-the-counter markets, while other REITs are privately held. Since the shares of most REITs are publicly traded, they represent a more liquid investment—a major advantage of REITs over other real estate investment vehicles.

Although REITs have been in existence since the late nineteenth century, they did not acquire the distinctive tax status they currently have until 1960. In that year Congress revised the Internal Revenue Code to exempt REITs from being taxed as corporations, thereby giving them modified conduit tax treatment like that for mutual funds. In essence, if the REIT satisfies rather exacting tax law requirements, the income it distributes to shareholders out of its earnings and profits will not be taxed at the REIT level—that is, it avoids the corporate burden of double taxation. Moreover, capital gains distributed in the year they are realized and designated by the REIT as a capital gain dividend are taxable to the shareholders as long-term capital gains.[18]

The conduit tax treatment of an REIT is only partial. Most significant from the point of view of the tax shelter-oriented investor is that, unlike a partnership, an REIT cannot pass through net operating losses to its shareholders, neither during periods of real estate construction nor at times when the REIT is losing money. However, REITs are now able to recognize operating losses and to carry them over to other taxable years. Also, a portion of the dividend may represent a return of capital, thereby lowering the tax basis of the investor's shares rather than being taxed currently as ordinary income or capital gains.

Basic REIT Types. There are two basic types of REITs, the equity REIT and the mortgage REIT. Those that combine the investments of both types are called hybrid REITs.

Mortgage REITs are primarily engaged in mortgage lending; equity REITs are primarily engaged in acquiring ownership of various categories of income-producing properties. The main source of income for equity REITs is from rents; mortgage REIT income comes principally from interest earned on mortgages, commitment fees, accretions of discounts on mortgages purchased at prices below face or maturity value, and commissions earned on mortgage purchases. However, newer REIT mortgage lending instruments also provide income from various forms of participation in the income streams or cash flow of mortgaged properties. Equity REITs obtain capital gains primarily from the sale of properties, whereas mortgage REITs obtain their capital gains principally from selling mortgages above their cost, usually when longer term interest rates drop. Other differences between the two

[18] The ordinary income dividends received by shareholders from a real estate investment trust are eligible for the full federal dividend exclusion if at least 75 percent of the gross income of the REIT consists of interest paid to the REIT. If less than 75 percent of the REIT's income is interest income, then the amount of the exclusion is proportional to the ratio of the interest income earned by the REIT to the REIT's gross income.

types of REITs relate to the types of benefits and problems associated with buying, selling, and holding each type of asset (i.e., mortgages versus real property).

Mortgage REITs have tended to concentrate their first mortgage lending on construction and land development loans—the more risky types of real estate mortgages—but at the same time the mortgages that generate the highest returns. Since the 1974–75 recession, there has been less of a concentration on these types of loans, as shown in Figure 11-4. A few REITs specialize in real estate specialty-type financing (and for this reason are sometimes referred to as specialty REITs) such as wraparound mortgages, second mortgages, or subordinated sale-leasebacks. A benefit of REITs to the real estate community has been their willingness and capacity to engage in a wide variety of financing and equity investment arrangements.

Historical Performance of REITs. In the years immediately following the 1960 tax legislation creating the current tax status of the REITs, REITs were overwhelmingly of the equity type. By 1968, however, REITs specializing in mortgage lending were becoming a significant part of the industry. In 1968, mortgages constituted 37 percent of industry assets and owned properties 53 percent. In 1973, the high water mark of the mortgage REITs, owned

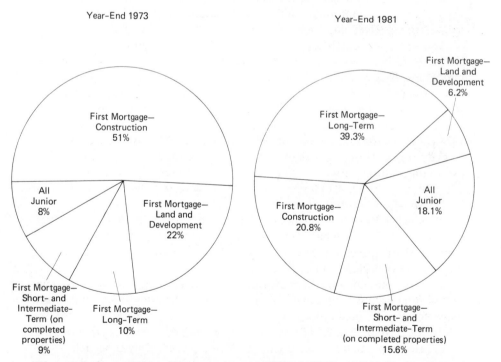

Figure 11-4. Composition of Mortgage Loans of REITs in 1973 and 1981. (SOURCE: National Association of Real Estate Investment Trusts (NAREIT) [1981])

properties fell to only 16 percent of industry assets, while mortgages accounted for approximately 75 percent.

The 1974–75 period was very difficult for the real estate community in general and disastrous for REITs in particular. Mortgage REITs were particularly hard hit due to a combination of economic conditions and industry practices including:

1. Overbuilding in many markets coupled with a slowdown in demand for rental space due to the relatively severe recession.
2. Accelerating construction and borrowing costs due to inflationary pressures and exceptionally (by historic standards) high interest rates. As a result many developers and builders were unable to complete their projects; those who were able to complete their projects were highly susceptible to default when they were unable to sell their units.
3. A concentration by security analysts on earnings per share and earnings growth rather than on cash flow, which led REIT managers to seek to increase visible (i.e., reported) earnings by increasing leverage and by lending more and more money at higher and higher rates on increasingly risky developments and ventures.

In short, the mortgage REIT debacle was due to a combination of adverse economic conditions, faulty security analysis, shoddy loan underwriting, and poor REIT management.

The equity-type REITs survived the 1974–75 recession in far better shape than their mortgage cousins, though they too experienced serious difficulties. Due partly to the fact that they had a better survival and performance record and partly to the difficulties REITs experienced during this period in obtaining money and backing to make mortgage loans, industry investment practices shifted back to property ownership following the 1974–75 recession. By the end of 1981, 58 percent of industry assets were in owned properties and less than 40 percent were in mortgages. The shift in asset composition between owned property and mortgage loans (all types) over the period 1968–81 can be seen in the aggregate balance sheet data for REITs shown in Table 11-14.

Although REITs have made a modest comeback from the reverses suffered in the 1974–75 debacle (at least up to 1981), they still suffer from its impact. Share prices have rebounded to some extent, but REIT industry assets have continued to decline.

To give some idea of the performance of REITs, the National Association of Real Estate Investment Trusts (NAREIT) has devised a total return index for REITs qualifying under the tax laws. This index computes the returns of tax-qualified REITs on the basis of both dividend distributions and share price appreciation over the initial period prices. Only those REITs for which share price quotations are readily available on a regular basis are

TABLE 11-14. Aggregate Balance Sheet Data for REITs ($ billions, year-end data)

	1968	1970	1972	1974	1975	1976	1977	1978	1979	1980	1981ᵇ
Assets											
Land, development, and construction loans	$0.26	$2.58	$ 7.56	$ 9.47	$ 3.86	$1.97	$1.25	$1.04	$1.07	$0.83	$0.71
Other loans[a]	0.12	0.64	3.07	6.78	3.28	2.67	2.13	2.03	1.85	1.89	1.93
Loan loss reserves	—	—	—	(0.73)	(0.76)	(0.64)	(0.37)	(0.21)	(0.14)	(0.06)	(0.05)
Property owned	0.55	0.95	2.48	4.06	4.74	5.08	4.24	3.99	3.88	3.77	3.89
Other assets	0.10	0.56	1.07	0.90	0.89	0.62	0.45	0.42	0.54	0.57	0.59
Total assets	$1.03	$4.73	$14.18	$20.48	$12.01	$9.70	$7.70	$7.27	$7.20	$7.00	$7.07
Liabilities											
Bank borrowings and commercial paper	$0.09	$0.80	$ 6.21	$10.29	$ 6.13	$3.96	$2.39	$1.79	$1.59	$1.21	$1.11
Mortgages on property owned	0.36	0.55	1.16	1.58	1.51	2.00	1.81	1.96	1.95	1.91	1.93
Other liabilities	0.11	0.49	1.70	3.95	1.21	1.10	0.89	0.92	0.87	0.96	0.94
Total liabilities	$0.56	$1.84	$ 9.07	$15.82	$ 8.85	$7.06	$5.09	$4.67	$4.41	$4.08	$3.98
Shareholders' equity	0.47	2.89	5.11	4.66	3.16	2.64	2.61	2.60	2.79	2.92	3.09
Total assets	$1.03	$4.73	$14.18	$20.48	$12.01	$9.70	$7.70	$7.27	$7.20	$7.00	$7.07

SOURCE: National Association of Real Estate Investment Trusts [1981].
[a] The category "other loans" includes intermediate- and long-term first mortgages on completed properties and junior mortgages.
[b] Preliminary figures.

included. The figures show large variability from one quarter to the next, often oscillating between large positive and large negative total returns.

One problem with these performance data is that no indication is given of how the different types of REITs (i.e., mortgage and equity) performed. Burns and Epley [1982], in a study showing how an investment portfolio previously consisting of all common stock can be made more efficient by including REIT investments, found that, in risk-return space, equity REITs dominated both hybrid and mortgage REITs over the period 1970–79. Utilizing a sample of 35 REITs (consisting of 10 equity, 8 hybrid, and 17 mortgage REITs), they found that equity REITs had the highest returns *and* the lowest risk and that mortgage REITs had the highest risk *and* the lowest returns of the REIT groups, with the hybrid type in between. On the basis of their findings, they conclude that little is gained by adding nonequity REITs, and especially mortgage REITs, to virtually any other portfolio. The general conclusion of their study is that a mixed portfolio consisting of equity REITs and common stock funds provided superior performance in risk-return space than a single-asset (i.e., all stock) portfolio over that period. This topic is discussed further in the section of the chapter covering risk and return analysis of real estate investment.

In sum, there is nothing basically wrong with the REIT concept, including the maligned mortgage REITs, as an investment vehicle. The difficulties that they experienced in the past were related more to poor management coupled with adverse economic conditions than to any inherent weakness in the concept itself. Indeed, changes in the mortgage market, as evidenced by various relatively new types of inflation-adjustable mortgage instruments (including creative financing arrangements being worked out between developers and builders, on the one hand, and lenders and suppliers of equity capital on the other), present new opportunities for the successful operation of mortgage REITs. The REIT remains a viable financial intermediary for the real estate industry and a potentially sound investment vehicle for individuals. But what kind of an investment vehicle does it offer tax-exempt investors, such as pension funds?

REITs as Pension Fund Investments. REITs are not necessarily tilted in favor of tax sheltered investments or the taxable investor. They are, in fact, oriented more to finding investments that provide a maximum of current cash flow as well as appreciation, with perhaps some differences in emphasis given to one or the other depending on the investment objectives of the REIT. The basic objective is to pay the largest dividends possible to the investor-shareholder. It is true that the tax-exempt investor does not care about the distinction between ordinary dividends and capital gains dividends. Thus, this investor will need to weigh the alternative investment policies of REITs in terms of maximum risk-adjusted before-tax cash flows.

A nontrivial advantage of the REIT vehicle for the pension fund investor in the past was that it enabled such an investor to indirectly invest in leveraged real estate without being subject to the tax on unrelated business income triggered by acquisition indebtedness under Section 514 of the Internal Revenue Code. However, the previously mentioned 1980 amendment to the tax law substantially eliminated this most prominent advantage of REITs over the tax-exempt commingled real estate funds by allowing commingled funds to invest in leveraged real estate without being subject to the tax on unrelated business income.

The REIT does have some disadvantages for pension funds. One is that of reconciling its checkered past with the prudent man investment requirements of pension funds. In addition to their past history, REITs do in fact seem to be riskier investment vehicles than at least the major commingled real estate funds, although no thorough study of this hypothesis had been done by mid-1982. Individual REITs have been observed to take on projects that appear to be more risky than the prudent man rule would seem to countenance, even assuming that a high level of risk is not inherent in the REIT concept. However, assuming the extra risk undertaken is essentially unsystematic in nature, adequate diversification coupled with sound investment decision making would alleviate this apparent situation. One source of the problem might be the inability of many present-day REITs to adequately diversify given their small asset base. On balance, return-risk experience with the REIT investment universe appears to be more variable than that with commingled real estate funds; thus, it would appear the pension fund investor needs to be more wary.

Aside from increased riskiness due to choice of investments, there is the added risk associated with the fact that most REITs make use of substantial leverage, usually a contributor to systematic risk. This means that REITs, to a greater or lesser degree depending on the type of REIT and its investment policies, are sensitive to high and volatile interest rates such as those experienced in the late 1970s and early 1980s.

Another consideration is the prohibition against tax-qualified REITs actively developing properties. Pension funds that seek an active involvement in real estate development, therefore, may not find the REIT vehicle compatible with their investment objectives.

Notwithstanding the above caveats, REITs are an inherently flexible form of investment vehicle that can be made attractive to pension fund investors. Indeed, in 1982 there were at least a few that were tailoring their portfolios specifically for pension fund clients.

REAL ESTATE VALUATION AND INVESTMENT ANALYSIS

Valuation vs. Investment Analysis

The purpose of real estate investment analysis is to evaluate real estate from the perspective of a particular individual or institution. It involves consideration of factors such as risk and the after-tax rate of return from the investment and how well the investment fits into an existing portfolio. The analysis is typically made relative to a presumed purchase price or estimated project construction cost. One of the primary considerations in investment analysis is whether the expected rate of return from an investment is sufficient to warrant the purchase by a particular investor or institution. Alternatively, one could determine the price necessary to provide an appropriate rate of return to justify the investment. This would indicate the value to that investor. This type of value is typically referred to as *investment value* and may be quite different from the *market value* (most probable current selling price) of the property. Investment value is affected by factors such as the investor's objectives and constraints as discussed in Chapters 4 and 5. Sometimes an investor will be willing to accept a lower return, if necessary, from one property versus another because it has other valuable characteristics for him (e.g., if the asset provides more diversification, liquidity, or tax benefits).

Real estate valuation is similar to investment or security analysis, but the term "valuation" usually implies *estimating* a market value or most probable selling price for the property since there is no national or regional exchange for determining the market value of real estate. According to the American Institute of Real Estate Appraisers [1973], market value is defined as "the highest price estimated in terms of money which a property will bring if exposed for sale in the open market, allowing a reasonable time to find a purchaser who buys with knowledge of all the uses to which it has been or could be adapted and for which it is capable of being used." This estimate can be thought of as *the* value for a "typical" investor in the type of property being evaluated.

Macroeconomic Factors Affecting Real Estate

Real estate prices and returns and risk for real estate investments are affected by a myriad of factors that determine the supply of and demand for different types of property (see Figure 11-5). First, values tend to be affected by the general level of business activity and particularly interest rate trends. However, the housing market and the market for commercial real estate differ as to the timing of their respective responses to changes in the overall economy. Historically, the housing market has tended to lead the rest of the economy into and out of a recession. The commercial real estate market, on the other hand, tends to follow rather than lead the overall economy. The difference in the reactions of these two segments of the market to conditions in the overall economy is due, in large part, to the fact that the housing market is very sensitive to interest rates which tend to peak near the crest of the boom portion of the business cycle and to bottom out near its trough. By contrast, the commercial real estate market is more responsive to the level of business activity. Second, real estate is perhaps particularly affected by the *expected* level of inflation or deflation. In an inflationary economy, such as that during most of the 1970s, real estate performed relatively well. In a deflationary or, more realistically, a disinflationary economy real estate

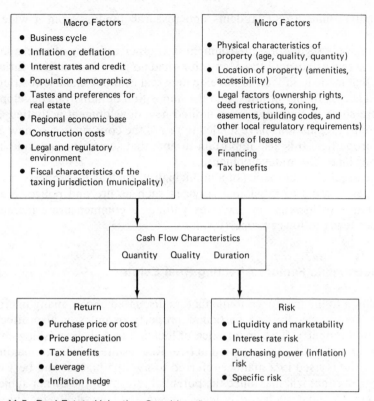

Figure 11-5. Real Estate Valuation Considerations.

might be expected to perform less satisfactorily and might have lower returns than bond and stock investments.

Another category of macro factors affecting the demand for real estate is population demographics. For housing, for example, this includes factors such as the birth rate; the average number of persons living in a household; the attitudes, tastes, and preferences about consumption of housing versus other goods and services; and the average income per household. Changes in life style coupled with higher energy costs could mean more households prefer to be closer to both work and shopping than in the past. This also has implications for the location of industrial and commercial space relative to residential property.

The economic base of the geographic region in which a property is located is still another factor affecting real estate values at a macro level. Some regional and local economies are stronger and grow faster than others. The health of a regional economy depends in part on the growth potential, stability, and diversity of its *base* employment—that is, employment in firms that export goods and services outside of the region. Examples are manufacturers who sell goods outside of the region, tourist-related businesses, large retailers or service industries that again sell outside the region, and even universities that attract students and research funding from a wide geographic area.

A region's regulatory environment is another category of macro factors affecting real estate activity. Many cities had no-growth strategies during the 1970s that made it difficult to develop new real estate. Land use restrictions, limited access to city utilities, and the imposition of numerous development fees are some of the ways cities limited new development activities. Also, rent control regulations have tended to retard the construction of new apartment properties. It is also important to note that some cities provide incentives for inner city redevelopment.

The fiscal characteristics of a municipality, such as its property tax base and rates relative to municipal services such as fire and police, are also important. An increase in tax rates without a commensurate increase in services tends to lower property values.

Microeconomic Factors Affecting Real Estate

In addition to the macroeconomic factors discussed above, many microeconomic factors specific to a particular property or investor also affect the value of a property. The importance of location as a distinguishing characteristic of real estate was stressed above. Real estate values are maximized when a site is used in a manner referred to as "the highest and best use." This is a use that will maximize the potential returns to the owner subject to the constraint that such use is legally permitted, physically feasible, and economically viable. The highest and best use of a site is determined by its location relative to other parcels of real estate and economic activities, uses permitted by zoning, the accessibility of the site, amenities on or near the site, availability of utilities, and the size, shape, and topography of the site. The value of an improvement placed on a site depends on such factors as the size and design of the structure, its age and ability to function well for its intended use, and its general physical condition.

The value of a property to an investor who has leased the property to another user (a *leased fee*) is also dependent on the nature of the lease. A lease that involves a below-market rent results in some of the value of the property accruing to the lessee. The value of this *leasehold estate* is the present value of the difference between the market rent and the contract rent. Leases vary in the way they deal with such considerations as who pays for future increases in operating expenses for the property (e.g., property taxes, insurance, and maintenance), when the lease will be renewed, and how the rate will be adjusted. Many leases also provide for lessors of retail property to receive a "percentage rent" that includes a percentage of the tenant's income over some base amount. All of these characteristics of a lease, in addition to the financial strength of the lessee, affect the value of a leased fee property as well as the extent to which it will be an inflation hedge.

If an investor has a below-market-rate mortgage on a property (perhaps because interest rates have risen), this can result in a higher selling price for the property if the loan can be assumed. That is, the favorable financing is "sold" along with the property. This assumes the absence of a *due on sale* clause in the mortgage which prohibits sale of the financing to the new owner; the enforceability of such clauses was reaffirmed by the U.S. Supreme Court in 1982.

An important economic motivation for many real estate investors, developers, and owner-users is the tax benefits received by investors in real properties relative to most other assets. The primary source of these benefits is the depreciation deductions that are permitted on the entire cost basis of property improvement—deductions that typically greatly exceed any economic depreciation of the value of the income property. This leads to deferral of income taxes until the property is sold. Furthermore, gain on sale of a property is usually treated as a long-term capital gain if the property was held long enough to qualify *and* if straight-line depreciation was taken. If accelerated depreciation is taken instead, then part of the gain may be subject to recapture as ordinary income. For residential property, the excess depreciation (the difference between the accelerated depreciation claimed and that which would have been taken using straight-line depreciation) included in the gain is reclassified as ordinary income. However, on nonresidential real estate *all* accelerated depreciation taken and included in the gain is subject to reclassification as ordinary income.

Another potential tax benefit received by real estate results from the tax credits for rehabilitation of older properties. The Economic Recovery Tax Act of 1981 greatly increased these benefits. The effect of taxes on the return for real estate will be discussed further in the next section.

Overview of Investment Analysis

When inflation was low and relatively predictable, typical financing included fixed rate mortgages, tax sheltering was not considered a primary investment motive, and the valuation of income property was relatively easy. Property value in this environment could often be estimated fairly well by simple capitalization techniques, and simple ratios could be used for measures of investment potential.

As uncertain inflation became more of a factor in the market, financing became more complex, and "bracket creep" increasingly affected investment behavior. At the same time, tax law changes favored real estate relative to other assets. In this changed environment, simple traditional models for income property valuation became inadequate. Most analysts now feel that it is necessary to explicitly project the cash flows expected from a real estate investment over the anticipated holding period. Discounted cash flow analysis is then used to evaluate the cash flows, including the financing and tax benefits. Figure 11-6 on page 492 shows a general model of income property evaluation.

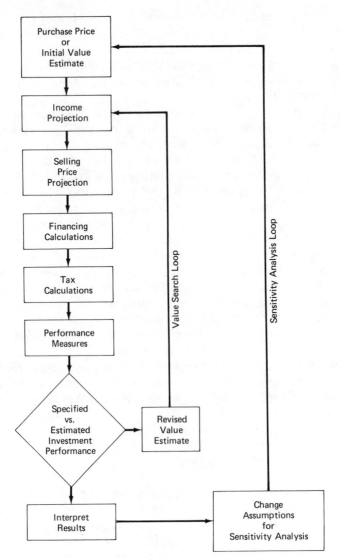

Figure 11-6. The Real Estate Valuation Process.

Cost or Value Estimate. The starting point of a real estate investment analysis is normally either an estimate of the cost of developing the project or the price at which an existing property might be acquired. The purpose of the analysis is, of course, to test the feasibility of this cost or price. If financing is being explicitly considered in the analysis, the focus will be on the return on equity invested in the project (cost or price, less any debt financing).

Income/Expense Projection. The next step is the projection of operating income. This involves projecting potential gross income, vacancy and collection loss, and operating expenses (property taxes, insurance, maintenance, and so on) over a projected holding period.

Projecting income requires consideration of the pattern of the income over time. This depends on the nature of the leases, the type of expenses, the expected increase in these expenses, and how they are related to lease income. Here analysts often make assumptions that essentially involve smoothing the income pattern.

Selling Price Projection. If the period of analysis (the holding period) is shorter than the economic life of the property, the property will have a value at the end of this holding period. This value depends, of course, on expected income that a potential buyer might receive beyond the holding period. Such income could exceed the value to the seller if the seller were to keep the property. One reason this could occur is that the buyer would be taxed differently from the seller because a new basis for depreciation would be established. In any case, the initial or current value of the property frequently depends substantially on the anticipated value (i.e., selling price) at the end of the holding period.

For simplicity, the selling price expected at the end of the holding period is often expressed in terms of a percentage increase or decrease from the initial value. Alternatively, to estimate the selling price, a capitalization rate could be applied to the future stream of income expected at the end of the holding period. Capitalization rates are discussed further in a later section.

Financing Projection. The next major step in the valuation process typically involves financing projections. This includes projection of mortgage payments and the loan balance at the end of the holding period. Other financing considerations could include loan points, refinancing costs, prepayment penalties, loan participations, and possibly a sale-leaseback of the land. An investment analysis could include many combinations of loans and participations. The analyst would be searching for the best available financing alternative.

Related to choosing the best financial alternative is determining whether favorable financial leverage exists. For leverage to be favorable, the rate of return before any financing (the unleveraged or all-equity return) must exceed the cost of the financing. For a taxable investor, this must be evaluated on an after-tax basis.

A sale-leaseback of the land, where the seller retains ownership of the building, can also be viewed as a way of increasing tax benefits. Since land cannot be depreciated but the entire building can be, such a sale-leaseback increases the proportion of the investment that generates a depreciation tax shelter. The lease payments on the land are tax deductible to the lessee and are taxable income to the lessor. As in the case of debt financing, it may be advantageous from a tax perspective for a lower-tax-bracket investor to purchase the land and lease it to a higher-tax-bracket investor.

It should also be pointed out that some investors, such as REITs and pension funds, do not explicitly consider financing in the analysis. They may prefer to value a project on an unleveraged (all-equity) basis.

Tax Calculations. The next step in the valuation process involves tax calculations. This can range from making no tax assumption—that is, doing a before-tax analysis—to doing a comprehensive after-tax analysis by explicitly considering the interaction of the real estate investment with the investor's or institution's other taxable income, recognizing such factors as ordinary income taxes, capital gains taxes, the regular minimum tax on tax preferences, income averaging, and so on. An intermediate position often taken is to use a *marginal* tax rate that assumes all taxes and tax benefits can be captured by a single tax rate. This may or may not be accurate depending on the nature of the investment and the investor's tax status.

If taxes are not explicitly considered (i.e., a before-tax analysis is used), one must know how the tax benefits of the property are reflected in before-tax yields for similar properties. For example, yields tend to be lower for tax-exempt municipal bonds versus otherwise equivalent taxable bonds because the prices of each reflect their tax status. The differential yield is, in effect, the price paid for the tax benefits received and reflects the marginal tax rate for the marginal taxable investor. The investor must evaluate whether he or she is in a position to receive enough tax benefits from the investment to offset the lower before-tax yield. So too, many real estate investments are more attractive to higher-tax-bracket investors than lower-tax-bracket investors. Deciding whether to include a real estate investment with a high degree of tax shelter versus one with less tax shelter in a portfolio is analogous to deciding whether to include stocks with high dividend yields (whose dividends are taxable as ordinary income) versus lower yielding growth stocks with the potential for long-term capital gains.

Valuation Measures. After the above projections are made, the analyst calculates various measures of expected investment performance. These range from simple ratios such as cash flow-to-equity and debt coverage, to measures such as the internal rate of return (the rate that equates future cash inflows with current outflows) and net present value. Valuation measures based on estimated cash flows would then be contrasted with specified investment criteria (e.g., a required rate of return) to evaluate the investment. For example, the after-tax internal rate of return would be compared with other investments of comparable risk. If a certain valuation measure (e.g., internal rate of return) is not equal to that required by the investor to justify the investment, a revised price estimate can be made and the process repeated, starting with income projections.

The valuation process suggested here is analogous to the dividend discount model and security market line (SML) approach originally developed by Wells Fargo Investment Advisors. Using this approach, a security's internal rate of return and systematic risk are estimated and, via the SML, compared to other common stocks in the sample to determine whether, at that stock's systematic or beta risk level, it is undervalued or overvalued.

Interpretation of Results and Sensitivity Analysis. After evaluating performance measures, the analyst must interpret the results in view of overall investment criteria and risk considerations. At this point, it is often desirable to evaluate the sensitivity of the results to alternative assumptions that could be made in any of the major valuation steps discussed above. This includes alternative financing, tax assumptions, and income projections. *Sensitivity analysis* is performed for two reasons. First, it is used to help determine an optimal financing or depreciation plan. Second, it is a step toward identifying the riskiness of the investment. Risk is discussed further in a later section.

Holding Period Considerations. Real estate income property is typically sold after a holding period of seven to ten years. One of the reasons for this is that the tax benefits of the property usually decrease over time. This occurs because (1) with accelerated depreciation, the depreciation deduction decreases over time, and (2) as the mortgage is repaid, the interest portion of the loan payment decreases while the total payment (principal and interest) usually remains constant. Since only the interest is tax deductible, tax benefits tend to decrease each year. Furthermore, as the mortgage is repaid, the investor's equity investment in the property increases and the leverage benefit decreases. After a period of time, more funds may be tied up in the property than the investor would prefer to have in a single project. Thus the investor may either refinance or sell the property to receive this equity buildup.[19]

Use of the Computer in Real Estate Evaluation

The valuation process outlined in the previous section is well suited for computer analysis for several reasons. First, once the input assumptions are made, the remaining steps involve applying mathematical calculations to the inputs to arrive at the various performance measures. Second, many of the calculations involve an iterative or recursive search process that can be quite time consuming even with the use of a hand calculator. Third, the computer can easily be used to recalculate all the performance measures based on

---

[19] The purchaser of a property can start depreciating the new basis in the property and also can use an accelerated method of depreciation. Thus, the depreciation tax benefits received by the buyer may exceed those given up by a seller. The tax benefits received by the buyer would be expected to be reflected in the price he or she is willing to pay for the property. This price may be higher than the value of the property to the current owner if the property is held. Thus a sale may be beneficial to both parties. One useful measure that can be used to help decide when to sell a property is the marginal rate of return. This is discussed further in the chapter appendix.

changes in one or more of the input assumptions, whereas the time and effort required to make such sensitivity analysis is difficult and time consuming without one. Fourth, using the computer to do the calculations makes it feasible to incorporate more complex and comprehensive assumptions into the evaluation process (e.g., taxes and financing) than might otherwise be considered. New software that will further standardize the valuation process for real estate applications is being developed.

The above discussion should not be construed to imply that all aspects of real estate evaluation can be computerized. One must still use personal and subjective judgment in arriving at the proper input assumptions and in interpreting the results. Rather, it is the design of the process and the conversion of the input assumptions into meaningful performance measures and summary statistics that is well suited to computer analysis.

The appendix to this chapter provides a case example to illustrate the basic steps in real estate investment analysis outlined above. This includes details of the procedures for calculating before- and after-tax cash flows and rates of return for real estate. It also shows how a computer model called REALVAL, which is used by many insurance companies and mortgage bankers, can be used to do this kind of analysis.

The Appraisal Process

When securities are listed on an exchange and traded fairly often in standard units, it is relatively easy to determine what the market believes to be the value of the investment. In the case of real property, no such national exchange exists. As discussed at the outset of this chapter, each parcel of real estate is unique and does not sell frequently. This reality creates the need for a means by which to estimate the market value of the property. For this purpose, the analyst must use a procedure known as the *appraisal process* to estimate the market value.

The appraisal process involves gathering information both about the property being valued (referred to as the *subject property*) and for other similar or comparable properties (referred to as *comps*) in the same market area. Three approaches are then typically taken to estimate the market value of the subject property.

Cost Approach. The first of these, the *cost approach,* starts by estimating the cost of replacing or reproducing the improvements as if new. A deduction is then made for factors such as physical deterioration in the structure, obsolescence in functional design, and loss of value due to economic factors external to the property that reduce its utility for its intended use. Finally, the value of the land site is added to arrive at an estimate of the total market value. The value of the site would have to be estimated by one of the approaches discussed below.

Income Approach. The *income approach* starts by estimating the income from the property. The income is then converted into a present value estimate. This process is referred to as *capitalization*. There are many capitalization techniques used by appraisers. One approach is to discount the future income to arrive at a present value estimate. This is conceptually the same as discounting future dividends or earnings to arrive at an estimate of the value of a stock. The appropriate discount rate would reflect the riskiness of the real estate. It represents the rate of return that can be earned on properties with comparable risk and tax characteristics.

When estimating market value, federal income taxes usually are not explicitly considered in the analysis. That is, the before-tax cash flows are discounted to arrive at the value estimate. In this case the discount rate (internal rate of return for comparable properties) must also be on a before-tax basis. One must be careful that such a rate is derived from properties of comparable tax treatment, since differences in taxation might be expected to result in much different before-tax rates of return for properties even though after-tax rates of return are comparable.

Income property appraisal techniques differ as to whether the income stream is valued before or after deducting financing costs. If financing costs (e.g., the mortgage payments) are not deducted, the rate of return is a return on the total property. This is analogous to return on assets. When financing is deducted, the rate of return used in the analysis is a return on equity and will reflect any financial leverage that results from the financing. This will be higher (lower) than the unleveraged return on the entire property if the leverage is favorable (unfavorable). Thus, as was the case with taxes, the choice of a proper discount rate depends on the assumption made regarding the income stream.

Market Data Approach. The third approach to appraisal is referred to as the *market data approach*. While all three approaches to appraisal rely on market data, this approach differs from the other two in that the data used are those directly observable in the market. There are two primary ways of applying this approach.

DIRECT MARKET METHOD. The first, the *direct market method,* takes sales prices from comparable properties that have recently sold and adjusts these prices for differences due to factors such as age, location, size of the site and improvements, market conditions at the time of sale, and so on.

GROSS INCOME MULTIPLIER METHOD. The second, the *gross income multiplier method,* involves calculating the ratio of the observed selling price to potential gross income for the coming period from comparable properties and using this ratio to estimate the value of the property being appraised. The critical assumption is that the properties used to develop the gross income multiplier ratio are truly comparable to the subject property in terms of risk, expense ratio, taxation, financing, and so on. If enough data on these key variables can be found that are truly comparable, this approach has potential merit. It is analogous to using a price/earnings ratio of a stock listed on an exchange to establish the value of other stocks of similar risk and growth prospects that should, since they have comparable key variable characteristics, have similar price/earnings ratios.

CAP RATE APPROACH. A similar approach involves the use of the pretax ratio of net operating income to selling price for comparable properties to estimate the value of the subject property. This ratio is referred to as the capitalization rate or *cap rate* for the property. When adequate actual or expected income and operating expense data are available, this rate can be observed directly from the market and used with an estimate of operating income to estimate the value of a specific property. Although using cap rates in making appraisals is usually considered an income approach, used in this fashion it could be considered another application of the market data approach to appraisal. Cap rates can also be derived algebraically based on assumptions about future income and the required return for the holding period. This approach is analogous to using discounted cash flow analysis, and is another method used as part of the income approach.

It is important to recognize that the cap rate is a *ratio* of the current operating income (before depreciation, taxes, and financing) to the value of the property. It is *not* a rate of return. Properties with the same expected after-tax rate of return over a holding period may have different cap rates due to differences in the expected future growth of income of the properties. A property that has a below-market interest rate loan that can be assumed may also justify a lower cap rate than a property that does not have such financing. This is because the financing can be sold along with the property.

To arrive at a final value estimate for a property, an appraiser usually uses evidence obtained by using all three major approaches discussed above (cost, income, and market data). If properly applied with sufficient and compatible data, each method should produce a value estimate that is comparable with any other. However, for income-producing properties being bought and sold as investments, which is the focus of this chapter, most analysts believe that the income and market data approaches usually produce a more reliable and useful value estimate than the cost approach because the former approaches more fully reflect what investors are seeking in future benefits from the property.

RISK AND RETURN ANALYSIS OF REAL ESTATE

The previous sections of this chapter have attempted to identify the major vehicles for investing in real estate and some of the more significant considerations in making such an investment. The major participants in the real estate market were also identified. This section introduces some of the important considerations in determining how much and what kind of real estate a particular individual or institutional investor should incorporate into a portfolio. First identified are the major factors that affect the risk and return characteristics of a real estate investment, with particular emphasis on real estate equity investments. The risk and return tradeoffs for the major real estate investment vehicles are then discussed.

Factors Affecting Risk and Return

As in the case of fixed income (Chapter 9) and corporate equity (Chapter 10) securities, the choice of an appropriate vehicle for a particular individual or institution depends on the risk and return objectives of the investor. These objectives must be matched against the characteristics of the particular investment vehicle and any constraints facing the investor, such as liquidity, taxes, investment holding period, regulatory and legal factors, or other unique considerations as discussed in Chapters 4 and 5.

We have already mentioned some of the objectives and constraints of different types of real estate investors, including those for pension funds, insurance companies, and individuals. Earlier in this chapter some of the reasons why real estate differs from other investments were offered. Several reasons were then given for considering real estate as an investment. These include its potential hedge against inflation, portfolio diversification benefits, and tax benefits. These factors ultimately affect the risk and return characteristics of real estate relative to other assets. Other risk and return modifying factors that are important for real estate include the potential for using a high degree of financial leverage, the need for professional management, and the relative lack of liquidity and marketability of many real estate investments.

In constructing an investment portfolio, one must determine the role that real estate can serve in terms of the overall risk and return characteristics of the portfolio. The optimal amount of real estate and the particular way of investing in real estate depend on the investment objectives and constraints of the individual or institution. The following factors might be considered:

- Existing portfolio mix
- Return requirement
- Desired level of risk
- Time horizon
- Liquidity needs
- Tax status
- Legal and regulatory considerations
- Amount of capital available

All portfolios must be tailored to meet the needs of a particular investor. This is particularly important for real estate, however, due to the heterogeneous character of real estate investments and the flexibility that is provided by structuring such investments. The remainder of this chapter considers the role of real estate in the asset mix decision in detail.

Diversification Benefits. An investor without any kind of real estate investments should be able to increase portfolio diversification by adding them, especially in the equity form. This is due to the fact that returns for equity real estate tend not to be highly correlated with those of more traditional portfolio investments such as stocks and bonds.

A study by Friedman [1971] showed that portfolios that include real estate investments may be more efficient than those that do not. That is, one may be able to reduce the degree of portfolio risk for a given level of expected return by including real estate. Figure 11-7 illustrates the benefit of adding real estate as a fourth asset type to a three-asset portfolio of cash equivalents, bonds, and common stocks using data supplied by Malcolm MacKinnon of the Prudential Insurance Company.

Burns and Epley [1982] found essentially the same results using equity REITs instead of the direct real estate investments used by Friedman. Using data for the 1970–79 time period, a mixed-asset efficient frontier consisting of both equity REITs and diversified common stock portfolios was found to be superior to portfolios of just stocks or just REITs at every risk and return level.

Other studies have also found relatively low correlation between real estate and other investments, suggesting that there might be diversification benefits associated with adding real estate to a portfolio. For example, Robichek, Cohn, and Pringle [1972] found that farm real estate had a negative correlation coefficient (ρ) with the S&P Industrial Index ($-.13$), the S&P Utility Index ($-.15$), and U.S. government securities ($-.19$) over the period 1949–69. Similarly, Hoag [1980] found negative correlation between a value-weighted index of industrial real estate and corporate bonds ($-.31$) and the S&P 500 Stock Index ($-.07$) over the period 1973–78.

Extending this concept even further, it may also be beneficial to invest both in different types of property (residential, office, industrial, and so on) and in real estate in different geographic locations. As pointed out earlier, real estate, which is fixed in location, frequently depends to a significant extent on local economic conditions that can often differ significantly from one location to another. Also, different types of property are affected by different supply and demand factors. At the level of a particular project, one would normally look for diversification among the types of tenants for similar reasons.

Tax Benefits. The tax benefits of real estate relative to other investments were previously mentioned. It was also pointed out that the price of real estate may reflect these tax benefits. Thus, a price is paid for tax benefits in terms of a lower before-tax return than might be expected for otherwise comparable fully taxable assets. This is illustrated in Figure 11-8 (page 502),

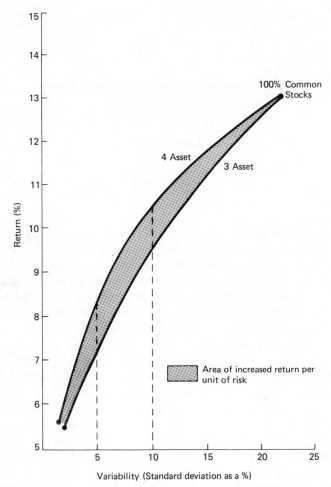

Figure 11-7. Comparison of Portfolios on a Three-Asset (Cash Equivalents, Bonds, and Common Stocks) Efficient Frontier with Portfolios on a Four-Asset (adding Real Estate) Efficient Frontier.

which depicts rates of return on a fully taxable and a tax-exempt investment as a function of investor tax benefits. The before-tax rate of return would be the same as the after-tax return for an investor with a zero tax rate. As the investor's marginal tax rate increases, the after-tax rate of return decreases for the fully taxable investment. However, the after-tax return for the tax-exempt investment is the same as the before-tax return regardless of the tax rate.

The before-tax return for the fully taxable investment must be higher than that for the tax-exempt investment because the returns for both investments would be expected to equate on an after-tax basis at a positive marginal tax rate t_m. The actual rate at which the after-tax returns equate de-

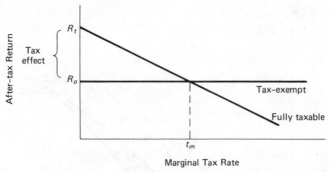

Figure 11-8. Comparison of Tax Effect on Returns to Tax-Exempt vs. Fully Taxable Investors.

pends on the supply of and demand for different sources of tax shelter. The difference in before-tax rates of return between the fully taxable and the tax-exempt investments would be the difference between the vertical intercepts $(R_t - R_o)$. This reflects the differential tax treatment. We would expect an analogous differential in before-tax rates of return between otherwise comparable fully taxable investments and real estate investments possessing tax benefits. Consequently, the extent to which an investor can use the tax benefits of a particular real estate investment should be weighed against the price paid for these benefits in terms of lower before-tax return.

Unfortunately there is little hard evidence as to the degree to which returns for real estate have reflected tax benefits. Some evidence of the price of a tax shelter might be found in the return differential for taxable and tax-exempt bonds. In an efficient market one would expect a similar price for comparable types of tax shelter. However, real estate has significant tax characteristics, such as the potential to shelter other investment income, that differ from those of tax-exempt bonds. Thus, it may be priced quite differently. For a particular real estate investment, an investor can identify the specific tax shelter benefits.

SELLING BENEFITS TO TAXABLE INVESTORS. For tax-exempt investors such as pension funds, it is possible to achieve the diversification benefits as well as the return benefits of real estate by selling the tax shelter benefits to taxable investors. Indeed, many partnerships are structured in a way to allocate tax benefits, such as depreciation and capital gains, to the investor most able to use them in exchange for allocating more cash flow to the lower-tax-rate or tax-exempt investor.

Similarly, the use of debt financing can be viewed as a way of allocating the cash flow from a real estate investment to two different investor clienteles. Since interest is tax deductible, debt financing tends to increase the amount of tax benefits relative to the equity invested in a property. Although the interest income to the lender is taxable, a lender in a lower tax bracket may find the after-tax return on interest income more attractive than the after-tax return that could be achieved on an equity investment (assuming the before-tax return on the real estate is lower due to the tax benefits).

PORTFOLIO POSITIONING OF TAX SHELTERS. Fisher [1980] has shown the effect of explicitly considering tax sheltered investments in a portfolio setting. An equilibrium model is developed in which there are market-clearing prices for each asset. However, each investor does not hold the same portfolio; rather, investors in different tax brackets see different after-tax efficient frontiers. Similarly, the after-tax risk-free rate also differs for investors in different tax brackets. Thus, instead of a single optimal (tangency) portfolio, as is the case for traditional portfolio theory, there is a unique optimal portfolio for each tax bracket. This is illustrated in Figure 11-9.

The line from R_f along the tax rate axis represents the after-tax risk-free rate, $R_f(1 - t)$. Similarly, there is a series of after-tax efficient frontiers at each tax rate along the tax axis. The optimal portfolio for an investor in a particular tax bracket would then be represented by the point of tangency between the efficient frontier and a line from the after-tax risk-free rate. By combining a portfolio of risky assets with the risk-free asset, the investor can select a level of risk and return anywhere along this line.

Note that due to tax effects the before-tax return-risk point, R_m, for the market portfolio, consisting of a value-weighted investment in each asset in the market, is no longer the optimal risk-return position for risk asset portfo-

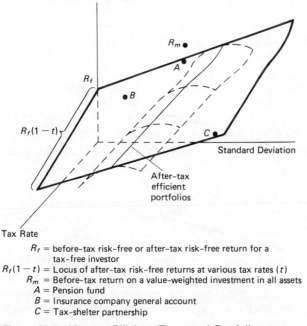

R_f = before-tax risk-free or after-tax risk-free return for a
tax-free investor
$R_f(1 - t)$ = Locus of after-tax risk-free returns at various tax rates (t)
R_m = Before-tax return on a value-weighted investment in all assets
A = Pension fund
B = Insurance company general account
C = Tax-shelter partnership

Figure 11-9. After-tax Efficient (Tangency) Portfolios.

lios for every investor. Because of differential taxation of asset returns, investors can maximize after-tax risk-adjusted returns by tailoring their portfolio to their tax situation. Since such tailoring may result in each investor holding a disproportionate share of certain assets, no one will hold exactly the same market portfolio.

Maximizing Benefits by Tailoring Portfolios. The importance of this result is that individuals and institutions should be aware of the possible benefit of tailoring portfolios to maximize tax benefits. That is, the optimal portfolio for a tax-exempt investor could be quite different from that of a high-tax-bracket investor. The former might be tilted more toward mortgages and land investments, while the latter might hold highly leveraged equity investments in depreciable property. However, it is not necessarily irrational for a tax-exempt pension fund to hold some depreciable income property, since the diversification benefits may outweigh the cost (in lower returns) resulting from purchasing a tax shelter that cannot be used. However, the diversification benefits of adding additional depreciable real estate would be expected to diminish much faster than for a taxable investor.

The model developed by Fisher implies that the pricing of assets can be explained in terms of their systematic risk and potential tax-shelter benefits (if any), as illustrated in Figure 11-10. The expected before-tax rate of return for an asset rises with additional systematic risk but decreases with additional tax-shelter benefits. Thus, a fully taxable bond or mortgage investment might be represented by point A on this investment market plane, whereas a tax-exempt municipal bond might be represented by point C.

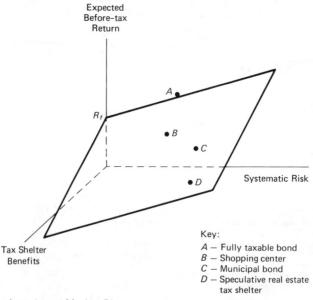

Figure 11-10. Investment Market Plane.

Similarly, points *B* and *D* might represent two different real estate equity investments, the latter containing more tax benefits than the former. The plane approach developed here is analogous to the security market plane used by Wells Fargo Bank to capture the differential taxation of dividends versus capital gains for stocks, but is more general.

Inflation Hedge. It has repeatedly been mentioned here that real estate was an excellent inflation hedge during the 1970s. Early in this period Hallengren [1974] found that returns from real estate were higher during inflationary cycles but lower during disinflation. Hoag [1980] found the correlation between the rate of inflation (as measured by the Consumer Price Index) and returns on his index of industrial real estate to be $+.50$ during much of the 1970s, while inflation's correlation was negative with stock $(-.41)$ and bond $(-.50)$ returns. Thus, it is not surprising that many institutional investors turned to real estate during the 1970s in an attempt to beat inflation. Whether real estate will continue to be an inflation hedge and how it will perform in future periods of disinflation are unresolved but important issues.

Measuring the Performance of Real Estate

Information as to the performance of real estate is not as readily available as that for assets like stocks and bonds, which are traded continuously on national exchanges or frequently in the over-the-counter market. This makes it difficult to evaluate the performance of real estate in general, and—perhaps more importantly—to evaluate how well a particular real estate portfolio did relative to other real estate portfolios or investments. Since a particular real estate investment may turn over only every five or more years, market price data typically are not available to develop the risk-return measures based on annual or shorter holding period returns that can be developed for other assets such as stocks and bonds. While appraisals are sometimes used to arrive at more frequent price information, this is not as objective as actual transactions data and may tend to smooth out the fluctuations that might be seen in actual values if they could be observed. Thus, for real estate, variance or standard deviation of returns calculated on the basis of these data may substantially underestimate the true value of these dispersion statistics based on actual transactions data. The longer average holding period for real estate investments relative to stocks and bonds adds to the apparent stability of market values for real estate.

One step toward better evaluation of real estate portfolios might be via a national real estate index as proposed by Hoag [1980] and being developed by him in 1982 and by the Frank Russell Company. The advantage of such an index is that it would provide information to develop annual total or holding period returns that could then be used to develop risk and return measures for real estate, as has been done for assets such as stocks using indexes like the S&P 500 or the Wilshire 5000. Such an index has the potential to give a more accurate indication as to how well real estate has performed, its covariance with other assets in the market, and how to optimally balance a portfolio with real estate and other assets.

Using his index, Hoag estimated the *quarterly* return and standard deviation for industrial real estate for the 1973–78 time interval as follows:

Asset	Quarterly Mean Return	Standard Deviation
Real estate—industrial properties	3.38%	8.61%
S&P 500	.92	10.38
Inflation	1.96	.61
Corporate bonds	1.55	4.02
Treasury bills	1.52	.31

The *annualized* returns would be roughly four times the numbers shown; annualized standard deviations would be about twice their size. These results contrast with those from another study by the Frank Russell Company that found the following annual returns and standard deviations for an 8-year time interval through 1981.

Asset	Annual Mean Return	Standard Deviation
Commingled real estate fund	11.9%	4.0%
S&P 500	8.0	18.6
Dow Jones Industrial Average	5.9	18.6
Long-term corporate bonds	2.9	14.1

Other than the difference in holding period, the dramatic difference in the relative amount of risk and return for real estate between these two sets of results is explained by the fact that Hoag used only transactional data in his study. Frank Russell's numbers include significant appraisal data and thus result in a substantially lower standard deviation for the latter. Hoag's results show real estate volatility akin to that of common stocks.

Additional Real Estate Risk and Return Modifiers

Many of the important characteristics of real estate equity investments in terms of diversification benefits, tax shelter benefits, and as a potential inflation hedge have already been discussed. These factors all impact the risk and return of real estate equity investments relative to mortgage investments and non-real estate investments. Several additional characteristics of real estate must be discussed to fully evaluate different types of real estate investments relative to each other and relative to other assets. These are leverage potential, liquidity and marketability, the relative efficiency of real estate markets, and the need for professional management.

Leverage Potential. Real estate has typically been financed with a combination of equity and debt. Leverage provides a risk-return extender as discussed in Chapter 10. It also increases the relative amount of tax shelter from a direct real estate equity investment because the interest is tax deductible. Real estate is not subject to the at-risk depreciation tax rules that limit the ability to gain tax benefits from leveraging other types of tax shelter. A real estate investor can therefore depreciate the entire cost basis of the building even though only a small portion of it is financed by *at-risk equity capital.*[20]

Liquidity and Marketability. Earlier we raised the fact that real estate is not traded on a national exchange (except indirectly via REITs), which limits its liquidity. Real estate properties cannot be moved from areas of excess supply to areas of excess demand. Moreover, at any given point in time there may be a limited number of investors in the market for a particular type of property in a particular price range and in a particular location. Thus, real estate tends to be less marketable than other investment assets. It may take several weeks or months to find a buyer for a property at a price close to what is estimated as its market value. In fact, recall that the American Institute of Real Estate Appraisers' definition of market value includes a reasonable time on the market.

The marketability of real estate depends on the restructuring of the terms of sale and the financing available. Since real estate typically cannot be sold for cash in a short period of time without (or even with) a large price concession, it is much less liquid than either equities or fixed income securities. This adds to the risk of direct real estate investments and would, of course, dictate a higher rate of return than otherwise comparable but more liquid assets.

Exchange funds, such as the 1982-incorporated Rexmoor Properties, Inc., may provide a new avenue for liquidating real estate. Rexmoor is seeking to acquire income-producing properties throughout the United States and is offering in exchange shares of Rexmoor common stock, which is expected to be listed on the American Stock Exchange. Rexmoor is also

---

[20] Furthermore, direct real estate equity investments are often classified as property held as a trade or business rather than property held as an investment. Such property is not subject to the nontrade or nonbusiness interest deduction limitation that typically applies to margin-financed securities purchases. Interest charges on funds borrowed to finance security purchases are limited to the lesser of $10,000, or one-half of net investment income—such as dividend or interest income—earned on those securities, a limitation that affects investors using leverage to purchase capital-gain-oriented stocks. In fact, Litzenberger and Ramaswamy [1979] argue that this limitation may result in some investors (who desire to use high leverage as a risk-return extender) preferring high-dividend-paying stocks to growth stocks because the former allow maximum deduction of interest expense.

seeking debt-free properties, but may acquire properties subject to mortgages if it deems the terms to be advantageous.

Efficiency of Real Estate Markets. The real estate market is often viewed as less efficient than many other markets. Several reasons for this have already been discussed, including:

- Uniqueness of each parcel
- Lack of a national exchange
- Difficulty of obtaining relevant information about prices and values
- Large size of typical direct real estate equity investments
- Importance of financing for many purchasers
- Necessity for professional management
- Difficulty of applying standard valuation tools applicable to real estate
- Potential legal complications

Thus, the real estate market appears to violate many of the conditions normally considered prerequisite to an efficient market. At the same time, it is unlikely that an investor can earn a higher than normal return simply by using information about past prices and without seeing the property or knowing anything about the local market—especially when the relatively high round-trip transactions costs of a typical real estate investment are considered. Such costs include brokerage commissions, legal fees associated with verification and transfer of title, costs of obtaining financing, and taxes associated with the sale. Thus, the real estate market is likely to be weak-form efficient in the sense discussed in Chapter 10.

However, an investor who has advance information about plans for future highway expansions, new plant locations, and the like may be able to make a higher than normal return by buying land before the information is publicly available and fully reflected in land values. The use of such inside information is *not* illegal in real estate transactions, as it is for trading corporate securities by those in possession of material inside information. Of course, excess returns earned by using such information may represent, in part, a return on time spent cultivating political and social relationships with the appropriate people and learning about the local market. There are also risks that time spent pursuing a strategy of trying to be at the right place at the right time will not pay off. Thus it is still not clear that the market for information is not relatively efficient for real estate markets. What is clear is that if one decides to follow a strategy of trying to pick properties that have the potential for windfall gains, then one should be compensated for the higher risk and costs associated with following such a strategy.

The Need for Professional Management. As we have discussed, direct real estate equity investments require professional management. Choice of tenants, negotiation of leases, proper maintenance, and so on are important to the success of a real estate venture. Professional property managers can be hired to perform such activities, but ultimately the owner-investor bears the responsibility. Even when professional managers are hired, the owner must monitor the performance of the property manager; not being in a position to do so poses an additional risk. For this reason, it may be desirable for an institution to have a local partner to oversee the operation of direct real estate investments.

Unsystematic Risk. We have seen that real estate is not highly correlated with stocks and fixed income securities and that adding real estate investments can increase overall portfolio diversification. Due to the local orientation of the real estate market, the uniqueness of each parcel, and the way socioeconomic factors affect different types of real estate, different parcels of real estate may react differently to changing economic conditions. Properties in one area of the country may be rising in value while others are falling or stable. Similarly, office buildings may be an attractive investment at times when apartment buildings are not. At the same time, real estate in general may behave differently than stocks and fixed income securities in response to changing economic conditions. This makes it possible to reduce total portfolio risk (variance of returns) at a given level of return for a well-diversified portfolio of real estate, stocks, and fixed income securities. But it also leads to the potential for special sources of unsystematic risk for a portfolio that is not well diversified, both geographically and by property type.

Unfortunately, there is little evidence as to just how important it is to diversify across geographic locations and property types in order to minimize unsystematic risk. Intuitively, it would seem that such diversification would be highly desirable. If so, an investor or portfolio manager who purposely attempts to concentrate investment in geographic areas or property types that he or she thinks will outperform the market may incur additional unsystematic risk. This is analogous to choosing particular industries and companies in which to concentrate common stock investment. To compensate for the higher exposure to unsystematic risk, a commensurately higher return must be expected to justify such a strategy. Unfortunately, knowledge about the future performance of different types of property or geographic locations may already be reflected in the current price of the property.

Given that it is desirable to diversify across property type and geographic location, the large amount of investment required for many properties (e.g., an office building in downtown Denver) makes it difficult for many investors to achieve such diversification with direct real estate investments, even if vehicles such as real estate limited partnerships are used. Thus, alternative vehicles such as REITs and commingled real estate funds may provide an important diversification service in this respect.

Risk and Return Tradeoffs for Alternative Vehicles

Earlier we said there is a myriad of real estate investment alternatives. The investor can purchase either a debt, equity, or hybrid debt-equity real estate position. Also, investment can be made directly in a property or indirectly through a number of intermediaries and security-like instruments. The major alternatives are shown in Table 11-15.

The risk and return characteristics of a particular investment vehicle depend on whether the vehicle is more in the nature of debt or equity and whether it is a direct or indirect investment vehicle. A summary of the various investment vehicles and their relative differences in potential risk and return benefits follows.

Equity Real Estate. The additional diversification benefits of real estate and its potential as an inflation hedge accrue to equity investment because the rate of return on equity depends directly on the residual performance—after leverage effects—of the property, just as it does for common stocks. Direct real estate equity investments such as proprietorships, joint ventures, and limited partnerships, and direct investment by institutions also provide the greatest potential tax benefits to the investor.

The disadvantages of direct investments include the need for professional management, the need for a significantly large investment fund to diversify across geographic locations and property types, and the relative lack of liquidity. The impact of these factors on return and risk was discussed previously.

Indirect investments such as equity REITs and commingled real estate funds should provide the investor with more liquidity and professional management, with open-end CREFs providing more liquidity than closed-end funds as mentioned earlier. Furthermore, the REIT or CREF frequently invests in a wide variety of property types and geographic locations and therefore provides diversification services. However, because of their risk-reducing properties, these more efficient vehicles are likely to be more effi-

TABLE 11-15. Matrix of Real Estate Investment Categories

Debt vs. Equity Spectrum	DIRECTNESS OF INVESTMENT SPECTRUM	
	Direct ←——————————→ Indirect	
Debt	Mortgage loans	Mortgage-backed securities Mortgage REITs
	Mortgages with participations Convertible mortgages	Hybrid debt-equity REITs
Equity	Joint ventures Limited partnership Sole ownership	CREFs Equity REITs

ciently priced (for the risk level assumed) than direct investments with commensurately smaller expected returns. Additionally, the investor may not be able to receive the same tax-shelter benefits through an indirect real estate investment. For example, REITs cannot pass net operating losses through to the investor as an offset to an investor's other taxable income. Also, a stigma associated with the poor performance and the investment practices of many REITs during the early 1970s may result in a possible systematic, continuing negative bias in their pricing.

Real Estate Debt Investments. A pure debt investment in real estate has few if any of the benefits of equity real estate investments, such as tax shelter, diversification potential, or inflation hedge. Of course, the real property is still the underlying collateral and thus has some impact on the underlying value of the debt instruments. Still, a mortgage investment is much like any fixed income investment, with much the same risk and return characteristics (except it is less liquid). A standard fixed rate mortgage is analogous to a bond with a constantly amortizing principal value resulting in a zero face value at the end of the loan term. However, the borrower can usually call the loan (like a corporation calling a callable bond) by selling the property or prepaying the loan (although there may be a penalty for early repayment).

Because mortgage payments include both interest and principal, the *duration* (a concept discussed in Chapter 9) of a mortgage will be less than that of a bond with the same term to maturity and coupon. As discussed earlier, mortgage loans in the early 1980s typically had a shorter term (e.g., 3–5 years) even though they were still amortized over a longer period (e.g., 20–25 years). Such loans are even more analogous to bonds, with the bond face value being equal to the balance of the mortgage.

As discussed previously, the use of a variable rate mortgage is a way of transferring some of the interest rate risk to the borrower. This is one way of adjusting the degree of risk exposure of the lender. A variable rate mortgage might therefore be expected to have a lower initial rate than a fixed rate mortgage unless there is a declining term structure of interest rates, because the ability to adjust the interest rate periodically produces an investment with lower risk.

A major disadvantage of direct mortgage loans is the lack of liquidity, although, as discussed earlier, by the early 1980s advances in the secondary market for residential loans had helped alleviate this disadvantage. Indirect mortgage investments, such as mortgage REITs or mortgage-backed securities, provide some liquidity and geographic diversification to the mortgage portfolio.

Hybrid Debt-Equity Investments. There exist several vehicles that allow for an investment that has the characteristics of both debt and equity. The main alternatives were identified earlier in this chapter. For example, direct real estate mortgage loans can be combined with participations in either the income or price appreciation of the property in return for a lower basic mortgage interest rate. Thus, the lender exchanges some of the return in the form of fixed interest payments for a return that depends on the performance of the property. This provides the lender with a potential inflation hedge and a return with a systematic risk component much like that of an equity investor. In addition, there are indirect investment vehicles, such as hybrid mortgage-equity REITs, that invest in both debt and equity, providing diversification both within and between asset categories.

Another relatively recent alternative is the convertible mortgage. These loans typically give the lender the option of converting the debt to an equity ownership in the property after a period of time—typically about five years. The price of the option is a lower interest rate on the loan. The loan is also typically interest-only as long as it is in debt form (i.e., participation is possible only via conversion from debt to equity). An interesting aspect of this arrangement is that the developer receives the tax benefits during the early years of the property (which may be more valuable to the developer than to the lender), and the lender receives an option that, like any option, is a risk-return extender but has the characteristics of a real estate equity investment.

Asset Allocation and Portfolio Optimization

In the immediately preceding three chapters the portfolio construction process was described in terms, first, of deciding how much of a portfolio should be allocated to different asset categories (e.g., equities and fixed income securities) and, second, of optimizing the composition of the subportfolio of assets within each of the asset categories. The investor's objectives and constraints and the expectations for the markets in general, and for individual securities or investments in particular, influence both steps in this process.

Adding real estate to the investment opportunity set increases the complexity of making these decisions. With the agglomeration of debt-like, hybrid debt-and-equity-like, and equity-like instruments as suggested in this chapter, it is almost impossible to treat all types of real estate as having a uniform set of risk and return characteristics. There are wide differences in the diversification potential (i.e., covariances with other assets), hedging benefits, leverage potential, taxation, and liquidity of the different real estate investment vehicles. Therefore, for real estate portfolio construction, it might be more practical to separate real estate into at least two major categories, such as those most like debt and those most like equity, and then optimize each of these subportfolios.

The debt-like real estate portfolio could then be viewed much the same as a portfolio of fixed income securities. In fact, these two portfolios might even be combined and managed as a single, debt or fixed income portfolio.

The equity-like real estate portfolio would ideally be optimized using the same portfolio methodology as applied to corporate equities in Chapter 10.

Alternatively, one could jointly optimize a portfolio consisting of both corporate equities and real estate equity. However, in either case it would be necessary to estimate the mean returns and standard deviations for different subcategories of real estate equity (e.g., by property type and geographic location) and either the covariances (or correlations) between all the assets in the portfolio or the covariance with a common index. Unfortunately, the data needed for such computations were either not available or not reliable in 1982.

This suggested approach does not provide a very satisfactory solution for quasi-debt, quasi-equity hybrid instruments such as shared appreciation or convertible mortgages. The only resolution possible is the same as that for convertible debentures or convertible preferred stocks: Rather than letting them remain a fixed-income-type asset, treat them as equity instruments either at the outset or as soon as the odds shift in favor of the instrument being converted into an equity-type asset by the end of the projected holding period.

Given the lack of frequent transactions data for real estate equities and the lack of real estate indexes, the approach suggested here is not currently possible. However, given its particular advantages and disadvantages, enough is known about the risk and return characteristics of real estate equities to make at least a rough subjective judgment as to how much equity real estate to include in a portfolio under various economic scenarios. (This was in fact done in Chapter 6.) That is, we know how real estate equity in general correlated with stocks, bonds, and cash-equivalent instruments during the 1970s (even though, as pointed out earlier, this very favorable environment may not soon occur again). What we don't know a lot about are the correlations among different property types and locations within the real estate category. Until the data and tools are such that more sophisticated methodology can be applied, one will have to rely largely on common sense to diversify among property types and geographic locations to optimize the real estate equity portfolio.

SUMMARY

This chapter has introduced the important considerations in real estate investment analysis, including its role in an individual's or institution's overall investment portfolio. The major vehicles for real estate investment were discussed, ranging from debt to equity investments and from direct to indirect forms of investment. The investment objectives of the major participants in the real estate market, such as individuals, limited partnerships, pension funds, and financial institutions were also described.

A primary purpose of this discussion has been to make the reader aware of the role that real estate can play in a portfolio, and to provide some guidance as to how one might decide how much and what type of real estate would be appropriate in a given investment situation. A framework has been provided for understanding the major factors that affect the risk and return for the different real estate investment vehicles.

As a final comment, recall that the primary reason for having a diversified portfolio is the fact that it is difficult, if not impossible, to predict what kinds of assets will outperform the market in the future. Thus, it is desirable to combine different types of assets in a portfolio in the expectation that all will not respond in the same way to changes in the economic climate. In this regard, real estate is an asset that was largely neglected by many institutional investors until the 1970s. While the unique conditions that made the returns on real estate unusually attractive during the 1970s may not be repeated in the future, there is still reason to believe that real estate should play a role in the structuring of investment portfolios—especially since the variety of alternative vehicles that have evolved are specifically designed to meet the needs of adding real estate to individual and institutional investment portfolios.

Thus, it is likely that most future portfolio managers will view real estate as a viable investment alternative. Although some adjustment of the size and composition of the real estate portfolio may be warranted on the basis of the macro and micro economic forecasts, real estate should be acquired with an eye toward its long-term investment potential.

FURTHER READING

The following texts provide an introduction to the study of real estate: Arnold, Wurtzebach, and Miles [1980], Bloom, Weimer, and Fisher [1982], and Ring and Dasso [1981]. A collection of 67 independently authored articles covering a broad range of real estate topics is found in Seldin [1980].

Real Estate Finance and Investment Analysis

For an introduction to the basic principles of real estate finance, see Beaton [1982]. A book with a number of independently authored articles on a range of real estate finance topics is Britton [1977]. Brueggeman and Stone [1981] provide a comprehensive treatment of real estate finance and investment analysis from both an analytical and institutional perspective. For a good introduction to the topics of real estate finance and investment, see Epley and Millar [1980]. Jaffee and Sirmans [1982] treat the study of real estate from the point of view of modern financial theory. For a text that provides a general introduction to a wide range of real estate investment topics see Pyhrr and Cooper [1982]. An introductory treatment of real estate investment analysis techniques is provided by Wendt and Cerf [1979]. The following texts introduce the topic of real estate appraisal principles and practices: American Institute of Real Estate Appraisers [1978] and Epley and Boyken [1983]. For a recent text with an orientation toward income property valuation, see Friedman and Ordway [1981].

Legal Aspects of Real Estate

The following texts provide a good reference to legal aspects of real estate: Atteberry, Pearson, and Litka [1978], Kratovil and Werner [1979], and Lusk and French

[1979]. The following texts provide a rigorous treatment of the legal aspects of real estate finance with a strong case orientation: Nelson and Whitman [1981], Osborne, Nelson, and Whitman [1979], and Steuben [1980].

Real Estate Portfolio Performance

The following articles are related to real estate investment performance from a portfolio perspective: Brinson [1982], Burns and Epley [1982], Curcio and Gaines [1977], Findlay, Hamilton, Messner, and Yormark [1979], Findlay, Messner, and Tarantello [1979], Friedman [1971], Hallengren [1974], Hoag [1979, 1980], Pellatt [1972], Robichek, Cohn, and Pringle [1972], Roulac [1976], and Sack [1980].

Real Estate Investment Vehicles

Various types of real estate investment vehicles are discussed in Allen [1977], Brachman [1981], Davis [1982], Lawless [1974], Miles and Esty [1982], Roulac [1974], and Smith [1980].

Institutional Investing

Issues and problems of importance to the institutional investor are covered in the following articles: Chadwick [1980], Cheng [1982], Davidson [1981], Eagle [1980, 1982], Ellis [1981], Garrigan, Sullivan, and Young [1981], Mamorsky and White [1981], McMahan [1981], Thorndike [1981a, 1981b], and Walters [1980].

Mortgage-backed Securities

For additional background in the area of mortgage-backed securities, see Bettner [1980], Clauretie [1982], Doehler [1980], Dunn and McConnell [1981], GNMA Mortgage-Backed Securities Dealers Association [1978], Peters [1980], Rush and Bolger [1981], Sessoms [1980], Sivesind [1979], Winger and Uth [1981], and Wynn [1982].

Alternative Mortgages and Mortgage Markets

Alternative mortgages and mortgage markets are discussed in the following articles: Cassidy [1981], Iezman [1981], Jacobe and Thygerson [1981], Jones [1981], Jones [1982], Lessard and Modigliani [1975], McKenzie [1982], and Strawn [1982].

Miscellaneous

For a discussion of how the accelerated cost recovery system (ACRS) created by the Economic Recovery Tax Act (ERTA) of 1981 affects real estate, see Brueggeman, Fisher, and Stern [1982]. For further examples of the use of the REALVAL computer model for real estate investment analysis and valuation, see Fisher and Stern [1981].

BIBLIOGRAPHY

Allen, Thomas F., *Real Estate Investment Trusts,* BNA Tax Management Portfolio No. 107–4th, Washington, D.C.: Tax Management Inc., 1977.
American Council of Life Insurance, *Life Insurance Fact Book, 1981,* Washington D.C.: American Council of Life Insurance, 1981.

————, "Mortgage Commitments on Multifamily and Nonresidential Properties Reported by 20 Life Insurance Companies, Fourth Quarter 1981 and Annual Data," *Investment Bulletin,* No. 836, April 1, 1982.

American Institute of Real Estate Appraisers, Textbook Revision Subcommittee, *The Appraisal of Real Estate,* 6th and 7th Eds., Chicago: American Institute of Real Estate Appraisers, 1973 and 1978.

Arnold, Alvin L., Charles H. Wurtzebach, and Mike E. Miles, *Modern Real Estate,* Boston: Warren, Gorham & Lamont, 1980.

Atteberry, William L., Kark G. Pearson, and Michael P. Litka, *Real Estate Law,* 2nd Ed., Columbus, Ohio: Grid, 1978.

Beaton, William R., *Real Estate Finance,* 2nd Ed., Englewood Cliffs, N.J.: Prentice-Hall, 1982.

Bettner, Jill, "Projected Yields on Ginnie Maes Lure Savers, but the Mortgage Pools' True Yields Are Elusive," *The Wall Street Journal,* October 20, 1980.

Bloom, George F., Arthur M. Weimer, and Jeffrey D. Fisher, *Real Estate,* 8th Ed., New York: John Wiley, 1982.

Board of Governors of the Federal Reserve System, *Annual Statistical Digest, 1970–1979,* Washington, D.C.: U.S. Government Printing Office, 1981.

————, "Financial and Business Statistics," *Federal Reserve Bulletin,* July 1977, January and June, 1982.

Brachman, William O., "Rating Commingled Funds," *Pension World,* September 1981.

Brinson, Gary P., "Intelligently Setting a Portfolio Mix," *Pension World,* March 1982.

Britton, James A., Jr., and Lewis O. Kerwood, *Financing Income-Producing Real Estate,* New York: McGraw-Hill, 1977.

Brueggeman, William B., Jeffrey D. Fisher, and Jerrold J. Stern, "Choosing the Optimal Depreciation Method Under 1981 Tax Legislation," *Real Estate Review,* Winter 1982.

————, **and Leo D. Stone,** *Real Estate Finance,* 7th Ed., Homewood, Ill.: Richard D. Irwin, 1981.

Burns, William L., and Donald R. Epley, "The Performance of Portfolios of REITs and Stocks," *The Journal of Portfolio Management,* Spring 1982.

Cassidy, Henry J., "Price-Level Adjusted Mortgages Versus Other Mortgage Instruments," *Federal Home Loan Bank Board Journal,* January 1981.

Chadwick, William J., "ERISA and the Portfolio Manager," in Sumner N. Levine, Ed., *The Investment Manager's Handbook,* Homewood, Ill.: Dow Jones-Irwin, 1980.

Cheng, Anna, "Marketing Real Estate to Pension Funds," *Real Estate Review,* Spring 1982.

Clauretie, Terrence M., "Why Do GNMAs Yield More than Treasuries?" *The Journal of Portfolio Management,* Spring 1982.

"Consultant Says Pension Funds Are Still Misunderstood," summary of speech by Blake Eagle to the 1981 annual convention of the Mortgage Bankers Association, *National Real Estate Investor,* January 1982.

Council of Economic Advisors, *Economic Report of the President,* Washington, D.C.: U.S. Government Printing Office, February 1982.

Curcio, Richard J., and James P. Gaines, "Real Estate Portfolio Revision," *Journal of the American Real Estate and Urban Economics Association,* Winter 1977.

Davidson, Harold A., "The Pension Funds' Increasing Real Estate Commitment," *Real Estate Review,* Spring 1981.

Davis, G. Abbott, "Real Estate Funds: An Alternative for Pension Managers," *Financial Executive,* June 1982.

Doehler, Steven P., "Private Mortgage Insurance—Its Expanding Role," *Mortgage Banker,* March 1980.

Downs, Anthony, "Two Contrasting Types of Real Estate Equity," *Pension World,* May 1981.

Dunn, Kenneth B., and John J. McConnell, "Rate of Return Indexes for GNMA Securities," *The Journal of Portfolio Management,* Winter 1981.

Eagle, Blake, "Delayed but Moving Right Along," *Pension World,* July 1980.

———, *Preliminary Real Estate Report,* Tacoma, Wash.: Frank Russell Company, March 9, 1982.

Ellis, Charles D., "On Pension Funds and Real Estate," *Pension World,* September 1981.

Epley, Donald R., and James H. Boyken, *Basic Income Property Appraisal,* Reading, Mass.: Addison-Wesley, 1983.

———, **and James A. Millar,** *Basic Real Estate Finance and Investments,* New York: John Wiley, 1980.

Findlay, M. Chapman III, Carl W. Hamilton, Stephen P. Messner, and Jonathan S. Yormark, "Optimal Real Estate Portfolios," *Journal of the American Real Estate and Urban Economics Association,* Fall 1979.

———, **Stephen P. Messner, and R. A. Tarantello,** "Risk Analysis in Real Estate," *The Real Estate Appraiser and Analyst,* July/August 1979.

Fisher, Jeffrey D., "An Analysis of Real Estate and Other Tax-Preferred Investments," unpublished doctoral dissertation, Ohio State University, 1980.

———, **and Jerrold J. Stern,** "Computer-Assisted Investment Analysis, Tax Analysis and Valuation of Income Property," Bloomington, Ind.: Foundation for Economic and Business Studies, Graduate School of Business, Indiana University, 1981.

"FNMA Unveils New Mortgage-Backed Security Offering," *Savings and Loan News,* June 1982.

Frank Russell Company, *FRC Property Index Fourth Quarter 1981,* 1982.

Freshman, Samuel K., *Principles of Real Estate Syndication,* 2nd Ed., Los Angeles: Parker and Son, 1973.

Friedman, Harris C., "Real Estate Investment and Portfolio Theory," *Journal of Financial and Quantitative Analysis,* March 1971.

Friedman, Jack T., and Nicholas Ordway, *Income Property Appraisal and Analysis,* Reston, Va.: Reston Publishing, 1981.

Garrigan, Richard T., Mark J. Sullivan, and Michael S. Young, "Financing Real Estate Investments of Pension Funds," *Real Estate Review,* Winter 1981.

GNMA Mortgage-Backed Securities Dealers Association, *The Ginnie Mae Manual,* Homewood, Ill.: Dow Jones-Irwin, 1978.

Hallengren, Howard E., "How Different Investments Fare During Inflationary Cycles," *The Commercial and Financial Chronicle,* June 23, 1974.

Hemmer, Edgar H., and Jeffrey D. Fisher, "Dealing With Uncertainty in Income Valuation," *The Appraisal Journal,* April 1978.

Hertzberg, Daniel, "Pension Funds Cut Real Estate Investment as Prices Level Off, Inflation Rate Slows," *The Wall Street Journal,* April 1, 1982.

————, and **Randall Smith,** "Prudential Property Fund Pinched as Slump Makes Investors Skittish," *The Wall Street Journal,* June 4, 1982.

Hoag, James W., "A New Real Estate Return Index: Measurement of Risk and Return," *Proceedings of the Seminar on the Analysis of Security Prices,* University of Chicago, May 1979.

————, "Toward Indices of Real Estate Value and Return," *The Journal of Finance,* May 1980.

Iezman, Stanley L., "The Shared Appreciation Mortgage and the Shared Equity Program," *Real Estate Review,* Fall 1981.

Jacobe, Dennis J., and Kenneth J. Thygerson, "Mortgages," in Frank J. Fabozzi and Frank G. Zarb, Eds., *The Handbook of Financial Markets,* Homewood, Ill.: Dow Jones-Irwin, 1981.

Jaffee, Austin J., and C. F. Sirmans, *Investment Decision Making,* Englewood Cliffs, N.J.: Prentice-Hall, 1982.

Jones, Baron A., "The Convertible Mortgage: Everyone Can Be A Winner," *Pension World,* March 1981.

Jones, Marcos T., "Mortgage Designs, Inflation, and Real Estate Rates," *Federal Reserve Bank of New York Quarterly Review,* Spring 1982.

Kratovil, Robert, and Raymond J. Werner, *Real Estate Law,* 7th Ed., Englewood Cliffs, N.J.: Prentice-Hall, 1979.

Larkins, Daniel J., "Recent Developments in Mortgage Markets," *Survey of Current Business,* February 1982.

Lawless, Harris, "Living With the Deal, or How to Manage the Real Estate Syndicate," *Real Estate Review,* Winter 1974.

Lessard, Donald, and Franco Modigliani, Eds., *New Mortgage Designs for an Inflationary Environment,* Boston: Federal Reserve Bank of Boston, January 1975.

Lewis, Stephen E., "Domestic Institutions Dominating [Real Estate] Investment Market; Foreign Fervor is Cooled by Rising U.S. Dollar," *National Real Estate Investor,* September 1981.

Litzenberger, Robert H., and Krishna Ramaswamy, "The Effect of Personal Taxes and Dividends on Capital Asset Prices: Theory and Empirical Evidence," *Journal of Financial Economics,* June 1979.

Lusk, Harold F., and William B. French, *Law of the Real Estate Business,* 4th Ed., Homewood, Ill.: Irwin, 1979.

Mamorsky, Jeffrey D., and Thomas M. White, "Pension Plans and Real Estate—A Legal Perspective," *Pension World,* June 1981.

MacKinnon, Malcolm D., "Pension Funds and Real Estate II: Making the Connection," Presentation at *Pension World* Conference, Atlanta, Georgia, June 18, 1982.

McKenzie, Joseph A., "A Borrower's Guide to Alternative Mortgage Instruments," *Federal Home Loan Bank Board Journal,* January 1982.

McMahan, John, "Institutional Strategies for Real Estate Equity Investment," John McMahan Associates, May 20, 1981.

Miles, Mike, and Arthur Esty, "How Well Do Commingled Real Estate Funds Perform?" *The Journal of Portfolio Management,* Winter 1982.

Money Market Directories, Inc., Ed., *Real Estate Investing By Pension Funds,* Charlottesville, Va.: Money Market Directories, Inc., 1982.

Mortgage Bankers Association of America, "Loans Closed and Servicing Volume for the Mortgage Banking Industry, 1980," Trend Report No. 29, July 1981.

National Association of Real Estate Investment Trusts, *REIT Fact Book,* Washington, D.C.: National Association of Real Estate Investment Trusts, 1981.

Nelson, Grant S., and Dale A. Whitman, *Real Estate Transfer, Finance and Development: Cases and Materials,* 2nd Ed., St. Paul, Minn.: West, 1981.

Olin, Virginia, "Secondary Mortgage Market Activity in the Fourth Quarter of 1981," *Federal Home Loan Bank Board Journal,* February 1982a.

———, "Secondary Mortgage Market Activity in the First Quarter of 1982," *Federal Home Loan Bank Board Journal,* May 1982b.

Osborne, George E., Grant S. Nelson, and Dale A. Whitman, *Real Estate Finance Law,* Hornbook Series, St. Paul, Minn.: West, 1979.

Pellatt, Peter G. K., "The Analysis of Real Estate Investments Under Uncertainty," *Journal of Finance,* May 1972.

Peters, Helen Frame, "Prices and Yields on Mortgage-Backed Securities," *Mortgage Banker,* September 1980.

PRISA 1981 Annual Report, Newark, N.J.: Prudential Insurance Company, 1982.

Pyhrr, Stephen A., "A Computer Simulation Model to Measure the Risk in Real Estate Investment," *Journal of the American Real Estate and Urban Economics Association,* June 1973.

———, **and James R. Cooper,** *Real Estate Investment: Strategy, Analysis, Decisions,* Boston: Warren, Gorham & Lamont, 1982.

Ring, Alfred A., and Jerome Dasso, *Real Estate Principles and Practice,* 9th Ed., Englewood Cliffs, N.J.: Prentice-Hall, 1981.

Robichek, Alexander A., Richard A. Cohn, and John J. Pringle, "Returns on Alternative Investment Media and Implications for Portfolio Construction," *Journal of Business,* July 1972.

Roulac, Stephen E., "Giving the Syndicator His Just Reward." *Real Estate Review,* Winter 1974.

———, "Can Real Estate Returns Outperform Common Stocks?" *The Journal of Portfolio Management,* Winter 1976.

———, "How to Structure Real Estate Investment Management," *The Journal of Portfolio Management,* Fall 1981.

Rush, Michael C., and Timothy J. Bolger, "Mortgage-Backed Securities: Producing Predictable Income," *Pension World,* November 1981.

Sack, Paul, "Management of Real Estate Portfolios," in Sumner N. Levine, Ed., *The Investment Manager's Handbook,* Homewood, Ill.: Dow Jones-Irwin, 1980.

Schloss, Nathan, "Real Estate's Financial Performance in the Marketplace," *Pension World,* June 1981.

Seldin, Maury, Ed., *The Real Estate Handbook,* Homewood, Ill.: Dow Jones-Irwin, 1980.

Sessoms, Fred M., "Pass-Through Securities," *Pension World,* October 1980.

Sivesind, Charles M., "Mortgage-Backed Securities: The Revolution in Real Estate Finance," *Federal Reserve Bank of New York Quarterly Review,* Autumn 1979.

Smith, Keith V., "Historical Returns of Real Estate Equity Portfolios," in Sumner N. Levine, Ed., *The Investment Manager's Handbook,* Homewood, Ill.: Dow Jones-Irwin, 1980.

———, **and David Shulman,** "The Performance of Equity Real Estate Investment Trusts," *Financial Analysts Journal,* September/October 1976.

"Speakers Present Opposing Views of Realty Record," *National Real Estate Investor,* September 1981.

Stephens, Paula S., "Pension Funds to Increase Real Estate Activity: Involvement to Include Development, Experts Predict," *National Real Estate Investor,* December 1981.

Steuben, Norton L., *Real Estate Planning: Cases, Materials, Problems, Questions and Commentary,* Mineola, N.Y.: The Foundation Press, 1980.

Strawn, Louis F., "The Convertible Mortgage—Is It Really Convertible?" *Pension World,* February 1982.

Thorndike, W. Nicholas, "Real Estate and the Institutional Investor," Part I, *Pension World,* June, 1981a.

———, "Real Estate and the Institutional Investor," Part II, *Pension World,* July 1981b.

U.S. Department of Commerce, *Survey of Current Business,* Washington, D.C.: U.S. Government Printing Office, 1982.

Vandell, Robert F., and Marcia L. Pontius, "The Impact of Tax Status on Stock Selection," *The Journal of Portfolio Management,* Summer 1981.

Walters, James L., "An Overview of Fiduciary Law," in Sumner N. Levine, Ed., *The Investment Manager's Handbook,* Homewood, Ill.: Dow Jones-Irwin, 1980.

"We Buy Equity Real Estate: A Symposium," *Real Estate Review,* Spring 1981.

Webb, James R., and C. F. Sirmans, "Yields and Risk Measures for Real Estate, 1966–1977," *The Journal of Portfolio Management,* Fall 1980.

Wendt, Paul F., *Real Estate Appraisal: Review and Outlook,* Athens, Ga.: University of Georgia Press, 1974.

———, **and Alan R. Cerf,** *Real Estate Investment Analysis and Taxation,* 2nd Ed., New York: McGraw-Hill, 1979.

Wiggin, Charles E., "How Equity Financing Works," *Real Estate Review,* Spring 1981.

Willis, Arthur B., John S. Pennell, and Philip F. Postlewaite, *Partnership Taxation,* 3rd Ed., New York: McGraw-Hill, 1981.

Winger, Alan R., and Madelynn Uth, "Savings and Loans and the Mortgage-Backed Security," *Federal Home Loan Bank Board Journal,* January 1981.

Wynn, Ronnie J., "GNMAs: A Success Story," *Mortgage Banking,* Special Issue, 1982.

APPENDIX

Sample Problems for Existing Property Investment Analysis

In order to illustrate the steps in a typical income property investment analysis, a case example called Oakwood Apartments is presented and discussed.

ASSUMPTIONS FOR CASE EXAMPLE

General Assumptions

Tables 11A-1 to 11A-5 show the input assumptions for this case using the REALVAL computer model developed by the author for investment analysis of real estate income properties. Although the assumptions are intended to be realistic, they are somewhat simplified in order to show all the calculations without becoming overwhelmingly detailed.

The purchase price of the property is assumed to be $360,000, of which 20 percent ($72,000) represents the cost of the land. An 8 percent annually compounded property value growth rate is assumed for the four years of the holding period. Selling expenses are anticipated to be 6 percent of the sales price. See the worksheet used for general inputs to the REALVAL model shown in Table 11A-1.

Income Assumptions

The leases offered by Oakwood fall into two categories. Lease type 1 is renewed annually. Potential gross income for this lease category is $40,000 for year 1, and is expected to increase 5 percent for year 2. In year 3 the annually compounded rate of growth is forecasted to be 3 percent; it is expected to remain at that level for the remainder of the holding period. Potential gross income for lease type 2 is $20,000. This is a 2-year lease and is level for these two years. However, in year 3, when the lease is renewed, the level of potential gross income for this lease category is anticipated to jump 10 percent and then remain level for the remaining years of the projected holding period. Figure 11A-1 on page 522 shows the pattern of the two leases over time. Vacancy rates for both lease categories are projected to be 5 percent. See Table 11A-2 (page 522).

TABLE 11A-1. General Inputs

Analysis code (Integer 0–2)	0
Holding Period (Integer 1–20)	4
Calculation years (Integer 1–20)	4
Required yield (Decimal)	.15
Number of loans (Integer 0–3)	1
Number of assets (Integer 0–7)	1
Number of lease types (Integer 0–4)	2
Selling expense, % (Decimal)	.06
Number of expenses (Integer 0–5)	2
Land lease payments (Dollar or decimal)	0
Growth rate of lease (Decimal)	0
Participation type (Integer 0–3)	0
Initial participation (Decimal)	
First incremental participation (Decimal)	
Starting at base $ (Dollar)	
Second incremental participation (Decimal)	
Starting at base $ (Dollar)	
Marginal tax rate (Decimal)	.40
Minimum tax (Integer 0–1)	0

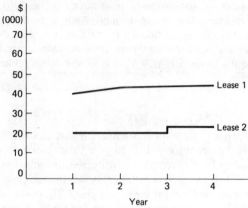

Figure 11A-1. Pattern of Gross Income for Two Leases Offered by Oakwood Apartments

TABLE 11A-2. Lease and Purchase Price Inputs for Oakwood Apartments

	Purchase Price	Lease 1	Lease 2	Lease 3	Lease 4
Amount	$360,000	$40,000	$20,000		
Initial change	.08	.05	0		
Year of change		3	3		
Change		.03	.1		
Year of change			4		
Change			0		
Year of change					
Change					
Year of change					
Change					
Vacancy, year 1		.05	.05		
Vacancy, year 2		.05	.05		
Vacancy, year 3		.05	.05		
Vacancy, year 4		.05	.05		

TABLE 11A-3. Operating Expense Inputs for Oakwood Apartments

	Expense 1	Expense 2	Expense 3	Expense 4	Expense 5
Amount, year 1	.25	8,000			
Amount, year 2	.25	8,000			
Amount, year 3	.25	9,000			
Amount, year 4	.25	9,000			
Initial change		.10			
Year of change					
Change					
Year of change					
Change					

Expense Assumptions

As with many types of income property, some of Oakwood's operating expenses vary with effective gross income and some are fixed in amount regardless of vacancy levels. Expense type 1, comprising all the variable operating expenses, is predicted to be 25 percent of effective gross income throughout the holding period. Expense type 2 includes all of the fixed expenses. These are planned to be $8,000 in years 1 and 2 and $9,000 in years 3 and 4. See Table 11A-3.

TABLE 11A-4. Financing Inputs for Oakwood Apartments

	Loan 1	Loan 2	Loan 3
Amount of loan	$252,000		
Rate	.15		
Term	25		
Year called	5		
Years interest only	0		
Points	0		

Financing Assumptions

The financing for Oakwood includes a mortgage for $252,000 (70 percent of the $360,000 purchase price); it carries a 15 percent interest rate that is fixed for the first four years, a 25-year term, and monthly payments. Thus, the investor's equity investment is $108,000 ($360,000 purchase price less net loan proceeds of $252,000). See Table 11A-4.

Tax Assumptions

For tax purposes, the Oakwood investor is presumed to be in the 40 percent tax bracket. Also for tax purposes, the improvements ($288,000, or 80 percent of the $360,000 purchase price) are depreciated over 15 years in accordance with the accelerated cost recovery system (ACRS) created via the Economic Recovery Tax Act of 1981. Straight-line depreciation is employed. See Asset Inputs in Table 11A-5.

Cash Flows—Operating Years

Table 11A-6 shows the pro forma operating statement for Oakwood Apartments. There are three major blocks of calculations: (1) before-tax cash flow, (2) federal income tax, and (3) after-tax cash flow.

Before-tax Cash Flow. The first step in the calculation of annual cash flow from operations is the before-tax cash flow. The potential gross income ($60,000 the first year, $62,000 the second year, and so on) is based on the two lease categories discussed earlier. An allowance for vacancy (5 percent per year) is subtracted to arrive at effective gross income. Operating income is calculated by subtracting the fixed and variable operating expenses from effective gross income. Operating income

TABLE 11A-5. Asset Inputs for Oakwood Apartments

Price of Land: $72,000

	Asset 1	Asset 2	Asset 3	Asset 4	Asset 5
Cost of Improvements	$288,000				
Recovery class	15				
Recovery period	15				
Method	1				
New? (1 = Y; 0 = N)	1				
Residential?	1				
Investment tax credit	0				

TABLE 11A-6. REALVAL Pro Forma Operating Statement, Tax-Related Cash Flows and Profitability Measures

Operating Statement

	YEAR			
	1	2	3	4
Potential gross income	$ 60,000	$ 62,000	$ 65,260	$ 66,558
Vacancy & collection	3,000	3,100	3,263	3,328
Effective gross income	$ 57,000	$ 58,900	$ 61,997	$ 63,230
Operating expenses	22,250	22,725	24,499	24,808
Operating income	$ 34,750	$ 36,175	$ 37,498	$ 38,422
Debt service	38,732	38,732	38,732	38,732
Lease payments	0	0	0	0
Participation	0	0	0	0
Before-tax cash flow	$ −3,982	$ −2,557	$ −1,235	$ −310
Operating income	$ 34,750	$ 36,175	$ 37,498	$ 38,422
Lease payments	0	0	0	0
Participation	0	0	0	0
Interest	37,733	37,573	37,386	37,170
Depreciation	19,200	19,200	19,200	19,200
Amortized points	0	0	0	0
Taxable income	$−22,183	$−20,598	$−19,088	$−17,947
Federal income tax	−8,873	−8,239	−7,635	−7,179

Tax-Related Cash Flows—Operations Only

	1	2	3	4
Before-tax cash flow	$ −3,982	$ −2,557	$ −1,235	$ −310
Federal income tax	−8,873	−8,239	−7,635	−7,179
After-tax cash flow	$ 4,891	$ 5,682	$ 6,401	$ 6,869

Tax-Related Cash Flows—Operations and Reversion

	1	2	3	4
Before-tax cash flow	$ 110,489	$ 142,311	$ 176,557	$ 213,148
Federal income tax	−4,926	3,459	12,187	21,171
After-tax cash flow	$ 115,415	$ 138,853	$ 164,371	$ 191,976

Profitability Measures

	1	2	3	4
Before-tax IRR	2.30%	12.96%	15.92%	16.92%
After-tax IRR	6.87%	15.67%	18.10%	18.90%
After-tax NPV	$ −7,639	$ 1,246	$ 8,626	$ 14,521

represents cash income before considering financing or federal income taxes. Operating expenses such as property taxes, insurance, and maintenance are considered. (Note that a reserve for replacements figure is not included in operating expenses since it is a non-cash expenditure. Such a reserve is usually deducted from operating income by appraisers when computing net operating income.)

Debt service (principal and interest) is deducted from operating income to produce before-tax cash flow. This is an estimate of spendable cash available from the investment before considering federal income taxes.

For Oakwood Apartments the mortgage interest rate is 15 percent with a 25-year term. The *mortgage constant* for this loan, used to determine the amount of the mortgage payment, would be .15370 or 15.37 percent. With a 70 percent loan-to-value ratio, the amount of the loan is $252,000 (.70 × $360,000). Multiplying this by the loan constant produces a mortgage payment of $38,732 ($252,000 × .1537). Since the debt service (mortgage payment) exceeds the operating income for the four years, as shown in Table 11A-6, before-tax cash flows are negative. Thus, the investor would have to put additional cash into the investment each year in an amount equal to the deficit cash flow in order to fulfill the mortgage payment requirement.

Federal Income Tax

To compute after-tax cash flow, two sets of calculations must be made. First, taxable income (loss) from the investment is identified. Next, the federal income tax increase (or decrease) is computed based on the taxable income (loss) from the investment. Before-tax cash flow minus (plus) the federal income tax increase (or decrease) equals after-tax cash flow.

Taxable income from the real estate investment each year is found by subtracting tax-deductible expenses from income. For most real estate projects, the deductible expenses include operating expenses, interest, and tax depreciation. Simplifying, we can use the following income statement format: operating income minus interest and depreciation equals taxable income.

In order to calculate the federal income tax liability (saving), it must first be known how the purchase of the real estate investment changes the investor's tax liability. Federal income tax rates in 1982 ranged from zero to 50 percent. The marginal tax rate is the rate the taxpayer pays on an additional dollar of income. In the simplest situation, the real estate investment either increases or decreases taxable income within a single tax bracket. For example, a married taxpayer would pay taxes at a 49 percent rate on taxable income between $45,800 and $60,000. Assuming the addition of the real estate investment does not cause the investor's taxable income to move outside this range, we can evaluate the investment using a 49 percent tax rate. (Note that it is also assumed that the investor is not subject to the regular minimum tax.) Recall, in the Oakwood Apartments example, a 40 percent tax rate is used.

Interest

For a standard fixed rate mortgage the mortgage payment (principal and interest) is constant each year. However, the proportion of interest and principal in each payment changes each month. Each time a payment is made, the loan balance decreases by the principal portion of the loan payment. Since interest is paid only on the balance of the loan, the interest portion of each payment decreases and the principal portion increases with the passage of time. The principal and interest portion of the loan must be separated in order to calculate taxable income. If the analysis were being done by hand, a schedule of monthly loan payments could be set up, but this would involve many calculations (12 for each year of the 5-year holding period). A shortcut is as follows: first, find the loan balance at the *end* of each year. This is done by dividing the loan payment by a loan constant at the same interest rate but for a loan term equal to the number of years remaining in the original loan. For example, after one year the balance is found by dividing the payment by a loan constant for a 24-year loan. That is, $38,732/.15432 = $251,000.

Since the loan balance is known to decrease each year by the principal portion of the loan payment, the principal the first year must by $252,000 − $251,000, or $1,000. Since the total of the payments is $38,732, the interest portion of the payments must by $38,732 − $1,000, or $37,732.

For the second year the loan balance is found by dividing the payment by the loan constant for a 23-year loan, since there are now 23 years remaining in the loan term. That is $38,732/.155028 = $249,839. The change in the loan balance from the previous year is $251,000 − $249,839, or $1,161. This is the principal portion of the payment during the second year. Subtracting this from the total payment we have $38,732 − $1,161, or $37,571, which is the interest for the second year.

This procedure can be used each year to calculate the total annual interest that is used in the calculation of taxable income. Table 11A-7 shows the loan amortization schedule for Oakwood.

Depreciation

Depreciation is a tax deduction that does not represent an actual cash expenditure. However, it can be used to reduce taxable income and thus reduce the investor's tax liability. This represents a tax shelter to the extent that the depreciation allowable for tax purposes exceeds any actual economic depreciation in the property.

The shortest allowable recovery period (depreciable life) under the accelerated cost recovery system for virtually all real estate investments is 15 years. Only improvements can be depreciated, not land. Investors can use straight-line depreciation or an accelerated depreciation method.

The tax basis of a property is generally its purchase price. From this the land is subtracted to arrive at the depreciable basis of the property. For straight-line depreciation the depreciable basis is divided by the recovery period of the property, producing an equal annual charge for depreciation. The recovery periods available for almost all real estate are 15, 35, and 45 years. However, the 35- and 45-year periods may be chosen only if the investor employs the straight-line method.

For Oakwood Apartments the building value of $288,000 is to be depreciated over 15 years. Thus, straight-line depreciation is $19,200 per year ($288,000/15). Table 11A-8 (page 528) shows the depreciation schedule for Oakwood.

Taxable Income

Recall that taxable income is found by subtracting the interest expense and depreciation deduction from operating income. The investor's tax liability can be calculated

TABLE 11A-7. Summary Loan Amortization Schedule for Oakwood Apartments

	YEAR			
	1	2	3	4
Interest	$37,733	$37,573	$37,386	$37,170
Principal	999	1,160	1,346	1,563
Total payment	$38,732	$38,732	$38,732	$38,732

TABLE 11A-8. Depreciation Schedule for Oakwood Apartments

	Year			
	1	2	3	4
Beginning basis	$288,000	$268,800	$249,600	$230,400
Depreciation claimed	19,200	19,200	19,200	19,200
Undepreciated balance	$268,800	$249,600	$230,400	$211,200
Net excess depreciation	0	0	0	0
Yearly excess depreciation	0	0	0	0
Basis for sale	$268,800	$249,600	$230,400	$211,200
Individual tax credit taken	0	0	0	0
Investment recapture	0	0	0	0

based on the investment's taxable income as follows: taxable income × marginal tax rate = tax.

For Oakwood Apartments taxable income is negative for the five years illustrated. This reduces the investor's other taxable income, which we assumed would be taxed at 40 percent. Thus, the investor has tax *savings* during these operating years because other income is sheltered, i.e., offset by tax losses from the investment. The tax savings are found by multiplying the tax rate by the amount of tax loss. For example, tax savings the first year amount to $8,873 ($22,183 × .40). This represents taxes that would have to be paid if the investor did not purchase the real estate.

After-tax Cash Flow

As noted earlier, after-tax cash flow is found by subtracting the federal income tax from before-tax cash flow. When taxable income is negative and tax savings result, as in the Oakwood Apartments example, the tax savings are added to the before-tax cash flow of $4,891 that results from adding $8,873 tax savings (subtracting a negative tax) to the negative $3,982 before-tax cash flow.

An alternative way of calculating after-tax cash flow is illustrated as follows for year 1:

Taxable income	$ −22,183
−Tax	−(−8,873)
Income after tax	$ −13,310
+Depreciation	+19,200
−Principal (loan amortization)	− 1,000
=After-tax cash flow	$ 4,890

Taxable income and the amount of tax are calculated as before. In this case, however, an additional figure called income after tax is calculated. This is an accounting concept that is not the same as after-tax cash flow. Two adjustments are necessary: first, depreciation is added back because it presents a non-cash expense that is deductible for tax purposes but does not affect before-tax cash flow available from the investment; second, principal is subtracted because it is a cash payment that was not deductible in the calculation of taxable income.

After-tax cash flow represents the cash the investor is projected to have after all expenses, mortgage payments, and taxes have been paid. To reiterate, it is not the same as income after tax. Note that for Oakwood Apartments the after-tax cash flow is positive but taxable income is negative. The difference is largely due to depreciation, which reduces taxable income and results in tax savings that, in turn, increase after-tax cash flow.

Reversion

Thus far we have only considered cash flows during the investment holding period. Upon sale of the property (reversion), there are also tax implications. The following steps can be followed to calculate the reversion cash flows for Oakwood Apartments after a 4-year holding period during which the market value of the property has grown at an annual compound rate of 8 percent.

Step 1—Calculate before-tax cash flow

Sales price	$ 489,776 [$360,000 × (1.08)^4]
−Selling costs	−29,387
−Mortgage balance	−246,932
=Before-tax cash flow	$ 213,457

Selling costs normally include commissions paid to the broker who was responsible for the sale and the seller's costs for title transfer. The mortgage balance is the payoff to the lender who provided the debt financing, including any penalties due. The before-tax cash flow represents cash received by the investor from the sale of the property. This is in addition to any before-tax cash flow from operating the property during the year of sale.

Step 2—Determine adjusted basis

Original cost basis	$ 360,000
−Accumulated depreciation	−76,800
=Adjusted basis	$ 283,200

Each year the property is owned, depreciation is used to reduce taxable income. This also lowers the adjusted basis (book value) of the property. The adjusted basis at the time of the sale is therefore equal to the original cost less the total tax depreciation.

Step 3—Determine total taxable gain

Selling price	$ 489,776
−Selling costs	−29,387
−Adjusted basis	−283,200
=Taxable long-term capital gain	$ 177,189

The total taxable gain at reversion is equal to the difference between the net sales proceeds (after selling costs) and the adjusted basis of the property. However, since accelerated depreciation was not used, the gain receives favorable treatment as a long-term capital gain.

Step 4—Compute taxable income

Taxable gain	$177,189
×40% (in 1982)	× .40
=Taxable income	$ 70,876

In calculating taxable income (in 1982), 60 percent of the long-term capital gain is excluded from taxation, with the remaining 40 percent being added to the investor's other taxable (ordinary) income.

Step 5—Calculate tax from reversion

Ordinary income	$70,876
×Marginal tax rate	× .40
=Tax from reversion	$28,350

The additional tax due as a result of sale of the property assumes the investor's marginal tax rate is still 40 percent after considering all other sources of income and tax shelter.

Step 6—Determine after-tax cash flow

Before-tax cash flow	$213,457
−Tax from reversion	− 28,350
=After-tax cash flow	$185,107

The additional tax from reversion is now subtracted from before-tax cash flow. The calculations in the above steps are summarized in Tables 11A-9 and 11A-10.

TABLE 11A-9. Oakwood Apartments Reversion Calculations

Selling price			$489,776
Selling costs			29,387
Mortgage balance			246,932
Before-tax cash flow			$213,457
Selling price		$489,776	
Selling costs		29,387	
Total cost basis	$360,000		
Accumulated depreciation	76,800		
Adjusted basis		283,200	
Total capital gain		$177,189	
Taxable portion		× .40	
Ordinary income		$ 70,876	
Tax rate		× .40	
Income tax			28,350
After-tax cash flow			$185,107

TABLE 11A-10. Reversion Information for Oakwood Apartments

	YEAR			
	1	2	3	4
Selling price	$388,800	$419,904	$453,496	$489,776
Selling costs	23,328	25,194	27,210	29,387
Mortgage balance	251,001	249,841	248,495	246,932
Before-tax cash flow from reversion	$114,471	$144,869	$177,792	$213,457
Selling price	$388,800	$419,904	$453,496	$489,776
Selling costs	23,328	25,194	27,210	29,387
Adjusted basis	340,800	321,600	302,399	283,199
Total gain (or loss)	$ 24,672	$ 73,110	$123,887	$177,190
Recapture—Sec. 1245	$ 0	$ 0	$ 0	$ 0
Recapture—Sec. 1250	0	0	0	0
Capital gain	24,672	73,110	123,887	177,190
Ordinary loss	0	0	0	0
Total gain (or loss)	$ 24,672	$ 73,110	$123,887	$177,190
Unamortized points	0	0	0	0
After-tax cash flow from reversion	$110,524	$133,171	$157,970	$185,107

Evaluating Cash Flows

In the preceding discussion the input assumptions and basic calculations for projecting before- and after-tax cash flows for a real estate income property investment were presented. In this section these cash flow projections are evaluated and interpreted, with the ultimate objective of making investment decisions. Discussion of the Oakwood Apartments example is continued to illustrate different measures of investment performance. The commentary below is based on Table 11A-11, the key ratios printout for Oakwood Apartments.

TABLE 11A-11. Key Ratios for Oakwood Apartments

	YEAR			
	1	2	3	4
Mortgage balance	$251,001	$249,841	$248,495	$246,932
Estimated selling price	388,800	419,904	453,496	489,776
Debt coverage ratio	0.90	0.93	0.97	0.99
Loan/original value	0.70	0.69	0.69	0.69
Loan/current value	0.65	0.59	0.55	0.50
Before-tax cash flow/equity	−0.04	−0.02	−0.01	−0.00
After-tax cash flow/equity	0.05	0.05	0.06	0.06
Current value/potential gross income	6.48	6.77	6.95	7.36
Operating income/current value	0.09	0.09	0.08	0.08
Marginal return	6.87%	25.63%	23.43%	21.53%

Debt coverage ratio. A ratio that is of importance to the lender is the debt coverage ratio (DCR). It is calculated by dividing operating income for a given year by debt service. It is a measure of the degree to which operating income exceeds required payments to the mortgage lender. A ratio of less than 1 indicates that operating income is less than the debt service.

For Oakwood Apartments the debt coverage ratios are:

Year	1	2	3	4
Debt coverage ratio	0.90	0.93	0.87	0.99

The ratio only comes close to 1 by the fourth year. Thus, the investor may have some difficulty obtaining the financing that has been assumed and thus more equity may be required. This example illustrates some of the shortcomings of the standard fixed rate mortgage in an inflationary environment. While the rate of return on this project appears to be adequate, most of it is based on tax shelter and price appreciation. Operating income is relatively low compared to financing requirements. Thus, an alternative to the standard fixed rate mortgage may be better for both the lender and investor. For example, one alternative might be a lower interest rate coupled with a participation in the future income of the property. This would reduce the initial mortgage payments and provide the lender with an inflation hedge.

Before-tax Cash Flow to Equity. The term *equity* refers to the initial cash invested in a property. For a property that is purchased, such as Oakwood Apartments, the equity is usually the purchase price less the loan proceeds. For Oakwood Apartments the purchase price is $360,000 and the loan is for $252,000. The equity investment is, therefore, $108,000.

One way of evaluating a real estate investment is to divide the before-tax cash flow for a given year by the equity investment. Also referred to as the *equity dividend rate*, or *cash-on-cash return*, this gives an indication of how much cash is available from a property before considering federal income taxes.

For Oakwood Apartments the before-tax cash flow to equity ratios are:

Year	1	2	3	4
Before-tax cash flow/equity	−0.04	−0.02	−0.01	−0.00

The ratio of before-tax cash flow to equity is negative for the four years shown, since before-tax cash flow is negative. This was somewhat typical during the early 1980s when financing costs were relatively high and debt service on fixed rate mortgages usually exceeded operating income. Alternatives to the fixed rate mortgages were often necessary to obtain financing. It should be clear from the ratio of before-tax cash flow to equity that the investor could not justify this investment on the basis of before-tax cash flow during the operating years only.

After-tax Cash Flow to Equity. The ratio of after-tax cash flow to equity is similar in concept to the before-tax cash flow to equity but considers the taxation of the investment.

For Oakwood Apartments the ratios are:

Year	1	2	3	4
After-tax cash flow/equity	0.05	0.05	0.06	0.06

In the first year, after-tax cash flow is 5 percent of equity. This increases to 6 percent by the fourth year. The after-tax cash flow to equity is positive because of the tax-shelter benefits of Oakwood Apartments. The ratio does not give a complete indication of the potential rate of return for Oakwood because it does not consider any increase in value over the holding period.

Current Value to Potential Gross Income. A ratio that can be estimated for real estate investments is the ratio of value to estimated potential gross income for the same year.

For Oakwood Apartments the ratios are:

Year	1	2	3	4
Current value/potential gross income	6.48	6.77	6.95	7.36

This ratio is most useful when compared with the same ratio for alternative investments that are very similar (i.e., have the same expense ratio) to the one being evaluated. It is often referred to as the *gross rent multiplier* and gives a rough indication of the expected relationship between the estimated rent and value.

Operating Income to Current Value. Another common ratio is found by dividing estimated operating income by the property's estimated value for a given year. This ratio is sometimes referred to as the *capitalization rate.* It should not be interpreted as a rate of return.

For Oakwood Apartments the figures are:

Year	1	2	3	4
Operating income/current value	0.09	0.09	0.08	0.08

As was the case for the gross rent multiplier, this ratio gives an indication of the expected relationship between income and value for a property. Its reciprocal is analogous to an earnings multiplier for common stocks.

Marginal Rate of Return. The marginal rate of return is similar to the after-tax internal rate of return insofar as it is a rate of return calculated on the investor's after-tax cash flow. However, the marginal rate of return is calculated each year and represents the return the investor earns by holding the property one additional year.

For example, if Oakwood Apartments were sold at the end of year 2, after-tax cash flow from reversion is estimated to be $133,171. If, however, the property is held one additional year and sold at the end of year 3, after-tax cash flow from reversion is estimated to be $157,970. In addition, $6,401 of after-tax cash flow is received from operating the property in year 3. This would not have been received if the property had been sold in year 2. Thus the marginal rate of return (MRR) resulting from selling in year 3 instead of year 2 can be calculated based on the incremental cash flows as follows: MRR = [($157,970 + $6,401)/$133,171] − 1 = 23.43 percent. Unless the investor expects to be able to reinvest the proceeds from a sale in year 2 at a return greater than 23.43 percent *with the same level of risk,* it is probably better to hold the property.

The marginal rate of return usually rises initially because the costs associated with a sale of the property are spread over a longer time period. That is, the return from selling after just one year is relatively low because any increase in property value is reduced by the selling costs. However, each year the investor may be losing some of the tax benefits from the property. This can arise from two factors: first, with a standard fixed rate mortgage, the tax-deductible interest portion of the payment decreases each year as the loan is repaid, even though the total payment remains constant. Thus, the tax shelter benefit from the interest deductions decreases each year. Second, if accelerated depreciation is being used, the tax benefit of the depreciation deduction also decreases each year.

In addition to the loss of tax benefits each year, *equity build-up* is another factor to be considered. As the loan is repaid, the investor has more equity in the property, assuming the investment is increasing in value. This reduces the relative amount of financial leverage over time. Unless the income and property value increase enough to offset tax benefit declines and equity build-up, the marginal rate of return tends to fall over time.

The marginal rate of return is related to the internal rate of return (IRR) in that the IRR for a given holding period is a weighted average of the MRRs for all the preceding years. The IRR rises as long as the MRR is greater than the IRR and falls when the MRR is less than the IRR. Thus the MRR is, in a sense, the force driving the IRR and a good indication of the future direction of the IRR. It is often desirable to sell a property when the MRR falls below the rate at which the funds could be reinvested.

Present Value and Rate of Return Calculations

The calculations described in this section are illustrated in the pro forma operating statement for Oakwood Apartments shown in Table 11A-6.

Net Present Value. To evaluate the investment potential of Oakwood Apartments over the 4-year holding period, we need to consider the cash flows from the operating years and reversion. Furthermore, due to the time value of money, we need to weight cash flows received in the early years of the investment more heavily than those received in later years.

One measure that meets these criteria is the *net present value* (NPV). It is found by discounting the cash flows at a specified rate. The NPV can be expressed mathematically as follows:

$$NPV = \sum_{i=1}^{n} C_i \frac{1}{(1 + r)^i} - E_0$$

where C_i is the cash flow in year i, and E_0 is the initial equity investment (in year 0). According to the above formula, the cash flow each year (C_i) is multiplied by a factor that represents the present value of $1 at a specified discount rate (r). The equity investment is then subtracted from the sum of the present value of the cash flows. We can calculate the net present value for either the before-tax cash flows or the after-tax cash flows. Of course, the discount rate would have to be chosen accordingly.

For investment analysis the net present value is usually calculated for after-tax cash flows. For Oakwood Apartments the after-tax NPV based on a 15 percent discount rate would be calculated as shown in Table 11A-12. At a 15 percent discount rate, the NPV is $14,530. Thus, since the NPV is positive, the investment earns a compound average return that is greater than 15 percent. The investor could have invested $14,530 more equity in the property and still achieved a 15 percent after-tax return with the same cash flows.

TABLE 11A-12. **Present Value Analysis—15 Percent Discount Rate**

	Year	Factor	Cash Flow	Present Value
	1	.8696	$ 4,891	$ 4,253
	2	.7561	5,682	4,296
	3	.6575	6,401	4,209
	4	.5718	6,869	3,928
Reversion	4	.5718	$185,107	$105,844
Total present value				$122,530
Initial equity investment				108,000
Net present value				$ 14,530

TABLE 11A-13. **Present Value Analysis of After-Tax Cash Flow for Oakwood Apartments Based on a 19 Percent Discount Rate**

	Year	Present Value Factor	After-Tax Cash Flow	Present Value
	1	.8403	$ 4,891	$ 4,110
	2	.7062	5,682	4,013
	3	.5934	6,401	3,798
	4	.4987	6,869	3,426
Reversion	4	.4987	$185,107	$ 92,313
Total present value				$107,660
Initial equity investment				108,000
Net present value				$ (340)

TABLE 11A-14. **Present Value Analysis of Before-Tax Cash Flow for Oakwood Apartments Based on a 17 Percent Discount Rate**

	Year	Present Value Factor	Before-Tax Cash Flow	Present Value
	1	.8547	$ −3,982	$ −3,403
	2	.7305	−2,557	−1,868
	3	.6244	−1,235	−771
	4	.5337	−310	−165
Reversion	4	.5337	$213,457	$113,922
Total present value				$107,715
Initial equity investment				108,000
Net present value				$ (285)

Internal Rate of Return. The *internal rate of return* (IRR) is the discount rate that equates the present value of the cash flows with the initial investment. Thus, when the IRR is used as a discount trade, the NPV is zero. Finding the IRR when there are several cash flows that differ over time involves searching for a discount rate that satisfies the above condition (zero NPV).

For Oakwood Apartments the after-tax IRR is known to be greater than 15 percent, since the NPV was positive at this discount rate. At a 19 percent discount rate, the NPV is $-340 as shown in Table 11A-13. Since this is just under zero, the IRR is slightly under 19 percent (it is actually 18.9 percent).

The internal rate of return can also be calculated for the before-tax cash flows. This return is about 17 percent as shown in Table 11A-14. At a 17 percent discount rate, the before-tax NPV is $-285. The exact before-tax IRR is 16.92 percent. Note that the negative cash flows are also discounted and act to reduce the IRR.

It is informative to note that in this case the after-tax return is higher than the before-tax return. This is due to the tax shelter benefits of Oakwood Apartments, which allow the investor to shelter other taxable income.

CHAPTER 12

Implementation Of Strategy: Execution

Jack L. Treynor

$\mathbf{A}$t this point the portfolio building process is almost complete. Investment policy based on the preferences of and constraints on investors has been developed. Macro and micro expectational factors relevant to investing have been identified. Investment strategy has been set through the joint consideration of investment policy and expectational factors. The strategy development process has been subdivided: asset categories have been allocated and portfolios in those asset categories—bonds, common stocks, and real estate, in this book—have been optimized.

Now we are faced with the last step in the building process: implementing the optimally prescribed portfolios within asset categories by selling existing assets and buying desired assets in the optimal amount. This is the execution step. Without it, there cannot be an implementation of portfolio management strategy. But it is not a costless step. And, as we shall see, the *true* costs of execution are complex in nature, larger than popularly believed to be, and difficult to ascertain. Yet because they can have such an important effect on investment results, an attempt to identify and measure these costs must be made.

THE COST OF TRANSACTING

Every holding in an active portfolio entails two transactions. If these transactions cost too much, or consume too much time, the performance of the portfolio is degraded. Yet it is perhaps not too much to say that, in view of the way in which orders are communicated to the trading desk and the sophistication with which the performance of the trading function is monitored, most institutions regard trading as a quasi-clerical function.

In the most rudimentary terms, conceptually the trading desk is merely a link in a two-way information chain connecting the decision maker in the investment organization with exchange specialists, over-the-counter dealers, and block positioners who bring together buyers and sellers of securities, often with a time lag that necessitates some financial exposure on the part of those specialists, dealers, and positioners. A more exalted view of the trading desk is provided by Beebower and Surz [1980] in the following excerpt from their paper.

> Trading in equity securities can be loosely compared to a poker game. The traders are the players at the house table. Commissions are the house fees. The investors or investment management organizations are the owners of the capital with which the traders play. The hands dealt are determined by the [capital] owners according to their longer term investment judgements and their short-term liquidity needs. The traders are concerned with the immediate interplay of the other traders with their respective hands. Judging and discovering [who has and who needs] liquidity is their primary function.
>
> Taking the [trading] table as a whole, the net profits and losses must equal zero after removing the house fees. That is, there are always two sides to every trade. If market makers are added but not explicitly observed at the table, their profits or losses disturb the zero net. In the current institutional [dominated] market, market maker net profits and losses are estimated to be very small relative to either the dollars played at the table or the commission fees.
>
> Expert traders should be expected to make short-term profits if unconstrained by investment directives. They profit by taking the opposite side from traders required to buy or sell specific securities within a short time period relative to [the amount of available] market liquidity. Trading urgency may be warranted if related to information of greater immediate value [in terms of subsequent price action] than the immediate cost [in terms of the total cost of transacting].[1]
>
> A super efficient trader should make money or reduce the costs of trading in a given situation by gauging the market in particular securities and by finding liquidity inexpensively. Larger trading costs are expected when conditions are most constrained.

EXPLICIT EXECUTION COSTS

In large part, of course, it is up to the investment organization whether the people manning its trading desk play a strictly clerical role, play the swashbuckling role envisioned by Beebower and Surz, or, indeed, play some other role in the investment process. The first step in determining that role is to

---

[1] Beebower and Surz make reference here to liquidity-based and information-based traders who will be treated in much greater depth later in this chapter.

answer the following question: What is at stake for portfolio performance in the management of the trading desk?

Beebower-Surz Results

A number of recent empirical studies shed light on the answer. The Beebower-Surz study [1980] examined the trading experience of 13 investment organizations that provided data on over $27 billion of equity trades, excluding odd-lot and client-directed trades which were analyzed separately. There were over 215,000 individual tickets covering nearly 2,500 individual equity securities. Purchases accounted for a rather consistent 52 percent of the principal dollar amount over the 18 months covered. Types of investment organizations included a broad cross-section of the institutional equity marketplace, including mutual funds, employee benefit separate accounts, personal trust accounts, pooled funds, market timing funds, and index funds.

Beebower-Surz's measure of explicit execution cost was designed to estimate to what extent a trade was made at a fair price by looking at price action, net of common price action for equities in the same industry grouping, after a trading program in a security was assumed to have ended. A positive percentage value indicated there was a trading disadvantage or cost and a negative value indicated there was a trading advantage or *anticost*. Excluding commissions and taxes, the average explicit execution cost for all trades should be zero unless the sample of transactors is biased with excess trading expertise (negative average cost) or a lack thereof (positive average cost). With commissions and taxes, the average execution cost would be the average of commissions and taxes.

The Beebower-Surz findings show that, relative to the 1979 median round-trip execution cost of −0.02 percent (slight expertise bias), the high cost participant paid 0.86 percent above the median while the two low cost participants paid 0.49 percent below the median. These explicit execution costs (or, when negative, anticosts) are of the same order—less than one percent—as the computed round-trip commissions costs, 0.66 percent. Beebower and Surz state that for an organization, execution costs can be as important as commission costs. For accounts within an organization, the execution cost range can be much wider, with some having costs well over 2 percent per round trip.

The 13 organizations studied tended to preserve their relative rankings over time. Beebower and Surz noted that the Spearman rank correlation coefficient (R) for the round-trip execution costs for the ten consistent participants is remarkably high for each pair of 6-month time periods and on average.

Last half 1978–First half 1979	R = 0.64
Last half 1978–Last half 1979	R = 0.76
First half 1979–Last half 1979	R = 0.77
Average correlation	R = 0.72

These correlations show that institutions with low explicit transactions costs in one period tend to be low cost institutions in the next period, with the same true for high cost institutions.

Less significant, but highly supportive of meaningful trading performance consistency, are the correlations between intraperiod buy and sell execution costs.

Last half 1978   R = 0.65
First half 1979   R = 0.15
Last half 1979   R = 0.42

These correlation results show that, in addition to remarkably stable round-trip execution rankings, organizations with good buy executions tend to have good sell executions and those that buy poorly tend to sell poorly.

Other Studies

Another recent study by Condon [1981] found what she termed "market impact" costs of about the same magnitude as did an earlier study by Beebower and Priest [1980], although her mean round-trip costs, which were measured somewhat differently than Beebower-Priest's, were higher (1.84% vs. 1.00%).[2] Condon also contrasted buy transactions with sell transactions. She found that, on average, buy transactions relative to sell transactions cost more (1.27% vs. 0.57%) and took longer to execute (5.7 days vs. 3.9 days).

A different kind of evidence is provided by studies of the performance of paper portfolios. In the classic study of Value Line's investment research, Black [1971] reported that Value Line's top-ranked stocks outperformed the market on a risk-adjusted basis by about 10 percent per year from 1965 to 1970—ignoring transactions costs.[3] More recently, Ambachtsheer and Farrell [1979] used Value Line research recommendations to manage an active "paper" portfolio that balanced the rewards of acting on research against the active extra risk incurred. Adjusted for systematic risk differential, the return increment over a market portfolio was 5.7 percentage points, much smaller than what Black estimated for a paper portfolio consisting of Value Line's top ranked stocks.

Figure 12-1 displays the so-called characteristic line for the Ambachtsheer-Farrell paper portfolio based on the Value Line recommendations,

[2] Condon's market impact factor was the price change of a stock from its *strike price* at the order's time stamp to time of execution, unless a one-day or more gap in trading occurred causing resetting of the strike price. Stock price changes were net of price changes of the S&P 500 Stock Composite Index. Her study covered 2,330 purchases and 1,172 sale transactions from December 1977 to May 1978 for employee benefit consolidated trades in portfolios managed actively by one large New York City bank.

[3] As reported in Chapter 10, a more recent empirical study by Lee and Nachtmann [1981] of the Value Line methodology produced much less favorable performance results.

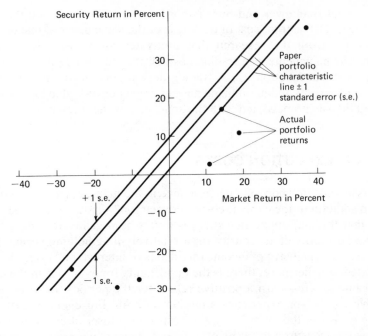

Figure 12-1. Characteristic Line for the Ambachtsheer-Farrell Paper Portfolio Based on Value Line Recommendations and Actual Return Experience of the Value Line Fund.

showing how that portfolio's return would behave given different levels of market return. (It is banded by two parallel straight lines, one standard error away in each direction.) The figure also displays the actual return experience for the Value Line Fund. Although any appraisal of the actual fund's performance is clearly subject to substantial sampling error, the performance difference—in terms of the average vertical distance of the actual portfolio plots from the characteristic line—appears to exceed 5 percent per year and may be as high as 10, not an insignificant differential for the length of the period examined.

In reckoning performance on their paper portfolio, Ambachtsheer and Farrell allowed for a round-trip transactions cost of 2 percent. Given the turnover they incurred (50 percent per year), a 2 percent in-and-out transactions cost reduces performance one percentage point per year. Relative to the findings of Beebower and Priest, Condon, and Beebower and Surz, 2 percent is generous. Yet it does not begin to explain the performance difference between paper and actual portfolios based on the same research. Nor is the difference unusual. While actual portfolios managed by sophisticated investment organizations strain to beat the market averages, paper portfolios based on the same sort of research commonly outperform the market by 10 to 15 percent a year.

If the sum of the explicit costs of execution—commission costs and transfer taxes—and the market impact costs measured by Beebower and Priest,

Condon, and Beebower and Surz is not large enough to explain the difference, then: (1) The total cost of trading is of the same order of magnitude as the benefits from the research that motivates most institutional trades. Clearly, the management of trading costs of this magnitude is not a clerical or quasi-clerical function. (2) A trading desk preoccupied with negotiating small commissions and minimizing market impact costs—shaving sixteenths and eighths—is preoccupied with the small end of the trading cost problem.

IMPLICIT EXECUTION COSTS

What is at stake for portfolio performance in the management of the trading desk in addition to the explicit costs of execution? First, it should be understood that trading, unlike investing, is a zero-sum game. Investing entails taking a position with a security for a relatively long holding period during which a return inclusive of income (dividends or interest) and price change is calculated. Furthermore, there is the opportunity for everyone in the investment game to win—earn a positive return for the period—or lose—earn a negative return—or experience a mixture of both. For every winner in the trading game, on the other hand, there must be a loser of equal magnitude. Returns are measured in terms of dollars or percentage price changes, frequently over very short time periods.

Second, it is important to understand the perception that traders on either side of a transaction have of each other. That is, traders expect to gain from each transaction whether they are on the buy side or on the sell side; otherwise, they would not be willing to transact. But given the nature of the zero-sum game being played, this implies that each expects the other to lose. Yet neither transactor gives more than passing consideration to the fact that the one expects the other to lose. And this occurs even though, on average, if both transactors are representative, the respective magnitudes of the expected gain motivating each transactor and the loss implied by the other transactor's motivation are necessarily equal.

Furthermore, in disregarding the motives of the transactor on the other side, active investors are tacitly assuming that the transactor is drawn randomly from the population of investors. This illusion is heightened by dealers and block positioners, who present a bland façade that tends to hide the motives of the investor on the other side. In actual fact, these investors are drawn not from the general population of investors but from that much smaller number of investors who have a reason to transact.

These investors' reasons for trading represents an element in trading cost that dwarfs commissions and transfer taxes. In general, active investors should be able to demonstrate that their research is valuable—gross of the cost of trading with other investors. Net of this cost, they will find it hard to outperform a passive portfolio consistently. And investors who transact without good research will incur this cost of trading without any offsetting benefits. Indeed, this is precisely how unsuccessful investors fail.

This hidden cost of trading explains why paper portfolios perform better than real portfolios. In a paper portfolio trading decisions execute whether or not a transactor on the other side has a motive for transacting. The successful executions in a paper portfolio that would fail to execute in an actual portfolio are precisely those trades for which the transactor on the other side had no motive. The superior performance of paper portfolios can be traced directly to those "costless" trades, which, in actual portfolio, would not have executed.

Estimating the Implicit Cost of Executing

Suppose that the gross return for each trade in the paper portfolio is the same, whether or not the trade actually executed in the actual portfolio. In theory, then, the difference in performance between trades that executed and trades that did not is the trading cost that is present in the former and absent in the latter. This represents the price one must pay to transact. In practice, of course, we are talking about the difference in return per dollar invested in the assumed executed securities in the paper portfolio and those that actually did end up in the actual portfolio.

If we know the return per dollar invested in the actual portfolio and the return per dollar invested in the paper portfolio—including both trades that executed in the actual portfolio and trades that did not—the implicit cost of trading, C, can be estimated using the following formula, which is derived in Appendix A. Note that this cost figure is stated as a percentage of dollars *traded, not* dollars invested.

$$C = \frac{tR_P - R_a}{tT(1 - t)}$$

where T equals the turnover rate on the paper portfolio, t equals the proportion of paper trades that actually execute in the actual portfolio (i.e., t is expressed as a fraction of T), R_P equals the net percentage return on investment in the paper portfolio, and R_a equals the net percentage return on investment in the actual portfolio.

This formula gives some indication of the maginitude of the problem. Suppose, for example, the turnover rate for the paper portfolio is 100 percent per year while the fraction of paper portfolio trades that execute in the actual portfolio is 0.5. The return from investing in the paper portfolio is 5 percent, as compared with a (risk-adjusted) return on the actual portfolio of zero. According to the formula the cost of trading (expressed, as noted, not per dollar invested, but per dollar traded) is 10 percent.

In practice, of course, the investor would need a more refined equation to make decisions regarding actual executions, since both the fraction of paper trades that execute in the actual portfolio and the cost of trading will depend on the investor's trading strategy. The above formula merely measures averages; every trading strategy has its own cost and its own probability of success.

THE KEY PLAYERS IN THE TRADING GAME

To succeed at the trading game, the active investor needs to understand the motives of the transactor on the other side. Generally speaking, active investors have two fundamentally different motives. One of these is information—not (presumably) the kind of overwhelmingly material information that gets him or her in trouble with the Securities and Exchange Commission's Rule 10b-5 (which prohibits the use of inside information), but nevertheless specific information that will change the outlook for a company and, hence, the market price of its shares. The other motive for transacting is value—a perceived discrepancy between market price and *justified price,* what the investor thinks a security is worth based on publicly available information.

Value-based Transactors

The first player to be identified is an individual or institution known as a *value-based transactor* (VBT). Value-based traders make absolute value judgments about (the probability distribution of) the justified price (JP_{VBT}) of a security based on extensive fundamental analysis of all the macro and micro expectational factors that might affect value, such as those covered in Chapters 6 and 7, the data for which are publicly available. The VBT, then, *analyzes* a security to determine its absolute, total worth in dollars, typically using a top-down, highly disciplined approach to select securities, usually for large trades for large portfolios at large, highly structured institutions. Once this is done, the VBT typically reassesses value only after a significant amount of new information has accumulated—a relatively infrequent event. The VBT, a team player, frequently compares research and justified prices with others for reinforcement, consistency, and compatibility.

In terms of market activity, the value-based transactor, in effect, makes the market for a security, determining the spread between the respective prices at which one can buy quickly and sell quickly. That is, the VBT considers the expected value of the probability distribution of justified price possibilities to be the best estimate of the true equilibrium value of the security and sets a bid price (BP_{VBT}) below JP_{VBT} and an ask price (AP_{VBT}) above JP_{VBT}, as shown in Figure 12-2.

The spread shown in this figure between BP_{VBT} and AP_{VBT} will be not so wide as to attract additional VBTs who are willing to transact at narrower spreads, nor will it be so narrow as to inhibit trading by the primary transactor on the other side of the market, the *information-based transactor* (IBT).

Spread Represents a Consensus. In actuality, the spread portrayed in the figure can be considered a consensus of the spreads of thousands of VBTs, a few of whom are depicted in Figure 12-3 on page 546. VBT_1, with a wider spread, will transact less, on average, because his ask price is higher and his bid price lower than the consensus. VBT_2, however, will transact more

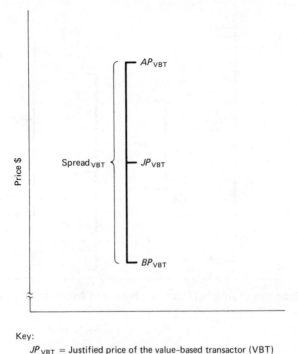

Key:

JP_{VBT} = Justified price of the value-based transactor (VBT)
BP_{VBT} = Bid price of the VBT
AP_{VBT} = Ask price of the VBT
$Spread_{VBT}$ = Difference between AP_{VBT} and BP_{VBT}

Figure 12-2. Justified Price, Bid Price, Ask Price, and Spread for a Value-based Transactor.

because of his smaller spread, lower ask, and higher bid. VBT_3 will get more sells but fewer buys; VBT_4 will get more buys but fewer sells.[4]

Hence Figure 12-2 has implied in it the contents of Figure 12-4 (page 546) where each of the three prices used by value-based transactors is portrayed as a distribution of VBT-based prices in the marketplace. Note that unless the distribution of ask prices *overlaps* that for bid prices, as in Figure 12-5 (page 547) there will be *no* transactions in a marketplace consisting only of VBTs.

In sum, the value-based transactor is the anchor or base for the trading system. The VBT places no value on time. In a market with dealers—to be considered later—VBTs would place limit orders to buy and sell with a spread that encloses justified price and that is wide enough to provide a cushion to offset losses from "getting bagged" by information-based trad-

---

[4] As Figure 12-3 might lead you to conclude, there should be distributions of justified prices and distributions of bid/ask spreads across transactors. These are not necessarily interrelated. The mean of the *JP* distributions would represent the judgments of the market participants about value, whereas the average spread around that mean would represent their risk judgment about the chances of getting bagged by other transactors.

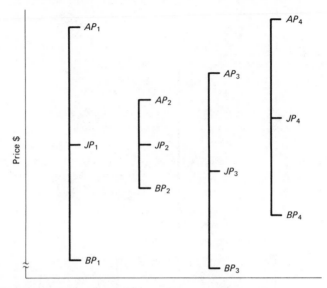

Figure 12-3. Examples of Justified Price, Bid Price, and Ask Price for Four Value-based Transactors.

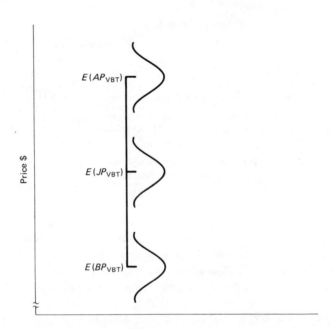

Key: $E(\ )$ = Expected value of a price variable

Figure 12-4. Probability Distributions of Justified Price, Bid Price, and Ask Price for a Value-based Transactor.

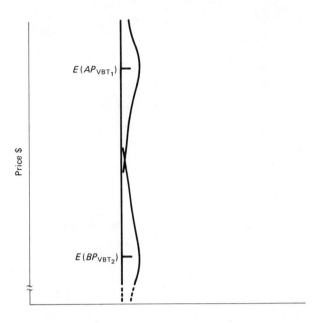

Key: $E(AP_{VBT_1})$ = Expected value of probability distribution of ask
prices for value–based transactor 1.
$E(BP_{VBT_2})$ = Expected value of probability distribution of bid
prices for value–based transactor 2.

Figure 12-5. Example of Overlapping Probability Distributions of Bid Price and Ask Price of Two Value-based Transactors.

ers. Ultimately, it is the VBT who establishes the framework within which dealers operate.

Information-based Transactors

Information-based transactors are traders who come into possession of new information that will have a substantial effect on a security's price, information that is not yet accurately absorbed by value-based transactors. Because this information has value only as long as it has *not* been fully discounted in the security's price, time is of the essence. Since the VBT cares only about value based on analysis of available information relative to market price, his or her only concern is how much price movement toward *JP* will occur. The IBT, on the other hand, cares more about how long it will take for market price to move up or down in response to the new information.

Diagrammatically, for a market consisting only of VBTs and IBTs, the situation is shown in Figure 12-6 on page 548. The VBT has ask, justified, and bid prices set as shown. The IBT comes into possession of adverse information on the security indicating a sharp drop should occur in all three

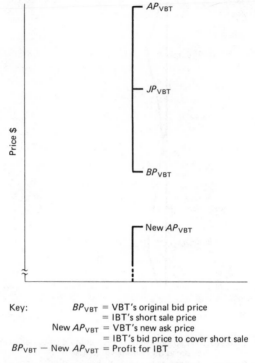

Key:

BP_{VBT} = VBT's original bid price
= IBT's short sale price
New AP_{VBT} = VBT's new ask price
= IBT's bid price to cover short sale
BP_{VBT} — New AP_{VBT} = Profit for IBT

Figure 12-6. Marketplace with Value-based and Information-based Transactors Before and After the Arrival of New Information.

of the VBT's prices. How far they will drop is not known and may only be roughly estimated by the IBT. All the IBT wants is a high degree of assurance that the VBT's ask price will drop substantially below his or her current bid price. That being the case, the IBT will sell or sell short the security to the VBT at the latter's bid price and will make a profit equal to the difference between this price and the VBT's new ask price when the market vindicates his or her beliefs about the value of the information.

Contrasting Analyses Used. Information-based transactors often use not only fundamental security analysis—although on an incremental basis—but also technical analysis since timing is such a critical factor and since price behavior reflecting the arrival of new information is so important. IBTs tend to *investigate* rather than *analyze* a security to try to reveal undiscovered material information. They cannot, however, determine whether fundamental analytical information is already impounded in the security's price because they did not assess the absolute value of the security. All they can do is assess the approximate marginal fundamental/technical combined impact on the security's price.

In contrast to VBTs, IBTs use a bottom-up, undisciplined, unstructured asset-picking (such as stock-picking) approach. They are usually found in small institutions that manage small portfolios and emphasize speed in their trading. Because they are not in the comparison business, they are frequently "lone wolves."

In sum, the information-based transactor is the principal adversary of the value-based transactor. The IBT places a high value on time because he or she needs to transact before unique information is widely known. As a result, the IBT will be willing to buy at a higher price (or sell at a lower price) than may have been quoted recently in order to establish (or eliminate) his or her position; specifically, the IBT will trade at the VBT's ask (or bid) price. This is one of the reasons why the IBT's actual portfolio returns are consistently below paper portfolio returns with the differential representing the cost of obtaining information from VBTs.

Trading Between VBTs and IBTs

Ultimately, in a market made up of VBTs and IBTs, VBTs establish *prices* and IBTs determine *volume*. How a market made up of VBTs and IBTs actually works is shown in the trading array in Figure 12-7.

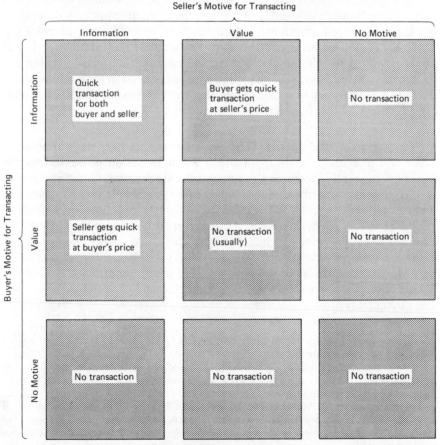

Figure 12-7. Trading Array for a Market Composed of Value-based and Information-based Transactors.

As shown in the array, transactions between two value-based transactors will not occur unless one of them is seriously in error, since neither will trade in the absence of a discrepancy between price and value, and such discrepancy cannot simultaneously be to the advantage of both buyer and seller. Transactions between an information-based buyer and an information-based seller will occur only when their respective information has contrary implications for price and neither transactor is aware of the other's information. In that case, the transaction will execute quickly and at a price that each transactor will consider a bargain.[5]

On average, however, both transactors will be disappointed—and by an amount equal (ignoring brokerage commissions, transfer taxes, and dealer spread) to the research-based expectation of the transactor on the other side. If one defines the cost of trading as the difference between what a transactor expects based on unbiased securities research and what he or she gets, then the principal element in the average cost of trading is the gross research advantage motivating the transactor on the other side.

This holds equally true for transactions between an information-based buyer and a value-based seller (or vice versa). The information-based buyer will want to transact before his or her information gets impounded in price, but the value-based transactor will be unwilling to sell unless the price exceeds his or her estimate of the security's value. If the information-based buyer is willing to pay the price, there will be a quick transaction, but the information-based buyer will be paying a price concession for it. He or she is likely to be disappointed to the extent that the concession absorbs the trading advantage of this information.

Trading Risk and Spread Size. As indicated earlier, the value-based seller will ultimately be disappointed if the information possessed by the buyer subsequently increases the value of the shares sold. Getting bagged—having price move in the direction inferred by the buying or selling activity and research of the party on the other side of the transaction—is the principal business risk of the value-based transactor. But because the value-based transactor sets the price at which the transaction takes place, he or she can exact a premium for assuming this risk. The value-based transactor, in effect, makes the market in the security; he or she determines the spread between the price at which one can sell quickly and the price at which one can buy quickly.[6]

---

[5] Up to now we have ignored an important complication—*limit order* competition between VBTs. The potential outcome of this competition is discussed in Appendix B to this chapter.

[6] So far we have treated value- and information-based transactors as polar opposites. The boundary between them is actually a gray area. For example, is a new, superior security valuation model merely a technique to improve the value-based transactor's estimates of value, or is it new information? Presumably its use will gradually spread through the population of investors until the consequences of the model are fully reflected in market prices. The source of VBT and IBT research errors and the nature of their respective error functions relative to the speed of information propagation are explored in Appendix B to this chapter.

This spread will vary with the likelihood of large price moves in a security. If a company has volatile sales, a high degree of operating or capital structure leverage, and a low degree of product diversification, which together produce volatile earnings, the risk of getting bagged by trading in its shares will be great. In equilibrium, the spread on the stock will expand until, on average, the discrepancy between its bid and ask prices and its justified price is just sufficient to compensate the value-based transactor for assuming the risk of taking a long or short position in the security. If the spread on the stock expands beyond this point, value-based transactors will be attracted to the stock, driving the spread back toward equilibrium. Conversely, if the spread shrinks, value-based transactors in the stock will withdraw. In equilibrium, therefore, the cost of trading on information will be closely related to the cost of trading on value.

The Trading Paradox

Alas, equilibrium in real world markets cannot be as simple as we have described it to this point. To see why, consider the information-based transactor. If the information-based transactor knew the size of the value-based transactor's spread, the IBT would never trade unless the value of his or her information exceeded the spread. But this implies that the information-based trader would trade only when it was to the value-based transactor's disadvantage. No matter how large the value-based trader's spread, therefore, it is never large enough to make value-based trading profitable if the information-based trader estimates the spread correctly. In effect, the IBT is playing a "heads I win, tails you lose" game with the VBT.

To be willing to trade, therefore, the value-based trader must believe that the transactor on the other side either (1) underestimates value-based research used in determining the value-based trader's spread, (2) overestimates the value of his own information, or (3) is trading for reasons other than investment advantage. Trading reasons 1 and 2 may seem to be errors the information-based transactor is unlikely to commit consistently. However, as our discussion of dealer markets later in this chapter suggests, these errors are surprisingly easy to make.

Liquidity-based Transactors

As regards reason number 3, many transactions entail no attempt to reap investment advantage. Securities are sold to make way for the purchase of other securities or bought to round out a passive portfolio and so on. Thus many transactors who have no information are not holding out for a transaction price more favorable than value; indeed, they may be willing to transact at an unfavorable price in order to transact quickly, even though they lack information.

These traders are called *liquidity-based transactors* (LBTs). Their role was originally described by this author writing under the name Walter Bagehot [1971]. They are transactors who trade to obtain or divest cash or, equivalently, to rebalance portfolios that have gotten out of balance relative to original dollar allocations because of price movements (up or down) of some securities.

In a market consisting solely of value-based and liquidity-based transactors, trades will take place quickly via LBTs buying at VBT ask prices and LBTs selling at VBT bid prices. Hence, with a positive spread, the VBT consistently makes a profit in such a market equal to the difference between the two prices.

Pseudo-Information-based Transactors

Still a fourth type of trader is Bagehot's [1971] *pseudo-information-based transactor* (PIBT). This is the trader who either exaggerates the value of new information or believes his or her information has value when, in fact, it has already been largely impounded in the price of the security.

In the case of adverse information, for example, the justified price of the security will fall little or not at all, and the PIBT will be forced to cover at the VBT's ask price, incurring a loss equal to the VBT's spread.

Winners and Losers

Given the above four categories of transactors, we can make some preliminary statements about who wins and who loses in the zero-sum trading game.

Basically, the value-based transactor always loses to information-based transactors. On the other hand, the VBT always wins in his transactions with liquidity-based and pseudo-information-based transactors. To the value-based transactor, however, information-motivated, liquidity-motivated, and pseudo-information-motivated traders are largely indistinguishable. In order for the VBT to survive and prosper, his combined gains from LBTs and PIBTs must exceed his losses to IBTs. The spread he sets between his bid and ask price affects each. If the VBT widens his spread, he loses less money to information-motivated transactors and he makes more from liquidity- and pseudo-information-motivated transactors—assuming that a wider spread does not discourage transactions and/or encourage competition from other VBTs. The reverse obviously holds for a spread narrowing.

When the role of the value-based transactor is as described here, he or she can be viewed as a conduit through which money flows from liquidity- and pseudo-information-motivated transactors to transactors with new, material information. That is, the VBT wins from LBTs and PIBTs and loses to

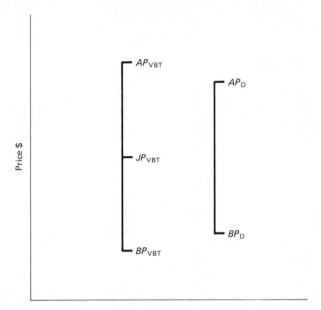

Figure 12-8. Bid and Ask Prices of a Dealer Relative to a Value-based Transactor.

IBTs with the hope that he or she has set spreads wide enough to win on balance.[7]

ENTER THE DEALER

Up to this point our discussion has ignored an important feature of most securities markets—namely, the dealer (D). Under this generic heading we include over-the-counter dealers, block positioners, and exchange specialists. Some markets will have several dealers. Others, like the New York Stock Exchange, will have only one. What is the role of the dealer and how does his or her presence affect the trading problem for institutional (or individual) information-based and value-based transactors?

In our view, the real market maker in securities markets is not the dealer, but the transactor whose decisions are based on his or her perceptions of value, the VBT. But if the dealer is not the real market maker, what does the dealer do? Basically, as shown in Figure 12-8, the dealer preempts transacting by setting a bid and ask price inside the prices set by value-based transactors, thereby creating a smaller spread than that of the VBT. By setting a bid price higher than the VBT's bid price and by setting an ask price lower than the VBT's ask price, the dealer causes all the transactors who would nor-

---

[7] Given the role of the dealer, to be discussed shortly, markets with large numbers of LBTs and PIBTs are likely to be markets characterized by a proliferation of dealers, since trading with these two types of transactors is so profitable.

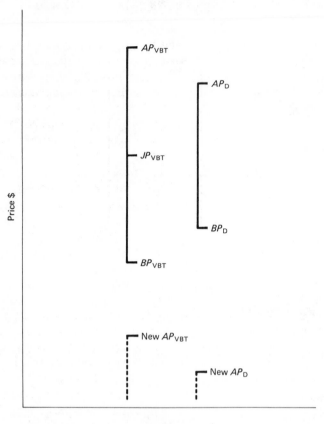

Key: $AP_D - BP_D$ = Dealer profit against LBT
$BP_{VBT} -$ New AP_{VBT} = IBT profit against VBT
$BP_D -$ New AP_D = IBT profit against dealer

Figure 12-9. Winnings and Losings in a Market Consisting of Value-based Traders, Information-based Traders, and Dealers.

mally sell to and buy from a value-based transactor to sell to and buy from the dealer.

What results, then, is a marketplace with dealers and three of four types of transactors operating as shown in Figure 12-9. The resulting market is a hard one in which to make consistent trading profits even though it is obviously less than perfectly efficient.

1. Assuming their information is substantiated by the market, IBTs win in their transactions with dealers, by an amount exceeding what they would have won against VBTs, unless the dealer's bid (ask) price is close to the VBT's bid (ask).
2. Dealers consistently win against LBTs by an amount equal to their bid/ask spread.

3. Dealers win against PIBTs, albeit in possibly lesser amounts.
4. VBTs transact very little, except when the dealer lays off to them. Legally usable new information tends to bag VBTs rather than the dealer.

Width of the Dealer's Spread

What are some other factors that have been identified in the literature as affecting dealer spreads? Garbade [1982] provides us with a systematic review, as summarized below.

Time Rate of Transactions. The literature views the dealer as providing a liquidity-in-depth service for transactors that bridges the gaps between the arrival of buy and sell orders. Since greater liquidity service is provided by dealers with relatively long gaps between offsetting orders, dealers in low volume securities, other things equal, will set a larger bid/ask spread than dealers in high volume securities. This inverse relationship between trading volume and spreads has been documented by a number of researchers, among whom Demsetz [1968] was the earliest.

Price of the Security. These writers argue that, other things equal, the bid/ask spread on a security should be directly proportional to the price of the issue. However, several empirical studies on common stocks have demonstrated that spreads are less than directly proportional. Demsetz [1968] and Benston and Hagerman [1974] attribute this phenomenon to the size of commission costs involved in trading a given dollar amount of a stock; that is, lower priced stocks incur larger costs than higher priced stocks. The result is a tendency of institutional investors to prefer higher priced stocks. With the larger volume thereby generated producing a faster time rate of transactions, spreads will be narrowed doubly.

Size of Trade. A third factor affecting the dealer's bid/ask spread is the size of individual transactions. The bid/ask spreads for standard-sized lots of securities—which vary from one type of security to another—have been empirically observed to be smaller than either larger or smaller transactions. Little or no explanation for this observation is available other than the hypothesis that the cost of the liquidity service provided by the dealer is greater in these circumstances.

For larger-than-standard-sized blocks, the arrival of market-order blocks indicates an imbalance in supply and demand that serves as a proxy variable for relevant information unknown to the dealer, who then widens his spread to reduce the impact of getting bagged. For smaller-than-standard-sized blocks, the dealer has an assembly problem—that is, finding enough additional nonstandard-sized small blocks on the other side of the market before he gets bagged by the arrival of new information.

Insider Trading. Bagehot [1971] has pointed out the losing nature of dealer transactions with new information available to transactors. Benston and Hagerman [1974] and Barnea and Logue [1975] carried the investigation further by demonstrating that the size of dealer spreads depends on the importance of the information affecting the price of the security. They assumed the importance could be measured by the security's specific risk as defined in Chapters 2 and 3. They found that variations across securities in specific risk explained a significant portion of observed variations in spread. The largest spreads tended to be those of nondiversified companies.

Laying Off by Dealers

What we have, then, is a market where the dealer attracts a good deal of trading volume, albeit at a necessarily smaller spread. If value-based transactors transact at a competitive spread—that is, at the smallest spread they can afford to charge information-based, liquidity-based, and pseudo-information-based transactors and still survive—how can the dealer afford to charge a still smaller spread?

The first thing to observe about the dealer is that, because of his relatively high trading volume and his practice—to be explained shortly—of laying off residual positions, he does not expect to be greatly exposed nor for any length of time. Whereas the value-based transactor may end up holding a position for months or even years, the duration of the dealer's position is likely to be measured in hours or at most days. Thus, information that takes more than a few days to propagate through the population of investors represents little or no risk to the dealer.[8]

The second thing to observe is that most of the securities acquired by the dealer in transactions with IBTs, LBTs, et al., who are selling will be dealt away in transactions with other IBTs, LBTs, et al., who are buying. Even if the transactions accommodated by the dealer are an entirely random mixture of purchases and sales, however, the dealer will occasionally accumulate (or decumulate) a position large enough that prudence compels it to be *laid off*. In order to lay off securities, the dealer must be willing to transact at a price that will be attractive to the transactors on the other side. These are, of course, the value-based transactors, since they are the only investors who respond to price relative to a security's absolute value. The threshold price at which VBTs respond is governed by their spread. Figure 12-10 depicts an example where the dealer has acquired either (1) an excess inventory and finds it necessary to lay off to a VBT, or (2) an excess short position and finds it necessary to lay off from or buy from a VBT to cover that short position.

As Figure 12-10 shows, at any given time the dealer has a desired inventory level (horizontal axis) at I_0. The VBT has a larger spread around the

---

[8] An excellent discussion of the distinction between information that represents a risk to the dealer and information that does not can be found in the case law on inside information. There, new information potentially damaging to dealers is referred to as "material."

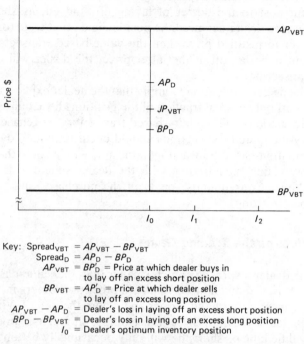

Key: $\text{Spread}_{VBT} = AP_{VBT} - BP_{VBT}$
$\text{Spread}_D = AP_D - BP_D$
$AP_{VBT} = BP_D' = $ Price at which dealer buys in
to lay off an excess short position
$BP_{VBT} = AP_D' = $ Price at which dealer sells
to lay off an excess long position
$AP_{VBT} - AP_D = $ Dealer's loss in laying off an excess short position
$BP_D - BP_{VBT} = $ Dealer's loss in laying off an excess long position
$I_0 = $ Dealer's optimum inventory position

Figure 12-10. Pricing Framework for Dealer Layoffs to Value-based Transactors Resulting from Excess or Deficient Securities Inventories.

justified price (vertical axis) than the dealer. Any buying, selling, or shorting activity that takes the dealer substantially away from his optimal inventory position increases the likelihood of his having to incur the cost of laying off at that spread. This, in turn, will tend to cause the dealer to shift the level of his own bid and ask relative to the VBT's bid and ask to reflect the resulting change in the expected cost of accommodating information- and liquidity-motivated buyers and sellers. In Figure 12-10, assume that the dealer experiences an imbalance of sell orders, accumulating inventory to undesired higher level I_1 relative to the optimum I_0. If sell orders net of buy orders continue to materialize, the dealer adjusts both JP and bid/ask prices to lower and lower levels until finally at inventory level I_2 he is able to sell (lay off) securities to the VBT because at this point the dealer's ask price, AP_D', equals the VBT's bid price, BP_{VBT}, at this high inventory level. The dealer's loss in laying off to the VBT will be BP_D minus BP_{VBT}.

If the process had gone in the opposite direction, with the dealer going more and more short, the dealer would finally be able to buy in from the VBT because at that point BP_D would equal the VBT's ask price, AP_{VBT}. The dealer's loss in buying from the VBT will be AP_{VBT} minus AP_D.[9]

[9] The potential behavior of dealers, called *specialists* on the organized exchanges for common stocks, in this type of scenario is interesting. When an influx of market sell orders begins to play out after forcing JP, BP, and AP downward, the specialist may execute the remaining value-based limit buy orders on his book for his own account, going short the stock in the

In sum, then, the spread imposed by value-based transactors represents the contingent cost to the dealer of laying off. Indeed, as shown in the example, since the dealer acquired the position laid off at a bid (or ask) price that was closer to justified price than the value-based transactor's bid (or ask) price, but must lay off at the latter price, the dealer will lose on the combined transaction.

What is the dealer's salvation? Simply that the dealer expects to incur the cost of laying off only a small fraction of the positions he acquires in accommodating information- and liquidity-based transactors. Purchases and sales from liquidity-motivated transactions should occur randomly over time; as regards information-based transactions, it is at least plausible that good and bad news motivating their trading with the dealer should also arrive randomly over time. Consequently, many of the purchases and sales by the dealer will be offsetting.

Dealer's Effect on the Trading Game

As noted, the dealer's spread is much smaller than the value-based transactor's spread. It is also much more visible to other transactors in the market. Should they concentrate on the former and ignore the latter? What does the presence of a dealer mean to these transactors? Although at any given time the dealer will be long or short, he will only occasionally be long enough or short enough to lay off to the value-based transactor.

We have noted that the longer or shorter the dealer is, the closer he is to having to lay off at the VBT's price; consequently, as layoff becomes more likely, he moves both his bid and asked price closer to the value-based transactor's price.[10] On the other hand, these movements in the level of the dealer's prices are virtually invisible to his clientele, since they are camouflaged by changes in the justified price of the security that alter the bid and asked prices of the value-based transactor. The value-based transactor's bid

---

process and moving justified price lower and making the spreads around this *JP* wider than they would otherwise have been. This allows the specialist to short the stock at relatively favorable ask prices (i.e., high relative to subsequent price action as described next). When pseudo-information-based market sell orders subsequently are received in response to whatever new information has been driving down the stock's justified price, then the specialist—who has by now cleaned out the limit buy orders at the bottom end of his book—will execute these sell orders at bid prices that are quite low, lower certainly than any of the bid prices formerly on the book. The end result, of course, is a covering of the specialist's short position in the stock at relatively favorable (low) purchase prices. Note that when all of this occurs, the specialist is not taking the usual dealer action of offsetting by accommodating other transactors or laying off. Instead, the specialist is deliberately using his semimonopolistic dealing position to create a situation of sizable profit.

[10] The rational investor will limit the position he takes on the basis of new information, thus limiting impact on price. In a world of such investors, information becomes fully impounded in price only when all investors in the market have received and acted on it. The speed with which price reacts to new information is thus limited by the speed with which that information propagates through the population of investors.

and ask are also invisible to the dealer's clientele. Unless the information-based transactor's information is being offset by information held by information-based transactors on the other side, however, the former is likely to end up paying a price for his transaction that is heavily influenced by the value-based transactor's spread.

The effect of the dealer on the value-based transactor is more subtle. Whereas, in the absence of a dealer, the value-based transactor would enjoy the offsetting transactions by information-based and other transactors—at a self-determined spread—when a dealer is present, the dealer gets the benefit of the offsetting transactions (albeit at the dealer's spread). This consideration suggests that the presence of dealers makes the game far less attractive to value-based transactors.

Information vs. Informationless Trading. Broadly speaking, the dealer's layoffs can be viewed as a result of the dealer's accommodating information-less trading (e.g., with VBTs or PIBTs) or information trading (e.g., with IBTs).

While the dealer rarely gets bagged by information trading because he or she either offsets in the accommodation of other transactors or lays off quickly with a minimum of price change damage, the value-based transactor almost always does get bagged. Needless to say, however, accommodating layoffs stemming from the dealer's informationless trading are pure profit for the VBT at his large spread.

On the other hand, the more successful the dealer is in offsetting informationless trading—so that he or she does not have to lay off—the larger the fraction of layoffs that will be information layoffs when they do occur, and hence the greater the hazard to the VBT in accommodating those layoffs. The only way the VBT can compensate for this increased hazard, of course, is to increase spread.

When the VBT fails to recognize this situation and simply maintains his or her bid/ask spread in the face of repeated layoffs from dealers, the value-based transactor can still realize a gross profit on the spread. But the question is: Will that gross profit compensate him or her for the cost of trading, i.e., the cost of getting bagged? These costs for the VBT are the exact counterpart to costs incurred by IBTs when they place too high a value on time.

It would hardly be necessary to stress the importance of this were it not so easy for both VBTs and IBTs to underestimate, for the reasons just noted, their true costs of transacting.

MANAGING THE TRADING DESK

In sum, one of the key elements in effective management of the trading desk is to know who the players are and why they behave as they do. The information-based transactor is buying time, and is interested in buying it as cheaply as possible—i.e., at the smallest possible spread. The value-based transactor is selling time, preferably at the highest possible price—i.e., at the largest possible spread. Thus, in this context, although the securities market ostensibly involves the exchange of securities for cash, it actually involves the exchange of money for time, with securities serving as incidental vehicles. A trading desk that either sells time too cheaply in executing value-based transactions, or buys time too expensively in executing information-based transactions, is failing in one of its most important tasks.

In order to perform this task well, the trading desk needs to fulfill two functions. First, it needs to determine how much time is worth in the current transaction. That is, what is the value of the research motivating the proposed transaction? Second, acting as a market intelligence unit, the trading desk needs to ascertain the going tradeoff between price and time. Otherwise, the trading desk is certain to goof by committing one of three errors: selling time too cheaply, buying time too expensively, or failing to trade at all.

Knowledge Needed to Succeed

The first and second steps in avoiding the mistakes just cited are for the trading desk to know what kind of player it is in each proposed transaction and, given this knowledge, what type of trades it should seek. For example, is research generating information-based recommendations where speed of execution (up to some maximum price) is the vital element? Or is research generating value-based recommendations where price is the vital element? Top-down organizations tend to be too large and ponderous to do information-based trading. Instead, they should be value-based transactors. Top-down organizations often say they are looking for efficiently priced securities, but this is exactly wrong. If you are a VBT, your profit opportunity depends on a discrepancy between true value and current price and you should, therefore, be seeking *inefficiently* priced securities.

Bottom-up organizations tend to be information-based transactors. Often they say they are looking for inefficiently priced securities, but this is also exactly wrong. If you are an IBT, you should be looking for securities that you can transact quickly and cheaply, i.e., efficiently priced securities or highly liquid securities. However, one important caveat is in order. Highly liquid securities tend to be securities with small specific risk and hence diversified across many industries. In these securities, the IBT's opportunity to use information is diluted across the many industries.

There is one further point with respect to the need for the trading desk to identify the kinds of input it is getting. Institutional behavior patterns tend to change over time. That is, just because the trading desk has been receiving value-based inputs, there is no assurance that the next input will be value-based. The trading desk must be actively and continuously inquisitive of research to determine the origin of recommendations.

Matching Transactions with Market Circumstances

The third crucial function of the trading desk is to match its transaction with the market's circumstances in terms of the current tradeoff between price and time. That is, the trading desk must assess the value of its research against that of opposing transactors and take appropriate action. This is an extremely complex decision-making process, one that will always be specific to current market circumstances and one that does not lend itself to resolution by appeal to principle.

In order to fulfill this function, the trading desk must know the nature of its potential losses and gains. For example, if you are a VBT, you will consistently lose to IBTs because of unrecognized information resulting in a substantial (eventual) change in security price. You will consistently gain from LBTs and PIBTs, respectively, because of their cash needs and incorrect judgments about the rapidity with which price impounds new information. On the other hand, you will occasionally get bagged in your transactions with the dealer. Hence, the most important question for the trading desk is what the dealer is doing. Is he or she dealing (i.e., accommodating information-based and liquidity-based transactors and setting his or her own bid and ask prices) or laying off at prices determined by value-based transactors? If the latter, is the dealer laying off to a value-based buyer or a value-based seller? The price at which layoffs occur can give the trading desk observing these transactions some idea of the location (in terms of price) of competition for its own offers to buy and sell.

Knowing Bid and Ask in Size

Specifically, the trading desk should make every effort to know at every point in time what a stock's *bid in size* and *ask in size* are, where size refers to tradeable lot size or the number of shares that can be traded instantly and at no price concession. An example of tradeable lot size might be 10 percent of the stock's float or average trading volume.

Realistically, bid and ask in size prices can never be known with certainty in advance of a trade; the trading desk can only make a judgment as to tradeable lot size prices.

But once that judgment is made, the trading desk can locate the price where the dealer has recently been dealing and compare it to its own estimates of bid and ask in size prices. If the dealer's price is close to either the bid or ask in size, he is close to laying off.

For example, if the dealer is long a stock and has a larger than desired inventory of it, the dealer will be accommodating information-based sellers at a price only slightly above the VBT's bid price (for example, just below inventory level I_2 in Figure 12-10), since there is a high probability that he will have to lay off to the VBT. If this is the case, IBT buyers would be able to buy the stock cheaply, but IBT sellers would be able to sell only at an expensive price. The continuum of tradeoff between time and spread has tilted strongly toward one end of the spectrum.

In this situation the price of time to sellers is very high. Therefore, if research comes in with a recommendation based on new information to sell quickly, the trading desk will be duly resistant, wanting to know if the value of the research was higher than the current high cost of selling. Only when this can be assured, perhaps with the portfolio manager as final arbiter, should the transaction be carried out.

It should be noted that the presence of a dealer, in effect, eliminates the possibility that an IBT anxious to buy and an IBT anxious to sell will *simultaneously* pay a high price for transacting quickly. Depending on the dealer's inventory position, one or the other—but not both—of the IBTs will pay that price. Within the framework of the VBT's bid/ask spread, therefore, there is in principle a price/time tradeoff that can run in either direction, but in only one direction at any given time. Figure 12-11 demonstrates how the dealer's prices are likely to respond to changes in his inventory position.

Locating the Price/Time Tradeoff

As the figure shows, the prime indicator of which way the price/time tradeoff is running is the location of the dealer's mean (or justified) price relative to the VBT's bid and ask prices. If, in fact, one of the key tasks for the trading desk is to estimate which way the tradeoff is running and how big it is, then it follows that the trading desk must attempt running estimates of the VBT's bid and ask prices. One clue as to their location is the dealer's layoff transactions. That is, if these transactions result in sharp changes in the dealer's inventory position, they should tend, according to the model discussed here, to result in sharper price changes than those accompanying routine transactions. As Figure 12-11 shows, note that the price change will be in the direction *opposite* to the price effects of the trading pressure that occasioned the layoff. In principle, the layoff transaction will be the one *preceding* the sharp price move. Since that transaction involves the VBT as well as the dealer, it establishes the VBT's bid or ask price at that point in time.

A subsidiary task for the trading desk is to estimate the VBT's bid/ask spread. Why? Because if the trading desk has an estimate of the spread, then every observation of either the VBT's bid or the VBT's ask, in effect, gives the trading desk estimates of both. Since the VBT's prices move only when new information gets into the public domain, the information necessary to update price estimates obtained from the dealer's last layoff is, in principle, always available to the trading desk's own research organization. By assigning an incremental value to the information and passing that value along to the trading desk, research can contribute significantly to the trading desk's effectiveness.

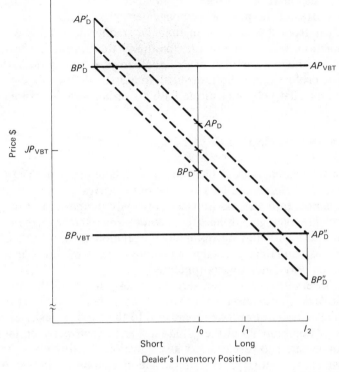

Figure 12-11. Potential Locuses of Dealer Bid, Ask, and Mean Prices Between Opposite Ends of His Layoff Spectrum.

Role of the Portfolio Manager

It should be apparent from the preceding discussion that communication between research and the trading desk—in both directions—is critical. Yet some investment organizations actually set up obstacles to this two-way flow. Facetiously, one may say that this obstacle is called an investment committee in some organizations and a portfolio manager in others. More seriously, the portfolio managers and investment committees may be an obstacle to the free flow of information between research and the trading desk unless they understand the importance of that flow and their role as the connecting link between the two.

Specifically, is portfolio management an administrative process or a control process? It should be a guidance process, with the portfolio manager controlling the portfolio via a steering function that calls on years of experience in the securities markets. Unfortunately, however, there is a distinct tendency for the manager to make the process an administrative one (complete with organizational pyramiding of people and titles) because he perceives that this enhances his role. But in so doing, the manager may hinder the effectiveness of the portfolio management process.

It is clear from this discussion that the trading desk function is not a clerical function. Given the complex nature of the transaction process and the potentially huge gains and losses involved, the trading desk should be staffed by a professional who thoroughly understands the process and who has a title and salary commensurate with his or her sizable responsibilities.

Evaluating the Trading Desk

Control of the trading desk is basically a statistical problem. The reason is that a substantial element of luck relating to the arrival of transactors on the other side enters into specific transactions. Only the pattern of trades over time will tend to average out the effects of luck and tell management whether the trading desk is behaving optimally in relation to the market tradeoff between money and time. Actual transactions—those of others as well as its own—are the only clues to this tradeoff.[11]

These observations lead to a series of questions about the operation of the trading desk. For example, how is research's opinion of the value of time on a particular transaction communicated to the trading desk? How is the trading desk's opinion about the going market tradeoff between money and time communicated to research? A key question is: How does the trading desk document the actual money/time tradeoff impounded in the completed transaction?

Application to Fixed Income and Real Estate Transacting

This discussion of execution has been limited to its application to equity securities and portfolios. However, the principles illustrated are applicable in whole or in part to fixed income and real estate investment transactions.

Since fixed income securities bear a high order of systematic risk, the discussion of value-based and liquidity-based transactors is most applicable to the execution of bond purchases and sales. Information relating to an

---

[11] How to specifically assess the performance of the trading desk is not a simple matter. One approach, used in studies cited earlier, might be to see if, over time and many transactions, price changes following the completion of buy trading programs—whether information-based or value-based—were sizably positive or not (and the reverse following sell trading programs). But even if prices rose after a buy trading program, was it the trading desk's trading activity that drove the price up or was research's research good, resulting in a quick and permanent upward impact on price? The key, of course, is how permanent the price change is. But this raises the issue of how long does it take to get and maintain a significant permanent price change? Under any circumstances, the necessary information must be collected transaction by transaction on a time-stamped basis to make a rational evaluation of the trading desk's activities. But even with these data, there is great difficulty in making evaluative judgments of trading desk performance on the basis of a buy or sell price versus the closing price after the end of a trading program.

individual security is of less importance because of the homogeneous nature of bonds.

Conversely, the individualized and unique characteristics of each piece of real estate places much greater importance on information-based transactions. In fact, inside information is not prohibited and is the basis for a portion of all real estate transactions. Thus, the trading characteristics of the VBT, IBT, and LBT can be identified and related to the execution aspects of the management of any investment portfolio.

CONCLUDING NOTE

Good research inputs are worthless to the portfolio manager unless the manager can persuade someone to transact with him or her *and* do so at a price that does not offset the value of research inputs (or worse). A critical judgment for the manager is how much investment advantage his or her counterpart on the other side is bringing to the transaction. In addition to trying to negotiate the best possible price, therefore, the manager must try to estimate the value of the other's research advantage and try to conceal the value of his or her own research advantage.

Although couched in terms of the price of the security being transacted, the negotiation on price really centers on the value of the respective managers' research advantages. The bids and offers in the negotiating process convey information about the advantages, very much in the fashion of bidding in contract bridge or betting in poker. Perhaps more than any other game, active portfolio management resembles five card stud; *in the long run, the cards that research deals the portfolio manager may matter less than his or her judgment about when to raise and when to fold.*

FURTHER READING

Generally speaking, readings on the subject of execution can be divided into three categories.

The first category includes empirical studies that provide evidence on how markets operate, principally via price behavior. They include Beebower and Priest [1980], Beebower and Surz [1980], Brealey [1969, 1970, 1971], Close [1975], Condon [1981], Kraus and Stoll [1972a, 1972b], Lorie and Hamilton [1973], Niederhoffer and Osborne [1966], Securities and Exchange Commission [1971], and Tinic and West [1972, 1974].

A second grouping of materials covers the legal and institutional settings in which securities markets operate. They include Farrar [1974], Mendelson [1973], Peake [1978], Smidt [1974], U.S. House of Representatives [1965], and U.S. Treasury–Federal Reserve System [1959].

A third topic area, the one with which this chapter is most concerned, is the economic principles of market-making. These readings include Bagehot [1971], Barnea [1974], Barnea and Logue [1975], Benston and Hagerman [1974], Demsetz [1968], Fama [1970], Fama and Laffer [1971], Garbade [1982], New York Stock Exchange [1968], Samuelson [1965], Smidt [1971], Tinic [1972], Tinic and West [1976], Treynor [1981], Treynor and Ferguson [1976], West [1975], and West and Tinic in their pioneering book on market-making [1971], the contents of which are updated in their investments text [1979].

BIBLIOGRAPHY

Ambachtsheer, Keith P., and James L. Farrell, Jr., "Can Active Management Add Value?" *Financial Analysts Journal,* November/December 1979.

Bagehot, Walter, "The Only Game in Town," *Financial Analysts Journal,* March/April 1971.

Barnea, Amir, "Performance Evaluation of NYSE Specialists," *Journal of Financial and Quantitative Analysis,* September 1974.

——, **and Dennis Logue,** "The Effect of Risk on the Market Maker's Spread," *Financial Analysts Journal,* November/December 1975.

Beebower, Gilbert, and William Priest, "The Tricks of the Trade," *Journal of Portfolio Management,* Winter 1980.

——, **and R. Surz,** "Analysis of Equity Trading Execution Costs," Center for Research in Security Prices Seminar, November 1980.

Benston, George, and R. Hagerman, "Determinants of Bid-Ask Spreads in the Over-the-Counter Market," *Journal of Financial Economics,* December 1974.

Black, Fischer, "Yes Virginia, There Is Hope: Tests of the Value Line System," *Financial Analysts Journal,* March/April 1971.

Brealey, Richard A., *An Introduction to Risk and Return from Common Stocks,* Cambridge, Mass.: M.I.T. Press, 1969.

——, "The Distribution and Independence of Successive Rates of Return in the U.K. Equity Market," *Journal of Business Finance,* Summer, 1970.

——, *Security Prices in a Competitive Market,* Cambridge, Mass.: M.I.T. Press, 1971.

Close, Nicholas, "Price Effects of Large Transactions," *Financial Analysts Journal,* November/December 1975.

Condon, Kathleen, "Measuring Equity Transaction Costs," *Financial Analysts Journal,* September/October 1981.

Cootner, Paul H., "Stock Prices: Random versus Systematic Changes," *Industrial Management Review,* Spring 1962.

Demsetz, Harold, "The Cost of Transacting," *Quarterly Journal of Economics,* February 1968.

Fama, Eugene F., "Efficient Capital Markets: A Review of Theory and Empirical Work," *Journal of Finance,* May 1970.

——, **and Arthur B. Laffer,** "Information and Capital Markets," *Journal of Business,* July, 1971.

Farrar, Donald E., "Toward a Central Market System: Wall Street's Slow Retreat into the Future," *Journal of Financial and Quantitative Analysis,* November 1974.

Garbade, Kenneth, *Securities Markets,* New York: McGraw-Hill Book Company, 1982.

Kraus, Alan, and Hans Stoll, "Price Impact of Block Trading on the New York Stock Exchange," *Journal of Finance,* June 1972a.

—— and ——, "Parallel Trading by Institutional Investors," *Journal of Financial and Quantitative Analysis,* December 1972b.

Lee, Wayne Y., and Robert Nachtmann, "The Informational Content of Value Line Ratings: An Empirical Anomaly," Working Paper, Indiana University School of Business, October 1981.

Lorie, James, and Mary Hamilton, *The Stock Market: Theories and Evidence,* Homewood, Ill.: Richard D. Irwin, 1973.

Mendelson, M., "The Martin Report and Its Aftermath," *Bell Journal of Economics and Management Science,* Spring 1973.

New York Stock Exchange, *Economic Effects of Negotiated Rates on the Brokerage Industry,* a report submitted to the Securities and Exchange Commission, 1968.

Niederhoffer, Victor, and M. F. M. Osborne, "Market Making and Reversals on the Stock Exchange," *Journal of the American Statistical Association,* December 1966.

Peake, J. W., "The National Market System," *Financial Analysts Journal,* July/August 1978.

Samuelson, Paul A., "Proof That Properly Anticipated Prices Fluctuate Randomly," *Industrial Management Review,* Spring 1965.

Securities and Exchange Commission, *Institutional Investor Study Report,* Washington, D.C.: U.S. Government Printing Office, 1971.

Smidt, Seymour, "Which Road to an Efficient Stock Market: Free Competition or a Regulated Monopoly?" *Financial Analysts Journal,* September/October 1971.

——, "The Changing Relative Roles of Individuals and Institutions in the Stock Market," *The Journal of Contemporary Business,* Winter 1974.

Tinic, Seha M., "The Economics of Liquidity Services," *Quarterly Journal of Economics,* February 1972.

——, **and Richard R. West,** "Competition and the Pricing of Dealer Service in the Over-the-Counter Stock Market," *Journal of Financial and Quantitative Analysis,* June 1972.

—— and ——, "Marketability of Common Stocks in Canada and the U.S.A.: A Comparison of Agent vs. Dealer Dominated Markets," *Journal of Finance,* June 1974.

—— and ——, "Economics of Market-Making: Regulation versus Competition," *Journal of Contemporary Business,* Summer 1976.

Treynor, Jack, "What Does It Take to Win the Trading Game?" *Financial Analysts Journal,* January/February 1981.

——, **and Robert Ferguson,** "In Defense of Technical Analysis," Chicago: Center for Research in Security Prices, 1976.

U.S. House of Representatives, 88th Congress, 1st Session, House Document No. 95, *Report of the Special Study of the Securities Markets of the Securities and Exchange Commission,* Washington, D.C.: U.S. Government Printing Office, 1965.

U.S. Treasury–Federal Reserve System, *Treasury–Federal Reserve Study of the Government Securities Market,* Washington, D.C.: U.S. Government Printing Office, 1959.

West, Richard R., "Two Kinds of Market Efficiency," *Financial Analysts Journal,* November/December 1975.

——, **and Seha M. Tinic,** *The Economics of the Stock Market,* New York: Praeger, 1971.

—— and ——, *Investing in Securities: An Efficient Markets Approach,* Reading, Mass.: Addison-Wesley Publishing Company, 1979.

APPENDIX A

The Cost of Trading

The cost of trading can be determined by defining the percentage net return on investment in the paper portfolio. This percentage net return is defined in terms of the percentage gross return, the percentage cost, and the frequency of portfolio turnover less the comparable percentage net return from the actual portfolio and is obtained by solving for the percentage cost. The paper portfolio formulation is:

$$
\begin{matrix}
\text{Percentage net} \\
\text{return on \$} \\
\text{assumed invested} \\
\text{in paper portfolio} \\
(R_P)
\end{matrix}
=
\begin{matrix}
\text{Percentage net return on \$} \\
\text{assumed traded in paper portfolio}
\end{matrix}
\quad
\begin{matrix}
\text{Paper portfolio} \\
\times \text{ turnover} \\
(T)
\end{matrix}
$$

$$
=
\left[
\begin{matrix}
\text{Percentage gross} & \text{Percentage cost} \\
\text{return on \$} & \text{on \$} \\
\text{traded in} & - \text{ traded in} \\
\text{paper portfolio} & \text{paper portfolio} \\
(g) &
\end{matrix}
\right]
\times T
$$

$$
=
\left[
g -
\left(
\begin{matrix}
\text{Percentage cost} \\
\text{of \$} \\
\text{traded in} \\
\text{actual portfolio} \\
(c)
\end{matrix}
\right)
\times
\left(
\begin{matrix}
\text{Ratio of} \\
\text{turnover} \\
\text{of actual} \\
\text{portfolio} \\
\text{to} \\
\text{turnover} \\
\text{of paper} \\
\text{portfolio} \\
(t)
\end{matrix}
\right)
\right]
\times T
$$

$$
= (g - tc)T
$$

In other words, only the trades in the paper portfolio that actually execute in the actual portfolio are assumed to experience trading costs in the paper portfolio, because they are the only trades in which the transactor on the other side is research motivated.

The actual portfolio's net percentage return on investment is:

$$
\begin{matrix}
\text{Percentage net} \\
\text{return on \$} \\
\text{invested in} \\
\text{actual portfolio} \\
(R_a)
\end{matrix}
=
\left(
\begin{matrix}
\text{Percentage net} \\
\text{return on} \\
\text{\$ traded}
\end{matrix}
\right)
\times
\begin{matrix}
\text{Actual} \\
\text{portfolio} \\
\text{turnover}
\end{matrix}
$$

$$
=
\left(
\begin{matrix}
\text{Gross percentage} \\
\text{return on \$} \\
\text{traded in} \\
\text{actual portfolio} \\
(g)
\end{matrix}
-
\begin{matrix}
\text{Percentage} \\
\text{cost on \$} \\
\text{traded in} \\
\text{actual} \\
\text{portfolio} \\
(c)
\end{matrix}
\right)
$$

$$\times \ \frac{\text{Actual turnover}}{\text{Paper turnover}} \times \ \begin{array}{c} \text{Paper} \\ \text{turnover} \\ (T) \end{array}$$

$$= \ (g - c)tT$$

Note the percentage gross return on dollars traded in either portfolio is g, whereas the cost of inducing an actual trade—not a paper trade—is c. Everything in these two equations is measurable except c and g, either of which we can solve for.

Multiplying out these two equations, we have

$$R_P = gT - tcT$$
$$R_a = gtT - tcT$$

Multiplying the first equation by t and subtracting the second equation

$$tR_P = gtT - t^2cT$$
$$-(R_a = gtT - tcT)$$

produces the remainder

$$tR_P - R_a = (t - t^2)cT$$

Solving for c, the cost of trading, gives

$$c = \frac{tR_P - R_a}{t(1 - t)T}$$

APPENDIX B

Research Error Distributions and Functions of Transactors

VBT Error Distributions

Even those value-based transactors using the most sophisticated and thorough evaluation methods will make large errors—of both omission and commission. The result will be (on the ask side, for example) the kind of cumulative distribution of offers to sell shown by the solid curve in Figure 12-B1 (page 570). In this diagram, price or value in dollars is measured on the horizontal axis and cumulative probability and cumulative frequency are measured on the left vertical scale. Such cumulative distribution curves begin at zero at the extreme left-hand side of the horizontal axis and rise to 1 on the extreme right-hand end of the horizontal axis. If such curves are both symmetric and unbiased, they will cross the vertical axis at a cumulative probability of 0.5—i.e., half the cumulative chances of occurrence will be below the true value or justified price and half will be above. All these comments apply as well to the cumulative distribution of errors made by competing value-based transactors represented in the diagram by the dashed curve.

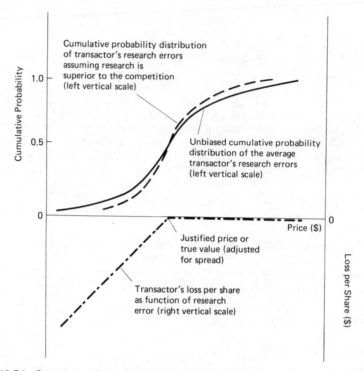

Figure 12-B1. Cumulative Probability Distributions of Transactor's Research Errors and Accompanying Transactor's Research Error-based Loss Function.

We have also shown on the same diagram, in terms of the dash-dot-dash line at the bottom, the possible losses for our transactor as a function of the research error. The amount of loss for all possible ask prices is shown on the right vertical scale. *If there is no systematic bias across competing transactors* in their estimates of value, then the consensus price will equal the true value or justified price, adjusted for that part of the spread between *JP* and the ask price. If our value-based transactor errs in the direction of the values above true value, then the VBT ask price will be above the consensus ask price and no transaction will take place. This result is shown by the horizontal portion of the dash-dot-dash loss function line located to the right of justified price. The more the VBT errs in the opposite direction, however, quoting too small an ask price, the larger his transaction will tend to be, the fewer competitors he will have at the resulting ask price, and the larger his transaction loss will tend to be, shown by the downward slope of the dash-dot-dash line to the left of *JP*. Since the transaction occurs at the VBT's ask price, it will reflect the VBT's estimation error. Two things should be clear from the diagram. First, no matter how good the VBT's research is (i.e., no matter how narrow and concentrated the resulting distribution of ask prices), the expected (i.e., the average) result of transacting on estimates of value subject to research error is a loss. Second, the larger the average error (i.e., the greater the spread and distribution of ask prices resulting from the VBT's research), the larger the loss will be when an error in the direction of a finite loss occurs.

Note that Figure 12-B1 assumes that our value-based transactor is better than the competition—i.e., he makes smaller estimation errors on average and hence has a "tighter" cumulative distribution curve. This is shown by the dashed curve being below the unbiased solid curve to the left of the justified price and above the unbiased curve to the right of *JP*. That is, in the area of the transaction's finite loss in the figure—the area to the left of *JP*—our hypothetical transactor consistently has below-average cumulative probability of transactor's research error; whereas in the area of no loss—to the right of *JP*—he has an above-average cumulative probability of making research errors.

What these observations ignore, of course, is the value-based transactor's gain from the spread. In effect, the VBT hopes to make enough money on the spread to cover losses on research errors.

VBT vs. IBT Error Functions

What is the relationship of VBT research errors to research errors of IBTs? As Richard Brealey has noted in discussions with the author, an information-based transactor will make far smaller errors if he makes incremental estimates—i.e., estimates based on the incremental implications of the information rather than "ground-up" estimates of the value of the security in question before and after impounding the new information. The problem with the incremental approach to estimating the value of new information is that, unlike the ground-up approach, it provides the transactor with no clue as to whether the information is already in the price. As pointed out in an unpublished paper by Treynor and Ferguson [1976], the information-based transactor's only recourse for answering the question is technical analysis. But the key to the usefulness of technical analysis for determining whether information is already in the price depends on the speed with which information propagates. If information propagates slowly, then the relevant "recent" price history may span several months or more and the power of statistical analysis to determine whether the information is in the price or not breaks down; the price jump (up or down) associated with new information will be indistinguishable from random price movements over such a lengthy time period. The situation is depicted in Figure 12-B2.

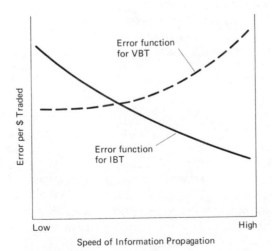

Figure 12-B2. Error Functions for VBTs and IBTs.

The value-based transactor makes a ground-up estimate of the value of the security and judges whether the information is in the price accordingly. The faster the information propagates, the more pressure on the value-based transactor to complete the estimate, which is necessarily elaborate and subject to error from a variety of sources. Thus, as a practical matter, the faster the information propagates, the larger the error the value-based transactor is likely to make. This is shown in the diagram by the broken curve that rises as the propagation speed of the information increases.

As a practical matter, of course, imponderables enter into the determination of both curves, with the result, as noted at the outset, that the boundary between value-based and information-based transactors is a gray area. To avoid circumlocution, however, we ignore this gray area, discussing trading behavior in terms of the polar cases.

Part V

Managing the Investor's Portfolio

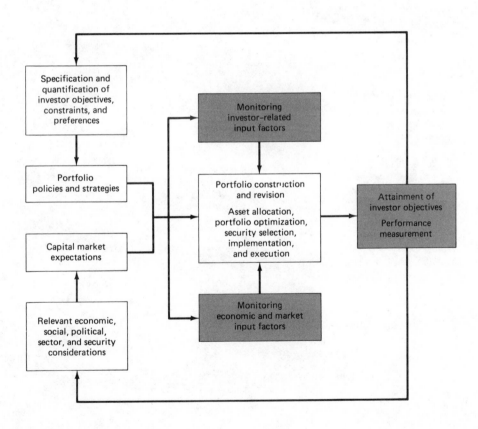

CHAPTER 13

Monitoring the Portfolio and Responding to Change

John L. Maginn, C.F.A.
James R. Vertin, C.F.A.

In the uncertain world of investment management one of the few things that practitioners truly know is that the optimal[1] portfolio, so carefully constructed yesterday, is already suboptimal to some degree and will become increasingly so with the further passage of time. We know, too, that this will occur even though our own expectations and forecasts remain intact, and the objectives of the investors for whom the portfolio was formed remain unchanged. We also understand the reason for this inevitable drift of portfolios toward a need for eventual revision. As new information enters the thinking of other market participants, changing prices both within and across asset categories, the risk-return profiles of our portfolios change. That is, they lose their currency, lose their firm connection with things as they were and as we expected them to be, and, therefore, lose their original optimality. Of course, any changes in our forecasts or in investor-related factors will surely accelerate the need for revision and the reestablishment of optimality.

Since capital markets are dynamic and investors are themselves a changeable lot, the need to cope with change in some orderly, systematic manner is a fundamental element of the portfolio management process. The coping mechanism can be formal or informal, hand driven or machine driven, plain or fancy, but it must be cost-effective for the investor involved. And, it must in some way be discerning in its prescriptions, continuous in its

---

[1] That is, the portfolio that (given a particular set of capital market and investor related input factors) maximizes expected return at a particular level of risk or minimizes risk for a given level of expected return.

application, and efficient in its execution. Otherwise, only approximations (and perhaps only gross approximations) of true optimality will be attained, opportunity will be wasted, and clients will seek more able, more productive managers through whom to pursue their various goals.

OBSERVATIONS ON PORTFOLIO REVISION

At the outset, practitioners should consider the following observations intended to highlight the many challenging aspects of the portfolio revision process:

1. Obviously, optimality with respect to a portfolio can only be achieved in a *portfolio* context. The monitoring and response process must therefore view the investor's assets as an integrated whole whose characteristics are evident and measurable (and, therefore, effectively addressable) only when seen as an entirety.
2. It follows that an adjustment process that focuses on individual issues or sectors within a portfolio cannot produce optimal rebalancing except by accident. It is not enough, for example, to have a view that this issue or that sector is now under- or overpriced as a result of economic and/or capital market changes and to make portfolio changes accordingly. Doing so will not necessarily restore optimality (it may merely shift suboptimality around), but it will surely incur two sets of transaction costs.
3. Transaction costs matter and, as pointed out in Chapter 12, matter a great deal. Not only do they reduce the client's current wealth immediately but they also reduce the portfolio's realized rate of return forever. Therefore, a truly effective adjustment process will, in addition to operating at the level of the portfolio as a whole, operate in a manner that integrates the penalty of transaction costs into the rebalancing decision. One that simply reaches a decision and hands it on to the trading desk for implementation (as if implementation were a free good having little or nothing to do with the value of the decision itself) will not be effective.
4. Investor-related factors are always of fundamental importance, and may sometimes be a decisive source of suboptimality, whether or not changes in our economic and/or capital market forecasts have occurred. Time horizon, risk capacity, return requirement, tax and/or legal considerations, and special circumstances are all client-specific (and even pooled and/or mutual funds require estimates of these factors for a typical or proxy client set). One cannot arrive at an optimal portfolio without these factors being dealt with at the portfolio level nor can one maintain optimality in the face of significant change in any one of them, regardless of stability in economic and/or capital market inputs.

5. It is apparent, then, that an efficient and effective adjustment process must contain a *monitoring* element that operates at the portfolio level on both the economic/capital market *and* the client factor input sides. Preferably, this monitoring activity should be continuous, since it is obvious that the longer the interval between sweeps across the entire range of relevant total factors, the larger the probability that the drift toward suboptimality has created a need to at least consider an adjustment. If one cannot make it continuous, one must provide for a disciplined, systematic, noncontinuous monitoring element that unfailingly addresses the issue at preset intervals that are as close to one another in time as possible. This point is stressed because the importance of an effective monitoring function is often overlooked or downgraded. We all find time to follow changes in our favorite stocks or sectors more or less continuously, but in a bigger picture sense find it very difficult to do the same for changes in the input factors as they affect expected return-risk relationships and, therefore, optimality.

6. None of the foregoing is new, of course; we already were aware of it. Typically, what we lack is not awareness itself or even some kind of method for attacking the problem. Rather, we lack a *current* methodology that: deliberately reflects the fact that portfolio management is a dynamic process; makes full use of the new knowledge now available to enhance the decision-making requirements of the process, particularly as to decision making at the "portfolio as an entirety" level; makes full use of the new technology now available in the form of affordable mini and micro computer systems that can convert piecework methods into continuous, real time attention to problems; and grants the importance of the monitoring and execution elements in a well-constructed, systematic process for portfolio revision.

TRADITIONAL APPROACH TO REVISION

The traditional investment literature has stressed the techniques of portfolio construction but has provided little insight into the ongoing aspects of investment management that occupy most of the typical portfolio manager's time. Indeed, the value of a portfolio manager is measured not simply by how well a portfolio is constructed but also by how effectively it is managed over time. In other words, portfolio managers are not simply architects who make a series of complex, one-time decisions that produce a single optimal mix of asset classes and individual securities or real estate properties. Rather, portfolio managers are responsible for the continuum of decisions necessary to maintain optimality over time within an uncertain and ever-changing environment. And it is in the opportunities for reassessment and revision that occur over time that the insights and skills of the practitioner can be harnessed to provide *value added*. This continuous decision-making responsibility is, then, the essence of portfolio management, as it is the essence of all managerial activities.

PORTFOLIO CONSTRUCTION

This practitioner-oriented book has recognized the importance and complexity of portfolio construction. In Chapters 4 and 5, investor objectives and constraints were identified and techniques for their quantification or specification were explained. In Chapters 6 and 7, macro- and microeconomic and capital market expectations were explained and illustrated. The process by which investor considerations and capital market expectations are integrated was developed in Chapters 8, 9, 10, and 11. Portfolios, like buildings, are only designed on paper and do not become real until the design is implemented and the resulting construction is subjected to the vagaries of the marketplace. Implementation requires order execution, the subject of Chapter 12.

Construction of a portfolio is only the beginning—an essential task, but a small portion of the portfolio manager's total responsibility. In fact, for most portfolio managers, opportunities to participate in the *initial* construction of portfolios may be quite limited, and most of their work will be concerned with matters of ongoing adjustment. Investors' objectives and constraints vary with the life cycle position and the economic circumstances of the individuals involved and/or with changes in operating conditions and circumstances for an institutional or corporate investor. Since capital markets are even more dynamic and complex, expectations concerning them are subject to more or less continuous modification and change.

RESPONSIVE PORTFOLIO MANAGEMENT

The portfolio manager must be alert to the potential for further change as well as to the fact of actual change, and must be prepared to respond to the new circumstances as they occur—continuously in the marketplace and periodically among investors. The process of portfolio revision should be systematic and parallel to the portfolio construction decision process outlined in Chapters 8, 9, 10, and 11. Indeed, the revision process is a modification of the initial construction process.

To respond effectively, a portfolio manager must have relevant information about both the portfolio and the outside world. Such information is provided by a monitoring element that is a basic and essential part of the revision process. Using the concept of feedback loops, it is now possible to complete the portfolio management process diagram. New information of major or minor significance that is relevant to the portfolio is gathered and evaluated through the monitoring process with analysts and portfolio managers and, to some extent, the investor interacting. The accumulated information warrants a response if it necessitates a change in the specification of investment policy or in capital market expectations. The process for systematic response should repeat the applicable portfolio construction process steps (see Figure 13-1 on page 560) to ensure the proper respecification of the portfolio.

Basic management and investment skills and controls are necessary to monitor, probe, and evaluate the interdynamics of investors and investments. This chapter will address the following questions:

1. What is portfolio monitoring and revision, and why is it desirable and necessary?
2. What are the essentials of the monitoring and revision process?
3. What are the causes of portfolio revision?
4. What are the portfolio revision practices of professional investors?

DEFINITION OF PORTFOLIO MONITORING AND REVISION

Portfolio monitoring is the continuous, ongoing assessment of the current portfolio relative to:

- Its original intent or goal
- Changes in investor preferences
- Changes in capital market conditions and expectations

The monitoring process involves:

- Periodic reinterviews with the client to keep up to date on any changes in needs or preferences
- Continuous review of these factors relative to (1) current investment policies as a reflection of investor preferences and (2) current investment strategy as a reflection of capital market conditions and expectations
- Ongoing assessment of the appropriateness and optimality of those policies and strategy
- Communication of the assessments to clients and other process participants

From this statement it should be clear that the efficiency of the portfolio monitoring process will be dependent on clear and understandable statements of portfolio policy and capital market expectations. Specification and, where possible, quantification of investor objectives and constraints as well as economic, market, and individual asset expectations is the *sine qua non* of portfolio monitoring.

Portfolio revision is the set of actions taken by the portfolio manager in response to the assessments and communication derived from the monitoring process. Also a continuous process, revision—responding to change—is

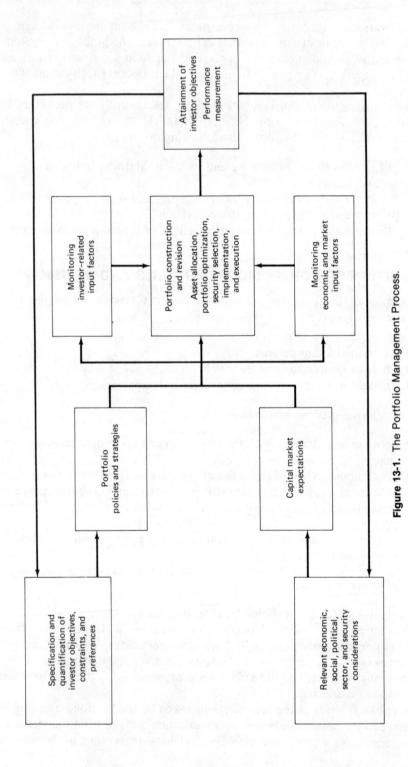

Figure 13-1. The Portfolio Management Process.

the most tedious, time consuming, significant, and potentially valuable contribution of the portfolio manager. It is and should be the value added by professional investment management.

Revision includes both rebalancing and upgrading. *Rebalancing,* or what Curley and Bear [1979] describe as reallocation, refers to the adjustment of the portfolio to bring it back to its original state assuming no change in investor preferences or capital market expectations. For multi-asset portfolios, rebalancing most often entails purchase and sale action to bring asset class and individual asset weightings back in line with the original portfolio plan.

Upgrading involves the revision of a portfolio on the basis of new information. Changes in investor objectives or constraints, which tend to occur periodically rather than continuously, may and often do require an upgrade in the portfolio to reflect the new circumstances. Meanwhile, on a continuous basis, analysts are searching out and assessing information, some of which is new and may warrant a change in the mix of asset classes or individual issues in the portfolio. And, of course, new information, whose significance may also require upgrading changes, is arriving from other sources that are external to the manager.

Goals and Objectives

As Sharpe [1981] defines it, the portfolio manager's "goal is to improve the suitability of a portfolio, net . . . of the required transaction costs." In addition, decisions to sell a portfolio asset and buy a new asset must be made in a portfolio context, not on a case-by-case basis. Each portfolio asset must be considered in relation to all other portfolio assets. Thus, portfolio revision decisions involve complex relationships and have repercussions not only on the asset or asset class in question but on the total portfolio.

True portfolio revision includes, in addition to asset selection considerations:

1. Recalculation of portfolio characteristics and assessment of how the suitability of the investor's portfolio will be affected by the proposed investment actions.
2. Determination of the expected effect on investor wealth, net of any applicable taxes, transaction costs, and investor's opportunity cost, of the proposed investment actions.

Given the changes that occur in investor considerations and capital market expectations, portfolio monitoring is expected to take cognizance of these changes and to trigger a revision process that prescribes movement toward a revised portfolio whose benefits, in terms of risk-adjusted expected returns, outweigh costs as measured by realistic transaction and income and capital gains tax expenses incurred. It is important to note that not all change will trigger an action response by the portfolio manager. If action is warranted, it will often be gradual and piecemeal. However, if the new information is momentous, the response will be commensurate in timing and impact.

PRINCIPLES OF THE MONITORING AND REVISION PROCESS

Portfolio management may be thought of as an ongoing process in which an investor revises a portfolio from time to time as changing conditions demand. Regardless of how the initial portfolio is built, it must then be managed through time.

In general, any portfolio monitoring and revision process should employ systematic methods for making a controlled transition from one portfolio to another. To maintain control and ensure an effective as well as responsive process, the monitoring procedure must be comprehensive, continuous, and documentable. Observation, data gathering, evaluation, and communication are each key elements.

Monitoring Investor Objectives and Constraints

In effect, the portfolio manager or other designated staff person must maintain contact with the investor to be aware of changes in objectives and constraints. One of the most obvious updating tools is a periodic review of the existing investment policy statement with the investor and portfolio manager. Periodic questions directed to the investor will also enable the manager or staff to be attentive to changes that may have portfolio implications. Communication is a joint responsibility of the investor and portfolio manager. However, the latter cannot depend on assumptions and generalizations. The more the specification and, where possible, quantification of investment policy, the less the chance for misunderstanding by either party.

Formalized investment policy statements and review procedures are well accepted among institutional investors, as described in Chapter 4. They have not yet gained wide acceptance with individual investors, even those whose accounts have been managed professionally by trust departments or investment counselors. However, a recent regulatory ruling requires bank trust departments to prepare and maintain an up-to-date investment policy statement for each trust account portfolio. In any event, portfolio managers serving the needs of the individual investor would be well advised to utilize monitoring procedures that are based on specifications of investor objectives and constraints, as described in Chapter 5.

Monitoring Capital Market Expectations

A traditional role of analysts and portfolio managers has been the monitoring of changes that could influence or alter forecasts of economic or market conditions or the outlook for a sector/industry and/or individual company. In fact, the professional analyst's or manager's stock in trade is the perceived ability to filter out and evaluate relevant macro- and microeconomic and/or market information and to arrive at informed conclusions as the basis for portfolio upgrading. Multiple-scenario forecasts, properly updated, as explained in Chapter 6, provide a means of tracking the macro factors. Utilizing different valuation techniques, as explained in Chapter 7, the analyst or portfolio manager can develop expected return and risk assessments for individual assets. In Chapter 11, real estate market expectations are discussed and a basis for informed revision decisions is outlined.

The Revision Process

The revision process must integrate a comprehensive but selective monitoring system with a well-defined decision-making system. The objective is to search out and communicate relevant information to those responsible for revision decisions, so that timely consideration can be given to an appropriate portfolio response. Two old sayings illustrate the importance and difficulties involved. "Garbage in—garbage out," a popular phrase among data processing people, applies equally well to the informational inputs to the revision process. "Many's the slip twixt cup and lip" aptly describes the frustration of effective monitoring of output that is coupled with an ineffective system for translating investor and market intelligence into portfolio decisions. To be effective, portfolio managers must be well informed and proficient decision makers, but not necessarily perfect ones. Good monitoring and communication systems are an important part of being effective.

Routine Revision or Rebalancing. The most frequent and commonplace circumstances emanating from the monitoring process involve the receipt of small amounts of new information that eventually trigger a rebalancing of the portfolio. The passage of time and the dynamics of the marketplace will inevitably impact the portfolio's original asset allocation and/or security weightings. Thus, it is to be expected that an out-of-balance condition will develop with respect to the original portfolio prescription. This out-of-balance condition can and does occur even though there has been no change in investor considerations or capital market expectations.

The resulting overweighting toward one asset group relative to another or toward individual securities relative to others within asset groups—producing nondiversification—can be corrected rather simply. In such cases, the rebalancing requires sales of securities that have earned higher returns in the past and redistribution of the net proceeds through purchases of securities that, to date, have had lower returns. However, this should only be done when the manager is convinced that the price trending that has occurred has essentially run its course. And it assumes that high expected return relative to risk is still forecast for the low-return-experience securities in the portfolio.

Allocation and weighting specifications can be defined in terms of fixed target percentages of the total or in terms of variable range targets, with the latter providing greater portfolio tolerance to changes in relative values. The use of targets for either revision or rebalancing is considered beneficial because:

1. Unsystematic risk is usually reduced when unintended concentration is avoided.
2. Systematic risk is restored to the original level established for the portfolio (unless all portfolio securities have the same beta).
3. Potential portfolio return may be enhanced, if all securities held are initially presumed to have been undervalued.

By controlling risk and reallocating funds to securities where attractive returns are still expected but have not yet occurred, future portfolio performance should benefit.

For taxable accounts, sale of securities that have realized a large return produces a capital gains tax liability. Conversely, selling an unprofitable holding could have favorable tax implications, particularly for an individual investor if it qualifies as a short-term loss (i.e., held less than one year) and thus is deductible from ordinary income dollar for dollar, subject to a limitation of $3,000 per year with any remainder carried forward. However, the sale of the least profitable or unprofitable holdings accentuates the concentration in the remaining investments. Thus, the portfolio manager must weigh the tax considerations against the portfolio considerations. His or her particular concern is an increase in unsystematic risk—and also possibly an increase in systematic risk if the sale candidate security's beta is at one end of the systematic risk spectrum or the other *and* if it is a heavily weighted security (large dollar value relative to the rest of the portfolio). Although the manager may suboptimize for a period by having the portfolio absorb some increase in unsystematic risk, the process should provide for the ultimate restoration of full diversification in its target specifications.

Nonroutine Revision or Upgrading. Upgrading revisions vary in complexity and are based on the receipt of significant new information regarding either investor considerations or capital market expectations. The result will be to change investment policies or strategies, which will necessitate changes in (1) the portfolio's asset allocation and/or (2) the composition of either the fixed income portfolio, the equity portfolio, the real estate portfolio, or some combination of the three.

New investor information can affect and alter the specifications of either investor objectives, constraints or preferences. Several brief examples are listed below:

An individual dies at age 57 leaving his entire estate to his wife as her only means of support. Whereas growth of assets for retirement was previously the primary portfolio objective, the widow now needs secure investment income for her support.

A company is acquired and control of its pension fund is assumed by the acquiring firm. The portfolio policies of the parent are prescribed for the acquired company's pension fund and this necessitates major revisions in the specification of return requirement and risk tolerance.

A casualty insurance company experiences severe underwriting losses and consequent income tax loss carryforwards. As a result, the company's marginal income tax rate drops from 46 percent to zero and this necessitates a shift in the need for liquidity and/or taxable interest income.

The capital markets are impacted by a constant stream of new information that primarily affects individual securities, industries, and/or sectors, but may affect whole classes of investments as well. Analysts and portfolio managers sift through and evaluate this information on a continuous basis: Some of it reinforces their earlier expectations; some of it modifies their expectations; and some of it may trigger significant changes in their expectations. The latter typically affects the expected return or expected risk of holdings and may warrant a series of portfolio revisions. Such revisions may be simple—affecting only a few portfolio holdings—or complex—affecting many holdings or even the asset allocation weightings of the portfolio's holdings of bonds, stocks, cash, or real estate, or major sectors within one of these asset categories.

Asset Allocation Changes

In investment management as in other managerial endeavors, timing is a critical element. Properly timed purchases and sales within asset classes and between asset classes are key decision variables for portfolio managers. Chapters 9, 10, and 11 discussed timing considerations in the construction and management of fixed income, equity, and real estate portfolios and in the use of cash reserves. Chapter 8 discussed the most important portfolio decision—asset allocation.

The decision to shift or change a portfolio's asset allocation is the most critical timing decision, expanding the investment problem to a new dimension far beyond the level of individual security selection. The choice is between fixed income, equity, real estate, and cash equivalents and is usually triggered by changes in perceptions about future economic conditions. In effect, the portfolio manager reacts to changes in economic expectations. In some cases, asset mix changes are triggered by changes in capital market conditions that have altered the expected return and risk relationships for one class of assets relative to another. This can be vividly illustrated by referring back to Figure 10-8 in Chapter 10, which shows the security market line at specific points in time. Both the level and the slope of the line are significant in evaluating the relative attraction of the equity market. For example, the steeply positive slope and level of the line at December 31, 1974, reflected the relative attraction of stocks versus bonds in terms of the potential return for the risk assumed. Furthermore, that particular configuration reflected the attraction of high beta versus low beta stocks, since large increases in expected return were possible with only a small increase in risk. Or, changes in investor circumstances may make reallocation desirable or necessary. In any event, the portfolio manager must concurrently analyze and select the best combination of asset classes to realize the highest possible risk-adjusted return, given a set of objectives, policies, and constraints.

The necessity for dealing with change through asset reallocation may be approached and/or met in either an active or a passive manner. The portfolio manager's response is shaped by confidence in the predictive inputs, the investor's attitude toward risk, the return needs of the investor, and assumptions regarding the efficiency of the market. Thus, there is no one proper response but, rather, the portfolio manager may choose to pursue one of three courses of action that best combines his or her skills and the investor's preferences.

Passive Response. A passive response, in effect, ignores the problem by arbitrarily deciding on a permanent asset allocation (such as 100 percent to common stocks or 100 percent to fixed income securities or 50 percent to both) and suboptimizes by selecting, monitoring, and revising the resulting portfolio. A passive attitude toward new information generates a response in which revision is undertaken without altering the basic asset allocation; changes in the capital markets are reflected in changes among securities held. A buy-and-hold policy generates no revision activities at all, and implicitly limits portfolio management to purchase transactions with available cash on the premise that the risks of upgrading exceed any potential rewards. For some investors, such as life insurance companies, regulation dictates the limits of asset allocation changes. For example, common stock holdings may be limited to 10 percent of assets of such companies.

Active/Defensive Response. A combination active/defensive response would assume a lack of forecasting ability, a belief that markets move in cycles either with or without a positive trend, and a high degree of risk aversion. This response usually involves active reallocation among asset categories to minimize the effect of market cycles on portfolio value. Formula plans, which allocate monies among portfolio assets according to a predetermined ratio of total fund or fixed dollar value, are examples of systematic approaches to limit the impact of timing factors on the portfolio's value. Dollar cost averaging is another systematic approach that is defensive and assumes a fixed dollar amount of new money available for periodic investment. In such response, the numbers of shares of stock or par value amount of bonds will mechanically adjust inversely to increases and decreases in the price levels of the markets. No overt attempt is made, however, to produce the optimal portfolio for an investor in these mechanical systems, except initially when the formula is established.

Active/Aggressive Response. This approach usually involves managing the portfolio by forecasting future values of key economic and other macro capital market variables, and determining their effect on the risk-return characteristics of individual assets and asset categories, reallocating accordingly. While success in an active/aggressive mode is difficult to predict, Curley and Bear [1979] point out that active market timing may have some real benefits:

1. Timing considerations will determine the asset categories to which interim cash flows (new funds, investment income, and so on) will be allocated.
2. A portfolio manager or investor may indeed be able to predict correctly major market variations with sufficient accuracy to justify timing strategies.
3. Although Sharpe's [1975] study on likely gains from market trading showed little net returns from a timing scheme that required a prediction at the same date every year, investors may make much more extra return from reacting to market cycles on a longer and more irregular basis.

Of course, the objective is to restore the portfolio to optimality whatever the approach or method. This point should remain uppermost in the portfolio manager's mind.

Security Selection Changes

Previous chapters have stressed the importance of the portfolio over the importance of any single security in the portfolio. The optimal portfolio achieves the highest expected return for a given level of risk through a properly diversified mix of assets based on the combined risk and return properties of each.

Given the dynamics of the capital markets, the opportunities for new information to alter the expected return and risk profile of a portfolio security are ever present. The portfolio manager must be prepared to deal with such changes insofar as changes in the profile of one or more portfolio securities significantly affects the expected return and risk profile of the portfolio. The important point is not the effect of these changes on the security, but rather their effect on the profile of the portfolio as a whole including the extent of the effect.

The standard textbook example of a response to new information of importance is a simple upgrading example wherein one security is sold and a security with identical systematic and unsystematic risk properties is purchased with the proceeds. In most cases, the textbook examples mention but do not adjust for transaction costs and any tax liability that is incurred. While these examples are illustrative, they are not realistic, since securities are unique. In the real world it is difficult to find securities (particularly common stocks) of companies that are in virtually identical circumstances. Furthermore, the effect of reinvesting cash flow or net proceeds itself produces distortions that must be recognized, particularly as it may affect the dollar weightings of the replacement security acquired and the asset class or sector of which it is a part.

Revision Benefits vs. Costs. Curley and Bear [1979] outline a more complex and correct *benefit-cost revision strategy* that does take risk, especially covariances, into account as well as transaction and tax costs. Their strategy assumes (1) a common investment horizon for all securities, and (2) a current optimal balance and diversification, which optimal condition is to be maintained. Their procedures are a sequential analysis of all changes necessary to progress from an existing portfolio to the new optimal portfolio, in which portfolio decisions involve only one security at a time and progress one step at a time.

Revision benefit is defined by Curley and Bear as the improvement in risk-equivalent expected return. *Revision cost* is defined as transaction and tax cost, where applicable, with all factors stated in dollar amounts. Pairings of sell/buy candidates are evaluated with a *benefit-cost ratio* of 1.0 representing the breakeven level. No revision is warranted if the ratio is less than 1.0; conversely, priority should be given to revisions having the highest ratio above 1.0.

The pairings procedure alone is inadequate without evaluation of the effect of the upgrading or switching decision(s) on the portfolio's risk and return. Every change in the portfolio affects the covariance relationship of individual securities. Thus, portfolio covariances must be recalculated after each step in the revision process. Transactions are continued until there are no sell/buy candidate combinations with benefits outweighing costs, including improved covariances.

To be effective, a revision strategy must provide increased opportunity for or probability of enhancing portfolio expected returns with the least or no increase in risk and without excessive turnover and attendant transactions cost. A systematic sell/buy evaluation procedure allows the portfolio manager to marshal all of the facts and information into a quantifiable decision-making matrix that encompasses all major dimensions—benefit-cost and covariance tradeoffs—of the revision process. In reality, portfolio revision is too often limited to a one-dimensional evaluation of the benefit-cost factors related to one or several sell/buy pairs. The effect on the total portfolio is considered but rarely quantified, evaluated, and integrated into the action decision set.

FACTORS CAUSING PORTFOLIO REVISION

It is important to focus on the causal factors that create the need or opportunity for revision in an existing portfolio. In fact, the continuous surveillance and evaluation of these factors should be the role of an effective portfolio monitoring system. The factors to monitor that could prompt portfolio revision are: changes in market or security price behavior patterns; changes in investor objectives, constraints, or preferences; and changes in the market environment.

Changes in Security Price Trends

Changes in security price trends are the most frequent causes of portfolio revision through rebalancing. Divergent intermediate price trends can and do lead to security price cycles with little or no secular price trend. If these security or sector price trends continue or persist rather than reversing themselves over time, then some securities or asset categories in the portfolio will dominate others. This would result in a lack of diversification within or imbalance among asset groups.

In the case of asset categories, if equities trend upward in price or have large returns in several successive time periods, while fixed income securities trend downward or have small returns, the asset allocation between these two asset classes will diverge significantly from that originally established. Such divergent price trends can and do occur within intermediate time periods without any necessary change in overall capital market conditions.

Alternatively, if a sector of equities (e.g., energy stocks in 1979–80) trend upward in price or have several large quarterly returns in a row, the equity portion of the total portfolio will become (1) overweighted toward that sector and (2) not adequately diversified in terms of original specifications. In both cases, corrective action would have to be taken to sell off the uptrending or large return asset(s) and invest the proceeds in the downtrending or small return asset(s) in order to restore the original apportionment of the portfolio or subportfolio.

Timing of Changes. Obviously, the timing of such decisions and their implementation can be critical since the intermediate trends or cycles can persist for many months. Witness, for example, the approximate two-year run-up in energy sector stock prices in 1979–80 and their sharp decline in the winter of 1980–81. As shown in Figure 13-2 (page 590), a move to rebalance too soon could cause significant opportunity losses. Conversely, to rebalance too late could cause significant realized or unrealized capital losses.

This is a classic example of the need for a systematic but nonmechanistic portfolio revision process as compared to either an eclectic or mechanical

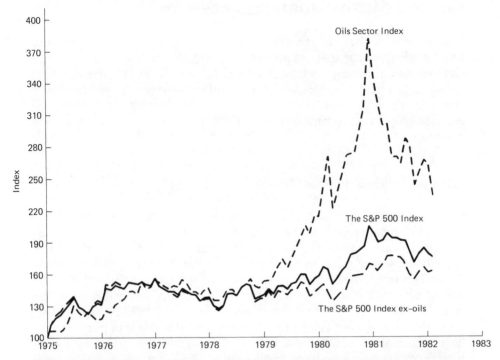

Figure 13-2. Performance of Oils Sector, S&P 500, and S&P 500 Ex-Oils Indexes, 1975–82. The oil sector index is a market-value-weighted average of the price index for crude producers, domestic oils, international oils, offshore drillers, and oil service equipment groups. The S&P 500 ex-oils is a market-value-weighted index of all S&P industry groups, excluding the above oil groups. (SOURCE: First Boston Corporation)

one. The latter represent two extremes—one essentially free-form and the other highly rigid. The temptation with the free-form process is to "ride trends" and ignore the portfolio imbalances, while the mechanical process ignores the persistence of the trends while maintaining portfolio balance.

The importance of a dynamic but systematic process is borne out by the important roles that market timing and portfolio balance play in determining a portfolio manager's success in achieving the investor's objectives.

Indeed, what is described here is not unlike the various cycle theories of the markets for equity and fixed income assets and the attempts at market timing to try to take advantage of these cycles, defined as intermediate term trends that ultimately do reverse themselves.

In modern portfolio theory (MPT) terms, this could be represented in a risk-return diagram as a temporary movement of the portfolio *along the efficient frontier* away from the desired asset allocation at point *A* or, for just the equity part of the portfolio, movement from optimal equity portfolio *M* on the efficient frontier to an *inefficient interior equity portfolio M'* (see Figure 13-3).

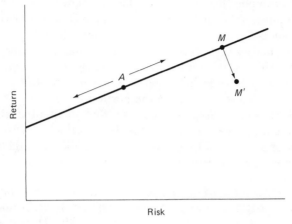

Figure 13-3. Possible Movement of Portfolios from Preferred Risk-Return Positions.

Portfolio Strategies and Rebalancing. In terms of the portfolio strategies discussed in Chapters 8, 9, 10, and 11, rebalancing is most closely identified with balanced funds where either the fixed income or equity portfolios have gotten out of balance because of large returns over several periods in one of the two components and small returns over the same periods by the other component.

Within equity portfolios alone, rebalancing may be necessary by rotators when they shift or rotate the areas of the equity market in which they wish to concentrate their holdings. Or it might occur for index fund managers when the fund does not behave as a mirror image of the index chosen for replication. This occurs most frequently for indexers who invest in only a sample of stocks drawn from the index universe. An example is Batterymarch Financial's use of the largest 250 stocks in the S&P 500 as an index fund in an attempt to replicate the S&P 500 Index.

Similarly, rebalancing will be required from time to time in bond portfolios that have been immunized. That is, even though asset and liability durations have been essentially matched, full and perfect immunization is usually not achievable. As cumulative net cash inflows or outflows develop over time due to coupon income and maturing principal not matching cash outflows, reimmunization via rebalancing will be necessary.

Changes in Investor Considerations

Changes in investor considerations encompass all the various factors that alter the location of an investor's utility function or change the utility function itself. They are changes that result in alterations in investment policy for individuals and institutions as discussed in Chapters 4 and 5.

The brief examples listed below reflect the effect of a change in the investor's circumstances on the investor's objectives—return requirement and risk tolerance—or the investor's constraints—liquidity, time horizon, and tax and regulatory considerations. Changes that occur abruptly tend to be obvious and are easily identifiable by the portfolio manager. More often, changes evolve slowly over time. All must be monitored by the portfolio manager and reflected in changes in the portfolio mix.

Following are some examples of changes that affect either the allocation of portfolio assets between asset classes—bonds, stocks, or real estate—or the allocation of assets within a class. The portfolio construction material outlined in Chapter 8 is pertinent.

Change in Wealth Position. Typically, an increase in wealth will allow the investor to undertake more risk, achieve better diversification, and perhaps even shift to a different type of utility function. Decreases in wealth usually produce the opposite result.

Change in Time Horizon. Not unlike a change in wealth position, a change that lengthens the investor's time horizon will enable the individual to undertake more risk, especially systematic risk. Usually, changes in the time horizon are gradual or evolutionary but they can also be abrupt. An example of the former might be the horizon involved in provision for retirement or college education for offspring. As time moves on, these phenomena have an ever-shortening horizon requiring a constant reduction of risk, especially systematic, in the investor's portfolio. An example of the latter, also involving a change in wealth position, is the unexpected death of the last life income beneficiary of a trust where the assets pass to a remainderman with significantly longer time horizons.

Change in Consumption and Savings Desires. This may be related to wealth position, income receipts, inflation, savings incentives, or other variables and may affect the investor's return objectives, risk tolerance, and liquidity needs.

Change in Liquidity Needs. When the market for sizable holdings of an investor is perceived to be less liquid (e.g., real estate in 1981–82), a larger liquidity provision or need for the portfolio may result.

Change in Tax Situation. Changes in tax laws or tax circumstances may shift investor needs and preferences. Examples include: larger exclusions of interest or dividends, leading to a preference for higher yielding assets; or reduction in the maximum tax rate or the required holding period for long-term capital gains, leading to a preference for assets with a potentially large price change component of total return.

Change in Legal or Regulatory Environment. Adoption of ERISA-type personal trust prudent man rules might mean more risky assets and/or more risky investment strategies are available for portfolios than previously. Recent interpretations of ERISA have stressed the importance of each security, not as an individual asset that might increase or decrease in value, but as a part of a diversified portfolio of investment assets where the suitability of the entire portfolio is of primary importance.

Change in Efficient Market Perceptions. Should investors believe that the market for an asset(s) has grown more efficient, meaning smaller rewards are likely for assuming unsystematic risk (i.e., for not diversifying fully), investors may desire more passive portfolio management relative to active.

Availability of New Securities. Investor acceptance of new forms of securities, such as options or financial futures, either as risk modifiers or as sources of leverage could change optimal portfolio specifications.

In MPT terms, these changes in investor desires or preferences can be characterized typically by the rightward (toward more risk) or leftward (toward less risk) movement of the investor's desired risk position (point *B* on a risk-return diagram such as Figure 13-4).

Changes in Market Environment

Changes in the market environment affect the analyst's and portfolio manager's macro expectations for the capital markets as discussed in Chapter 6. Ultimately, such changes also affect the micro expectations for sector/industry and/or company changes as discussed in Chapter 7. Within a portfolio context, the portfolio manager's value is importantly determined by the ability to upgrade on a timely basis the portfolio mix across asset classes or within an asset class. The scope of the upgrading required is dependent on

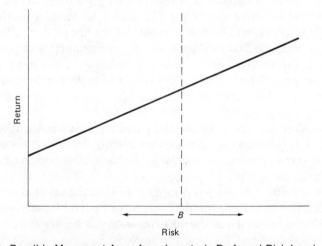

Figure 13-4. Possible Movement Away from Investor's Preferred Risk Level.

the magnitude and significance of the market changes and their effect on portfolio expectations.

The brief examples below reflect the effect of macro or economywide or marketwide changes on the expectations that have formed the basis for the portfolio's current asset allocation and individual investment selection. Generally, such changes are momentous and engender a major upgrading opportunity. Numerous studies have validated the hierarchy of portfolio decisions with respect to ultimate portfolio performance as follows:

1. Allocation of assets among classes of investable assets.
2. Allocation of assets to sectors within a class of investable assets.
3. Individual asset selection and weighting.

Economywide Changes

Federal Reserve Policy Shift. If, for example, the Federal Reserve (Fed) tightens the money supply, this will probably (but not necessarily) result in a forecast of higher interest rates and a possible increase in investor uncertainty about the future. Together these changes will usually result in an increase in the rate at which estimates of common stock dividends are discounted and thereby increase the probability of a fall in stock prices, if not actually trigger such a fall. Bond prices should also fall as coupons and maturity value are discounted at higher rates. The prices of equity and income real estate would be expected to be affected in a manner similar to equities.

An active portfolio manager anticipating such a change in Fed policy would be expected to consider, at the least, changes in asset allocation and portfolio construction that generally would preserve portfolio values. Such changes might be to increase holdings of cash equivalents, shorten the maturity of fixed income portfolios, and reduce equity portfolio exposure, especially to interest-sensitive securities. The degree to which a portfolio manager actually responds will be based in part on the interaction of the revised expectations with the investor's objectives, constraints, and preferences. For example, the shorter the investor's time horizon, the more likely the portfolio manager will be to make major revisions in the portfolio in response to a shift in Federal Reserve policy.

Inflation Rate Changes. As unanticipated increases in the rate of inflation occur, or as inflation expectations rise rapidly, interest rates and uncertainty will also rise, leading to essentially the same effect on stock and bond prices as described above.

The primary effect of macro changes is to shift the optimal asset mix of the portfolio. The end result, in MPT terms, of Federal Reserve-induced or inflation-induced increases in the risk-free rate can be illustrated in Figure 13-5. As the risk-free rate increases from R_F to R'_F, the slope of the capital

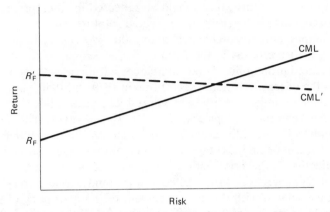

Figure 13-5. Example of a Shift in Level and Slope of Capital Market Line (CML).

market line (CML) will shift significantly, even to the extent that it slopes downward. This is an illogical, irrational, and perverse slope for the CML, but it has been observed on several occasions in recent years, at least temporarily.

Sector/Industry/Company Changes

Bond Rating Changes. In the fixed income area, bond ratings are being continuously updated by the various services to reflect improvement or deterioration in a company's debt-carrying and repayment ability. A change in the rating of a bond may result in a change in expected return because of an expected change in the bond's price. The effect of a change in a bond's rating on the subsequent price of the bond will obviously vary with the direction of the change (upgrade or downgrade), the level of the change (such as from Baa to A or Aaa to Aa), the magnitude of the change (one or more than one rating level), and whether the change is in the same or the opposite direction to the general trend of bond prices.

Active bond portfolio managers will attempt to anticipate such changes and may aggressively acquire potential upgrade candidates or may defensively dispose of potential downgrade candidates. For bond portfolios with specific quality rating limitations reflecting investor risk tolerance, changes in quality ratings must be monitored and may trigger revisions. Even if the portfolio is managed passively, a change in a bond's rating that removes it from the minimum acceptable category should generate an upgrading revision by the portfolio manager.

Equity Changes. In the equity area, changes in sector/industry/company circumstances may result in changes in expected earnings and dividend growth resulting from the impact of these circumstances on the expected profitability trend. In turn, this should be reflected in stock prices. The net effect is an increase or decrease in expected total return.

For example, perceived changes in an industry's ability to pass through inflationary cost increases in the form of higher selling prices will directly impact expected profitability of the companies within that industry. A classic example is the energy/petroleum sector that in 1979 and 1980 was considered to have almost unlimited ability to raise product prices in line with increases in world market crude oil prices. In 1981–82, however, a decline in oil consumption and a rapidly growing supply necessitated major downward revisions in the expected earnings of the oil industry. As illustrated earlier, a dramatic decline in the prices of oil company stocks ensued.

Conversely, increases in expected returns and a rising trend of stock prices are associated with the announcement of the marketing of profitable new discoveries or inventions, such as occurred in the early 1980s in the personal computer area, and had occurred previously in many other areas.

These changes can affect an entire industry or sector or may be limited to an individual company. For example, a new drug discovery may significantly affect the expected returns of a single drug company. Also, unanticipated merger/acquisition news such as the 1981 battle between Seagrams, Mobil Corporation, and DuPont for control of Conoco Inc. drastically altered the expected returns of the latter. Ironically, but not unexpectedly, as the bids for Conoco increased, the expected return and market price of the successful bidder, DuPont, declined.

It is important to note that the primary effect of micro changes is to shift the security selection of the portfolio or the sector/industry weightings within an asset class. In MPT terms, the holdings of securities that now have become inferior relative to other (superior) assets will make the portfolio inferior or inefficient relative to the potential efficient frontier represented by the straight line R_FMZ in Figure 13-6. This portfolio can be represented by movement from the efficient frontier to point W. With the elimination of inferior securities in portfolio W and their replacement with superior risk-return securities, the portfolio can be moved to point X or Y or any point on the efficient frontier in between, depending on the desire to minimize risk and maintain return, maintain risk and maximize return, or adopt an in-between risk posture, respectively. The distance YW represents the return improvement possible if risk posture B is maintained. This improvement would be net of transaction costs and tax effects. The distance WX represents the risk improvement possible if the return of portfolio W is maintained under the new circumstances.

TECHNIQUES FOR PORTFOLIO REVISION

We have seen that the passage of time activates many factors serving to move a portfolio away from its (assumed) original position on the efficient frontier of return-risk relationships. If the degree of change is severe

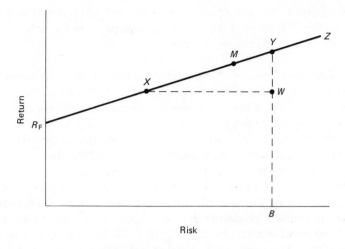

Key:
W = Inefficient portfolio
X = Efficient portfolio with same expected return
    as W but less risk
Y = Efficient portfolio with same risk as W but
    more expected return
M = Equities market portfolio
R_F = Risk-free rate
B = Preferred risk level
$R_F MZ$ = Efficient frontier with borrowing and lending

Figure 13-6. Alternatives for Making an Inefficient Portfolio Efficient.

enough, the existing portfolio may now even be perverse relative to the investor's current objectives. Effective revision is required. What techniques do professional managers employ to accomplish this end?

Wells Fargo System

One of the most comprehensive systems for monitoring and revision, introduced in Chapter 8 in the context of asset allocation, is discussed in detail below. The key to the system is the interaction of the portfolio managers, clients, and computers, which requires a significant commitment of skilled professionals and capital resources by the management organization.

Client Updates. Through the organization's portfolio managers, the scope of whose job has been expanded to include specific responsibility for ongoing contact with its investor clients, new information about investor circumstances is routinely collected and analyzed. A quantified profile exists for each investor-client, expressed in terms of specifications that reflect each one's time horizon, risk aversion (in the form of a utility function that serves to place the investor on the efficient frontier of risk-return relationships), return requirement, and special considerations, including unique preferences and tax and legal factors, if any. As the portfolio manager's monitoring turns up changes in these investor factor circumstances, the quantified profile is adjusted and new specifications are put in place. At any point in time, then, these quantified specifications will provide the investor-related inputs to the portfolio revision process.

Capital Market Updates. Meanwhile, monthly or more frequent updates of conditions and relationships in the capital markets are captured and put on paper for use by a policy group that includes analysts and portfolio managers among its decision makers. Among the inputs are the expected return on the organization's large universe of common stocks, derived from its analyst's forecasts and the operation of a dividend discount valuation model; the expected return on the aggregate fixed income asset class, derived from the yield to maturity on long-term, Aa-rated corporate obligations; an analysis of the spread in expected returns between these asset classes and the cash (equivalent) alternative; and information concerning the level and trends of expected returns among various categories of equities including analyses by capitalization size, yield, risk, liquidity, and economic/ market sectors. In addition, economic forecasts are considered; an analysis is made of the slope and position of the Security Risk and the Security Yield Lines, both derived from the Security Market Plane, an expansion of the security market line concept that treats the tradeoffs among risk, yield, and total return across the equity market; the performance of the equity coding process is displayed and discussed; conditions in the fixed income markets are examined and forecasted; and portfolio performance—both absolute and relative—is reported and analyzed. From this monitoring and evaluation activity come the capital market inputs to the asset allocation element of the revision process, together with certain judgmental modifications of the raw quantitative information that would otherwise have flowed to the portfolio optimization model.

Account Status Report. With one additional input, the portfolio manager has in hand all of the information and data needed to revise a given portfolio. The missing piece, which is extracted from several data bases via an interactive information system accessed by the manager through an on-line terminal at his or her desk, is called an *account status report*. This report, using current prices, allows one to examine the existing portfolio relative to the market; to measure its relationship to policy and strategy guidelines (targets) for accounts with this set of investor specifications; and to display differences in actual versus optimal composition relative to ideal positions. The latter is determined by multifactor screens on the basis of such classifications as risk, economic sector, liquidity, capitalization, growth ratio, yield, and industry group.

If these differences are, singly or in the aggregate, beyond certain tolerance levels, the portfolio will be revised immediately to return it to the efficient frontier of available portfolios. If the differences are within the tolerance bands, revision is optional with the portfolio manager, who will use his or her client knowledge as a key in the decision to proceed with or defer the revision. If the investor is particularly sensitive to turnover, for example, the decision may be to defer revision until a more marked suboptimality is observed. On the other hand, if the investor understands the coding process and tends to be critical of less-than-maximum levels of relative coding attractiveness across the equity holdings and if substantial improvement of aggregate coding "goodness" (i.e., either increase expected return at the same risk or lower risk with the same return) can be obtained within the constraints imposed by a trading costs penalty, the revision will probably proceed. The point is that the revision decision is controlled by the portfolio manager and will be made from a position of current knowledge about the investor's attitudes, the degree of suboptimality now present in the given portfolio, the degree of improvement that can be effected, and the costs involved in obtaining it.

Revision Process. A decision to proceed with the revision moves the portfolio through a sequence of further steps. First, the portfolio manager will utilize an asset allocation program that, given the investor-client factor inputs and the capital market inputs (which include expected returns, expected variances, and expected covariances for the asset classes involved), will generate the stock/bond (and/or other asset) mix that maximizes the investor's utility. Next, the portfolio manager will—for the equity component—utilize an optimization program, starting with the existing holdings and constrained by a transaction cost penalty (and perhaps by other constraints generated from the portfolio manager's knowledge of the investor client's objectives and preferences), that will produce a list of recommended purchases and sales that maximizes the equity component's *measure of relative attractiveness* (i.e., its expected excess return or alpha at a given level of risk). A similar procedure is followed on the fixed income side to obtain a list of recommended bond purchases and sales.

Trading Desk Role. Assuming that the portfolio manager is ready to proceed to execution of the revision program (after examining the trade lists and perhaps finding substitutes for any issues whose appropriateness is questioned for a given client situation), he or she will now work directly with the trading desk. Here, market information will be examined and decisions made about individual issues and transactions in the light of current knowledge and opinion from the traders. Aspects of the original buy/sell program will be qualitatively modified by an experienced portfolio manager to fine tune computer-generated data, if necessary. And the revision process goes on until an appropriate set of transactions has occurred that completes it, restoring the portfolio to optimality.

Manual vs. Automatic Revision. In most cases, this examination/decision/execution sequence takes one or two days to complete under the portfolio manager's hands-on control. The system can also operate on automatic pilot if desired, using various data sources to compare the existing portfolio to an optimal alternative, compute the differences (in expected return versus risk terms), estimate the degree of improvement possible for a given level of cost and, if warranted, generate buy/sell lists for implementation/execution, all in a matter of minutes. The difference, of course, is the degree of involvement of the portfolio manager and the application of his or her knowledge and skills. On many occasions, the system operates simultaneously in both modes, the portfolio manager deciding which situations require (or can benefit most from) his or her direct involvement and which situations can be appropriately handled without it. Or, the portfolio manager may choose to be involved in one or another aspect of a given revision situation, although not in other aspects. The system is sufficiently flexible to permit whatever degree of manager involvement is chosen, from full hands on to none.

Tax Considerations. For taxable account situations, the process takes the fact of taxes into consideration at each point where they affect decision making. Again drawing on the portfolio manager as a monitoring entity and an investor-client profile as the source of information for specifications, each account is assigned a tax-cost penalty equivalent that reflects state as well as federal income and capital gains taxes. The equity coding process also takes taxes, decomposed into their income and gain elements at each level of marginal rate change, into account. Thus, for taxable investor-clients, the portfolio manager is armed with information and tools for making the required revision process decisions in the same orderly, systematic manner as in tax-free situations. Output from the process will often be much different, since the fact of taxes creates much different solutions to the optimality problem, but the basic process is essentially the same and portfolio managers can move comfortably across it from one type of tax situation to the other.

Active vs. Passive Management. This example of a management organization's portfolio monitoring and revision process is a relatively comprehensive one. Since the organization makes extensive use of concepts and techniques drawn from capital market and portfolio theory, in combination with more fundamental and traditional approaches, it is primarily focused on the portfolio as a whole and on the management of portfolio risk. To facilitate the integration of information and the interaction of practitioner staff with its extensive data resources, the process is heavily computerized and utilizes an in-house time sharing network to bind the process participants together. While the process was designed to fully accommodate the needs of portfolio managers pursuing active strategies on behalf of their investor-clients, the organization also manages assets in a variety of passive forms for which the process is equally accommodative. In contrast to the sometimes very complex set of portfolio manager activities involved in a fully hands-on situation, the monitoring and revision process can be quite uncomplicated in some passive management situations.

For example, assume that an investor wishes only to shift monies between equities and fixed income obligations in response to changes in spreads between expected returns for the two asset classes, utilizing a passive portfolio without concern for issue selection, industry/sector, or other standard active strategy elements. The investor-client's profile will provide the necessary specifications and data for this side of the asset allocation model's input needs, while the organization's ongoing information collection and data base maintenance activities will provide the inputs required on the capital markets side. The portfolio manager simply accesses the relevant information, inputs it to the asset allocation model, and receives back a stock/bond mix recommendation based on current expected return spread data as conditioned by constraints and specifications. Since the portfolio optimization step is by-passed in this example (because the decision has already been made not to use individual issue data in constructing the portfolio), the portfolio manager's next step is simply to order up the movement of the monies needed to achieve the desired mix, shifting funds into or out of an indexed equity portfolio to or from a passive bond portfolio. At either a predetermined interval of time or upon the happening of a predetermined change in spread relationship, the process is repeated: A new asset allocation run is made and the prescribed change, if any, from the original portfolio is ordered up in the form of transfers between the passive portfolio elements. Such a strategy is, of course, a simple one to operate and to execute.

Cumulative Performance. Figure 13-7 (page 602) shows the cumulative outcomes from several variations of this approach over the nine years 1973–81. The "control" mix, a constant 60 percent in stocks and 40 percent in bonds, serves as a benchmark; the "unrestricted" mix permits 100 percent in stocks or 100 percent in bonds or any combination in between as prescribed by the organization's asset mix optimizer; the "30% range" mix permits any level up to 30 percent above or below the benchmark 60/40 mix (i.e., up to 90 percent in stocks to as low as 30 percent in stocks); while the "15% range" mix permits any level up to 15 percent above or below the benchmark 60/40 mix. In calculating the data used in the figure, transaction costs of one-fourth of 1 percent were charged on movements into and out of the indexed equity portfolio component (consistent with transaction cost experience on such portfolios), while transaction costs of one-half of 1 percent were charged on movements into and out of the pooled fixed income vehicle. Obviously, the portfolio revision problem here is a simple one: a quarterly rebalancing to specified stock/bond levels that depend entirely on the output of the asset allocation model.

Other portfolio revision techniques are easily identified. For example, the system's stock coding process produces rankings from 1 (maximum attractiveness) to 5 (minimum attractiveness). You could set up an active strategy involving a revision program that would automatically keep the coding level of a given portfolio at a level of 1.5 (or any other number), rebalancing monthly (or at any other interval). Or, you could constrain such

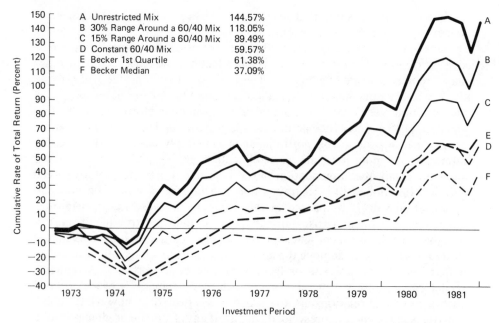

	A	Unrestricted Mix	144.57%
	B	30% Range Around a 60/40 Mix	118.05%
	C	15% Range Around a 60/40 Mix	89.49%
	D	Constant 60/40 Mix	59.57%
	E	Becker 1st Quartile	61.38%
	F	Becker Median	37.09%

Figure 13-7. Cumulative Quarterly Performance Results—Comparison of Stock/Bond Mix Strategies. (SOURCE: Wells Fargo Investment Advisors)

a program at some arbitrary turnover level, or at some arbitrary beta level, or at some arbitrary yield level, or by any combination of such factors. Using an optimizer, you could maintain—at the same time—any relative-to-market (S&P 500 or other bogey) configuration that your judgment, insight, intuition, or quantitative method called for. Portfolio optimizers are highly versatile and efficient tools, capable of extending and enhancing the skills of good portfolio managers significantly.

Value Line System

For 50 years, Value Line and its founder, Arnold Bernhard, have been dedicated to the calculation and publication of an objective standard for the current evaluation of common stocks. At Value Line in 1982, each of the 1,700 stocks in their universe is ranked or scored on the basis of three tests:

1. The "nonparametric value position," which is based on three factors:
   a. relative earnings rank
   b. relative price rank
   c. relative price momentum
   and for which a stock is ranked between 1,700 (highest) and 1 (lowest).

2. The "earnings momentum test," for which a stock is scored 400, 800, or 1,200.
3. The "earnings surprise factor," for which scores range from −400 to +400.

Based on the cumulative test scores, a final test score ranging from 1 to 3,300 is computed for each stock. Value Line's computer then lists the stocks in the order of their final scores. The top 100 stocks in the universe are ranked 1 (highest); the next 300 stocks are ranked 2 (above average); the middle 900 are ranked 3 (average); the next 300 are ranked 4 (below average); and the bottom 100 stocks are ranked 5 (lowest).

Since this scoring and ranking system was first introduced in 1965, the record of performance shows that, on average, group 1 stocks outperform all other groups, and group 2 stocks tend to have the next highest average performance with the other three groups following in succession. These results were confirmed at an early point by Black [1971].

As the above brief discussion suggests, the rank of each stock is subject to change within and between groups. In fact, there are three sets of circumstances that could cause a stock's rank to change: (1) changes caused by a new earnings report, (2) changes caused by weekly stock price movements, and (3) changes caused by the dynamism of the ranking system—that is, a rank change could occur because of changes affecting other stocks in the universe, even if a company's relative earnings and price trend did not change.

Performance Record. Even from this brief synopsis, it is obvious that Value Line's system is complex and dynamic because everything is relative to what is happening to the other companies in the universe. In this respect it provides an example of the importance of portfolio revision based on changes in the "timeliness" rank. Figure 13-8 and Table 13-1 (pages 604 and 605) reflect the performance record of Value Line rankings for the period April 16, 1965 to June 30, 1982, rebalancing weekly on the basis of changes in rank. In effect, five portfolios, one for each group of stocks, have been maintained. The holdings within each portfolio are equal dollar amounts of each of the stocks within the respective group. Figure 13-9 and Table 13-2 (pages 606 and 607) show the same phenomenon based on portfolio rebalancing for changes in rank only once annually rather than once weekly.

Since the timeliness rankings are updated weekly, rebalancing to maintain the integrity of each group results in average turnover ratios for group 1 of about 5 percent per week or 250–300 percent per year. In this connection, it should also be noted that Value Line's performance figures are not adjusted for transactions costs, including market impact costs as described in Chapter 12. And there is some recent evidence, provided by Lee and Nachtmann [1981], that the Value Line system tends to produce equity portfolios with small excess returns net of transactions costs and then primarily in down markets.

TABLE 13-1. Record of Value Line Rankings for Timeliness—April 15, 1965–June 30, 1982 (rebalancing weekly on the basis of changes in rank)

Group	1965[a]	1966	1967	1968	1969	1970	1971	1972	1973	1974
1	+28.8%	- 5.5%	+53.4%	+37.1%	-10.4%	+ 7.3%	+30.6%	+12.6%	- 19.1%	-11.1%
2	+18.5	- 6.2	+36.1	+26.9	-17.5	- 3.2	+13.7	+ 7.4	- 28.9	-29.5
3	+ 6.7	-13.9	+27.1	+24.0	-23.8	- 8.0	+ 9.3	+ 3.5	- 33.6	-34.1
4	- .4	-15.7	+23.8	+20.9	-33.3	-16.3	+ 8.4	- 7.1	- 37.9	-40.6
5	- 3.2	-18.2	+21.5	+11.8	-44.9	-23.3	- 5.5	-13.4	- 43.8	-55.7

Group	1975	1976	1977	1978	1979	1980	1981	1982[b]	1965 through mid-1982
1	+75.6%	+54.0%	+26.6%	+32.6%	+54.7%	+52.6%	+13.6%	+ 1.3%	+3112%
2	+47.4	+31.2	+13.4	+18.3	+38.0	+35.7	+ 1.8	- 6.4	+ 335
3	+40.7	+29.0	+ 1.3	+ 3.0	+20.7	+15.4	- 3.3	- 9.6	+ 16
4	+39.3	+28.8	- 6.9	- 3.8	+12.8	+ 7.4	- 8.7	-17.1	- 62
5	+40.9	+26.7	-17.6	- 3.2	+10.4	+ 2.9	-21.4	-27.5	- 92

SOURCE: Value Line "Selection & Opinion" [1982].
[a] April through December
[b] First six months

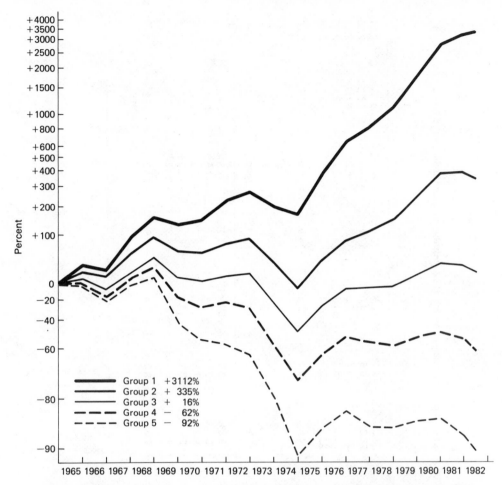

Figure 13-8. Record of Value Line Rankings for Timeliness—April 16, 1965–June 30, 1982 (rebalancing weekly on the basis of changes in rank). (SOURCE: Value Line "Selection & Opinion" [1982])

To illustrate the problems of excessive rebalancing, Table 13-3 (page 608) reflects the year-to-year difference in portfolio performance for group 1 between weekly and annual rebalancing based on changes in rank. In most years transactions cost differentials would have largely, if not completely, offset the spreads shown between the two rebalancing approaches.

Mellon Bank

A fledgling portfolio called the Fundamental Equity Fund has been designed for small- and medium-sized pension fund clients of the Mellon Bank. The

TABLE 13-2. Record of Value Line Rankings for Timeliness—April 15, 1965–June 30, 1982 (rebalancing annually on the basis of changes in rank)

Group	1965[a]	1966	1967	1968	1969	1970	1971	1972	1973	1974
1	+33.6%	- 3.1%	+39.2%	+31.2%	-17.7%	- 8.9%	+26.5%	+10.1%	- 17.1%	-23.1%
2	+18.9	- 6.0	+31.9	+26.3	-16.3	- 4.0	+17.4	+ 7.5	- 26.2	-27.8
3	+ 8.9	- 9.7	+30.1	+21.4	-20.7	- 5.5	+12.2	+ 6.2	- 27.0	-28.5
4	+ .8	- 7.2	+25.1	+25.1	-26.8	-11.7	+14.2	+ 3.2	- 29.1	-33.6
5	- 1.2	-12.4	+28.4	+25.9	-35.7	-13.1	+10.5	+ 2.9	- 43.1	-36.8
Average	+10.1	- 7.9	+29.9	+24.6	-22.1	- 7.5	+14.9	+ 5.5	- 27.7	-29.6

Group	1975	1976	1977	1978	1979	1980	1981	1982[b]	1965 through mid-1982
1	+51.6%	+35.3%	+15.8%	+19.8%	+25.6%	+50.2%	- 1.9%	- 1.5%	+721%
2	+53.0	+36.3	+12.7	+16.1	+30.8	+37.4	+ .7	- 7.5	+358
3	+52.9	+33.8	+ 5.2	+ 9.2	+27.6	+20.8	+ 2.7	- 6.3	+152
4	+48.4	+36.1	- .2	+ 2.4	+23.1	+13.2	- .9	-12.3	+ 30
5	+42.1	+38.2	- 2.8	+ 4.0	+39.9	+ 8.4	- 4.2	-20.2	- 31
Average	+51.2	+35.1	+ 5.8	+ 9.6	+28.0	+23.4	+ .9	- 8.2	+152
Dow Jones Industrials									- 15
N.Y. Stock Exchange Composite									+ 31

SOURCE: Value Line "Selection & Opinion" [1982].
[a] April through December
[b] First six months

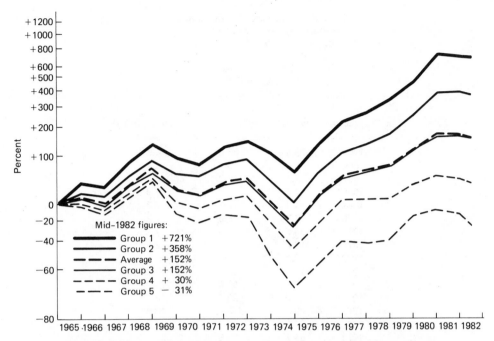

Figure 13-9. Record of Value Line Rankings for Timeliness—April 16, 1965–June 30, 1982 (rebalancing annually on the basis of changes in rank). (SOURCE: Value Line "Selection & Opinion" [1982])

fund invests an equal dollar amount (2 percent of assets) in 50 industries, choosing a leading company in each industry category. The objective is to hold these leaders unless the company's fundamentals change. The interesting aspect of this portfolio is the rebalancing discipline that is designed to limit losses as well as gains through maintenance of target weightings.

The fund reduces any holdings that increase in market value by 20 percent above the target weighting of 2 percent. In effect, this discipline forces the fund to realize gains, rather than take a chance on further gains. Conversely, the fund adds to holdings of any stock that falls below the 2 percent target by more than 20 percent, unless the fundamentals have deteriorated to the point that the company is not the industry leader in Mellon's opinion. A fallen leader must be sold, the loss realized, and the proceeds reinvested in the new industry leader to maintain the original 50-industry representation.

Mellon's industry leaders serve as a proxy for an entire industry and are screened on the basis of such fundamental characteristics as high market share, proprietary products, pricing flexibility, advantageous cost structures, success in dealing with government intervention, and superior management. This combination of analytical and portfolio management discipline is representative of portfolio rebalancing techniques, which are varied in their application but are premised on the maintenance of target weightings as a means of controlling the day-to-day management of the portfolio.

TABLE 13-3. Value Line Group 1 Annual Total
Return Performance—April 16,
1965–June 30, 1982

	REALLOCATION ALLOWING FOR CHANGES IN RANK		
Year	Weekly	Annually	Difference
1965[a]	28.8%	33.6%	− 4.8%
1966	− 5.5	− 3.1	− 2.4
1967	53.4	39.2	14.2
1968	37.1	31.2	5.9
1969	−10.4	−17.7	7.3
1970	7.3	− 8.9	16.2
1971	30.6	26.5	4.1
1972	12.6	10.1	2.5
1973	−19.1	−17.1	− 2.0
1974	−11.1	−23.1	12.0
1975	75.6	51.6	24.0
1976	54.0	35.3	18.7
1977	26.6	15.8	10.8
1978	32.6	19.8	12.8
1979	54.7	25.6	29.1
1980	52.6	50.2	2.4
1981	13.6	− 1.9	15.5
1982[b]	1.3	−1.5	2.8

[a] April through December
[b] First six months

SUMMARY

This chapter has only touched the surface of the myriad of portfolio revision situations that face the portfolio manager. The importance of portfolio monitoring and revision cannot be overstated. Given the fact of more or less continuous changes in the marketplace and of at least periodic changes in investor circumstances, the portfolio manager's effectiveness will reflect not only the ability to construct an optimal portfolio in the first place, but, more importantly, the ability to manage or guide that portfolio through time and changed circumstances to the attainment of its objectives.

The task may appear simple to the casual observer, but the experienced investor—amateur or professional—is cognizant of the difficulties. Instinctive judgments, while important, cannot take the place of a systematic process for monitoring and revising portfolios in response to changes in investor considerations or capital market expectations.

Successful portfolio management is characterized by relatively smooth transitions in the portfolio over time, effected with the controlled maintenance or modification of expected return and risk characteristics at minimum cost in terms of transaction fees and taxes. Attainment of objectives, a primary measure of manager effectiveness, requires a disciplined and efficient response framework using at least some of the principles and examples illustrated in this chapter. If the realization of investor objectives is to be maximized, pragmatic practitioners will recognize the value of the tools presented as enhancements of their intuition and their judgmental skills.

FURTHER READING

Despite the importance of monitoring and rebalancing a portfolio, very little literature is available on the subject. The following textbooks provide background for understanding the process and certain of the procedures discussed in this chapter: Curley and Bear [1979], Jones, Tuttle, and Heaton [1977], and Sharpe [1981].

Several sources of portfolio information provide historical evidence of the value of rebalancing and/or practical procedures for monitoring and rebalancing. They include *Business Week's* "Following the Leader" [1982], Value Line's "Selection and Opinion" [1982], and Wells Fargo's "Institutional Counsel Service" [1982].

BIBLIOGRAPHY

Black, Fischer, "Yes Virginia, There is Hope: Tests of the Value Line System," *Financial Analysts Journal*, March/April 1971.

Curley, Anthony J., and Robert M. Bear, *Investment Analysis and Management,* New York: Harper & Row, 1979.

"Following the Leader," *Business Week,* March 22, 1982.

"Institutional Counsel Service," Wells Fargo Investment Advisors, San Francisco, 1982.

Jones, Charles P., Donald L. Tuttle, and Cherrill P. Heaton, *Essentials of Modern Investments,* New York: John Wiley, 1977.

Lee, Wayne Y., and Robert Nachtmann, "The Informational Content of Value Line Rankings: An Empirical Anomaly," Working Paper, Indiana University School of Business, October 1981.

"Selection and Opinion," *The Value Line Investment Survey,* New York: Arnold Bernhard & Co., July 16, 1982.

Sharpe, William F., "Likely Gains from Market Timing," *Financial Analysts Journal,* March/April 1975.

———, *Investments,* 2nd Ed., Englewood Cliffs, N.J.: Prentice-Hall, 1981.

CHAPTER 14

Evaluating Portfolio Performance

Peter O. Dietz
Jeannette R. Kirschman

From the investor's viewpoint, the purpose of performance measurement is to identify skill at portfolio management, to provide evidence that favorable performance coincides with the investment skills that were claimed by a particular manager, and to monitor the investment strategy that has been developed based on investor objectives. Some of the possible objectives of investors include:

- High total rate of return
- A large real (inflation-adjusted) rate of return
- Maximization of current income or yield
- A high after-tax rate of return
- Income growth equal to or greater than the increase in inflation
- Preservation of capital
- Superior risk-adjusted return

MONITORING INVESTMENT STRATEGY AND MANAGER SKILLS

The portfolio strategy developed to meet the defined investment objectives takes into account the investor's time horizon and tolerance for risk. For example, a maximum total rate of return objective probably would suggest a 100 percent equity (common stock and/or real estate) portfolio, as equities are generally expected to provide the highest rate of return over

multi-year or multi-decade time periods. For investors with a higher tolerance for risk, the portfolio manager may wish to attempt to "time" the
market by selling stocks when he believes they are overvalued. However, if
the investor does not have a relatively high tolerance for risk, then the equity
percentage should be reduced and part of the portfolio invested in less risky
assets. At the other end of the spectrum, you have preservation of capital,
which implies very safe investments such as U.S. Treasury bills. However,
if the investor has some tolerance for risk, then the strategy might call for
adding risky assets to the portfolio mix.

In addition to monitoring investment strategy, from the investment manager's perspective, performance measurement should provide feedback as to
whether results coincide with expectations.

Prior to the mid-1960s, little performance measurement existed, even in
the institutional market, and what did exist was primarily a measure of
internal rates of return, generally computed for periods of one year or
longer. Internal rates of return compute the actual return earned on the
initial portfolio and on any net contribution for the time held in the portfolio.
For that reason, internal or dollar-weighted rates of return are appropriate
for such purposes as actuarial assurance of meeting pension obligations.
However, because they are to a large degree influenced by cash flow (such as
contributions to or distributions from a retirement fund), they are not appropriate for comparison to other portfolios or to market indexes, and may
obscure measurement of the portfolio manager's skill.

EVOLUTION OF PERFORMANCE MEASUREMENT

Standing back and looking for long patterns in the evolution of the art
suggests the following ten-year calendar for portfolio management and performance measurement cycles:

Years	Action Taken by Portfolio Managers	Performance Measurement
1945–1955	Buy bonds	None
1955–1965	Buy stocks	None
1965–1975	Switch to last year's best investment vehicle	Risk-adjusted measurement
1975–1985	Diversify the investment portfolio	Adjust for economic/ statistical/theoretical limitations of measurement systems

Since 1966, time-weighted rates of return have been the standard comparative measure in the industry. They are used to compute the return
earned on the beginning portfolio for any given time period, with a number of

methods existing for diminishing the impact of cash flows. As such, time-weighted rates are much more appropriate than internal rates for comparative purposes. Although time-weighted rates are currently accepted, we can gain insight into the problems of performance measurement by the historical discussion below.

Time-weighted rates were first introduced by one of the authors of this chapter,[1] followed by the first major study of performance measurement by the Bank Administration Institute [1968]. At that time the concept of time-weighted rates of return was a major breakthrough for pension fund sponsors as well as other institutional investors. The mutual fund method of unit value accounting, which puts everything on a dollars-per-unit-purchased basis and automatically provides data for calculating time-weighted returns, became universally accepted.

Since the late 1960s, the initial time-weighted return formulas have been expanded upon as computer developments have allowed for much more sophisticated, detailed, and accurate measurements. However, the basic theory has continued in force. Later developments include risk-adjustment procedures introduced by Treynor [1965], Sharpe [1966], and Jensen [1968], which arrive at risk-adjusted returns and capital market statistics such as alpha (α), beta (β), standard deviation (σ), and correlation coefficient (ρ) as discussed in Chapters 3 and 10.

Prior to 1965, returns were seldom related to a measure of their riskiness. The author's work relating returns to their standard deviation was subsequently more fully justified theoretically by tying return to risk, which is defined as (systematic) return covariance with a market portfolio of all assets. This final definition is based upon the capital asset pricing model (CAPM) espoused by Lintner [1965], Mossin [1966], and Sharpe [1964], and is represented by relating return to beta such as in Figure 14-1(a) on page 614. Figure 14-1(a) shows a security market line (SML) drawn between the risk-free rate (R_f) and the expected return on an economy-wide market index security (R_m), such as the S&P 500, that is given a beta of 1.0 as developed in Chapters 3 and 10. Figure 14-1(b) shows a characteristic line that relates portfolio return to market return. A detailed discussion of capital market risk-adjusted performance statistics, such as alpha, beta, standard deviation, and correlation coefficient, appears later in this chapter.

However, before a fuller discussion of the advantages and limitations of the various risk-adjusted measures can be made meaningful, it will be useful to develop the basic principles of measuring rate of return on a non-risk-adjusted basis. In the next two sections, we shall describe the basic issues involved in performance measurement, including valuation methodology, accounting basis, length of time period, and the problems associated with multi-asset portfolios.

---

[1] Dietz, in his initial work [1966a], called the time-weighted return method the average return method.

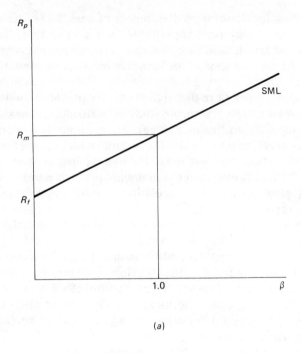

(a)

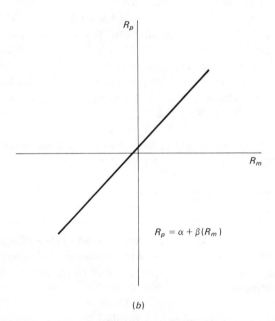

$$R_p = \alpha + \beta(R_m)$$

(b)

Figure 14-1(a). Illustration of the Security Market Line Based on the Capital Asset Pricing Model; **(b)** Illustration of a Characteristic Line Relating Individual Security Return to Return on the Market.

PRINCIPLES OF PERFORMANCE MEASUREMENT

Portfolio management begins with a portfolio of securities and an investor; performance measurement begins with portfolio valuations and transactions. In other words, performance measurement starts with accounting data and translates that into rates of return. Although neither performance measurement nor accounting is an exact science, because performance measurement is based on accounting data, it is important that the accounting data be accurate and consistent.

Even an educated first-timer into the real world of performance measurement is generally surprised at the amount of judgment that can go into the computation of the finished accounting product that becomes the raw data for performance measurement. The areas subject to interpretation are discussed in this section.

The real world of performance measurement, in addition to statistics such as alphas and betas, deals with the raw accounting data fed into programs that relate to valuation methods, accrual basis versus cash basis, and trade-date accounting versus settlement-date accounting. This chapter will highlight where the differences occur and the views of each side in any controversy.

Recording the accounting data is not difficult. Basically only four types of transactions occur: purchases, sales, income, and contributions or distributions. On occasion, a conversion, merger, stock dividend, or stock split may occur. None of these transactions is difficult to account for. The subjects discussed here are not bookkeeping entries but more theoretical issues.

Valuation Methods

Equities. Investment portfolios should be valued at their current market value; however, it is difficult to determine exactly what current market value is. In general, investments are valued at the "best available" price. For listed common stocks, preferred stocks, and convertible preferred stocks, this is generally the closing composite price. The composite includes trades on the American, Midwest, New York, Pacific, PBW, Boston, and Cincinnati stock exchanges and as reported by the National Association of Securities Dealers.

Most mutual funds continue to use the New York Stock Exchange closing prices so that they can determine their net asset value and process that day's investments and liquidations prior to the close of their business day at 5:00 P.M. Eastern time.

For over-the-counter issues, the generally accepted source for prices is the National Association of Securities Dealers Automated Quotation System (NASDAQ). The NASDAQ prices printed in the *Wall Street Journal* and picked up by the pricing services are the 4:00 P.M. Eastern time intradealer bid and asked prices for actively traded issues and the best bid-ask ranges as of 2:00 P.M. Eastern time for less actively traded issues. Most mutual funds use the mean between the bid and ask prices, while most other investors use the more conservative bid price.

Bonds. Bonds have continually provided a valuation problem for portfolio managers and recordkeepers, as most bonds are not traded on exchanges (even though many are listed) and dealers are reluctant to report trade prices to any central data gathering organization. Bonds traded on exchanges are generally small lots of less than $10,000 par value, and therefore prices are not necessarily representative of those at which the $100,000 and $1,000,000 (and higher) par value trades of institutional investors occur.

Obviously, the bond dealer community is the best source for prices. Some mutual funds arrange with bond market makers to receive price quotations on a routine daily basis. Most institutional investors rely on pricing services such as Telstat, Interactive Data Corporation, and Merrill Lynch. Telstat's pricing service for bonds provides closing exchange prices for bonds traded on an exchange. For other corporate bonds, which is the vast majority of corporates, prices are obtained from market makers. U.S. government and agency issues are usually priced at the prices listed in the *Wall Street Journal,* which are defined as "mid-afternoon over-the-counter quotations; sources on request."

MATRIX PRICING METHOD. Interactive Data Corporation (IDC) and Merrill Lynch use a matrix pricing method. A *matrix* is a multidimensional representation tracking a number of different variables, depending on the complexity of the pricing algorithm. Such variables might include coupon rate, maturity, sinking fund characteristics, call feature, the issuer's industry/ sector, quality rating, and liquidity. The matrix method groups bonds according to their values along the various matrix scales. Merrill Lynch and Lehman Brothers Kuhn Loeb traders provide input to the pricing matrix by using actual trader quotes for pricing a key bellwether issue in each cell. These prices are then used to estimate the price of other cell-inhabiting bonds with similar features.

It should be noted that Telstat in 1982 developed a "bond valuation model," which uses actual trade prices reported by banks and bond dealers in a more detailed matrix, taking into account other bonds of the same issuer, to arrive at bond values.

At various times in the past, the Frank Russell organization has compared bond prices reported by pricing services and found that most often, although prices on individual issues may vary, for a total bond portfolio they will be quite close. Occasionally they are not and this has been the cause for some controversy. However, there is at least a partial analogy to the stock market that can be used to temper this controversy. Suppose an investor held a $200 million portfolio invested in 50 different issues. That would mean that at least 100,000 shares of some issues would be held, a lot size so large that it is unlikely that it could be sold at the closing composite price. Hence, even with accurate, readily available pricing data, the aggregate value of large blocks of stocks is not estimable with assured accuracy. On the other hand, with bonds the problem is even worse because of the lack of a central source for pricing for the valuation process.

SIGNIFICANCE OF PRICING ERRORS. It is apparent from the preceding discussion that the valuation process is not exact, even with actively traded issues. From a pragmatic view, in the long run the issue will be sold and the pricing *error term* previously included in the performance measurement process will wash out during the period the issue was held. For example, if a bond purchased at $90 is priced at $85.5 and $95, respectively, at the end of the two subsequent quarters, and is then sold at the end of the third subsequent quarter for $98, the returns, based on price change only, will be −5.0, 11.1, and 3.2 percent, respectively, which compound to 8.9 percent. The same result is achieved by measuring point-to-point from $90 to $98. In other words, in this example it does not matter—for rate of return purposes— whether the intervening quarter-end prices were accurate. Inaccurate interim pricing, on the other hand, may artificially magnify or reduce volatility measures. When one takes into account income and the effect on the remainder of the portfolio, some amount of distortion exists. By default, this is accepted from a performance measurement viewpoint, but obviously the pricing error term is a constant source of frustration for those charged with the responsibility of computing unit values for pooled funds and per share net asset values for mutual funds.

Real Estate and Other Assets. Now let us turn to the issue of real estate, private placements and other infrequently traded securities, and venture capital investments.

Real estate held in institutional portfolios is generally appraised by an outside appraiser on an annual basis. Because that appraiser generally has been educated and trained in the profession, his expertise is respected and his appraised values are generally accepted. However, to compute acceptable time-weighted rates of return requires valuations at least quarterly. Most real estate management firms have developed internal methods of determining market values on an ongoing basis for properties held in their portfolios, taking into account the state of the economy, inflation, income, and capitalization rates, among other items. While the only practical approach is to rely on the valuations determined by the professional real estate manager, the appraisal process does tend to smooth out price changes that might be reflected in actual transactions. As discussed in Chapter 11, this has the impact of reducing volatility in any measurement process.[2]

Private placements of bonds whose issuers also have publicly traded bond issues are not as controversial. The prices of the publicly traded issues can be readily converted to the coupon rate and maturity of the private

[2] For a detailed description of this issue and a suggested solution, see Chapter 11.

placement. Generally, a discount is taken from such an inferred value for the illiquidity inherent in the private placement feature. The amount of the discount varies and is dependent upon the individual circumstances. In those cases where the issuer has no publicly traded bonds, then the valuation involves a review of prices for bonds of similarly rated companies, coupon, maturity, sinking fund requirements, and so on, applying, again, an appropriate discount for the private placement feature.

For infrequently traded bond or stock issues, you must do what you can. For audit purposes at year-end you will probably be required to request, in writing, a reliable value from a market maker. For non-year-end periods, one or more market makers should be called for current quotations.

Portfolio valuation sounds easier than it is. You can see from the preceding discussion that several methods can be used, and each would be considered correct. Valuation is one of the most important factors in performance measurement and is often overlooked in theoretical discussions. It is entirely possible that two identical portfolios could have different computed returns due solely to the market valuation methods employed.[3] However, we do believe that consistency is extremely important; in the long run, valuation differences tend to wash out.

Accrual Basis vs. Cash Basis

Accrual basis refers to an accounting method that includes accrued income (income earned but not yet received) in the portfolio value and also records security transactions, with offsetting receivables and payables, on the trade date rather than on the settlement date. The cash basis accounting method recognizes income only as cash is received and also records security transactions on the settlement date when cash is received or paid.

It is extremely important to include accrued income in portfolio valuations and performance measurement, particularly in bond portfolios where income is a primary determinant of the portfolio return. The return may be significantly distorted (see Table 14-1) by including cash in income only as it is received. Accrued income is not material for common stock portfolios where income is a lesser portion of return and is generally received on a quarterly basis.

Table 14-1 compares the two treatments of income on a single bond portfolio. It shows that the return would have been distorted by 5 percent (i.e., 3.0 versus −2.0 percent) for the first quarter and by 3.2 percent (i.e., 2.9 versus 6.1 percent) for the second quarter using the cash basis accounting method. It should be noted that this difference will continue to exist until the bond is sold and the accrued income is received.[4]

---

[3] An interesting example of this situation is provided in Dietz and Williams [1970].

[4] The only argument we have seen against including accrued income in portfolio valuation for performance measurement is that it is not available for the manager to invest. Using the example of Table 14-1, at the beginning of the second quarter, the portfolio actually had a bond

TABLE 14-1. Comparison of Bond Returns on Accrual vs. Cash Basis

	Accrual Basis	Cash Basis
Portfolio at beginning of quarter 1: 12% short-term issue	$1,000,000	$1,000,000
Transactions at end of quarter 1: Short-term issue matures: principal	$1,000,000	$1,000,000
interest	30,000	30,000
Buy: $1 million 12%, 10 yr. Treasury bond principal	(980,000)	(980,000)
+5 mos. accrued interest	(50,000)	(50,000)
Portfolio at end of quarter 1: $1 million 12%, 10-yr. Treasury bond	$ 980,000	$ 980,000
Accrued interest	50,000	0
Total market value	$1,030,000	$ 980,000
Quarterly return (first period):	$\left(\dfrac{1,030,000}{1,000,000}-1\right) \times 100 = 3.0\%$	$\left(\dfrac{980,000}{1,000,000}-1\right) \times 100 = -2.0\%$
Transactions during quarter 2: Interest received	$ 60,000	$ 60,000
Portfolio at end of quarter 2: $1 million 12%, 10-yr. Treasury bond	$ 980,000	$ 980,000
Cash	60,000	60,000
Accrued income	20,000	0
Total market value	$1,060,000	$1,040,000
Quarterly return (second period):	$\left(\dfrac{1,060,000}{1,030,000}-1\right) \times 100 = 2.9\%$	$\left(\dfrac{1,040,000}{980,000}-1\right) \times 100 = 6.1\%$
2 quarters' return:	$\left(\dfrac{1,060,000}{1,000,000}-1\right) \times 100 = 6.0\%$	$\left(\dfrac{1,040,000}{1,000,000}-1\right) \times 100 = 4.0\%$

Trade Date vs. Settlement Date

When should a trade be reported—when it is executed, or when money changes hands? As stated previously, this is actually a part of the accrual versus cash basis controversy.

Our experience has been that it makes little difference in the rate of return, as it is seldom that a major market price change will occur during the five days between trade date and regular settlement. Occasionally, however, a material change will occur. On that basis, and with the realization that once a purchase has been executed, the buyer benefits from any price increase (or suffers any price decline) regardless of what was actually paid for the purchase (and vice versa for a sale), we strongly recommend that trade date basis be used for accounting and portfolio valuation purposes.

---

value of $980,000 plus accrued income of $50,000. The accrued income does not earn any return, so the investor actually had only $980,000 working for him or her in the first month of the next quarter. During the following quarter, the investor earned $30,000 (i.e., 12 percent on $1 million par value), *but* earned it on $980,000, not on $1,030,000, so the return (on an "adjusted" accrual basis) should have been 3.1 percent ($30,000 ÷ $980,000) rather than the 2.9 percent computed using the (standard) accrual method.

To alleviate this error term, Rosenberg [1980] has suggested discounting the accrued income to the payable date. Assuming 12 percent is reflective of current short-term rates and is therefore appropriate for the discount rate, the portfolio valuations using the accrued income method would have been:

Beginning	$1,000,000
End of first quarter	1,029,500
End of second quarter	1,060,800

It is assumed the $60,000 income received was also reinvested at 12 percent, thereby earning $1,200. Using the standard accrual basis, the portfolio valuations would have been:

Beginning	$1,000,000
End of first quarter	1,030,000
End of second quarter	1,061,200

The resulting rates of return could be compared as follows:

	Accrual	Accrual with Discount
First quarter	3.00%	2.95%
Second quarter	3.03	3.04
Two quarters	6.12	6.08

As can be seen, the difference is quite minor. The authors believe the discounting of accrued income brings a dimension into performance measurement that confuses the issue. The resulting minute performance differences are overshadowed by the potentially much larger differences in valuation amounts, not only due to varying methodologies used in portfolio valuations but also to the potential transaction cost—that is, the difference between valuation amounts and the amounts that might be realized if the total portfolio were sold.

METHODS OF PERFORMANCE MEASUREMENT

Calculation of Rate of Return

The basic purpose of all rate of return calculations is for return to account for changes in asset value plus dividend and interest income plus realized capital gains or losses. These changes are then expressed as a percent of initial capital value, adjusted for net contributions or withdrawals. As noted earlier, time-weighted rates of return are used in performance measurement because they eliminate the impact of external cash flows—over which the portfolio manager has no control—on the rate of return calculation.

Internal Rate of Return. An example of this is shown in Table 14-2. The only two factors affecting the output of the internal or dollar-weighted rate of return method are: (1) beginning and ending market values and (2) the timing of net contributions. That is, this rate of return calculation is heavily dependent on the level of portfolio assets during the various subperiods comprising the overall period. In the example, it is assumed that both portfolios were invested in the same assets. An examination of hypothetical portfolios A and B in time period X shows the results of an internal rate of return calculation. During period X, portfolio A had an internal rate of return of 5.16 percent while portfolio B's return was 2.72 percent. Since the two portfolios were invested in the same securities, the difference in the internal rates of return is accounted for by two facts: (1) portfolio A benefitted to a greater extent than did portfolio B by the high 30 percent rate of return during the first subperiod, when A's asset value was roughly six times that of B's, (2) portfolio A also benefitted as compared with B in later periods when much lower returns were experienced by A at a time when A was only three or four times the size of B.

The internal rate of return method, then, weights the final (overall) return figure by the values of the portfolio in each subperiod. As a result, different dollar size and growth of the portfolios have a strong influence on the final return figure. This example indicates that even though portfolios A and B

TABLE 14-2. **Hypothetical Portfolios A and B in Market Period X**

| Investment Subperiod | PORTFOLIO A | | | PORTFOLIO B | |
	Contributions	Market Values	Return	Contributions	Market Values
Beginning		$1,000.00			$100.00
1	$100.00	1,415.00	+30%	$100.00	245.00
2	100.00	1,661.50	+10	100.00	374.50
3	100.00	1,419.20	−20	100.00	389.60
4	100.00	1,666.12	+10	100.00	533.56

were invested in the same securities and in the same proportions, the internal rate of return method gives inappropriate results if the purpose is to compare the performance of two portfolio *managers,* despite the fact that it does give the exact rate earned on funds invested. The latter is frequently important when comparisons to a minimum acceptable return are made—for example, to a pension fund's actuarial return rate.

Time-weighted Rate of Return. The time-weighted approach computes a rate of return for each subperiod. As shown in Table 14-2, the subperiod rates are the same for each of the two portfolios, since the names and weightings of the securities held are the same for each. These individual subperiod rates of return are then compounded together (or chainlinked) to get a return rate for each portfolio for the entire period X. Thus, during period X a dollar invested in either portfolio A or B at the beginning of the period grew to $1.26, as will be more fully developed below. A compound rate of return for period X can be found by taking the nth root. In this case, it is the 4th root and the 4th root of 1.26 gives a compound rate of 5.9 percent.

All algorithms in use currently are based on the original Dietz and BAI formulas.[5] Both methods assume all contributions occur at the midpoint of the specified time period. However, the Dietz method does this by assuming that one half of the net contributions are made at the beginning of the time interval and one half at the end of the time interval. This is done by adjusting portfolio beginning and ending values by adding and subtracting half the contribution, respectively. The BAI algorithm solves for the return by the process of iteration and assumes midperiod compounding.

For example, given the following information for a portfolio for a specific time interval:

Portfolio value at beginning of time interval	$10,000,000
Portfolio value at end of time interval	12,050,000
Net contributions during time interval	1,000,000

the Dietz method arrives at a return of 10 percent via this calculation:

$$R_i = \left(\frac{\$12,050,000 - .5(\$1,000,000)}{\$10,000,000 + .5(\$1,000,000)} - 1 \right) \times 100 = 10.00 \text{ percent}$$

---

[5] The *Dietz algorithm* is

$$R_i = \left(\frac{P_i - 5C_i}{P_o + .5C_i} - 1 \right) \times 100$$

where: P_o = portfolio value at beginning of time interval i
P_i = portfolio value at end of time interval i
C_i = net contribution(s) during time interval i
R_i = rate of return for time interval i

The *BAI algorithm* is $P_o(1 + r_i) + C_i(1 + r_i)^{1/2} - P_i = 0$. By iteration solve for r_i and then $R_i = r_i \times 100$.

while the BAI method arrives at a return of 10.01 percent via their calculation:

$$\$10,000,000 \ (1 + r_i) + \$1,000,000 \ (1 + r_i)^{1/2} - \$12,050,000 = 0$$

$$R_i = r_i \times 100 = 10.01 \text{ percent}$$

Time Intervals

It is generally agreed that more frequent measurement periods (shorter time intervals) result in more accurate returns. Ideally, portfolio valuations should be calculated whenever a contribution or distribution takes place. This would eliminate the necessity of making assumptions as to the timing of cash flows and would simplify return computations. However, as a practical matter trustee/custodian banks and investment management firms usually do not have systems in place that allow for valuation more frequently than monthly, nor has there been a great demand for such services from institutional investors.

Because employee benefit funds, other institutional investors, and individuals do not generally make contributions to or receive distributions from portfolios on a daily basis, monthly computations are normally sufficient. Computations at monthly intervals and never less frequently than quarterly are strongly encouraged.

On the other hand, registered investment companies (mutual funds) generally value their portfolios on a daily basis in order to arrive at the net asset value (NAV) per share to be used for shares of the fund that were purchased or redeemed on that day. Therefore, assuming their data are more reflective of actual market values, rates of returns computed for mutual funds are the most accurate; all other methods are simply estimates.

There should not be a direct relationship between the time interval for valuation and the time horizon of the portfolio. The time horizon of the portfolio may be three, five, or perhaps fifty years. Certainly the investor would not want to wait fifty years to find out whether or not objectives have been met. Therefore, the time-weighted returns for shorter time intervals are computed and compared to objectives and alternative portfolios.

Other Methods

Day Weighting. Recognizing that cash flows do not all occur at the midpoint of a time interval, and in an attempt to minimize the distortion that might result from such an assumption, some performance measurement algorithms day-weight cash flows. For example, if a contribution is made on the tenth day of a month, rather than assuming it was made at the midpoint of the month, the return algorithm is adjusted to treat it as having been in the portfolio for two-thirds of the month.

Using the previous example and the Dietz algorithm, the revised calculation would be

$$R_i = \left[\frac{\$12,050,000 - \left(\frac{30 - 20}{30} \times \$1,000,000 \right)}{\$10,000,000 + \left(\frac{30 - 10}{30} \times \$1,000,000 \right)} - 1 \right] \times 100 = 9.84 \text{ percent}$$

Beta Adjustment. In an attempt to recognize that the market (and consequently portfolio value) does not move up or down smoothly during any given month but instead fluctuates daily, some algorithms include a beta factor. By applying the portfolio beta to the market return and the result to the beginning portfolio value, an assumed portfolio value is computed as of the date of the cash flow. This assumed portfolio value adjusted for the cash flow is the denominator used for computing the return for the next subinterval.

For example, assume the portfolio has a beta of 1.05 and the market increased by 5 percent from the beginning to the tenth of the month. The portfolio value on the date of the contribution is computed as: $[(1.05 \times .05) + 1] \times \$10,000,000 = \$10,525,000$.

In other words, while the market increased by 5 percent from the beginning of the month to the date of the contribution, it is assumed that the portfolio increased on a beta-adjusted basis by 5.25 percent (1.05×5) during the same period so that the portfolio value at the point of the contribution was $\$10,000,000 + 5.25$ percent of $\$10,000,000$, or $\$10,525,000$.

This estimated value is then used in computing the return for the last twenty days of the month as follows, with the contribution amount of $\$1,000,000$ and actual portfolio valued at $\$12,050,000$ at the end of the month.

$$R_i = \left(\frac{\$12,050,000}{\$10,525,000 + \$1,000,000} - 1 \right) \times 100 = 4.56 \text{ percent}$$

The returns for the two subintervals for the month are chainlinked (compounded or time-weighted) to arrive at the return for the month of 10.05 percent.

$$R_j = [(1.0525 \quad \times \quad 1.0456) \quad - \quad 1] \times 100 = \quad 10.05\%$$

Return for first 10 days + 1	Return for last 20 days + 1	Monthly return

No one method as described here consistently arrives at the most accurate time-weighted return. In any event, recall that the purpose is to determine how well the manager is doing his or her job; therefore, small error terms in the rate of return calculations are tolerable, especially in view of the valuation problems discussed previously and the risk-adjustment issues still to be discussed.

Annualized Returns

Once the returns for individual time intervals are arrived at, to compute the time-weighted rate of return for sequential time intervals, you merely need to chainlink the results of the individual time intervals. If the sequential time intervals involved in the computation in total cover more than a one-year period, then the appropriate root is found to determine the annualized (compound) rate of return. For example, if the total time period is three years, then the 3rd root is taken to arrive at the annualized rate of return.

To compute a quarterly time-weighted rate of return from the returns of the three individual months, the returns are changed into return relatives (decimal form plus 1) and multiplied together to arrive at the quarterly return.

Month 1	+3.06%
Month 2	−1.95
Month 3	+5.01

Thus, $R_i = (1.0306 \times .9805 \times 1.0501) - 1 = 1.0611 - 1 = .0611$ for a quarterly time-weighted return of 6.11 percent.

An annual rate of return is computed by chainlinking the results of the twelve individual months, or the results of the four individual quarters. For example, for the following four quarter returns,

Quarter 1	6.11%
Quarter 2	4.06
Quarter 3	−3.54
Quarter 4	+2.95

the annual return calculation is

$$R_i = (1.0611 \times 1.0406 \times .9646 \times 1.0295) - 1 = 1.0965 - 1 = .0965$$

or an annual return (compounded quarterly) of 9.65 percent.

Annualized returns are computed by chainlinking monthly, quarterly, or annual returns in the same fashion and taking the appropriate root of the result. The root should be the number of years in the total time period (for three years, the 3rd root; for $4\frac{1}{2}$ years, the 4.5 root, and so on). An eight quarter example, involving the 2nd or square root, is shown below:

Quarter 1	+6.11%
Quarter 2	+4.06
Quarter 3	−3.54
Quarter 4	+2.95
Quarter 5	+8.34
Quarter 6	+5.20
Quarter 7	−1.95
Quarter 8	+4.86

$$R_i = \sqrt[\overline{}]{1.0611 \times 1.0406 \times .9646 \times 1.0295 \times 1.0834 \times 1.0520 \times .9805 \times 1.0486} - 1$$
$$= .1335$$

The result, 13.35 percent, is the annualized or compound annual rate of return for the period measured. Because of extreme fluctuations in monthly or quarterly returns due to market movements, annualized quarterly returns should never be computed with fewer than four quarters of data. The following example shows the unrealistic results of annualizing quarterly returns where only one quarter's return is used: the annualized rate of return based on a 20 percent positive quarter would be $[(1.20)^4 - 1] \times 100 = 107.36$ percent, while the annualized return based on a one quarter return of minus 20 percent would be $[(.80)^4 - 1] \times 100 = -59.04$ percent.

Portfolio Segment Measurement

The preceding section addressed the various methods of performance measurement for total portfolios. Errors are possible in using these methods as long as valuations are not performed at the time of each new cash flow. In dealing with portfolio segments such as stocks, bonds, convertibles, and so on, these estimation errors may be even greater because accurate performance measurement would require valuations each time a purchase, sale, or income transaction took place. In general, cost-benefit analyses have shown that the additional accuracy does not warrant these costly computations so long as monthly asset valuations take place.

Segment measurement helps explain the total portfolio return and how it was achieved. For example, suppose the return for an equity-oriented portfolio was only 5 percent for a quarter in which the equity market return was 10 percent. If the return on the equity segment of the portfolio were 12 percent, then that would indicate the manager was probably right about the stocks bought for the portfolio (stock selection); however, the fact that the portfolio was about 70 percent in cash had a detrimental effect on the return (e.g., the manager made a wrong timing decision). On the other hand, if the equity segment return were only 7 percent, then the manager would have been wrong on two counts, stock selection *and* timing.

When dealing with a segment of the total portfolio, such as the equity and/or the fixed-income portion, it is impossible to determine how the cash contributions were allocated between the specific portions of the portfolio. That is, there is no way to know what portion of contributions were invested in common stocks versus what portion in bonds. However, since net security purchases must equal the sum of contributions and cash investment income to the fund, an equivalent can be developed. The algorithms for total portfolio performance are thus altered so that the contribution term is replaced by the term net security purchases (gross purchases less sales) minus income.

The returns for portfolio segments can be chainlinked to arrive at quarterly, annual, and annualized longer period returns using the same algorithms as for total portfolio returns.

Annual returns are those computed for individual one-year periods, whereas the term *annualized returns* is used to designate the compound average annual return for periods longer than one year.

Adjusting for Risk

A well-accepted theorem is that rate of return and risk are positively correlated. Therefore, no performance measurement process is complete without some attempt to measure the riskiness of the portfolio. In this section we provide a discussion of the major methods currently used to calculate risk-adjusted performance measurement.

The most fundamental notion of both security and portfolio risk is variability; that is, variability of interperiod results compared to average results over time. Basically, the notion is simple; that is, a security with a return stream of .05, .05, .05, and .05 is more predictable (less risky) than a security with a return stream of .03, .07, .01, and .09. Both securities have a mean return of .05. Most approaches to measuring variability or risk use the standard deviation of return distributions following the method originally suggested by Markowitz [1959] and discussed in Chapter 3.

Although we do not attempt to prove it here, the standard deviation of return for securities follows our general notions of riskiness. That is, securities with high degrees of fundamental riskiness, having characteristics such as poor market liquidity, cyclical industry, high financial leverage, small capitalization, or long duration, have tended to have higher standard deviations than securities with the opposite characteristics. Thus, time series of Treasury bill returns generally have smaller standard deviations than returns on long-term bonds and much smaller than returns on equities; among stocks, there is a fairly wide range of risk, with utility stocks, for example, usually having return distributions with lower standard deviations than stocks in the airline industry.

Standard deviation measures total risk, or variability. As demonstrated in Chapter 3, an alternative and more theoretically elegant approach is to partition total risk into its component parts, systematic and nonsystematic risk. Systematic risk (measured by beta) is the component of a security's or a portfolio's volatility related to the market in general, while the nonsystematic risk (total risk net of beta risk) measures the residual variability of a security after market-related risk is removed.

Having once measured the riskiness of a portfolio, it becomes necessary to relate risk to return in order to determine whether the return earned was sufficient to reward the investor for the degree of risk incurred. This is most generally done by use of a single index model such as those proposed by

Treynor [1965], Sharpe [1966], or Jensen [1968]. These single index models are described briefly below.[6]

Treynor Measure. Treynor suggested that the appropriate risk measure of a portfolio is its systematic risk (i.e., beta). The Treynor measure (T) relates the rate of return earned above the risk-free rate to the portfolio beta during the time period under consideration. Thus,

$$T = \frac{R_p - R_f}{\beta_p}$$

or, in words,

$$\text{Treynor's measure} = \frac{\text{excess return on portfolio } p}{\text{beta on portfolio } p}$$

$$= \frac{\begin{array}{c}\text{average rate} \\ \text{of return for} \\ \text{portfolio } p\end{array} - \begin{array}{c}\text{average rate of} \\ \text{return on a risk-free} \\ \text{investment}\end{array}}{\text{beta on portfolio } p}$$

where portfolio p's beta is the slope of the portfolio's characteristic line, which measures the portfolio's volatility relative to the market—that is, its systematic risk. An example of a characteristic line was shown earlier in Figure 14-1(b).

The numerator of the T ratio ($R_p - R_f$) is the risk premium earned by the portfolio and the denominator the measure of risk. Therefore, the T ratio indicates the portfolio's return per unit of risk. Since the risk measured is systematic risk, it assumes nothing about the portfolio's diversification. The Treynor measure, then, implicitly assumes that the portfolio being measured is fully diversified.

Using this measure, numerous portfolios can be ranked relative to one another and to the market portfolio. Since higher T values give higher returns per unit of risk, risk averse investors would seek to maximize this value. Since the market beta equals 1.0 (by definition), the market risk premium ($R_m - R_f$) becomes the slope of the SML as shown earlier in Figure 14-1(a). Portfolios plotting above the SML have superior risk-adjusted performance.

Sharpe Measure. The Sharpe measure (S) is also based on the capital asset pricing model (CAPM) and relates return to the capital market line (CML). This measure is the same as the Treynor measure except that the

[6] For our discussion of Treynor, Sharpe, and Jensen we have closely followed Reilly [1982]. For a more detailed discussion see his Chapter 23.

denominator used is the standard deviation, which measures total risk or variability. Thus,

$$S = \frac{R_p - R_f}{\sigma_p}$$

That is, excess return on portfolio p is now measured per unit of σ_p, which is the standard deviation of the portfolio's rate of return during the measurement period.

Since the numerator is the risk premium earned in the portfolio, the Sharpe measure indicates the return per unit of total risk. Both the Treynor and Sharpe measures assume a linear relationship between return and risk. For perfectly diversified portfolios the two measures will give identical rankings because the total variance of the portfolio would be the same as its systematic variance. If a portfolio is poorly diversified, it is possible for it to have a Treynor ranking different from its Sharpe ranking relative to other portfolios included in the rankings.

Jensen Measure. The Jensen measure, Jensen's alpha, also is based on the CAPM. It is based on the theory that the realized rate of return on a portfolio should be a linear function of the risk-free rate plus a risk premium that is a function of the portfolio's systematic risk during the period of review plus a random error term. Thus, using a time series linear regression format for realized rates of return, we have

$$R_{pt} - R_{ft} = \beta_p(R_{mt} - R_{ft}) + U_{pt}$$

In words,

$$\begin{pmatrix} \text{Realized} & \text{Risk-} \\ \text{return on} & - \text{free} \\ \text{portfolio } p & \text{return} \end{pmatrix} =$$

$$\text{function} \begin{pmatrix} \text{Realized} & \text{Risk-} \\ \text{return on} & - \text{free} \\ \text{market index } m & \text{return} \end{pmatrix} + \begin{matrix} \text{Random} \\ \text{error} \\ \text{term} \end{matrix}$$

or

$$\begin{matrix} \text{Excess return} \\ \text{on portfolio } p \end{matrix} = \begin{matrix} \text{function} \\ \text{(beta)} \end{matrix} \begin{pmatrix} \text{Excess return on} \\ \text{market index } m \end{pmatrix} + \begin{matrix} \text{Random} \\ \text{error} \\ \text{term} \end{matrix}$$

In equilibrium, in an efficient market one would not expect an intercept for the regression. However, if some portfolio managers can consistently select superior portfolios, they will consistently plot above the average represented by the regression line; that is, their actual returns will consistently be above expected returns. This can be measured by the regression intercept (alpha) term of the regression equation as follows:

$$R_{pt} - R_{ft} = \alpha_p + \beta_p(R_{mt} - R_{ft}) + U_{pt}$$

or verbally,

$$\begin{array}{c} \text{Excess return} \\ \text{on portfolio } p \end{array} = \begin{array}{c} \text{Unique} \\ \text{return} \\ \text{(alpha)} \end{array} + \begin{array}{c} \text{function} \\ \text{(beta)} \end{array} \left(\begin{array}{c} \text{Excess return on} \\ \text{market index } m \end{array} \right) + \begin{array}{c} \text{Random} \\ \text{error} \\ \text{term} \end{array}$$

That is, α_p represents the unique return experience of portfolio p over time relative to market index m.

Given enough time periods, the significance of alpha can be measured. The Jensen measure, like Treynor, assumes fully diversified portfolios.[7] An additional problem with the Jensen alpha is that it is unique to a particular portfolio beta level. In other words, Jensen alphas in different risk classes should not be compared with one another. As will be discussed later, we recommend segregating portfolios into different management styles, each of which tend to have different systematic risk parameters.

All three of the methods just discussed assume (at least in their simplest form) that the relationship between risk and return is linear and remains linear throughout its entire range. Much academic research has shown that the relationship is not as simple as capital market theory would suggest, and sophisticated methods for improving risk-return measurement have been recommended. Further, although we will not be discussing the detailed mathematics, important insights are gained from understanding the following empirical problems inherent in the simplistic use of the CAPM methodology for ex post risk adjustment:

1. The intercept of the empirically derived SML often differs significantly from the risk-free rate as approximated by actual Treasury bill return experience.
2. There is no generally accepted and universally applicable economy-wide market index.
3. Statistical error is so large, because of large fluctuations observed in a limited sample of data, that statistically significant alphas seldom occur.
4. Errors in estimating beta may (or may not) produce offsetting errors in alpha, the measure of excess portfolio return.

[7] To correct for this deficiency, Camp and Eubank [1981] argue for a new risk measure, the *beta quotient,* which is defined as the portfolio beta divided by the correlation coefficient of the characteristic line. The authors believe this correction may be helpful, but have not had sufficient empirical experience to comment further at this time.

5. Residuals from the characteristic line calculation frequently are not statistically independent across securities.
6. Residual risk appears to be nonconstant over time.
7. Beta estimates for individual stocks appear to be nonstationary.
8. Capital market line analysis does not tell how a manager achieved his return.

We believe that the combination of ex post return measurement errors, ex post risk measurement errors, and the nonlinearity of the total true risk-reward function are such as to strongly recommend a two-parameter measure such as the rate of return/standard deviation diagrams used in the remainder of this chapter. While portfolio rankings are less precise than those provided by single index models, the probability for drawing erroneous conclusions is also lessened. The theory that one prefers the highest return for any given level of risk still holds.

While great strides have been made in ex post return measurement and risk adjustment, we believe that use of the CAPM methodology is most successful when augmented by the methods discussed below, as well as by personal knowledge of the manager's organization and detailed analysis of how the portfolio was invested.

EVALUATION OF PERFORMANCE

The evaluation of portfolio performance must be made in light of the purposes of portfolio measurement which were stated in the introduction to this chapter. That is, from the point of view of the investor, the performance evaluation system should monitor investment strategy, which is based on client objectives and risk tolerance; identify skill at portfolio management; and provide evidence that favorable performance coincided with skills that were claimed in advance.

From the investment manager's viewpoint, the system should provide feedback as to whether the results coincide with his or her expectations. Inherent in these purposes is the necessity of comparing results both on an absolute and on a risk-adjusted basis. Let us first address the issue, from the investor's viewpoint, of appropriate measures at the three levels identified above.

Investment Strategy Monitoring

This is one of the more straightforward performance areas to evaluate. Presumably the investor would have allocated assets based on predetermined objectives and at that point should have determined how he or she was going to evaluate the success or failure of that strategy. For our purposes here, we will assume that the investor had previously determined objectives and allocated assets accordingly.

Suppose, for example, the investor's objective was an annual return of 13.0 percent, and on that basis 65 percent of assets had been allocated to equities and 35 percent to bonds. Then, if equities returned 15.0 percent and bonds returned 10.0 percent, the objective would have been met. The comparison for the total fund of an investor should be the allocated percentages invested in appropriate market indexes versus the investor's objectives. Any excess or deficiency between the index composite and actual returns can then be determined as due to the portfolio manager's action, either through security selection or through weightings of selections within asset categories. It will also give the investor an indication of the general marketplace in which the portfolio manager was operating and what might consequently be expected in the area of individual portfolio returns.

Another example: If for the given time period above, an unmanaged bond index result was 5.0 percent and an unmanaged equity index result was 8.5 percent, then, given the investor's allocations, the composite index result would be 5.7 percent, well below the objective of 13.0 percent. That should not concern the investor too much in the short run. Since in this case his portfolio return was actually 10.0 percent, he would have outperformed his naive unmanaged portfolio and would need to look further to determine where the incremental return came from. If total return was below 5.7 percent, then the investor should look closely at the individual segment returns to see if the poor results were due to (a) poor timing of commitment to asset classes, or (b) poor selection of assets within a given asset class. As introduced in Chapter 8, Stolte [1981] develops an entire analytical system expanding on the framework just presented.

Problems with Strategy Monitoring Analyses. However, there are several severe practical problems that need to be solved before a Stolte-type system can be implemented. This is especially true in a system where multiple managers are used to manage a large portfolio, a practice very common to the pension fund industry. To implement such a system the investor would need to set objectives in terms of (1) normal stock/bond/Treasury bill ratios, (2) agreed-upon benchmark yardsticks for managers of various portfolio segments, and (3) standard cash reserve positions of equity managers. This is rarely laid out in such detail. Furthermore, while there were reasonable indexes for Treasury securities, equities, and bonds in 1982, there were no publicly available indexes for a fourth asset category frequently encountered in institutional portfolios, real estate. Even the market index for equities is subject to considerable controversy; in mid-1982, for example, there were no acceptable benchmarks for managers given specialty assignments such as small emerging growth stocks.

Evaluation of Bond Strategies

In Chapter 9, bond management strategies were divided into three broad categories: income maximization using a passive buy-and-hold strategy; accumulation maximization using immunization techniques; and total return maximization using active bond management strategies.

An approach to differentiating among *active* bond management strategies further divides bond managers into three groups: (1) those who anticipate changes in interest rates and modify bond portfolio structure accordingly, principally by shortening or lengthening maturity or duration when rates are expected to rise or fall, respectively; (2) those who always invest in long-term bonds and swap between various sectors of the fixed income market depending on the relative attractiveness, usually in yield spread terms, of those market sectors; and (3) those who anticipate interest rate changes to a lesser degree and search for undervalued sectors or individual issues, sometimes with a focus on a specialized segment of the fixed income market (such as mortgage related securities). There are numerous variations of these strategies.

Assuming the investor made the decision that a manager in each of these categories was necessary to cover his or her objectives, then each one should be compared to different yardsticks. Over the long haul, each of them should provide a higher return than that available from an unmanaged bond index of similar composition (in order to make comparisons among equally risky portfolios) *and* a higher-than-average return relative to actively managed portfolios using a similar strategy.

Appropriate Benchmarks for Active Managers. Over an interest rate cycle, an actively managed bond portfolio should provide a return greater than an unmanaged bond index in order to justify the cost of active management. An example of a yardstick that would provide an appropriate benchmark for the second strategy—the manager who always invests in long-term securities—would be the Salomon Brothers High-grade Corporate Bond Index. An appropriate benchmark for the third strategy might be the Lehman Brothers Kuhn Loeb Government/Corporate Bond Index or the Merrill Lynch Master Index, because they are both more broadly representative of the overall fixed income market than the Salomon Brothers Index; the latter index is composed of longer term to maturity and higher quality bonds than the other two indexes. Figures 14-2 (page 634) and 14-3 (page 635) show all three indexes plotted against the pooled fixed income accounts for 112 banks for the time period 1975–77 (a rising market) and 1978–80 (a declining market), respectively. As is evident, selection of the index against which performance is compared can be a critical decision.

In addition to comparison with a passive benchmark, the bond portfolio's results should be compared to a broad universe of actively managed bond portfolios. Consistent above-average returns based on a comparison with other active bond managers investing in similar types of fixed income securities would demonstrate good fixed income portfolio management skills.

Analyzing Sources of Returns. For shorter time frames, analysis of sources of returns can provide the investor with evidence that performance

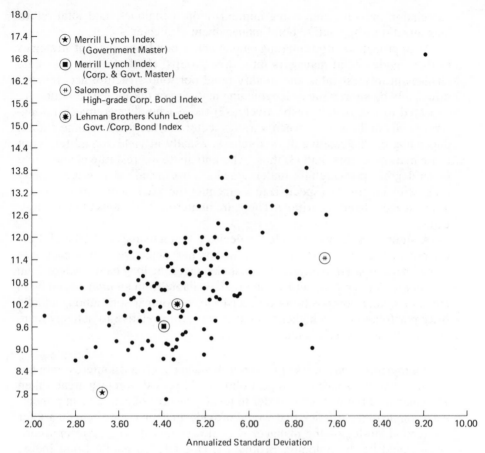

Figure 14-2. Risk-Return Performance Comparisons of 112 Bank Fixed Income Pooled Accounts 1/1/75–12/31/77. (SOURCE: Frank Russell Company)

coincided with skills that were claimed in advance, and can provide the investment manager with feedback as to whether the results coincided with his expectations.

For example, if the bond manager had claimed skill at interest rate forecasting and subsequently was fully invested in 20-year bonds during a holding period when long-term interest rates soared from 10 to 15 percent, the investor would obviously question the manager's skill at interest rate forecasting. Obviously the results did not coincide with his expectations.

On the other hand, if the manager had claimed that his skill was in swapping long-term bonds for incremental return and that he would always be invested in long bonds, then even if he had a poor absolute return for any given (short) time period, an analysis of return relative to yield curve changes might indicate that the low return was due entirely to increasing

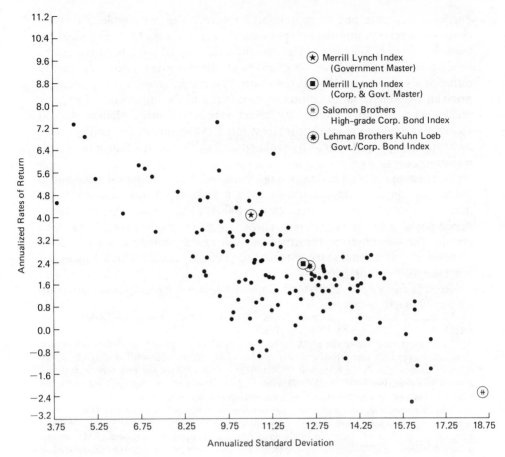

Figure 14-3. Risk-Return Performance Comparisons of 121 Bank Fixed Income Pooled Accounts 1/1/78–12/31/80. (SOURCE: Frank Russell Company)

interest rates and that he had actually added value via swapping long-term bonds. The investor should not be unhappy; the manager actually performed well in terms of his advertised skills. Likewise, the bond manager should not be disappointed in that his results coincided with his expectations. Both of them may be unhappy because interest rates increased and the value of the portfolio declined, but that is an external circumstance they cannot control nor, unless a change in basic strategy occurs, adjust for.

Making Decomposed Returns Comparisons. There are several commercial services that attempt to examine fixed income returns on such a micro level. One consulting firm, for example, has developed a model that isolates the impact on portfolio results of changes in the term structure of interest rates, both from the effect of sector and quality selection on the part of portfolio managers and from unrelated return.[8] The methodology decomposes bond returns into the components shown in Figure 14-4. The yield-to-maturity effect is the *a priori* known return that would have been earned by an investor had there been no changes in interest rates, sector or quality differentials, and so on. This is the return that results from accruing income, price change due to amortization toward par, and the impact of "riding the yield curve."[9] The interest rate effect represents price change due to changes in the general level of interest rates, while the sector/quality effect measures return contributed by yield spread shifts due to change in sector/quality differentials.[10]

In order to assess a manager's results against a broad-based unmanaged index, the decomposed returns of each managed portfolio are measured against the decomposed returns of a 2,100-bond universe. The universe is decomposed into its constituent parts using the methodology described above. The decomposed returns from the index provide a set of return components on a benchmark unmanaged portfolio against which a managed portfolio may be compared.

Results for a very short-term portfolio and a long-term portfolio com-

---

[8] For a full description, see Dietz, Fogler, and Hardy [1980]. For a slightly different approach, see Fong, Pearson, and Vasicek [1982].

[9] The effect from riding the yield curve assumes a stable upward- or downward-sloping yield curve over time and a buy-and-hold bond strategy. With an upward-sloping curve, for example, as time passes the bond will constantly move leftward toward zero time to maturity and, in so doing, the bond's yield will automatically drop and its price will automatically increase. The opposite would be true of a downward-sloping yield curve.

[10] An alternate approach has been suggested by Fong, Pearson, and Vasicek [1982]. Their approach partitions total bond portfolio return into five components: the effect of interest rate level (RI), the effect of interest rate change (RA), the maturity management (RM), sector/quality management (RS), and selectivity (RB). The first component can also be interpreted as the expected return on default-free securities, and the second as the difference between the actual and expected return on the default-free Treasury market index. The first two components are the effect of external factors beyond the control of the portfolio manager, namely, the interest rate environment (RE). Their sum is the actual return on the Treasury index. The last three components reflect factors within the control of the manager, that is, the management skill (RC). Together they add up to the total management contribution. The sum of all five components is the actual return on the portfolio (R). An alternative way of looking at the composition of the total return given by the following equation which will reflect the way these components are actually calculated, is to consider the cumulative totals.

$$R = \underbrace{RI + RA}_{RE} + \underbrace{RM + RS + RB}_{RC}$$

The first total, RI, is the expected return on a randomly selected portfolio of Treasury issues, calculated assuming no change in interest rates. The second total, RI + RA, is the actual return on a randomly selected portfolio of Treasury issues. The third total, RI + RA + RM, is the return on the actual portfolio (including all activity) as if all securities were Treasury issues priced on the term structure (that is, no sector/quality effects and no specific returns). The fourth total, RI + RA + RM + RS, is the return on the actual portfolio as if all securities were priced according to their issuing sector and quality (that is, no specific returns). Finally, the fifth total, RI + RA + RM + RS + RB, is the actual portfolio return.

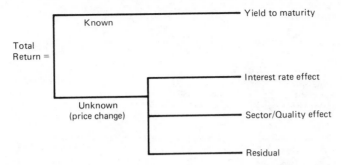

Figure 14-4. Model for Decomposing Fixed Income Portfolio Returns. (SOURCE: Dietz, Fogler, and Hardy [1980])

pared against the 2,100-bond universe are presented in Table 14-3 for the fourth quarter of 1981. Since the fourth quarter of 1981 was a period during which interest rates declined, analysis of the long-term portfolio return attributable to interest rates shows a positive differential relative to the universe benchmark. Conversely, the portion of return in the short-term portfolio attributable to interest rates indicates that the short-term portfolio underperformed the 2,100-bond universe in this respect, but the manager added value through sector/quality weighting and other factors, though not enough to offset the interest rate effect and outperform the universe on a total return basis.

Evaluation of Equity Strategies

Within the universe of managers of equity portfolios, there are a number of management styles. Since Chapter 10 of this book is one of the first efforts at categorizing these styles, there is little in the established literature concerning standardized equity investment management styles. The result is that there is a multiplicity of possible logical breakdowns. Figure 14-5 is a sche-

TABLE 14-3. **Value Added by Active Management**

	Total = Return	Yield to Maturity	+	Interest Rate Effect	+	Sector Quality Effect	+	Residual
Short-term portfolio return	8.30%	4.06%		3.94%		−0.58%		0.88%
Less: Index return	10.44	3.92		8.20		(−1.68)		0.00
Management differential	−2.14%	0.14%		−4.26%		1.10%		0.88%
Long-term portfolio return	16.25%	3.63%		9.76%		−1.37%		4.23%
Less: Index return	10.44	3.92		8.20		(−1.68)		0.00
Management differential	5.81%	−0.29%		1.56%		0.31%		4.23%

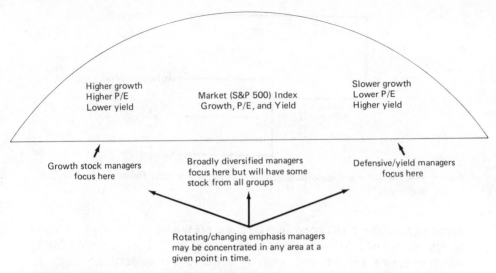

Figure 14-5. Diversification by Equity Style Across a Universe of Stocks Represented by a Market Index. (SOURCE: Frank Russell Company)

matic that shows one logic of identifying the main investment themes employed by equity managers. The two most distinctive styles can be termed *aggressive/growth* and *defensive/yield*. The manager of the aggressive/ growth stock portfolio tends to invest in companies with above-average

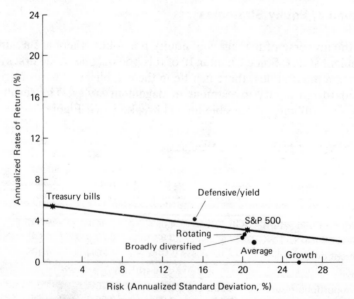

Figure 14-6. Group Risk-Return Performance Comparisons of 98 Mutual Funds for the Five Years Ended 12/31/75. Groupings included 34 growth, 25 broadly diversified, 16 rotating, and 23 defensive/yield funds. (SOURCE: Frank Russell Company)

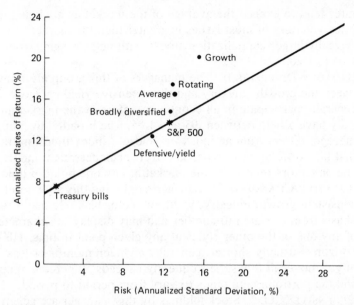

Figure 14-7. Group Risk-Return Performance Comparisons of 98 Mutual Funds for the Five Years Ended 12/31/80. Groupings included 34 growth, 25 broadly diversified, 16 rotating, and 23 defensive/yield funds. (SOURCE: Frank Russell Company)

projected earnings growth, whereas the manager of a defensive/yield portfolio tends to invest in stocks with higher-than-average expected dividend yields. These two portfolios would normally also be at opposite ends of the systematic risk spectrum; therefore, differences in performance may well be explained by a beta effect. Because of measurement errors in equity market indexes, it is preferable to compare portfolios with those of similar objectives. In any event, these differences in intended equity market sectors must be taken into account in comparing and evaluating performance.

Figures 14-6 and 14-7 show this effect for a group of 98 mutual funds measured for the 5-year period ended December 31, 1975 and the 5-year period ended December 31, 1980, respectively. Note that in the first five years the ex post capital market line is negative and that for the later period it is steeply positive.

Identification of Styles. The funds were segregated into five styles:

1. AGGRESSIVE GROWTH. Managers classified in this group would, as a general rule, hold more than 70 percent of their portfolios in companies of under $1 billion market capitalization and with a historical beta at least 20 percent greater than the broad market.
2. QUALITY GROWTH. Managers falling into this category usually hold stocks with low dividend payout and a heavier emphasis toward technology than basic industry. The earnings and dividend growth

rates tend to exceed the average of the market as a whole, and the price volatility of most issues is greater than the market. They are typically larger capitalization stocks with betas ranging from about 1.05 to 1.20.

3. BROADLY DIVERSIFIED. The managers of this group are found between the growth category and the defensive/yield category. They generally participate in all economic sectors of the market and typically have a beta between .95 and 1.05. The broadly diversified manager differs from an index or "closet" index fund[11] in the sense that his portfolio may somewhat over- or underweight industries and/or sectors relative to the market at any one point in time.

4. ROTATING/CHANGING. A manager employing this style rarely has a consistent growth industry, yield, or sector bias. He may shift emphasis from one area to another and may display the characteristics of any one of the other styles at any given point in time. His time horizon is usually shorter, generally eighteen months or less. Equity turnover in this style frequently exceeds 50 percent annually and the portfolio beta tends to vary from period to period.

5. DEFENSIVE/YIELD. Stockholdings by this manager are generally found among noncyclical necessities industries, such as food, liquor, and tobacco and sometimes cyclical industries, such as steels, autos, chemicals, and so on. The price/earnings ratios are generally lower than the market and dividend payouts are usually higher. Frequently the companies have lower earnings growth rates and sometimes they are of lesser quality. They are in sharp contrast to issues defined in the growth category. Portfolio betas are typically .95 or less.

Figures 14-6 and 14-7 show that the defensive/yield portfolios were the best performers in the earlier period and the worst performers in the latter period. The aggressive growth portfolios had exactly opposite results.

As indicated previously, we have measured riskiness by use of the standard deviation of quarterly returns. Although beta (systematic or market risk) is only one portion of the risk measured by standard deviation, a pronounced beta effect is evident. That is, higher standard deviation/higher beta portfolios performed worse than the market in bearish market years (1971–75) and better than the market in bullish years (1976–80).

In theory, one would expect optimally diversified portfolios to fall on the capital market line in an efficient market. The fact that they do not indicates either superior (inferior) security selection, excess positive (negative) returns due to nonmarket risk, or measurement error. It is likely that all three factors are present. The aggressive/growth portfolios typically contain the greatest nonmarket risk as measured against the capitalization-weighted S&P 500 Index.

[11] This is an extensively diversified fund—essentially an index fund—masquerading as a truly actively managed fund.

The methodology applied here does not imply superior or inferior selection of issues within each segment of the market in which the portfolio is invested, but instead relative to the market as a whole. For example, in the 5-year period ended December 31, 1975, the aggressive growth style portfolios performed poorly in comparison with those of the other styles. The portfolios may have displayed superior selection of aggressive growth stocks, but because they selected aggressive growth stocks, selection relative to the market was poor. In the same vein, the term *measurement error* does not refer to computational errors, but instead implies that it may not be appropriate to measure aggressive growth stocks against a capital market line determined by the rate of return on Treasury bills and the return and risk on the S&P 500. A different, better-tailored market index would be more appropriate in this instance, although such an index was not publicly available in 1982.

Over a market cycle the investor would expect each type of actively managed portfolio to perform better than a passive market portfolio in order to demonstrate evidence of the manager's skill at portfolio management. The investor would also expect an even higher return from growth stock portfolios to compensate for the additional systematic or market risk assumed.

Performance Comparisons Within Styles. The evidence provided in Figures 14-6 and 14-7 suggests that the performance of a portfolio should be compared with a universe of portfolios of the same investment style. These universes may be made up of mutual funds, pooled accounts, such as at commercial bank trust departments, or separately managed portfolios. Figure 14-8 shows the 4-year moving average returns of the same set of mutual funds plotted in Figures 14-6 and 14-7. However, in this case we have removed the market by showing the returns relative to the S&P 500. As can be seen, portfolios (stocks) tend to move in groups based on short-term market preferences. Thus, aggressive growth stocks did very well relative to the market in the 4-year periods ending in years up through 1969 and again in the

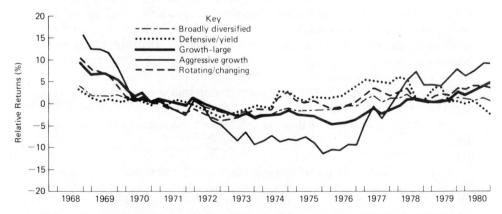

Figure 14-8. Four-year Moving Average Returns of Grouped Mutual Funds Relative to the S&P 500, 1969–80. (SOURCE: Frank Russell Company)

periods ending after mid-1977. However, they seriously underperformed the market in the 4-year periods ending in 1972 through 1977. This could not be explained by the beta effect, as the average annual return on the S&P 500 during this period was 15.4 percent, giving the capital market line a steep positive slope. The defensive/yield portfolios in the sample were primarily comprised of large capitalization, low beta stocks. These style or peer group universes give a good indication of relative management skill for periods that are less than full market cycles.

By contrast, traditional risk-adjusted measures such as the Sharpe or Treynor indexes or the Jensen alpha could be misleading, even over time periods as long as four years. For example, due to the nature of traditional risk-adjustment methods, the defensive/yield managers would have appeared to have earned superior results for the 4-year period ended 1978 when, in fact, the results were primarily due to investor preferences as a whole, and not to superior security selection.

On the issue of how style or peer groups are formed, this is perhaps more an art than a science at the current time. However, at one large firm peer groups are formed by careful analysis of each manager's historical beta, current beta, degree of portfolio diversification, portfolio composition, and turnover, together with an analysis of their decision-making process based on lengthy in-person interviews. More recently, factor analysis of portfolio returns has been successfully used to segregate managers by style.[12]

Portfolio Analysis

Portfolio analysis helps both the investor and the investment manager to determine the reasons for over- or underperformance. One approach that has been found useful is a combination of equity profiles and an analysis of management effect. As an example, suppose the industry profile of portfolios A and B and the market were as shown in Table 14-4.

In the analysis of management effect shown in Table 14-5, the return for each economic sector is calculated and its impact (return × portfolio weight) on the total results for portfolio A, portfolio B, and the market is shown.

A quick glance at the total equity returns shows that portfolio B earned a superior return while portfolio A's return was almost ten percentage points lower than B and almost five percentage points lower than the market. A cursory judgment might arrive at the conclusion that the manager of portfolio B was the superior manager.

However, an analysis of these two tables shows the following was true for portfolio A:

1. Diversification in terms of percentage distribution among sectors was very close to that of the market portfolio.

---

[12] Dietz, Fogler, and Smith [1982].

Table 14-4. Market Value Weightings of Two Hypothetical Equity Portfolios and the Market Index

	PORTFOLIO MARKET VALUE WEIGHTINGS		
Sector Profile	Portfolio A	Portfolio B	Market Index
Consumer	28%	40%	30%
Energy	24	30	26
Technology	8	20	10
Basic industry	25	5	22
Interest rate sensitive	15	5	12

2. Three sectors of the portfolio (consumer, basic industry, and interest rate sensitive) performed better than the counterpart market sectors. These sectors included 68 percent of the portfolio versus 64 percent of the market portfolio.
3. Only two sectors of the portfolio (energy and technology) performed worse than the market sectors.

If we add to this the fact that the manager of portfolio A had said in advance that the stocks in the portfolio (1) would have market diversification and (2) would have high dividend yields, *and* we knew that during this time period the stellar performance of the energy sector was in low-dividend-paying issues, then our overall conclusion might be that portfolio A's manager did a pretty good job. By comparison, the following was true for portfolio B:

1. In comparison to the market, the portfolio was overweighted in the combined consumer and technology sectors at 60 percent, versus 40 percent for the market portfolio.

Table 14-5. Analysis of Active Management of Two Hypothetical Equity Portfolios Relative to a Market Index

	ANALYSIS OF MANAGEMENT EFFECT					
	PORTFOLIO A		PORTFOLIO B		MARKET INDEX	
Sector Profile	Absolute Return	Impact[a]	Absolute Return	Impact[a]	Absolute Return	Impact[a]
Consumer	21%	5.9%	19%	7.6%	20%	6.0%
Energy	30	7.2	70	21.0	50	13.0
Technology	10	0.8	8	1.6	20	2.0
Basic industry	28	7.0	22	1.1	25	5.5
Interest rate sensitive	15	2.2	30	1.5	10	1.2
Total equity return		23.1%		32.8%		27.7%

[a] Market value weighting from Table 14-4 multiplied by absolute return

2. Sector returns were all lower than the market except for the energy sector where the manager had approximately a market weighting and the interest-rate-sensitive sector with a smaller-than-market weighting.
3. Essentially all of the portfolio excess return came from the energy sector.

If we add to this the fact that the manager said in advance that he would (1) invest the portfolio in growth stocks and (2) over- and underweight the portfolio in accordance with his anticipation of economic trends, we might question whether the portfolio's performance was as good as the absolute return would indicate or simply lucky stock selection in the energy area.

From the manager's viewpoint, A would probably be pleased that the results coincided with his expectations. Manager B should review his economic analysis to determine why the consumer and technology sectors did not meet expectations as evidenced by their portfolio weightings.

Timing vs. Selection

Finally, there is the subject of market timing. While there are a number of methods employed to determine the return gained or lost due to market timing, putting any of them on a risk-adjusted basis via beta adjustment is problematic because of a lack of sufficient stability of beta coefficients.

Ignoring the issue of risk adjustment for equities, the return due to market timing for a portfolio made up entirely of some combination of equities and cash can easily be computed as the difference between the total portfolio return and the return of the equity segment. For example, if the equity segment return were 10 percent for a given time period, the assumption is made that if the entire portfolio had been invested in equities, then the total portfolio return would also have been 10 percent. If the total portfolio return were only 8 percent, this would indicate that the portfolio lost 2 percent (opportunity cost) by not being fully invested in equities. Thus, −2 percent is presumed to be the timing return.

Calculating the Timing Return. For balanced portfolios invested in some combination of fixed income and equity securities, the process is more difficult and a factor termed *benchmark allocation,* which is the "normal" allocation of equities and bonds, can be used. Those asset allocation percentages applied to the equity and bond segment returns give the return of the benchmark portfolio. The difference between the actual total return and the benchmark portfolio return is the timing return.

For example, assume the following:

- Benchmark portfolio (determined by client and based on objectives): equities 60%, bonds 40%
- Actual segment returns: equities 35%; bonds −4.0%
- Actual portfolio return: 21.8%

The timing return is computed in two steps:

1. Determine the benchmark portfolio return

Equities:	.6 × 35% =	21.0%
Bonds:	.4 × −4% =	−1.6
Benchmark portfolio return		19.4%

2. Determine the timing return

Actual portfolio return	21.8%
Less: Benchmark portfolio return	19.4
Timing return	2.4%

However, this process does not indicate whether the positive timing return was the result of good timing in the equity or the bond market.

Decomposition of Returns Approach

Before concluding this section on evaluation of performance, two integrated systems of performance attribution should be noted. The first, involving decomposition of portfolio returns, was suggested by Fama [1972]. As indicated in Figure 14-9 (page 646), he proposes that return can be attributed to (1) returns from the investor's targeted systematic risk level above the risk-free portfolio, (2) returns from the actual systematic risk the manager chose to take, and (3) returns from selectivity. The latter, in turn, are attributed to diversification, the additional return that would just compensate the investor for the diversifiable risk randomly assumed by the manager, and net selectivity, the actual results of (nonrandom) security selection compared to a naive portfolio at the chosen level of diversification.[13]

Analysis of Extra-market Risk Approach

The second is a system developed by Rosenberg, initially discussed in Chapter 10 and developed at length by Rudd and Clasing [1982]. Rosenberg subdivides a portfolio's total return into market risk, industry risk, and six fundamental measures of extra-market risk, as follows:

- Market variability
- Earnings variability
- Low market valuation and unsuccess
- Immaturity and smallness
- Growth orientation
- Financial risk

Extra-market risk arises from common factors of residual return. In this diagnostic system, one economic event might have a market-wide (system-

[13] Fama's methodology is more fully explained in Elton and Gruber [1981].

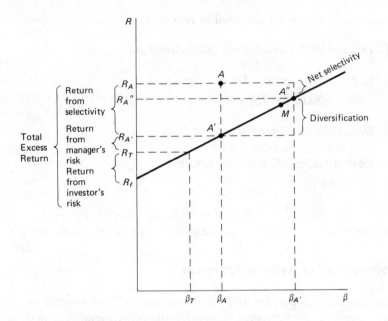

Key:

Part 1: Components of return from selectivity (all returns are excess returns)

$R_A - R_{A'}$ = Return from selectivity = Jensen differential return or Jensen measure of performance
    = Return from incurring diversifiable as well as systematic risk
    = Return from incurring the equivalent of $\beta_{A'}$ minus β_A of systematic risk

$R_{A''} - R_{A'}$ = Return from random non-diversification or from incomplete diversification but naive security selection
    = Return for randomly bearing unsystematic risk

$R_A - R_{A''}$ = Return from net selectivity
    = Return from incomplete diversification and deliberate security selection

Part 2: Components of return from (systematic) risk bearing

$R_{A'} - R_f$ = Return from bearing systematic risk level β_A

$R_T - R_f$ = Return from bearing systematic risk level β_T where β_T is investor's target risk level given to manager

$R_{A'} - R_T$ = Return from bearing systematic risk level β_A' chosen by manager, rather than target level β_T

Figure 14-9. Decomposition of Portfolio Return. (Source: Fama [1972])

atic) effect, another event might have an impact on all stocks with high financial risk (extra-market risk), and a third event might have an additional effect on a specific stock (such as to cause company bankruptcy). The system calculates the specific risk assumed by the manager. A portfolio's source of return can then be attributed to the following: (1) the risk-free return, (2) the level of systematic risk, (3) residual return from common extra-market factors, industry factors, and specific factors.[14]

[14] For a more detailed explanation of the Rosenberg methodology, see FRS Associates [1980] and Rudd and Clasing [1982].

Although both of the systems just described are fully integrated and theoretically appealing, they are subject to many of the empirical criticisms of the CAPM and test results using them are often difficult to interpret.

PROBLEMS WITH PERFORMANCE MEASUREMENT

Client Pressures

One of the major problems with performance measurement is that some investors (especially pension plan sponsors) tend to measure results too often and to make judgments based on a time frame that is too short to be a true measure of significantly good or poor portfolio management. While it is agreed that for accuracy of computations, performance should be computed as often as practical, results should not be taken as significant by the investor or the investment manager until a reasonable period of time—such as a market cycle for equities or an interest rate cycle for fixed income securities—has elapsed. The reasons why results may be random in short time frames have been enumerated previously.

It has been our experience that a plan sponsor often puts pressure on a portfolio manager because the portfolio's return is lower than other portfolios, especially in a comparative framework. At other times, the manager may perceive such pressure even if it does not exist. This may lead the manager to change management style or take more risk than he or she is comfortable with in order to catch up. Very often this leads to disastrous results; much more will be said about this in Chapter 15. Although it cannot be proven statistically, one of the reasons why some mutual funds outperform pension funds with similar goals and objectives is because the purchasers of mutual funds are less sophisticated and therefore have less influence over the activities of the portfolio manager.

Choice of Comparison Measures

A critical consideration in the area of portfolio performance evaluation is the choice of comparison measures. That is, as indicated earlier, the market indexes for comparison should be chosen carefully. Comparison of a manager's portfolio return to an inappropriate universe may result in a mistaken termination. For a number of years, the Standard & Poor's 500 Composite Stock Index has been generally accepted as the comparative index for institutional portfolios. This is the so-called Roll/Rosenberg controversy, which centers around the determination of an appropriate market index for performance evaluation. Since all portfolio characteristics (alpha, beta, standard error, and rho) are computed by a regression of portfolio returns against the market index, Roll's contention that the S&P 500 is not representative of the market is material. Also, in the regression technique, U.S. Treasury bills are generally used as the risk-free rate. Roll contends this is also inappropriate. For a more detailed discussion see Roll [1980, 1981].

Figure 14-10 depicts the importance of the choice of a market index in performance measurement. For illustrative purposes, the capital market line has been drawn from the return on Treasury bills to the return on both the NYSE Composite Index and the Wilshire 5000 Index. Both indexes are capitalization weighted. Portfolios plotted in the space between these lines would have a negative alpha (or unique return) using the NYSE Index as a market proxy and, simultaneously, a positive alpha compared to the Wilshire 5000.

Appropriate Risk-free Rate

To further complicate matters, the compounded 90-day Treasury bill rate may not be appropriate as a risk-free rate. In Figure 14-10, an ex post Treasury bill rate provides the basis for the capital market lines. In fact, the only risk-free investment available to the portfolio manager for the period January 1, 1977 to December 31, 1980 would have been a Treasury note or bond with a 4-year maturity and a return of 5.86 percent. This is the only ''riskless'' security with that particular maturity that could be bought and held to maturity with a relatively assured return. Since the portfolio manager is always measured after the fact over a time period beyond his control, the risk-free rate more likely plots out as a narrow ellipse lying along the vertical axis of a risk-return diagram like Figure 14-10 rather than just as a single point. The ellipse traces out the sharp fluctuations in return and the small but finite risk of the riskless asset. Thus, one can think of a whole series of capital market lines against which to measure performance.

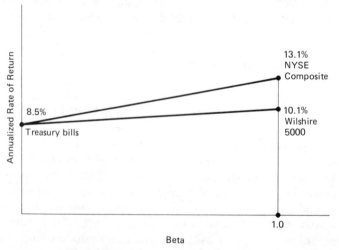

Figure 14-10. Capital Market Lines for the Period 1/1/77–12/31/80 Using Two Different Equity Market Indexes. (Source: Frank Russell Company)

Comparison with an Unweighted Index

Most measurement services use a market capitalization index against which to measure performance. This is normally appropriate for institutional portfolios where invested assets are in large amounts. However, a number of studies have shown that in various recent periods, smaller capitalization issues tended to outperform larger issues even on a risk-adjusted basis. Therefore, it may be more appropriate to compare the performance of a portfolio invested in emerging growth stocks against an unweighted index of small companies with large earnings growth over the last several years. Due to size limitations, it would be inappropriate to measure most institutional portfolios against such an index; but for small portfolios managed by small money management firms, an unweighted index may well be more appropriate.

Performance in Perspective

Finally, as one investor well put it, "You can't eat relative performance." For many investors, such as pension funds, performance has direct cash flow implications. Shortfalls from the actuarial return rate may require alternate funding, such as increased contributions from the pension sponsor. In the case of an endowment fund, such shortfalls may require the invasion of principal to meet current budget requirements or reductions in the budgeted disbursements themselves. Theoretical portfolio work has led many to define risk as variability of returns; however, many investors would agree that the more relevant risk is the probability that the portfolio will not achieve a stated rate of return objective—a concept introduced in Chapter 8.

An investor's primary objective should be to obtain a real return—one that maintains or increases the purchasing power of the portfolio relative to its funding requirements. In other words, the portfolio objective stated in nominal terms must incorporate current cash flow needs, an adjustment for current and prospective inflation, and, where applicable, a margin of safety for forecast errors. While this should be inherent in the asset allocation determination as discussed in Chapter 8, not enough attention has been paid to setting portfolio objectives in real return terms or measuring performance in those same terms.

Liabilities are funded and cash is disbursed in absolute, not relative, terms.[15] In essence, then, the most basic measure of portfolio performance is in absolute terms—the actual realized return for the time period involved measured against the portfolio's return objective. As stated above, this measurement primarily reflects the appropriateness of the asset allocation decision or how well the investor's needs have been integrated with expecta-

---

[15] For an interesting alternative approach to performance measurement, see Jeffrey [1977], in which it is argued that the ultimate test of investment expertise is the ability of the manager to produce a growing dividend/interest stream.

tional factors. Relative return performance is primarily a measure of the appropriateness of individual asset selection and weighting—portfolio construction within asset categories—as compared with an appropriate market or asset index or bogey.

SUMMARY

Writing this chapter has forced the authors to reflect on the process of performance measurement and portfolio analysis. As we have indicated, there are many pitfalls and unresolved issues. Experience has taught us that there are many decision makers who place great emphasis on the niceties of quantitatively defined results. Blind use of performance numbers can lead to erroneous conclusions and poor decisions. A whole industry has developed around ex post measurement. Given how it has sometimes been used by client-investors, we question whether it has really improved the return of the mutual fund investor or decreased the cost of providing pension benefits.

On the other hand, while a quantitatively based approach to performance evaluation has its shortcomings, the available alternatives are almost always worse. We believe that performance measurement, judiciously analyzed in conjunction with other factors, can aid the careful investor, showing him how the decision-making process may be improved through time.

FURTHER READING

Rate of Return Calculations
Time-weighted and dollar-weighted rate of return concepts are developed and explained in Dietz [1966a, 1966b] and Bank Administration Institute [1968].

Risk-Adjusted Performance Measures
There are many approaches to risk measurement and risk-adjusted performance. The seminal works are: Jensen [1968, 1969], Fama [1968], Sharpe [1966], and Treynor [1965].

Performance Attribution
Performance attribution (the analysis of performance) is becoming more important to pension plan sponsors. Academic work in this area has been sparse, with most methods developed commercially. Fama [1972] and Rosenberg [1978] deal with equity portfolios; Dietz, Fogler, and Hardy [1980] and Fong, Pearson, and Vasicek [1982] deal with fixed income performance attribution.

Critique of Generally Accepted Measurement Techniques
Current methods of portfolio measurement and risk adjustment are widely used in the investment industry. However, there are both practical and theoretical limitations to these methods. These are highlighted in the following references: Jeffrey [1977], Ferguson [1980], Roll [1980, 1981], and Stolte [1981].

BIBLIOGRAPHY

Arditti, Fred D., "Risk and the Required Rate of Return on Equity," *Journal of Finance*, March 1967.

Bank Administration Institute, *Measuring the Investment Performance of Pension Funds*, Park Ridge, Ill.: Bank Administration Institute, 1968.

Bower, Richard S., and Donald F. Wippern, "Risk-Return Measurement in Portfolio Selection and Performance Appraisal Models: Progress Report," *Journal of Financial and Quantitative Analysis*, December 1969.

Camp, Robert C., and Arthur A. Eubank, Jr., "The Beta Quotient: A New Measure of Portfolio Risk," *The Journal of Portfolio Management*, Summer 1981.

Carlson, Robert S., "Aggregate Performance of Mutual Funds, 1948–1967," *Journal of Financial and Quantitative Analysis*, March 1970.

Cohen, Kalman J., and Bruce P. Fitch, "The Average Investment Performance Index," *Management Science*, February 1966.

———, **and Jerry Pogue,** "Some Comments Concerning Mutual Fund Versus Random Portfolio Performance," *Journal of Business*, April 1968.

Cranshaw, T. E., "The Evaluation of Investment Performance," *Journal of Business*, October 1977.

Dietz, Peter O., "Pension Fund Investment Performance—What Method to Use When," *Financial Analysts Journal*, January/February 1966a.

———, *Pension Funds: Measuring Investment Performance*, New York: Free Press, 1966b.

———, "Components of a Measurement Model: Rate of Return, Risk and Timing," *Journal of Finance*, May 1968.

———, **H. Russell Fogler, and Donald J. Hardy,** "The Challenge of Analyzing Bond Portfolio Returns," *The Journal of Portfolio Management*, Spring 1980.

———, ———, **and Madelyn Smith,** "Factor Analysis of Manager Returns," unpublished working paper, 1982.

———, **and George P. Williams, Jr.,** "Influence of Pension Fund Asset Valuations on Rate of Return," *Financial Executive*, May 1970.

Elton, Edwin J., and Martin J. Gruber, *Modern Portfolio Theory and Investment Analysis*, New York: John Wiley, 1981.

Fama, Eugene, *Measuring the Performance of Pension Funds. A Supplement: Risk and the Evaluation of Pension Fund Performance*, Park Ridge, Ill.: Bank Administration Institute, 1968.

———, "Components of Investment Performance," *Journal of Finance*, June 1972.

———, "A Note on the Market Model and the Two-Parameter Model," *Journal of Finance*, December 1973.

Ferguson, Robert, "Performance Measurement Doesn't Make Sense," *Financial Analysts Journal*, May/June 1980.

Fong, Gifford, Charles Pearson, and Oldrich Vasicek, "Bond Performance Analysis," presented to the Institute of Quantitative Research in Finance, May 1982.

Fox, Edward A., "Comparing Performance of Equity Pension Trusts," *Financial Analysts Journal*, September/October 1968.

Friend, Irwin, and Marshall Blume, "Measurement of Portfolio Performance Under Uncertainty," *American Economic Review*, September 1970.

———, ———, **and Jean Crockett,** *Mutual Funds and Other Institutional Investors*, New York: McGraw-Hill, 1970.

———, and Douglas Vickers, "Portfolio Selection and Investment Performance," *Journal of Finance*, September 1965.

FRS Associates, *Pension Asset Management: The Corporate Decision*, New York: Financial Executives Research Foundation, 1980.

Gaumnitz, Jack E., "Appraising Performance of Investment Portfolios," *Journal of Finance*, June 1970.

Grant, Dwight, "Portfolio Performance and the 'Cost' of Timing Decisions," *Journal of Finance*, June 1977.

Gumpetz, Julian, and Evertee Page, "Misconceptions of Pension Fund Performance," *Financial Analysts Journal*, May/June 1970.

Horowitz, Ira, "The 'Reward-to-Variability' Ratio and Mutual Fund Performance," *Journal of Business*, October 1966.

Jeffrey, Robert H., "Internal Portfolio Growth: The Better Measure," *The Journal of Portfolio Management*, Summer 1977.

Jensen, C. Michael, "The Performance of Mutual Funds in the Period 1945-1964," *Journal of Finance*, May 1968.

———, "Risk, the Pricing of Capital Assets, and the Evaluation of Investment Portfolios," *Journal of Business*, April 1969.

———, "Capital Markets: Theory and Evidence," *Bell Journal of Economics and Management Science*, Autumn 1972.

Joy, Maurice, and Burr Porter, "Stochastic Dominance and Mutual Fund Performance," *Journal of Financial and Quantitative Analysis*, January 1974.

Klemkosky, Robert, "The Bias in Composite Performance Measures," *Journal of Financial and Quantitative Analysis*, June 1973.

———, "How Consistently Do Managers Manage," *The Journal of Portfolio Management*, Winter 1977.

Kon, Stanley, and Frank Jen, "Estimation of Time-Varying Systematic Risk and Performance for Mutual Fund Portfolios: An Application of Switching Regression," *Journal of Finance*, May 1978.

Lee, Cheng, and Frank Jen, "Effects of Measurement Errors on Systematic Risk and Performance Measure of a Portfolio," *Journal of Financial and Quantitative Analysis*, June 1978.

Levy, Haim, "Portfolio Performance and Investment Horizon," *Management Science*, August 1972.

Lintner, John, "Security Prices, Risk, and Maximal Gains from Diversification," *Journal of Finance*, December 1965.

Mains, Norman E., "Risk, the Pricing of Capital Assets, and the Evaluation of Investment Portfolios: Comment," *Journal of Business*, July 1977.

Markowitz, Harry, "Portfolio Selection," *Journal of Finance*, March 1952.

———, *Portfolio Selection: Efficient Diversification of Investments*, New York: John Wiley, 1959.

McDonald, John, "Objectives and Performance of Mutual Funds: 1960–1964," *Journal of Financial and Quantitative Analysis*, June 1974.

Mennis, Edmund A., "A New Method for Evaluating Pension Fund Portfolios," *The Journal of Portfolio Management*, Winter 1979.

Meyer, Jack, "Further Applications of Stochastic Dominance to Mutual Fund Performance," *Journal of Financial and Quantitative Analysis*, June 1977.

Mills, D. Harlan, "On the Measurement of Fund Performance," *Journal of Finance*, December 1970.

Mossin, Jan, "Equilibrium in a Capital Asset Market," *Econometrica*, October 1966.

Reilly, Frank K., *Investments,* Hinsdale, Ill.: Dryden Press, 1982.

Robinson, Randall S., "Measuring the Risk Dimension of Investment Performance," *Journal of Finance,* May 1970.

Roll, Richard, "Performance Evaluation and Benchmark Errors (I)," *The Journal of Portfolio Management,* Summer 1980.

————, "Performance Evaluation and Benchmark Errors (II)," *The Journal of Portfolio Management,* Winter 1981.

Rosenberg, Barr M., "Performance Measurement and Performance Attribution," Research Program in Finance, Working Paper #75, Berkeley, Calif.: University of California, May 1978.

————, "Bond Performance Measurement," presented to the Institute for Quantitative Research in Finance, April 1980.

Rudd, Andrew, and Henry K. Clasing, Jr., *Modern Portfolio Theory: The Principles of Investment Management,* Homewood, Ill.: Dow Jones-Irwin, 1982.

Sarnat, Marshall, "A Note on the Prediction of Portfolio Performance from Ex-Post Data," *Journal of Finance,* June 1972.

Sharpe, William F., "Capital Asset Prices: A Theory of Market Equilibrium Under Conditions of Risk," *Journal of Finance,* September 1964.

————, "Mutual Fund Performance," *Journal of Business,* January 1966.

————, "Reply to (West [1968])," *Journal of Business,* April 1968.

Smidt, Seymour, "Investment Horizons and Performance Measurement," *The Journal of Portfolio Management,* Winter 1978.

Smith, Keith V., and Dennis A. Tito, "Risk-Return Measures of Ex-Post Portfolio Performance," *Journal of Financial and Quantitative Analysis,* December 1969.

Stolte, Myron O., "Pension Plan Sponsors: Monitor Yourselves," *Harvard Business Review,* March/April 1981.

Treynor, Jack, "How to Rate Management of Investment Funds," *Harvard Business Review,* January/February 1965.

————, **and Kay K. Mazuy,** "Can Mutual Funds Outguess the Market?" *Harvard Business Review,* July/August 1966.

West, Richard, "Mutual Fund Performance and the Theory of Capital Asset Pricing: Some Comments," *Journal of Business,* April 1968.

Williamson, Peter, "Measurement and Forecasting of Mutual Fund Performance: Choosing an Investment Strategy," *Financial Analysts Journal,* November/December 1972.

CHAPTER **15**

Management Skills for Investment Managers

_____ *Daniel J. Forrestal, III, C.F.A.*

Portfolio management is a dynamic activity that combines knowledge, skill, and innovation to achieve certain objectives of asset management. Previous chapters have discussed various investment skills that are central to the portfolio management process.

The intent of this chapter is to shift the focus to identifying and discussing the managerial skills applicable to portfolio management, that is, to managing the investment management process. The definition of management as used here refers to activities and methods of making investment resources productive, of providing an environment in which creative professionals combine to do useful work that achieves the investment objectives of their clients. Success in this profession does not automatically flow to firms that assemble the best people or spend the most money. Something else seems to be at work in the good firms, and it is the identification and discussion of this set of factors that is the subject of this chapter. Managerial skills, as applied to portfolio management, are a critical consideration for any investment organization in which one or more people take the responsibility of directing the efforts of other investment professionals.

The discussion will approach specific managerial skill applications from two perspectives. First, the analysis will concentrate on observable skills that have been tested in actual practice by managers of successful portfolio firms. The approach will not be based on theoretical management models nor will it focus on inborn personality or behavior traits common to good investment leaders. Rather, the interest here is on some common management skills displayed by investment professionals who perform their jobs effectively. Skill is intended to imply an ability that can be identified, observed, and, most importantly, developed by the investment practitioner. The application of skills is manifested in the actual, not merely the potential, performance of an investment organization.

The second objective is to address unique environmental factors that affect the dynamics of portfolio management and examine how such factors impact the effective administration of the investment firm. Portfolio management, being a service activity dominated by interaction of creative people, resembles a number of other disciplines in the scope and substance of required managerial skills. What sets portfolio management apart, however, is its confrontation with a unique set of external factors that, in the absence of effective managerial action, can impose conflicting, destabilizing threats to the long-term perspective and effectiveness of the organization.

After setting a managerial perspective for skill requirements and operating environment, the discussion will focus on some common management strategies used in different degrees by successful firms to achieve desired results. In the profession of portfolio management, the ultimate test of effective management is the ability to make investment resources productive in the actual achievement of goals and expectations of the organization and its clients. The final sections will deal with specific issues encountered in the management of growth and organizational change, and with specific managerial strategies employed by two large firms to cope with these most important aspects of managing the portfolio management process.

COMMON MANAGEMENT SKILLS

In observing the activities of successful groups of investors, one can group effective management action into three basic categories of developable skills. The definitions and basic parameters for these categories were first described by Katz [1974].

Effective administration of portfolio management can be broken into three basic classifications of *conceptual, technical,* and *human* skills. Given the dynamics of the profession, it is unrealistic to assume that each category is practiced separately by successful investment firms. However, for the purpose of analysis, we shall address each skill category independently.

Conceptual Skills

Conceptual skills involve the ability to see how creative people, who are the essence of portfolio management, can blend together as an effective unit to add investment value and provide needed services to investment clients. There are two dimensions to effective implementation of conceptual skills. The first is the ability to step away from the daily activities of portfolio management, to appraise the business risks and opportunities of the enterprise from a long-term perspective, and to articulate goals and investment direction with precision and clarity.

The second element is to recognize how the various functions of the organization depend on each other to build and maintain an effective portfolio process. The good conceptual manager is sensitive to the priority and challenges of combining structure and creativity in a firm to achieve investment results, and how changes in one part of an organization can affect all the others. He or she is conscious of and responds effectively to the impact of growth and organizational change on the quality of execution of the firm's investment style.

Conceptual skills are of crucial importance to effective management throughout the life cycle of an asset management firm. These attitudes are a reflection of the administrator's leadership ability, that is, the way the administrator adjusts the direction and methods of his or her organization in response to growth, competitive development, and the changing needs of the marketplace.

Technical Skills

Of the three categories of management skills, technical skills are probably the most familiar subject of analysis because they are the most concrete and, given the trend toward specialization in portfolio management, are the skills required of the greatest number of people. Technical skill refers to an understanding of and proficiency in specialized activities that are a part of the portfolio management process. Technical skills involve specialized knowledge required for implementation of the specific investment style of a firm and facility in the application of this knowledge to client objectives.

Technical skills can be further broken down into two subgroups: *tactical* and *procedural*. Tactical skills refer to specific disciplines or divisions of labor that are part of the investment services offered by the firm. Examples of activities requiring tactical skill are formulation of investment policy, analytical research of investment securities, and portfolio construction in concert with client objectives.

Procedural skills refer to procedures and methods used by the firm to combine its tactical skills in a way that optimizes the talents of the firm and its professionals. Examples of procedural skill would be how to respond to a new analytical insight germane to a firm's prevailing investment strategy, or how to exploit a sudden price disparity in the marketplace that accommodates a specific portfolio objective.

Whereas tactical skills relate to *what* is done by the firm, procedural skills deal with *how* to do it. Procedural skills apply to the flow of production in portfolio management—from awareness and analysis of investment ideas to the execution of portfolio decisions. Within the arena of technical skills, management will likely devote increasing attention to procedural skills as the firm grows in size and complexity.

Human Skills

Technical skills are primarily concerned with the "things" of portfolio management: investment tasks, investment methods, and determining and satisfying client needs. Human skills, on the other hand, deal with understanding and motivating creative people as they relate to each other and the goals of the organization in the daily conduct of investment management. Human skills are demonstrated in two ways: in a manager's ability to work effectively as a team member in the portfolio process and in his or her ability to provide leadership in building cooperative effort from a group of subordinates. In both cases, effective action is manifested by providing and participating in an environment where creative people feel comfortable and are motivated to apply their talents to the stated goals of the organization.

Human skills imply an awareness by the manager of his or her own attitudes and personality characteristics and how these are perceived and interpreted by others in the organization. The manager must also be aware of the needs and motivations of others within the firm in order to judge the likely reactions to, and outcomes of, various courses of action being considered. Real skill in working with others is not a manufactured or occasional effort; it must be a continuous, natural activity not only at times of decision making but also in the day-to-day behavior of the manager.

Because of the dominant role played by people and the quality of their judgments in asset management, human skill application is of paramount importance for achieving success and continuity in portfolio management.

ENVIRONMENTAL AWARENESS

Portfolio management is a process of forming judgments on the investment worthiness of financial assets, as measured against client return expectations and risk tolerance. In daily application this is not a static activity, but rather a dynamic process in which creative people interact with each other to combine knowledge, skill, and innovation for the purpose of achieving certain objectives.

Effective management of any endeavor requires environmental awareness, or an understanding of the climate in which the business or activity combines resources to add value and satisfy customer needs. This takes on profound significance in the conduct of the portfolio process and in the proper application of conceptual, technical, and human managerial skills. Unless these factors are understood and controlled properly, the series of environmental factors that are constantly at work can frustrate or even destroy the basic mission of portfolio management.

Contrary Judgment

The effectiveness of portfolio management rests on the quality of human judgments about future uncertain outcomes. This, in turn, depends directly on the ability of the practitioner to engage in independent, unemotional thinking, to apply skill and knowledge in a disciplined, consistent manner, and to form judgments with conviction and long-term perspective. More specifically, portfolio management favors the disciplined individual who is comfortable in becoming detached from consensus thinking, searches out undiscovered value, and makes contrary bets based on sound, informed analysis.

In providing direction to such a process, the investment leader must recognize that this facility for detached, unemotional judgments runs counter to a basic psychological human need for acceptance and recognition by one's peers and associates. Portfolio management is unique among major disciplines in that the elements for successful execution of the process are in basic conflict with fundamental human tendencies to seek conformity and acceptance by other people.

Effective managerial response to this conflict in values is complicated by several external factors that impact on investment people in the daily application of their skills. The daily pricing of securities, the growing volatility of investment markets, and the short-term performance orientation of many of its participants lead to a confrontation of time horizons in the strategic decision making of many investors. Due either to self-imposed or client pressures, investment firms may find themselves in the perverse position of being long-term investors, subject to short-term performance measurement.

Portfolio management is characterized by a high ease of entry by new organizations, above-average mobility of clients, and effective marketing skills from a variety of competitive products and services. These factors can exert subconscious but powerful pressure on professionals for short-term deviations from sound investment principles and/or the stated goals of the organization. The temptation for reactive, ill-founded decisions is often greatest at just the time when perseverance to stated objectives is most needed—that is, when short-term investment performance is faring poorly.

A disciplined long-term perspective is also threatened by the pace of change and instant communication of massive amounts of information that characterize the industry. Management must recognize that the basic human response when subjected to a constant barrage of new information is to react to short-term events rather than long-term logic.

Gut Feelings and Emotional Excesses

The major threats to integrity of the portfolio process stemming from this combination of pressures are twofold. First, investment staff will be tempted to engage in erratic, "gut feel" decisions that are at variance to the stated investment philosophy and style of the organization. The tendency toward such actions will likely be strongest when short-term investment performance is faring poorly or when the firm's philosophy is out of phase with popular investment concepts of the day.

Second, the temptation to find the comfort of consensus judgment often leads to emotional excesses and periods of exaggerated trends in the valuation of securities or entire market sectors. This danger is at its greatest when groups or committees of investors with similar philosophical biases converge to make unified investment judgments. The more cohesive the decision-making group, the more the members respect each other and are attached to each other's thinking, the more likely are concurrence-seeking tendencies that will result in following the prevailing consensus. Under the strain of short-term external pressures unique to their profession, the temptation for professional portfolio managers to follow the crowd can be overwhelming.

Investment professionals appear especially susceptible to the danger of what was described as *groupthink* by Janis [1972]. As Janis put it, "The most frequent behavior of individuals in groups is to show instances of mindless conformity and collective misjudgment of serious risks which are collectively laughed off in a clubby atmosphere of relaxed conviviality." Groupthink helps explain the recurring theme of investment professionals liquidating securities rapidly at market bottoms, even when their valuation methods indicate prices are at very attractive levels; or why favorite institutional stocks usually do worse than the overall market; or, of major significance to management, why a large percentage of professional portfolio firms seem unable to outperform an index of unmanaged investments.

The issue of environmental awareness is critical to the successful management of portfolio activities. The administrator must understand the impact of operating climate on the portfolio methods, internal dynamics, and investment mission of his or her firm. Only then can managerial strategies be developed that lead to productive effort and combat external pressures inherent in the portfolio process.

EFFECTIVE SKILL APPLICATION

The discussion now proceeds from defining skills and environmental setting to observation of how successful groups of investors combine these elements to cause effective action. Attention will focus on observable patterns of success in applying the dynamics of portfolio management to the investment expectations of the client, and hence to the profit and personal reward expectations of the firm, its owners, and its employees. To simplify the analysis, the approach will address each of the managerial skill areas separately, although again it is stressed that actual application of these skills is a dynamic, coordinated process customized to prevailing needs for making resources productive and managing for results, not potential.

Conceptual Skills

The successful conceptual manager demonstrates his or her skills by employing some combination of three special abilities:

1. An unusual ability to perceive the essential attributes of successful investing and transmit these standards to professionals.
2. An ability to step away from the dynamics of the portfolio process and visualize the potentials of his or her resources from a business perspective; and to be opportunistic in responding to market needs and creating investment services that add value and can be effectively delivered.
3. A talent to combine the potentially conflicting elements of structure and creativity within the portfolio process. This is normally due to deliberate managerial effort, and is often accomplished in the face of substantial growth in assets under management.

Investment Direction. Possibly the most important conceptual skill is the recognition and communication of the true essentials of achieving superior investment results. The process begins with a strong personal conviction in a particular style of investing by the founder or group of senior professionals leading the organization. Successful investors transmit tremendous enthusiasm and self-confidence toward the destiny of their investment style which is often contagious to those around them.

Good investment people understand the necessity of patience and staying power for their philosophy to succeed. They also understand that knowledge and hard work lead to conviction, perseverance, and the strength to withstand the pressures of the environment. The more knowledge and fundamental analysis one applies to a portfolio process, the less likely one will be to rely on gut feel or intuitive judgments. In fact, many successful investors depend on the weakness of others, manifested in the crowd behavior and exaggerated trends of security prices, to effectively and unemotionally apply their particular philosophy.

Good conceptual investors know their weaknesses as well as their strengths. They are honest with themselves, their clients, and their associates. Good investors know what they can do well and what they cannot do well, and they are good at communicating these values both to people inside and outside their organizations. The successful portfolio management firms are those that develop and stay with a particular style of investing, with the foreknowledge that they will periodically be out of phase with the investment markets and with their competitors.

Investment Philosophy. Consequently, in the formative stage of a firm, a fundamental first question to be answered is, "What part of the investment business do we want to be in and how can we provide added value?" Even the smallest of firms should answer this question as precisely as possible. Management should establish broad, simple statements outlining the values they intend to offer to clients and where the firm wants to position itself relative to its competitors. The perspective should be long term and permanent in scope, focusing on issues of investment style and policy rather than on shorter term strategies the firm might apply to adapt its philosophy to current market conditions.

The recognition of and response to intermediate and shorter term events is of critical importance to effecting a dynamic, responsive portfolio process. However, these types of inputs lose relevance or become destructive to successful investment management if they are not applied within a permanent framework of investment direction.

By articulating its investment philosophy, senior management sets a foundation to the internal purpose and dynamics of daily portfolio functions. A well-developed philosophy provides an identity for the firm as it communicates its role to clients and prospects. It provides direction and a strong sense of motivation to the firm's professional staff. Finally, it offers added protection and encouragement to withstand the pressures of external environmental factors and the related tendencies to deviate from a disciplined predetermined investment style.

Work Environment. Another common characteristic of successful firms is their ability to perceive the importance of maintaining an internal work environment conducive to the achievement of superior investment results. The leaders of these organizations seem to be managers who see their jobs as managing innovation and consciously providing an environment that seeks out and rewards creative effort. These organizations are aware of the importance of managing time as well as knowledge in portfolio management, and thus put special emphasis on establishing methods and procedures that allow investment ideas to flow quickly, freely, and boldly into portfolio decisions.

Specialization. Drucker [1980] has said that when a company permits itself to become marginal, it is on its way to destruction. This seems particularly relevant to the portfolio management profession. The successful firms are usually market leaders or occupy a special market niche with their investment approach. Often the firm has targeted one central business value or investment concept and has committed the organization to performing this one function extremely well. There is a continual development, refinement, and perfection of the organization's basic strengths.

Coping with Growth. Growth can have a corrosive, sometimes devastating impact on the creative energies of investment firms. (There will be specific discussion of the challenges of managing growth and organizational change in the next segment of the chapter.) Successful firms seem to cope well with this problem, retaining their innovative and entrepreneurial spirit despite significant increases in their asset base. Managements of such firms usually anticipate and plan for growth and know the size that can be attained without sacrificing quality or competence. Special attention is placed on the issue of refining and improving investment methods and decision flow, allowing ideas to flourish into effective value-adding investment decisions.

Adding Value. Successful managers recognize the importance of profitability and direct the firm with a professional business perspective. As a strategy for ensuring product quality and the ability to attract creative talent, management makes deliberate efforts to position the firm as a provider of high value-added services to its clients. Decisions on resource allocation are client driven, not product or marketing driven. Successful firms generally avoid lower fee services, preferring to capitalize on the willingness of portfolio management clients to pay a premium fee for a superior product that truly adds investment value.

Creativity. Many effective investment leaders pursue a business strategy of creating new investment products and services that respond to market needs and offer the opportunity for providing quality, proprietary investment expertise. Conversely, less time is spent on harnessing internal resources to generate above-average investment results from traditional portfolio services. An emphasis on product and service innovation and intensive client service finds a warm response in a marketplace that is increasingly receptive to new solutions for satisfying investment needs.

Personnel Policies. Conceptual managers recognize the paramount importance to the organization of selecting and retaining superior professionals. As part of this effort, successful firms recognize the leverage of high productivity and structural leanness to ensure product quality, enhance creativity, and motivate professionals. Good firms err on the side of quality rather than quantity of their investment staff. A highly productive, lean organization of superior individuals has the greatest odds of generating high, sustainable levels of profitability from portfolio management activities. Equally important to motivating its people, such firms offer professionals a better chance for involvement in key investment decisions, as well as retaining a stimulating, creative working environment.

Creative people, if properly motivated and involved in key decisions, have more fun being overworked than being underworked. This is one of the reasons why outstanding service organizations seem to operate at about twice the productivity rate of their average competitors. An investment firm can receive incredibly powerful leverage, for both performance and profitability, from well-utilized, well-motivated investment talent. The successful firms recognize this and seem to allocate man-hours more efficiently and generally work "smarter" than their competitors.

Directional Assessment. Conceptual skills imply formal and periodic reassessment of the firm's direction and internal effectiveness in executing its stated investment philosophy. Management must engage in a rigorous analysis of quality control, with attention to the question: "Do we as a firm do what we say we do?" This is a critical issue for maintaining the consistency and performance of the firm's investment approach, and for preventing adverse short-term deviations from longer term goals and objectives. As part of this analysis, management should review its own record at reinforcing the values and disciplines of its investment approach, particularly during periods of high emotional stress or adverse investment performance.

A unique element confronting portfolio managers is the constant series of temptations to divert attention away from the larger decisions that truly impact investment performance. The psychological comfort of making smaller, daily decisions, or the nonpostponable nature of solving sudden crises, takes time away from the significant policy or strategy issues that comprise the essence of investment management.

Investment leaders must recognize that they can unconsciously succumb to the same type of deviations concerning their role of reinforcing the direction of the organization. It is a natural human reaction to seek diversions or ignore problems when a commitment to a specific course of action seems to be going astray temporarily. However, this is precisely the time when practitioners and clients of portfolio management need reinforcement that an organization is committed to its stated investment style.

Communication. Management must recognize this fact and make a special effort to communicate the firm's goals and objectives during periods of performance shortfall. For some organizations, the need for policy reinforcement may be just as great when things are going well, when performance momentum is strong and staff morale is particularly high. This might be an excellent time to remind both clients and staff of the longer term objectives of the firm's investment style and of the possible unsustainability of recent results.

Management may want to consider periodic meetings of its senior people away from the offices, possibly joined by outside board members or other qualified advisors, to discuss the firm's destiny in an informal, uninterrupted forum. The important issue is to address the questions of investment direction and organizational purpose regularly, formally, and objectively. Major points of discussion would include:

1. Is our stated investment philosophy being implemented in the portfolios under our management? Are we being honest with ourselves and our clients in the actual execution of our firm's investment style?
2. Have we been effective in communicating the direction of the firm to our people, our clients, and our prospective clients? Do we explain ourselves as clearly and simply as possible?
3. Do we retain the capability to perform our particular investment services extremely well?
4. Do our services satisfy real investment needs of our clients? Are we truly client driven rather than product driven?

Style Effectiveness. As part of its review process management should continually monitor the responsiveness and efficiency of its portfolio methods. Is the organization retaining its creative spirit and ability to respond to change? Is it still structured to capitalize on opportunities? Are the creative professionals truly involved with the investment process? Are the long-term disciplines of its portfolio style, so essential to achieving investment success, being retained? These questions become particularly important as the firm becomes larger or adds additional portfolio services. Management must recognize and initiate any required changes in procedures and methods necessary to maintain effective coordination of the firm's resources.

The explicit purpose and long-term direction of the firm should be reviewed periodically to ensure its vitality and the competitiveness of services offered. Management should reaffirm its commitment to its investment philosophy and objectively analyze the merits of its strategies to attain stated goals in light of prevailing competitive conditions. To maintain structural soundness, management should be willing to abandon unproductive or unprofitable services and concentrate its creative resources in areas where the firm can become a market leader and retain a reputation of providing value-added services to its clients.

Conceptual skills represent the unifying, coordinating ingredient to defining and controlling the basic direction and purpose of portfolio management. These skills are of undeniable overall importance in making investment resources productive.

Technical Skills

Technical skills involve the application of specialized knowledge to achieve the stated goals and directions of the firm. They are a natural extension of investment style or philosophy, and as such depend on identification and understanding of this philosophy by the firm's professionals. Technical skills extend beyond the execution of specialized tasks to embrace the methods and procedures employed to unite these tasks into an efficient, dynamic portfolio process. Technical skill is demonstrated by a firm in two ways: its proficiency in tactical skills—or *what* is to be done to achieve stated goals and objectives—and the efficiency of its procedural skills—or *how* resources and tasks are combined to achieve productive effort.

Tactical Skills. Tactical skills refer to specific disciplines or tasks to which resources are allocated to enable an organization to accomplish its stated purpose. The composition and relative importance of tactical skills relate directly to the investment vehicles and management style contained in the portfolio services offered by a firm. Tactical skill can be limited to the specialized activities required in traditional portfolio services, such as the management of stocks and bonds, or be applied to more specialized functions such as the management of real estate, oil and gas, or venture capital.

Management must carefully appraise the tactical skills required to build and maintain a leadership position in its chosen field of portfolio services. The skills associated with traditional active management of stocks and bonds may not apply to every firm's specific investment direction. Obvious examples would be investment groups committed to real estate management or common stock management based exclusively on quantitative methods or modern portfolio theory. In both cases, tactical proficiency in fundamental equity research would be of much less value to the portfolio management process, and these firms would have to build specialized types of expertise unique to their needs. Identification of tactical skill requirements is a highly customized managerial decision. Apart from the issue of unnecessary costs stemming from superfluous staff, poorly conceived job descriptions usually lead to unproductive or inconsistent activities somewhere within the organization, activities that sap the creative energies and the operating effectiveness of a firm's investment process.

The Core of Tactical Skills. While identification and development of tactical skills is customized to organizational needs, there is a basic core of tactical abilities that apply to virtually every portfolio endeavor. These are different and specific disciplines, although their daily application becomes intertwined and difficult to isolate as proficiency builds and applications become routine. In smaller firms it is not uncommon for all of these tactical abilities to be practiced by each member of the organization. Nonetheless, management should carefully examine the talents and accountabilities of the firm's investment staff to ensure that the following core of basic tactical abilities is properly addressed and controlled:

1. STRATEGY FORMULATION. The determination of key strategies or investment themes to be used in portfolios to maximize the effectiveness of the firm's investment philosophy and to optimize investment policy based on the investor's objectives and constraints.
2. ANALYTICAL RESEARCH. The evaluation of return and risk characteristics of individual assets and groups of assets to determine their attractiveness within the framework of the firm's investment philosophy and prevailing investment strategy.
3. PORTFOLIO CONSTRUCTION. The decisions concerning asset allocation and the actual selection, timing, and weighting of individual investments in portfolios.
4. EXECUTION. The step that actually carries out the implementation phase of the portfolio process via the trading desk function.
5. MONITORING AND REVISION. The ongoing, continuous process of monitoring investor needs, capital market conditions, and individual asset attractiveness, and of implementing changes that are required to restore portfolio optimality.

The formulation of strategy is of special significance to the portfolio management process. It represents the attempt to interject responsiveness and shorter term market relevance into the firm's investment style, which is properly defined as a more permanent, longer term perspective. Strategic decisions translate investment philosophy to specific portfolio recommendations, or investment themes, that can be applied throughout an organization to achieve distinctive, superior investment results. The design, communication, and firm-wide implementation of selected investment themes strongly imply that there is merit to a consistent application of individual style by all of a team's professionals. An even more basic premise is that the internal resources of a firm can be harnessed to make judgments that, indeed, add value within the guidelines of its investment philosophy.

Strategy vs. Execution. Strategic abilities add creativity and a shorter term currency to investment style. However, management must recognize the limitations of strategic decisions as applied to the dynamics of daily portfolio judgments. In addition to direction received from the firm's investment philosophy and prevailing investment strategy, there is a third layer of inputs which impact the actual construction of portfolios by a member of the organization. These are the nuances of *market feel,* or the sensitivities developed through experience for capitalizing on opportunities provided by random price disparities, the actions of other investors, and other events that occur in the daily pricing of securities.

These types of factors, if effectively controlled, can add significant value to a creative, dynamic portfolio process. By definition, sudden price disparities or the purchase and sale intentions of other investors occur randomly and with little or no advance notice. Hence, the value-added opportunities contained in such factors are beyond the control of a centralized investment strategy function, particularly if this function is providing direction to a number of portfolio managers.

It is for this reason that strategic inputs should normally be confined to aggregate terms of portfolio construction (such as asset allocation, recommended emphasis in various maturity segments of fixed income investments, or industry or market sector equity exposure). Attempts to carry strategic decisions down to security selection and timing will normally lead to a ponderous, unresponsive portfolio process with predictably negative impact on investment performance.

Balancing Structure and Creativity. A well-constructed system for bridging strategy inputs with selection and timing decisions for security selections provides a healthy balance between structure and creativity in the portfolio process. Uniform execution of major strategies offers an essential degree of consistency and organizational identity to all portfolios under management. At the same time, strategy can be designed to enable individual team members to apply their creative talents to the flow of ideas and opportunities that occur randomly but cannot be controlled from a centralized strategy committee.

One way to accomplish this is to confine strategy decisions to key basic parameters such as asset allocation percentages, cash reserve position, market sectors, or industry weightings. Given the dynamics of investing, management should guard against preconditioning its staff to any fixed classification of assets when considering changes in strategy. Rather, strategic investment themes could be defined to embrace any fundamental or valuation criteria applicable to a group of investments that, when included in or excluded from portfolios, is expected to have a major impact on achieving superior results. Given this type of direction, the timing and selection of issues used to reflect prevailing strategies would be the responsibility of individual portfolio managers and traders. The universe of eligible issues could be controlled in some fashion, such as through the use of an approved list, but the final decisions on purchase and sale would be determined by the translation of strategy to client objectives and prevailing market conditions.

This combination of strategic investment themes and individual portfolio judgment provides a centralized direction to the investment process, while retaining the creative advantages of personal involvement and real world sensitivity to client objectives and prevailing market conditions. This approach will inevitably lead to some dispersion in investment results within the firm. While this dispersion must be continually monitored and controlled within some acceptable range, a small potential variance in performance may be a price worth paying if the offsetting advantage is retaining the dynamic, creative spirit so critical to the achievement of superior long-term investment results.

Strategy Formulation. The tactical skill of investment strategy formulation should be established as one of the critical functions of the organization and the professionals it assigns to this task. The strategy unit should have a bias toward action and recognize the dynamic, ongoing nature of its responsibilities. Consideration of strategic changes does not lend itself to a predetermined schedule but, rather, should be taken up whenever dictated by changes in valuation, fundamentals, or other relevant factors. The strategy unit should take special care to ensure the integrity of the firm's commitment to its specific investment style and not allow its strategy recommendations to contradict or dilute its stated investment philosophy.

Management should reinforce the priority for consistent, uniform execution of strategy by portfolio managers with appropriate adjustments to accommodate specific client needs. The best designed strategy is of little value if it does not find its way into portfolios. Procedures should be implemented for ensuring timely, effective communication of strategic themes throughout the firm and for reviewing conformity to these themes by all portfolio managers.

Portfolio Construction. The tactical skill of portfolio construction is demonstrated in two ways. First, the portfolio manager is responsible for translating the firm's philosophy, strategies, and research judgments into actual portfolio formation. The manager accomplishes this task by applying specialized knowledge of the investment markets to the selection, timing, and weighting of individual investments.

The manager's second role is to customize and adapt firm-wide policies and strategies to the specific needs of the clients. Only the portfolio manager in the field can seek out, update, and respond to the needs of individual clients in the execution of the organization's portfolio services. A precise understanding of return expectations and risk tolerances does not come easily. The first step in understanding objectives is for the portfolio manager to truly care about the client, to take the time to ask and listen, and to recognize that objectives will differ, despite initial appearances or pretenses of similarity. A second important factor to recognize is that, contrary to the ever-changing dynamics of portfolio management, client objectives tend to be relatively static once they are honestly communicated by the client.

A possible reason for the apparent difficulty experienced by many portfolio managers in the objective-setting process is this potential clash between the permanency and stability of client needs and the dynamic and psychological pressures of portfolio management. Effective portfolio construction implies the ability to recognize this conflict, to overcome it, and to seek out individual client needs in a caring and personalized manner.

Tactical Skills Delegation. As it considers the merits of specialization and delegation of tactical skills, management must balance the potential advantages against the risks of reducing the coordination and responsiveness of its investment efforts. When practiced effectively by a group of investors, portfolio management is a finely tuned dynamic process that can deteriorate quickly in the absence of a clear understanding of respective roles and responsibilities. The ability to respond to change and to implement decisions quickly can erode as the decision process adds new components. In approaching tactical skill delegation, investment leaders should pay special attention to several key factors to preventing organizational decay:

1. Assignment of activities should optimize the special talents of everyone in the organization. Their specific contribution to the total effort should be understood and properly recognized in the attainment of the firm's investment objectives. There must be a continued effort to know what everybody is doing and why.
2. Management should specifically address the subject of building and maintaining an effective communications network throughout the organization. It should work to build an environment that encourages frequent, random, informal expression—a talking and listening to each other.
3. Senior management must stay involved with the investment process. While some delegation of tactical skill is proper and perhaps necessary as the firm grows larger, management must stay attuned to changing events that pertain to the organization's investment style. Information on both the external and internal investment environment must stay fresh and current for management to provide effective, credible leadership.

Procedural Skills. Procedural skills shift management attention from what should be done, or tactical abilities, to how these abilities are unified to create maximum effectiveness in delivering value-added portfolio services. Procedural skills are dedicated to determining the best way to get things accomplished and making this process of "doing" a matter of routine. Procedural skills deal with processes and methods or, more specifically, with the internal organization of the firm and its resources. They are demonstrated by how decisions are actually made, and by what methods are used to transfer knowledge and ideas that originate in various tactical skill areas into productive portfolio action. Finally, procedural skills imply quality control—the ability to assess, and adjust when necessary, the methods actually used by team members in executing the portfolio process.

Organizational Effectiveness. The organization of a firm should be deliberately structured to accommodate early recognition of change, creative analytical insights, and prompt implementation of portfolio decisions that respond to opportunities as they occur. Effective procedural skills are particularly challenging to large organizations where many professionals impact the decision process. The issues of creativity and responsiveness seem more difficult as jobs become more specialized and the total portfolio process becomes more diffused. Organizational inertia is a major problem in larger firms. The path of least resistance often is to do nothing or to continue doing what has been done even after conditions change.

A precise, formal specification of portfolio methods is complicated by the fact that portfolio decisions are often not made the way the policy manual or organization chart says they are. This stems from the creative, dynamic nature of the portfolio process. Williams [1980], for example, addressed the problems of traditional organizational structure in achieving investment success.

TOP-DOWN APPROACH. The multilayered, hierarchical, *top-down* organization can be detrimental to new ideas and insights because it places too much emphasis on a few at the top and provides too little motivation to the people at the bottom. Good investment ideas come from all sources, and at times the most junior analyst may have better insights than the most senior investment officer. In addition, reserving all responsibility for key decisions to one or just a few people works against early recognition of change. This is true because individual investors or portfolio managers are prone to biases that develop out of their most recent successes. Only the multiple perspectives of a variety of people, operating with many viewpoints in an environment that encourages the expression of ideas, can overcome this problem and pick up the weak signals that are the first indication of significant change.

BOTTOM-UP APPROACH. On the other hand, the traditional, democratic, *bottom-up* approach also has organizational shortcomings for effective portfolio management. In firms where all members share major decision making with equal voice and vote, it is often too late to respond to an opportunity by the time everyone in the organization agrees on a course of action. In addition, the dynamics of the portfolio process seldom yield investment decisions that are answered with a simple yes or no. If implementation of new ideas must wait for a broad consensus to form, the result will usually be paralysis—an inability to translate ideas into effective portfolio action.

Informal Structures. There is an alternative to organizational design for a large portfolio firm. The starting point is to observe and copy the best features of portfolio management as practiced in smaller, informal firms. Management explicitly recognizes that in portfolio management, as in most creative group endeavors, many decisions are made informally; if formal structure exists, it is frequently ignored. Management in the large, informal organization deliberately attempts to combine the advantages of large-firm ample resources and information flow with the creative, entrepreneurial spirit normally associated with smaller investment entities.

LATERAL ORGANIZATIONAL DESIGN. Successful implementation of an informal operating structure involves two key elements. First, the organization is deliberately designed and communicated (borrowing from the literature of business organizational behavior) as lateral or horizontal, i.e., antihierarchical. It would be characterized by open communication that cuts across the usual hierarchical lines. Within the process of making portfolio decisions, organizational status or title would be no measure of the value of an individual's opinions, observations, or ideas.

MATRIX MANAGEMENT APPROACH. Secondly, the informal organization is—again using the words of management science—a matrix. Each person has more than one investment task to perform. The individual does not just stay in a single box on the organizational chart, practicing one tactical skill.

It is important to note that the informal lateral-matrix organization is the result of specific managerial action, is often seen in large firms, and is not the by-product of financial or other organizational limitations. It is rather a specific offensive strategy designed to stimulate creativity and responsiveness in the portfolio management process.

The objective of the lateral-matrix organization is to enable investment professionals to cut across the classical distinctions between security analysts, portfolio managers, and investment policy committee members. The organization thus becomes a matrix in that all of its professionals are encouraged to cross over rigid reporting channels and take an active role in creating strategic and individual selection ideas which become part of the firm's overall investment policy. It is lateral in that final portfolio construction is dispersed horizontally, with the portfolio manager responsible for implementing the strategy he or she personally has helped to forge, within the confines of individual client objectives and firm style.

Assigning people to their proper roles within an informal organization structure can be a difficult process, subject to possible trial and error. In addition, establishment of proper accountabilities can be a problem for management. Because productive portfolio decisions are seldom the result of one precise judgment by only one person within an informal organization, it may be difficult to properly reward the truly deserving individuals. The best solution for management in both of these situations is to be involved, observant, and unbiased when approaching its investment process. Given the dynamics of portfolio management, there is a special need for ongoing surveillance of internal methods in informal organizations. Experimentation and change are often necessary to fit people into the roles that are right both for them and for the firm as a whole.

Quality Control. Given the dynamics of the portfolio process, it is often difficult to evaluate the effectiveness of internal skills and methods without giving undue emphasis to recent success or failure in achieving desired performance goals. Nonetheless, management must recognize the urgency of maintaining freshness and vitality within the daily activities of the firm. Even in the best managed investment entities, the dynamics of translating ideas to action within a specific long-term focus is constantly subjected to subtle but powerful threats of erosion. Management must counter this potential problem of organizational slippage by specifically addressing the quality control of the firm's portfolio process, as manifested by its observable patterns of execution in all important tactical and procedural skill areas.

While relevant measures of control will vary from firm to firm, some common checkpoints applicable to most portfolio endeavors deserve attention by management. As discussed earlier, the really important investment decisions have a tendency to be postponed, particularly against the time pressures of daily events and problems that appear to need immediate solutions. Given the daily confrontations of new information and price changes inherent in the business, certain staff members appear to work at a feverish pace, often with a strong personal sense of accomplishment, but they avoid critical decisions that will truly impact the value added to clients. Management must also be sensitive to tendencies of team members to "wing it"—to approach major decisions without appropriate analysis. This problem is more likely in times of performance shortfall, or after an individual has served in one role for a considerable period. Knowledge and analysis lead to conviction, patience, and staying power, all of which are essential to consistent execution of investment style.

OVERMANAGING PORTFOLIOS. Again, and particularly in volatile market environments, management must guard against tendencies to overmanage portfolios. Often the best strategy during turbulent markets is to do nothing. Management should use such periods to reaffirm the firm's values and priorities and stress the merits of capitalizing on distressed valuations for enhancing the long-term effectiveness of its stated philosophy. There is a subconscious tendency for portfolio people to become internalized and risk averse just when values are most attractive and opportunities most plentiful. The reverse occurs in favorable market environments; aggressiveness builds and pressures develop for adding new products, new investment ideas, and a few selected exceptions to the investment direction of the firm. Management must be sensitive to such pressures and offer offsetting encouragement for stimulating creativity during adverse periods and emphasizing control and discipline during favorable markets.

DISCARDING GOOD IDEAS. There are several additional monitoring points especially appropriate for quality control within larger organizations. As growth occurs, management must evaluate the effectiveness and job satisfaction of individuals assigned specific tasks in the firm. If a valued employee loses effectiveness in a specific assignment, can his or her talents be employed better elsewhere in the process? One signal for the need to change procedural skills is the incidence of greater instances of good ideas not finding their way into portfolios. Is the process too complex? Has it lost its effectiveness due to additions to staff? Are we attempting to command too much of the portfolio effort from a centralized level? Are persons in control too rigid and unyielding to new ideas?

PORTFOLIO CHOICES WITHOUT CONVICTION. Two signs of lack of conviction by portfolio managers in the quality of their decisions are an acceleration in asset turnover and an increase in the number of issues in portfolios. Management should determine if such factors are symptoms of more significant potential problems, such as diffusion of effort to peripheral activities or a lack of confidence in the strategic and research inputs that affect portfolio construction.

EMPLOYING EXCESSIVE INPUTS. Management should make a special effort to control the quantity and quality of external information impacting the portfolio process. The profession is subjected to a massive array of inputs, some of which are totally irrelevant to the investment style of the organization. Investment leaders should address this problem directly and attempt to limit both the volume and content of information to that which is germane to its specific philosophy and strategies.

Human Skills

Whereas technical skills are primarily concerned with the "things" of portfolio management (investment tasks and processes), human skills deal with working with people. Human skill is the manager's ability to work effectively as a group member and his or her ability to provide leadership in building cooperative effort from a group of subordinates. As applied to portfolio management, human skill is the ability to provide and participate in an environment where creative people can do productive investment work.

Considering the dominant role played by people and the quality of their judgments in the portfolio firm, human skill application is of paramount importance for achieving managerial success.

Managing Creative Professionals. The portfolio management profession attracts a group of people as creative, energetic, and interesting as can be found anywhere. The business needs this type of person to execute effectively, but must work hard to provide an environment that both stimulates and controls its internal resources. This requires an action orientation by management, a willingness to stay involved in the investment process, a willingness to listen to others in the firm, and a willingness to implement action that is designed to maintain creativity within some sense of structured, coordinated environment.

Successful firms seem to blend a consistent, stated investment direction that is understood by their people with an atmosphere of challenge and excitement. They provide warmth, friendship, and often a refreshing sense of humor and humility that encourage expression of ideas and innovative thinking. Good people seem to be drawn to investment firms having a sound sense of purpose and direction. Conversely, creative people are dissuaded by a sense of regimentation and routine or a lack of inquisitive or curious minds to interact with.

CAREFUL PERSONNEL SELECTION. Successful firms also set extremely high standards in selecting individuals to join their team. The long-term economics and value added by such an approach are compelling, since above-average people have unusually high productivity potential for portfolio management. Conversely, unproductive people can have a disproportionately negative impact on the dynamics and creative energies of other team members. Management must pay special attention to the quality of compatibility. Does the new employee understand and personally believe in the investment style of the firm? Is there strong confidence that this individual can identify and really care about what the firm is doing? Incompatibility within a portfolio team can be particularly disruptive to the internal efficiencies needed for investment success.

BEHAVIORAL SENSITIVITY. Human skill requires an awareness by the manager of his or her own attitudes and personality characteristics and how these are perceived and interpreted by others in the organization. The manager must also be aware of the needs and motivations of others in the firm in order to judge the likely reactions to, and outcome of, various courses of action he or she may undertake. Real skill in working with others is not a manufactured or occasional effort; it must be a continuous, natural activity, not only at times of decision making but also in the day-to-day behavior of the manager.

On the subject of motivating employees, human skill is demonstrated in three ways:

1. A display of effective leadership by senior management.
2. A commitment to providing involvement and participation in key decision making to all professionals.
3. An equitable and competitive compensation philosophy.

Leadership. To stimulate motivation, senior management must display strong leadership to its staff by setting an organizational direction for the firm that others want to be a part of. Creative people identify with and respond to a strong sense of purpose. John Wareham, in his book *Secrets of a Corporate Headhunter* [1980], lists some general attributes of a leader that seem quite germane to directing portfolio management:

- Look like a leader
- Have a dream
- Set a goal and begin advancing toward it
- Develop specific knowledge
- Have a little mystery about you
- Be prepared to bend internal rules
- Be well organized
- Be ruthless, without trepidation, when necessary

Creative people also respond well to recognition. Feedback and rewards should be prompt and recognition should be for effort, not merely for the success of an idea. Motivation of creative people also requires a willingness to systematically ask employees about their jobs, and to listen to their suggestions for improving their own productivity or that of the firm. Particularly in larger investment firms, the management must accept the fact that many subordinates know more about their own jobs and tactical skills than the manager does. To provide a catalyst for this type of dialogue, an excellent question that all managers should be required to ask their subordinates in every review is, "What would you like to be doing here that you are not doing now?" The question is posed in qualitative rather than quantitative terms, and is asked of everyone down to the lowest nonprofessional level. While the company obviously cannot hope to satisfy all requests, such a question engenders discussion and suggestions useful to the employee and the company, and gives a sincere impression of care and concern by management toward each individual.

Compensation Policy. Financial rewards are obviously important, but their impact on employee motivation and happiness and, hence, on retention rates probably receives exaggerated significance. The personality and leadership of the organization and recognition of the individual's involvement with it by peers and superiors are at least as important. Over and over again, a key theme of people departing an organization is the feeling of being unappreciated. The larger and more impersonal the firm, the more difficult it may be to offer participation and involvement with key decisions and, hence, the greater the likelihood for some personnel turnover.

Size in and of itself is not necessarily an obstacle for attracting and keeping creative professionals. Many highly productive, innovative people prefer the comfort and security of larger, more structured firms. A more common motivation problem stems from the potential inequity that may exist in salary levels between investment and noninvestment people in multi-purpose organizations such as banks, industrial corporations, and insurance companies. Too often such institutions fail to recognize that they are competing for investment accounts and talent nationwide, against all comers, not just against similar companies in their region or industry.

Multipurpose organizations can also be disadvantaged by equity participation or profit sharing arrangements offered by many firms exclusively devoted to portfolio management, or by a bonus system offered to investment staff in which rewards are tied to performance standards unrelated to results achieved in the portfolio function. The management of such entities should attempt to construct a compensation program having two critical parts. First, the investment staff should be able to derive meaningful financial rewards for achieving above-average but realistically attainable goals; and second, such goals and the resulting reward for their achievement should be independent of the financial progress of the total firm and its other endeavors.

THE CHALLENGE OF GROWTH AND ORGANIZATIONAL CHANGE

As we discussed in a preceding section, the effective manager must be sensitive to external environmental events that continually confront and threaten the long-term perspective and creativity of the firm. In the course of daily activities, there is a second, more subtle, and hence more difficult layer of environmental awareness required for effective management of the dynamic portfolio process. Contrary to external pressures, these forces are born within the firm and center on the challenges of managing the impact of growth and organizational change.

The Problems of Growth

The management of growth and organizational change has special significance to portfolio management. There are countless instances of firms that have lost their momentum and effectiveness over time, often following a period of success and impressive growth. There are other firms that seem to sustain their special market niche and creative energies despite increases (sometimes substantial) in their asset and employee base. Lack of marketability of investment holdings and physical ability to implement major strategic changes are often offered as a major impediment to success as firms grow larger. While there obviously is some relevance to this, there are enough exceptional larger firms around to make one think that the primary obstacles to success are located deeper in the fabric of an organization. Specifically, two problems that accompany growth offer unique challenges to effective management of portfolio firms.

First, successful portfolio management is a finely tuned balance of creative people anticipating and responding to opportunities, creating a flow of ideas through the cycle of awareness, analysis, and execution of portfolio decisions; growth can be disruptive to this process. Growth is associated with an increase of staff and accounts that impact the established order of the firm. The dynamics and special culture of the organization are tested, sometimes overwhelmed, as internal procedures incorporate more people and more diffusion of important tasks.

Second, the skills and behavior patterns that work in one phase of organizational growth may be of limited value in later periods. The job satisfaction of creative people may be penalized by their own success and contribution to the firm. A transition of needs and talents may not be detected, or worse, may be actively resisted by people in the organization, leading to deterioration in performance, morale, and managerial effectiveness.

By understanding and planning for change as it relates to portfolio management, the effective manager can enhance the quality and growth of the organization and begin to prepare for the environment that will likely accompany success. Focus can be placed on the specific managerial skills required at different organizational life stages, and the relative importance of each to the total management process.

Shifting Phases of Activity. Aplin and Cosier [1980] describe two distinct phases of activity that can be identified in most organizations. They include a relatively stable, internally oriented *maintenance* period and a dynamic, externally oriented *creative* period that includes, but is not limited to, the start-up phase of an organization. A series of common behavior patterns is demonstrated as a firm cycles from one phase to another, both in terms of the values, directions, and priorities of the firm and the change of effective managerial skills that must be implemented to sustain organizational vitality. Aplin and Cosier also point out that transitions between these phases cause special managerial problems due to, among other factors, the potential inability of managers to excel in the activities required in both of these distinct organizational stages.

These concepts seem unusually relevant to effective management of investment asset management firms. The pressures of organizational change should be expected and anticipated by the growing firm. In addition, the larger slow-growing firm will occasionally require a pruning and revitalization of its efforts, with such renewal requiring many of the management skills associated with new or emerging firms.

The rest of this chapter will discuss characteristics of the creative, mature cycle that seem particularly relevant to the portfolio process and, of singular importance, how successful firms have treated this phenomenon in their strategies of managing for results.

Key Organizational Phases

Portfolio management seems to go through recurring cycles of what will be defined as creative and mature organizational phases. Given the pace of change within the industry, the frequency of transition between these two phases can be expected to be high, but the length of the creative and mature periods varies considerably depending on the management philosophy and investment style of the firm. Mature periods, with their generally greater sense of stability, usually last longer than creative periods.

Creative Phase. Creative and mature investment organizations have distinctly different characteristics in terms of internal culture and working environment, values and priorities, portfolio methods, and the impression they transmit to clients and the outside world. An organization enters a creative phase at its formative stage and on those occasions when management makes a deliberate effort to change the destiny of the firm by the introduction of new organizational strategies. These changes might embrace a change in the total investment thrust of the firm, but more often involve an adaptation in philosophy or style, the introduction or abandonment of a specific portfolio service, or major changes in portfolio methods or procedures.

Portfolio management firms in the creative organizational phase tend to exhibit a set of common characteristics:

1. The firm displays relative immunity from the external pressures of the business. Investment philosophy and direction are well understood internally and externally, leading to high perseverance and staying power of conviction.
2. The thrust is externally oriented and aggressive. There is a willingness and comfort in dealing with long-term concepts and ambiguities in setting investment strategy. The managerial emphasis is on creating business through new services as opposed to maximizing internal efficiencies and controlling costs.
3. Employees are motivated by the momentum of the firm and a creative, growth-oriented job content. There are few, if any, people problems.
4. In addition to directing the firm, senior management retains a strong and active role in the portfolio management process.
5. Investment methods and procedures are relatively simple and internal communications are effective. The firm exhibits an action orientation and a willingness to experiment, to implement, and to re-

spond to change. Given this combination, new ideas seem to flow freely and are quickly translated into portfolio decisions.

Mature Phase. An investment firm has a tendency to enter a relatively stable mature phase after its direction and style have become established and formalized procedures have become routine. An influx of business and/or new professionals increases the priorities of consistency and quality control, and this also leads to evolution away from the creative phase into a mature phase.

Characteristics of a mature investment organization would include:

1. The organization takes on an internal focus, with primary interest in improving and refining existing services and methods. There is less inclination to change direction or consider new strategies and a greater emphasis on product improvements.
2. There is a more regimented, task-oriented environment, which often leads to frustrations in job content and turnover of creative and younger people.
3. Senior management relinquishes some involvement in the investment process as more of its time is spent on other duties.
4. The portfolio process becomes more complex, with more steps involved between idea awareness and execution of decisions. This is usually accompanied by greater use of committees or group judgments on important investment decisions.
5. The organization puts greater attention on efficiencies and cost control. The working environment becomes more formal, often accompanied by more use of long-term planning, budgets, and written reports.
6. With expansion of staff, good communications become more difficult, both internally and externally. Confusions arise as to the true purpose and direction of the firm, leading to greater instances of deviation from stated investment style.

It should be evident that the innovative and crisp behavior required for effective portfolio management find a much more conducive environment in a creative rather than in a mature organizational setting. Portfolio management requires an environment that encourages the expression of ideas, the seizing of opportunities, and the prompt implementation of investment decisions. It is crucial for investment leaders to recognize that, in the absence of deliberate managerial action, mature organizations will develop tendencies that can stifle the initiative and flow of ideas central to value-added portfolio management.

Since effective portfolio management is a dynamic, finely tuned process, firms with expanding staffs and client bases have a natural tendency to gravitate to a mature state. However, the industry is replete with smaller firms exhibiting mature organizational symptoms due to a failure by their leaders to recognize the need for effective managerial direction.

Cycle Transition. The impact of organizational conflict, augmented by the intensely competitive environment of portfolio management, eventually leads to a recycling of mature organizations to new creative endeavors. The impetus for such change can originate from either self-initiated management decisions or intense external pressures on the firm and its portfolio services. This sets in motion an alternating cycle between creative and mature periods for portfolio management firms, with the frequency of change dictated by the integrity and staying power of a particular organizational strategy to add investment value.

In addition to the characteristics of the creative and mature phases, management should address specific issues that arise during the transition between such stages. This problem is particularly acute in portfolio management, since the skills required for investment success during the creative phase contrast considerably with the talents needed for superior results in a mature organization. A problem commonplace in portfolio management is the inability or unwillingness of individuals to excel in the managerial abilities required in *both* creative and mature organizations.

SPECIAL TRANSITIONAL PROBLEMS. Effective management of organizational transition is further complicated by events unique to creative-to-mature (C–M) as contrasted with mature-to-creative (M–C) transitions. C–M transitions can creep up on an organization, since these often require no direct managerial intervention. Portfolio management entities can easily get caught up in the momentum of their own success. The frenzy of activity eventually wanes as growth materializes and is naturally replaced by a desire for stability and quality control. Conversely, M–C transitions can prove to be disruptive and unpleasant for the firm and its management; hence, there is often a subconscious tendency to delay needed decisions. Resistance to change developed during the mature period can become so intense that the staff may refuse to consider new strategies, even in the face of potentially devastating consequences. The following hypothetical examples highlight two investment situations in which organizations were unable to successfully complete their needed transitions.

> **Situation A:** On the basis of above-average equity performance and a unique, disciplined investment style, an investment counseling firm had experienced growth in assets under management from $25 million to $500 million over the past four years. The firm's founder remained active in the investment process while taking personal responsibility for all marketing efforts. Rapid expansion of accounts and personnel was leading to slippage in performance versus the market averages, serious variance in performance among accounts, and more frequent instances of exceptions from the firm's stated investment philosophy. In response, the founder of the firm tightened control over major

investment decisions and became unwilling to delegate major duties to his other professionals. Employee turnover accelerated, particularly among senior people, and the long-standing rapport of the firm with a number of major clients deteriorated rapidly, ultimately leading to several account terminations.

Situation B: The investment management division of a large multipurpose financial institution had generated moderately above-median performance from a high-quality, diversified equity philosophy over the past decade. The philosophy was strongly fundamental in approach, and the firm conducted its own research with a staff of ten highly qualified analysts. Despite achieving respectable performance, the firm had recently been losing pension accounts and revenues to smaller equity managers that offered more specialized investment styles and more intensive client service. To counter this trend, management decided to focus its resources on two distinct styles of equity management that optimized the analytical talents and creative abilities of the division. This effort proved successful in temporarily arresting account defection and in attracting the attention of prospective new pension clients. Internal criticism, however, was intense. Analysts, sensing a change from their original "mission," opposed a change in direction. Portfolio managers were upset by the more concentrated thrust of the philosophy. After 18 months of internal organizational turmoil, management reversed its strategy and returned to offering its initial equity investment style. Account terminations reaccelerated, and attention turned to installing greater budgeting and cost control as a means of stemming erosion of profitability.

The two organizations were unable to evaluate changing conditions that impacted their effectiveness, and hence were unable to make needed organization transitions. In situation A, the counseling firm was unable to anticipate the consequences of growth and could not shift its orientation to the requirements of a mature organization. In situation B, the investment division had become so maintenance-oriented it could not respond to the need for restructuring to counter the effects of a new competitive climate.

Many successful investment firms have found it difficult or impossible to make the transition between cycles of creative and mature phases, partially because of their unwillingness to shift from managerial and investment methods that have worked in the past. Particularly in light of the creative, dynamic nature of portfolio management, failure to manage a transition can lead to reduced performance, morale problems, and a major decline in the momentum of the organization.

MANAGING FOR RESULTS

The portfolio management profession includes a number of exceptional organizations that have been quite successful in coping with growth, absorbing fairly significant increases in assets with no apparent dilution of their investment skills. These firms vary considerably in their personalities and specific approaches to investment management, but do seem to fall within two basic patterns of organizational behavior.

Retaining Creativity

First and more numerous are firms that seem to retain their creative status despite the experience of growth and organizational change. These entities recognize and preciously guard their creative energies against the natural tendencies to evolve into a more regimented, mature status. Conceptually, the founder or leaders of such a firm have tremendous personal conviction and involvement with their stated investment style. Of equal importance, they are effective in transmitting their values and priorities to others internally, leading to consistency of execution and perseverance in the face of distracting external events.

These firms seem to have extremely high standards for selection of staff; this in combination with the momentum accompanying their growth results in superior people who are more likely to make superior investment judgments. In many cases there is a deliberate leanness to the organization's staffing, accompanied by the high productivity and profitability that results from a unified, consistent application of superior investment people. These types of creative organizations retain their characteristics longer than many of their competitors by knowing precisely what they are trying to do, accumulating quality resources to execute their role, and concentrating on doing a few things extremely well.

Responding to Change

The second type of organization that copes well with growth is the firm that has deliberately developed the facility to respond to external changes in its competitive environment and in the investment needs of its clients and prospects. As opposed to resisting change, such organizations seem to relish the challenge and opportunity provided by sensing new client needs that can be satisfied by leveraging new investment applications upon a core of knowledge and expertise that has already been assembled. The management of such firms builds an organizational spirit that responds positively and quickly to environmental change and is proficient in effecting mature-to-creative transitions.

The conceptual skills of such firms are manifested in their ability to envision new services that can draw upon the tactical skills and creative talents of their people. These organizations are particularly adept at resisting the inward orientation that burdens many larger investment organizations, and they retain a truly client-driven approach in providing services to their clients.

While the leader or leaders of such a firm may relinquish some personal involvement in the investment process, this is more than offset by their comfort and proficiency in dealing with customers and their ability to perceive investment needs that can be competently and profitably met by the organization. These firms are normally blessed with above-average application of human skills, particularly in the area of retaining entrepreneurship and a small team environment for various functional activities.

Illustrations of Managerial Success

As proven examples of managerial skill in accommodating growth and change, we have chosen two firms that have pursued distinctly different managerial strategies to achieve success. These firms have been unquestionably successful in combining superior growth with a retention of creative dynamics which characterize their specific investment style.

Alliance Capital Management. Alliance is a firm that has defined and executed specific strategies to enable it to apply the skills of its creative organizational phase to a progressively larger base of clients and investment assets. Through deliberate managerial action, the firm has avoided transition to a mature organizational phase while experiencing exceptional growth since its inception in 1972.

Management has focused on the importance of procedural skill development as the key to sustaining its success, specifically on building an environment that captures and retains the attributes of smaller, informal investors and the way they actually make portfolio decisions. Many of its professionals have joined the firm from larger, more structured organizations, and this fact facilitates an awareness of the potential problems of inertia and lack of creative insight that burden many larger investment entities.

The firm has a participative, dynamic internal flow of ideas that involves all of its professionals in a daily interchange of information and an active involvement in setting policy and strategy. No one individual or committee dictates policy, but rather all of the firm's professionals are encouraged and evaluated on their initiative to express ideas and bring forth faintly held beliefs for active and frequent discussion.

The company has retained the elements of creative organizational behavior by providing an environment that allows a frequent flow of information and ideas among its investment professionals. The intellectual appeal and stimulating work content provided by the environment have enabled the firm to attract a high caliber group of professionals that has remained essentially intact despite enjoying above-average growth and high recognition of success by its competitors. Two other related managerial strategies have been important to the firm's success.

UNIQUE ORGANIZATIONAL STRUCTURE. First, management has implemented a specific and unique organizational structure to accommodate future growth and change. The firm has positioned its portfolio managers in six different U.S. locations, plus a London office, to further attempt to retain the advantages of smallness in its investment process. All of these offices take an active role in formulating strategy, and the key elements of the firm's asset mix and portfolio composition are implemented uniformly among all offices and investment managers.

The major purpose of the firm's regional office commitment is to combine the wide flow of information and organizational stability one associates with larger firms with the creativity and entrepreneurial spirit normally seen in smaller groups of investors. Management has recognized the unique features of this combination and has taken deliberate action to achieve and retain a specific organizational style. The small team environment of its regional offices also allows the firm to assimilate further increases in its asset base without disruption to its style of investing.

MANAGERIAL AUTONOMY. A second important strategy is management's commitment to providing portfolio managers considerable autonomy in timing and selecting investments, within the parameters of broad portfolio themes that are implemented consistently in all accounts with similar objectives. The firm is committed to the concept of delegation as a major tool for retaining creativity and freshness of ideas.

Management is equally aware of the critical importance of high quality professionals if delegation and dispersion of investment responsibility are going to work. The firm gives major attention to the task of selecting its personnel, and specific jobs will often go unfilled for months as senior management screens applicants to select those that fit the personality, investment style, and quality standards it has set.

COMMUNICATION PRACTICES. Communication of policy and internal procedures are deliberately unspecific in many areas, in order to provide sufficient leeway for superior professionals to apply their own judgment to a given investment question. Conversely, all levels of management are actively involved with the investment process, which allows the firm to take responsive and uniform portfolio action when this is dictated by market events.

Alliance has addressed and overcome the potential problems stemming from organizational growth by implementing managerial strategies to retain a small, creative environment for its professionals. The success of its efforts has been demonstrated by its ability to deliver consistently above-average results on an asset base exceeding $10 billion of discretionary and nondiscretionary funds in 1982.

Provident National Bank. As the result of deliberate managerial action, Provident has developed and demonstrated a facility to respond to change that is unusual in the investment field. Its strategy for success has been different from that of Alliance, in that it recognized its movement toward mature organizational tendencies and took specific action on several occasions to effect a transition back to a creative state. The bank has evolved to an organizational state that is comfortable in responding positively to change; this, in turn, has allowed it to enjoy above-average growth and profitability despite an investment asset base that today totals over $16 billion.

CREATING NEW PRODUCTS. Approximately 15 years ago, management took stock of its market position, which at that time included reasonable investment skills, a high-caliber trust administrative and financial planning ability, and a good local franchise in traditional trust services. By building on this position and introducing specialized added technical skills, management sensed an unexploited opportunity to distinguish itself by creating new investment products to satisfy unfulfilled client needs on a national basis.

The bank demonstrated a degree of conceptual skill that was unique in the mid-1960s, by committing itself to identifying and fulfilling true investment needs rather than simply attempting to generate maximum investment performance from traditional portfolio assets.

MARKETING QUALITY RESEARCH. Its first action was to enhance and expand its commitment to a quality investment research capability and to make its research product a profitable, self-sustaining entity. The bank decided to sell its investment research to other institutions who were either in need of a fiduciary research product or unwilling or financially unable to assemble one themselves. After developing an initial market for its research with other institutional trust departments, the bank found that a second demand for its service resided in brokerage firms who found it more economical to purchase a quality investment research capability from an outside source than to commit their own internal resources to such an effort. By offering this wholesale research capability, the bank was able to derive incremental revenues on a very minimal increase in costs and resources devoted to this activity.

LEVERAGING DISTRIBUTION CHANNELS. As a second or separate transition to a creative organizational phase, management then perceived that a new layer of investment opportunity rested in the wide distribution networks of brokers to whom the bank was supplying its research package. The bank decided to leverage the marketing channels of other financial institutions by offering them value-added services with relatively low variable cost that could be sold by the institutions directly to their customers.

MONEY MARKET FUND ADVISING. Management also had the foresight to be one of the early industry leaders in recognizing the tremendous potential of offering to investors prevailing money market yields in commingled form and at a constant unit value. The bank redirected a portion of its trust investment resources to researching and eventually overcoming legal and regulatory hurdles to serving as investment advisor to open-end money market mutual funds.

A subsidiary of the bank served as investment advisor to a $50 million money market fund that was offered to the public in 1972, thus marking it as one of the first funds in what was in 1982 a $220 billion industry. Among other cash equivalent funds for which it serves as advisor, the bank was again one of the first in offering a tax-exempt fund consisting of Federal Project Notes and other short-term state and municipal obligations. Similar to its earlier research service and other money market funds, this is another example of management's conceptual skill in identifying and exploiting unfilled demands of institutional and retail investors. Total cash equivalent assets for which the bank and its subsidiaries serve as advisor now total over $12 billion.

LEVERAGING ADVISORY SERVICES. Having established a franchise with brokerage firms, bank trust departments, and other institutions, management has set its sights upon opportunities that are emerging from the growing trends toward deregulation of financial and investment services. Given certain regulatory changes, management envisions its fiduciary money market activities growing from a role as advisor of its own sponsored money market funds to being an advisor to money market mutual funds offered by other banks and financial institutions. Similar to its earlier activities of leveraging the fixed costs of its research effort into incremental earnings, the bank is now applying the same business strategy to its established reputation as an advisor to short-term money market investment vehicles. The opportunities for additional earnings sources are considerably enhanced by the growing trend toward deregulation of financial services and the growing sophistication of investors and savers seeking quality, convenience, and access to competitive interest rates for their short-term investment vehicles.

As impressive as its strategy for sustaining growth is management's control of its traditional services over this dynamic 15-year expansion phase. The bank has restructured its investment activities into three distinct business units to better manage its major activities of traditional trust services, institutional investment counseling, and investment advice to mutual funds.

MARKET-DRIVEN ORGANIZATION. Change in organizational direction has been evolutionary, well researched, and confined to investment areas where the bank had technical expertise and could offer services of demonstrated value to clients. Provident is truly a market-driven organization that has developed an unusual expertise in perceiving gaps between what investment customers need and what they are offered, and then creating value-added services that fill those gaps. As a testimony to its success, assets under management by the bank have grown from $1 billion to over $16 billion during the past 15 years.

Contrasting Alliance and Provident. It is interesting to note that there is a major organizational commitment to growth at both of these firms, despite their already impressive levels of assets and profitability. Both management and staff understand the very direct and self-sustaining linkage between client satisfaction, organizational success, and the ability to attract and retain exceptional people. These two firms demonstrate that the dynamics of portfolio management are consistent with, and perhaps even dependent upon, a mandate for sustainable, well-founded growth in profitability and momentum.

By contrast, there is a noticeable distinction in the job content at the executive level of the sustainably creative firm (Alliance) and the accomplished transitional firm (Provident). The leadership of Alliance makes a point of retaining active involvement in the firm's investment process. It devotes considerable attention to reaffirming the essentials of its investment style, both internally and externally. And it constantly focuses on the application of technical and human managerial skills that are crucial to its ability to retain the advantages of a creative, flexible investor.

On the other hand, the senior management of the Provident investment group has made a willing and conscious effort to depart from the daily rigors of the portfolio process. It recognizes the importance of applying conceptual managerial skills for successful achievement of its chosen role as a transitional, client-driven investment organization.

This conceptual skill is only partially manifested in the bank's ability to recognize and exploit unfulfilled client needs. Of equal importance is its ability to translate these opportunities into quality investment services capable of sustaining a leading competitive position, while at the same time providing a creative, stimulating environment for the firm's professionals.

SUMMARY

The intent of this chapter has been to isolate and define common managerial skills displayed by investment professionals who perform their jobs effectively.

One central conclusion is that there is no single model or set of procedures that characterizes success in managing investment managers. One of the more fascinating, and in a sense predictable, aspects of the profession is the wide variety of managerial strategies that leading firms have developed to control their particular investment strengths, market niche, and growth potential.

In observing these strategies, as practiced by successful groups of investors, one detects a consistent foundation of management activities that can be classified as conceptual, technical, and human managerial skills. The chapter discusses various components of activities within these skill levels and how they are applied to the portfolio process by leading investment firms.

Particular emphasis is placed on the application of conceptual, human, and technical skills within two environmental settings that are unique to the dynamics of portfolio management. Effective leadership must address and overcome a set of external factors that impose a continual destabilizing influence on the ability of an organization to maintain a long-term perspective and form clear unemotional judgments on the investment worthiness of securities. Secondly, management must confront the challenge of retaining the integrity and responsiveness of its portfolio process as the organization grows in asset base and number of professionals.

Firms that meet these challenges successfully seem to demonstrate two underlying characteristics. First, the good firms understand themselves and their commitment to a specific investment philosophy extremely well. This normally results from the impact of one or a limited number of leaders who have strong personal conviction in a certain style of investing and, of equal importance, have the personality and communication skills to instill their beliefs throughout the organization.

Successful firms understand their limitations as well as their strengths and have the discipline to confine their activities to investment alternatives they know well. A strong sense of organizational direction breeds permanence and confidence through different market environments that generally enhance investment performance and client rapport.

A clearly stated investment philosophy builds motivation and job satisfaction among the firm's professionals and also raises the prospect for compatibility from subsequent staff additions. Firms committed to this managerial approach seem to retain the characteristics of a creative, entrepreneurial organization despite the absorption of relatively large sums of assets and clients under their management.

A second common management trend of successful firms is their understanding of the power and productivity of superior investment professionals and the importance of remaining lean and efficient in the portfolio decision-making process. In many industries, smaller firms have an important advantage if they can avoid the costs and inertia embedded in the sizable overhead of their larger competitors. This statement seems particularly appropriate to the dynamics of professional portfolio management. As a general rule, the leading firms spend considerable time and effort on the selection and retention of their investment staff.

There are probably few other professions in which the decisions of one or a limited number of truly superior people can have such leveraged impact on the performance and profitability of the organization. Conversely, the efforts of nonproductive or incompatible staff, or the results of an inefficient or cumbersome decision-making process, can have abnormally adverse consequences to a portfolio management activity.

Leading investment firms are usually characterized by a structural soundness of the organization and a lean staff and they make a deliberate attempt to focus on quality rather than quantity of investment professionals. This management philosophy normally results in higher profitability both for the firm and its employees, which further reinforces the organizational commitment to providing a leadership role in its particular investment endeavors.

FURTHER READING

The classification of major managerial skills for investment leaders is drawn from definitions and basic parameters first described by Katz [1974]. Another source of insight in this area is Skinner and Sasser [1977].

For additional discussion of the qualifications for successful leadership and organization of the portfolio process, readers are encouraged to read Peters [1980] and Drucker [1980].

The importance of setting a permanent investment style for the portfolio firm drew largely from the definition and ramifications of groupthink that were described by Janis [1972]. This was supplemented by the work of Drucker [1980].

The chapter discussion on the challenges of organizational growth and change in investment firms drew upon the definitions for creative and maintenance organizations described by Aplin and Cosier [1980]. A discussion on the key elements of a creative investment management organization is further amplified by Williams [1980].

BIBLIOGRAPHY

Aplin, John C., and Richard A. Cosier, "Managing Creative and Maintenance Organization," *Business Quarterly,* Spring 1980.

Drucker, Peter F., *Managing in Turbulent Times*, New York: Harper & Row, 1980.

Janis, Irving L., *Victims of Groupthink,* Boston: Houghton Mifflin, 1972.

Katz, Robert L., "Skills of an Effective Administrator," *Harvard Business Review,* September/October 1974.

Peters, Thomas J., "Putting Excellence into Management," *Business Week,* July 21, 1980.

Skinner, Wickham, and W. Earl Sasser, "Managers with Impact: Versatile and Inconsistent," *Harvard Business Review,* November/December 1977.

Wareham, John, *Secrets of a Corporate Headhunter,* New York: Atheneum, 1980.

Williams, Dave H., "Organizing for Superior Investment Returns," *Financial Analysts Journal,* September/October 1980.

Index

Accident plans, 64
Account status reports, 598-599
Accounting statements, portfolio, 29
Accrual basis, 618, 619
Accumulation-maximizing investors, 309
Active/aggressive response, 587
Active/defensive response, 586-587
Active management, 600-601, 633
  asset allocation, 282-283
  decisions, 19-21
  equity stocks, 402-415
  fixed income securities, 320-326
  and optimal systematic risk, 15-16
Active portfolio optimization, 331, 334, 410-415
Actuarial assumptions and methods, 68-69, 71-73
Actuarial return rate, 67
Adjustable rate mortgages (ARMs), 467-468
Adjustments, return, 28-29
Adverse outcomes, real risks of, 14-15
Advisors, managers as, 284-285
Age, average, of employees, 73
AICPA (American Institute of Certified Public Accountants), 369
Allen, Thomas F., 515
Alliance Capital Management, 683-684, 686-687
Alpha factors, 16, 52, 613
Alternative mortgage instruments (AMIs), 456-458
Ambachtsheer, Keith P., 5, 56, 282-283, 287, 397, 429, 431, 540-541, 566
Ambrose, James H., 5
American Council of Life Insurance, 515-516
American Institute of Certified Public Accountants (AICPA), 369

American Institute of Real Estate Appraisers, 488, 507, 514, 516
American National Bank (Chicago), 401
American Stock Exchange, 507, 615
AMIs (alternative mortgage instruments), 456-458
Ammerman, Robert C., 287
Analytical research, 666
Annual returns, 627
Annuities, pension, 64
Anticost, 539
Aplin, John C., 677, 689
Appraisal process, 496-498
APT. *See* Arbitrage pricing theory
Arak, Marcelle, 177, 204
Arbitrage pricing theory (APT), 49-50, 281-282
Archer, S. H., 56
Arditti, Fred O., 65
Arithmetic mean return, 28
ARMs (adjustable rate mortgages), 467-468
Arnold, Alvin L., 516
Ask in size, 561
Asset allocation, 22, 261-290
  and active management, 282-283
  considerations in setting asset mixes, 264-271
  for employee benefit funds, 80-81, 288-290
  importance of mix decisions, 261-262
  maker of mix decisions, 262-264
  and monitoring/revision, 585-587
  and nonlife insurance companies, 111
  optimal mix selection, 271-280
  and portfolio management, 283-286
  for real estate, 512-513
  reconciliation of different models, 280-281
  and tax arbitrage theory, 281-282